Public Life in
Renaissance Florence

Public Life in Renaissance Florence

RICHARD C. TREXLER

CORNELL UNIVERSITY PRESS
Ithaca and London

First published, Cornell Paperbacks, 1991.
Originally published 1980 by Academic Press.

International Standard Book Number 0-8014-2694-4 (cloth)
International Standard Book Number 0-8014-9979-8 (paper)
Library of Congress Catalog Card Number 91-55259

Printed in the United States of America

Librarians: Library of Congress cataloging information appears on the last page of the book.

⊛ The paper in this book meets the minimum requirements of the American National Standard for Information Sciences—Permanence of Paper for Printed Library Materials, ANSI Z39.48-1984.

Contents

List of Plates

Preface

This book describes the way in which Florentines from Dante to Michelangelo interacted with one another, with foreigners, and with their divinities. The writers, artists, and politicians of Florence need no press; their accomplishments have long been part of the human heritage. Yet genius in Florence as elsewhere emerged from a collective way of life, from systems of formal communications that focused, identified, and evaluated the actions of its residents. The city has its own formal life. This book recognizes that fact, and studies one past city from that point of view.

I wrote this book in part for those who want to know more about Renaissance Florence. Yet from the start I wrote for another group—for those social scientists interested in social action and in the forms that give such actions their meaning in an urban context. This book examines general questions, therefore, from a particular historical experience: in its original topical format, through its study of individual and small-group psychology, to its analysis of Florence's collective forms, and finally in its historical account of the revolution of ritual forms during the Medici period.

All students of Florence bring to their work some familiar guide, some Virgilian spirit who first revealed Florence's importance to their own inner experience. Mine has been Niccolò Machiavelli. Machiavelli allowed me to see the primordial problems of urban life then, and now. We live in modern cities, yet Florence's incomparable historical resources—the great political scientist among them—permit us the shock of recognition in the midst of an enchanted past. This book is about history, system, and identity.

Acknowledgments

My greatest debt is to student colleagues who marched with me in the protest movements of the 1960s. This activity awakened and has sustained my interest in public behavior; our common actions and reflections upon those actions taught me much about political motivations and behavior.

I wish next to acknowledge members of the professional community who, a gleam in their eye, have shared knowledge with me. There were "think groups" at Frankfurt am Main when I was a student, and at El Paso and Urbana since I have been a teacher. Single individuals have inspired me by their pedagogy: Theodor Adorno, Clifford Geertz, Herbert Marcuse, Donald Preziosi, Gloria Ramakus, and John Rechy. The community of the Florentine archives, finally, has my special gratitude. It is a distinct thrill to discover the past embedded in total contexts, and I cherish the experiences I have shared with that *buon'uomo* Gene Brucker, with my cohorts Rab Hatfield and Anthony Molho, with younger scholars like Samuel Cohn and Ronald Weissman, and with many other colleagues. None of that excitement would have been possible, of course, without the help of the personnel of Florence's archives and libraries; I thank them all.

This book has been read at different stages in various parts by several colleagues. Charles Trinkaus and Donald Weinstein read the work when it was only an essay, and told me to go back and write a book. Linda Duchamp, best of students, read the whole manuscript, and Cynthia Bouton assisted me in its final preparation. Natalie Davis, John Elliott, Rab Hatfield, Christiane Klapisch-Zuber, Randall Kritkausky, Carolyn Schmidt, and Philip Steedman critiqued different chapters, and their contributions are deeply appreciated. The many colleagues who furnished particular references and unpublished papers are thanked in the text. Charles Tilly's editorial suggestions were cogent and wise, and his encouragement was crucial.

Institutional support was important in making this book. It came from the Harvard Center for Italian Renaissance Studies at Villa I Tatti (formerly presided over by Sheila and Myron Gilmore); from the Institute for Advanced Study (through NEH grant H5426); from the Center for Advanced Study at Urbana, Illinois; and, at the end, from the Centre de Recherches Historiques of the École des Hautes Études en Sciences Sociales, Paris.

I reproduce the paintings in this book by permission of the museums and galleries indicated in the captions, and with the assistance of their photographic services and those of Fratelli Alinari in Florence (Plates 3, 4, and 7), Guido Sansoni (Plates 10 and 26), and the Gabinetto Fotografico, Soprintendenza Beni Artistici e Storici di Firenze (Plates 6, 17, 21, 23, and 24).

Finally, I want to express my thanks to associates at the State University of New York, Binghamton: to Roxanne Vavra, who typed the manuscript, and to the Educational Communications Office, for its photographic assistance.

The final word belongs to a singular friend and critic. Bernice J. Trexler has given and taught me more than I can say, so I shall only gesture: This book is dedicated to her.

R.C.T.

Introduction

Since the city is large, it needs ceremonies.*

In a revolution, said Hegel, heaven and earth are one. Commenting on the French Revolution, the German philosopher paid witness to the vitalism of the civil procession when the structure of government has collapsed, when backstage, onstage, and audience unite and act out reality together. In the revolutionary street, mass action is a play structuring reality.

Hegel's enthusiasm for creative ritual has not been shared by most moderns, for the specter of dancing processional politicians restructuring and redistributing power frightens weak and strong. The beliefs that the individual is not defined by a socially active self, that the search for one's identity takes place in the mind of the individual, not upon the streets of cities, disguise a basic fear of change. Purposeful combined action in the streets is in this view the work of a mob, of show-offs, of beasts without interior sensibilities. *Civilisation* or *Kultur* excludes mass action. The Protestant Reformation's denial of the meaningfulness of action, the Scientific Revolution's objectification of physical and social processes, and the Industrial Revolution's theft of the personal identity of work have all contributed in a general way to the modern, "civilized" view of street action. Today few

* *Filarete's Treatise on Architecture, Being the Treatise by Antonio di Piero Averlino known as Filarete*, ed. J. R. Spencer, I (New Haven, 1965), 44.

social theorists consider Hegel's city more than an illusion, for even revolutions have been found to have anatomies. It is difficult to find a theorist of religion who views processional religiosity on a par with the "real religion" of the contemplative, or a student of diplomacy who takes etiquette seriously. Indeed, one (fruitful) school of social psychology views all interpersonal relations in terms of theater.[1]

Ritual persists, however, in the teeth of an unfriendly universe of discourse. Although some academicians resist the study of religion because "religion is a childhood disease," Japanese tea service is taught to sophisticated Occidental women, and Oriental religious forms to their men. Religious cults emphasizing mnemotic gestures spring up among social groups unsuspected of "superstition"; eminent anthropologists impressed by the ritual solidarities of less complex cultures convert to Catholicism; business managers go to Aspen, Colorado, to learn the ritual of social behavior. Some established economists even recommend returning to the ritual solidarity known to tribal cultures as part of salvation from ecological catastrophe.[2] Ritual is at the base of religion, after all. Our ancestors were right when they defined religion as common behavior, and we deceive ourselves to think of it as a community of belief. A religion is a system of reverential behavior shared by a sworn community, and group authority is rooted in the normative replication of that decorum.

The survival of ritual is noticeable not only in the interpersonal and small-group realms. Political change continues to stimulate general processional activism: The parades of the Red Guards, of the Petrograd Soviets, of the French Commune, and of the Great French Revolution have all demonstrated an acceptance of the religious behavior of the past, even though the past's beliefs have been rejected. In the United States, demonstrations against the Vietnam war were as exhilaratingly creative to their participants as they were frightening and confusing to their opponents. As the war progressed, many of those who opposed the conflict but disdained demonstrations ended by taking part. This was an object lesson that something was wrong with a world view that rejected the public stage as a fitting forum to display and form beliefs and emotions, that something was askew in a concept of identity that excluded *homo politicus*. Humanity's need to congregate had blithely ignored the long intellectual and police campaign waged against it. In the course of these antiwar demonstrations, bemused

---

1. See the works of E. Goffman, including *The Presentation of Self in Everyday Life* (Garden City, 1959), *Interaction Ritual* (Garden City, 1967), and *Asylums* (Garden City, 1961). For critiques, see A. Gouldner, *The Coming Crisis in Western Sociology* (New York, 1970), 378–390, and R. Sennett, "Two on the Aisle," *New York Review of Books* (hereafter *NYR*), Nov. 1, 1973. P. Rosenberg's review of Goffman's *Frame Analysis* (Cambridge, Mass., 1975) suggests that Goffman has somewhat revised his earlier position; *New York Times Book Review*, Feb. 16, 1975, p.21.

2. R. Heilbroner, "The Human Prospect," *NYR*, Jan. 24, 1974. The same message stressing the value of a renewed ritual vitality is in M. Douglas, *Natural Symbols* (New York, 1973), 19–60, and in J. Shaughnessy (ed.), *The Roots of Ritual* (Grand Rapids, 1973), especially the article by M. Mead, "Ritual and Social Crisis," 87–101. A sympathetic study of contemporary ritual is R. Bocock, *Ritual in Industrial Society. A Sociological Analysis of Ritualism in Modern England* (London, 1974).

bystanders, the merchants of apolitical identity, lent first their names, and then for a fleeting moment their bodies, to the better reality of the political procession.

Ritual lives. It is not simply a tribal or village phenomenon, but an integral part of established urban life. This book defends that proposition. It returns to the urban culture of the medieval and early modern period to study ritual before its efficacy was challenged: ritual with no questions asked. We shall discover that conditions in the traditional European city were conducive to intense public ritual behavior, that ritual was in fact at the core of the city's identity. It played a central part in a recurrent, powerful political process by which major urban groups competitively created and asserted the primacy of their own definitions of the city's rationale and structure to their compatriots, and to the world at large. A principal task of the present work is to explain how ritual life created and resuscitated urban life, order, and values.

The best vehicle for studying ritual forms and attitudes is a city that is both a cultural and a political unit, and the Italian city-state of Florence during its republican period meets this test. An outline of its history is in order.[3] Benefiting from the investiture struggle between the papacy and the Holy Roman Empire, Florence established itself as an independent commune in the twelfth century, and emerged as an important commercial center during the thirteenth. With this growth came a series of internal convulsions between the city nobility on the one side, and the non-noble families and gilds on the other, a clash terminating in the victory of the latter two parties and the establishment of the classical government of the priorate in the later thirteenth century. The history of the city from that point until the second third of the fifteenth century was dominated by strife between the "optimate" non-noble families and the propertied artisanate gathered in the gilds, with recurrent changes of regimes reflecting the increasing weakness of the republican order. In 1342 the optimates called in a foreign prince to aid them, but he soon allied himself with the lower artisanate and even with the nonpropertied, nongild proletariat (the Ciompi). Walter of Brienne failed to establish such an illegitimate one-man government, though almost everywhere else in northern Italy similar Signorias were engulfing old republican communes. In 1378 some optimate families allied themselves with these same Ciompi, and only the threat of a social revolution from below persuaded families and established gilds to unite against this proletariat and preserve the community of the possessing classes. The elitist, neoaristocratic character of the subsequent regime alone seemed capable of preserving the city's independence in the fifteenth-century world of *Signorias*, yet that regime prepared the way for the quasi-princely leadership of the Medici. Returning from banishment in 1434, the Medici in the following three gen-

---

3. The best overview of Florentine history remains
F. Schevill, *Medieval and Renaissance Florence* (New
York, 1961).

erations prepared the principate. Yet to the amazement of the world, optimates and gildsmen united shortly after the death of Lorenzo the Magnificent in 1492 to drive out the first family. For eighteen years, under the leadership first of the friar Savonarola and then of Piero Soderini, they maintained a refurbished republican regime. Returning to the city in 1512, the Medici were again driven out in 1527, only to return once more after the collapse of the Last Republic in 1530, claiming the city as their birthright and establishing a duchy during the same decade.

During much of this time, Florence was one of the cultural arbiters of Italy. The language of its great fourteenth-century (Trecento) writers was on its way to becoming the classical literary language of all Italians, the philology of its humanists led the way in the discovery of antiquity, and the canons of representational art established by its fifteenth-century (Quattrocento) artists would last into the twentieth century. Finally, Florence produced the leading political artists of the age, men whose brilliant reflections on the relation between the cultural and the political unity of their city make Florence not only a natural but an exciting choice for this study.

Europe possessed many types of cities; this book shows the relation between the conditions of life and ritual within one type. It first deals with the social problems generated by the political and economic structures of the city, and then examines the resulting civic cosmos as manifested in social relations and in religion at the individual, small-group, and civic levels. Finally, the exchange theory at work in this society is extracted from the behavioral sources. Once this analytical framework is established, it is possible to examine the classical commune at its ritual work: its response to the stimulus of celebration, the stimulus of foreigners, and the stimulus of danger. In the fifteenth century major changes took place in Florentine society, and we will see their impact upon classic public ritual: the movement of marginal social groups toward the center of the political stage, the Medicean challenge to traditional social and ritual organization, and the reactive but creative restructuring of ritual in the period after that family was expelled in 1494. A revolution in ritual behavior occurred during the period from 1470 to 1530. The final chapters of this book attempt to explain these events in the context of Florentine history.

More is attempted here than a study of Florentine formalism, however, for we shall look at Florentine affairs in the light of larger questions about the nature of history, space, and behavior—with caution, but with no apologies. In the course of this first systematic study of the formal life of an urban society, a new way of periodizing the past according to behavioral epochs will be offered. Students in search of a new mind's eye for social spaces can find in these pages a perspective and approach to the urban procession and theater that may encourage them to look again at their own modern streets and churches. For those interested in behavioral processes, this book, by examining not only group but also individual dynamics on the urban stage, provides a thespo-religious approach to the problem of the creation and diffusion of power, authority, and status in the city. Throughout, this book asks what ought to be among the philosopher's questions: What is the relative weight of action and of thought in establishing and changing individual and group identity?

It is my belief, and the perspective of this work, that premodern urban ritual was an important means of creating, maintaining, and transforming life among populations forced to govern their own relations with foreigners, gods, and each other. The vital association of ritual with civil life declined as power and communications passed to the early modern state or dynast. The process unfolded as follows: In the Middle Ages, the urban laity shared with its clergy the task of maintaining life through ritual. They joined in prayer and procession to preserve their communities because they were sovereigns of their destinies.

Early modern absolutism witnessed the decline of local sovereignties, the integration of urban economies into world and national ones, and the outside regulation of civil precedence and order. As a result, the court assumed responsibility for maintaining life through ritual; the old rationale and sacrality of local ritual vanished, to be replaced by new meanings. Not accidentally, the attention paid to court ritual increased by quantum leaps; the peculiar modalities of the French word *civilisation* perhaps best suggest the thirst for a definitive ritual that contemporaries quenched by watching the absolutistic prince.[4] The city in the meantime turned from processions to theater, featuring as likely as not *les gestes du roi* and, more recently, the spectator sports that enact territorial rites for depoliticized male citizens. The decline of public ceremonies in the cities marked the cities' political decline.

Centralized monarchies and their courts took over the ritual work of their subjects; no wonder that Protestant reformers rejected work theology in this heyday of the thaumaturgic kings. Not only had the king become the charismatic lawgiver or orator representing order to his subjects, but his

4. L. Pfandl, *Philipp II* (Munich, 1938), ch.8, is one of the few historians who, with cross-cultural evidence, have examined absolutistic court ceremonial in terms of its religious and sacral roots. See also M. Bloch, *Les Rois Thaumaturges* (Strassburg, 1924), and E. Kantorowicz, *Laudes Regiae* (Berkeley, 1946), and *The King's Two Bodies* (Princeton, 1957). N. Zemon Davis' superb studies of ritual constellations in sixteenth-century France are group-functionalistic in thrust. They do not examine social rites in relation to crown or political ritual or power; *Society and Culture in Early Modern France* (Stanford, 1975). See also her forthcoming and indicatively titled "The Sacred and the Body *Social* in Sixteenth-Century Lyon" (my italics), *Past and Present*, no. 90 (1981), 40–70. Two exchanges on works about early modern European history are especially interesting in this regard. In the first, a sociologist's book relating the character of central political structures to religious beliefs (G. Swanson, *Religion and Regime: A Sociological Ac-* count of the Reformation [Ann Arbor, 1967]) is critiqued by historians generally favoring local, non-political emphases; "Reevaluating the Reformation: A Symposium," *Journal of Interdisciplinary History* I (1971), 379–446. In the second, a historian's anthropologically informed book on "magic" (K. Thomas, *Religion and the Decline of Magic* [London, 1971]) is criticized by anthropologist Hildred Geertz, in part for explaining ritual as personal need fulfillment rather than in reference to social and ultimate meanings, in part for disputing that things (e.g. political structures and kings) have symbolic meanings in complex societies; "An Anthropology of Religion and Magic, I, II," *Journal of Interdisciplinary History* VI (1975), 71–109. On the relation of courts (not cities) to the new economic systems, see I. Wallerstein, *The Modern World-System. Capitalist Agriculture and the Origins of the European World-Economy in the Sixteenth Century* (New York, 1974), 133–162, especially 145f.

everyday interaction ritual with courtiers had become sacred behavior. The life-giving procession of the medieval city or village became the equally significant daily behavior of the king.[5] Reading a description of a medieval procession and then Saint-Simon's narration of a day at the court of the Sun King, one traces a common thread of concern for the welfare of the country emerging from these two different types of participatory ritual.

For all the political revolutions of modern times, we modern political pluralists have inherited the legacy of this absolutistic work ethic. Closet Jacobins in our behavioral assumptions, all but the rarest among us accept the principle, if not the distribution, of state power, presume without questioning that decorum is a virtue, and instinctively perceive the political center as the ultimate seat and stage of decorum. Ritual has become cognitively unimportant to the modern individualist—that gracious throwaway of the absolutistic state—because it is now supremely important and communicable through state agencies. The bureaucratic process, fostered at first by absolutistic state ceremonies and subsequently by nationalistic parades of soldiers and now by the television performances of high state dignitaries, is ritual at its core, a repeated exercise of political power effective because affective, a force said to be impersonal because it is rooted in the consensually accepted authority of a fascinating, righteous executive.

This historical perspective relating urban power and authority to urban ritual leads us to reexamine certain presuppositions about city space, and to arrive at some new hypotheses. Was and is the city per se antiritualistic and disenchanted, as Max Weber tended to believe, rationalized by the nature of its associations and economic activity? My approach questions this point of view, and suggests that it was through ritual that the medieval city achieved its identity, which it then lost when it surrendered its sovereignty and was subordinated to international markets and court ritual monopolies. Far from witnessing a decline of public sacred behavior, the emerging medieval city spent enormous sums on prestige economy and processional salvation. It had many of the attributes that Fustel de Coulanges ascribed to the ancient city, but denied to his own Christian towns.[6]

Has the city, as one school of American urban and psychological sociologists argues (Park, Goffman, Sennett), been emptied of the rich public life of yesteryear, but saturated with personal and small-group rituals because the "impersonal" nature of most urban contacts necessitates elaborate

5. The concept of ritual as life-generation is in A. Hocart, *Kings and Councillors* (Chicago, 1970), 33–40, 245. On the decline of urban festive life see Y.-M. Bercé, *Fête et Révolte. Des Mentalités Populaires du XVIe au XVIIIe siècle* (Paris, 1976), 93–125. This process was slow, as was the centralization of the state. See N. Davis's warning against oversimplification in "Deforming the Reformation," *NYR*, Apr. 10, 1969.

6. M. Weber, *The City* (New York, 1958), distinguishes between the ancient city, with its social order characterized by ritual exclusiveness, and the medieval city, where ritual social identity was absent; especially 144, 149. Partly as a result of this absence of ritual separateness, free men exchanged more easily and rationally together; see further 93f, 111f, 155, 183, 223. F. de Coulanges, *The Ancient City* (Garden City, 1956), 394, believed that Christianity represented a revolt against the state, and that politics could govern man without reliance on sacred usages or the consulting of auspices or oracles. That this was not the case will be made clear in this book.

distancing mechanisms to preserve individual privacy and identity?[7] Although these thinkers follow Georg Simmel in rightly noting the importance of ritual in micro-urban life, their derivation of such behavior from the alleged impersonality of the city at large, and their inattention to the devotional roots of all gestural systems (including silence), lead them to neglect the complex fashions in which such intimate ritual did and still does relate to the personality, the honor, and the shame of the political order.[8] The very urban boundaries of distance and intimacy are furnished to city dwellers by authoritative precedence-setters in the public press. At home in the city, individuals learn from modern priestesses of decorum the public behavior that is expected of them in private. Leaving that home for the beach, the football game, the demonstration, or the church, our domestic denizens understand that the street and city remain personal, not cold, and, with some original trepidation, they use the public language of signs to find, and strengthen their place in the social hierarchy of the public stage.[9] We know little of the state of public ritual life in the modern city, and can scarcely judge the extent to which it builds, and transforms, our social structures; a preoccupation with the concept of impersonalism, itself an achievement of a personalistic political order, has kept modern public life from being seriously studied. Yet I suspect that public man has not declined, but has merely added the home as another locus for nationally syndicated behavior.

Was it, or is it, only among the unintegrated groups in the city that ritual has flourished, as Mary Douglas, Harvey Cox, and to some extent Max Gluckman suggest, established groups' ritual having yielded to the abstract and rational forms of communication said to be characteristic of technopolis?[10] As I have indicated, I believe that, although ritual responsi-

7. See Martindale's characterization of Park in Weber's *City*, 22, also R. Sennett, *The Fall of Public Man* (New York, 1976), and the same author's critique of Goffman cited earlier, n. 1. An underlying assumption of some sociopsychologists is that private life can be sincere and spontaneous, but public life is by definition role oriented, routinized, and duplicitous. Why specific cultures make this romantic division is one of the questions posed by J. Shklar, "Let Us Not Be Hypocritical," *Daedalus*, Summer, 1979, pp. 1–25. An astute demolition of the idea of public routine is C. Tilly, "The Routinization of Protest in Nineteenth-Century France," and "The Web of Collective Action in Eighteenth-Century Cities," respectively Working Papers nos. 181, 74 of the *Center for Research on Social Organization*.

8. Weber was aware of the importance of such so-called irrational considerations as honor in the Italian cities; *City*, 95, 102, 222. Scholars have given close attention to the importance of honor and shame in the Mediterranean area, emphasizing, however, the cultural more than the social sources of the phenomenon; J. G. Peristiany (ed.), *Honour and Shame. The Values of Mediterranean Society* (Chicago, 1966); and

a special issue on social and political processes in the Western Mediterranean, *Anthropological Quarterly* XLII, no. 3 (1969).

9. For an absorbing comparison of a German soccer match and a religious and diplomatic ceremony, see M. Lasky, "One Nation, Divisible," *New York Times Magazine*, Sept. 22, 1974, 20 seq. A study of sexual territorialism in sports is A. Dundes, "Into the End-zone for a Touchdown: A Psychoanalytic Consideration of American Football," *Western Folklore* XXXVII (1978), 75–88.

10. Douglas, *Natural Symbols*, 59–76; H. Cox, *The Secular City* (New York, 1965); M. Gluckman, "Les Rites de Passage," in *Essays on the Ritual of Social Relations*, ed. Gluckman (Manchester, 1962), 35. The association of ritual first with "primitive peoples" and of late with the Western lower classes continues to bedevil the best social science long after the traditionally negative attitude of the clericoscholarly world has become history. At first Westerners thought, and primitives did; then the Western upper and lower classes both thought, the former rightly, the latter vestigially "superstitiously," if interestingly;

bility has shifted to the state, ritual activity continues in the establishment that scorns it. As for the earlier period, the evidence in this book suggests that at a certain level of urban development toward organization, coercion, and legitimation, ritual patterns were more evident among established groups than among immigrants. In the medieval city, establishment ritual predominated, and the public ritual of urbanizing groups was inhibited because they were excluded from the streets, from organizations, and from citizenship. Ritual was not an activity of the periphery.

Finally, what *is* this behavior called *ritual*? Distinctions abound in the literature of the social sciences. Liturgy and devotional customs are different, we are told. Ceremony and ritual have been distinguished, as have secular and religious ritual. Public and private formal behavior have been the subjects of separate discourses, and scientists attempt to discover the distinction between language and speech, and between conscious and unconscious behavioral patterns.[11] Yet when we examine the results of this ongoing attempt to classify formal activities, we find among historians only parochial treatises on one isolated ritual process or the other, and absolutely no consensus among social scientists as to what constitutes the essential divisions among these various distinctions. This diversity in the understanding of ritual tempts me to cast the net wide, and leads me to believe that only by interrelating these different aspects of ritual can we arrive at a general comprehension of the role of form in urban life of the premodern period. By ritual I shall mean formal behavior, those verbal and bodily actions of humans that, in specific contexts of space and time, become relatively fixed into those recognizable social and cultural deposits we call behavioral forms. The purpose of ritual, I believe, is to achieve goals; it is not obsessive or irrational, but ecologically adaptive. The mode of ritual is simultaneously

and today the lower classes are said to have a belief system ("popular culture") equally as valuable as, if sealed off from, that of the technopolis, and often from its politics. A sophisticated view of a distinct "popular culture" is given by E. Thompson, "The Moral Economy of the English Crowd in the Eighteenth Century," *Past and Present* L (1971), 76–136, and "Patrician Society, Plebeian Culture," *Journal of Social History* VII (1974), 382–405. K. Thomas' pathfinding *Religion and the Decline of Magic* provides a good example of the uncertainty about the "lower classes" in contemporary historical writing; the original subtitle (*Studies in Popular "Beliefs"*—my quotation marks) was dropped from the later paperback edition. Two brilliant studies that avoid disintegrating culture by group, and succeed in studing meaning through general societal behavior, are P. Brown, "The Rise and Function of the Holy Man in Late Antiquity," *Journal of Roman Studies* LXI (1971), 80–101, and "A Dark-Age Crisis: Aspects of the Iconoclastic Controversy," *English Historical Review* LXXXVIII (1973), 1–34.

11. Ritual as action and ritual as belief are examined by C. Crocker in "Ritual and the Development of Social Structure: Liminality and Inversion," in Shaughnessy, *Roots of Ritual,* 47–86. The relation between conscious and unconscious ritual is discussed in many articles edited by J. Huxley, "A Discussion on Ritualization of Behavior in Animals and Man, *Philosophical Transactions of the Royal Society of London,* ser. B, CCLI (1966), 247–526. R. Firth distinguishes between communicative and acommunicative ritual in "Verbal and Bodily Rituals of Greeting and Parting," in J. La Fontaine (ed.), *The Interpretation of Ritual* (London, 1973), 2. J. Goody distinguishes between ceremony and ritual in "Religion and Ritual: The Definitional Problem," *British Journal of Sociology* XII (1961), 157 seq. The Burg Wartenstein Symposium no. 64 addressed itself exclusively to this topic: *Secular Ritual Considered: Prolegomena toward a Theory of Ritual, Ceremony and Formality* (Aug. 24–Sept. 1, 1974). R. Rappaport derives religious ritual viewed as communication from the sacred viewed as unquestioned beliefs; "The Sacred in Human Evolution," *Annual Review of Ecology and Systematics* II (1971), 23–44.

contractual and conflictual. The result of ritual action is, finally, the small- or large-scale transformation of both the actor and the audience to the transaction.

Source limitations have admittedly forced three particular emphases. This work deals more with consciously adopted than intuitive behavior, more with group than individual activity, more with public than private display. Despite these limitations, however, the interrelated nature of different types of formal behavior remains a central thesis of this work. It is definitely necessary to break down the subject–object, viewer–artifact bias of Western studies. As Peter Brown has correctly insisted, it is impossible to understand what is happening in a work of art without giving attention to "the crowd beneath the mosaics";[12] neither can we analyze a festival or procession and ignore the audience. It is just as important to refuse an artificially imposed divine–human or religious–secular dichotomy: The behaviors of one person kneeling before the Christian image and another bowed before a secular ruler are symmetrical, and should be studied as such. In rejecting the polarizing objectifications of modern science, the student has on his side the mind-set of the urbanites he now approaches. They too recognized the public utility of private devotion and the private effects of public processions. They knew that sacred and profane acts had profane and sacred implications, that the game could be ominous and the Mass frivolous, that pomp and intention were inextricable. They were sure that no essential quality distinguished manifestations of effective form, for all took place beneath the sacred canopy.

Our subject then is that chironomic prescription of form that leads animals and man to greet in a like manner;[13] moved Quintilian to recommend certain finger positions if exhorting;[14] encouraged our ancestor to bare his left shoulder while kneeling before the king if he desired to avoid death;[15] and today governs the proper way to enter audience with the pope; requires the Christian, Hindu, Buddhist, or Mohammedan propitiator to assume different prayer attitudes for different ends and deities;[16] and prescribes different movements to cure our different diseases.[17] Our setting is a communal life where private emotions unfolded in public rituals to save the whole and each of its parts.

Formal behavior was as alive with meaning in the Renaissance as in any other culture. Yet this simple fact has long been ignored by historians,

12. P. Brown, "The View from the Precipice," *NYR*, Oct. 3, 1974, p. 3.

13. I. Eibl-Eibesfeldt, *Love and Hate* (New York, 1971).

14. *Institutio Oratoria* (London, 1922), bk. XI, ch. 3.

15. Pfandl, *Philipp II*, 122.

16. T. Ohm, *Die Gebetsgebärden der Völker und das Christentum* (Leiden, 1948).

17. As, for example, the gestural recommendations of the Florentine physician Antonio Benivieni; L.

Thorndike, *A History of Magic and Experimental Science*, 8 vols. (New York, 1923–1958), IV, 588. Physical actions for dealing with the problems of pregnancy were known to the Florentines through the work of Soranus, *Gynecology* (Baltimore, 1956), 45–68. See also vol. III of Hippocrates, *On Joints*, in Loeb Classical Library (Cambridge, Mass., 1959), 201–397. P. Laín Entralgo has a suggestive study of *The Therapy of the Word in Classical Antiquity* (New Haven, 1970), with many references to motor therapies.

heirs of a tradition that speaks of the period as one of individualism, in which men shattered forms to achieve "the ego revolution par excellence."[18] It was a seductive message for the modern world. Despite the fact that no period of Western history was more preoccupied with correct behavior than this one, its students have preferred to follow Luther and avow the meaninglessness of what men formally did. If verbocentric historians of humanism and the arts have followed the German reformer's avocation for the Word, they have pursued the history of thought, not rhetoric. That waif of the historian's progeny has been studied not to find its meaning, but to dispute whether rhetoric had one, whether words were sincere. In the nineteenth century, Renaissance humanists were viewed as servants of tyrants; their verbal forms meant nothing. In the twentieth century Hans Baron has maintained that Florentine rhetoric was related to politics, and did have content. Now late in the century of Wittgenstein, some critics of Baron want to return to the older and primitive view of verbal and bodily formalism as "mere forms."[19]

There is of course no such thing as "mere form," and inversely there never has been a factuality without form, a "politics of force" where forms were or could be ignored.[20] Viewing the Renaissance individualist as anti-form always has been silly science; now it is manifestly dated nineteenth-century liberal ideology. This book will leave most questions unanswered. But as it hopes to bring historical dimension to urban and behavioral studies, so it intends to modernize the discourse among Renaissance historians.

18. The term is E. Erikson's; *Young Man Luther* (New York, 1962), 193. The standard work on Renaissance historiography is W. Ferguson, *The Renaissance in Historical Thought* (Cambridge, Mass., 1948). For study of the "Renaissance question" see W. Bouwsma, "The Renaissance and the Drama of Western History," *American Historical Review* LXXXIV (1979), 1–15.

19. See, for example, P. Herde, "Politische Verhaltensweisen der Florentinischen Oligarchie, 1382–1402," in *Geschichte und Verfassungsgefüge. Frankfurter Festgabe für W. Schlesinger* (Wiesbaden, 1973), 161–249. More sophisticated opponents of Baron's views see humanistic rhetorical forms as evolving, but in response to the internal laws of style rather than those

of politics; see, for example, J. Seigel, *Rhetoric and Philosophy in Renaissance Humanism* (Princeton, 1968). Others have pursued the Renaissance thinkers' insight that forms can persuade and thus change those exposed to them, but have limited themselves to verbal forms and not studied how the orators thought their bodily motions affected and transformed audiences; H. Gray, "Renaissance Humanism, The Pursuit of Eloquence," *Journal of the History of Ideas* XXIV (1963), 497–514. Baron's fundamental work is *The Crisis of the Early Italian Renaissance* (Princeton, 1966).

20. Presumably an operative concept of Machiavelli and his time; F. Gilbert, *Machiavelli and Guicciardini* (Princeton, 1965), 131 and *passim*.

Public Life in
Renaissance Florence

PART I

THE FRAMEWORK
OF RITUAL

Rituals do what words cannot say. . . .
*Actions speak louder than words.**

Elaborate public ritual was one of the distinctive elements of the European city during the Middle Ages and the Renaissance. Many differences separated the religious life of the city from that of the countryside and villages of Europe, but the most important one was this: The city developed a separate processional identity, a technical apparatus maintained by citizens and professional religiothespians appointed to protect, expand, profit, and honor the commune.[1]

The mature city's sacrality had humble beginnings, probably to be located in the private purchase of relics by its merchants and clerics.[2] Civic cultivation of holiness,

*D. Pocock in the Foreword to M. Mauss, *A General Theory of Magic* (New York, 1972), 4.

1. Differences between urban and rural or village religion are considered by D. Pocock, "Sociologies: Urban and Rural," *Contributions to Indian Sociology* IV (1960), 63–81; P. Hauser, "Observations on the Urban–Folk and Urban–Rural Dichotomies as Forms of Western Ethnocentrism," in Hauser and L. Schnore (eds.), *The Study of Urbanization* (New York, 1965), 503–517. See also Trexler, "Ritual Behavior in Renaissance Florence: The Setting," *Medievalia et Humanistica*, n.s. IV (1973), 130, 136.

2. On relics in cities, P. Geary, *Furta Sacra. Thefts of Relics in the Central Middle Ages* (Princeton, 1978), 106–

131. The predominantly private nature of relic acquisition in Florence before about 1300 is evident from the information in R. Davidsohn, *Storia di Firenze*, 8 vols. (Florence, 1956–1968), VI, 485f; VII, 115ff. At this early point, relics obtained by the bishopric of Florence were not considered obtained by the commune; the two were separate entities, with separate patrons. Evidence: In the twelfth century epileptics came to the tomb of S. Zanobi; Davidsohn, *Storia*, I, 1059. But this first bishop of Florence was the patron of the bishop of Florence and not of the city; cf. *Archivio Arcivescovile, Firenze* (hereafter *AAF*) *filza cartapecore* 1321–1389, ff. 10v–11r, dated Dec. 1321, which

the conversion of the city into a ceremonial center, came later, when farsighted burghers and lords saw that their profits could be enlarged and the quality of the center heightened if foreigners came for worship as well as trading.[3] *Civil self-identity grew up around the civic altar which came to harbor the precious possessions of patron saints.*[4] *Contracts were made there, since the trust necessary for commercial transactions often rested upon the altars of the relics.*

names Zanobi as a patron of the see, but omits St. John the Baptist, with *Archivio di Stato, Firenze, Provvisioni* (hereafter ASF, *Prov.*), 1, f. 12r (1284), a governmental document, which lists the Baptist as one of those under whose name the city is governed, but omits Zanobi. Only in the course of the fourteenth century did Zanobi become a communal saint, and Giovanni an episcopal one. While recording the first offering made by the Parte Guelfa to Zanobi (1392), a diarist explains the reason for the latter's tardy incorporation into the civic pantheon: The saint had been a member of the Girolami family, whose members were "all Ghibellines"; *Biblioteca Nazionale, Firenze, fondo Panciatichi* (hereafter BNF, Panciatichi), 158. f. 170r, now edited by A. Molho and F. Sznura, *Alle Bocche della Piazza. Diario di anonimo fiorentino (1382-1401)* (Florence, 1986).

3. P. Wheatley, *The Pivot of the Four Quarters* (Chicago, 1971), ch. 3, examines the nature of the ceremonial center. On the relations of relics to civil identity, see H. Peyer, *Stadt und Stadtpatron im Mittelalterlichen Italien* (Zurich, 1955), 5–11 and *passim*. Unlike Florence, Milan seems to have prepared chamber of commerce–type books listing the location of bodies and the indulgences attached to them. See the 1288 boast of Bonvesin de la Riva that Milan and its countryside (*contado*) possessed seventy saints' bodies; *Storia di Milano (Fondazione Treccani degli Alfieri)*, IX, pt. 2 (Milan, 1961), 568f; also P. Borella, "Corpi Santi in Milano e Diocesi," in *Studi in onore di Carlo Castiglioni* (Milan, 1957), 131–158; C. Cattaneo, "I 'libri indulgentiarum' di Milano nei secoli XIV–XVI," *ibid.*, 253—257. There were of course lists of relics prepared for separate chuches in Florence, as required by canon law, and there is one indication of a list of indulgences attached to a painting:

> *E vidi le lasagne*
> *Andare a Prato a vedere il Sudario*
> *E ciascuna portava l'inventario*

Burchiello, *I Sonetti*, ed. A. Viviani (Milan, 1940), 12. But Florence's relics seem rather to have been listed only in rituals, books not intended for tourists. See, for example, ASF, *Carte Strozziane*, II, 56; *Ritus in Ecclesia servandi, Biblioteca Riccardiana, Firenze* (hereafter *Riccardiana*), 3005; D. Moreni (ed.), *Mores et Consuetudines Ecclesiae Florentinae* (Florence, 1794), all three antedating 1350.

4. A review of the communal acquisition of relics shows first that the patrons S. Reparata and the Baptist, if not Zanobi, were apparently long

adored before their relics were obtained, and second that although the commune was active in buying relics throughout our period, the peak efforts were between 1300 and 1450. Here is an overview of communal activity: In 1311 the Guelfs of Florence obtained relics of S. Barnabas, on whose day in 1289 Florence had defeated the Guidi at Campaldino; *Croniche di Giovanni, Matteo, e Filippo Villani*, 2 vols. (Trieste, 1857), G. Villani, bk. IX, ch. 13. The civil festivities surrounding the translation or movement of the relics of S. Zanobi took place in 1331; *ibid.*, X, 171. In 1334 the city obtained relics of S. Jacopo and S. Alesso, and part of Jesus's loincloth; *ibid.*, XI, 9. It purchased in 1352 (faked) relics of S. Reparata because, said one contemporary, its cathedral church had had other names, but hers was the normal one; *Cronaca Fiorentina di Marchionne di Coppo Stefani* (hereafter Stefani), ed. N. Rodolico, *Rerum Italicarum Scriptores*, n.s. (hereafter RIS), XXX, pt. 1, rub. 241; also M. Villani, III, 15, 16. In 1357 the remains of Pope Stephen were found; *ibid.*, VII, 91. The first relics of the Baptist, along with those of others, were obtained in 1393 from a Florentine merchant and a widow in Venice; *Cronica Volgare di Anonimo Fiorentino dall'anno 1385 al 1409 già attribuita a Piero di Giovanni Minerbetti* (hereafter, P. Minerbetti), ed. E. Bellondi, RIS, XXVII, 172f. In 1411 the commune almost bought the Baptist's head from Pope John XXIII for 50,000 florins; Filarete, *Treatise*, 45, n. 5. Shortly thereafter it obtained a finger of the same saint from that pope; ASF, *Prov.*, 110, ff. 204rv (Jan. 27, 1420 Florentine style, 1421 modern style, the Florentine year starting Mar. 25; hereafter, e.g., 1420/1421, with all nondifferentiated years in the modern style). In the 1440s the architect Filarete apparently tried to steal the Baptist's head in Rome, seemingly acting as an agent of the commune; *Treatise, loc. cit.* Relics acquired after 1450 were of nonpatrons: In 1451 the arm of S. Verdiana was obtained from a dominion rector; G. Richa, *Notizie Istoriche delle Chiese Fiorentine*, 10 vols. (Florence, 1754–1762), II, 230. In 1454 the commune bought relics purportedly emanating from Constantinople; *Priorista di Paolo di Matteo Pietrobuoni* (hereafter Pietrobuoni), BNF, *Conventi Religiosi Soppressi*, C-4-895, ff. 167rv. Council debates on the purchase of these relics are in ASF, *Consulte e Pratiche* (hereafter CP), 53, ff. 86r–89v; also on this purchase see *Ricordi Storici di Filippo di Cino Rinuccini dal 1282 al 1460, colla continuazione di Alamanno e Neri suoi figli fino al 1506* (hereafter Rinuccini), ed. G. Aiazzi (Florence, 1840), lxxxii. In 1532 many containers of relics were pre-

On their name days, the city saints were lifted from their occult sources and shown to the populace and to visitors. These days commonly were or became fair days, when business activity was particularly marked.[5] The clergy who lifted the veil to reveal the naked sanctity of the holy developed for this unveiling a theatrical setting, which became the movable or processional identity of the city.[6] Visitors from the countryside and sometimes from afar entered the city on these days to view this sight while pursuing their interests.

To foster the religious fame and commercial wealth of the city, rulers granted safe-conducts to all those in their dominion, and procured them for all travelers within the lands of surrounding nobles. The stated reason for such safe-conducts was a desire to make indulgences and blessings available to those who visited the churches containing the saints. Persons coming on the saints' days could not be arrested, even for debts previously incurred.[7] Nonviolence and safety were associated with urban religion as well as with trade.

As the city became a sacred asylum with its own civic calendar and sacred objects, the surrounding countryside was robbed of shrines and thus of indigenous religious elements. The religious significance of the countryside to the city declined as the

sented to the city by Pope Clement VII; Luca Landucci, *Diario Fiorentino dal 1450 al 1516 continuato da un anonimo fino al 1542*, ed. I. Del Badia (Florence, 1969), 370; B. Varchi, *Storia Fiorentina*, 2 vols. (Florence, 1963), bk. XIII, ch. 9.

At Venice the acquisition of the relics of St. Mark coincided with the development of an ecclesiastical and political center; A. Galante, "Per la Storia Giuridica della Basilica di S. Marco," *Zeitschrift der Savignystiftung für Rechtsgeschichte, Kanonistische Abteilung* XXXIII (1912), 283f. On the relation between holy bodies and civil identity at Milan, see *Storia di Milano*, IX, pt. 2, 553, 567f. And on the altar of the city (*ara civitatis*) at Strassburg as a focal point of civil identity, see L. Pfleger, "Die Stadt und Rats-Gottesdienste im Strassburger Münster," *Archiv für Elsässische Kirchengeschichte* XII (1937), 4.

5. A feast of Mary was a fair day at nearby Prato; Ser Lapo Mazzei, *Lettere di un Notaio a un Mercante del secolo XIV con altre Lettere e Documenti*, ed. C. Guasti, 2 vols. (Florence, 1880), I, 34. More on this relationship in V. Turner, "The Center Out There: Pilgrim's Goal," *History of Religions* XII (1972), 204, 208. Linguistically, trade days and sacred days are linked: *foire, feria*; *Messe*, market, Mass.

6. Civic mobile identity around relics with clerics as masters of ceremonies can be glimpsed clearly at York; J. Fowler, "The Life and Miracles of Saint William of York," *Yorkshire Archaeological and Topographical Journal* III (1875), 198–348. See also C. Phythian-Adams, "Ceremony and the Citizen in the Communal Year at Coventry," in P. Clark and P. Slack (eds.), *Crisis and Order in English Towns, 1500–1700* (London, 1972), 57–85. On the procession as a reenactment of the translation of saints (an equivalent of taking the saint for a walk), see G. Moroni, *Dizionario di erudi-*

zione storico-ecclesiastica, 103 vols. (Venice, 1840–1879), LV, 257; LXXIX, 168 seq.

7. For early evidence of safe-conducts for trade, see *The Cambridge Economic History of Europe* III (Cambridge, 1963), 128–131. Debt collection was suspended on feast days for ostensibly charitable reasons: "Since we want to ask God's grace, we ought to be liberal to our neighbors"; *L'Ordine delle Processioni che hanno a fare per la Città e Distretto di Firenze*, BNF, Custode, B-9, f. 2 (1518). Such suspensions are encountered in Siena in 1296; W. Bowsky, *The Finance of the Commune of Siena, 1287–1355* (Oxford, 1970), 32. The first statutory safe-conducts for attending the feast of the Baptist in Florence that I encountered were in 1407, probably much later than in fact; ASF, *Prov.*, 96, ff. 23rv (Apr. 29). Subsequent ones are in *Statuta Populi et Communis Florentiae*, 3 vols. (Fribourg, 1778), I, 190 (1415) (hereafter *Statuta*); ASF, *Prov.*, 110, ff. 122r–123r (Oct. 16, 1420); 117, ff. 48rv (June 6, 1427); 117, ff. 92r–93r (June 13, 1427); 128, ff. 279v–280r (Mar. 13, 1437/1438); 131, ff. 293rv (Jan. 28, 1439/1440); 136, ff. 260v–261v (Feb. 17, 1445/1446); 139, ff. 186rv (Dec. 30, 1448); 140, ff. 298v–299r (Feb. 29, 1449/1450); 172, ff. 132r–133r (Dec. 21, 1481); 172, ff. 145r–146v (Feb. 7, 1481/1482); 182, ff. 15v–16v (Apr. 26, 1491).

Cities commonly used these safe-conducts when a famed preacher was in town, evidently for both religious and economic reasons. Thus S. Bernardino of Siena urged the Sienese authorities to do this, since many other cities had done the same for him; *Le Prediche Volgari* (Siena, 1425), ed. C. Cannarozzi, 2 vols. (Florence, 1958), II, 90; *Le Prediche Volgari* (Siena, 1427), ed. P. Bargellini (Milan, 1936), 373. A Milanese safe-conduct is recorded in Cattaneo, "Libri Indulgentiarum," 264f (1480).

religious and economic attraction of the central place grew. There developed a geography of ritual: Hundreds of shrines competed for the prayers of devotees in the Tuscan town of Prato, said one contemporary, but the countryside was almost empty of holy places.[8]

As cities expanded militarily, their soldiers added ritual ridicule to military action so as to destroy the sacrality of neighboring towns. During sieges they minted coins outside the walls and ran horse races around the perimeter, while whores raced each other past the enemy's gates. The intent was to frighten and bring despair upon the surrounded community, convincing it that not even its patron saints were capable of saving it from such insults.[9] Could a town ignored by the heavens be saved? Indeed, the besiegers sometimes disarmed those foreign saints by praying to them to support their cause and not that of the antagonists. They urged the native saints to withdraw (evocatio). Thus in 1260 the Sienese could brag that "it had been of little worth [to the defeated Florentines] to ask S. Zanobi and S. Reparata to aid them."[10]

8. Mazzei, I, 106 (1395). J. Russell uses Central Place theory in his *Medieval Regions and their Cities* (Bloomington, 1972). A theoretical review is in B. Berry and C. Harris, "Central Place," *International Encyclopedia of the Social Sciences* II (1968), 365–379. The theory does not, to my knowledge, comprehend centrality as a religious phenomenon. R. Brentano notes the meager number of distant Italian pilgrimage goals in *Two Churches. England and Italy in the Thirteenth Century* (Princeton, 1968), 225, 233f. At Lyon, citizens did publicly visit outside shrines; Davis, "Sacred."

9. See the Dragomanni edition (1844–1845) of the *Cronica* of the Villani, I, 555, for information on such insult rituals. Coining of money, consecration of knights, dances, and the like by the Pisans under the walls of Lucca in 1263: Davidsohn, *Storia*, II, 758f; also VII, 568f. At the siege of Arezzo in 1288–1289 the Florentines ran a horse race (*palio*) around the city and mocked the Aretines with mitered ass-heads representing the besieged's ex-bishop; G. Villani, VII, 120, 132; Davidsohn, *Storia*, III, 465. In 1292 the Florentines ran the *palio* near the gates of Pisa; G. Villani, VII, 154. In 1325 the Luccan general Castracani "in dispetto e vergogna de' Fiorentini [fece] correre tre palii delle nostre Mosse infino a Peretola, l'uno a gente a cavallo, e l'altro a piede, e l'altro a femmine meretrici"; *ibid.*, IX, 317. In 1386 a German mercenary captain had a painting of the Anziani of Bologna made with them hanging by the feet and then had a prostitute carry it around the Bolognese *contado*; Ps. Minerbetti, 24. In 1363 the Florentine captain at the gates of Pisa had "all possible vituperations done": coining, races of gamblers and whores, and so on; Giovanni di Pagolo Morelli, *Ricordi*, ed. V. Branca (Florence, 1956), 308. Further evidence of insult ritual is in A. Pucci, "Guerra Pisana," in *Delizie degli Eruditi Toscani* (hereafter *Delizie*), ed. I. da San Luigi, 24 vols. (Florence, 1770–1789), VI, 193f, 223, and 235 on Pisan

rituals *in dispetto di Firenze*; also F. Villani, XI, 97. During the 1530 siege of Florence, the besiegers solemnly buried the Marzocco (figured lion) of Florence outside the city, with bells ringing; Varchi, XI, 58. Another example in Bologna in 1488: Landucci, 55. For paintings done before and during battles in order to harm the enemy, see Davidsohn, *Storia*, IV, 323f, 330f.

10. Peyer, *Stadtpatron*, 50. On the *evocatio* of St. Ambrose by the Florentines in 1423, see page 287, this volume. The (presumed) Florentine attempts to steal the most important Pratese relic during the war of 1313 are described in Davidsohn, *Storia*, IV, 616ff; VII, 424. In the twelfth century pro- and anti-Roman parties in Milan accused each other of trying to neutralize, respectively, St. Ambrose and St. Peter; Peyer, *Stadtpatron*, 31. In 1476 in Milan plotters against the Sforza urged Ambrose to prove he was not in favor of tyranny; N. Machiavelli, *History of Florence* (New York, 1960), 353 (bk. VII, ch. 6). The religious orders used evocation against each other. Thus the Dominicans tried to protect their leader Savonarola at his fire trial by praying to Franciscan saints; J. Schnitzer, *Savonarola und die Feuerprobe (Quellen und Forschungen zur Geschichte Savonarolas*, 4 vols. [Munich, 1902–1910]), II, 105. Conversely, it was thought that Florence had been freed from Savonarola through the prayers of St. Francis; E. Sanesi, *Vicari e Canonici Fiorentini e il "Caso Savonarola"* (Florence, 1932), 19. Information on the Roman practice of *evocatio* is in G. Wissowa, *Religion und Kultus der Römer* (Munich, 1912), 39, 321f. In 1269 Florentines spared the Sienese war wagon (*Carroccio*) from their destructive fury "chè v'era entro dipinta la Nostra Donna." Instead they brought the wagon to Florence and hung it in the Baptistry; *Cronica di Paolino Pieri Fiorentino delle Cose d'Italia dall'Anno 1080 fino all'Anno 1305*, ed. A. Adami (Rome, 1755), 37 (hereafter Paolino Pieri).

Spoliation followed victory: The victors wheeled their sacred wagon through the streets of the fallen town, whose holy objects were carted off to the capital, thereby robbing it of its sacrality.[11] *In a gesture of magnanimity the conquering city might return the town's saint to prevent complete despair, but the understanding remained that the conqueror had the right to desacralize his conquered hinterland, and that the subject town preserved its identity only through the grace and intercession of the conquerors; the capital might even prescribe on what feast days the satellites could unveil their relics.*[12] *Thus divine services in the hinterland lost their local meaning, though relics of former community might remain in place.*

The conquering city replaced the old local ritual of community with its own, introducing the cult of its patron saint into the countryside, which in worshiping this new saint effectively celebrated its own loss of sovereignty.[13] *It was not just the object of worship that became the same, however, but the worship itself. Subject towns and villages celebrated the capital's feasts on the same days and hours with the same prayers as did the capital.*[14] *Ambitious citizens of the conquered towns, deserting the fraternity of their birth, had their children baptized not at their own baptismal font but at that of the new rulers. Thus the city-state was born from the city: a holy enclave surrounded by a desacralized country, a center whose altars dictated the motions of suburban satellites.*

The Florentines achieved this desacralized landscape despite major obstacles. During the rise of the commune, for example, the Tuscan countryside was one of the most sacred areas of Europe, a fact that could have diminished the attraction of the capital. The homeland of the Camaldolan founder and miracle-worker Romualdo was in the distretto, *as was that of the Vallombrosan founder Giovanni Gualberto de'*

11. In 1362 Florentines dismantled the great chains across the port of Pisa, dragged them to Florence "per dirizione" and "per dispetto de'Pisani e per rispetto della nuova vittoria de' Fiorentini," and hung them in front of San Giovanni; M. Villani, XI, 30. They are visible in Plate 10. In 1422 the head of S. Rossore came to Florence from a church in Pisa after the latter had fallen to Florence in 1406. In the words of a sixteenth-century writer, Pisa, after being "deprived of liberty and of its ancient honors, was further abandoned by its saints, and there against the city of Florence filled itself with pomp, with glory, with riches, and with benediction"; S. Ammirato, *Istorie Fiorentine* VI (Florence, 1826), 429; also Pietrobuoni, f. 107r. In 1430 the vestry (*opera*) of the cathedral considered the acquisition of the relics in the Pisan *distretto* town of Vada; A. Doren, *Le Arti Fiorentine*, 2 vols. (Florence, 1940), II, 244f. In 1503 the tunic of St. Francis was brought to Florence after the commune seized Aretine Monte Aguto; Landucci, 253f; see also the description of Filepepi in P. Villari and E. Casanova (eds.), *Scelta di Prediche e Scritti di fra Girolamo Savonarola* (Florence, 1898), 473.

12. Thus the head of S. Donato of Arezzo was first "stolen" by the mercenaries when they conquered

the city for Florence in 1384, and then obtained by Florence. It was borne in the entry procession of the new Florentine bishop on Jan. 29, 1386, then ostentatiously honored by placement alongside S. Zanobi's head in the cathedral, before finally being returned to Arezzo in March; Panciatichi, ff. 150va; also *Diario d'Anonimo fiorentino dall'Anno 1358 al 1389,* in *Cronache dei Secoli XIII e XIV*, ed. A. Gherardi (Florence, 1876), 463. The case of Florence controlling the unveiling of Prato's main relic is documented on page 98, this volume.

13. For the extension of S. Zanobi into the rest of the diocese, see R. Trexler, *Synodal Law in Florence and Fiesole, 1306–1518* (Vatican City, 1971), 30f. On Venetian use of the *laudes* as part of its imperialization of Dalmatia, see Kantorowicz, *Laudes Regiae*, 153–156. The Florentines had paintings made showing the Pisans at the feet of S. Giovanni, the conquerors' patron; see page 124, this volume.

14. See the mandate in *ASF, Missive*, 22, f. 139v (June 3, 1391). To complement the Florentine celebration of the Sforza conquest of Milan, the government "mandossi a notificare a tutte le terre e amici che ne facessino festa"; Pietrobuoni, f. 152r (1450).

Bisdomini, the mother-house of the Servites, and the stigma-friary of the Franciscans. Florence fostered these orders' growth, in part because of the strategic military importance of their houses' locations. Yet the latter did not become important pilgrimage centers until mid-Renaissance, a fact that can be attributed in part to a conscious policy of the city. Until the political identity of the city was irreversibly established, burghers preferred that visitors come to Florence, and citizens' alms made the urban monasteries of these orders the center of their activities.[15]

The city competed for pilgrims as it competed for trade, excluding only those who were part of mass movements that might endanger urban stability. Rome of course was an overweening competitor, but Florence welcomed Rome-bound pilgrims and encouraged them to stay.[16] It kept its own citizens at home. By buying Roman jubilee indulgences the city fathers enabled residents and prospective visitors to receive the same indulgence in seven Florentine churches as they would have obtained by visiting the seven churches of Rome. The success of these efforts can be judged by communal receipts from wine gabelles, which far exceeded the norm in these indulgence years.[17]

Fundamentally antagonistic to the sacralization of its own countryside, the city never sponsored a pilgrimage or procession to a place outside the walls, and required Florentine pilgrims to return by sunset and spend the evening in town. As in the field of education and spas, so in the religious realm the city developed resources calculated to discourage citizen tourism and encourage visitors.[18] The republic never ceased the systematic acquisition of holy things and the development of a staggering ceremonial calendar to honor them.

In the fifteenth century this picture was modified. Encouraged by a more tolerant

15. Especially Servite and Camaldolan activities were centered in the city. For the latter, see J. Schnitzer, *Peter Delfin* (Munich, 1926), 29–32.

16. Davidsohn, *Storia*, VII, 153. As early as the mid-twelfth century, Florence was impeding the efforts of pilgrims to visit even nearby relics; see the papal warning to the bishop of Florence *ibid.*, I, 1058.

17. C. de la Roncière, "Indirect Taxes or 'Gabelles' at Florence in the Fourteenth Century: The Evolution of Tariffs and Problems of Collection," in N. Rubinstein (ed.), *Florentine Studies* (London, 1968), 167. Communal activity in obtaining Roman indulgences may have started as late as the Black Death; see the indulgence of May 16, 1348, in C. Guasti and A. Gherardi (eds.), *I Capitoli del Comune di Firenze* II (Florence, 1893), 489. Among the innumerable later indulgences negotiated by the commune was that of 1414, "like [the one at] St. John Lateran in Rome"; "Diario Fiorentino di Bartolommeo di Michele Del Corazza" (hereafter Del Corazza), ed. G. Corazzini, *Archivio Storico Italiano* (hereafter *ASI*), ser. 5, vol. XIV (1894), 253. Florentine repetitions of Roman jubilee indulgences were purchased in 1476: Rinuccini, 235, 237f, 238f, 241f, 246ff; in 1501: Landucci, 218, and in 1526. *Ricordanze di Bartolomeo Masi Calderaio Fiorentino dal*

1478 al 1526 (hereafter Masi), ed. G. Corazzini (Florence, 1906), 281f. In 1481 six Florentine churches were listed for a Roman pardon; Landucci, 37. In 1516 Pope Leo appointed seven chapels in the cathedral as equivalents of the seven churches of Rome and set out a series of Stations equivalent to the Roman ones; Masi, 189–192. In 1526 Pope Clement appointed seven equivalent Florentine churches for the Florentine jubilee; *ibid.*, 281f.

18. The government advertised the city's one-time indulgences to its subjects, so that the latter would journey to Florence; *Ser Giusto d'Anghiari, Memorie, 1437–1488* (hereafter ser Giusto), BNF, Class XXV, codex 496, f. 138v (1481). Prohibitions against citizens taking the baths or education abroad are described in A. Molho, *Florentine Public Finances in the Early Renaissance* (Cambridge, Mass., 1971), 134f. A prohibition against remaining outside the city overnight is in Ps. Minerbetti, 241f; an exception is noted on page 148, this volume. Davidsohn gives a meager list of pilgrimage goals in the area compiled from testamentary bequests; *Storia*, VII, 147–154. I have no present evidence of immigrants periodically returning to their home parishes for the *sacra*, or for prayers to and favors from such extra-Florentine divinities.

governmental attitude, dominion and rural shrines slowly started to take hold. This was part of a more general social phenomenon: Florentine patrician circles were emphasizing the rural villa as the appropriate residence of the leisured bourgeoisie. Not surprisingly, patrician rural churches often became miracle-churches in the process. If in the old days pilgrims from the dominion streamed into Florence to visit the Lady of Or San Michele, and the Lady of the rural village of Impruneta had to be brought to the city to work her wonders, now Florentines increasingly visited Bibbiena, Prato, Pistoia, Loretto, and La Verna, areas in the dominion or beyond where miracles occurred.[19]

The traditional civism of sacrality was, however, by no means destroyed. The fifteenth century was after all the golden century of the Lady of the Annunziata, a city cult fostered by the Medici that drew visitors from throughout Europe.[20] *And with the overthrow of that family in 1494, the Florentines turned against the dominion shrines, urged by their preachers to spend their time, prayer, and money in the city.*[21]

The sacred was then directly involved in the development of the European city. It was no mere pawn in the profit and power game, but a fundamental part of civic identity. Religion in practice was a union of utility and salvation: The pilgrim coming for the indulgence while selling his wares at the market did not lay aside his bargaining techniques when he approached the altar. The city became a center of trade in salvation as it did for material commodities. The gods who responded were city gods.

Was the desacralization process replicated in other areas of Europe? Can one discover a decline in the importance of public religious ritual in conquered areas around other medieval cities? What is the nature of the ritual interchanges inhabitants of the hinterlands did continue to live by? The answers to these questions will depend on

19. When in the early fourteenth century the preacher Giordano da Rivalto spoke out against pilgrimages, he had in mind a mere trip to San Gallo just outside the walls; *Prediche del beato fra Giordano da Rivalto dell'Ordine dei Predicatori: Recitate in Firenze dal MCCCIII al MCCCVI*, ed. D. Moreni, 2 vols. (Florence, 1831), sermon 23 (hereafter Giordano da Rivalto–Moreni). Sometime before the 1440s the practice of group pilgrimages from Florence to nearby Impruneta grew (see page 408, this volume) and by the mid-fifteenth century rural miracles were increasingly drawing Florentine attention to distant goals in the dominion. In 1446 a Virgin-image at Montevarchi became real; H. Aliotti, *Epistolae et Opuscula*, 2 vols. (Arezzo, 1769), I, 187. In 1459 a host in the Mugello would not melt; *AAF, Atti Straordinari*, ser Domenico da Figline, I, ff. 155r–170r. At the end of the century miracles came thick and fast: the Bibbiena Virgin started to change colors in 1482; Landucci, 41. The miracles at S. Maria delle Carceri started at Prato in 1484; *ibid.*, 47. The Queen of Heaven started sweating at Pistoia in 1490; P. Vigo (ed.), *Una Confraternità di Giovanetti Pistoiesi a principio del secolo XVI (Compagnia della Purità)* (Bologna, 1887), 84. This proliferation was accompanied by the commune now entering into the business of regulating rural shrines. La Verna came under its protection and administration in 1431; *ASF, Prov.*, 123, ff. 136rv (June 28, 1432); 124, ff. 169v–172r (Aug. 11, 1433), and in 1476 the government obtained a pardon for visitors to La Verna; Rinuccini, 228, 241. On the association between rural patrician homesteads and miracles, note the remark of the legist Piero degli Ubaldi (c. 1400) that many magnates and nobles had rural possessions "at the entrance of which are walls in which is depicted the image of the Blessed Virgin Mary and other saints. And miracles are said to have happened at them, because of which men stream to this place for devotions, [and] they offer much [charity] both *inter vivos* and in the last will"; *Tractatus*, in *Tractatus . . . Universi Iuris . . .* , XV, pt. 2 (Venice, 1584), c. 211rb.

20. The defeat of Charles the Bold at Nancy, for example, was a miracle of the Annunziata, for in the heat of battle his opponents had vowed to the miraculous painting (to which, of course, Charles himself had dedicated a pompous votive statue—*evocation*); Landucci, 15.

21. Landucci, 47.

geographical, political, and economic circumstances and ritual systems often very different from those of northern Italy.[22] *But it seems certain that this highly concentrated urban life went hand in hand with extensive rural and subject areas poor in shrines.*

---

22. For Coventry see C. Phythian-Adams, "Ceremony"; for Lyon see Davis, "Sacred"; and for a general theory of European shrines in their relation to land, cities, and courts, see L. Rothkrug, "Religious Practices and Collective Perceptions. Hidden Homologues in the Renaissance and Reformation," *Historical Reflections* VII (1980); "Popular Religion and Holy Shrines. Their Influence on the Origins of the German Reformation and Their Role in German Cultural Development," in J. Obelkevich (ed.), *Religion and the People, 800–1700* (Chapel Hill, 1979), 20–86. An equally important work on Spanish shrines is forthcoming from W. Christian, *Local Religion in Sixteenth-Century Spain* (Princeton, 1980).

Chapter 1

Institutions

Firm and solid columns maintaining
*this sublime Republic and its liberty.**

A city so vile that one . . . gave
dowries to males . . . not females.†

The visitor entered the city, his senses at a high pitch, unable as yet to distinguish the worthy and unworthy, envious of the inhabitants, who knew where one could be at ease. He did not yet know how to act. An important foreigner received orientation in behavioral geography from worthy men. Led first to the shrine of the Annunziata to worship, then to the city hall for a reception (or during the Medici period first to the family palace), he learned urban political geography: The city was divided into quarters (after the 1340s) named after their principal churches.[1] On the north side of the Arno River he made his way from San Giovanni to Santa Croce to Santa Maria Novella quarters over the traditional processional route linking the main *sacra*, then crossed to the other side of the river (Oltrarno) to the quarter of Santo Spirito.

Along with other symbols, the cross led the way in acclimatizing the stranger, for it identified churches, convents, and rectories. It also showed

*Cited in Trexler, "The Foundlings of Florence, 1395–1455," *History of Childhood Quarterly* I (1973), 259.

†*Istorie di Giovanni Cambi, Cittadino Fiorentino,* vols. XX–XXIII of *Delizie* (hereafter Cambi), XXII, 316.

1. From the later fifteenth century, dignitaries normally went "the first thing" to the Annunziata, who would be unveiled for them: the duke and duchess of Milan in 1471 (Rinuccini, cxv); the duke of Ferrara in 1504 (Landucci, 270); Giuliano de' Medici in 1512 (Masi, 99f); Ippolito de' Medici in 1524 (Cambi, XXII, 265); Baccio Valori in 1530 (Varchi, XI, 136).

where one could not urinate. The city had placed crosses on those surfaces it wanted to keep clean, as well as on the walls that marked the community off from the outside world.[2] Other symbols provided further orientation. The visitor could learn much about the city's politics by noting the positioning of statuary, for certain saints were placed so as to cast their portentious gaze in the direction of political danger. Just as Mars facing the wrong way could invite natural disaster, so David placed brashly in the open more assertively represented the commune than one hidden under a loggia, where its political meaning was muted.[3] At the judicial palaces the visitor encountered the collection of defamatory paintings that represented the foreign and domestic enemies of the community, and in churches as well he saw paintings that clarified the policy of the government in foreign and domestic affairs.[4] The visitor learned how and where to act as the planners had intended. He cultivated reverence and repugnance, formality and casualness in certain presences. He was drawn toward the freestanding statue, held at a distance by the enveloped one, attracted by the cross, yet repelled by it.[5]

It took but half an hour to walk across the city, but much longer to acquaint oneself with that curious urban combination of solemnity and irony, sacrifice and deception. To comprehend this urban society the visitor started with the phenomena confronting him, but the reader does not have the time, and must understand from the beginning some of the basic social and cultural forces that explain the phenomena the visitor witnessed. For the moment, therefore, this discussion turns away from observable behavior and toward some characteristics of the city that vitally conditioned ritual behavior. To describe modern theater, one may limit oneself to the actors, their props, their audience, and their house. To describe the vital ritual of the traditional European city, the distribution and organization of force in the whole of society must be understood, for all urban dwellers were actors, one way or the other, in the ritual drama. The city is the theater; the play presents the past, present, and future of participants and audience.

The Human Body

Florentine population trends resembled those of other European cities during this period, increasing until about 1300 and stagnating or decreasing

---

2. "What an abominable thing that you put crosses in the alleys so people don't piss there. Have the crosses freed of piss!"; Bernardino of Siena, *Prediche* (Siena, 1425), II, 231; Trexler, *Synodal Law*, 130.

3. On statuary as a political compass, read with caution S. Levine, "The Location of Michelangelo's *David*: The Meeting of January 25, 1504," *Art Bulletin*

LXI (1974), 34f. For Mars, see A. Pucci, *Centiloquio,* in *Delizie* IV, 129f.

4. On the defamatory paintings, see pages 122 seq., this volume.

5. See the remarks of the communal counselor Andrea Il Riccio on the David coming to the viewer or the viewer coming to the David; Levine, "Location," 40.

from that point until the mid-sixteenth century. From a peak of about 95,000 the population slumped to about 30,000 during the 1340s (Black Death) and stabilized around 40,000 to 55,000 until the later fifteenth century, when it showed signs of a secular increase. The great pestilences of the 1520s again decimated it; however, these were the last such natural disasters to reduce the population to the base level. Thereafter the population tended to rise steadily. By 1550, it had reached 59,000.[6]

The population was predominantly young in a society where age, at least male longevity, counted politically and socially, and male youth below thirty were considered imperfect "idiots," as were all women.[7] Early fifteenth-century figures show the population inordinately skewed with young widows, orphans, and a large number of teenagers without fathers. Usually marrying only in their late twenties or early thirties, males frequently died before their wives were thirty and when their legitimate offspring had barely reached adolescence. Daughters of upstanding families were placed in nunneries, which was cheaper than marrying them, and adolescent boys often found themselves cut off from the patronal backing necessary to settle down.[8] When the father of Bartolomeo Masi died in 1526 at the age of 73, his son noted that his father had left eight sons: "Not one of us eight children, males, ever had a wife or children."[9] Plague, marriage patterns, the monachizing of young and widowed women and the footlooseness of young males all go to explain the inability of the city to reproduce itself. This young population was constantly being revitalized by immigrants from the dominion.[10]

The citizens or political community of Florence came from that minority of the population that was male, had survived the first thirty years of life, had resided in the city for a substantial period of time, and paid taxes. Thus of the approximately 20,000 males in the 1427 population, some 8,000 were thirty years of age or over and thus politically mature—Aristotle's "perfected men." Of this group perhaps 30 percent had no taxable wealth, reducing the potential political group to about 5,600 men in a population of about 40,000 souls.[11] Other considerations excluded still more males from rights to political office: One had to be a member of a gild; many men were in tax arrears and thus

6. E. Fiumi, "La Demografia Fiorentina nelle Pagine di Giovanni Villani," *ASI*, CVIII (1950), 112–118; D. Herlihy, "Mapping Households in Medieval Italy," *Catholic Historical Review* LVIII (1972), 5f. P. Battara, *La Popolazione di Firenze Metà del Cinquecento* (Florence, 1935), 9.

7. Attitudes toward youth are discussed in ch. 13, this volume.

8. D. Herlihy, "Vieillir à Florence au Quattrocento," *Annales E.S.C.* XXIV (1969), 1341f. The richest men in Florence were about 31.2 years of age when they married; those with no fortune, 27.7 years; D. Herlihy and C. Klapisch-Zuber, *Les Toscans et leurs Familles* (Paris, 1978), 411.

9. Masi, 284.

10. J. Plesner, *L'Émigration de la Campagne qa la Ville Libre de Florence au XIIIᵉ siècle* (Copenhagen, 1934).

11. In 1343, when the population was still very substantial, 3346 men were admitted to the scrutiny for communal office, and of these about one-tenth were actually imbursed; G. Villani, XII, 22. In the 1382 scrutiny, about 5000 were considered; G. Brucker, *Florentine Politics and Society, 1343–1378* (Princeton, 1962), 67. Assuming a population of 50,000 at the time this means 10 percent were loyal, male, thirty years of age or older, tax-clear, and gild members. The age proportions in 1427 are in Herlihy–Kapisch, *Toscans*, 374–382.

barred; many were absent from the city for business reasons. In the colony of Avignon alone in 1371, some 300 Florentine males were in residence.[12]

The area of the city within the third and final set of walls easily accommodated the reduced populations of the Renaissance. The construction of large Renaissance palaces in the center city during the fifteenth century certainly complicated the lives of displaced artisans, but it does not seem to have brought about any significant housing development in the sizable open areas within the walls. In 1530, the large garden areas in the city and the generally uninhabited hills in the southeast quadrant remained intact. Population density, conceivably an important element in explaining why men gathered together so often in ritual order, was never a pressing problem in late medieval or Renaissance Florence.

The Social Body

Medieval historians often view neighborhoods as the building blocks of civic organization, and Florence offers some justification for this view. The tax and elective system had geographical axes: Imposts were divided between the quarters (sixths before the 1340s) of the city to facilitate collection, and each of the quarters had a number of flag companies, usually four, a vestige of the old days when military squadrons assembled in parishes before coming together as the urban mass to face a foreign enemy. City offices were chosen on the basis of legal residence; two of the ruling Signoria (executive committee of the commune) came from each of the quarters, and the Standard Bearer of Justice (nominal head of the republic) was rotated among them. The political divisions instituted in the fourteenth century did not, to be sure, overlap the more ancient parishional map of the city. Most of the former were rectilinear or triangular in structure, radiating out from the city center to the walls with Cleisthinian disregard for chthonic solidarities; the parishes, with some notable exceptions, were more circular in form, and therefore more neighborly.[13] Thus civil society was by definition the sum of Florence's political sections and, to a much smaller exent, of its neighborhood parts.

Students of Florentine affairs long neglected the importance of such geographical infrastructures, for they were concerned with civic more than social questions. Historians are correcting this oversight, showing, for example, that the Niccolini and Corsini families chose most of their infants' godparents from those who lived in their own ward or a contiguous gonfalon, and left cross-city and extra-Florentine spiritual cognation to a few great families.[14] Local alliances were also forged at the time of marriage, and

12. Trexler, "A Medieval Census: The *Liber Divisionis*," *Medievalia et Humanistica* XVII (1966), 82–85.

13. A map of the political subdivisions has been done by R. Weissman, "Community and Piety between

Renaissance and Counter-Reformation, Florentine Confraternities, 1200–1600" (diss. Univ. of California, Berkeley, 1978), 42, and see his *Ritual Brotherhood in Renaissance Florence* (New York, 1982).

14. On the Niccolini, see C. Klapisch, "Parenti, Ami-

Samuel Cohn has demonstrated that exogamy was generally limited to the patriciate; among the lower classes and some sections of the middle class endogamy within the *parish* was the rule.[15] Finally, Ronald Weissman has suggested that the four quarters of the city may have replicated each other's occupational variety; presumably, a significant part of the work force labored in the same *quarter* it inhabited. So striking do all these facts appear to Weissman that he has characterized Florence as a group of "villages."[16]

This is an idea whose time will not come, for the city's parishes, as distinct from its family turfs, were not community centers. In 1202 a border dispute between two parishes ended with one family's males being assigned to one parish and its females to another,[17] so weak was the sense of *popolo* or parish even in the thirteenth century. Yet that century would bring still stiffer challenges. Parish rectors could not compete with the footloose Mendicant friars for the corpses and thus alms of parishioners. Few patricians spent their money on parish churches, and only the exceptional parish had a vestry or fabric organization (*opera*) of parishioners.[18] Contests between neighborhoods in the early fourteenth century were considered revivals of old customs rather than living rivalries, and until the late fifteenth century no neighborhood had a processional character of its own.[19] Parishes had no baptismal fonts, as they did in other Italian cities, and those neighborhood godfathers who christened infants left their parishes for the one central Baptistry of San Giovanni. There was but one public stage in Florence, the city stage.

Because of their lack of tradition and artificial construction, the political sections of the city might seem poor settings in which to form endogamous unions. Yet on those few occasions when Florentines did recommend a geographic endogamy to their heirs, they almost always referred to the gonfalon and not the parish. Their motivations were transparently fiscal and political rather than chthonic in nature: Godparents and marriage stood members of a gonfalon in good stead when the latter met to distribute taxes.[20]

ci, e Vicini: il Territorio Urbano d'una Famiglia Mercantile nel XV secolo," *Quaderni Storici* XXXIII (1976), 953–982, and for the Corsini see Weissman, "Community and Piety," 47–50. Examples of foreign *compari* are given on page 320, this volume.

15. S. Cohn, "Community and Conflict in the Renaissance, 1340–1530" (diss. Harvard Univ., 1978), 83 and *passim*, with important chronological limitations upon my summary statement.

16. Weissman, "Community and Piety," 37ff, 50.

17. P. Cianfogni, *Memorie istoriche dell'Ambrosiana R. Basilica di S. Lorenzo di Firenze*, with the *Continuazione* of D. Moreni, 3 vols. (Florence, 1804–1817), II, 339ff.

18. The *opera* of S. Maria Maggiore was typical of the six or seven parish churches that had such bodies; *ASF, Prov.*, 55, ff. 170rv (Apr. 28, 1368). The *Ricordanze* of Francesco di Tommaso Giovanni (*ASF, Carte Strozziane*, II, 16, and 16 bis) detail the workings of the

opera of Santo Spirito (a Mendicant friary, not a parish); *ASF, Acquisti e Doni*, 292, at the date Apr. 1436. I will throughout refer to this C. Carnesecchi transcription of Giovanni's *ricordi*. The deliberations of that *opera* from 1439 to 1461 may be studied in the *BNF, Strozzi ms. foglio*, no. 70. See also *Filippo Brunelleschi. L'Uomo e l'Artista. Mostra Documentaria* (Florence, 1977), 72f.

19. The very number of parishes in Florence, about 56, mitigated against such local identities. The data on the emergence of local processional and confraternal identities are given on page 405, this volume. The 1304 festival was described by G. Villani, VIII, 70.

20. D. Kent, *The Rise of the Medici. Faction in Florence, 1426–1434* (Oxford, 1978), 62f. Also F. Kent, *Household and Lineage in Renaissance Florence. The Family Life of the Capponi, Ginori, and Rucellai* (Princeton, 1977), 172–185.

Doubtless these sections pursued the interests of their members, and yet how seldom did constituents identify themselves as such. Rarely indeed did a Florentine express pride or "affection for one's gonfalon and quarter."[21] In this city, one was either a member of a family and a Florentine, or nothing at all. No significant voluntary organizations were to be found in the parishes or sections. Confraternities, gilds, even factions were citywide in scope, for that was what the interests of the ruling merchants required.

The social profile of these citywide groups was carefully controlled to prevent unrest. In the confraternities, for example, the taxpaying, non-noble, fully emancipated male population twenty-five years of age and up was generally the only group allowed to form a legal association, a policy modified in the fifteenth century when youth and adolescent confraternities appeared, and these in turn were carefully monitored by elders. Women's sodalities were not unknown, but they played no perceptible civic or neighborhood role. The exclusion of workers and artisans without gild status was then the basic policy. Still, the commune, from fear of cabal, could reverse itself, and ban from confraternities those who had the right to hold governmental office.[22] Confraternal membership rolls are only now being seriously studied, but on the whole they probably consisted of lower-middle-class, taxpaying but not politically significant elements, leavened by control elements of patrician leadership.[23]

Further evidence of communal control is found in the fact that few confraternities' membership came exclusively from single occupations. Some gilds had chapels and typical social-welfare benefits for their members, but these organizations were more sociopolitical than religious in nature, and their membership was limited to property owners. The fact that confraternities were not occupationally based reflects the same fear of conspiracy that necessitated tight control of the legal status of their members: The ruling class of Florence was determined to render common cause among the producing elements all but impossible.[24]

The gild structure of Florence developed in the thirteenth and early fourteenth centuries out of a long conflict between the society of international merchant–bankers and the emerging associations of producers and shop-owning artisans whose genius was converting Florence into an important exporter of industrial goods. The resultant gild structure absorbed the

21. D. Kent, *Rise of the Medici*, 61.

22. Doren, *Arti*, I, 210f; Davidsohn, *Storia*, VI, 209–212. An example of confraternal exclusion of the *veduti*, those examined for office: ASF, *Prov.*, 134, ff. 208v–209r (Feb. 19, 1443/1444).

23. See, for now, Weissman, "Community and Piety," and the careful study of the confraternities in the Val d'Elsa by C. de la Roncière, "La Place des Confréries dans l'Encadrement Religieux du Contado Florentin: l'Exemple de la Val d'Elsa," *Mélanges de l'*

École Française de Rome LXXXV (1973), 31–77. See also A. Benvenuti Papi, "L'impianto Mendicante in Firenze, un Problema Aperto," *Mélanges de l'École Française de Rome, Moyen Age, Temps Modernes* LXXXIX (1977), 597–608.

24. Foreign artisans whom the Florentines wanted to keep were allowed to organize into confraternities. Otherwise occupational confraternities were very rare; Davidsohn, *Storia*, VI, 209–212. Doren points to the fundamental difference between the essentially non-confraternal *arti* of Florence and the German gilds; *Arti*, I, 210f.

merchant–bankers as senior partners, and made membership in one of the twenty-one gilds a requirement for political office. Representation in government was apportioned according to the status of the gilds: A 5–2–1 ratio for the Signoria, for example, was considered an equitable division between the major, middle, and minor gilds.

Theoretically, therefore, Florence might seem a republic of workingmen organized by occupation. Practically, however, gilds continually manifested preference for those who did not work with their hands. The major gilds that dominated political life were composed not of handworkers, but usually of merchants or rentiers who lived off land or commercial investments. Prospective members chose a particular gild less because of occupational affinity than because one offered a better chance for political and social influence and government position than another. Conversely, exercising a gild trade did not give a right to gild membership, and research in the rolls of the banker–changers gild suggests that, at times, only a small percentage of changers belonged.[25]

Thus the gild structure in Florence not only excluded all but self-employed shopkeepers; it may have excluded a majority of the latter as well. Perhaps this was less true in the politically less significant lower and middle gilds.[26] But the import is clear: The gild was not the occupational organization it seemed, but a filter mechanism for controlling access to political office. The classical gild defended the interests of powerful generalists, the power brokers of Florentine society, whose affinity to their gild brothers was based more on family and patronal ties than on occupational ones.

In summary, the nature of extrafamilial, citywide associations in Florence was as follows:

- Gilds: the upper gilds composed of substantial citizens of property with diversified interests and investments, the lower containing more specialized shop owners with political ties to major gildsmen
- Confraternities: preponderantly made up of taxpaying nongildsmen, but led by members of important gilds[27]
- Women, adolescents, youths, and adult salaried workers: excluded from occupational associations and, generally, from religious groups until the later fifteenth century.[28]

25. J. Najemy, "The Guilds in Florentine Politics, 1292–1394" (diss. Harvard Univ., 1972), 147, 238. See now his "Guild Republicanism in Trecento Florence: The Success and Ultimate Failure of Corporate Politics," *American Historical Review* LXXXIV (1979), 53–71.

26. Doren, *Arti*, I, 192–198.

27. Florentine gilds and confraternities both maintained constitutional distinctions between major and minor members. For the gilds, see *ibid.*, I, 199. For the Confraternity of the Misericordia, see *Documenti Inediti o Poco Noti per la Storia della Misericordia di Firenze*

(1240–1525) (Florence, 1940), 60, 88. On the division in the Venetian confraternities, see B. Pullan, *Rich and Poor in Renaissance Venice* (Cambridge, Mass., 1971), 72–83.

28. References to women's confraternities are in Trexler, *The Spiritual Power* (Leiden, 1974), 131 (1377); ASF, *Notarile Antecosiminiano*, G 676 (1300–1303), f. 150v (*societas mulierum S. Laurentii*); *ibid.*, B 2126 (1300–1304), f. 114r (*societas virginis Marie in Sancta Reparata* "quem est de mulieribus"); *ibid.*, S 690 (1440–1449), no. 144 (*domine societatis Annunziate in Sancta Croce*). On the later adolescent and plebeian confraternities, see ch. 11, this volume.

The last category of inhabitants had no legally incorporated identity, although they made up a majority of the population. They were not part of the *cittadinanza* or *communità* properly speaking, which was limited to the political males. In the language of contracts, members of this category were objects of trade, being *locati*, "placed" or rented in countless agreements.[29] To them was attributed a more or less common psychological character. Young males, for example, "because of their youth no less than because of their nude knowledge . . . [are] equal to the vile females."[30] Women and the young in turn were comparable to the male rustics and working "multitude," for all were drawn to excess and passion, ignorance and sin. The moon, said Alberti, controlled "feminine and plebeian movements."[31]

Political society was composed of "grave" or mature males whose sexuality was under control. Yet if this group was charged with what Nancy Munn has called "transgenerational continuity," the preservation of gods, social orders, and family names, the "intergenerational" or biological force of the polis was found in its despised apolitical majority.[32] Women produced male descendants, boys and youth manifested male vitality, and ignorant working people through their "mindless" faith and religious excitability saved honorable persons through the prayers they said for their betters. They were political liminal groups living on the edge of the *communitas* of mature males, groups whose presumably innate qualities of vision, generation, and destruction frightened a stable commune but were invaluable in crisis.[33] Because of the large number of young widows and fatherless adolescents in Florentine society, and the endemic economic want and unemployment of working people, the Florentine community of males feared the limina's unorganized potential for disorder. Aggravating this concern was the conceptual equation of *all* women and *all* children within one psychological box: From the sexual point of view the honorable Strozzi widow had more in common with the

29. Treating these groups as commodities was practiced by the nonrepresented themselves. On the monetary value of infants, see Trexler, "Foundlings," 279. Mothers insisted they had to "demonstrate" their girls in church if the latter were to win husbands; Bernardino of Siena, *Prediche* (Siena, 1425), II, 88. Genoan girls' corporal measurements were taken in church, according to Bernardino of Siena, *Le Prediche Volgari* (Florence, 1425), ed. C. Cannarozzi, 3 vols. (vols. III–V of the 1425 sermons) (Florence, 1940), V, 88. At a conservatory for girls projected by the architect Filarete, the walls would be filled with openings so that prospective husbands shopping for wives could see them at work; *Treatise*, I, 242ff. A hint that pictures of girls may have been placed in churches for marital shopping is in G. Savonarola, *Prediche sopra Amos e Zaccaria* (*Edizione Nazionale delle Opere di Girolamo Savonarola*, general editor R. Ridolfi [Rome, 1955–continuing]), II, 25 (hereafter I refer only to this edition and only to Savonarola's Old Testa-

mental source, volume, and page number). For vivid descriptions of young girls' physical features, see the letters of the important Florentine matron Alessandra Macinghi negli Strozzi to her marriageable son; *Lettere di una Gentildonna Fiorentina del secolo XV*, ed. C. Guasti (Florence, 1877), 458f, 464, 470, 485, 489 (hereafter Strozzi, *Lettere*).

30. G. Cavalcanti, *The "Trattato Politico-Morale" of G.C. . . .* (*1381–c. 1451*), ed. M. Grendler (Geneva, 1973), 115.

31. L. Alberti, *I Libri della Famiglia*, eds. R. Romano and A. Tenenti (Turin, 1969), 358.

32. N. Munn, *Walbiri Iconoraphy* (Ithaca, 1973), 27f.

33. On the concept of liminality, see A. Van Gennep, *The Rites of Passage* (Chicago, 1960). On the particular functions of these groups in crisis, see ch. 10, this volume. As far as I know, a concept of political liminality in an urban setting is new.

lower-class urchin than she had with her own family. Two normative systems stood in endless tension. The Strozzi boy was a Strozzi, but he was, after all, a mere boy. The mature worker might be a worker, but he was at least a man.

From the bottom of the social hierarchy through the confraternities and gilds to the halls of government, groups gained respectability only when they were headed or at least patronized by members of leading and preferably ancient families. These consorteries were independent social groups, but, just as important, they were sources of honor through which all extrafamilial political and social groups legitimated themselves. Preachers might with only slight exaggeration tell their audiences that no Florentine could trace his ancestry to the fifth generation, but the family was all the city had to lend its institutions honor and legitimacy.[34] Perhaps in the remote past the few families with proper surnames and fitting pretensions had preserved a quasi-sacred ritual identity; in central Italy several families retained totemic identifications with animals.[35] In the early days of the Florentine commune, family appurtenance certainly brought with it important privileges. The Uberti, Ubaldini, Guidi, Alberti del Giudice, and similar consorteries had been laws unto themselves, their good the good of the commune. But with the emergence in the latter part of the thirteenth century of a communal identity greater than that of any single family, with the development of a rich corporate life in the city, and with the increased desire of nameless men to develop a surname, the traditional rights and authority of the older families came under continual challenge. The victory of the ignoble *popolo* over the noble *magnati* and the establishment of the gild system at the end of the century made nobility a political liability. Nobles could not hold a series of important political offices, including the legislative council of the *popolo* and the priorate or executive. It became as much a curse as a blessing to be a member of an honorable family. Laws punishing any member of a consortery for the crimes of one individual made family members cautious: A peaceful artisan Acciaiuoli might change his name because he found it dangerous to be nominally linked with his powerful relatives, who were always in the public eye. A rich Bardi did not want to be associated with a distant criminal cousin who lived on the edge of indigence, and forced the cousin to desert the name. Designation as a magnate became the political penalty for nonconformity: The Ricasoli, faced with a communal law banning them from civil participation for past crimes, soon found their honored name a distinct disadvantage, and changed it.[36]

---

34. I. Origo emphasizes the citizens' illegitimacy, lack of roots, and racial admixtures, citing the early fourteenth-century preacher Giordano da Rivalto; "The Domestic Enemy: Eastern Slaves in Tuscany in the Fourteenth and Fifteenth Centuries," *Speculum* XXX (1955), 339.

35. A distant echo of family sacred identity was the Pazzi's customary portage of the sacred fire from the Baptistry to the family chapel on Holy Saturday, a practice ended in 1478 after the Pazzi conspiracy; A.

Fabroni, *Laurentii Medicis Magnifici Vita*, 2 vols. (Pisa, 1784), II, 113 (law of May 23, 1478). On the "cult exclusiveness" of the great families, see Weber, *City*, 98. On familial identifications with animals, see V. Lanternari, "La Politica Culturale della Chiesa nelle Campagne: la Festa di S. Giovanni," *Società* XI (1955), 64–95.

36. For examples of such actions, see Brucker, *Politics*, 22f, 51.

Thus nobility, the prime European hallmark of honor, became suspect. Doubtless there were advantages for the *popolo* in demeaning its ancient families, but the cost to the victors was great. The loss of the group that embodied honor, and from which flowed credit and trust, was ever after keenly felt by this plebeian city. Machiavelli spoke of the burden: In the beginning nobility had brought the city not only the military virtue needed to maintain independence, but a certain "generosity of feeling," which was soon to be completely foreign to the *popolo*.[37]

The ambiguous attitude of this city toward nobility, the constant "contention of liberty and dignity," was one of Florence's most distinctive characteristics.[38] Citizens feared aristocrats but needed them, primarily because the city had no other "natural" honor acceptable to feudal Europe. "Here [in Florence] they are considered persons *da bene*," said a parent characterizing the family of a prospective bride for her son, "[but] I don't know about [their status] abroad."[39] Even in civil life the nobility was important. Lower ranks deferred to aristocrats, conceiving their presence as the embodiment of the honor and power of the commune. Citizens bemoaned the demise of an honored family as a depletion of the city's own nobility. Government used its meager number of honorable men in ambassadorial posts because it knew how important honor was to the outside world. It revered a sociopolitical organization—the Parte Guelfa—that vaunted aristocratic values, and reveled in the display of its few nobles' prowess. This weakness for finery was no vestige of the past, and it certainly was not some venial sin or pardonable peccadillo of a progressive bourgeoisie. It reflected an ignoble social body's ingrained need for corporate dignity.

Put on the defensive in such a complex urban society, yet conscious of bourgeois society's market for their wares, honorable families defended themselves by broadening their identity beyond the consanguinal to the adoptive and spiritual realms. In Genoa this process of adopting outsiders into the family circle reached its logical conclusion: New members ceremonially changed their names to the surnames of their patrons, and wore livery identifying them as family members.[40] Such practices were not unknown in Florence. In the later fifteenth century a Salviati changed his name to Riario and a Becchi sought to become a Medici.[41] Because of the aforementioned antifamilial laws, however, Florentine patricians could not usually take this route to broaden their base of support. Instead they created *familiae* (called "factions" by enemies) through marriage and baptismal sponsorship, through business associations (unrelated members of companies might be

37. *History*, 107, 109.

38. This Roman concept was known to Leonardo Bruni in the early fifteenth century; N. Rubinstein, "Florentine Constitutionalism and Medicean Ascendancy in the Fifteenth Century," in Rubinstein, *Florentine Studies*, 449.

39. Strozzi, *Lettere*, 313.

40. J. Heers, *Le Clan Familial au Moyen Age* (Paris, 1974), 107.

41. Lorenzo de' Medici, *Lettere*, eds. R. Fubini and N. Rubinstein (Florence, 1977–continuing), I, 428; II, 182, 267.Pope Leo X (Giovanni di Lorenzo de' Medici) bestowed his family name upon foreigners; L. von Pastor, *Geschichte der Päpste seit dem Ausgang des Mittelalters*, 16 vols. (Freiburg, 1955–1961), IV, 681ff (1515).

known by the name of the family that controlled the company), through association with churches, confraternities, charities, religious orders, and gilds. The greater the family's patronal extension, the greater its own protection and—most important—the greater the honor of the commune, which relied on the honor of its families for its own. Family honor was the essence, and the bane, of communal and group honor.

Government

Without family honor, there was no commune. Florence lacked a king, an emperor, or a developed knightly ethos to embody morality and ideals. It even lacked its own army. Without titled men at the helm, the acts of untitled men carried less authority. Governmental decisions were made and executed by mere men, politicians by necessity, traders by profession. Certainly in Florence, as elsewhere, a consensual fiction common to all representative groups was present: Money was no part of governmental ethics, for government was not business; representative groups sacrificed rather than bargained. But in merchant republics like Florence claims that the government stood above mere business and pursued a high purpose were palpably hollow. It was evident to anyone who looked that Florence was full of citizens who insisted, as one pained citizen put it in the early fifteenth century: "Let us make money and we shall have honor."[42] Decades of civic humanism in the late fourteenth and early fifteenth centuries failed to dignify government, for the humanists were no more capable of imagining traders as ideal citizens than were European nobles. Instead of ennobling trade, they generally played down the merchant roots of the citizenry as something unclean. Their Good Citizen was not a merchant. Nor was the Signoria of Florence a fitting model for humanistic or other moral biographies. Apparently few republican artists portrayed Florentine governmental groups, and rare representations of single officials were limited to private devotional paintings.[43] Florence offered

42. A 1424 condemnation of his compatriots by Domenico da Prato, cited in Baron, *Crisis*, 383. The tensions created by this alleged mercantile attitude toward government are examined in ch. 13, this volume.

43. Not until the *Vita* of the 1527–1528 Standard Bearer of Justice Niccolò Capponi, written around 1550 and attributed to Bernardo Segni, is there a literary biography of a Florentine concentrating on his official life. For a personal diary that emphasizes political involvement, however, see *Cronica, o Memorie di Iacopo Salviati dall' Anno 1398 al 1411, in Delizie*, XVIII, 177 seq. (hereafter Salviati). In the figurative realm, comparisons to other cities are suggestive. In Florence there were no group portraits of governments until

Pontormo's *Holy Family* (Plate 1) of the 1520s, and only occasional representations of individual officials in devotional paintings, such as Lenzi in Masaccio's *Trinity* and what is probably an (anonymous) Standard Bearer of Justice in an altar painting of the early fifteenth century (Plate 8), on which see M. Meiss, "An Early Altarpiece from the Cathedral of Florence," *Metropolitan Museum of Art Bulletin*, n.s. XII (1954), 302–317. See the jacket of this volume for an uncommon example of government in a historical scene. When Giovanni de' Medici died in 1353, he was of course buried as a Hungarian knight, not as the Standard Bearer of Justice, which office he held at the time. Sword and spurs similar to Medici's are shown in P. Bargellini, G. Morozzi, and G. Batini, *Santa Reparata. La Cattedrale Risorta* (Florence, 1970). The

PLATE 1. Pontormo. *The Holy Family* (detail). c. 1525. Paris, Louvre.

PLATE 2. *St. Bernardino Preaching.* Attribution: Vecchietta. c. 1450. Liverpool, Walker Art Gallery.

21

PLATE 3. *The Annunciation.* **Anonymous. Fourteenth century.**
Florence, SS. Annunziata.

PLATE 4. *The Story of Antonio Rinaldeschi* (detail). **Anonymous. c. 1501.**
Text: "Cursing, he throws dung in the face of the Blessed Virgin,
and flees to [his] villa."
Florence, Museo Stibbert.

PLATE 5. *Opus Penitentiale Petri Pictaviensis.* **Anonymous Prayer Gestures.
Thirteenth century.**
Venice, Archivio di Stato; *Scuola Grande S. Maria della Misericordia in Valverde,* b. 1.

PLATE 6. Ignazio Hugford.
Our Lady of Impruneta
(faked, 1758).
Impruneta, S. Maria.

PLATE 7. Giotto. *St. Francis at Greccio.* c. 1300.
Assisi, S. Francesco.

PLATE 8. *The Intercession of Christ and the Virgin.* **Anonymous. c. 1402.**
Texts: "Dearest Son, because of the milk I gave you, have mercy on them";
"My Father, let those be saved for whom you wished me to suffer the passion."
New York, The Metropolitan Museum of Art. The Cloisters Collection, Purchase 1953.

no mirror of princes, and Erasmus' ideal Christian knight never governed Florentine habits. In other bodies politic, the authority of a king or doge might help to concentrate policymaking in the political arm and legitimate its proceedings. In a self-governing republic like Florence, politics constantly responded to subsystems that lent governments their charisma.

Conceived as a fraternity of equals regulating merchants and governing the liminal groups of society, the government of Florence actually radiated distrust in its structure. Offices were short-term, attained through a complex system of scrutinies and lot designed to guard against inequality. The eight priors and the titular head of the republic, the Standard Bearer (*gonfaloniere*) of Justice, governed for two months, and the associated executive colleges sat for three and four months. The approval of legislation was in the hands of short-term councils (six to four months) composed of citizens.[44] Justice was done by foreigners brought in for six-month terms to distribute equal justice among the fraternity of merchants. In emergencies, special six-month commissions called *balie* received broad powers.

Trust and long-term commitments in Florentine society could not be provided by short-term governments of ignoble men. A complex subgovernmental system of clientage built upon concepts of *familia* was one of the social instrumentalities that filled this gap. *Familia* possessed a more sacral binding force than did the government contract; defiance of government brought only banishment, but violation of personal allegiance to a patron led to fatal vendettas. To understand Florentine government one must, to borrow Karl Morrison's words, conceive of it as "a league of Mafia families."[45]

In theory Florentine governors were disinterested. They were said to represent sections and gilds (the basis of their selection) rather than persons. In fact government was interested; it consisted of a group of "fathers," "friends," "godfathers," or clients whose decisions were determined time and again by clients or patrons to whom they were wed much more intimately than they were related to the *buon comune*. The merchant left his family, his confraternity, his clients and patrons for a short period of government office. Within months he would return to those groups, and his knowledge of that fact induced the anxiety toward governmental service that can still be noticed in the Mediterranean area.[46] Florentines asked too much of their public

tomb was brought to my attention by F. Toker, who is preparing the definitive work on the recent excavations of S. Reparata; Medici's grave is no. 42 in Toker's catalogue. In Siena, another city without a permanent head of state, Ambrogio Lorenzetti's mid-fourteenth-century *Buon Governo* portrays government officials, in the same diminutive devotional position. Although no historical painting of a Florentine official being invested with regalia is documented, a Sienese painting of the investment of a condottiere is shown in Plate 14. In Venice, dogal portraits emerged in the fifteenth century, as did representations of governmental officials in ceremonial processions; see, for now, E. Muir, "Images of

Power: Art and Pageantry in Renaissance Venice," *American Historical Review* LXXXIV (1979), 16–52. E. Muir, *Civic Ritual in Renaissance Venice* (Princeton, 1981), makes a solid contribution to these comparisons. M. Meiss contributed to my understanding of Florence's minuscule official painting tradition, which I plan to study in a separate place.

44. Brucker, *Politics*, 59.

45. *Europe's Middle Ages* (Glenview, 1970), 82. Florentines did not customarily use the word *famiglia*, but instead used *sette, parte, fazione, amici,* and so on.

46. The problem of governmental officials in societies with strong "familial" patronage networks is well

servants, expecting them to be both objective in office and loyal to friends. No cry was more common than that one should be guided by the *buon comune*, but nothing was more a staple of Florentine political reality than vote trading and lending based on patronal interest,[47] nothing more characteristic of political commentary than the ledger-like reports of "friends" and "enemies" in government, no law more common than those favoring individuals and groups when enough "friends" were in government.[48]

Formal government maintained the fiction of equality among brothers because it was a condition of civil life. In order for this horizontal conception of government to be plausible, however, merchants who filled governmental posts as brothers had to know their place as fathers and sons in another system, which, different from government, allowed them to act out the factual differences in their social and financial status. This subgovernmental system was the patronage network, the everyday lines of communication regulating social relations. In this network, as in formal government, men styled themselves each other's true *amici*, and despised "the love of the merchant: You help me, and I'll help you." In it the client might insist that he was a free and equal partner of the patron. But here the client could also call himself "son," his patron "father" as well as "friendly equal" or "fellow father," his patron's wife *comare* or "mother," and his wife could become a "daughter" to the patronal couple.[49] The essential characteristic of the patronal network was behaviorally to combine equality and inequality, inducing fraternal solidarity while vertically integrating factual inequality. And this vertical integration of merchants made plausible the horizontal, fraternal conception of government.

Patronage established trust in a deceitful world. Being a godfather, said Giovanni Morelli, was one of the duties of a man seeking to protect himself.[50] "For I calculated," said Buonaccorso Pitti, "that if I were to become a connection of [Guido Del Palagio] and could win his good will, he would be obliged to help me obtain a truce with the Corbizi family."[51] To avoid being harmed by government, said Giovanni Rucellai, one had to avoid enemies, for one

---

stated in J. Boissevain, *Saints and Fireworks. Religion and Politics in Rural Malta* (New York, 1965), 121.

47. The *ricordanze* of Francesco di Tommaso Giovanni record vote "exchanges," "obligations," and "promises," as one might register financial debits and credits; Giovanni–Carnesecchi, Feb. 24, 1439/1440, Jan. 1441/1442, and Jan. 31, 1441/1442.

48. For examples, see Mazzei, I, 172f, 360. One contemporary told how the vestry of the church of Santo Spirito waited till its colleague Capponi was Standard Bearer of Justice before requesting a subsidy; had Francesco Giovanni himself not procured one for the vestry when he was a prior?; Giovanni–Carnesecchi, Apr. 1436. The only reason Francesco's family lost another case, he wrote, was that his Rucellai antagonist was a *gonfaloniere* and three of five officials were *stretti parenti; ibid.,* Jan. 16, 1443/1444. From a foreigner's report, we know that the priors customarily

reserved the first six weeks of their office for public business, and used the last two to pass laws favoring friends and clients (*cose di loro amici et particulari persone*); G. Brucker, *The Civic World of Early Renaissance Florence* (Princeton, 1977), 283. On the rhythm of petitions to government for private ends, see M. Becker, *Florence in Transition,* 2 vols. (Baltimore, 1967–1968), I, 21.

49. Mazzei, I, 425; II, 57, 92ff, 185, 194. For the values sought in clients, see L. Martines, *The Social World of the Florentine Humanists 1390–1460* (Princeton, 1963), 18–84.

50. G. di Pagolo Morelli, *Ricordi,* 149f. On Mazzei's attitude toward godparents, see *Lettere,* I, 151.

51. *Two Memoirs of Renaissance Florence, the Diaries of Buonaccorso Pitti and Gregorio Dati* (hereafter Pitti or Dati, *Memoir*), ed. G. Brucker (New York, 1967), 46.

enemy hurt more than four friends. Nevertheless, he told his descendants, to survive government, stay close to *consorti, parenti, amici*.[52] Francesco Datini did not believe kin could be trusted: "One sees brothers betray each other every day; but good friends do not thus."[53] Spiritual brotherhood was more valuable than blood relations, it seemed. A good client, said Morelli, "had friends and not relatives to help and sustain him so he was not harmed."[54] Some Florentines, therefore, did not trust relatives as patrons. Leon Battista Alberti's ideals aside, the patronal *familia* often seems to have been designed to protect oneself from kin as well as from outsiders.[55]

While regulating merchants by hierarchically ordering the fraternity, the patronage system also bridged the gap between merchants and the nonpossessing male population that was excluded from the political realm altogether: not only the nontax-paying salaried workers, but the sons of the merchants as well. By accepting as his *garzone* either a mature male of lower-class provenance or the son of his *amico*–client, the *padrone* fostered vertical integration and allowed the representation of nonpolitical segments of the population. Though the patron did not call his *garzone* an *amico*—poverty was the enemy of friendship—the aim of cross-group patronage was the same as that within the merchant class: protection in exchange for service. Its effect was also the same: The patronage system made government possible by ordering the obligations of unequals.[56]

It is difficult to imagine a Florentine citizen having said, "I am governed by the commune," for the "fathers," as Florentines sometimes called their governors, did not conceive of themselves as governed so much as self-regulated. "Let us not say," proclaimed one counselor to his brothers in 1427, "that we cannot emulate the Venetians, for we are men, and we can and ought to live and govern ourselves as they do."[57] *Governo* was the condition under which everyone except the political males had to be if the commune was to prosper, and the fact that the word referred to familial rather than governmental functions reflects the importance of the former. *Governo* was the control exercised over someone *subject* to obedience. Thus women were *sotto governo* of their fathers, husbands, or abbesses; workers were under the governance of the gilds even though they were not members; religious were *sotto governo* of their superiors; and the elderly were often under the governance of the city hospital or their sons. "Because I am old, I need *governo*," says one of Arlotto's characters.[58] Dependence was *governo*'s hallmark: Savona-

52. G. Rucellai, *Zibaldoni. I: il Zibaldone quaresimale*, ed. A. Perosa (London, 1960), 9.

53. I. Origo, *The Merchant of Prato* (New York, 1957), 103.

54. G. di Pagolo Morelli, *Ricordi*, 150. Spiritual relationships (godparenthoods) are used in Guatemalan villages to counteract the more stressful kin ties, according to S. Gudeman, "The *Compadrazgo* as a Reflection of the Natural and Spiritual Person," *Proceedings of the Royal Anthropological Institute of Great Britain and Ireland for 1971*, 45–54. See also my *Synodal Law*, 382, at "Cognitio spiritualis."

55. Cf. Alberti, *Famiglia*, bk. 5: "de amicitia."

56. On horizontal and vertical integration, see D. Levine, "Integration, Cultural," *International Encyclopedia of the Social Sciences* VII (1968), 379f.

57. Brucker, *Civic World*, 445f.

58. *Motti e Facezie del Piovano Arlotto*, ed. G. Folena (Milan, 1953), 66. When one was sick he was "governed"; Giovanni–Carnesecchi, Dec. 22, 1436.

rola's explanation to his audience that "if you pray to a saint, he governs you" reflects this point of view. Citizens obeyed the law because they were brothers; the *soggetti sotto governo* did so because they were governed. "Know how to govern yourself," Morelli instructed a future citizen, "govern yourself and your family."[59]

Government, then, can best be conceived as a fraternity of fathers, each man representing his clientele before those brothers, the cement of government being furnished by the trust through obligations generated below the level of formal government. Government could function only as long as it permitted the defense of these patronal and client interests, and only when those otherwise politically excluded were *sotto governo* either of private patronal networks or of the government itself (widows, orphans, foundlings, the destitute poor).

Such a personalistic system of power made governmental objectivity more fictive than factual. Curiously, government gained from this state of things. Its honor rested upon the patronal honor of its members. It drew what social esteem it had from the private sphere, and could achieve fraternity and effectiveness only because of the commitments to clients that its officials had made: The trust the patron brought with him was one reason his governmental brother could trust him. Formal government, more in need of trust than of objectivity, was a parasite of patronal honor.

Still, a patronal ethos of honor was not enough, for the best merchant, patron, or client was not fully convincing in the role of governor of the *buon comune*. Direct representatives of the principle of ethical objectivity were needed in government, for the best of burghers might steal. The problem with fraternal government was not, however, merely corruption. These "brothers" constantly voted for or against their fellow citizens and assessed each other's taxes. How could they remain "equal" if, by the nature of their governmental tasks, they raised or lowered the fortunes of their colleagues? There was a real danger that civil discourse would be infected by mutual suspicion if secrecy could not be maintained in such matters. To maintain this secrecy, and prevent theft, a government composed of grave fathers had to be mediated by men obligated to a higher patron: clergymen. Trust among laymen was only possible if certain key governmental posts were manned by men of God.

The first of three areas where clergy held communal office was in the reception, preservation, and disbursement of communal wealth. One religious official, the bursar of the camera of the commune, sat in the palace of the *podestà*. Before this office was at least temporarily abolished in 1436, Cistercian choir monks and lay brothers, Umiliati priors and lay brothers, Benedictines, Servites, and Carmelites held sway alongside lay bursars. They swore their oath not to the commune, but to their religious superiors, and did not post bond as did the lay bursars.[60]

---

59. G. di Pagolo Morelli, *Ricordi*, 279, 294; Savonarola, *Ezechiele*, II, 233.

60. Trexler, "Honor Among Thieves. The Trust Function of the Urban Clergy in the Florentine Republic," in S. Bertelli and G. Ramakus (eds.), *Essays Presented to Myron P. Gilmore*, 2 vols. (Florence, 1978),

Another office, the treasury or bursary of the camera of arms, was housed in the city hall; it was manned throughout the republic by two Cistercian lay brothers. The chapel of the priors in the Palace of the Signori was named after the Cistercian St. Bernard, and the most precious possessions of the Signoria were stored there and guarded by these brothers. The arms bursars served for life and held their office alone; there were no lay bursars of the camera of arms.[61]

The laws of Florence do not spell out the reasons for religious bursars, nor should one expect them to. But in sermons delivered to the citizens of Siena in 1425 and 1427 the Sienese Franciscan Bernardino went right to the heart of the problem there and in Florence:

> You are also giving your offices to friars and priests. It might seem you are right in doing so, since you say that they steal less. . . . You may say: "[The religious] rob less." That is one sorry compliment to pay your citizens.![62]

> Oh tell me citizens, who are calculating your taxes. . . . You give yourselves to believe that your lay bursars of the commune have stolen communal income, and thus you want to put friars in that office. You think the friars don't steal? Oh, it is a bad sign that you want a religious bursar for this reason. How blessed it is, that each of you suspects the other.[63]

These religious officials, in short, made honor possible among thieves.

No less important than acting as recipient and disburser of communal funds were other religious men's duties at the center of the tax assessment mechanism. Throughout the republican period, different clerical groups took the several assessments of each taxpayer in the city, threw out the highest and lowest assessments, and averaged the remainder. The resultant figure was the definitive assessment, so that no lay assessor knew what his fellows had done, and no citizens knew how his fellow citizens had acted.[64] One monastery whose monks long acted in this capacity became, in the words of a contemporary the "depository of all the secrets of the Florentine Republic."[65] The Camaldolans kept the chits of the tax assessments, said one law, "since they are religious and honest, and also for the peace and quiet of citizens," and, said another, to execute that assessment "better and more cautiously."[66] Looking back on the ashes of the republic in the 1550s, the historian Varchi reacted to these complicated tax assessment methods:

> This process was praised by some as ingenious and reasonable, and condemned by many as too long and overly complicated and bothersome. I am satisfied to let everyone hold his own opinion on the matter, and will only say that in well-ordered republics, one ought not use religious persons in secular offices.[67]

I, 321f. Early evidence of religious communal bursars is in G. Villani, VII, 16 (1267).

61. Trexler, "Honor," 325ff.

62. *Prediche* (Siena, 1425), II, 231f.

63. *Prediche* (Siena, 1427), 863f.

64. Trexler, "Honor,"322f.

65. E. Martène and U. Durand (eds.), *Veterum Scriptorum et Monumentorum . . . Collectio* III (Paris, 1724), cc. 1131f. (letter of Pietro Delfin of Aug. 27, 1485).

66. Trexler, "Honor," 322, 329.

67. *Storia*, VI, 10.

For similar reasons of secrecy, religious persons assumed central positions in electoral procedures and in communal scrutinies. The ancient method by which voters whispered in the ears of clergymen was replaced by more sophisticated, but equally clerical, procedures. In scrutinies to determine the names of qualified officeholders, religious collected the black (yes) and white (no) beans in a secret fashion, counted them, and reported the results. Franciscans, Dominicans, Augustinians, Camaldolans, and Olivetans did this at various times.[68] The registers containing the names of accepted candidates were kept in one church, the bags containing the name chits for lot in another. Since religious personnel controlled most of the keys (*signori delle chiavi*) to the chests containing these records, they were constantly involved in the governmental process. The bimonthly selection for office was executed by religious lifting name chits from the bags.[69] Finally, a Cistercian *converso* or lay brother, the Friar Secretary, functioned at the heart of government, collecting the beans on all votes by the communal executive in the course of everyday business, counting them, and reporting the results. Again, the explanation for this procedure was patent: "so that . . . citizens . . . of good life and manner come to office," and to "guard the honesty" of scrutinies.[70]

Thus clergy operated in government in positions no layman could hold; clerical participation allowed men, in Bernardino's words, to suspect each other less. Clerks permitted government to function in the best of times; they were an absolute necessity during periods of civil strife. When in 1429 a faction-ridden regime sought to end sects through the extreme measure of allowing each new government to ostracize the one citizen it thought most "scandalous," all counselors agreed that religious had to be utilized every step of the way. First, the new government took an oath to end scandal upon a Bible held by a friar. Then that friar, standing before the altar of the Palace chapel, collected in a basket the chit of each voter naming the one person he wanted ostracized. Next these names were examined in secret by two lay functionaries, by the friar of the communal seal, and by two other friars who, according to one recommendation, were to be foreigners of different orders appointed by the Signoria specifically for this task. Finally, this group was to report to the Signoria whether any citizen had been ostracized by the minimum number of required votes, leaving unnamed all others who had received votes.[71]

The clerical participants in government were able to serve the city because they were representative of an ethical ideal, and constantly ennobled

68. Trexler, "Honor," 323f. Until 1328, this election was done by one of the two bursars of the camera of arms, a Cistercian; *Statuti della Repubblica Fiorentina*, ed. R. Caggese, 2 vols. (Florence, 1910, 1921), vol. I: *Statuto del Capitano del Popolo degli Anni 1322–1325* (hereafter *Statuto . . . Capitano*), 86f.

69. Trexler, "Honor," 324

70. *Ibid.*, 329. The commune of San Gimignano first seems to have used religious to collect voting beans around 1278, shortly after it came under Florentine control; R. Davidsohn, *Forschungen zur Geschichte von Florenz*, 4 vols. (Berlin, 1896–1908), II, 210, no. 1550. This practice may therefore have been adopted from the Florentines.

71. *Commissioni di Rinaldo degli Albizzi*, ed. C. Guasti, 3 vols. (Florence, 1867–1873), III, 167ff (c. Nov. 21, 1429).

the ignoble Signoria and its entourage by their objective innocence. Complaining in 1451 that the dignity of the priors of Florence was disturbed at meal by the loudness of their familiars, petitioners urged that Vallombrosan monks be appointed to certain posts near the Signoria so that governmental fraternity at meals could proceed with the requisite poise. Formal government, the petition stressed, needed "persons of good life and example . . . like religious men."[72]

The Clergy

The clergy's role in government reflected its position in society at large. Considered essential in mediating types of social relations, the professional religious of Florence were at the same time expected to be separate and distinct from the lay estate. We must understand this paradox.

Separation from the world was the foundation of clerical utility; celibacy, legal immunity, and privilege were necessary if the clergy was to fill its role. Clerical vestments might be the finest products of the tailor's art, but they like their bearers had to be purified of the lust for gain that had inspired their lay donors; clerical lands had to produce for God and not man; clerical persons had to be subject to divine and not human courts. Sacrifice and contract, in short, had to be distinguished if either were to be possible.

Once properly immune from the *saeculum,* the clergy could tap the multiplicity of powers in the divine realm. Whether they formed part of the ceremonial, monastic, curative, or prophetic clergy, they could draw into the city the grace and sacrality, the honor and power so necessary to social life. The city in turn drew from this acquired power—for example, by using clerical functionaries in government to legitimate central exchange procedures between citizens, or by confraternities' regular hiring of chaplains to facilitate their fraternal life. The clergy therefore functioned not only outward toward God, but into the commune, mediating power; its separateness was the quality that made both possible.

The way any particular ecclesiastical person performed these conductive tasks depended upon his or her position in the clergy. The approximately fifty-six parish churches of Florence each had its rector and clerk. About ten of these were collegiate churches supporting not only a clerical prior but between two and ten canons, the latter mostly minor clerks not irrevocably committed to the religious life. In addition to this secular clergy, the city housed an average of six friaries (including Franciscans, Dominicans, Carmelites, Servites, and Augustinians) and four monasteries (Benedictine, Vallombrosan, and Camaldolan) of males, plus from twenty-two (1427) to fifty (1551) nunneries. The male secular and religious clergy, which alone was able to wander freely through the streets, represented perhaps 2 percent of the

72. Trexler, "Honor," 328.

general male population. The total clerical population was about 2.5 percent of the general population in 1427 and 7 percent in 1551, due to a radical increase in the number of nuns.[73]

The term *religious person* also included scores of hospital workers who were bound by the statutes of their hospitals if not by formal ecclesiastical codes. They too appeared dressed in distinctive habits and were protected by law, as were the clergy. Still, their identification with the clergy was at best nebulous; they lived together under *governo* and were thus religious, but contemporaries did not conceive of them as having more than caritative functions within the city. They were therefore clearly enough distinguished from the consecrated clergy.[74]

Within the clergy an unwritten but evident distinction existed between the ceremonial clergy of canons and prelates recruited mainly from the sons of solid citizens, and the curative or sacramental clergy, which heard confession, served communion, said Mass, and consoled the laity. The former, like their families, did not work with their hands: A prelate who said Mass when he did not have to was considered a rarity.[75] They represented the commune—that is, the families of their prestigious fathers—by parading relics, dressing finely for processions and other ceremonial occasions, lending their presence at solemn Masses said by lesser clerks. They also served the commune as ambassadors, charged with bearing the honor of the commune abroad.

The curative clergy, generally of lower-class or non-Florentine origins, was responsible for most of the work of sacramental life. Its secular wing was sometimes beneficed but mostly salaried, because the ceremonial clergy accumulated all valuable prebends and titles. Members of the religious wing—friars and monks—were held in greater esteem than the curative secular clergy because of their education. Although most of them were occupied with simple confessions, Masses, and consolation, their numbers could occasionally produce an important preacher.[76] Such a preacher had to ration his time. One of them instructed his listeners to be brief when they came to seek his advice during office hours (six to nine each evening). Come to the

73. Preliminary population results in my "Le Célibat à la fin du Moyen Age: les Religieuses de Florence," *Annales E.S.C.* XXVII (1972), 1337.

74. Lapo da Castiglionchio, *De Hospitalitate*, in *Tractatus . . . Universi Iuris . . .*, XIV, cc. 162–167. The position of the tertiaries or third-order religious was more complex; C. Piana, "La Posizione Giuridica del Terz'Ordine della Penitenza a Firenze nel secolo XIV," *Archivum Franciscanum Historicum* L (1957), 49–73.

75. Contemporaries marveled at the Camaldolan general Traversari, who remained with his monks, celebrated all offices, and even washed feet, since this was so uncommon; A. Dini-Traversari, *Ambrogio Traversari e i suoi Tempi* (Florence, 1912), Appendix 3 (*Hoedoeporicon*), 56. A contemporary called Arch-

bishop Antonino the prelate "who celebrated Mass every day he could"; R. Morçay, *Saint Antonin. Archevêque de Florence (1389–1459)* (Paris, 1914), 427. A contemporary pointed out that the *pievano* Prospero Pitti "did not think it vile to administer the sacraments with his own hands, and preach to his parishioners," even though he had a chaplain; P. Ginori Conti (ed. attrib.), *La Vita del beato Ieronimo Savonarola* (Florence, 1937), 21 (hereafter Ps. Burlamacchi).

76. Once their son has become a friar, said Savonarola, parents want him to become a preacher and a worthy man for the glory of the world, so they can tell others: "I have a son, I have a relative who is doing great things"; Savonarola, *Amos e Zaccaria*, III, 30.

point, he urged them: " 'Father, this is the situation.' I will answer you: 'Do this.' And [then] go away without further ado."[77] Another told his audience that bringing every little problem to him "is a waste of time, for I could sit and study and write a little sermon."[78] When one did gain success as a preacher, therefore, the curative role had to be balanced with ceremonial and dramatic ones comparable to those of the priors and abbots of the religious houses.[79]

The female monastic clergy was distinguished by its sex, locus, and function. It formed a cloistered holy city that through its exemplary group socialization encouraged virginity among lay virgins and confidence within a less socialized general population. Violation of cloister neutralized its effectiveness. Thus the commune instituted an office to keep males out of the nunneries, and was responsive to the nuns' assertion that paying taxes was an intrusion upon that separation.[80] The prayers of a nunnery that could maintain such celibacy were, in the words of one proud abbess, "more useful, coming from persons of such great religion, than are two thousand horses."[81] A city that preserved all its nunneries immaculate was a powerful one. "Day and night they consecrate their prayers to the most dignified Signoria of Florence," wrote one admiring citizen; "Open your eyes and appreciate this!"[82]

The nunneries' ability to preserve Florence was thought to be dependent on the quality of their inhabitants. Though servant sisters were of lower-class and generally foreign origin, the choir nuns, whose holiness mattered, were predominantly recruited from the "honest" middle and upper levels of the city's population. The prayers of "honest virgins" were considered more efficacious than those of some lesser group.

In its basic social composition, therefore, the clergy as a whole reflected the society from which it was drawn. Its public ceremonial was performed by men of good family; its private monastic group was drawn from the females of the same group; its curative element was normally drawn from the lesser social ranks. Lay principles of corporate hierarchy reigned in the clerical body despite the ideal of fraternal community that inspired the estate. Justice was different for clerks of good family than it was for those of mean origins, as was deference, and position within the religious hierarchy.

In unstable times, a fourth type of clerk appeared in the city, one distinguished not by sex, social origins, or dignity of title, but by prophetic qualities.[83] In such periods of stress distinctions between honorable and ignoble clergy were obscured. Under the impress of the prophet or visionary, rich clerks shed their robes and assumed the life-style of the lay brother, and

77. Savonarola, *Ruth e Michea*, I, 8, 98.

78. Bernardino of Siena, *Prediche* (Siena, 1427), 615f.

79. Though like other ecclesiastics Savonarola spoke of the importance of the priest, he himself had not originally wanted to become one; *Aggeo*, 324f. Hearing confession was considered an encumbrance for the preacher, and the Mendicants in general released preachers from this duty and from begging.

80. Trexler, "Célibat," 1329, 1349.

81. *Ibid.*, 1329.

82. *Ibid.*

83. On the prominence of nonstatus or liminal persons during crisis, see ch. 10, this volume.

clerks of humble origin were ennobled by the needs of the time. But such prophetic clerks were few and far between, and formed no part of the normal organization of civil life. During normal times, the city did not maintain a priesthood of visionaries, but rather one of ritual and technical capacities.

The specific services these different types of clerks rendered to society were, consequently, neatly political; they were clearly directed toward the preservation of masculinity, lineage, and order. By placing his sons as ceremonial canons in the main churches of the city, a father could provide for their upkeep, keep them out of trouble, and, perhaps most important, make them long-range representatives of family honor in a society where governmental representation was short term. The nuns' role in preserving the family was no less important. The majority of girls who became nuns did so because their fathers could not afford to marry them without destroying the family patrimony and eventually the family name.[84] The city's honor was directly affected by the honor of families, so that the latter's preservation sustained communal honor and authority. In churches and in the streets, the honorable canons mirrored their fathers' riches, authority, and honor. Within the nunneries, daughters exemplarily socialized into a divine community at once preserved family and communal capital, name, and authority. Parents' gifts of land and personal wealth to their clerical sons and daughters further protected these families, for gifts were tax-exempt. Such charity protected the families from God, but it also protected them from a commune in need of money.

Thus, although the clergy was expected to protect all inhabitants of the city by procuring them grace, it principally served the upper classes; its mission was selective. This was not yet the age of the internal mission to the lower classes and to the peasants, nor the age of careful attention to children and young people.[85] The clergy was predominantly intended for the gov-

---

84. In 1471 the paternal decision to monachize was taken at around six years of age, and actual entry during the Renaissance occurred at about ten years of age; Trexler, "Célibat," 1342f. Christiane Klapisch's reading of the Florentine *ricordanze* tends to confirm my finding: The average vestition age of twenty-four girls entering nunneries between 1332 and 1524, according to her records, was ten and a half years. I would like to thank Professor Klapisch for her personal communication; see also her "Zacharie, ou le Père Evincé. Les Rites Nuptiaux Toscans entre Giotto et le Concile de Trente," *Annales E.S.C. XXXIV* (1979), 1216–1243. My findings have been disputed by A. Molho and J. Kirshner, who sketch a meritocratic society giving its girls until eighteen years of age to "win a man"; "The Dowry Fund and the Marriage Market in Early Quattrocento Florence," *Journal of Modern History* L (1978), 423. In fact, as Klapisch's reading of the Minerbetti *ricordanze* also shows, Florentine fathers either invested in the state dowry fund before their girls reached six years, subsequently to marry them, or did not do so, and subsequently monachized them. Such entrants almost always brought a (lesser) dowry to the nunnery—raised through means other than the state dowry fund—*because* girls were almost always below the minimum legal age for vesting when they entered, as is indicated by Bernardino of Siena, *Prediche* (Siena, 1425), II, 90, and by the notarial documents accepting such minors, such as *ASF, not. antecos.*, P 351 (1470–1472), Mar. 28, 1470.

The clergy also protected the family by absorbing sickly children; see Trexler, "Célibat," 1343, for several examples. Boys were also commonly consigned to the clergy for this reason. Note the humanist Salutati's decision to make his son a clerk "because he had weak eyes and because he was not judged suitable for the active life"; E. Sanesi, "Canonici Fiorentini dal secolo XIII al secolo XV," *Atti della Società Colombaria di Firenze (1928–1929)* (Florence, 1933), 45. And Bernardino of Siena criticized fathers who procured abbeys or a bishopric for relatives who could not govern three snails; *Prediche* (Siena, 1427), 546f.

85. G. Strauss, *Luther's House of Learning. Indoctrination of the Young in the German Reformation* (Baltimore, 1978).

ernors and not the governed. When civil war threatened, as it did in 1295, this functional direction and the overlapping lay–religious sociology were strikingly apparent. To avoid civil war between two camps, Villani tells us, the Florentines used the mediation "of friars of good family from one side and the other. [As a result] each side disarmed, [and] the city pacified itself without a riot."[86] These were the social strata that had built the churches and should attend them; preachers urged churchgoing upon the well-to-do and their wives, not upon salaried workers.[87] The same clergy directed its best literary efforts, of course, to the same group: Upper-class society figures were the almost exclusive recipients of edificatory letters from religious advisors.[88]

Even in its mission to the wives of political men, however, the clergy was really aiming at the mature males who governed these women. Thus a rector could say that he had only two or three parishioners, by which he presumably meant not the working people of the parish, nor the wives of citizens, but the few male heads of honorable families.[89] Even though the majority of an audience at a sermon might be female, preachers addressed their sermons to males.[90] In church, laymen came nearest the *sancta sanctorum*, familiarly approaching and surrounding the altar.[91] In paintings of sermons, we find the civil governors, males all, iconically framing the pulpit and altar.[92] Their canon-sons represented their fathers' masculinity, their daughters in nunneries prayed for it. It was the usury of the fathers that was purified in their children's sacrifice.

The very narrowness of the clergy's ministry to the male political class provides the key to understanding the more general social roles of the religious specialists. The clergy concentrated upon politicians because they had the money and influence to foster and protect the religious; that goes without saying. But is this not another way of saying that patrician charity and good behavior were the clergy's main weapons in defending the common good, the sins of the male politicians the greatest enemies of the *respubblica*? Conceiving of itself as the defender of the populace at large, the clergy viewed the male political class as the cause of good times and bad, and concentrated its efforts upon this body. In bad times the clergy, much like the other social groups that were excluded from political life, protectively encircled its males to shield them from God; only if the males were safe could the populace at large hope for surcease. In more normal times the clergy, unlike society's lay liminal

86. G. Villani, VIII, 12.

87. Trexler, *Synodal Law*, 65.

88. An exception was the letter of the hermit Giovanni da Celle to the carpenter Maso; F. Tocco, "I Fraticelli," *ASI*, ser. 5, XXXV (1905), 344.

89. S. Bastiano was the parish; I have unfortunately lost my reference.

90. A late-fifteenth-century French preacher estimated four women to each man at sermons; A Krails-

heimer, *Rabelais and the Franciscans* (Oxford, 1963), 20.

91. Giotto's *St. Francis at Greccio* (Plate 7), shows the burghers familiarly inside the screen separating nave from altar, whereas the women in the nave peer through the opening. I would like to thank Marcia Hall for bringing this to my attention. See her "The *Tramezzo* in Santa Croce, Florence, Reconstructed," *Art Bulletin* LVI (1974), pl. 17.

92. See Plate 20 for a standard representation of officials framing a preacher.

groups, continued its vigilance. The clergy was, so to speak, an institutionalized rite-of-passage group continually passing all the inhabitants of Florence
through uncertainty and danger by ministry to the males.

Among the many roles of the clergy that affected the general population,
four deserve special mention. First, as professional generalists they defended
the city against natural forces. Even more than today, when states still hold
(televised) prayer services in the face of uncontrolled nature, the European
cities of past ages were like arks afloat in a troubled sea. The walls of Florence
could not disarm these forces. Catastrophes of wind, rain, and lightning were
as omnipotent as plague. The city was an easy target for an angry God, and
the clergy was its essential ally in combating a wrathful deity.

Laymen were scarcely less expert in manipulating persons than they
were in fighting natural forces. Diplomatic usage and vocabulary, for example, were still rudimentary. Bankruptcy proceedings and a host of bureaucratic tasks were done by skilled but unspecialized notaries. Lawyers were
simply divided between canonists and civists.[93] There was no police profession as such. The medical profession was unspecialized, both its practitioners
and therapy elementary.[94] And at the peak of the political order stood
amateurs with no calling. Thus a second task fell to the clergy: They served as
generalistic person-manipulators in a society that distrusted whatever division of labor there was. People approached counselors like the Dominican
Giordano da Rivalto and asked not only "if it is better to say Our Fathers, or
fast; better to say Our Fathers, or go on trips for indulgences; better to give
alms, or serve in hospitals . . ."[95] but also how to reach a negotiated settlement
of a business dispute, how to settle an argument between husband and wife
or father and son, how to collect debts, and how to get well. To us this range
of problems seems within the world of psychology and communication, but
to the Franciscan Bernardino of Siena it seemed that any tribulation at all
landed in his lap. When he protested that he was not qualified to deal with
many of these problems, and that "everyone should deal with his own
specialty," he received the answer, "It seems to me that you are bishop,
pope, and emperor."[96]

A third clerical role was to provide and maintain a consecrated center that
could withstand the varied transformations the city underwent. Men fled the
city during the plague; they followed profits and courts and maintained dual
citizenship. There was no incontrovertible argument against deserting Florence, and as a result, wealth and talent in the city one day was gone the
next.[97] Bankruptcies were common. This mobility of urban fortune and status
meant that domestic associations, always fragile, were constantly being re-

93. Note L. Martines' qualifications to this view in
Lawyers and Statecraft in Renaissance Florence (Princeton, 1968), 91–95, 170.

94. Bernice Trexler, "Hospital Patients in Florence:
San Paolo, 1567–1568," *Bulletin of the History of Medicine* XLVIII (1974), 41–59.

95. Giordano da Rivalto–Moreni, *Prediche,* 184.

96. Bernardino of Siena, *Prediche* (Siena, 1427), 615f.

97. An example of this threat is in Trexler, *Spiritual
Power,* 22f.

constructed. From one point of view, the clergy was a societal broker constantly facilitating new civil associations and thus a new civil identity. From another, it *was* that identity, providing a stable center in the swirl of changing faces and social bonds.

The final role of the clergy that I shall mention was its role as a moral beacon for society, the one most often stressed by contemporaries: "*Popolo*, if you want to be good, seek to have good priests."[98] The clergy was a publicly maintained representation of society's highest expectations and lowest realities. It was a unity, incorporating for critics Hypocrisy, Ignorance, and Cleverness, for its champions Altruism, Humility, and Saintliness. It was the primary repository of the vices and virtues native to the society it protected, and this is why treatises on vices and virtues so commonly have "the clerk" or "the clergy" as their descriptive vehicle.

Thus, although contemporaries thought of different segments of the clergy as providing different models for emulation—individualistic hermits as images of unorganized holiness, monks and nuns as ideals of contemplation, secular clergy and friars as examples of civic participation—they expected all clergy to adhere to either a universal or a corporative moral code so as to form through example general patterns of lay behavior. They taught individual ethical lessons, of course: friar X does not steal, layman Y should not. But they taught formal behavior as well. By the relative solemnity and reverence of their own bearing, the ideal clergy, within which ethically ambiguous activities were excluded as they could not be in the world of business and sexuality, taught city dwellers the right places and times at which behavior had to be rigidly patterned. The Christian clergy of Florence incorporated both attitudinal and legalistic ethical models for the laity, which expected of its clergy a combination of reverence and normative conformity.[99] Thus as an immune body separate from the populace, the clergy could be part of the solution to the social and governmental problems of Florence. But as an integral part of that society, the Florentine clergy was also a part of those problems.

Facing the Outside World

Ritual was a centripetal force drawing pilgrims to and holding inhabitants around the communal altars. Yet the sacred ashes under the city altars were recent and imported—Zanobi alone among the city's patrons was a hometown product, whereas Milan had long boasted of a saint from almost every family in the city.[100] The Arno city was a latecomer in the business of building a native center, and for most of its republican history it relied on

98. Savonarola, *Esodo*, I, 42.

99. Elaboration on page 471, this volume.

100. *Storia di Milano*, IX, pt. 2, 567.

older, better established political and spiritual entities for its traditions and values. Gods and the immune clergy who manipulated them, the central resources for vivifying a spiritless commune, all came from abroad or drew their authority thence. To hold its center the Tuscan town catered to foreign tastes.

Florentines faced the assumed inadequacy and hollowness of their own culture with a mixture of civic boosterism at home and fawning acquiescence abroad. They knew that their merchants exported a wealth of merchant technology and expertise to the rest of Europe, yet the merchants were the first to admit their social and occupational inferiority to those whose courts they provisioned. These traders were despised: by wealthy and noble clients for the unseemliness of the Florentines' occupations, by whole peoples for their assumed rapacity. "In the whole world I don't think two sins are more abominable than those the Florentines commit. The first is usury and infidelity, the second [homosexuality] is so abominable I don't dare mention it."[101] Pope Gregory XI's animus was that of any number of Europeans against Tuscan traders whose political system was so ephemeral and ignoble that sodomy might seem indigenous to it.

Florentines wanted to be like their betters. Most sought no higher goal than to convert themselves into rentiers, their political system into that of the nobler Venetians, their manners into those of the finer people in princely states. In Machiavelli's words, the Florentines, "having destroyed [their] nobility, and their republic being wholly in the hands of men brought up in trade, followed the usages and examples of others."[102] Only the appearance of Medici leaders in the fifteenth century, combined with the skillful exploitation of another foreign resource—antiquity—gave Florentines some respite from a sense of cultural backwardness. For in Lorenzo de'Medici, the city would see embodied those foreign ideals for which it had so yearned but not found.

Until Lorenzo's golden age, the city imported its ethos, for burghers had none of their own. Provence and its Neapolitan appendage were the principal sources: sweet *courtoisie*, concepts of masculinity and femininity, of correct form, speech, and action, of reverence and deference, of sublimated violence in the joust and tourney. Francesco da Barberino from the end of the thirteenth century and Boccaccio in the second third of the fourteenth were urban litterati who in the *Documenti d'Amore* and in the *Decameron* created an imaginary Florentine society whose tenor had little in common with the violent reality of the Arno city—Barberino could actually bring himself to speak of Florence "where there is always peace and unity among the citizens"—and everything to do with a romantic ideal from the other side of the

---

101. Trexler, *Spiritual Power*, 38. On the strong ultramontane scorn of Italian military ability, see R. Truffi, *Giostre e Cantori di Giostre* (Rocca S. Cacciano, 1911), 19–22; and for other Italians' scorn of Florentine military ability, see the quote on page 531, this volume.

102. *History*, 45.

mountains.[103] They created an imaginary courtly world in a city with a weak political center. Institutionalized in the Parte Guelfa, that union of finer men, this ethos sought its and the commune's charisma in Rome, the natural center of spiritual honor, and in the French court, the center of courtly honor.

The city adopted the *giglio* or fleur-de-lis of the Capetians, just as the Parte Guelfa made the blazon of a pope its own. Its citizens sought and obtained the right of their canon-sons to wear the official vestment of the papal court.[104] And to become an imperial knight! That was the desire of the proudest Florentine businessman. Asked by King Rupert to carry out a dangerous mission, Buonaccorso Pitti insisted he be knighted, and explained why:

> A more glorious memory would survive me and more honor reflect on my family if I were to die bearing arms in his service than if I were to be killed as an agent on my way to pick up funds.

Pitti got his armorial quarter and promptly composed a verse that vividly reflects its significance for a Florentine burgher:

> The current year of fourteen one,
> King Rupert, in his town of Trent,
> Decreed my scutcheon might henceforth present
> An armorial emblem of his own:
> The golden lion rampant and, thereon,
> Caused to be written in a document
> My brothers' names and mine with his assent
> So each of us might bear the lion on
> His wavy field. Thence our privilege comes,
> With lasting patents of nobility,
> To bear this symbol bravely on our arms
> Wherever such heraldic emblems be
> Borne: here or in other realms,
> And to hold land from kings in fee.
> So, sons and brothers, nobly cultivate
> Virtue, as befits our new estate.[105]

Not only this genteel ethos came from abroad, but ethics as well: from the realm of the Roman and canon law, and from the moral theologians interpreting the scriptures. After the second half of the fourteenth century, eminent lawyers could be heard to say that a municipal statute was as valid as any law or canon, and Florentine legislators warned against suggesting otherwise;[106] the

103. *I Documenti d'Amore di Francesco da Barberino*, ed. F. Egidi, 4 vols. (Rome, 1905–1927), II, 218.

104. A late case of a common practice is in W. Roscoe, *The Life and Pontificate of Leo the Tenth*, III (Liverpool, 1805), 67 (1515).

105. Pitti, *Memoir*, 70ff. On the importance of Maso

degli Albizzi's knighting (1388/1389) to his political future, see Brucker, *Civic World*, 274. Piero Pazzi's knighting was also significant in this respect; Vespasiano da Bisticci, *Vite di Uomini Illustri del secolo XV* (Florence, 1938), 396ff.

106. For example, *Statuta*, I, 763.

city law was in fact never sovereign. Interpreted by canonists and legists, Florentine urban statutes bent again and again to broader principles of justice. The municipal law never developed its own jurisprudence. Laws were regularly abjured because they violated the canon law, suits constantly won on the basis of the Roman law.[107] How could it be otherwise if Florentines were to have credit beyond their borders?

The city secured faith in itself by appeal to foreign authority, for its own solidity was tied to foreign approbation as well as limited by it. The actions of the commune in the 1340s are a case in point. With general bankruptcy of its great business houses in process, the commune sought a way to assure foreigners of Florentine credit, and convince its own citizens of governmental continuity. The answer was to allow foreigners and citizens to sue in the Roman court if the commune did not fulfill its political and financial commitments.[108] Reaching out toward more trustworthy sources of credit in this fashion was inherent in the political and social system. When a century later Cosimo de' Medici set about establishing his de facto authority in the city, he may as papal depositor have been able to promise his backers access to the Roman judicial system to settle contract difficulties, thus avoiding Florentine courts.[109] When in the mid-fifteenth century the commune stopped paying interest on its clergy's investment in the public debt, the clergy had less reason to maintain its loyalty to Florence, and looked to Rome.[110] The laity followed, because their interest payments were soon compromised. By the end of the century, it seemed to humiliated Florentines that the papacy was as involved in rendering justice in Florence as was the commune.[111] Ethos, ethic, faith—all had their ultimate sources abroad. Evidently, the importation of relics was but a reflection of a broad cultural fact: Associated with Florentines or their institutions, foreign nobility bestowed on the former an authority and legitimacy they did not otherwise possess.

Political dependence went hand in hand with cultural eclecticism, for the city's well-being depended upon the foreign business activity of hundreds of its citizens. The city was constantly hostage to its merchants, who, isolated in their small confraternities in so many European cities and courts, were exposed to the whim of local authorities.[112] To increase their chances for gain and to protect their investments, these men subjected themselves to foreign courts, took out citizenship in foreign centers to avoid being treated as Florentines, sought honors and ennoblement, and invested in local undertakings.[113] They could easily change loyalties. Such considerations dic-

---

107. On cancellation of laws violating ecclesiastical liberty, see Trexler, *Synodal Law*, 22f.

108. Trexler, "Florence, by the Grace of the Lord Pope . . .," *Studies in Medieval and Renaissance History* IX (1972), 115–215.

109. Such speculation must await further study of Cosimo's role, now being undertaken by Anthony Molho. Neither G. Holmes ("How the Medici Became the Pope's Bankers," in Rubinstein, *Florentine Studies*,

357–380), P. Partner ("Florence and the Papacy in the Earlier Fifteenth Century," *ibid.*, 397–401), nor R. de Roover (*The Rise and Decline of the Medici Bank* [New York, 1966]) hints at this possibility.

110. Trexler, *Spiritual Power*, 168f.

111. Martines, *Lawyers*, 246–310, especially 282f.

112. On this danger, see Trexler, *Spiritual Power*, 44–108.

113. "The Venetians took reprisal on our goods in

tated a Florentine foreign policy closely geared to these merchant and foreign princely interests.

Thus the city sent out its merchants for gain, but lost its hold on them and some of its freedom in foreign affairs. It treasured the foreign honors that young Florentines won abroad—papal and royal bureaucracies recruited scions of the best families as officials—but realized that those honors drew honor away as well. Yet citizens vaunted the honor one of their own had received abroad, as if they could not do without it. In 1515 Giuliano de' Medici was firmly entrenched in Florence as the representative of his brother Pope Leo X. One would have thought that such honor would have been all Florence could have imagined. Yet Guicciardini wrote that in that year King Francis of France "gave status" to Giuliano by bestowing a French fief upon him.[114] On the eve of the Medicean principate, educated contemporaries obviously still felt that "status" came from the feudal order: It was such an honor for a hometown boy to be a French duke!

The previous pages have sketched the material and cultural background to which ritual would respond. First of all, the Florentine political and social order was illegitimate; formal behavior had to make that order legitimate. Second, the city, even with its patronal system, lacked honor; formal behavior had to create it. Third, inhabitants did not trust each other and foreigners did not trust Florentines; ritual had to provide the setting to encourage trust. Finally, Florentines lacked self-confidence, and were more convinced that the republican and merchant order was necessary than that it was culturally defensible; men acting in common form would have to infuse each other with pride and thus individual identity. Formal behavior could not be merely a mask or front, for Florence was not an insular court complete in itself. Drawing upon the authority of its families, however meager, upon its clergy, foreigners, and gods, Florentine action would have to combine expressive and ideal elements, technique and heartfelt conviction, tradition and creativity, if it were to vivify. Ritual, meant to generate life, could not afford stultification in an ignoble merchant community. Generating life, it had to embody it.

their territory. But that did not do much harm, because the property of most Florentine merchants there could not be touched, since they had the privileges of citizenship"; F. Guicciardini, *The History of Florence* (New York, 1970), 178.

114. As part of the accord with Leo, Francis I "desse stato in Francia e pensione a Giuliano"; F. Guicciardini, *Storia d'Italia* IV (Rome, 1968), 1120 (bk. XII, ch. 16).

Chapter 2

Cosmos

God is the republic, and he who
governs the republic governs God.
Thus God is justice, and he who
*makes justice, makes God.**

Florentines acted to counter the institutional conflicts of their society and, over time, perfected patterns of behavior they found efficacious in dealing with those conflicts.

Through observing their own formal behavior, they developed conventional attitudes toward space, objects, and time, attitudes that in their totality we call cosmology; this cosmology, in turn, predisposed subsequent behavior. Having studied the institutions that begat ritual, we turn now to the Florentine cosmology, which was a result and a cause of formal behavior.

The Florentines would not have agreed with our approach, which derives their cosmology from ritual without even mentioning ideas, beliefs, or dogmas. Called upon to reflect on the matter, they would have given primacy to the realm of creed, and tried to explain their actions as an effect of their beliefs, much as intellectual historians like J. H. Plumb still give ideas primacy.[1] In fact, however, dogmas and beliefs in this as in all societies were often inconsistent with actions, and with the attitudes toward the cosmos that one must deduce from those actions. Today, for example, men vilify and even

---

*"Deus est Respublica, et qui gubernat Rempublicam gubernat Deum. Item Deus est iustitia, et qui facit iustitiam, facit Deum"; statement of a Florentine counselor on July 31, 1431, cited in F. Pellegrini, *Sulla repubblica fiorentina a tempo di Cosimo il Vecchio* (Pisa, 1880), cxxxiii.

1. *New York Times Book Review*, Feb. 9, 1975, p. 1.

physically attack objects while insisting they are inanimate. In the days of the republic, Florentine citizens professed monotheism, yet their behavior and often their speech were convincingly polytheistic. They dogmatized that the commune did not die, but their ritual actions showed a preoccupation with preventing its demise.[2]

Conceptions often contradict actions, but perceptions are always part of the frame of ritual, for they derive directly from action. The most direct approach to understanding the nature of ritual, therefore, lies not in the study of theological or liturgical treatises, nor in the study of any other type of reflective documentation; these sources tell us what men believed. We shall instead read historical sources that were intended to tell us what happened, and gather from them the reporters' offhand, often unintended perceptions of why things happened. From these fragments, we will reconstruct the Florentine cosmos.

The cunning tension of any cosmology is the relation between tribal and universal, subjective and objective force; our approach will recognize the power of self *and* otherness. Asked where the holy was that his space, time, and objects seemed to consume, our Florentine would after reflection have replied that the sacred was divinely and objectively outside; he would have denied that men made the holy. An older historiography did much the same. It explained local religious actions and institutions from the vantage point of what Robert Redfield called the Great Tradition, which in Western Europe meant the Roman church and the royal court.[3]

By studying historical sources rather than treatises, however, we will have no difficulty seeing that the Florentines perceived themselves at work on the stuff of holiness. They did have a percept of civic religion, one so marked that cosmology could be studied purely in terms of their Small Tradition.[4] There is no gainsaying the importance of civic religion, and in a subsequent chapter we will study men making holiness.

Still, the Florentine cosmology cannot be understood only in local terms. Inhabitants of the city acted as if they were worked upon by outside forms; they imported their forms, norms, and ethos to such an extent that their behavior is inexplicable if its universalistic sources are ignored. Even more important is the fact that the Florentine ritual actor sought a spiritual experience neither describable nor apprehensible in local terms; we must recognize and treasure that impulse. No less than the mystic, the Florentine ritual actor reached out to infinity, to a common human experience of oneness with nature and self that no merely intramural approach can fully explain.

---

2. On the undying commune, *Istoria di Firenze di Gregorio Dati dall'anno MCCCLXXX all'Anno MCCCCV* (Florence, 1735), 69.

3. R. Redfield, *The Little Community and Peasant Society and Culture* (Chicago, 1960), 42 seq.

4. See the symposium on civic religion in the *Journal for the Scientific Study of Religion* XIV (1975), 385–414. A. Soboul has fostered the study of the subject in modern times with his "Religious Sentiment and Popular Culture during the Revolution," in J. Kapplow (ed.), *New Perspectives on the French Revolution. Readings in Historical Sociology* (New York, 1965), 338–350.

Florentine attitudes toward the cosmos reflected this universalistic urge, for the ritual actor did not live encapsulated in theatrical space.

Space

There was no holy earth in Florence. The visitor watching the more or less formal behavior of inhabitants in order to learn right action himself soon discovered that it was not any particular space, but the buildings and more particularly the objects within them that brought about that rigidification and formalization of behavior, called ritual, which signifies the presence of the holy. To become pregnant, Florentine women went to the baths of Petriolo, not to the Arno. Men sought the healing air of their villas, not the city.[5] No sacred woods or streets graced the city. Its natural elements were profane and, unless mediated by human authority, were legitimate dumping grounds for material and body waste; a ditch without a coat of arms or a cross was a place to urinate.

Inhabitants created worshipful space by enclosing it. The emerging medieval city consisted of small clusters of houses built around powerful protectors living in towers. Each protector built a church or chapel and if possible obtained relics of its titular saint. As the tower had provided asylum to nearby inhabitants for their persons, goods, and deceased during crisis, so now the church near or affixed to the tower also assumed such functions. At the very end of the Florentine republic, churches were still used to harbor precious belongings during siege, and the government itself kept its most precious objects in the Palace chapel.[6] Such buildings were less profane than the area about them; attackers were inhibited by sacred associations from invading them to grab the loot inside. The builders of these tower churches realized this quality of the church and fostered their identification with it by placing their escutcheons both on the churches and on the relics inside.[7]

The building of the city walls marked an important turning point in the development of worshipful space, for it manifested an impulse toward common experience and protection, to some extent shifting the area of behavioral formalism away from the local tower and toward the center that would emerge within the walls. The walls themselves became the first ritual edifice of the new commune. Built by "religious officials" rather than by mere

5. F. Sacchetti, *Il Trecentonovelle*, ed. V. Pernicone (Florence, 1946), 288. Molho, *Florentine Public Finances*, 134. Individuals returned to the land for its curative values, we see, despite the government's aforementioned determination to desacralize its sacred things. For human spatial organization as analogous to language, see D. Preziosi, *The Semiotics of the Built Environment* (Bloomington, 1979).

6. In 1529, the Peruzzi emptied the bones of their ancestors from their chapel so as to hide the chapel's silver there; Richa, *Notizie*, I, 64. The practice of burying wealth with the deceased in turn stimulated grave robbing.

7. On the significance of this practice, see page 94, this volume.

laymen, and sanctified by attaching to them images and "public symbols," they were regularly lustrated by priests to preserve their virtues, and exorcized when it was thought devils had infiltrated them.[8] Processions touched the gates as part of the *via sacra*, military forces had to pass under them at propitious times, and visiting dignitaries could not traverse them without solemn preparations and ceremonies.[9] Furthering the city's protection from the natural world outside, nunneries sprang up at most of the city gates.[10] But salvation too could show its face there, as when in 1530 a preacher promised inhabitants that angels would appear at the bastions to save the city from its besiegers.[11]

Having joined into a commune, the lords of the towers set about creating its monuments. The octagonal church of San Giovanni became the citizens' exclusive baptistry and the fundamental place of brotherhood for protectors becoming citizens. Dino Compagni recorded how in 1301 he had hit upon the "holy and honest thought" of bringing these fractious men together in the place where they had been born in Christ. "Dear and capable citizens," he addressed them in that auspicious setting,

> who have each of you taken holy baptism from this font, reason forces and constrains you to love each other like brothers; also, you possess the most noble city in the world. . . . Over this sacred font, from whence you received holy baptism, swear to good and perfect peace among you, so that the [foreign] lord who is coming finds all the citizens united.[12]

The Baptistry, like the nearby cathedral of Santa Reparata (also conceived of by the citizens as a primal center—constitutional crises often led to plebiscites, *parlamenti*, in its wide bays), achieved its eminence by the willingness of protectors to bestow their family arms upon the walls of the structure. But once they had attained a symbolic value apart from the families that had graced them, these two churches represented a danger to the primacy of family honor. Regimes at the beginning of the fourteenth century forbade family arms to be placed in the cathedral and removed the bodies of private citizens buried there. At about the same time, the government insisted that the towers of family palaces not exceed the height of the communal palace— all evidence of an attempt to separate and protect the identity of the commune from that of its parts.[13]

8. The *segni publici* fell off in 1501; Schnitzer, *Quellen*, III, 12. The Sienese exorcized Florentine maleficence from the walls of their city in 1230; Davidsohn, *Storia*, II, 242. On religious officials building the walls, see my "Honor," 319f.

9. On processions to gates, Davidsohn, *Storia*, I, 1070. In 1362 Florentine troops broke order and ran to get through the gates in time; M. Villani, XI, 3. On visitors entering, see ch. 9, this volume.

10. Trexler, "Célibat," 1332.

11. Varchi, XI, 105.

12. D. Compagni, *Cronica delle Cose Occorenti ne'tempi suoi* (Milan, 1965), bk. II, ch. 8.

13. The cemetery between the two churches was ordered removed in 1296; Richa, *Notizie*, V, xv. In 1357 the *operai* of the cathedral moved to prohibit all burials in the church without their approval; C. Guasti, *Santa Maria del Fiore* (Florence, 1887), 93. In 1385 they decided to remove all private coats of arms from the church; *ibid.*, 277. Legislation limiting the size of

Building the Mendicant churches and the public edifices in the late thirteenth century provided a partial solution to the tension between civic and familial identity. Many important families, their numbers and traditions increasing, built chapels and burial lots in the Franciscan, Dominican, Augustinian, Carmelite, and Servite churches, their past and future wealth being placed in the vaults of their chapels, their arms signifying possession. The masculine towers of the Mendicant churches became the cultic homes of the protectors' citizen descendants, whereas the city churches of San Giovanni and Santa Reparata struggled valiantly to rise above such individuality. In the process, the old tower churches, now part of the parishional structure of the city, declined in importance as families bore the remains of their deceased to the Mendicants' temples.

Government buildings rose at the same time as the great Mendicant churches, and this second complex of worshipful space seems at first glance to express secular not ecclesiastical ideals, communal not familial goals. Yet these communal buildings of Florence will be found to embody the goals and charismata not only of the one commune, but of its familial parts: The Florentines' inveterate habit of pasting their family arms on public buildings is evidence enough that families, in dedicating these monuments to a power greater than their own, intended them to heighten their own power. Deeper examination will also show that within the perimeters of these buildings much the same type of behavior could be expected from citizens as from churchgoers. It will show that government buildings, far from being profane, had themselves been converted into sacred places.[14]

Before the construction of the city hall (started in 1298), the priors of Florence had met in churches and had used the latter's altars as the backdrop and seal of government's executive actions. Doubtless these churches had been honored by the association, just as the government itself had been able to strengthen its authority by accomplishing its sacred business in sacred places. Thus the move to the new, secular, Palace of the priors heightened rather than eliminated the need for an altar of submission, communion, and contract; the city hall had to be partly church. The sacramentals of political power—the myriad of flags, the high tower, seals, chairs, and batons—functioned in one sense to "frame" the exercisers of power, to define and limit communal power without extinguishing it. The raised platform (*ringhiera*) that was added to the building in the 1320s gave the effect of an altar, and commonly served as such during festive occasions, with Mass, displays of relics, and sermons making it the main outdoor shrine in Florence.[15] Upon these steps each successive Signoria took its oath or "sacra-

private towers goes back to at least 1250; G. Villani, VII, 39. On its failure, Davidsohn, *Storia*, V, 401f.

14. Martines has reviewed the legal practice of calling government buildings sacred; *Lawyers*, 93.

15. N. Rubinstein notes the ceremonial motivations

behind the building of the Piazza della Signoria in Florence, in E. Hubula and G. Schweikhart (eds.), *Festschrift H. Siebenhüner* (Würzburg, 1978), 19–30. An extensive description of the platforms and their arrangements for a propitiative procession in 1390 allows the following reconstruction:

ment" of office in full view of the *popolo*. On the rare occasions when civic turmoil made it necessary to solemnize this contract out of the people's view, chroniclers of local events recorded such privacy as never having happened before.[16] These altar steps were also the stage where the subjects of Florence displayed their annual signs of submission to the public authority.

The new Palace was not a church merely in the metaphorical sense, however. Inside the building, a chapel built to St. Bernard served the brother priors for their obligatory divine services and much of their governmental business, as a sacred depository for communal treasures, and as a new center for hierarchical ordering around Bernard's altar. The saint's altar soon acquired importance as one of the "sacred stones" upon which communal contracts were sealed.[17] New subjects of the Signoria made their offerings on this saint's altar and feast day, as well as on that of the city's patron, John the Baptist.[18]

The Palace was, consequently, more than an administrative center, a profane place whose inhabitants sought salvation elsewhere. Imbued from the beginning with the authority of the city's political families, it sought the greater authority of St. Bernard, and a cult of hierarchical exchange was created around his altar. In the process, this saint emerged as a competitor of the Baptist: The Signoria, that is, distinguished itself from the city as government sought to distinguish itself from the families that composed it.[19] The new building harbored a new ritual; it created new means for relations between citizens and subjects. In the future there would be disputes as to whether the Palace, or the church of S. Giovanni, should be the home of new relics purchased by the city.[20] Thus the city hall added to, rather than elaborated upon, the sacrality of Florence. When the steps of the Palace became a regular stopping place on the standard processional route—the priors were joined to the procession much as the relics were fetched from churches and added to the procession—the building had definitely become one of the centers of ritual activity within the city.

Churches and governmental buildings were public places, the departure and terminal points of most manifestations of public unity. The third complex of space within which the behavior of Florentines became codified, the nun-

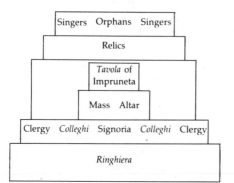

The source is Panciatichi, f. 160r (Oct. 12).

16. G. Villani, XII, 8 (1342); *Cronache e Memorie sul Tumulto dei Ciompi*, ed. G. Scaramella, *RIS*, XVIII, pt. 3, 17 (1378) (hereafter *Tumulto dei Ciompi*).

17. Compagni, II, 12; N. Rubinstein, *The Government of Florence under the Medici (1434 to 1494)* (Oxford, 1966), 157.

18. *ASF, Prov.*, 153, ff. 163v–165r (Oct. 27, 1462).

19. This continued a tradition of sovereign separateness, since in Florence, the *popolo* was formally distinct from the commune.

20. *ASF, CP*, 53, ff. 87v–88v (July 3, 1454). I would like to thank Julius Kirshner for this reference.

neries, was apart from society. Secular patrons might support the nunneries and compete to affix familial coats of arms to monastery walls. They certainly looked upon the nunneries as merit-making establishments that would contribute to their salvation. Yet laymen afforded this help in order to keep the houses apart from the world, not to absorb them into it. These were the city's holy enclaves, places where constant ritual sacrifices by virgins were thought to guarantee the continuity of public life. Utility to the commune depended on their ceremony being carried out in seclusion. The nunneries were not on the processional routes.

On the other hand, they were not indiscriminately scattered about the city. When at the end of the thirteenth century several groups of nuns moved their quarters within the city walls and when in the subsequent century and a half some two score more nunneries were consecrated, they followed the tendency of professional groups to concentrate their houses near each other. Agglomerations could be found near the city walls and along certain streets. For example, in 1552 from the Piazza San Piero Maggiore, site of an ancient nunnery, up the Borgo Pinti, four nunneries were found. Again, from the church of San Lorenzo, up the street called for most of its distance Via San Gallo, to the gate of the same name, hundreds of nuns lived in the seven monasteries that lined the street, and many more lived in the side streets off this busy thoroughfare. To the Florentine antiquary Richa in the eighteenth century, this street was not so much "the holy street"—as it must have been called at the time—but "the street of confusion."[21] Other concentrations of nunneries could be viewed around the meadow (*prato*) near the church of Ognissanti, along the Via Ghibellina, and around the gate of San Piero Gattolino (the present Porta Romana).[22] Thus, their holiness hidden behind facades distinguished only by the crosses and family arms attached to their fronts, these nunneries were nonetheless grouped into regional blocks of sacred space, within whose perimeters a more reverential behavior was required by law and civic convention.

These worshipful places—churches, governmental buildings, and nunneries—had this in common: They were all covered by Florentine laws prohibiting "profane" behavior in their vicinity. Gambling, whoring, and drinking were outlawed thereabouts,[23] the laws to protect their inhabitants forbade blasphemy,[24] all three had some right of asylum or immunity attached to them,[25] and industrial activities that by their smell and noise profaned the

21. Cited without reference in E. Viviani Della Robbia, *Nei Monasteri Fiorentini* (Florence, 1946), 7.

22. More information on this distribution in my "Célibat," 1332.

23. Such regulations for the area around churches and nunneries were so common they need no verification. For prohibitions concerning the city hall, see *Statuto . . . Capitano*, 238 (taverns and alimentation); *ASF, Prov.*, 65, f. 71v (June 22, 1377) (prostitution); *Statuti . . .*, II: *Statuto del Podestà dell'Anno*

1325, 379f (actors and buffoons in the Palace) (hereafter *Statuto . . . Podestà*).

24. The chronicler Stefani complained in 1376 that the laws against blaspheming the Signoria were not enforced, whereas persons blaspheming the Parte Guelfa came off worse than those blaspheming God; Stefani, rub. 767. Statutes against those vilifying the Signoria are in *Statuto . . . Capitano*, 90; *Statuta*, I, 257f.

25. On the asylum problem as it concerned churches and monasteries, see *Statuta*, I, 360f; Trexler, *Synodal*

area were prohibited.[26] The fundamentally similar intent of laws mandating behavior around all these buildings is attested by the procedures followed when they were profaned. The ecclesiastical ceremonies by which churches and nunneries were purified of sacrilege are well known, but it is less known that inhabitants were just as concerned about the purity of the city hall. When in 1527 the city was freed from the Medici, the Hall of the Great Council in the Palace could not be used until it had been purified of Medici "filth"—the hall had been used as a stable. Zealous republican youth in a fury of energy cleaned and burnished the sacred hall, but that was not enough:

> The hall being [already] clean and having been purged of every filth, it was none the less [again] purged and expiated by the priests with holy water, according to the holy ceremonies.[27]

Once this had been accomplished, a Mass of the Holy Ghost was sung before a packed, highly wrought citizenry. At the exalted moment of the elevation of the host, the distraught crowd made the hall resound with its unified tears of joy.[28] As it was customary to purify the area around a statue that had been profaned, so the halls of government were lustrated to provide a fitting setting for a ritual act of fraternity.

Contemporaries would have thought it mad to ask why behavior in such areas should have been reverential, and would have responded much as today's ritual actors react: "It's a tradition." When assassins murdered Giuliano de' Medici in the cathedral of Florence on the Sunday before Ascension, 1478, the outrage at this "brutal and uncivilized act" was all the greater because, in Guicciardini's words, it had been committed "in church on a holy day." In short, there was a right time and place for everything.[29]

Why should these areas have been reverential? Specifically, one wonders if priests and citizens ceremonially purged the Hall of the Grand Council because of what it was or, as seems more probable, because it was to be a setting in which men came together in fraternity to regulate their political order. Space, one suspects, had to be clean because of the nature of the activity transpiring within it. The hall was not a church or chapel; that it had to be sacerdotally purified can have no other explanation than that certain types of human actions transformed spatial character: "The place does not sanctify man but man the place. Nor does the *cathedra* make the priest, but the priest the *cathedra*."[30]

Law, 60. On the immunities of the Signoria, see *Statuto . . . Capitano*, 89–91.

26. No further *stabula beccariorum* could be built near a nunnery because of the smell; ASF, *Prov.*, 133, ff. 300v–301v (Feb. 4, 1442/1443). Grass and herbs could not be sold near S. Giovanni; *Statuta*, II, 39. Those selling comestibles could not ply their trade near the main government buildings; *Statuto . . . Capitano*, 238. There are, of course, many laws on such activities around these *sacra*.

27. J. Nardi, *Istorie della Città di Firenze* (Florence, 1858), bk. II, ch. 128. This is the one known case of a formal ecclesiastical purification rite following defilement of a basically secular building.

28. U. Dorini, "Ragguagli delle cose di Firenze dal 1524 al 1530," *Rivista Storica degli Archivi Toscani* III (1931), 58.

29. *History of Florence*, 34.

30. Francesco da Barberino, *Documenti*, I, 123.

Having already determined that lands within the city preserved no sacred patina, this line of inquiry slowly leads to the possibility that buildings, in and of themselves, were profane, and were made attitudinally sacred by the activities they housed, by the time, and most important by the objects they encased: churches their sacred things, government buildings their officers, nunneries their virginal activism.

A church might seem the least likely place to prove such a view, yet an examination of the evidence will show it to be so. In a sermon on sacrilege delivered to the Florentines in 1424, for example, the Franciscan Bernardino of Siena displayed just such a conception of sacred space when he listed seven reasons for being reverent in church:

1. The church was the "place and hotel of God."
2. The body of Christ was present.
3. Angels lived in the church.
4. The faithful received grace in church through the sacraments.
5. The relics of the saints were in the church.
6. The faithful received grace through praying to these saints in church.
7. The church, or at least its altar, was consecrated.[31]

The church was holy, so their friar taught the Florentines, because it housed things and persons. Its primary residents were God and the titular saint of the church; the idea was that the saint who resided in the church was its possessor.[32] Then the body of Christ was there, which is to say Christ himself. Next angels lived in the church, as did other saints. Clearly, the primary ritual-inducing element in the church was sacred presence, and not abstract enclosure of space. Certainly the sacred numen that these objects radiated reached a limit of sorts at the walls of the church, nunnery, or governmental palace. But the *sacer locus* focused on the area occupied by *cose sacre*, holy things: The church contained a guardian angel for each person there, said Bernardino, suggesting that empty of people, it was empty of these guardian spirits.[33]

In the same sermon Bernardino distinguished the primary and secondary locus of the holy, thus furthering our inquiry. The worst sin, he said, was sacrilege against holy things in holy places. The second gravest sin was that against holy things in nonsacred places.[34] The preacher's emphasis was obviously upon objects, not place. The least sinful act, he concluded, was sin against nonsacred things in a sacred place. Two important facts emerge from this ranking. First, holiness resided in objects (divine persons and things) and therefore these objects could be removed and carried about the streets in procession without losing their sacrality; obversely, the emptying of the church in effect radically if not completely desacralized it. Second, the church

31. *Le Prediche Volgari* (Florence, 1424), ed. C. Cannarozzi, 2 vols. (Pistoia, 1934), I, 211f.

32. "Don't you see that the church belongs to the saint of the church?"; Bernardino of Siena, *Prediche* (Siena, 1425), II, 89. A typical Latin documentary formulation runs: "St. X et eius ecclesia."

33. *Prediche* (Florence, 1424), I, 212.

34. *Ibid.*, 214–217.

was not a unified ritual space. Closer to prized sacred objects, devotees would be brought to their knees, but further away their behavior would slant toward the profane. The Christian needed to know where in the church were "the things consecrated with the red cross," to follow Bernardino's words.[35] Thus within the church the cross located the holy, as, in Bernardino's vivid admission, on the walls of the city it served to restrain urination.[36] The church, much like any other place in the city, was a patchwork of ritual spaces marked by holy objects.

It is in part because things more than places were holy that preachers like Bernardino were never successful in convincing their listeners that churches should be used only for divine services. Bernardino listed some of the excesses he disliked most: dances staged in church, business negotiations being carried out there, girls being paraded before prospective suitors during so-called "banquets," school and club meetings being conducted in them.[37] The list of secular activities could be extended at will: government commissions continued to meet in church until the end of our period;[38] the local church was the normal meeting place for citizens when taxes had to be divided or a new rector elected;[39] mercenaries were garrisoned in them; plays and orations were held there.[40] Boys played in the aisles, dogs wandered back and forth, urinating against the pillars, completely unimpressed by the geography of the sacred.[41] In sermons, members of the audience corrected, made fun of, and seconded the preachers. Throughout, the selling of candles, statuettes, and charms of different sorts proceeded apace.

The well-known fact that churches in traditional Europe were variously used has usually been stated without commentary, when not condemned. Yet the fact that men and women acted irreverently and used the church for more than divine business is of central importance in determining their attitude toward space, objects, and time. The realization that reverence was due to Mass and not to natural or architectonic volume, to the relic or image not the church, to the Signoria not the Palace, to the nuns not their nunneries, leads us to a closer examination of the power of divine objects.

Objects

Traditional Europeans thought certain objects had power. In the belief structure they were either made so through priestly consecration, or they had

---

35. *Prediche* (Siena, 1425), II, 231.

36. *Ibid.*

37. *Prediche* (Florence, 1424), I, 211, 271; *Prediche* (Siena, 1425), II, 88; *Prediche* (Florence, 1425), V, 207; *Prediche* (Siena, 1427), 886.

38. The *Ufficiali dell'Onestà* (prostitution regulators) met in the church of S. Cristoforo from the fifteenth century into modern times; see now Trexler, "La prostitution florentine au XVe siècle: Patronages et

clientèles," *Annales E.S.C.* XXXVI (1981), 983–1015.

39. Election to rector of S. Leo; *ASF, not. antecos.*, L 76 (1298–1327), ff. 61rv (1303). For tax division, see *ASF, Prov.*, 190, ff. 52r–53v (Nov. 6, 1499).

40. In 1391 the churches of Florence were full of mercenaries; Panciatichi, f. 162rb.

41. On boys playing in churches, Arlotto, *Motti*, 176. I have lost Bernardino's complaint of dogs urinating in churches.

always been powerful; the attitude of devotees was irrelevant to objects' power. Although this analysis will ultimately show that laymen created that power, retained it, and finally destroyed it, the citizens of Florence were more humble, and believed that all power came from God. That humility was itself part of human power.

These same Europeans believed that the relics of all saints were holy. Yet as we watch the faithful behave, we see that of the hundreds of images and relics in a major church, only a few triggered that reverent rigidification of behavior that interests us, and they were, generally speaking, different objects for different persons and groups.

Again, these Europeans believed that Christ was superior to any other numen, especially since he lived body and soul in the church; the images and relics, if doctrine was to be believed, merely represented spirits who were not present. Despite these beliefs, on entering a church many persons "went first to some figure dear to them and nowhere else. In the presence of the consecrated body of Christ they leave the Lord to visit the servant."[42] Bernardino urged a different posture: "Go to a high altar when you enter a church, and adore it, rather than stand before painted images. First give due reverence to the body of Christ, then show your devotion to the other figures which represent to you other devout saints."[43] All in vain, for in practice the reverence due objects was as much subject to the identity of the worshiper as it was subject to time and place. Persons identified with representations just as much as with the host. This section examines what qualities Florentines attributed to different holy objects. And of the three objects that were perceived and handled as sacred—the host, images, and relics—the least probable of the three, the host, requires our immediate attention.

Like most Europeans of the late Middle Ages, the Florentines were "carnal illiterates," the colorful term used by the theologian Berengar of Tours to describe those who insisted on the fullest implications of the doctrine of the real presence.[44] A Florentine law of 1425 enshrined the orthodox view of the nature of sacred objects:

> All those things pertaining to the cult of God are revered in this world not for themselves, but rather refer figuratively to God. The exception is the most precious body of our lord Jesus Christ, which is in truth our god, without reference to anything else.[45]

Thus church doctrine recognized the existence of an urban power source that was unmediated; not a representation, but Christ himself. Florentines were receptive to the idea. People spoke of "going to see the body of Christ" as today's Catholic says "I'm going to Mass," and moralists recommended that citizens "go see God" before starting their business day.[46] Clergy were

42. Bernardino, *Prediche* (Siena, 1425), II, 226.

43. *Prediche* (Florence, 1424), I, 212. Note the wording: to adore the altar.

44. Cited in D. Devlin, "Corpus Christi: A Study in

Medieval Eucharistic Theory, Devotion, and Practice" (diss. Univ. of Chicago, 1975).

45. *ASF, Prov.*, 115, ff. 129rv (Aug. 24, 1425).

46. Trexler, *Spiritual Power*, 126. Paolo da Certaldo, *Libro di Buoni Costumi* (Florence, 1945), 223.

especially intolerant of anyone who quibbled about this complete realism in discourse and perception. When in the 1370s a preacher at Santa Croce told his audience that the common language usage "going to see God" was actually inaccurate, since the eyes still perceived bread, another friar denounced him to the Inquisition.[47] Laymen shared this insistence on directness. In one of Sacchetti's *novelle*, a group of laymen who had just been helped across a raging stream by a host held high above the water by a priest admonished the latter: "Ser Diedato, we want you to sincerely thank our lord Jesus Christ, whom you hold in your hand."[48]

The real presence was one dogma that struck deep roots in inhabitants' attitudes, the host taking on most if not all of the qualities of the living person it was said and perceived to be. It bled when stabbed, and wine changed to blood—one of the first great miracles in the civic tradition at the church of S. Ambrogio in 1229 involved such a change; it saw, heard, smelled, had its feelings hurt and soothed, and so on.[49] Since the real presence once infused was ineradicable, hosts, from the communion wafers (*communichini*) "small like a groat," to large models displayed for adoration, became important power objects for laymen.[50] They were used to find love, money, and health; they were buried in building foundations; and they were used to seal friendships, private, public, and diplomatic.[51].

Accepting the cult of the Corpus Christi certainly strengthened rather than weakened the reverential attitude of the average Italian toward the figures of saints and their bodily remains. If the host was the image of God, an icon of Mary was her very likeness. The cult of the body of Christ validated one of the strongest religious tendencies: to give form to power on the principle that power was imputable to objects:

> I think . . . that those ancient sages who sought to secure the presence of divine beings by the erection of shrines and statues showed insight into the nature of the All; they perceived that, though this Soul (of the world) is everywhere tractable, its presence will be secured all the more readily when an appropriate receptacle is elaborated, a place especially capable of receiving some portion or phase of it, something reproducing it and serving like a mirror to catch an image of it.[52]

We might add to Plotinus: if in so improbable a place as bread, how much more plausibly in the bones or effigy. The undiminished propensity of Florentines to impute power to relics and images reflected a healthy realism

---

47. Sacchetti, *Trecentonovelle*, 161f.

48. *Ibid.*, 232. Characteristically, the story goes on to show how the men afterward argued whether the priest had helped God or God the priest.

49. G. Villani, VI, 7. On the cult in general, see P. Browe, *Die Verehrung der Eucharistie im Mittelalter* (Munich, 1933).

50. "Tutte quelle ostie sagrate che sono picccoline come un grosso"; Del Corazza, 262. On the *com-munichini*, see G. Rondini, "I 'Giustiziati' a Firenze," *ASI*, ser. 5, XXVIII (1901), 225. A typical reference to those *maladette maliarde* who steal hosts to use them for their own ends, Bernardino of Siena, *Prediche* (Siena, 1425), II, 226.

51. See the striking use of the host discussed on page 116, this volume.

52. Plotinus, cited in F. Yates, *Giordano Bruno and the Hermetic Tradition* (New York, 1969), 64.

existing alongside the less probable, if authoritative, dogma of the real presence.

By virtue of the dogma of the real presence, preachers and theologians were actually quite amenable to devotional realism. Bernardino objected to people praying to their favorite images, not so much because they were only figures and Christ was real, but because worshipers reversed the correct procedure of first the Lord, then his servants. Any objections to such realism were pallid in comparison with contemporaries' thoroughgoing antagonism to those who rejected the idea of power in objects. When in 1489 the philosopher Pico della Mirandola denied that the cross of Christ or any image or actual picture of a person should be adored with *latria,* the highest form of adoration, the curial bishop Garcia insisted that the image was to be adored.[53] If it were said, he argued, that God could be worshiped *in* all things, it followed that one could worship him in unshaped wood as well as in the image that recalled his actions and visage. But such behavior would be idolatrous. Furthermore, if the physical world contained nothing but *signs* of divinity (as Pico had argued for images), then it followed that *man* should be adored more than any sign, since in a real way he was more God than any image—an equally horrendous idolatry. Without saying so, Garcia was effectively defending the principle of power in this world (the real presence) by guarding the power of the images and relics at the side altars.

The relic is the second vessel of holy content requiring our attention, and it is a curious combination of personality and impersonality. On the one hand it shared a common morphology with the devotee: Genuine relics were actual parts of past living persons or, if secondary relics, had been in contact with those persons. A devotee praying to a relic was one person praying to another. Still, such specks of matter communicated no personality or moral character, since they were inert and, so to speak, without content—very different from images, which through the artifice of man could teach and edify. Relics, said their carnival hawkers, operated "not through cunning or false incantations, but through their divine powers."[54] This "divine power" of the relic, corporal but nonexemplary, proves when observed in action to have been of a peculiar and limited character.

Different from the host or image, the normal domiciled relic—a speck of hair, a coat, a drop of milk, an arm—rarely performed miracles in Florence. Furthermore, Florentines do not seem to have entered into familiar relations with them. No devotional prayers to relics seem to have survived; there is no evidence of worshipers talking to relics and, just as important, little tradition of relics talking to devotees, or otherwise manifesting their corporality, as for example by bleeding. In the language of the time, Florentines do not seem to have had "devotions" to relics.

Relics were valuable despite their nonmiraculous nature; in fact, indi-

---

53. The Latin text of the following is reproduced in my "Florentine Religious Experience: The Sacred Image," *Studies in the Renaissance* XIX (1972), 40.

54. C. Singleton (ed.), *Nuovi Canti Carnascialeschi del Rinascimento* (Modena, 1940), 54f.

viduals and communes sought to purchase and possess relics more than any other objects. In scores of cases Florentines went to great trouble, expense, and intrigue to buy a speck of holiness from Rome or elsewhere, but no case is known of an image or host being sought or obtained from outside the city.[55] Obviously some other type of power was found in them, something that would not miraculously transform life but sustain and augment it. It is exactly this sustaining quality of the relic that was most valued. Whether it was a relic of the Baptist maintaining and augmenting the city, or a more humble relic of some local saint helping a woman through labor pains, these remnants of the past can be seen as sustentative rather than transformational *sacra*.[56] In processions relics went before images in a protective fashion. When in 1358 the church tower of Santa Maria Novella was repeatedly struck by lightning, the prior finally decided to replace the images in the tower with the relics, apparently because the relics were a superior protective agency.[57]

The protective nature of relics reveals itself nowhere more clearly than in the Florentines' fear that these revered objects were forgeries, and that they had been honoring "nothing." At such a point they called for a miracle from the relic of a quite specific type; not a miracle that would transform the group, or nature itself, but one that would keep the group together by proving the relic's ability to protect itself against natural agents. Thus a Florentine confraternity placed its piece of the true cross in fire to once and for all settle questions about its genuineness. Even here, the sense that it was wrong to expect, let alone demand, miracles was strong, and as the notarial document relating this event concludes,

> In the future no one will again dare or presume to try at his pleasure the fire experiment, since the divine power is not submitted to the will of sinners. It is not licit to any man to test the holy things of God and his miracles.[58]

The oldest relics were the most valuable. The city sought protection in the remains of those saints whose age when linked to the city could reconstitute an extensive communal ancestry. Thus in 1311 the commune of Florence went to great lengths to obtain relics of the apostle Barnabas, who had been held responsible for the Florentine victory at Campaldino in 1289.[59] Furthermore, the commune was always on the lookout for remains of old saints long identified with the communal past. Thus in 1362 it purchased what it thought were relics of the patroness Santa Reparata, who had allegedly saved the commune from the Goths in the sixth century, and in 1393 and *c.* 1415 it bought some of its ancient advocate the Baptist, who, as Florentines liked to

---

55. A list of communally obtained relics is on page 2, this volume.

56. They were especially important in binding men together; see page 113, this volume.

57. M. Villani, VIII, 46 (1358). The prior was the famous canonist Piero degli Strozzi. In the fifteenth

century a favorite tower protector was an "*agnus dei* of the type the pope makes," "for they have the property that lightning never strikes where they are"; Filarete, *Treatise*, 69.

58. Richa, *Notizie*, VII, 204f.

59. For references, see n. 4, page 2, this volume.

point out, was older than Jesus and had baptized him.[60] Certainly remains of
an ancient saint were more liable to be fakes than those of a more recent saint,
but this did not deter the Florentines. The chroniclers record only one case
where the commune sought and obtained a relic of a modern saint (three
centuries old), the cloak of St. Francis in 1502. Even in this case a close tie to
communal traditions was present: The Franciscan father was thought to have
saved the city from the deceptions of the Dominican Savonarola, who had
been executed in 1498.[61] Thus, a relic's value depended first on its antiquity,
then on long association with the city (usually reflected in the saint's previous
incorporation into the festive calendar), and finally on its association with
communal victories. All these relics established Florence's spiritual antiquity,
since they linked the city with the apostolic and even preapostolic age. An
apostle's participation at Campaldino suggested that the victory was already
presaged in the apostolic age.

A relic's previous owner and location were almost as important as its
antiquity, for provenience also gave the commune an honorable paternity.
Rome was doubtless the most desirable city from which to obtain a relic, not
only because there could be no question of its authenticity, but also because
the Eternal City was Florence's spiritual and material parent. Imperial relics
were desirable as well; perhaps the most expensive relics the city ever purchased came from the treasure of the last Byzantine emperor. They were bought
because, in one counselor's words, Florence to become ornate had to benefit
from the misfortune of cities like Constantinople.[62] Such considerations led
the city to procure relics from a third source: the treasures of conquered cities.
The relics, and thus the power, of these sources strengthened Florence's
position in the world. The need was great, and the commune stooped to theft
if purchase or dominion failed. In the 1440s, for example, the city apparently
commissioned an agent in Rome to steal the head of its patron St. John, and
then had to obtain the agent's release from prison when he was caught in the
act.[63] In the 1380s the sardonic republican Sacchetti referred to both the
acquisition and creation of relics when he said that "it always seems that
where *Signori* have ruled there are quite a few bodies of saints, especially
martyrs."[64] Yet the same writer, typical of his race in bemoaning the decline
of Florentine nobility, would have given his lifeblood for a genuine finger of
the ascended Virgin.[65]

Thus the sacrality of normal relics was not of a miraculous but of a
protecting, maintaining, and augmenting nature. The Florentines' zeal in

60. *Ibid.* References to the Baptist as a patriarch and prophet are in *ASF, Prov.*, 145, ff. 75v–76r (June 6, 1454). The Florentines had chosen him their "de- fender and protector," said Dati, because he was first among the saints and was born sanctified; *Istoria*, 127.

61. Sanesi, *Caso Savonarola*, 19.

62. "Nec civitas illius modi de rebus posset ornari, nisi alia destructa. Casus Constantinopoleos facit illas esse venales"; *ASF, CP*, 53, f. 88r (July 3, 1454). My thanks to Samuel Cohn for checking this passage.

63. Filarete *Treatise*, 45, n. 5.

64. *Trecentonovelle*, 375.

65. Unfortunately, I know of no private memoir in Florence that describes the private acquisition of a relic by its writer.

procuring these partial elements of holy people showed a desire to strengthen the city rather than to provide it with elements that would miraculously heal the city in crisis. The city's main patron, in fact, had never performed miracles while on earth.[66] His ashes were sought for other purposes. Relics were one medium through which the city attempted to draw the outside world into itself by incorporating the sacred wealth and pasts of both stronger and weaker neighbors. Its preference for ancient relics clearly reflected a belief that to consume the world of the sacred, one would have to consume all the past as well, bring into the city all those objects around which all human— that is, Christian—groups had ever gathered in prayer and common behavior. The core of the relic's sacrality was protection, and protection could only be generated through the antiquity, the continuing stability, of regimes, and the relics that linked them to all historical regimes.

Relic accumulation aimed at the ultimate reconstruction of bodies, and consequently of the civic past and ancestral lines. The Osirian myth that to be impregnable a political entity must gather parts to reconstitute a whole, must re-create the image of the sacred past, lurked behind much of the activity of the communes. Preaching to the faithful in Santa Maria Novella in 1303 and 1304, the Dominican Giordano da Rivalto made just this point. He told of the anxious citizens of a town under siege who could not divine why their protector S. Bartolo was failing them.[67] Presently the saint appeared to one of them in a vision and explained: God no longer heard his mediation, because the saint's relics had been scattered by enemies. If he were to function as patron, the saint admonished, the citizens of the town would have to gather these relics. Giordano was in effect suggesting that only the fully reconstituted body could bring about the miracle of the town's resurrection, recreating it as a utopic community, for only an integral relic had the voice to speak to God. Miracles were possible if whole bodies could be built. And as Bartolo wished his fragmented self reconstructed, so the devotee believed that his own fragmented self could be miraculously transformed if he could pray to another whole self. The miraculous rather than merely protective relic was an image.

It was easier to keep newly dead bodies and hope they would remain integral than it was to reconstruct scattered ones; the struggle between Siena and Aquila over possession of the body of S. Bernardino reflected this conviction. When cities were able to retain a cadaver of saintly repute, the months immediately after death were critical, for they would determine whether the body would remain intact or decompose. The colorful scenes of mayhem around these corpses, with crying men and women seeking a hair, a piece of cloth, and the like, must not distract us, for the reputed saint only proved his or her status if the body remained intact, and only intact saints performed miracles.[68] With amazing regularity, Tuscans of this period inspected such

---

66. Pointed out to the Florentines in 1303; Giordano da Rivalto–Moreni, *Prediche*, I, 123f.

67. *Ibid.*, I, 122f; II, 98f.

68. See for example Richa, *Notizie*, I, 364f (body of the *beata Umiltà*, 1311). Sacchetti pointed out how silly it was to believe both this and the threats of the priests

corpses to make sure that the signs of decay did not appear.[69] The function of this body-image was the same as that of material images: to integrate the past with the present, to tie the living to the dead, to achieve the miracle of immortality. The bridge between past and present was the transformation of the relic into an image.

Relics too fragmented to show a body were converted into images to heighten their power. Giovanni Villani tells us, for example, that when in 1331 the skull of the patron of the Florentine church, S. Zanobi, was found buried in the apse of the cathedral, it was put in a reliquary of silver "in the likeness of the face and head of the said saint, in order that on his feast it could be shown annually to the people with great solemnity." The fragmented relic was insufficient; the whole image was necessary to tie Florentines to their spiritual Adam.[70] Laymen used the same mechanism to identify with their own familial ancestors, charging artists to produce death masks that would be "true reproductions of [their] ancestors."[71] Members of religious orders sought to benefit from the mysterious power of their spiritual fathers' images. In a deep observation, the Camaldolan general Delphin, after detailing his efforts to obtain a true death mask of his predecessor Ambrogio Traversari, described his joy on receiving it as that of a man who had found the fountain of life:

> Everyone entering to see me observes and honors [Traversari's image] *pro numine*. I have it daily before my eyes. Through gazing at it, I am aflame to be bound to emulate and imitate such a father, wishing to be transformed into that same image, which this celestial image mirrored when he was alive.[72]

The third of the sacred objects, the image, was miraculous in more than a strictly religious sense. The most enlightened men of the age recognized the mysterious power of images to evoke human activity, and wondered at the human propensity to personalize visual representations. To prove the "truly divine power" of painting, Leon Battista Alberti told the story of Cassander's violent shaking as he contemplated the likeness of Alexander. It lay in the nature of things, Alberti noted, to "cry with the crier, laugh with the laugher, sorrow with the sorrowful," to kiss and talk to images.[73] Each image had its special utility, the merchant Francesco Giovanni knew when he gave his church "a painted *tavola* in glass with Our Lord on it with the cross on his neck": "one used it to give peace." A picture was "dead," even "double dead," said Leonardo, if it did not affect the viewer.[74] Elaborating on Alberti's

that the excommunicate's body would not decompose; *Trecentonovelle*, 377.

69. See the *locus classicus* for such scenes in Tuscany, the death of one *beata* Antonia, in Richa, *Notizie*, IV, 171f.

70. Villani, X, 168.

71. Vasari, cited in A. Warburg, *Gesammelte Schriften*, 2 vols. (Leipzig, 1932), I, 119.

72. *Ambrosii Traversarii . . . Latinae Epistolae*, ed. L. Mehus, 2 vols. (Florence, 1759), II, 1105.

73. M. Barash, "Der Ausdruck in der Italienischen Kunsttheorie," *Zeitschrift für Ästhetik und Allgemeine Kunstwissenschaft* XII (1967), 36, 38.

74. *Ibid.*, 44. Giovanni's specifications are in Giovanni–Carnesecchi, Sept. 14, 1425.

observation that, through art, men dead for centuries seemed to live again, Leonardo in two "prophecies" brilliantly suggested that one function of images of the dead was to give life to the living:

> Men will speak to men who will not hear, who will have their eyes open without seeing. They will speak to them but receive no response, ask favors of those with ears who hear not. They will light candles for the blind.[75]

> Those dead a thousand years will give a living to many of the living.[76]

The art historian Vasari marveled repeatedly at the wondrous ability of images "more real than life itself" to bring tears to viewers' eyes. Both he and Alberti would have agreed with Leonardo that no medium could match the emotive power of the picture: "Write up the name of God in one place and place his figure over against it, and you will see which will be more revered."[77] The affective power of the image was so much a matter of course that persons seeking to establish a cult immediately had the picture of the holy man or woman painted and exposed:

> *Then so as not to lose the devotion,*
> *One had the Virgin Mary made*
> *On a pilaster for that reason.*[78]

Obviously, power was not limited to corpses or death masks of spiritual or secular fathers. Sacred potential could be created *ex nihilo*, by simply painting an ancestor and breathing life into it by various means. The procedure was liturgically preserved in the ceremony by which a church was consecrated. On the eve of this event at the church of Santa Maria Novella in 1420, for example, the Florentines painted a different apostle on each of the columns of the nave. Then at the beginning of the ceremony of consecration, a cardinal proceeded solemnly from column to column, attaching a lit candle to each of them. (It is unclear whether these were placed in the hands of the images or before them.) After the pope had placed the requisite relics in the main altar, the cardinal again turned his attention to the apostles, going to each and christening the red cross that each held in his hand.[79] Through this procedure, the church was effectively filled with living presences. The images had been brought to life and thus new potential for miracles had been generated.

Images such as these were clearly not simple instrumentalities, mere objective materials devoid of spirit; they were not idols. In our period Florentines witnessed or discussed miracles involving images etched on

75. *The Notebooks of Leonardo da Vinci*, ed. J. Richter, 2 vols. (New York, 1970), II, 357. Alberti's remark is in Barash, "Ausdruck," 36.

76. Leonardo, *Notebooks*, II, 370.

77. *Ibid.*, I, 328.

78. Antonio Pucci, cited in S. La Sorsa, *La Compagnia*

d'Or San Michele (Trani, 1902), 12. In such paintings an exact replica of the dead person was obviously desirable, just as an exact replica of saints' features was required of painters; M. Baxandall, *Painting and Experience in Fifteenth-Century Italy* (London, 1972), 56–59.

79. Del Corazza, 270f.

wood, canvas, stone, and coins, representing the names or figures of Christian and pagan deities. Some were great cult Madonnas; others were bedside figures enlivened by much the same procedure the cardinal had used in Santa Maria Novella; and still others were common coins, bearing the image of the Baptist, which men exchanged with each other. The city was filled with thousands upon thousands of potential miracle-workers, powerful, intimate vessels of love and hate, spiritual ancestors dynamically affecting the civic cosmos. It is this vital quality of the image that must be examined.

One image, Our Lady of Impruneta, has left behind the kind of historical record that allows us fully to sense the Florentines' attitude toward the sacred image, and we shall follow her in her centuries-long procession through the city. Her origins were lost in time, and some Florentines thought St. Luke had painted her. Alas, Florence, unlike Rome, did not possess a sacred face or *volto santo* from apostolic times;[80] Our Lady was actually painted in the late thirteenth or early fourteenth century. Like many sacred images and unlike relics, which were kept in the city, Our Lady resided outside, at the suburban *pieve* or baptismal church of Impruneta six miles from Florence. Although pilgrimages to her were common, she was in general that type of image that did not manifest her power *in situ*, but had to be brought out. No rooted tradition of miracles was attached to her temple in the desacralized *contado*, and she seems to have remained veiled while there. Florence was her field of action, and whenever she was needed the Signoria ordered she be brought. It was in the procession, in motion, and not in any enclosed sacred place that she performed. "This blessed *tavola*," said one chronicler in 1372, "made many miracles in coming and leaving."[81]

When she came to the city, the Florentines kept one eye on her and another on the sky; this Lady was primarily a rain image. Their expectations were consequently material in nature—the control of weather conditions— though psychological benefits might also be derived from her presence.

Her material effects were of primary importance, and Florentine senses were pitched to notice the slightest sign of her effect. In one case, the rain stopped the moment the vote to call her was taken.[82] In another, an olive branch became stuck to a star on her coat as she was being carried through the countryside toward the city. This was quickly interpreted as a good omen for a victory the Florentines were seeking over the Pisans.[83] Generally, however,

80. G. Villani visited the Roman Veronica; M. Meiss, *Painting in Florence and Siena after the Black Death* (New York, 1964), 36. Meiss also sketches the creation of a painterly genre in Tuscany. Tradition held that Lucca had been definitively converted when the *volto santo* arrived; *Capitoli della Compagnia della Madonna dell'Impruneta*, ed. C. G. (Florence, 1866), 9.

81. *Cronichetta d'Incerto*, in *Cronichette Antiche di varii Scrittori del Buon Secolo della Lingua Toscana*, ed. D. Manni (Florence, 1733), 199. The painting's original power, however, had been manifested in the rural

setting of Impruneta around 1340; *Capitoli . . . Impruneta*, 10f. By 1758, the ancient painting had vanished, and a new Lady was painted *ex novo* by Ignazio Hugford to perpetuate the cult; J. Fleming, "The Hugfords of Florence," *Connoisseur* CXXXVI (1955), 200f, kindly brought to my attention by John Shearman. The new cult figure is shown as Plate 6. The (retouched) cult painting of the Annunziata is shown as Plate 3.

82. Landucci, 375 (1538).

83. *Ibid.*, 199 (1499).

it would seem that results were expected after she had entered the city and, with her eyes opened and veil removed, recognized her temporary habitat. An example or two will bring out the flavor of expectation. Matteo Villani reported that in 1354 the sky clouded up during the procession. The next day the cloudiness held, "which many times previously had been consumed by the excess heat." On the third day a steady drizzle started. On the fourth it began to rain abundantly. It seemed to bring dead fields of grain back to life. "The steady and useful [nature of the] rain was no less a wondrous gift of grace than the rain itself."[84]

The amazement with which Villani followed the peregrinations of Mary might conceivably be explained by the fact that the Virgin's incredible powers were just being recognized in these decades. Yet subsequent witnesses to these presumed miracles managed to combine that same amazement with a confidence born of her history. Almost a century later, in the autumn of 1444, the *priorista* Pietrobuoni recorded how the citizens called on Our Lady after five months of drought. "Ipso facto it rained so much that one could sow."[85] Pious confidence informed the deliberations of men at the end of this century as well. Giovanni Cambi recorded how the Florentines decided to use her in 1499 to help in the city's defense:

> The last time she came to us, she made us the very special grace of getting Livorno from the Venetians. . . . And thus we hope this time she will give us [the merit] to choose a good path honorable to God and in salvation of the liberty of the *popolo* of Florence.[86]

In 1509, the surety of the Florentines knew no end. Landucci told how rain followed the day after the procession, "as it pleases God, who always graces us through the prayers of the Blessed Virgin."[87]

Sometimes the Florentines became aware of her effectiveness in retrospect rather than on the spot. Thus 1496 witnessed a palpable miracle when the moment she arrived in Florence joyful military news arrived from Livorno. But only later, Landucci tells us,

> was it discovered that when the government had deliberated sending for her, in that same day the ships had left Marseilles; and when it had been decided upon, the ships arrived at the port of Livorno. And it was believed that truly, the Virgin Mary wanted to help Florence, and that this was a sign. The explicit miracle is self-evident.[88]

In sum, the abilities and actions of *Nostra Donna* were almost foolproof, stretching from those the inhabitants witnessed to the many they could only discover in retrospect or not at all. If as early as 1419 the government pointed to the "evidence" that "experimenting" with her brought results in the most evident fashion, by the sixteenth century the historian Segni was positively

84. M. Villani, IV, 7.

85. Pietrobuoni, f. 147r.

86. Cambi, XXI, 137f.

87. Landucci, 291.

88. *Ibid.*, 140.

ecstatic about the history of power that the Virgin had erected: "Our city has never, and I'm quite serious, publicly placed itself in the hands of this mother of God in any adverse situation without being answered."[89]

Mary brought other than material benefits to Florence, however. Her numen was psychologically positive, a fact of which the Florentines were perfectly aware, even if they did pay more attention to the weather. Three examples will illustrate this quality.

In February 1499 Our Lady was brought in order to inspire the Signoria to choose the correct political course. An astute contemporary, however, suggested that the real motivation lay elsewhere. He believed that the followers of the martyred Savonarola had procured her coming, and this for no other reason than the secret goal "of bringing about the resurgence of their sect and letting people know they were still a force."[90] In short, the result of her coming was to have been the revitalization of a political group and a change in political attitudes.

A second example: In October 1529, with the republic under siege by imperial forces, the government decided to bring in the Virgin, concerned first of all that such an important source of power not fall into the hands of the besiegers. She was smuggled past the enemy, through the suburbs and into the city. Solemnly met at the gate and accompanied to the cathedral, she was placed in the chapel of S. Zanobi. Why? "So that she would protect her city from the war being forced upon it." Her power was immediately shown. "Once she had arrived, fear and fright fled from the whole city."[91] It is crystal clear, we may conclude, that the Florentines valued her positive emotional effect upon them.

The Lady's material benefits could be gauged by watching the sky, but to validate her emotional benefits, one had to watch the behavior of devotees. Thus when in 1511 she was brought in to end the rain, the fact that she received so many gifts, "more than ever before," proved her ability to touch the Florentines. "She received eight very rich coats, many chasubles and altar frontals and cloth pieces, twenty in number; there were ninety white and yellow tapers, and one lovely silver cross."[92] Again in 1513 "the greatest honor was made to her; she received nine coats, seven of which were of gold brocade, from the Signoria and from the Medici. And there were many other gifts," the diarist reported, "more than ever before."[93]

These gifts were made in the expectation that because of them Mary would do the givers' bidding: "So that through them Madonna would be amenable to praying her son God to pardon and aid us."[94] It followed that the more Mary gave, the more the Florentines should give.[95] But popular devo-

89. *Storie Fiorentine di messer Bernardo Segni Gentiluomo Fiorentino dall'Anno MDXXVII, al MDLV* (hereafter Segni, *Storie*) colla Vita di Niccolò Capponi (hereafter Segni, *Vita*), 3 vols. consecutive pagination (Livorno, 1830): *Storie*, 44.

90. Parenti, cited in Landucci, 193.

91. Varchi, X, 37, who says the government feared it

would fall into the hands of the Lutherans; also Landucci, 368.

92. *Ibid.*, 308.

93. *Ibid.*, 337.

94. Masi, 260f (1522).

95. ASF, *Prov.*, 109, ff. 159r–160r (Oct. 19, 1419).

tion and divine response were not only consecutive realities, cause and effect. Both were considered effects of the power of the image. The Savonarolans who imported her in 1499 to revive their sect were relying not on popular credulity but on the efficacy of Mary. The chronicler who in 1389 reported on the 25,000 Christians jamming the main piazza and hanging from windows to see her viewed such devotion as a reflection of the charisma of the image.[96] Again, the besieged of 1529 would not have distinguished the power of the Lady in her chapel, forced by her continued presence to confront the horrors of the siege, from the emotional stability she engendered. The spirit with which the Florentines offered themselves to the Virgin was itself the product of Our Lady's power.

Florentines verified Mary's corporal functionality, therefore, by measuring her material and psychological power. Having established this, we turn inward toward her person, seeking to establish her character. What was Mary's power, and how was she related to the image, the Lady of Impruneta? We know the theological response, but this is only a skeleton to be fleshed with belief, attitude, and above all, behavior.

Setting aside for a moment Mary in the image, we must determine what the extent of Mary's power was as a person. Was she, as dogma would have it, simply a mediator possessed of no power herself? The answer is that Mary's power, like any saint's, was determinate. A conception of power transmission from divinities to humans dealing with effective causes finds that she and the saints essentially operated apart from God, both in the popular view and in the theological. Wise men had decided that God could not refuse Mary's and the saints' requests, and preachers passed this on to the Florentines.[97] Such tidings simply confirmed, rather than formed, a rooted, individualistic attitude toward sacred power.

A willful God could divest humans of what power they had; saints like Mary regained that power and dispensed it among their favorites. Because of men's sins, Giordano da Rivalto told his audience in Santa Maria Novella in 1303, the "vendetta of God" always appeared ready to plague the Florentines, but the saints combated God and the devil to protect the city. They harried God with their prayers so insistently that God had to obey them. God, Giordano told his listeners, always gave the saints what they wanted.[98]

Indeed, God had divided up the governance of individuals and groups among his saints. At the end of the fifteenth century Savonarola told his flock that diverse saints had diverse governances. Mary had greater governance of the world than any other saint, and she had specifically been "given power over the city of Florence."[99] She was not alone in having control of the City of the Lilies. Giordano had long before pointed out that, *ratione protectionis,*

96. Naddo di Ser Nepo di Ser Gallo, *Memorie Storiche,* in *Delizie,* XVIII, 106f (hereafter Naddo da Montecatini).

97. St. Bernard had established this point once and for all. Giordano da Rivalto passed it on in Giordano da Rivalto–Moreni, *Prediche,* I, 122.

98. *Ibid.,* and II, 84. On God's vendetta, see also Compagni, III, 38.

99. *Ezechiele,* II, 233; *Salmi,* I, 287, 295.

Florence was Santa Reparata's city because she was more recognized and honored there, and Savanarola, when he urged the Florentines to turn to saints who would intercede with God, mentioned the Baptist, Zanobi, and Antonino.[100] Each group from the commune downward had its own governing saint, and the individual's favorite saint governed him. Given this conception of relations with divinities, it is small wonder that God was so little in evidence except when it came to explaining evil. The words of a student of a modern south Italian village cannot be bettered: "Many think of God as a hostile, aggressive force. . . . Some [people] pray more to the saints than to God. Candles are rarely left before the main altar; most people think it more economical to leave them before the statue of a saint or Madonna."[101] Florentines had no doubt about it, for they knew that God *always* responded favorably to the prayers of his mother for the Florentines.[102]

The effective source of power was the saints, and all effort had to be made first to choose the right ones. Before "going to the saint," that is, to church, one had to know whom to visit. "You studied with the priests for eight years," said a modern peasant woman to a seminarian, "and you haven't even learned the differences between the Madonnas!"[103] The devotee had to cultivate the skill of a woman like Caterina de' Ricci, who could quickly determine when her St. Vincent was ineffective and switch to other saints.[104]

Once the saints were chosen, one had to convince them of the need and judiciousness of the request. Giordano explained to his audience that though God always obeyed the saints, the saints never asked for anything unpleasing to God; indeed by the very fact that they were saints they were incapable of wanting what God did not.[105] Thus the saints appear again to have been the determining factors in the transmission of power. The preacher's reasoning inexorably led to the view that God could not want anything the saints did not want. God, in the Florentine cosmos, never refused Mary and, more important, there is no evidence that he *exercised his will after contemplation*. The transfer of power was automatic in the moment the eye of the Virgin of Impruneta met the mind's eye of the supplicant. She was the power.

We arrive now at the heart of the matter, the relation between image and sacred person. The evidence we will examine suggests that, whatever contemporaries said when not active in the supplicatory process, in that act a practical identity existed between Mary and image. This is not surprising: It is in the nature of a sufficient power—either corpse or image—to embody itself perfectly and integrally in whatever form it happens to take. Let us consider the evidence for her animation.

First, linguistic usages point to the identity. Images were "adored,"

100. Giordano da Rivalto–Moreni, *Prediche*, II, 89; Savonarola, *Ezechiele*, I, 223; *Esodo*, 222.

101. E. Banfield, *The Moral Basis of a Backward Society* (Chicago, 1958), 130.

102. See page 59, this volume.

103. Banfield, *Moral Basis*, 131. *Andare al santo* was still another term for "going to church."

104. S. Razzi, *Vita di Santa Caterina de' Ricci con Documenti Inediti Antecedenti l'Edizione*, ed. G. Di Agresti (Florence, 1965), 104f.

105. Giordano da Rivalto–Moreni, *Prediche*, I, 123f.

there being no common language distinction between reverence (*dulia*) and worship (*latria*). That is, common language, in keeping with church doctrine, made no devotional distinction between image and representation. The image was referred to not always as "the image of Our Lady," but often simply as *Nostra Donna*, "the Virgin Mary," and so forth.[106] It may be argued, of course, that "the Virgin Mary came to Florence" was simply verbal shorthand, much as we find in such remarks as "the Virgin in the wall at S. Frediano," *una Nostra Donna*, and other statements of this type. No doubt we are dealing with ambiguity here, heightened by the fact that both painting (*tavola*) and *Donna* are feminine nouns. But that is the point. The ambiguity extended into the grammatical structure itself.[107]

Next, the image, rather than Mary, was regularly identified as the miracle-worker. Since Florentines never attributed miracles to objects they considered inanimate, the identity between Mary and image is clear. Thus the Florentine archbishop Antonino spoke of "the miracles in Florence from a certain figure of the glorious Virgin," and a sixteenth-century Dominican describing a Virgin in his church spoke of "this most devout figure of the Virgin [which] did not cease performing daily miracles."[108]

Third and perhaps most central to this animated view of the image is the wealth of evidence that the Lady of Impruneta, like so many other images, was thought to possess sensory attributes. The Signoria itself called the image "immaculate."[109] Coins with images of the divinities bled when mishandled by gamblers, as did other images when danger lurked.[110] "Among other things," wrote the chancellor Salutati in 1399, "four simulacra of the crucified have sweated live blood in places under our jurisdiction."[111]Few doubted that images spoke to devotees as well as bled, though credulity was warned against.

But when one "saluted the Madonna," the sensory quality most frequently noted was her sight. A law of 1466 prescribed double penalties for those who committed murders "almost in the face of the said image [of Impruneta]," while she was being carried through the city. Such crimes were in contempt of "the divine presence," his mother, and the government and people of the city, "the devotion of whom is disturbed by the criminality of such [people]."[112] Mary's vision was *in* the image. Both Bernardino in the 1420s and Savonarola at the end of the century warned Florentines against

106. For example, "venne in Firenze la Vergine Maria"; Landucci, 368.

107. In antiquity Plutarch in his *Isis and Osiris* had protested against the modes of speech that permitted the identification of the image with God; E. Bevan, *Holy Images* (London, 1940), 22.

108. Antonino cited in Richa, *Notizie*, I, 8; "Venerabilis Coenobii Sanctae Mariae Novellae de Florentia Chronica," *Analecta Sacri Ordinis Fratrum Praedicatorum* XII (1915–1916), 180ff (hereafter "Chronica . . . S. M. Novellae," with volume and page number).

109. Landucci, 322.

110. A famous case of 1393 is mentioned by Richa, *Notizie*, IX, 40, and by Bernardino, *Prediche* (Siena, 1425), I, 149. On the subjective value of money, see M. Mauss, *The Gift* (New York, 1967), 93, n. 25.

111. *Epistolario di Coluccio Salutati*, ed. F. Novati, 4 vols. (Rome, 1891–1911), III, 362. This remark may be compared to Salutati's concept toward images cited in Baxandall, *Painting*, 42.

112. *ASF, Prov.*, 137, ff. 79v–80v (June 13, 1446). On "saluting," see Arlotto, *Motti*, 20f.

committing sins "in the eyes of the Virgin Mary" of the Annunziata, another important Florentine Virgin, "as if to say to the Virgin there: 'I do it to insult you.' "[113] Savonarola assured Florentine women that the same Virgin did not take kindly to their appearance in the church heavily cosmeticized and dressed like prostitutes: "I tell you that the Annunciation doesn't want to see them dressed like that."[114] Bernardino extended the warning to the domestic realm, condemning women who appeared before their bedroom image shamelessly dressed, their cosmetic containers and ampules placed all around the figure.[115] One Virgin, looking out from her perch over a church entrance upon the unseemly behavior in the street, closed her eyes.[116]

It was only natural for the Florentines to punish defilers of particular Virgins in the presence of those Virgins. The punishment meted out to a Jew convicted in 1493 of defacing several Madonnas is particularly instructive in this regard, for it shows the individuality and animism of each Madonna. It was said that the iconoclast had covered with filth the face and body of "Our Lady on the corner of [the hospital of] Santa Maria Nuova, at S. Nofri, where those infected with plague are housed"; his hand was severed before that Lady. He had ruined a painted Pietà at Santa Maria in Campo; his other hand was removed there. He had not only besmirched the marble Donna at Or San Michele, but had stabbed her in the face and God in the eye; his eyes were extracted in the presence of this Mary and God.[117] The Virgins might have been satisfied, but the crowd was not. Some 2000 youth so pelted the officials accompanying the convicted man to the place of execution that they gave up the iconoclast to the fury of the youth, who completely mutilated him. This was the revenge of the Florentines—and the Virgins—upon the Jewish boy who, in the chronicler's revealing words, "had sullied and wounded these our ladies."[118]

A fourth evidence of these Virgins' animation was their psychic power and personal sensibility. The images' own personalities obviously accounted for their ability to dispel human fear and anxiety. The Lady of Impruneta, for example, was unhappy when the Medicean tyrants brought her to the city in 1526, for they wanted her to protect them against the citizens, rather than to protect the citizens from the threat of approaching armies. Giovanni Cambi was secretly delighted, therefore, when the whole procession was ruined by thunder and rain—the very elements that Our Lady infallibly controlled. "Thus," reported Cambi, "we can imagine how welcome her calling was to *Nostra Donna*."[119] Our Lady of Impruneta was her own woman, with an individual psychology. Varchi tells us that during the siege of 1529 the citizens brought her in for the duration despite her well-known dislike of being domiciled away from Impruneta: "The *tavola* of the Madonna

---

113. Savonarola, *Esodo*, I, 52.

114. *Amos e Zaccaria*, III, 233. Note: The Annunciation . . . sees.

115. *Prediche* (Florence, 1425), V, 206f.

116. Landucci, 279 (1506).

117. *Ricordanze Tratte da un Libro Originale di Tribaldo de' Rossi*, in *Delizie*, XXIII, 283ff (hereafter Rossi).

118. "Queste nostre done"; *ibid.*

119. Cambi, XXII, 296ff.

of Impruneta did not want to room overnight within the walls of Florence, [and] once [before] she had invisibly fled at night."[120] Her subsequent success in banishing fear and anxiety proved that citizen confidence in her malleability had not been displaced. If willful, she was also merciful.

The material and psychological benefits that she conferred, as well as the sensory and characterological qualities the Florentines ascribed to her, demonstrate conclusively that the Florentines communed with a complete fusion of image and divinity. The single recorded case in which the painting might be said to have failed republican Florence serves as a conclusive illustration of its identity with Mary. Rain had been falling for two months when, on December 30, 1435, the Signoria had the Lady brought in. In reporting the results, the *priorista* Pietrobuoni seems to be separating image and reality: "For one day the rain held back; and then it started again. God does that which is necessary, and it is better to turn to him first before [turning to] images."[121] Pietrobuoni was not actually separating image and reality, of course; he was no iconoclast. He meant that the reason the image of Mary had not worked was because God had not been prayed to first. The Florentines had, in short, forgotten what they had learned a century before: The correct procedure was to pray first to God, and then to the Virgin of Impruneta.[122] Pietrobuoni was therefore not objecting to the importation of the image, but protesting incorrect procedure. We are reminded of Bernardino's admonition to the Florentines only a few years earlier: "Always first to God and then to them, for the love of God."[123]

We have examined the benefits that could be expected from a sacred image, and analyzed the content of the Ladies as well as other saints. Impruneta was special; her prodigiousness lasted for centuries. But each image with a devotee had its own biography, no matter how short. The image was born of devotion and dead in its absence. At any instant of time through Florence's long republican history, crowds gathered before different sets of objects. Before Impruneta came on the scene, they had honored as a weather deity an equestrian representation called Mars, surrounding him with tabus and watching for portents of "great danger and change. And this was not empty talk, since experience had proved it [to be true]."[124] Impruneta's success did not satisfy Florence's lust for power sources, and the citizens constantly uncovered new ones. Writing in the 1380s, Sacchetti thought the Lady of Impruneta would be just another victim of popular inconstancy:

> How many changes there have been in the figure of Our Lady! There was a time when everyone ran to Santa Maria da Cingoli. Then one went to Santa Maria della Selva. Then the fame of Santa Maria in Impruneta grew. Then at Fiesole to Santa Maria di Primerana, and then to Our Lady of Or San Michele. Then all were deserted.[125]

120. Varchi, X, 37.

121. Pietrobuoni, f. 137v.

122. M. Villani, IV, 7, had made the same discovery (1354).

123. See page 47, this volume.

124. G. Villani, XI, 1. More in Trexler, "Image," 24.

125. Cited in La Sorsa, *Compagnia*, 54. Primerana was also tenacious; along with Impruneta, she was brought to the city during the siege of 1529; Varchi, X, 37.

Sacchetti was right in believing that the holy was highly volatile, transforming the ritual landscape of the city with great regularity. Any vessel, from a coin to a great Madonna, could be an outlet for this power, and this meant that even if one had no devotion to a particular image, a decent reverence was due to all. Most important, care had to be exercised that images not be indiscriminately made and placed, for every artifice of a holy face carried the danger as well as the benefit of such vessels. It was for this reason that the preachers objected to crosses in the streets, that opponents of Bernardino protested violently against his talismanic *IHS* being placed everywhere, that citizens showed such great care in maintaining the street-corner shrines or *cenacoli*.[126] The civil order needed these images—the Baptist was not on the florin for nothing—yet they created blasphemy and danger as well as reverence and power.

In this world of images, what was an idol? The problem is a serious one. Bernardino for example recognized the tendency of humans to personalize any object, and pointed out to his listeners that gamblers were idolators when they spoke to their dice: "O Lord Dice, etc. . . ."[127] Yet nowhere in his sermons or elsewhere did he object to praying to a coin image, for example, and we heard him warn women to behave in their bedroom if they had a Lady there. The potential for good and evil, it seemed, was everywhere. If any representation was a vessel for good or harm, what could be an idol? Around which images did citizens dare not congregate and which did they dare not personalize? We have seen that pagan images were not necessarily idols, for the statue of Mars was wreathed and laureled in the fourteenth century. Nor was the worship of all sacred images idolatry, as Protestants of early modern times ranted—all the time handling their Bibles gingerly—for any Florentine would have insisted they adored the face not the decoration, the initials of Jesus' name, as Bernardino insisted, not the gold and colors.[128] Only the worship of *some* sacred images was idolatrous, Florentines would have replied. What exactly was it that made a picture an idol?

An idol, when the term referred to a sacred representation, was no more nor less than a representation that was not working. To accuse a person of worshiping idols was to denounce him for worshiping something that possessed no *virtù*, no spiritual power—a coin image, for example, that despite rumors had not bled or given some sign of work. Proving an image prodigious disproved the charge of idolatry. The *image* was a valid, participatory intelligence; the *idol* was pure object, without spirit, without efficacy. From our modern point of view, therefore, iconoclasm was practiced against images, not idols. For who would bother to smash a pure thing?

In late thirteenth-century Florence, the pillar image of the Virgin of Or San Michele started to perform miracles, and this naturally caused great excitement throughout Tuscany. That was most inconvenient to the Mendicants of Florence, however, since it meant that devotion was directed to an

126. On Bernardino's difficulties, see I. Origo, *The World of San Bernardino* (New York, 1962), 120–126.

127. *Prediche* (Siena, 1425), I, 178.

128. Origo, *World of S. Bernardino*, 120–126.

image beyond their sphere. The poet Guido Cavalcanti tells us that the Franciscans accused the populace of idolatry:

> *A figure of My Lady Guido adores*
> *At San Michele in Orto. . . .*
> *Its fame passes along the far highways and byways.*
> *But the friars minor say this is idolatry*
> *From jealousy, that it is not near their churches.*[129]

Two generations later Giovanni Villani described the same events. The friars minor and the Dominicans "because of jealousy or some other reason, did not recognize the validity [of the miracles] and for this they were despised by the Florentines."[130] The motivational identity between Cavalcanti's "Friars minor say this is idolatry" and Villani's "did not recognize the validity [of the miracles]" is patent. Neither reporter felt any need to pursue the charge of idolatry beyond the assertion that the miracles were famous, and that the Florentines had faith in them. Only if the miracles proved fraudulent did the image become an idol. When that happened, Florentines showed not only anger at being duped, but anxiety for having threatened themselves and the city through worshiping nothing. The same anger for the same reasons surfaced when fake relics were uncovered. Thus Matteo Villani ruefully reported how the false relic of Reparata had been worshiped for four years and four months before the forgery was discovered: "At Florence for all this time that simulacrum was honored like a sanctuary. The abbess [responsible for the forgery] was the reason for all this [idolatrous] evil, since she was able to conceal her false religion."[131]

Idolatry therefore involved not only a picture that was inanimate, but a behavior that was fruitless, foolish, and dangerous. Many images required no particular devotion; coin images for example demanded but decent respect, for it was only when the saint in the coin was challenged or defamed, and thus stimulated, that its latent power became mandatorily adored.[132] In church a layperson could leisurely stroll past the image of a Virgin to which he had no devotion as long as, being a citizen, he was sure that decent regard was taken to dust her. In both cases, our uninvolved citizen had few if any obligations. Risk began when he sought the friendship of patrons. Would he choose his individual saint well? In the presence of an image revered by many devotees because of miracles, should he kneel and pray with society? It was a question crucial not only to his own salvation, but to that of the city, for what he really asked was this: Was ritual space correctly ordered? Was power being adored, or a worthless mirage of power?

---

129. Cited in La Sorsa, *Compagnia,* 12.

130. G. Villani, VII, 155.

131. M. Villani, III, 15, 16.

132. Thus a coin that bled after being mistreated by a gambler in 1392 became an object of veneration in the Augustinian church of Santo Spirito; Richa, *Notizie,* IX, 40; the notarial document on the case is in *ASF, Diplomatico,* Santo Spirito, 1392.

The land of the city lay fallow and profane. The buildings upon it competed for holy things to honor their own abstractness. Their fortunes were made and undone by the relative holiness of the images and relics they harbored. All major churches kept lists of relics, and visitors mentioned relics first in describing a church.[133] The value attached to these sacred objects, especially relics and images, did not, however, transfer itself to the physical area of the church, chapel, or palace. The main occasions for the demonstration of sacred things were in fact outside the church, when they were carried in procession through the city. Inside or out, it was the proximity to the holy object that modified behavior. I have summarized the Florentine perceptions of holy space and objects, and must now turn to time. For the fact was that these objects and spaces forced a ritual bearing only within a certain chronological setting. Time itself was significant and insignificant, not abstract and linear; it was sometimes sacred and sometimes profane. Men did not make it so; we continue to concede the humble Florentine protest that men did not make the holy. We shall look at how time worked on the city, and not—for now—how the city worked on time.

Time

When a male child was born, parents carefully recorded the day, the hour, and the minute, for this moment's astrological character could reveal the child's future. The infant often took the name of the saint of his birth day and, until the fourteenth century, was baptized on Holy Saturday.[134] Time was a public and divine thing to which the individual geared his own. Forty was the age at which individuals were supposed to convert and prepare for death, so although forty-two, Goro Dati called himself forty when he made the change of life.[135] Marriages were put off so that they would coincide with important feast days.[136] On whatever numerical date an important communal event might have occurred, the historian made it happen on the day of a saint near that event.[137] All time was significant—there was no accident—but that significance lay in world, not individual, biography.

133. These lists are to be distinguished from lists mentioned earlier which encompass the whole city, found at Milan but not at Florence.

134. For the influence of neighboring friaries upon names (e.g., Dominic, Francis), C. de la Roncière, "L'Influence des Franciscains dans la Campagne de Florence au XIVᵉ siècle (1280–1360)," *Mélanges de l'Ecole Française de Rome: Moyen Age, Temps Modernes* LXXXVII (1975), 27–103. The system of family nominal reproduction in Florence (*rifare*) has been studied by C. Klapisch, "L'Attribution d'un Prénom à l'Enfant en Toscane à la fin du Moyen-Age," *L'Enfant au Moyen-Age. Actes du Colloque d'Aix-en-Provençe, Mars, 1979* (Aix-en-Provençe, 1980). A na-

tivity astrologer first asked for information on the time of birth; Filarete, *Treatise*, 22. Typical are two futures read by the important astrologer Alessio: "Due Responsi Astrologici dell'Anno 1382 resi da Maestro Allesio da Firenze concernante due Pistoiesi," ed. A. Chiappelli, *Bolletino Storico Pistoiese* XXIV (1922), 133–138. The same astrologer was used by Datini; Mazzei, I, 187.

135. Dati, *Memoir*, 125.

136. Dati cited in C. Guasti, *Le Feste di San Giovanni Battista in Firenze* (Florence, 1884), 4f.

137. For example, if it happened on the vigil of some important saint's day, that saint would be chosen instead of the day's saint.

Segments of time were sacred to certain powers. Most commonly a day was associated with the saint whose feast was celebrated then, but mixed with the influence of the saint was the moral configuration of the stellar spheres on that day; both exerted either a malevolent or friendly influence upon the city. The gambler enraged at his losses shot an arrow into the sky, and the arrow fell back to earth bloody.[138] Had it wounded the day's saint or some celestial body? Both were agents that could do personal good or evil. With that commonality of saints' time and star time in mind, we turn to a separate examination of first calendrical, and then astrological, perceptions of time.

Preachers professed to find no rhyme or reason for the Florentines' organization of months, days, and even hours according to their relative auspiciousness. Apparently citizens predicted weather for each month by observing climate on each day of the fortnight before and after Christmas and January 1.[139] Certain days were unlucky: Mondays, Tuesdays, Fridays, and Saturdays are mentioned by different sources. Saturday was a day on which people could get away with sins, for, as the proverb ran, "God doesn't pay on Saturdays."[140] Perhaps for this reason the government executed criminals on this day.[141] On the other side of the ledger, Wednesday was thought auspicious, one belief holding that prayers offered to San Lorenzo on Wednesdays were worth more than those offered on other days, since it was on Wednesdays that the saint rescued souls from purgatory.[142]

Why should God hear San Lorenzo better on Wednesdays than on other days, asked the archbishop Antonino in criticizing such beliefs and their associated practices. All days were good days, the Franciscan Bernardino repeated again and again, and none were unlucky.[143] Savonarola ridiculed a visionary who had the Virgin's promise that the faithful could avoid the coming plague if they would fast the first Saturday after hearing the news of the vision and abstain the following Sunday: "Especially to say: 'The first Sunday,' etc. Doesn't this seem superstitious to you?"[144] To hear these preachers tell it, one would think their message was in fact the irrelevance of time to behavior.

The facts were altogether different. Preachers sought only to personalize all time within the Christian cosmos, dividing it according to the Christian saints. One stunning point in a sermon Bernardino gave to the Florentines in 1424 shows how effortlessly a preacher could take and give:

> Some avoid being asked for money on Mondays: Plain avarice! Some won't begin anything on Tuesdays, others won't touch cloth on Fridays. All this is an illusion of

138. L. Zdekauer, "Il Giuoco in Italia nei secoli XIII e XIV," *ASI*, ser. 4, XVIII (1886), 68.

139. "One says that such as are the days after S. Lucia, so are the months of the year"; note as well the three different lists of weather conditions in Naddo da Montecatini, 1ff, 28.

140. Today's simplified meaning is: "In the end your sins catch up with you." See Varchi, X, 70; also III, 9.

141. "Quelli cattivelli che sono in pregione, e aspettansi d'essere guasti quando odono sonare il sabato mattina la campana"; Giordano da Rivalto–Moreni, *Prediche*, II, 132 (1304).

142. Antonino cited in Cianfogni–Moreni, *Memorie . . . San Lorenzo*, I, 158f.

143. *Prediche* (Florence, 1424), II, 169.

144. *Amos e Zaccaria*, I, 330f.

the devil. All days are good. Do everything in reverence to God, but be careful not to work on mandatory feast days, and fulfill all your needs on the other days in reverence to God.[145]

Bernardino's transformation of one set of auspices into another continued. He branded as mortal sin the practice of writing at only a certain time of day, then turned around and insisted that sins committed on the feast days of the church were graver than those committed on other days, and acts of charity were more rewarding.[146] The transformation became complete when Bernardino admitted that those damnable inauspicious days, in which people believed by demonic illusion, were unlucky after all. But it was their own fault; if people *believed* certain days of the week or even certain feasts of the church were unlucky—the feast of the Baptist's decapitation and Good Friday were especially "evil feasts"—the "spiritual and temporal evils" that in fact befell them happened because God allowed them to.[147]

The basic position of Florentine doctors of the soul was that time was highly significant and unequal in value. Even Savonarola, after damning astrologers, explained that since the city was within the octave of the feast of Mary's Annunciation, the citizens should pray to the Virgin so that she would be the one to placate God's ire toward Florence.[148] In the same years the Camaldolan general Delfin warned against taking communion on just any day, when sex, gluttony, and drunkenness polluted the host. The Eucharist was only intended for three solemn days: "Doctors control the time when they give medicines to sick bodies, for those given at the wrong time often do harm." And so it should be for doctors of souls.[149] No one doubted that behavior had to be rigidly formalized according to time; the only difference was why. Those who professed the Christian calendar insisted that "God is the one who sanctifies days and things; days do not sanctify things."[150] The average layman like Paolo da Certaldo easily melded abstract and saints' time into a behavioral program:

> The sin committed on Sunday or other *pasque* and solemn feasts is greater than one committed on workdays. And thus when you want to celebrate a great feast in honor of a male or female saint, never do it with gambling or banquets or other mundane things. Do it with alms and prayers, and guard against sins. These are the feasts acceptable to God and to his blessed saints.[151]

The commune took up where preachers and individual laypersons left off, over the centuries creating and constantly refurbishing a calendar of shaped times when specific types of behavior were permitted or required. On the one hand, legal norms regulating behavior did not apply objectively to all times. Sumptuary laws were not enforced during celebrations; indeed it was a

145. *Prediche* (Florence, 1424), II, 76.

146. *Prediche* (Siena, 1425), I, 275.

147. *Prediche* (Florence, 1424), II, 169.

148. *Amos e Zaccaria*, III, 123.

149. Schnitzer, *Delfin*, 394, in the midst of a long discourse on sacred time.

150. Bernardino of Siena, *Prediche* (Florence, 1424), II, 182.

151. Paolo da Certaldo, *Libro*, 157.

mark of honor to the personage being honored that the normal rules of dress were waived.[152] Prohibited games were legal on some days of the year.[153] And what might seem oddest in a city so dedicated to merchandising, debts were suspended on some feast days.[154] On certain days, all these departures from normal rules were permitted.

On the other hand, the solemnity of the feasts caused the commune to suspend activities like usury, which, though in violation of divine law, were licensed in daily life. Every Thursday and Saturday evening and on the vigils of other solemn feasts, for example, the usurers' *tabulos et discos* had to be removed from the streets and from the divine view.[155] Streets were swept and prostitutes banned; the city was purified for the approaching sacred time.

The commune complemented its permission or requirement of special festive behavior by rigorously prosecuting those who committed grievous crimes on the sacred day. To murder or scar the face of an adversary on such days risked double punishment for the crime in question, for it was a principle of communal law as well as of the preachers that on those days when "one ought to be more modest," serious transgressions were twice as bad as on another day.[156] Just as it was forbidden and dangerous for civil officials to shed the blood of criminals on certain saints' days, so it dishonored a saint when a private person shed the blood of another of the saint's supplicants. It has always been important to prevent a sacrificer from becoming a victim.[157] How dishonored the saint was if one of his supplicants was severely wounded or murdered while basking in the security of that saint's day! On any particular day, a particular saint was alive, looked upon the city, and controlled its destiny. One had to "be sure," in Bernardino's words, not to offend him or her.

The shape of the city's calendar preserved the memory of the past, when certain saints had shown their beneficence, and at times their maleficence, to the Florentines on their days. True, a core of feasts requiring modest behavior had few civil associations: most prominently, the main feasts of the Savior and of Mary, as well as Sundays. Yet even some well-established feasts common to the universal church became special to the Florentines because of

152. Certainly sumptuary laws were not enforced on the feast of the Baptist, though I have found no official suspension. When Pius II entered the city in 1459, the laws were suspended; *Ricordi di Firenze dell'anno 1459, RIS,* XXVII, pt. 1, 19, 55 (hereafter *Ricordi . . . 1459*). The same suspensions were used at Venice; F. Bentivegna, *Abbigliamento e Costume nella Pittura Italiana. Rinascimento* (Rome, 1962), 12, citing Molmenti.

153. Zdekauer, "Giuoco," 33.

154. See page 3, this volume. An early Florentine chronicler explained the jubilee of 1300 by recalling that each fifty years the *antichi* released all prisoners, and "ogni debito o promessioni, et . . . ogni misfatto corporale e temporale" was forgiven;

Paolino Pieri, 66. For the relevant Jewish tradition, see J. Hastings (ed.), *Dictionary of the Bible* (New York, 1963), 208.

155. *Statuto . . . Podestà,* 367

156. "Certis diebus deberent homines modestius se habere"; *ASF, Prov.,* 79, ff. 238v–239v (Oct. 26, 1390); 137, ff. 79v–80v (June 13, 1446).

157. On the complexities of these roles, see ch. 3, this volume. A typical example of communal caution in executing criminals occurred in 1393, when an execution was postponed "so that the feast of Sant'Antonio was not spoiled." Antonio was one of the two saints who had helped put down the gild regime of 1378–1382; Panciatichi, f. 172ra (Jan. 17, 1392/1393).

specific civic associations. The feast of San Giovanni, for example, was certainly a major feast of the whole church. But it was especially important to the Florentines, Stefani believed, because on the Baptist's feast in A.D. 401 the city had been liberated from the Goths.[158] And many other feasts of lesser importance in the church calendar became civic occasions for the same reasons of Florentine victory. Stefani goes on to tell us that the Goths were completely defeated later in the same year on the feast of S. Reparata, and that S. Zanobi was the bishop of Florence during these events—a charming way of involving all three city patrons in one magnificent act of protection. The apostles Peter, Paul, and Barnabas, as well as Saints Victor, Augustine, Benedict, and many others, deserved special reverential behavior on their days because they had behaved well toward the citizens of Florence.[159] Florentines owed them eternal gratitude. On these *benedetti dì* the saints watched to see if these mortals would honor them or be incautious enough to forget the past. If the latter, catastrophe could follow, as one cleric warned the citizens when St. John was not duly honored on his day: "St. John the Baptist and the other saints, deprived of their accustomed honors, will justly turn against us, and then ruin will follow."[160]

Thus the Florentines watched the events of the day, and consistently interpreted them in the light of the saint who controlled these events. Always ready to highlight the efficacy of the day's saint when fortunate communal or political events occurred, they rarely reacted explicitly and literally to evidence of an association between misfortune and a saint, as they did when back-to-back misfortunes in 1433 and 1434 involving the feast of the beheading of St. John led the commune to change its own official calendar.[161] More commonly, chroniclers simply noted the bad news and mentioned the saint involved, allowing the reader to draw his own conclusions. It was not simply that they feared provoking the saint by making such an accusation in writing. They had qualms about how a saint could be responsible for such evils, a responsibility they were much more willing and found much more reasonable to attribute to God, who made no promises.

Precisely the absence of obligation distinguished the Florentines' relation to the stars from their links with the gods. Astrologers and the many chroniclers influenced by them could without fear of retribution attribute goodness to the divinities, and evil to the conjunctions of the planets. The dangers and potentials of astrological time could only be understood, not propitiated.

158. Stefani, rub. 25.

159. For Florentine attribution of civic fortune to the saints, see U. Dorini, "Il Culto delle Memorie Patrie nella Repubblica di Firenze," *Rassegna Nazionale* CLXXIX (1911), 3–25.

160. Francesco Altoviti, *in Defensione de Magistrati, et delle Leggi et Antiche Cerimonie al Culto Divino della Citta di Firenze contro alle Invettive et Offensione di Fra Girolamo* (Florence, 1497), c. a-v recto. The term *benedetti dì*

was used by *Diario d'Anonimo*, 298 (1365).

161. Guicciardini, *History of Florence*, 4. The disdain for a malevolent saint could be more direct. Salimbene tells us that St. Anthony was big in Padua since he had brought victory, but "the Bolognese, who were on the side of the church, did not sing [his praises, and] they did not want to hear this saint named in Bologna" because they had lost on his day in 1275; Salimbene de Adam, *Cronica*, ed. G. Scalia, 2 vols. (Bari, 1966), I, 573.

There was no mutuality of love and hate between men and the stars, only the abstract communion of cognition. The stars had no memory, and no capacity for willful vengeance. They could be blamed because they could not punish. Their seduction was great. Giovanni Villani's great chronicle was partially built on astrological models;[162] Pietrobuoni followed in the fifteenth century. Luca Landucci, although committed to the antiastrological Savonarola, could not avoid explaining the plague as resulting from the eclipse of the sun or phases of the moon.[163] Another Savonarolan, Giovanni Cambi, truer to his spiritual leader, generally managed to avoid stellar causality in writing his Florentine history. Thus in converting the chronicle of Pietrobuoni into the first books of his own history of the city, Cambi usually copied the latter's inveterate astrological explanations of misfortunes, but in his own record usually skirted such an approach.[164] Yet how he must have envied Pietrobuoni. For the only other way to explain misfortunes was to record the saint's name on whose day a misfortune had taken place, and thus imply his or her guilt.[165]

For obvious reasons of religious orthodoxy, the Florentine commune downplayed its use of astrological time. No communal law required the modification of behavior during certain stellar conjunctions; no public monuments to favorable conjunctions were raised in the city, though in at least one case a private person memorialized the constellation of a favorable event.[166] There were of course other than dogmatic reasons for this inattention to the stellar past. The significance of a conjunction rested on a complex of planetary positions that rarely recurred; most important, public monuments and laws memorializing the stars were fruitless because neither building nor laws could propitiate or serve as prayers, for the stars had no will.

Precisely because of these qualities of calculability rather than passion and intellectuality instead of memory, astrological time was the predominant instrument used by those who could afford it to plan and execute personal and political actions. Significant stellar times *were* occasions of formalized action, despite the silence of the communal law. In its pure state, such planetarily conditioned formalism differed from ritual for saints in being expressive, not demonstrative: The stars were sightless and could not be moved; the actor had to move correctly, but he did not have to combine this with any particular internal state.

---

162. V. Stegemann, "G. Villanis Historische Charakterbilder und die Astrologischen Texte der Planetarischen Anthropologie," in B. Bischoff *et al.* (eds.), *Lebenskräfte in der Abendländischen Geistesgeschichte* (Festschrift Walter Goetz) (Marburg, 1948), 125–199. Also L. Green, *Chronicle into History* (Cambridge, 1972), 29–35.

163. Landucci, 152, 155, 173, 220.

164. Based on a comparison of Cambi, XX, with Pietrobuoni.

165. Sometimes the chronicler could be explicit. Thus

when a jouster was accidentally killed in 1501, Cambi said this would be an example to those who played such games "on the feast of two such apostles [Peter and Paul], cousins of Christ"; Cambi, XXI, 160. The jousters were apparently punished by the saints. For his part, Guicciardini insisted on the fact that the fall of the Medici and the loss of Pisa both happened on the day of San Salvatore; *History of Florence*, 92–95.

166. Citing Warburg, Davidsohn says the small cupola over the sacristy altar of San Lorenzo is decorated with the constellation of the day the altar was consecrated; *Storia*, V, 31 (1422).

The ritualization of behavior around astrological points is one of the better known motifs of Florentine formal life. The baton of command could not be given to a condottiere, troops could not leave the city, battles could not be started, except at the right moments.[167] The new house, the new city, the scrutiny that redefined potential officeholders, could only be initiated in time. Florentines thought themselves distinguished by their attention to rational time, indeed Villani claimed that nearby Fiesole had been the first European city started in this fashion.[168] Unfortunate events were blamed on astrological sloppiness: One communal counselor complained that Donatello's statue *Judith and Holophernes* brought the city nothing but harm since it had been placed in position under an evil constellation.[169] When in 1458 the moon's unusual positions led some men to celebrate Carnival on February 14 and others to wait another week, Pietrobuoni recorded the confusion with evident concern for its implications.[170] When astrologers predicted bad times ahead, precautions were taken by the whole city, as in 1524 when all who could, hoarded food to circumvent the expected heavy rains.[171]

This attitude is well known; what has been obscured is the ease with which astrological time was combined with Christian time. Watching what Florentines did rather than what they and their preachers said shows that the two times were complementary rather than antagonistic. Citizens planned, then prayed.[172] Like most human beings, Florentines sought to combine reason and will, objectivity and manipulation; they tried in short to create a time that was planetarily just yet sacrally caring.

Savonarola exaggerated when he said that the Florentines believed more in astrology than in God.[173] Their actions suggest they believed that divinities were more responsive at some times than at others. Astrologically auspicious points were as much a part of that propitious time as were saints' days. Thus private persons prayed to the saints at astrologically auspicious points.[174] The posture was the same in the public sphere, with priests, images, and relics awaiting the point with the same anticipation as laymen. A scrutiny to determine the list of officeholders began, we are told, at the twenty-third hour of May 27, 1385, and was completed at the very same hour on June 10. The Palace bells rang out, and the citizenry held a procession to thank God for its completion. Not only had the times of this scrutiny been determined by an astrologer, but the astrologer was the abbot of San Benedetto in Alpe. Most significant, the same abbot then timed the following procession from start to

---

167. On the baton, E. Casanova, "L'Astrologia e la Consegna del Bastone al Capitano Generale della Repubblica Fiorentina," *ASI*, ser. 5, VII (1891), 134–144; troops leaving the city in M. Villani, XI, 3 (1362); on battle timing see Davidsohn, *Storia*, II, 241; IV, 1079.

168. G. Villani, I, 7.

169. Levine, "Location of *David*." 36.

170. Pietrobuoni, f. 176v. See also the sixteenth-century Carnival song on celebrating that feast on the

same day; C. Singleton (ed.), *Canti Carnascialeschi del Rinascimento* (Bari, 1936), 169.

171. F. Frediano (ed.), *Della Cronica di Firenze di fra Giuliano Ughi*, in *ASI, Appendici*, vol. VII (1849), *Appendice* 23, 135f.

172. E. Garin has stressed this combined approach; *Medioevo e Rinascimento* (Bari, 1966), 150–169.

173. *Giobbe*, I, 234 and repeatedly.

174. Garin, *Medioevo*, 165.

finish.[175] More: In 1427, three days of clerical processions preceded the astrologically timed consignment of the communal baton of command to the condottiere.[176] There were rare individuals who thought this effortless fusion of astrology and divine propitiation indecorous. The Savonarolan Giovanni Cambi, for example, after recording how the 1534 ceremonies surrounding the laying of the cornerstone at the Fortezza da Basso started with a Mass, and concluded with astrologers—a Carmelite general among them—armed with astrolabes ordering the first rocks kicked into the foundation at the right point in time, complained with the greatest disdain that "they did this in the name of God!"[177] The normal attitude, much different from Cambi's, was an easy approval of all available means suggesting that, in some way, the saints listened not only on their days but at certain junctures of the heavenly bodies. Astrologers too considered themselves Christians, and were the first to thank God when their dire predictions did not materialize. The fusion of the two times was so close in citizens' minds that they could refer to saints as "auspicious," their feasts as occurring under "happy auspices," and act accordingly.[178]

We have examined two types of sacred time, the calendrical and the astrological. Both were expected times, futures that could be planned and pasts whose events were better explained in the light of the time's significance. There was a third type of sacred time, however: a cunning time that was unexpected and not susceptible to planning. This unexpected time can be divided into times sacralized by physical omens, times sacralized by calendrical omens, and times heightened by the chronological coincidence of seemingly unrelated events.

Omens cross almost every page of Florentine history, making secular events sacred, formalizing and concluding most chapters of the civic past. Machiavelli did not really understand why "no great events ever occur in any city or country that have not been predicted by soothsayers, revelations, or by portents and other celestial signs." But he suggested that certain philosophers were right in explaining that "the air is peopled with spirits, who by their superior intelligence foresee future events, and out of pity for mankind warn them by such signs, so that they may prepare against the coming evils."[179] Whatever the explanation of this curious fact, its importance to the historian was indisputable: "Be that as it may, however, the truth of the fact exists, that these portents are invariably followed by the most remarkable events." The great political writer simply repeated a truism of the age.

"The significance," said one anxious chronicler in recording an omen,

175. Naddo da Montecatini, 78f; Panciatichi, f. 150r.

176. Pietrobuoni, f. 116r.

177. Cambi, XXIII, 141; J. Hale, "The End of Florentine Liberty: The Fortezza da Basso," in Rubinstein, *Florentine Studies*, 518ff.

178. Salutati called a meeting of the Holy League for Feb. 2, 1378, "quod felicibus auspiciis Purificationis Beatae Virginis factum sit"; *Lini Coluci Pieri Salutati Epistolae*, ed. J. Rigaccio, 2 vols. (Florence, 1741–1742), II, 92f.

179. Machiavelli, *The Prince and the Discourses* (New York, 1950), Discourses, bk. I, ch. 56. Note that Machiavelli does attribute moral attributes to non-Christian celestial spirits.

"cannot yet be interpreted."[180] Astrologers and ecclesiastics—often one and the same person—and a variety of soothsayers set about determining it. Those like the astrologers who believed such events were "in the course of nature" rather than judgments of God could be fatalistic. "I am a dead man!" Lorenzo the Magnificent is reported to have exclaimed on being told that the collapse of part of the cathedral's cupola in 1492 had sent boulders careening northward toward his palace.[181] Those who, on the contrary, leaned to volitional explanations of these phenomena returned to humility and faith. Machiavelli, in interpreting the hurricane of 1456, said,

> It was doubtless the design of the Omnipotent rather to threaten Tuscany than to chastise her; for had the hurricane been directed over the city, filled with houses and inhabitants, instead of proceeding among oaks and elms, or small and thinly scattered dwellings, it would have been such a scourge as the mind, with all its ideas of horror, could not have conceived. But the Almighty desired that this slight example should suffice to recall the minds of men to a knowledge of himself and of his power.[182]

Machiavelli had suggested that omens occurred "so that [people] may prepare against coming evils." Astrologers combined their talents with those of the priests to prepare the people. Giovanni Villani gives a remarkable example of such cooperation, telling how before the great flood of 1333 he had stood in church and listened to priests and astrologers explain from the pulpit a partial eclipse of the sun. The meaning of the omen was interpreted differently by the two, but the recommendation to the faithful was the same: Repent and pray.[183] Ominous time called for right action, both the scientific astrologers and the religious specialists agreed. In practice, they worked together to save the community.

A second type of ominous time resulted from peculiar configurations of the calendar. The saints' days were moral quanta, each calling for a specific emotional posture, and the faithful planned their emotional lives around these moral occasions. But the movable feasts of the church occasionally fell on fixed feasts with completely different attitudinal requirements, resulting in weird combinations difficult for contemporaries to act out as they were supposed to. The result was certainty that something was awry. Thus Naddo da Montecatini noted in 1383 that for the first time in many years Easter came before the feast of the Annunciation and that "because of this it appears that great novelties ought to be in the world, from which God in his piety guard us."[184] And Cambi more than a century later, rejecting astrology but firmly committed to auguries, noted that in 1502 Good Friday and the Annunciation fell on the same day. In a simple but eloquent testimony to his city's commitment to the richness and fullness of time, he added: "So there was sorrow and joy at the same time."[185]

180. Cambi, XXII, 245f (1523).

181. Landucci, 64.

182. Machiavelli, *History*, 303.

183. "Per savi religiosi e per mostramento d'astro-

laghi fu sermonato in pergamo in Firenze, il quale noi udino'; G. Villani, XI, 2.

184. Naddo da Montecatini, 62.

185. "Che ffu passione e ghaldio in un medesimo tempo"; Cambi, XXI, 170.

We turn now to a final type of ominous time, hours rendered sacred by the occurrence at one moment of two actions whose purposes were identical. For example:

> On June 2, 1509, the Pisans ratified the accord at the fourteenth hour. And almost miraculously at the same fourteenth hour, a dove entered the Palace through the gate of the Palace of the Signori, circled around the whole courtyard, and then flew over the heads of a part of the Ten who were at the entrance of the Palace. And wanting to alight upon the wall, it fell down at the feet of the said Ten in such a way that the provost, who was Giovacchino Guasconi, took it in his hand but could not hold on. Some feathers remained in his hand. It was judged a good sign, and especially because at that hour the Pisans had ratified the accord. Thus it was a sign that the accord was good, that an end had come to such evil [between the cities], and that the peace would be a good one. Even though some said these [events] had a natural [explanation], it was truly remarkable that [the dove] went to the Ten, who had negotiated the accord, and especially, that it went in the hand of the provost.[186]

Miracles of this sort were common, and were especially important in interpreting and explaining the past. Thus when the Signoria discovered in 1432 that the feast of San Rossore had been celebrated "with the most wondrous devotion" in the church of Ognissanti at the same time the Florentine forces had defeated the Visconti, it was believed that this conjunction of intents had caused God to give victory.[187] Coincidences such as this led inexorably to the view that the time of necessary acts in everyday life, acts that could not be geared to calendrical or astrological time, could be sacralized through prayer. Citizens could waken and alert the gods outside the calendar by matching the intent of their ritual actions to the intents of the actions whose outcome they hoped to influence. Thus Masses were said for condemned criminals in the moment of their execution;[188] Michelangelo asked that Masses be said in Florence at the same time that he was pouring a bronze statue in Bologna;[189] the mercenary general and astrologer Vitelli requested that a procession propitiating the miraculous *tavola* of Impruneta be advanced to coincide with the day on which he was to attack Pisa.[190] And in the most striking case of creating sacred synchronized time in the annals of Florence, the Signoria on November 2, 1529, issued the following decree to a besieged city:

> Hoping that the arms of our militia, if accompanied with prayer and divine help, will always lead to victory and everything good, [the Signoria] therefore causes to publicly announce to and notify whatever person not able and not suitable for arms, such as priests, friars, monks, nuns, boys, and women of any age, that every time our soldiers come to battle with the enemies, this signal will come from the Palace: one will sound the Ave Maria with the great bell of the Palace, the one with which the Great Council

186. Landucci, 294.

187. *ASF, Prov.*, 123, ff. 112v–113v (June 13, 1432).

188. L. Passerini, *Storia degli Stabilimenti di Beneficienza e d'Istruzione Elementare Gratuita della Città di Firenze*

(Florence, 1853), 493.

189. *Le Lettere di Michelangelo Buonarotti*, ed. G. Papini (Lanciano, 1913), 27.

190. Landucci, 199 (1499).

is usually called. And then when they hear this signal, all the above named persons not able and not suitable for arms are held and obligated to kneel either in the churches, in the religious houses, or in their homes, and make continuous prayer as long as the said battle lasts, praying almighty God that he give force and *virtù* to the arms of the soldiers and Florentine militia and victory against the enemies of the city of Florence, hoping that through the infinite mercy of Our Lord King of our city, and through the intercessions of his most holy mother, our aforesaid city will receive the above named grace.[191]

The discussion has come full circle. Starting with the basic attitude that time was predictably personalized and significant according to the saint of the day or the configuration of the stars, we then noted that certain types of unexpected time were sacralized by omens or calendrical quirks. Now, far from the world where the significance of time was determined apart from the volition of the Florentines, this examination has arrived at the creation of significant time by the Florentines themselves. The humble Florentines have been left behind, and we meet citizens pressed to act outside determinate time, constrained to force the divinities.

There is no further delaying an examination of the role the Florentines themselves played in sacralizing their world. It is time to clothe the image, surround the relic with precious stones, create time through ritual, even sanctify space through retinue. But before turning to the dialectic of manipulation, a summary of what has been learned is in order.

There were many relics and images in a church, yet reverence was accorded only a few of them. This past chapter has not fully explained why this was so, but it has begun the task by exploring Florentine attitudes toward the sacred. We found space not holy, but rather filled with holy objects around which men knelt and prayed. Particular buildings were only associated with particular concentrations of holy objects; the attributes of the objects did not penetrate the space around them. Behavior within these areas depended on the objects, not upon the space.

We saw that relics came almost entirely from abroad, and that their source was an integral part of their holiness. For the accumulation of relics was a process by which the power of the outside and its past time was consumed inside the city. By consuming the past and the outside within the city—relics remained in the city—the commune and individual relic gatherers protected themselves by weakening others. The result was stability and tradition. The relic was not miraculous; it did not edify or move its owner or supplicant, because it was faceless until converted to an image. Instead, it fostered maintenance and augmentation of identities.

Images were completely local; famous ones were never sought from abroad presumably because they were ineffective outside their hometowns. The power of the images was discovered within the city, and their autochthonous powers could there be used miraculously to transform one's material

---

191. Cited in full in C. Roth, *The Last Florentine Republic* (London, 1925), 220.

and psychological identity. Significantly, it was these nonconsumable holies with which one established intimate relations. The God that one ate at communion was "spiritual food" with whom one did not commune; the God in the monstrance, inedible, was a source of intimacy. Similarly, the fragmentary relic, flesh of one flesh with the devotee, was not an object of intimacy, but the image, apart and inedible, was. The secret of the miraculous image was that it had been made by devotees but could not be consumed by them.

A holy image was one that gave evidence of its corporal integrity and functionality to any one devotee. An image holy to one was not necessarily holy to another, and consequently the kinetic motions of devotees within a church were usually far from unified. Rather, they were an almost indecipherable mixture of awe and unconcern meaningful only to one who understood first that each devotee *knew* only one or perhaps two images, second that layered on top of many individual devotions to individual saints were group devotions to single images, and finally that both of these were topped by the general devotion of the city to its few central images. Cutting through and unifying all these devotions were the facts that all these images spoke to individuals because the holy was individual, yet prayers before any of these images were social in nature. All images were relations, all opened the doors to the wider world of feelings, all promised the transformation of self and society. The supplicant heading for his own image passed another image with seeming indifference, yet was undoubtedly gratified to see a devotee before it. It meant that another image was alive and functioning for a co-citizen, indirectly for himself, and finally for the city at large.

We found that time fundamentally conditioned behavior. Instead of passing another's image, our devotee might stop to pay his respects if it was the anniversary of that saint's birth, further complicating the ritual dynamics and the holy loci of the church. Thus ritual dynamics responded to the calendar of the Florentines' saints, especially those who had proven they cared for the city or its groups, to the warnings of the stars, to the omens of nature, to surprising chronological concurrence between the Florentines' actions and the movements of the heavens.

Finally, our study of the Florentine cosmology has made it apparent how deeply the Florentines were actually involved in making their own *sacra*. It has suggested, in short, that when and where the ranks of citizens formed, there was the holy: not only in the place, time, or object, but in the ritual of devotees. Now we shall place the devotee at the center of the holy.

Chapter 3

Exchange

*"Messer S. Ugolino, I pray you
for the love of God to do me neither
good nor harm." And he said this
three times, crossing himself continually.**

People talk best when eating and society functions best during a banquet, for food, going in and out all men the same, creates equality. In Christian practice men divided and ate God in the host when they wanted to join in solemn promises; in Christian theory the greatest love (*agape*) was fraternal participation in the divine meal of the Eucharist. This chapter introduces and probes the ritual of social exchange in the city, that Babel whose many languages and interests make every greeting an effort, each contract a ceremony. It will study the three constituent parts of social exchange—the image, its frame, and the devotees—and find that they existed together, or not at all. It will study worship, that process by which devotees made images, in its purest urban form: around the altar of communion. It will utilize the metaphor of Holy Communion as the banquet of society at which men might communicate their most intimate thoughts, where society might exchange its highest values.

An image, we say, is a figure that imitates something else. A frame, our categoric mind conceives, is some visually distinct material that encloses an object and separates both the object and itself from outside space. Mediating between inside and outside, the frame seems the central element in a spatial totality that includes the image, the frame, and the devotee, who is a person singularly attracted to the image. Yet such spatial totalities are moral quanta as well, and it is Leonardo who describes the origins of values in spatial organizations:

> If you meet with anyone who is virtuous, do not drive him from you. Do him honor, so that he may not have to flee from you. . . . If there is such a one among you, do him honor, for these are our Saints on earth; these are they who deserve statues from us, and images.[1]

Images are the hypostatized virtues of civil society, the Renaissance image-maker suggests, and their frames are social honors. The highest honor one can pay virtue is to frame it honorably and enduringly; the image is honored by association with the honorable traditions and social orders men treasure most. What are devotees, our Tuscan genius continues, if not the people who make the images so as to keep their saints?

This is a creative, even heretical view of the background to communion, but it has nothing in common with the dynamic aftermath of communion that this chapter will reveal. Iconoclasm is bad, in the artist's view. Having made the divine, men must not destroy it but must consistently maintain their devotion to it. What could be more repulsive, Leonardo continues, than those Indian nations whose priests cut the images of their saints into little pieces and distribute them, each devotee taking a piece home to devour, "believing that by faith he has eaten his saint who then preserves him from all perils."[2] The good society is like a banquet at which an undefiled image sits at the head of a table of honorable devotees who eat with, but not of, the image of unchanging social values. The bad society, Leonardo seems to think, is one where devotees eat the god alone rather than at the social banquet. This is a perishable society digesting and recasting its values, rather than a civil society whose lord, and the nimbus of honor that frames him, persist so as to make the gestures of devotees continually effective in perpetuating the one and future social contract.

Wishful thinking. The exchange society we now study did not operate in this fashion. It may have seemed so when the Florentine cosmos was viewed as through the eyes of a foreign visitor, but a different picture emerges when we perceive Florentine action first at the hands and then with the eyes of the native child. That child entered not into the artist's world of timeless statues and eternal values, but into a world of manipulable mothers and values that he molded to his needs. Accompanying that child into the adult world of images in their frames, as he watched adult devotees preparing their com-

1. Leonardo, *Notebooks*, II, 413. Modern science's relative inattention to behavior in churches and other sacred places would have made no sense to Leonardo; note this neglect in A. Kendon, "The Role of Visible Behavior in the Organization of Social Interaction," in M. von Cranach and I. Vine (eds.), *Social Communication and Movement* (London, 1973), 29–74 and in Kendon's bibliography.

2. Leonardo, *loc. cit.* See the summary of exchange theory in J. Chadwick Jones, *Social Exchange Theory: Its Structure and Influence in Social Psychology* (London, 1976). In what follows, I emphasize collective exchanges, viewing them as contractual processes constantly redefining the social order. On the sacred at table, see G. Greenewalt, *Ritual Dinners in Early Historic Sardis* (Berkeley, 1978).

munion, we shall witness as did he the fact that communion itself was often aborted. Society did break down and devotees did refuse social exchange with one another. Leonardo da Vinci could not describe the iconoclastic consequences of this fact, for he was like those modern Catholics who eat the mere wafer-god but flinch at the idea of digesting the host in the monstrance. Our native child, on the contrary, watched while his elders blamed their inability to exchange on their images' lack of effectiveness, and smashed them. Iconoclasm, we shall find, was a continuing ritual through which men made new images for civil communion; it was part of the historical dialectic of worship.

In the previous chapter we studied what the cosmos did to man. In the present one we watch man acting on the cosmos. The metaphor of Holy Communion will reveal itself as a social process of mutual manipulation. We shall witness not merely a liturgical commemoration, but the ritual of social transformation.

Childhood

The Florentine child first learned of the sacred as children still do, through the relationship between his own motor activities and those of the people he lived with. Augustine remembered his own childhood, when his parents

> named some object, and accordingly moved toward something. . . . Their intention was shown by their bodily movements, as it were the natural language of all peoples: the expression of the face, the play of the eyes, the movement of other parts of the body, and the tone of voice which expresses our state of mind in seeking, having, rejecting, or avoiding something.[3]

The Florentine infant, we may presume, acted first upon the nurse's breast, then upon other images such as family members' faces, hands, and so forth, with the purpose of obtaining food, pleasure, and more complex gratifications. The infant saw these objects of manipulation not as objective things, but rather as a series of feelings projected onto its surroundings so that it might enjoy its own self-created images. A child says; "Let that thimble be God," and it is.[4] Still, the infant learned that the manipulation of these images required a certain type of behavior, a wealth of gestures geared to the emotional individuality of the images it projected. Conflict developed between the gods of the child and the manipulated objects of the external world, between the child's motions and those of the adult world.

3. A passage of the *Confessions* analyzed by L. Wittgenstein, *Philosophical Investigations* (New York, 1953), 2.

4. Rilke, cited by G. van der Leeuw, *Religion in Es-* *sence and Manifestation*, 2 vols. (New York, 1963), 37. On the numinous quality of the nurse, see E. Erikson, "Ontogeny of Ritualization in Man," in Huxley, "Discussion," 337–340.

The child learned as well that this active identity was a "sometimes thing": The right time, space, and accompaniment were necessary to act gratifiably. Even more decisive, the young individual learned that within that perfect setting, *persona* depended upon his becoming an image projecting a unity of expected gestures. To gain their own wishes, the boy and girl not only had to use themselves, but had to be used. We recognize this process of the child moving from manipulator to manipulated in Giovanni Dominici's description of the young boy made into a play-priest, placed by his parents before a make-believe altar with "sacred" dolls, the remainder of the family then playing an audience that provided admonition and encouragement.[5] In this presentation ceremony, the presenting persons constructed the parameters of the child's values.

Developing a vocabulary of gestures having definite meaning remains an important part of human growth; neither the family nor society can have identity without such codes. Yet in infancy, childhood, adolescence, and youth, the Florentine youngster was thwarted in the attempt to imbibe only one code of communication. The Tuscan infant of the middle and sometimes lower classes was put out to nurse at birth and then changed wet nurses frequently. Since the infant usually went where the wet nurse lived, it changed environments as often as it changed nurses.[6] Thus the urban child lacked a stable maternal numen and a stable family and home context. This constant mobility must have resulted in massive difficulties in manipulative orientation and a vivid thirst for ritual stability; modern research on foundlings has established the devastating effects upon children of an absence of this stable numen.[7] When we see a sixteen-year-old Florentine nun being given a Christ-doll along with sets of doll clothing and an altar, when we see nuns fondling images, and we read Savonarola's protests against the women's "idolatry" with these *bambinetti,* and when, finally, we encounter Tuscans of all ages and sexes referring to their popes, patron saints, gods, and mother superiors as *mamma, santa mamma, babbo,* and *mammina,* we are in part witnessing the strong residual traces of manipulative instabilities in childhood.[8]

5. G. Dominici, *On the Education of Children,* ed. A. Coté (Washington, 1927), 42f. The infant's development of spatial and chronological paradigms has been examined by J. Piaget. I have used J. Flavell, *The Developmental Psychology of Jean Piaget* (Princeton, 1963), 135–151. S. Chevalier-Skolnikoff has compared primate and human manipulation in early life: "Kids," *Animal Kingdom* LXXXII, no. 3 (July, 1979), 14 seq.

6. In the Florentine income and census Catasto of 1427, 90 of 234 infants said to be with a wet nurse were of families below the authors' definition of rich: Herlihy and Klapisch, *Toscans,* 340, and 432ff for possible relations between wet nursing and fertility. Because of the practice of giving one's own infant to a wet nurse so as to be able to feed another child for

pay, however, the percentage of infants of lesser class with nurse was probably higher than these figures. On this practice, and for general comments on wet-nursing, see Trexler, "Foundlings." The extent and import of this circulation of infants are difficult to measure at Florence, but its enormous impact on pre-revolutionary Russia has been pointed to by D. Ransel, "The Women of the Foundling System," in Ransel (ed.), *The Family in Imperial Russia: New Lines of Historical Research* (Urbana, 1978), 189–217.

7. L. Gardner, "Deprivation Dwarfism," *Scientific American,* July, 1972, 76; Eibl-Eibesfeldt, *Love and Hate,* 212–224.

8. The gift of the doll is cited in R. Goldthwaite, "The Florentine Palace as Domestic Architecture," *Amer-*

Childhood insecurity continued into the school years and adolescence (from about thirteen to twenty-four years of age). Teachers changed as rapidly as wet nurses had in early years.[9] But children and young adolescents often did not remain in school continually, moving instead from shop work to school and back to the shop.[10] Predictably, Florentine adults only rarely remembered their school experiences. Villani's pride in the number of Florentine children in school must be balanced, after all, against the almost total absence of school memories from the voluminous *ricordi* of Florentine burghers.[11] How children must have yearned for family stability, yet in vain. Statistics gathered by David Herlihy show that the average Florentine father died when his oldest child was about twelve, just at the point, that is, when male children expected to be taken under their fathers' wings.[12] The plague was the final element in this catalogue of anxiety. It usually attacked the young most violently, forcefully impressing upon them the incalculability of life and friendships. "Boys are naturally terrified of death by plague," one contemporary wrote matter-of-factly. In the light of such an ecology, Lloyd deMause speaks with reason of the "abandonment mode" typical of this age.[13]

Early youth, which began at about twenty-four years of age, continued these patterns. Young men were excluded from political participation until they were twenty-five or until they came of age at thirty. Elders preferred that their sons fornicate rather than pretend to a right of political participation, and, to prevent their virile scions from disturbing the political order, tried to keep them isolated from each other.[14] The city fathers were basically antagonistic to the formation of age-specific confraternities or clubs. Youth did not even have the socializing benefit of camaraderie at arms, for the republic was defended by mercenaries.

I believe that this absence of a stable referent language of bodily communication in childhood affected the behavior of Florentines at maturity. Piaget's dictum of a relation between environmental variety and intelligence might augur a high level of adult intelligence and adaptability as one such result. Although a monochromic environment and intelligence are

ican Historical Review LXXVII (1972), 1011 (1452). Catherine of Siena called the pope *babbo;* the Bridgettines called St. Bridget *nostra mamma;* G. Hasenohr-Esnos, "Un Recueil Inédit de Lettres de Direction Spirituelle du XVᵉ siècle," *Mélanges d'Archéologie et d'Histoire* LXXXII (1970), 14. Dominican novices talked to a statue of Mary, calling her *nostra mamma;* Ps. Burlamacchi, 45f. Savonarola constantly called the Virgin *mia mamma* and *mammina* and St. Dominic his *babbo; Amos e Zaccaria,* III, 122f; *Ruth e Michea,* II, 61; *Ezechiele,* II, 130. Bernardino of Siena used the same language.

9. J. B. Ross, "The Middle-Class Child in Urban Italy, Fourteenth to Early Sixteenth Century," in L. de-

Mause (ed.), *The History of Childhood* (New York, 1974), 213.

10. This is clear from the movements of Lapo Mazzei's son Piero; Mazzei, I, 215ff, 233; II, 16, 243f, 262.

11. Gino Capponi describes a school memory in his "Ricordi," ed. R. Sereno, *American Political Science Review* LII (1958), 1122. See also G. di Pagolo Morelli, *Ricordi,* 212.

12. Herlihy, "Vieillir," 1341f.

13. Mazzei, II, 27; DeMause, *History,* 32–35, 51. On abandonment by young widows, see page 165, this volume.

14. On the generation gap, see ch. 13, this volume.

in no way mutually exclusive, it is certain that Florentines and their admirers celebrated quick wit and ingenuity.[15] This instability may also have resulted, however, in a marked receptivity to a definitive language of gesture once youngsters entered society, in a strong motivation for adults to provide such a language for each other, and in a social consensus that the public stage was a proper and necessary setting for the continual manifestation of this language. I am not suggesting that adult ritual merely compensated for personal identity not being achieved in childhood; adult ritual had social functions unrelated to compensation. I am instead speaking of this ritual's public concentration and uniformity as in part resulting from childhood patterns. The absence of a stable behavioral language in Florentine childhood may have been a cause of that society's perception of individual and collective identity as embodied in highly formal, public, activity.

This public identity was not pathologic. The psychological doctrine that adult identity is exquisitely personal and set, and that its modification through public activity represents a deindividualizing regression to infantile modes, may encourage political quiescence, but it is bad science.[16] Modern developmental psychology furnishes a better model: The Florentine infant's process of identification through action and participation continued into adulthood. Thus the characteristic public ritual mode through which Florence, like most traditional societies, mediated individual creativity was one historical alternative for creating, maintaining, and changing individual and group identity.

The Florentine young person entered a society that had behavioral rigidities of impressive dimensions. There was a right way to do everything, a set of images before which to do it, and a right frame encompassing these images, objective canons of decorum that honorable knights and saintly ascetics of old had found to "work." These procedures had not been invented any more than the image's power. Rather, they had been discovered; historical figures had found out God's behavioral plan.[17] Despite men's awareness that customs changed in time and place, some deep need convinced them that there was a link between cosmic and human order, between divine activity and men's gestures in the presence of the framed image. Only through such "natural" conventions was communication possible between man and man, between man and God. A moralist might argue discursively that bad manners and sins were different things, but in the end he perceived that they were essentially the same:

15. On Piaget, see J. McV. Hunt, *Intelligence and Experience* (New York, 1961), 308ff, 347 seq., 356. I would like to thank Carol Dweck for bibliographical aid and for discussion of this subject with me. On children seeking "new communal sponsorship" through disciplining their bodily expression, see E. Erikson, *Toys and Reasons. Stages in the Ritualization of Experience* (New York, 1977), 44.

16. A good example of this approach is P. Greenacre, "Crowds and Crisis. Psychological Considerations," *Psychoanalytic Study of the Child* XXVII (1973), 143, who speaks of demonstrators' "inevitable regression to pregenital levels."

17. Barash neatly isolates the meaning of "natural" behavior in such writers as Alberti and Leonardo; "Ausdruck," 40, 54.

Although [God] does not require that men observe certain manners, in the sense that violating them would mean committing a sin in the eyes of God, He nevertheless desires that all His servants live morally and customarily, if not because it is right to do so, at least for the reason that [a person] does not want to displease others, horrified by his bad manners. For since unanimity pleases God, and since through bad manners the relations between men are not conserved, unanimity is damaged, and consequently [God] is offended.[18]

We want to disturb but not shatter Francesco da Barberino's sense of cosmic decorum, dismantling this felt unity into its component parts of image, frame, and devotees. Without severing the image's moorings in the divine world, which we have studied in the previous chapter, we must draw it toward the world of manipulation and place it within the network in which men and women talked to each other. The image was in fact empty and dead apart from men; it awoke only in their presence, and lived because of the personal and group identities of devotees. The individual formed a society through breathing life into his private image; the confraternity unveiled its image only to its members; the commune as well lived through city icons. Wherever one of these images was worshiped, there was a group that shared civil conversation, common interests, fraternity. Where men framed the image, there was divine power. The image had the face of God, but the features of man.

Frames

Florentine children first learned formalities as children do, by trial and error. Then came the age for churchgoing, and Francesco da Barberino in the early fourteenth century described the Florentine mother taking her daughter to church so she could learn the right way to act. The adults had it all planned: The child would learn in the accustomed fashion, by watching and imitating those around her:

> *And if with her mother*
> *She goes perhaps to church,*
> *Little by little she learns*
> *To stand respectably and ornately*
> *And to pray, and say Our Fathers*
> *As she sees her mother*
> *And the other women act;*
> *Always following the instruction*

18. "Nota per istam gobulam et sequentem quod quamvis amor iste divinus non exigat quod homines servent certos mores in quibus si excedimus quo ad deum non committimus peccatum, delectatur tamen quod omnes servi eius moraliter vivant et si non propter se adminus ut non displiceat quis aliis ex orrore malorum morum nam si unanimitas placet deo et ex hiis homines alter alterius conservationem cesset unanimitas leditur et per consequens amor iste offenditur"; Francesco da Barberino, *Documenti*, I, 80.

> *Of her nanny or manservant*
> *As far as is praiseworthy and decent*[19]

Yet what does a child know of decency, how long can she be expected to concentrate on mimicking, especially when the glitter and brilliance of priests' gowns and gilded pictures catch her eye as she looks about? There were specks of bone—adults called them relics—completely dwarfed by the flashy incrustations of precious metals around them, pictures whose frames of ribbons and jewels and colors competed with the figure for the child's attention. Renaissance frames were elaborate affairs whose material and labor costs often far exceeded the market value of the enclosed objects.[20] From a purely material point of view, therefore, frames of paintings, statutes, and even architectural spaces such as chapels told the young viewer how valuable adults thought the objects were. Before learning where and how to kneel, therefore, the child had to evaluate the frames.

The Renaissance frame contained more than rich materials and craftsmanship, the child learned. It was often studded with discrete objects like jewels—not only valuable commercially but possessing a characterological value—and coats of arms, which were valuable because of the social honor of the families they represented. The spatially mediating frame thus also mediated material and moral values between devotees and enclosed images. In Leonardo's terms, the honor due the *virtù* of the objects was the frame: The more honorable the materials, the more valuable the object was to the patron; the more honorable the patron whose arms stood on the frame, the more valuable the object to those who viewed it. Michael Baxandall has said that paintings were deposits of social relationships;[21] the frame, it is clear, mediated those relationships. The honor of the frame was a fundamental part of the *virtù* of the image.

The conception of the frame explains the enormous attention Florentines paid it. A testator might leave a bed to the hospital of Santa Maria Nuova; he also left instructions that his family coat of arms be placed on it.[22] Family arms were directly attached to every type of sacred paraphernalia; they were embossed onto chalices and pyxes, sewn into altar cloths, maniples, and the like. As the priest celebrated Mass, kneeling devotees saw on his chasuble the ostentatious family blazon of its donor.[23] They genuflected before images that had been dressed in rich clothes bearing family emblems. When the indi-

---

19. *Del Reggimento e Costumi di Donna*, ed. C. Baudi di Vesme (Bologna, 1875), 33f.

20. Baxandall notes the increased use of gold in frames rather than in paintings, oddly attributing this "in part to a distaste for license"; *Painting*, 14f. A concentration of contemporary frames may be viewed in the church of Santo Spirito.

21. *Ibid.*, 1.

22. *ASF, not. antecos.*, R 316 (1320–1332), Apr. 14, 1331.

23. An unusual legacy of a chalice *without* insignia: *AAF, Contratti 1397–1507*, testamental abstract of Apr. 17, 1491, of Bernardo di fu Andrea de' Minerbetti. Also Bernardino of Siena, *Prediche* (Florence, 1425), IV, 334, which contains the standard defense of the practice: so the object would not be stolen; *ibid.* (Siena, 1427), 945. Again on a chalice: Mazzei, II, 111. For the arms on chasubles: Savonarola, *Amos e Zaccaria*, II, 26, and for a record of a garment with coat of arms once worn at a joust then given to a church as a chasuble, see Giovanni–Carnesecchi, Oct. 31, 1429.

vidual stopped to salute a saint in church, he found not only sets of family arms painted on the image, but often the donors themselves painted as devotees at the foot of the saint, beckoning their co-citizen to the same pious posture.[24]

If not directly attached to objects, such honorable elements were found at various removes from them. Crowded on the borders of relics and images, the ubiquitous arms of honorable civic groups vied for attention. Citizens exerted themselves beyond measure to attach their coats of arms to the baldachin covering the Corpus Christi or the visiting prince, if indeed they were unsuccessful in placing insignia upon the image itself.[25] Was a particular preacher or prophet of uncertain quality? His image was enormously strengthened if he had a noble youth about him rather than riffraff, if a noble woman held his hand, if the arms of honorable families decorated the walls of his friary.[26] To the side of a chapel statue or painting sat candles or torches and sometimes oil lamps donated to the saint by some living or dead person.[27] At certain times gifts lay at its feet, a further comment upon the value honorable men placed upon the image. Chapel walls were covered with the arms of the patronal groups, and the most sacred space was separated from the rest of the church by such identifying marks.

Every significant holy object or person had patronal associations. Our Lady of Impruneta was the Buondelmontes', a relic of the cross belonged to the Pazzi, the Girolami possessed the enchanted ring of their ancestor S. Zanobi, the Cerchi enhanced their fortune by housing a saintly recluse, the Palagi and Soderini patronized holy persons, the Ruspi possessed renowned relics, Francesco Datini of Prato had housed kings, and the Bardi and Mozzi had hosted popes.[28] Conceivable apart from group life, therefore, the holy was not in fact perceptible apart from the society that courted it.

We know that the moral content of image and frame was distinct because we can follow the process by which the holy entered society. Unpredictable in a natural setting, the anarchic holy to be of use to social groups was transformed into a predictable cult object. The frame both captured the holy and ordered it; in need of the holy, the social group defended itself through framing it, keeping the image's power while controlling its excesses. But once

24. It is easy to imagine the scene where the patrons represented kneeling in the painting come to church and kneel in the same fashion before the painting, surrounded by clients. So patrons in paintings, and their patrons, beckoned to passersby to kneel before them and the image. On such active invitations to devotion, see Meiss, *Painting*, 123.

25. In Gentile Bellini's *Procession in Piazza San Marco*, one can see coats of arms hanging from the baldachin. A characteristic placing of Florentine family arms on symbols of authority can be seen on a marriage chest (*cassone*) described by E. Callman in a paper to the 1975 convention of the College Art Association.

26. Catherine of Siena, Giovanni Dominici, and Savonarola all prospered in part because eminent men associated with them. Caterina de' Ricci had her hand held by honorable visitors to her nunnery; Razzi, *Vita*, 144.

27. Giovanni Rucellai, for example, endowed two lamps to be constantly lit before the Holy Sepulcre; Rucellai, *Zibaldone*, 25ff.

28. Hundreds of such associations are noted in such works as Richa, *Notizie*. The friars of S. Maria Novella presumed that if an object did not have family arms, it had been commissioned by the friars rather than by private patrons; "Chronica . . . S. M. Novellae," XII, 47, 313.

in society, the honor of the frame and the *virtù* of the image became indistinguishable. The devotee could not compartmentalize his experience of the image and of the frame, and in determining whether an object could be adored, the Florentine devotee like our child considered the quality of the frame. To Florentines there was scant difference between the value of the one and of the other. Describing relics or images they had visited or touched, they usually put as much emphasis on the frame as on the image. Indeed the word *relic* could be used to refer indiscriminately to the relic, its simulacrum, or the signs of esteem attached to it.[29] The Florentine could not worship God without worshiping man.

The centrality of the social frame explains why a relic or image of a minor saint could have more stature among devotees than that of a major figure. Guided by the candlelight that told where the action was in these shadowy temples, the individual inhabitants of Florence could ignore the self-sufficient host on the high altar and throw themselves at the feet of a minor saint because that saint was dear to an honorable family, as one could plainly see by the frame of lit wax, gilt, and arms. In a confraternity, members could consign an image of the Christ Child to a closet and cry in unison before his more earthly mother because the honor of the group was part of her *virtù*. The commune, finally, could expect unimpeachable deference before Our Lady of Impruneta rather than another Lady because the government and the families who composed it had surrounded that image with the highest values of the social whole and its most honorable parts.

Who framed the sacred, therefore, was a question of eminent political importance and one for which the Florentine government had no easy answer. City officials had the task of "maintaining and augmenting devotion," and that meant providing the group settings within which important families could maintain honor. Regimes encouraged these families' identifications with virtuous images, and thus preserved the familial basis of their own honor. By keeping individual frames of family honor at discrete distances from each other, the government could regulate family competition for space and thus contribute to civil order.

At the same time, however, the commune had to protect its own image, for only by providing an indisputably superior center could the weak government protect its constituent parts. Thus the early-fourteenth-century decision of the communal government to remove family remains and arms from the two central churches of Santa Reparata and the Baptistry was only part of a long struggle to maintain and extend its authority. By a law enacted in 1329, communal officials were forbidden to paint or sculpt their family coats of arms in or on their official residences or on the city walls.[30] At the same time, the commune favored all attempts to spread its arms into other sections of the

---

29. See, for example, Ps. Minerbetti, 172f.

30. The original law was passed on June 20, 1329; G. Gaye (ed.), *Carteggio Inedito d'Artisti dei secoli XIV,* *XV, XVI,* 3 vols. (Florence, 1839–1840), I, 473, and was still in effect in the fifteenth century; *Statuta,* I, 314f. For similar regulations at Venice, see Muir, "Art and Pageantry," 26f.

city, on or near holy objects. In 1340 the Confraternity of the Miraculous Blood in the church of Sant'Ambrogio told the government that "certain citizens" had offered to pay for a vault and tabernacle over the sacred object, but only if their arms and insignia were sculpted on them. From the confraternity's point of view, however, this miracle-working blood was "dowered with a grace of such divine attitude" that only the arms of the city, which had authority over all men, should be placed there, rather than the blazons of single persons.[31] In the early fifteenth century, the commune again insisted that "the arms and insignia of the Florentine *popolo* and commune and Parte Guelfa and of no one else" be placed on the ceiling of San Marco.[32] The technique was also used to protect the commune's image from foreigners. Just as a curial cardinal could prevent the commune from exercising its authority over buildings within the city by placing his arms on them, so the commune could prevent a hospital from going into commend by having its own arms placed on the church, hospital, and all other buildings of the *spedale* of San Gallo.[33]

For their part, individual families constantly sought to retain association with honorable objects by excluding other families. The Medici rose to power in part by challenging communal identification with objects, or by joining the communal identification to the exclusion of all other families. Thus when in the 1420s and 1430s that family increased the number of dignitaries in their parish church of San Lorenzo beyond the number in the city's cathedral, it was a sign that the Medici, having bought out other families' rights to display their arms in San Lorenzo, thus converting this parish church into a quasi-family chapel, now sought to challenge the image of the commune itself. The commune responded by increasing the number of cathedral dignitaries, and sought to limit the dignity of San Lorenzo.[34]

Greater calculation succeeded Cosimo's early brashness, and from that point on the family cultivated an identification with the communal frame. A document cited by Gombrich shows how Cosimo proceeded. In 1447 the Calimala gild of international merchant–bankers, charged by the commune with maintaining the church of San Miniato, was told that a certain "great citizen" was prepared to finance a tabernacle of great splendor and cost in the church, but only on the condition that no arms other than those of the gild were shown—doubtless a noble civic gesture. But the family's intent soon became clear. After having successfully excluded other families' arms, Piero di Cosimo de'Medici in the following year managed to add his own device,

31. *ASF, Prov.*, 30, ff. 49rv (Feb. 8, 1340/1341).

32. *Ibid.*, 107, ff. 52v–53r (Apr. 26, 1417).

33. *Ibid.*, 153, ff. 163v–165r (Oct. 27, 1462). Coats of arms were commonly placed on buildings as a sign of possession, and as a warning not to enter them. For the case involving the cardinal, see Vespasiano da Bisticci, *Vite*, 345 (Piero Acciaiuoli). A commend was a benefice whose revenues went to an outsider during its vacancy.

34. In 1419 Giovanni di Bicci de' Medici, with other parishioners, undertook the refurbishment of church; Cianfogni–Moreni, *Memorie*, II, 341–345. In 1427 the Signoria increased the number of canons in the cathedral; *ASF, Prov.*, 117, ff. 119r–120r (July 26). But the commune could not keep pace with Medici largess, and in 1432 it protested the diminution of the cathedral's honor; *ASF, Missive*, 34, ff. 56v–57r (Oct. 15).

and the family arms, to those of the gild.[35] The struggle for place around the holy images continued, with the Medici imperceptibly emerging as the prime communal frame of the city's holy objects. If in the early days the Signoria of Florence had sat during sermons in an arch around the preacher, framing him and heightening both their power and his, by the sixteenth century it would be the Medici saints Cosmas and Damian, and the Medici persons themselves, who would blend their honor with the *virtù* of holy men and objects. By then, the *palle* or balls of the Medici had gathered the ritual community around its images.

Devotees

A devotee is a worshiper making and destroying gods while searching for holy action. If we forget their mobile, god-making character, it is possible to think of devotees as extrinsic to the ritual action that has been described, and it becomes feasible to watch the mass of poor or undistinguished Florentines as if they, in turn, merely witnessed a vast patrician drama in which rich or honorable families and social groups competed with each other in locating the holy. Such a view would be fundamentally mistaken.

During the 1480s and 1490s, for example, Giovanni Tornabuoni agreed to repaint a chapel belonging to the Ricci because the latter family could not afford to, and promised to have the arms of the Ricci placed in an even more prominent place in the chapel than they had previously been. Commissioned by the Tornabuoni, Domenico Ghirlandaio proceeded to paint large arms of that family on the prominent columns on either side of the chapel entrances, while painting a miniscule set of Ricci arms on the tabernacle where the Corpus Christi was kept. The Ricci's protest at being placed so far from the devotees was in vain, for the Signoria on being consulted agreed with the Tornabuoni that it was indeed more dignified to be near the host than on the (remote) pillars.[36] Family honor, it might seem, depended on the quality of the divine object framed, not on the face the family showed the devotees.

Alas, the Ricci did not agree, for they realized full well that the competition to attach oneself to the holy was only part of the ritual act. The Ricci did not dismiss the honor of being near the host; they merely maintained that it was just as essential for families to attract devotees. The sense of holy presence did not result only from interaction between image and frame, nor only from the interaction between family honor and devotees. The spiritual and political experience of the holy was triadic.

Patrons sought devotees because they increased family status; if a "tail without a head" was worthless, so was a "head without a tail."[37] But a retinue

35. E. Gombrich, "The Early Medici as Patrons of Art," in E. Jacob (ed.), *Italian Renaissance Studies* (London, 1960), 299.

36. "Chronica . . . S. M. Novellae," XII, 49f.
37. The word *tail* was slang for *retinue*; Parenti, cited in Schnitzer, *Quellen*, IV, 101, 155.

was essential for another reason. The very salvation of the good people of Florence depended on those with less status.[38] Francesco Datini wanted to build a chapel around a Virgin so that people seeing his arms—Datini had his arms on all the *cose sacre* he had donated—would pray for him. His friend Lapo Mazzei recommended that he build the chapel outside the city if he hoped one day to enter heaven:

> A million persons might pass your house after you die; only a few will pray God for you from noticing your house. But if you have that figure [of the Virgin] placed at that corner [outside the walls], someone will kneel there daily for centuries without end, and there won't be one day when a prayer is not said for you. This is not to mention the fact that you will have honor from those who love you, and you confuse those who hate you. And if you say: "I had Our Lady placed at my corner in Prato," I say to you: It is in a town full of churches, hospitals, and figures [of Virgins and saints], but in the whole countryside of Prato, there isn't one.[39]

Mazzei moved from salvation to honor back to salvation because, in fact, the material element of personal honor was spiritual and the spiritual goal of salvation was material. How was it possible, a Florentine would have argued, for God to save an individual, family, or city that did not show him honor? Yet was not honor in the first place evident in the retinue good families brought to their altars? Without devotees there was no salvation, and without family honor there was no worship. The devotees' inability to worship God without worshiping man was a regrettable but necessary price that had to be paid.

The very centrality of devotees to both political status and religious authority made them extremely dangerous. If they were not controlled, they could attach themselves to an image and thus attach the image to themselves. When Walter of Brienne became the Signore of Florence in 1342, many people quickly displayed his arms on all their possessions.[40] The same thing happened when Giovanni de' Medici was elected Pope Leo X in 1513: Men rushed to attach their families' arms to Medici buildings, and stuck Medici arms on all the walls of the city and upon their own houses.[41] Such excesses were not in the interest of the city or its political families. In their view, social order consisted in prohibiting dishonorable men from framing the image, for this weakened that order. The task of identifying the location and quality of the holy for the mass of devotees belonged to honorable men. The common devotee, in this view, should prove quality, not identify it. Common artisans, workers, and women might modify the status of the patron and image by their devotion or lack of it, but only honorable families and corporations were expected to provide the outlets for the holy.

38. The poor said many prayers for the rich, since they received alms in exchange for promises to pray; Bernardino of Siena, *Prediche* (Siena, 1425), II, 284. Bernardino meant that many prayed for the rich in purgatory, few for the poor. Cf.: "The rich are necessary to the state, and the poor to the rich"; Origo, *World of San Bernardino*, 110.

39. Mazzei, I, 106. Datini's arms on everything: *ibid.*, II, 111.

40. "*[chi] per aver la sua benivolenza, e chi per paura*"; G. Villani, XII, 3.

41. Cambi, XXII, 8, 48f, 73.

Views of this sort were a prescription for a balanced, unchanging social order. In order to keep the image, the frame, and the devotees together, it was necessary to keep them apart. These views were also a prescription for maintaining the life of the image, and thus of the commune. Images lost efficacy if besmirched by commonality, and this could happen if the images were too easily accessible—that is, to common people.

Florentine law lucidly illustrates the view that exposure of images had to be limited. In a law of 1435 the government addressed itself to the repeated importation of the Virgin of Impruneta:

> Sacred objects and those dedicated to God are normally respected and held in greater reverence if they are rarely seen. The magnificent priors . . . , wish therefore to prevent the singular devotion . . . toward the figure of Our Lady of Impruneta from being diminished by her being brought to Florence too frequently . . .[42]

A law of 1460 turned its attention to the Signoria's own excessive public appearances, which were diminishing devotees' respect: "Considering . . . that all citizens are at one in holding that when this high authority goes outside too often, traversing every street and place as often happens, its reputation declines. . . ."[43]

When the Signoria and the Virgin of Impruneta did go about, they were surrounded by an honorable frame of imposing dimensions, for like all images they lost power if too close to the vulgar throng. Their potential prodigiousness depended on the quality of their viewers, and there were some cult images whom the devotees, in their own interest, were scarcely allowed to see at all. For only in the most noble surroundings would certain Virgins protect all the people.

This observation lies behind a Florentine law of 1448 regulating the public showing of the belt of the Virgin in nearby Prato. The Signoria had earlier approved a procedure allowing the belt to be shown to the general public on certain days of the year, but the belt was at other times kept hidden. Later, novelty had set in:

> In addition to these ordained times, for many years it has very often been and continues daily to be shown to many persons, especially on the authority of letters of the magnificent lord priors of the gilds and of the Standard Bearer of Justice of the city of Florence. And it often happens that it is specially shown to lesser known persons on the pretext that they are noble or dignified persons, who later are discovered to be vile persons of disreputable and evil fame. Because of this the devotion to this belt has been seen to decrease; in the future devotion will be still less. Such errors can happen if it is shown often, easily, and outside the ordained time.[44]

The same caution was essential in unveiling the Virgin of the Annunziata of Florence. She was normally not shown "to any but the greatest personages."[45] Indeed only honorable statues could look upon her: The

42. *ASF, Prov.*, 125, ff. 207rv (Feb. 17, 1434/1435).   44. *Ibid.*, 139, ff. 196v–197v (Dec. 30, 1448).

43. *Ibid.*, 151, ff. 242r–243v (Sept. 14, 1460).   45. U. Dorini (ed.), "Storia di Firenze dal 1526 al 1529

Annunziata was surrounded by gleaming life-size wax figures of grateful Florentines who had received favors from her. These *ex votos* were like the candles and lamps; they kept the Virgin company and thus kept her alive. Significantly, by a law of 1401 these *ex votos* were restricted to citizens who had a right to the highest communal offices.[46] Only they could be near the Virgin; only that quality of person could, in normal times, gaze upon her face. The ignoble had killed Christ, said the Franciscan Salimbene; noble men preserved him.[47] Without restrictions devotion would decline, and Florentines knew from their preachers what that would lead to: The church would be profaned by whores and dogs, and the Virgin would be displeased.[48] The city could not afford to dry up the milk of the Virgin's kindness; it could not tolerate a society unframed by honor. Without honor, there would be no devotees to activate the triadic sensation of the holy presence.

The devotees now step to center stage, armed with the power to augment or destroy the holy person and honorable family. The numbers in which they flocked to an image were important, and observers of devotions always assessed the size of the crowd. But mere presence in numbers was only the first step in creating a holy atmosphere; the formal comportment and inner state of the devotees were even more important. From within their hearts came the spark, through their bodily movements came the coded love that, inseparable, could illuminate the framed image. Let us step back and examine the formal behavior in church and in secular society that could activate image and augment frame. Now the child heard the preacher. He was intoning a code of behavior for her and for everyone else as well. The preacher said that there was but one God, and thus there could be but one language with which to address him. For the first time, the child was exposed to a conscious, articulated, universal "right way" of behaving, one that drew its authority from written texts and the experiences of great men. The preachers she watched were the transmitters of this knowledge.

She saw them give specific directions for body language, and first of all the right way to hold one's hands and kneel, perhaps directing the attention of the faithful to the movements of the priest celebrating Mass.[49] She learned that one should imitate Christ, perhaps by tying one's hands behind the back, or placing them upon a cross, or letting them hang motionless at one's sides, as the Observant Franciscan Giacomo Mazzo recommended. From Francesco d'Argenta the child could learn different physical positions for one's Our Fathers for each day of Holy Week, and from one Fra Cherubino a program of

di Baccio Carnesecchi," *Rivista Storica degli Archivi Toscani* III (1931), 108f (hereafter "Storia . . . Carnesecchi").

46. Warburg, *Gesammelte Schriften,* I, 116.

47. *Cronica,* II, 938.

48. See page 69, this volume.

49. See these positions in Plate 5. More on prayer attitudes in L. Gougaud, *Devotional and Ascetic Prac-*

tices in the Middle Ages (London, 1927), ch. I: "Attitudes of Prayer," with extensive references to patristic and hagiographical literature of the type preachers and laymen relied upon. Also G. Ladner, "The Gestures of Prayer in Papal Iconography of the Thirteenth and Early Fourteenth Centuries," in *Didascaliae. Studies in Honor of A. M. Albareda,* ed. S. Prete (New York, 1961), 245–275; Ohm, *Gebetsgebärden;* Baxandall, *Painting,* 61–66.

twenty-five Our Fathers with different body postures for each five of them.[50] Savonarola owed a good part of his fame to such new "devotions" or cultic programs, the best known of which consisted of holding a white candle in one hand and a red cross in the other during procession.[51]

The young churchgoer came to expect authoritative instruction in verbal gesture as well. Not only did many of the mass movements of the time attach uncanny significance to particular prayers (such as the Alleluja and the Stabat Mater), but in every crisis devotees looked to their clergy for verbal signs appropriate to the situation. A woman tormented by a demon asked a Dominican for help, and the religious specialist wrote out the text of an exorcism that freed her from possession when she read it aloud. The words of the efficacious exorcism were then copied down word for word by the memorialist recording the incident, for he wanted to pass the procedure on to his readers, and not forget it himself.[52] Listening to Savonarola's sermons, one regularly heard him pass on verbal formulas: certain prayers, certain numbers of them, at certain times, and under certain conditions.[53] There was a specific verbal gesture for each different life-threatening situation, and the preachers regularly provided old and young devotees with their texts; some elders transcribed them for use when such occasions arose.[54]

A child of good family could, therefore, learn some of this technology at home as well, either from such records of sermons or from manners books. One of the latter, the *Documenti d'Amore* of Francesco da Barberino, taught all the prayers for rising in the morning and retiring at night, a special prayer for avoiding dreams and death, prayers for walking, and prayers used on encountering a crucifix.[55] Whether one understood the meaning of such verbal talismans was not so important. After all, the young Florentine girl learned the Our Father by rote without understanding the meaning of each phrase, yet no one doubted that prayer's independent efficacy. What did matter was to utter these prayers just as they had been said by the authoritative and experienced men who had discovered their power, or at least to have them written down exactly to be carried about on one's person. The author of the *Documenti* was careful to describe to his readers the authority of each recommended prayer. The prayer to avoid death, for example, came from "a certain writing of great efficacy. Those who have carried it have never been known to have perished in war."[56]

After sufficient exposure to the mores of the church, Florentine children

50. M. Petrocchi, *Una "Devotio Moderna" nel Quattrocento Italiano?* (Florence, 1961), 41ff.

51. Ps. Burlamacchi, 116f.

52. Villari and Casanova, *Scelta . . . Savonarola*, 511f (Filipepi).

53. On prayer regimens for homes, *Aggeo*, 74; *Salmi*, I, 78; *Amos e Zaccaria*, III, 35f; *Ezechiele*, II, 60, 73. Also Ps. Burlamacchi, 91

54. This widespread practice can be seen in the note-book of a fifteenth-century devotee where these verbal recipes are copied: Z. Zafarana, "Per la Storia Religiosa di Firenze nel Quattrocento," *Studi Medievali*, ser. 3, IX (1968), 1076, 1107. See also Bernardino of Siena, *Prediche* (Florence, 1424), II, 236. Pico della Mirandola, of course, considered Hebrew a more efficacious language for such rituals than Latin.

55. *Documenti*, I, 147ff.

56. *Ibid.*

felt at home there, having learned the "certain order" to follow from the time they entered till departure.[57] The prayer for entering the church had been committed to memory. By now it was automatic to genuflect, bow the head, and remove one's hat (if one were male) when one approached the altar. How many signs of the cross should the devotee make on the breast and face while there? That had not yet been determined, as was clear from the fact that some authoritative churchmen blessed themselves often, others only once.[58] But most behavior was unambiguous. The accomplished devotee knew the times to genuflect during Mass, and knew as well that beyond those ordained times, "virtuous [men] genuflect whenever they hear the name of Christ or the Blessed Virgin or any saint to whom they have a devotion."[59] The importance of time was impressed on the neophyte, for what one said had special force at certain moments:

> Because although the Father, Son, and Holy Ghost are everywhere, nevertheless because of the *virtù* of the transubstantiation, at this point more valid and more efficacious prayers with greater compunction are directed and are admitted to grace.[60]

Finally, initiated Christians learned that, at the end of the Mass when the priest sprinkled holy water on the faithful, they were expected to bless themselves, and as they left church, say the appropriate prayer.

The young churchgoer learned not only an enormous amount about how to act both in church and in every life situation, but three principles: First, churchmen taught universal ways of getting things done through right action; one could not act casually in the divine presence or in meaningful life situations. Second, there was only one right behavior for any particular communication with divinities; different saints might compete for devotees, but all answered to the same vocabulary of bodily and verbal signs. Third, although the purpose of this behavior was utilitarian, the action was not spiritless. One might not have to understand what one did or said, but what one did had to be personally pleasing to the divinity, and thus add to his honor. There could be no communication without reverence; casualness was irreverence and irreverence was harmful. Church behavior was utilitarian, unitarian, and personalistic.

Preachers and lay moralists did not simply teach a vocabulary of right action, however. They also explained and defended the language of gesture itself, a practice all the more necessary because churchgoers were often disrespectful of the divine presence. Good church behavior had to be made to seem as important as secular right behavior. In defending the former, consequently, moralists presumed with their audiences that there was an elemental unity between church and street behavior, based on one principle of order

---

57. Note that the "certain order" Barberino outlined was meant to regulate one type of gesture, the sign of the cross, but in effect is a total program; *ibid.*, I, 141.

58. *Ibid.*

59. *Ibid.*, 141f.

60. *Ibid.*, 147. This idea partially explains why Florentines rushed into church at the time of the elevation of the host, and left afterward, on which see Arlotto, *Motti*, 81f.

and utilitarianism. Giovanni Della Casa thought this unity had developed historically, that men had learned manners from watching divine services;[61] preachers and ordinary moralists, less interested in the origins than in the functional equivalence itself, fostered respect for the divine by using the faithful's unquestioned respect for human behavioral customs. They built upon a contemporary mentality that effortlessly blended the divine and the human: like Giovanni Morelli, who spoke of a person "always intent on acquiring the love of God his creator by his alms and good works, and also the friendship of good men of power and good name."[62]

One way teachers encouraged good behavior toward God was to speak of Christ as a partner at dinner. In his book on table manners, the late-thirteenth-century Milanese writer Bonvesin de la Riva first condemned those who lacked *cortesia* toward their fellows at table, then criticized those "villains and malignant toward Christ" who did not courteously thank God before and after meals.[63] The Florentine Francesco da Barberino made a direct comparison between secular banquet and church communion. After an extensive prescription of table manners, he turned directly to the subject of behavior in church, saying: "Above he talked of the temporal table, now he teaches us about the celestial table." Through good behavior at table, he continued, we acquire only temporal things, but through correct manners in church we obtain eternity.[64]

But the most common way of fostering right behavior in church was to ask the faithful to reflect upon why they behaved reverentially in society, and then ask if the same motivations did not apply in church. A popular Franciscan like Bernardino of Siena came right to the point, for he thought everyone understood that the purpose of reverence was to gain something in return: "Through reverence you will have grace."[65]

> For example, if you went to the pope or to the emperor, wouldn't you take off your hat? I think so. And if you didn't take it off, wouldn't he ridicule you, and not listen to you nor grace you? Now think what you ought to do before the Corpus Christi, and what scorn not only the angels but also people of the world will subject you to [if you behave without manners].[66]

For Bernardino, one showed reverence to get something, as well as to avoid being shamed by bad form.

Preaching in the church of Santa Maria Novella, the more erudite Dominican Giordano da Rivalto believed these motivations needed more careful scrutiny if the faithful were to learn good behavior in church. One Lenten Friday in 1306 he announced; "Now this morning we will preach a little about this word [reverence]," and then led his Florentine audience through a remark-

61. Giovanni Della Casa, *Galateo* (Milan, 1950), 39.

62. G. di Pagolo Morelli, *Ricordi*, 149.

63. Bonvesin de la Riva, "De Quinquaginta Curialita-tibus ad Mensam," in *Le Opere Volgari di* . . . , ed. G.

Contini (Rome, 1941), 316, 322.

64. *Documenti*, I, 136, 138f.

65. *Prediche* (Siena, 1425), II, 226.

66. *Ibid.*, II, 227.

able analysis of the effect of behavioral forms upon God and man.[67] Is it not true, Giordano began, that a secular lord is impervious to what you do?

> You can't offend a great lord in any way, since you can't take either field or vineyard from him, nor [do him] the injuries which [lesser people do] receive. Nor can you do him harm with your tongue, since he doesn't pay you any attention: That can simply get you killed. Nor does he care about your malevolence of heart.

There seems, in short, no way a subject can disarm a lord impervious to heart, tongue, and political or economic action, for apparently the great lord and the lesser person have no relations but those the lord chooses to recognize. Yet Giordano relieves this dismal picture of powerlessness in a class society by showing that there was, after all, one way to activate a lord, and that was by offending him in being casual in his presence and not doing him reverence. Giordano implies that in a class society a formal behavioral setting was the only one in which the relations between men of different stations could be affected, for behavior in that setting affected the honor of the lord.

> But in one thing [a great lord] can be offended: that is, not to do him honor, not to do him reverence. And it is no small injury but a great one if, for example, you pass him without saluting him, without standing up, without honoring him. This injury is so great that you almost can't do a greater one to hurt him. One sees an example of this in the Scripture about Mordecai, who did not do reverence to Haman when [the latter] passed. [Haman] was done such injury by this, that he hated [Mordecai] more than his [military] enemies.[68]

For Giordano, passing from the honorable frame to the virtuous image, the lesson was clear:

> If a lord is greatly injured when you do not pay him the reverence you ought, then the greater, more noble, and more powerful the lord, the greater is the injury.

God, the greatest lord of all, was affected in exactly the same way as a secular lord. For all his power and distance, he too was at the mercy of the devotee's formal behavior:

> And this is [exactly the injury] you can do God. For you can't hurt him or do him harm either by your [political and economic] behavior, by your language, or in your heart, for he does not fear you. But in one way you can injure him, and in one way alone: This is not to do him honor.[69]

Giordano defended good church behavior, then, not only by pointing out as would Bernardino that through reverence one got what one wanted, and

67. I follow Giordano da Pisa, *Quaresimale Fiorentino. 1305–1306*, ed. C. Delcorno (Florence, 1974), 166f (sermon of Mar. 4) (hereafter Giordano da Pisa, *Quaresimale*).

68. The reference is to Esther, 3.

69. "Ché ttu non gli puoi nuocere né fare danno né in opera né in lingua né in cuore, ché non ti teme, ma in uno modo il puoi ingiurare, e non in più: questo è non farli reverenza"; *ibid.*, where Giordano, though equating the effects of the irreverence upon man and God, calls the latter action a sin as well as an injury.

through irreverence one was shamed and harmed. The Dominican put the very principle of order at the mercy of the ritual actor: Since Almighty God was injured by wrong behavior no less, indeed more, than were secular lords, there *was* no power outside the reach of the behaving devotee, no sovereignly indifferent force merely amused by gaucheness. Giordano would have disagreed with Bernardino's presumption that the only person one hurt through being discourteous was oneself. In fact, the target of discourtesy was immeasurably more injured than the subject. Intended or unintended, bad form diminished honor, and honor, as any Florentine knew, was power. The person in Santa Maria Novella that morning was effectively being told that he had the power to disempower God just as he knew he could disempower man, and that the farther away from God his station was, the more power he had to offend his Lord's honor. Did the faithful really want to exercise that power, disturbing the honors and virtue of the world order? Preserve the very principle of honor, Giordano insisted, through carefully executed forms of reverence.

One central argument could be used against the compelling logic of the preachers and moralists who maintained that addressing God incorrectly impeded communication with him. If one were a friend of God, an *amicus Dei*, were not forms unnecessary? If Giordano were right and forms were more important the greater the distance between actor and acted-upon, did it not follow that the closer one was to another, the fewer forms were necessary? Since the whole point of worship was to come close to God, were not devotional forms evidence that man and God were apart, not together? There were those who by their actions and words suggested that casual, erratic, or spontaneous behavior in church—and in society—was a higher, because closer, level of communicating with God or man.

Giordano's contemporary Francesco da Barberino confronted this conflict between normative and atypical behavior every time he watched people behave in church. Instead of abiding by a "certain order," particular devotees insisted on holding their arms up and extended for long periods. Others prostrated themselves and kissed the earth, still others beat their breasts loudly and repeatedly.[70] Barberino was obviously unsettled by this religious enthusiasm, which, since it sprang from devotion, could not be easily dismissed or condemned. On the one hand Barberino thought that the language for moving God was unambiguous, proven by experiment, and attested to by specialists. "Praised be he who holds to the common manner of signs and of prayers," he could proclaim, and

> Signs are external gestures in man indicating the internal state . . . , which demonstrate what we cannot represent with words. . . . The sign of the cross [blessing oneself] is the best of all signs.[71]

70. *Documenti*, I, 147. Note that this behavior's "freedom" is obtained by exceeding established norms, not by ignoring them.

71. "Elodo chi communa maniera tien di segni edorationi"; *Documenti*, I, 14, 143, 182.

Although dismayed by overgesturing in church, Barberino could not ignore the spirit that moved those who acted abnormally, for example those who thought that vividly imitating the Crucified was better than blessing oneself. Retreating to the scholastic habit of naming without explaining, he ended by condemning unusual behavior *moraliter*, but not *devotionaliter*.[72]

Trying to defend behavior against those who acted as though closeness to God diminished its necessity, Barberino had put himself in an untenable position. For how could socially (*quo ad moralitatem*) condemnable behavior be acceptable to God (*quo ad devotionem*), indeed be the result of God's infusion of spirit? Barberino did not take the customary position that any deviant behavior in church was mere posturing and repulsive to God. He understood that unusual behavior among devotees was often a mark of the divine presence.

Barberino's dilemma can be explained. By agreeing with Giordano da Rivalto that reverential behavior was necessary, he had been forced by enthusiasts to explain why their abnormal behavior was not reverential. But there could be no satisfactory answer as long as one harbored the utopian view that man could actually escape forms in relations with the divinity. As long as Barberino believed that free behavior could be good behavior or, expressed differently, that God could make men mad at will, the author could not escape his dilemma. The problem remained: Did not closeness negate the forms governing inequality? Was not love formless?

The brilliant sixteenth-century writer Stefano Guazzo was the first modern thinker fully to understand the psychology, if not the sociology, of formal behavior, and he provided far-reaching answers to these questions. Guazzo finally overcame his predecessors' weakness for enthusiasm, and was able to spell out the full implications of the traditional doctrine that, in both the secular and the spiritual realms, there were only good forms and bad forms leading to good results and bad results; that we live in one universe of communications. The insight at the center of his study of formalism was that God could be flattered, and that deception was moral.

True to the traditional principle that there was an elemental unity in relations between men, and between man and God, Guazzo progressed from the study of common secular experience to comment on behavior in church. He asked why it was that his century's most ornate figures were the very ones to condemn its florid richness of manners. Why did people like Giovanni Della Casa rail against the "artificial manners" of those who "kiss hands as if they had been consecrated like a priest's," as if ceremony was acceptable in church but bad in society?[73] Traditionally enough, Guazzo thought they should look at the whole range of human actions as unified, and not act as if what men did in a sacred setting was socially and psychologically distinct from what they did with each other. In a dialogue with an acquaintance who

72. Speaking specifically of too many signs of the cross, he says that "quod licet ex devotione proveniat quo ad moralitatem non laudo, quo autem . . . [lacuna in text: *ad devotionem* added by editor] non dampno"; *Documenti*, I, 141.

73. G. Della Casa, *Galateo*, 39.

documented his conviction that formalities were unnecessary between friends, Guazzo delivered a stunning defense of forms: they are deceptive but moral for man and God:

> Believe me, these [persons] are enemies of [ceremonies] in public and friends in secret. And if you reflect upon the whole in your mind, you will recognize that ceremonies don't displease anyone of any class. For it is quite certain that they use [ceremonies] as a sign of honor, and there is no one who does not like to be honored, or who ought to be displeased at honoring someone else. For those rays of honor that one sends toward [others] return to him, through a certain reflection, a large part of that honor. And although as you say someone who uses ceremony can fall under suspicion of simulation, he who ignores [ceremony] can give off the odor of a rustic, an uncivil [person] or [one who] despises [the other]. I don't want to say that they do bad who tell you they don't want you to use ceremony with them; indeed I praise it. Because to say this is [itself] another type of ceremony and [mark of] breeding, with which one suppresses ambition. And one follows the style of the doctors, who from modesty sometimes refuse money with the mouth, but accept it with the heart, and take it with the hand. Just as the sacred ceremonies have power in the sight of God and excite our spirits to devotion, so worldly [ceremonies] achieve the benevolence of the friends and lords to whom they are directed, and show us to be civil men, different from peasants.[74]

In Guazzo's view, therefore, behavior is nothing less than the identity of civil society; those who do not act formally are simply outside society. Furthermore, Guazzo suggests, men are brought together by the very forms that keep them apart. When his partner in the dialogue retreats from the totality and remorselessness of Guazzo's analysis, and tries by every means to preserve a realm of equality between friends where forms are unnecessary, Guazzo again presses him to consult not ideals, but the actual dynamics of interpersonal communications:

> You may as a sign of true love address one equal to you as "brother." But perhaps he is not moved to address you in the same way. To discourage the thought and the use of such familiarity, he will call you "lord."[75]

When that happens, Guazzo informed his perplexed partner, one is forced to withdraw and "treat him in a more honorable than loving fashion." The problem, Guazzo maintains, is not love; one *does* feel love. The problem is how to maintain communications between men, and that is accomplished by disguising feelings, by "abstaining from that security and from those free acts, through which one [can] lose their benevolence." Follow the example of the flies, Guazzo concludes on a sardonic but telling note. They eat with us, but they do not want to live with us.[76]

Thus verbal language and the body gestures that "speak while silent" were primarily used to communicate information about the object and his

---

74. *De Civili Conversatione domini Stephani Guazzi libri quatuor* (Strassburg, 1614), 255f. The work was dedicated by Guazzo in 1574. It is used here to exemplify this age's psychological sophistication.

75. *Ibid.*, 258.
76. *Ibid.* Note that these "free acts" are accomplished by diminishing expected behavior, as against exceeding it; cf. n. 70.

relationship with the subject rather than to express the moral condition of the subject. Guazzo was not saying that behavior was purely instrumental and unfeeling. Quite the contrary: From forms springs the sensation of honor, which is then fed back, "through a certain reflection," to the original subject. Guazzo leaves no doubt that this feedback system encompasses God as well as man, for God too responds to ceremony by honoring us. We see divine services, God sees us seeing them, thus "exciting our spirits to devotion." With one deft blow Guazzo brought God into society and ended his always tenuous special position. The author had absorbed the ultimate desire for communion with God into the very real, ambiguous world of communion between men. He argued that the ability to say what one meant and act as one was, which is the heart of the desire for communion, could only be approached if one said and acted what one was not. For deception, "suppressing ambition," itself made men moral and civil. Florentines had always known that to be true in society. Guazzo was saying that there was no more ultimate communion than the social banquet; there was only the social banquet.

Guazzo forces us to leave the church, and we turn now to the study of behavioral forms in secular society. Yet we depart with some sense of loss, for we have left behind not only the hope of a free love in God, but the chimera of a formless *vera amicizia* between classless men as well. The defense of right behavior in church through analogy to secular right behavior has ended all too convincingly. We now comprehend that all along the church was the only possible theater, not only of a religious but of a secular interaction emotive rather than formal in content, human rather than sociological in quality.

Preparing to instruct his readers in secular behavior, Francesco da Barberino perhaps had those wildly gesturing churchgoers in mind when he asked, once more, if the behavior of a loving, interacting, secular society would not have to be common to all God's children. It seemed clear to him, as it would to Guazzo, that men must know how to act: "Love is offended . . . when man, to whom reason and intellect are given, [lives] like a brute animal which lacks these [qualities]."[77] Yet the Bible and the Fathers seemed to contradict this view that the actions of one were as valid as those of another in civil society:

> "Blessed are the poor in spirit, for theirs is the kingdom of heaven" appears to be contrary [to my view]. And also this [statement] of Augustine in his commentary on Matthew 11: "The uncultured come and seize heaven, and we with our books descend to hell."

Barberino resolved his doubts with a brutal act of faith in honorable men: "There is no contradiction, for we cannot believe that God is more drawn to the illiterate and uncultured . . . than to men of learning and those more lettered."[78] This was a faith based on the very notion of law. World order,

---

77. This and the following quote, in *Documenti*, I, 80.   78. This and the following quote *ibid.*, I, 80f.

Barberino concluded, was based on orderly gestures: "Otherwise absurdity and illegality would follow, the foolish being of better condition than the experts, the uncultured [of better condition] than the judicious."

There would, then, be no room in Barberino's secular society for these *rudes*, "sinners in manners" who were guilty, in his characteristic equation, of sin and commonness (*peccatum et vilitas*).[79] The society that Barberino would instruct in manners was of a better sort, and he defined its parameters. It excluded "those completely base" but included many who were unequal to each other in social status. There were "superiors" and "inferiors," whose distance from each other Barberino defined to the superiors as "less than you by a little."[80] Each of the levels within this gesturing world would have its own distinct behavior in relation to the other groups. Barberino specified these subgroups of the gestural society, and he included a surprisingly wide range of social levels. Men's and women's behavioral forms were of course carefully distinguished, but so were the behaviors of young, nubile, married, and widowed females. Among men, Barberino distinguished a decorous behavior for nobles, professional people, merchants, and even laborers.[81]

Barberino laid out a vast scheme of "courtesy" for this range of social actors. There was a right behavior for each social actor in every conceivable social situation: crossing a bridge, walking, and dining; at home and in public; in small groups and large ones. The author spared no effort in prescribing authoritative actions for each circumstance. But I must be more selective, and so will build this examination of secular behavior around the greeting, which was the crux of Barberino's whole gestural machine.

A courteous man sees someone approaching. Having mastered the language of society, he recognizes the person's type at once: "The gestures of men and their speech will quickly indicate to you their quality and status."[82] He then acts on that knowledge with one intention in mind: to facilitate subsequent communications or, in the author's words, to prevent the "placated" person approaching from becoming *implacata*.[83] This was only possible if the bodily and verbal gestures of the greeting were absolutely appropriate to one's social standing. The correct verbal greeting for a great lord, for example, was this: "God give you life"; for an elderly man, "God save you"; for a healthy member of the middle classes, "God make you joyful"; and so forth for each social combination.[84] How one said these things was even more important, and Barberino urged each reader to adopt the *via media* of his own social class. Certainly no one should stand like a statue, for that would in itself damage communications.[85] At the other extreme, too much bowing,

79. *Ibid.*, I, 121, 278.

80. *Ibid.*, I, 110.

81. For the women, see the *Reggimento*, especially 61f. For the men, *Documenti*, I, 157 seq. and *passim*.

82. *Ibid.*, I, 83.

83. *Ibid.*, I, 168.

84. Barberino adopted these from Ugolino Buzola's *De Salutandi Modis*, written in Faventine rhyme. He uncovered a disquieting disagreement between Ugolino's recommendation for addressing the religious and Raymond of Toulouse's Provencal *Tractatus de Sotietate Fraterna*. He also cites Johannes de Bransilva's *Libellum de Benignitate* on how to interpret the response to a greeting; *Documenti*, I, 168–176. Further references to his sources at I, 108, 110.

85. *Documenti*, I, 102.

waving one's arms and feet, and shifting one's eyes about were bad practices. Also, one should embrace another only if both are "truly one."[86] Citing the Tuscan proverb; "He who embraces too much, commits himself but little," Barberino would have understood Guazzo's idea that forms keep us together by keeping us apart.[87]

Having set forth the correct forms for each social station, Barberino examines the actual dynamics of two unequal persons interacting with each other. The superior should step forward and take the lead. Being better than his opposite number, his actions should be more solemn;[88] paradoxically, what he does must be humble. Since for Barberino only equals can be "truly one" with each other, the superior's greeting must equalize the parties if further communication is to be possible. There is, in short, a definite implication that although the inferior must keep the placated superior from becoming implacable, the superior must placate a naturally implacable—because unequal—inferior. Thus the social superior with humility or courtesy (*humilitas seu curialitas*) should take the lead and invite the inferior to equality. Barberino cites the example of the pope, who writes to his bishops as brothers, and the queen, who "raises you up by addressing you in the plural."[89]

A lesser analyst might have protested that the reason the pope called other bishops "brothers" was because he was in fact a bishop (of Rome) like them. Barberino, however, dealt with phenomena, not cold institutional distinctions; he was a student of interpersonal dynamics, not merely a lawyer. And when he turns his attention to a meeting between equals, his remarkable insight is fully displayed. The closer in social station an inferior is to a superior, he suggests, the more the latter's greetings approach actual protestations of inequality. Thus a curious fact may be noticed when two equal lords meet; they do not call each other "brother," but "father." For equals to communicate, they must generate inequality rather than equality. Barberino shows us, for example, that when a king meets another king or a bishop meets another bishop, they claim filial status.[90] He had discovered that two or more equals have to construct a superior image between themselves if their honor is to be equally preserved.

Although it is true that the lord's verbal and bodily gestures invite the inferior to equality and the equal to superiority, they are not intended to cause the opposite party to act out those roles. Barberino in fact insistently cautions his readers against "emulating."[91] Opposite numbers do not accept the invitation, but keep their station: The king or bishop called "father" by his brother does not then call the latter "son." The queen does not expect her

---

86. *Ibid.*, I, 166 seq.

87. *Ibid.*, II, 210. Another proverb: "Chi sa carezzar le persone, con picciolo capitale fa grosso guadagno"; Della Casa, *Galateo*, 45.

88. Francesco da Barberino, *Documenti*, I, 65. In the sixteenth century Della Casa assumed throughout that the upper classes were the solemn classes; see, for example, *Galateo*, 45.

89. Barberino, *Documenti*, I, 110, 121; *Reggimento*, 160.

90. *Documenti*, I, 110.

91. *Ibid.*, for example.

equalized subject to respond as an equal. Barberino warns; "You well know that it is unseemly for a lesser woman to adopt this manner."[92]

Barberino's world of secular gesture is certainly saturated with artifice. He advises a bride to be rigid at the marriage ceremony, keeping her eyes down and not offering her hand for the ring. She should allow her hand to be taken "as if forced," but should not in fact resist.[93] On the wedding night the bride's action should be guided by her age; the younger she is, the more resistance she may seem to offer to consummating the union.[94] The irony is evident enough: Barberino had set out with the view that only "honest" people were ritually efficacious, and ended with the realization that efficacy was possible only through artifice. This was a strong position for someone who believed that a person skilled in courtesy could determine the status of another by his clothes, color, hands, bearing, indeed even by the way he offered gifts. Yet there was no turning back. At one point he admitted that bodily and verbal gestures sometimes became so inflated that they bore no resemblance to feelings. To combat this tendency, Barberino implied, one should try to remain speechless; if one had to choose between bodily and verbal dissimulation, it was better to mislead with the body than with the voice.[95] Teaching good behavior in both church and society, Barberino had maintained that the acts of decent folk were authoritative, because world order rested upon the reason and intellect they embodied. Yet in church he could not condemn the movements of the rude, and now in society, he had *had* to teach dissimulation as good behavior to "honest" society.

Barberino and Guazzo created part of this genuine intellectual problem through their class hatreds; the different ritual languages of the *rudes* seemed mere anarchy to them. Barberino also hesitated to confront a central contradiction in his approach. We saw him maintain that "signs are external gestures in man indicating the internal state," and at another point he asserted that attitudes were reflected first in man's physiognomy and then in gestures, a view he shared with later art theoreticians.[96] But he also taught that those internal states could be disguised through gestures, that manners were in part the science of artifice. Having said this, however, we must note that Barberino, like all his contemporaries, remained doggedly convinced that some relation between form and intent *did* exist.[97] Gestures, he understood,

92. *Che ben savate che non si conviene,*
    Perchè Reina talora si lodi,
    E perchè si tenga alta nel parlare,
    E perc' ancora ella parli in plurale,
    Che minor donna tal maniera tengnia;
    Reggimento, 160; also *Documenti,* I, 110. Barberino discusses the problem of the inferior who, being treated as an equal by a superior, assumes he is as the superior has treated him; *ibid.,* I, 106, 110.

93. *Le man non porga a colui chella tiene,*
    Quando l'anelo allei si dona;
    Ma prima aspetti, che quasi sforzata
    La man sia presa; e poi chella piglia

Non si conviene allei contesa alchuna;
    Reggimento, 119.

94. *Ibid.*

95. Barberino encourages servants to bow rather than address their lord; *Documenti,* I, 168. He pinpoints the conflict between his recommendations of sincerity and duplicity, *ibid.,* I, 180.

96. He refers to physiognomy and to the works of Arnold of Villanova and one Maxentius *ibid.,* III, 60f.

97. L. Trilling provides a literate sketch of the problem in his *Sincerity and Authenticity* (Cambridge, Mass., 1971), 6–25, especially 16. See also the issue of *Daeda-*

not only instrumentalized the environment; they first brought man's spirit into the world, and were never separable from that spirit. Men should accompany words with bodily gestures, said Guazzo, as they dance to music—not the words of a mere technician of gesture. Men's actions never left the space about them undisturbed, their frames and images unaffected; the sick took pills and drugs while performing certain acts and prayers to interact with that environment.[98] For in acting, men sought care, *cura*: "In the end," one student of gestures has stressed, "all actions between men express something spiritual."[99] The sacred and the profane look to each other; priests adopt feudal gestures, and secular men use liturgical forms from the same conviction that movements matter:

> And Moses, Aaron, and Hur went up to the top of the hill. Whenever Moses held up his hand, Israel prevailed; and whenever he lowered his hand, Am'alek prevailed. But Moses' hands grew weary; so they took a stone and put it under him, and he sat upon it, and Aaron and Hur held up his hands, one on one side, and the other on the other side; so his hands were steady until the going down of the sun. And Joshua mowed down Am'alek and his people with the edge of the sword.[100]

Preparing Communion

Daughter: But which of these is sacramental?

Father: Oh Lord, here we go again. I can only say this: that it is not one of these statements but their combination which constitutes a sacrament. The "pretend" and the "pretend-not" and the "really" somehow get fused together into a single meaning.

Daughter: But we ought to keep them separate.

Father: Yes. That is what the logicians and the scientists try to do. But they do not create ballets that way—or sacraments.[101]

The Florentines had learned to exchange honor through pretense, and honor, as these traders knew, was the precondition for exchanging things. Yet was the creation of honor through dissimulation not self-defeating? Did one's word not have to be one's bond in the marketplace, one's body language say what one meant? If the paradox of artifice and honor in exchange troubled the genteel subjects of Barberino and Guazzo, it was the more haunting in a society of merchants, where calculation for profit reigned

---

lus, Summer, 1979, *Hypocrisy, Illusion, and Evasion,* disappointing especially because it ignores the relation between animal and human deception. See the excellent book of R. Dawkins, *The Selfish Gene* (Oxford, 1976), 130f, 140f, 149, 166f, 171 seq. On the relation between form and intent in our sources, see Barberino, *Documenti,* I, 195f; Guazzo, *De Civili Conversatione,* 191.

98. *Ibid.,* 192.

99. Ohm, *Gebetsgebärden,* 10.

100. *Exodus* 17: 10–13. The iconographic tradition of this *locus classicus* for the efficacy of formal behavior has been examined by M. Schapiro, *Words and Pictures* (The Hague, 1973), 17–26. Mutual copying of gestures by laymen and ecclesiastics is treated in Ladner, "Gestures," 258f, 261ff.

101. G. Bateson, *Steps to an Ecology of the Mind* (New York, 1972), 37.

supreme. How could two traders, their confraternity, and their merchant community live in contract without grace?

The actions of men brought forth spirit, but was that spirit meant to augment the honor of a trading partner, or serve only oneself? The objective judicial, bureaucratic, and police institutions, which might have ensured both profit and honor through external coercion, were inadequate. So were the subjective frames of contract available in secular society. How meager and uncertain the prospects, for example, of finding some honorable man who by gracing a contract with his presence would successfully inhibit its violation; how inadequate were the honorific resources of a city without a substantial nobility, one governed by other merchants. Thus at the institutional, cultural, and individual levels of secular society, the trusting spirit necessary to community was inadequate. There was but one choice: To make contract, one had to "go see God"; one had to be religious. Without the grace of God, few Florentines could share their grace in contract.

Guazzo taught us that all communion was social in nature. Yet the only possible setting for the social banquet was around the honored images of the world of religion. Outside the church, Florentines knew, pretense abounded and gestures were always ambiguous; pretense in fact was one basis of a functioning civil society. Inside the ecclesiastics' house of dreams, they hoped, was reality, a place where men could profit from honor through feeling the spirit of what one did because, like Barberino's wildly gesturing women, God could make one act as one felt. Only in a religious setting, where the bad rituals of secular society, no longer merely "injuries," became "sins," only in a place where the equal exchange between unequal men we call contract was converted to the unequal exchange with God that we call sacrifice, could men communicate important business and make the exchanges necessary to the social contract. Without devotion, there could be no contract. The city and its families provided the images and frames to make this conversion. It remained for devotees seeking firm contract to choreograph spirit, to bring the *virtù* of their images, the restraining honor of their frame, to life, through artifice. The Florentines first gathered their *sacra*, then prepared them for the event, and finally swore their contract as a sacrifice. To create a setting suitable for contract, they first gathered together the sacred things they would handle in the act. Personal, business, and governmental relations between inhabitants of Florence, and between them and foreigners, were constantly established through holy objects. From the statesmen solemnizing an international treaty "over the host," "over the altar," "over the relic," "over the Bible," over the sacred stone," to the small group like the *operai* of the cathedral swearing "on the missal," or "on the gospels," to the individual promising under the most dire strictures to reward his image-saint for a favor, Florentines used sacred things to obligate themselves to each other.[102]

---

102. For examples of the use of host and Bible, see G. Villani, XII, 2, 3; Ps. Burlamacchi, 74; Guasti, *S. Maria* *del Fiore*, 188, 229. For the sacred stone of the cathedral, Guicciardini, *History of Florence*, 100; Rinuccini,

These *sacra* were not simply inserted between the contractors, like dead dolls; they first had to be prepared or worked up by devotees who had no doubt about their ability and power to fashion the spirit needed to make a contract a sacrifice. Taught by preachers like Giordano da Rivalto that it lay in their power to offend divinity or reap its generosity, Florentines saw themselves as experimenters who, once they could catch the Virgin's eye, might maintain her power through technique.[103] Nowhere is their confidence more glaring than in the laws Florentines made regarding the Lady from Impruneta. It was their will that controlled her *virtù*:

The will of the supplicators tempers and reduces too little or superfluous rain, against the order of . . . the heavens . . . .[104]

and it was their action that made her effective:

Carrying about the most sacred tabernacle . . . may be the cause of well-being.[105]

Contemporaries might speak of images as if they themselves facilitated the spirit necessary to inviolate community. There were visual representations that "increased devotion," "induced men to tears," "ignited and inflamed," provided "stupor and sweetness of body and mind," "marvel and tenderizations."[106] But these same contemporaries clearly sensed that these images would remain empty without human care, without careful procedures that were other than haphazard. There were certain forms that, if incorporated into images by mortal men, were known to have particularly efficacious impacts upon the attitudes of devotees. There was, in short, an aesthetic based on knowledge of psychological attitudes toward different types of representations. Preparing for community, devotees had to put this knowledge to work if their devotion was to be sufficient to contract.

One technique used was to surround a figure with signs of secular authority (Plate 2). Thus in 1397 a group of citizens conferred with the *opera* of the cathedral on how to adorn and where to place a Virgin that, though inappropriately located, had "grown in devotion." Convinced that the figure "had been honored by the growing devotion," the group considered how that devotion and the honor of the Virgin could be sustained. They decided to move the figure out of its cramped quarters, and to surround the new altar

clvi. On oaths over relics, F. Del Migliore, *Firenze Citta' Nobilissima Illustrata* (Florence, 1684), 487, and on the duke of Athens holding relics to force civic peace, I. Del Lungo, "Una Vendetta in Firenze. Il Giorno di San Giovanni del 1293," *ASI*, ser. 4, XVIII (1886), 392.

103. The experimentation was, of course, based on different models and recommendations from authoritative sources. On protoscientific experimentation, see Davidsohn, *Storia*, V, 26f.

104. *ASF, Prov.*, 107, ff. 110r–111r (June 28, 1417). Texts of both in Trexler, "Image," 23.

105. *ASF, Prov.*, 135, ff. 32rv (Aug. 7, 1444).

106. In order, one finds these terms: page 114, this volume; *Confraternità . . . Pistoiesi*, 26f, and P. Luotto, *Il Vero Savonarola e il Savonarola di L. Pastor* (Florence, 1897), 138; Ps. Burlamacchi, 91f, 117; R. Scholz, "Eine Humanistishe Schilderung der Kurie aus dem Jahre 1438," *Quellen und Forschungen aus Italienischen Archiven und Bibliotheken* XVI (1913), 124; Varchi, IV, 4.

with scepters. Furthermore, they recommended that "the figure be adorned [in the area] above and around [it] . . . with a heaven of shields"[107]—perhaps a painted vault or baldachin, or a radiant halo around the figure. In any case, the painting was retouched in order to increase its impact upon the viewers.

Frames of secular authority could also be combined with technically efficient sacred motifs, a procedure used in a striking sequence of events at Santa Maria Novella in 1470. A Virgin there started to complain loudly that she was not being properly cared for, and her plaint was heard by a group of boys who were playing outside. This miracle brought a rush of devotees to Mary's feet. Members of the Ricasoli family, whose boys had first heard the Virgin, decided to refurbish both the painting and the area around it:

> In the meantime however this most devout figure of the holy Virgin did not cease to radiate miracles. Because of this, and so that the devotion of the people would grow, these most pious men illustrated this [figure or Virgin] with a gold crown, and with gold images of angels becomingly holding [scrolls with] the angelic salutation. [The Ricasoli] completed this chapel perfectly and in good faith within the agreed-upon time, placing the organ and the seats of the choristers above, and their insignias on the doors, windows, and vaults.[108]

Clearly, the Ricasoli intended to heighten devotion not only by framing the painting with their arms, but also by placing on the Virgin herself objects they thought would maintain and augment the devotion of the faithful.

Further elements in this manipulation of the image by aesthetic means were common. Painters' contracts tell us that the face, eyes, hands, and feet of images were considered most important; consequently they had to be done by the master rather than by his associates.[109] On these expressive parts of the body the most expensive materials were used, such as metals and ultramarine blues.[110] If working with wax, that material that permitted the most exact texturing of the human form, the master working on a frame applied his material only to those active parts of the images, again revealing the tendency to reserve the best materials for expressive purposes. The hands that reached out, the eyes that wept and beheld devotees, the head that heard wishes—all were created and shaped by masters so that humans could then reach out to them.[111]

107. "Sopra il provedimento e modo dell'anornare la figura . . . e in che luogho si pongha più onorevole e acto. . . . Allora parea che la decta figura s'onorasse per la devotione che vi cresce, e perchè il luogo ov'è non è acto, si levasse di quello luogho e ponessesi nella faccia della chiesa dallato dentro tra le due porti della chiesa . . . e . . . si faccia uno altare circundato di bastoni al presente, . . . e la detta figura s'adorni con cielo d'assi di sopra e intorno, come parrà agli operai"; Guasti, *S. Maria del Fiore*, 293.

108. "Interim autem devotissima illa sacratae Virginis figura quotidianis non cessabat coruscare miraculis. Eapropter piissimi illi viri, *ut maior accederet populorum devotio*, ipsam aurea corona auratisque angelor-

um imaginibus, angelicam salutationem decenter tenentibus, *multisque aliis ornamentis illustraverunt*. Organa insuper et psallentium sedes apposuere, ac suis insignibus, ad ianuas, ad fenestras, ad testudines collocatis, sacellum ipsum plena fide, perfectum et absolutum statuto tempore resignarunt, quod ob puritatem a beatissima Maria virgine ab illo puero postumatam, *puritatis* obtinuit nomen"; "Chronica . . . S. M. Novellae," XII, 180f (italics mine except for the last).

109. Baxandall, *Painting*, 11.

110. *Ibid.*, 23.

111. On the wax members, see Warburg, *Gesammelte*

Differences of opinion certainly existed on the proper techniques for forming and framing an image to evoke the devotion necessary to contract. Archbishop Antonino and the preacher Savonarola insisted that certain pictorial trends in contemporary art did not increase devotion but instead generated laughter and amusement.[112] The younger Lapo da Castiglionchio believed that a good cultic act with hymns and psalms of polyphony would move anyone with the least religion to stupor and sweetness of body and mind, but his opponent in a dialogue favored simpler fare.[113] Rigorists like Savonarola believed that polyphony and organs, as well as the new styles of painting, drew attention to the performers and artists but not to God.[114] Yet all were concerned with the problem of how to increase devotion; all understood that every representation either defamed or honored the person represented and thus the attitude of the devotee; all agreed that the instruments for increasing devotion were at hand. All were aware of their constituent role in manipulating the object of their veneration.

Thus in order to contract, Florentines gathered images that they knew had the potential power to come alive and affect them. This potential spirit of the images then had to be activated so as to induce spirit in the devotees; the whole point of the preparation of the image, after all, was to fashion an object that would stimulate in the devotees those internal states necessary to communing. These states in turn would result in verbal and bodily gestures that would affect the image and release her *virtù*. Now the results of successful religious experience could be expected. People might "go around for a long time lost in thought, without saying a word, and occupied only with themselves."[115] Gestures, words, the whole bodily and spiritual attitude of the contracting group was no longer like calculated, mechanical clockworks of people "without spirit"; instead, their actions could now radiate "enamorative *virtù*."[116] Touched by such spirit, they were ready to do inviolable business. The spirit of communion was present, and the oath of contract could be pronounced.

The Spirit at Communion

In the right time and holy space, with sacred things and their frames correctly prepared and positioned, men exchanged things and values at the

Schriften, 99f, 116ff; E. Borsook, "Art and Politics at the Medici Court. I: The Funeral of Cosimo I de' Medici," *Mitteilungen des Kunsthistorischen Instituts in Florenz* XII (1965), 38.

112. C. Gilbert, "The Archbishop on the Painters of Florence, 1450," *Art Bulletin* XLI (1959), 76; Savonarola, *Salmi*, I, 189; R. Steinberg, *Fra Girolamo Savonarola, Florentine Art, and Renaissance Historiography* (Athens, Ohio, 1977), 47–52.

113. Scholz, "Eine Humanistische Schilderung," 124.

114. Savonarola, *Giobbe*, I, 393; *Salmi*, I, 189.

115. J. Schnitzer, "Die Flugschriften-Literatur für und wider Girolamo Savonarola," in *Festgabe Karl Theodor von Heigel* (Munich, 1903), 201.

116. Without spirit: Cambi, XXII, 44–49; Savonarola, *Giobbe*, II, 33. Enamorative *virtù*: *Ezechiele*, II, 168.

business and political levels of social life. Their instrument was the oath or promise, an eminently personal commitment of honor far from the impersonality and disenchantment usually ascribed to the city. Bargaining in traditional society, Edward Hall has stressed, is a technique of interpersonal relations.[117] And bargaining continued to be the very action of the exchange. As businessmen exchanged their florins—coins themselves, the medium of such exchanges, were images—they pronounced their "sacrament" (*sacramento*, the common word for "oath") to the attentive ears of cautious partners, who insisted that a sacred legitimacy be evoked: "I want to affirm that all loyal men, all those who swear by the body of Christ . . . are regal, just, and good. But . . . watch out for . . . he who swears 'by my conscience.' "[118]

To heal political wounds, and render the implacable placable, Florentine factions gathered at the altar like priests, and made contract sacrifice. They did the unmentionable, pushing the abilities of their sacred things to the farthest limits in their search for fraternity. Thus in 1466 terrible tensions in Florence between the Medici and Pitti factions were resolved through a solemn oath of peace between them. Two contemporaries recorded the private scene but did not dare reveal the technique: "One made that terrible obligation among all that each would not offend the other . . . ." "It would not be decent for me to tell the means used for the sacrament."[119] But another contemporary, equally horrified at the procedure, reluctantly revealed what acts had been necessary for communion between the principals:

> The leaders on each side took the holy body of Christ together, before the [dissension came to a head], and they divided it into pieces through the agency of a priest at Mass, intending this act as an oath that they would be as one, and would not deceive each other.[120]

This was not India, but Leonardo's Florence, where the large host of the Mass, and not the mere wafers, was divided up and eaten by devotees. In other realms kings might settle such disputes, but in Florence men made their figured hosts and ate them in order to maintain factional order.

Finally, when society at large gathered itself together to renew and revise its contract, the same common feedback system by which the Florentines simultaneously related to themselves and to God was employed, but on a vast scale, equal to the challenge of keeping a whole city together. To close this

117. E. Hall, *The Silent Language* (Garden City, 1973), 106f, 127ff.

118. Arlotto, *Motti*, 64f.

119. Cited in Rubinstein, *Government*, 157.

120. Vespasiano da Bisticci, *Vite*, 384 (Agnolo Acciaiuoli). Interestingly, Vespasiano argued that it was this "mixing of sacred things" that was responsible for the pact's failure and the continued civic turmoil. We owe the history of this event to the fact the

process failed. If it had been successful, Vespasiano would have accepted what happened as normal, and not mentioned it. The words of the oath, despite Vespasiano, survived through still a fourth source: "And whoever did the contrary should be duly held a perjurer, be stricken by the ire of God as were Judas and his followers. And he ought to be abandoned, chased, persecuted, and ridiculed by all other citizens"; A. Munichi, *La Fazione Anti-Medicea detta "Del Poggio"* (Florence, 1911), 116f. See further Rubinstein, *Government*, 156ff.

examination of the spirit of communion at work, we may watch the banquet of society unfold.

The city came to church to work on its arsenal of images and frames, and to be worked upon by them. Properly coming through separate doors into the church, men and women proceeded to their distinct places.[121] For Mass men went to the front of the church near the image and altar, and women remained in back (Plate 7), separated by a wall from their men.[122] The socially prominent of either sex preceded those of lesser estate, and sometimes had chairs to sit on.[123] During sermons, the seating was different; separated by a screen, men were on the right-hand side of the church (the honorable side), and women were on the left. Within each sex, groups might be discerned: confraternities, business associates, gild members, pupils with teachers among the men, neighbors and friends among the women. In all ceremonial settings the family was sundered, for sex-specific groups were the contracting elements in society. The social order had arranged itself before its images. And behind the priest or preacher, the government sat in a semicircular frame.[124]

His crucifix or image hidden for the time being behind the pulpit, the preacher stepped forward to bring out the devotional spirit of the devotees. "I will tell you how you have to dispose yourself, first externally and then internally," a master-preacher would assure them.[125] When he started to preach, the crowd responded vocally to cues from the pulpit. Devotees raised their voices with questions for the preacher, slowly effecting a dialectic of emotion and intellect between them and bringing the church to life. Cries of *Amen!* and *Misericordia!*, rhythmic and tearful wailing, and agitated but increasingly coordinated bodily movements closed the psychic distance between pulpit and audience, between one devotee and another, between all present and the spirit for which both reached—the image yet to be unveiled. Building toward a climax of emotion, the preacher would try to end his homily when these ritual responses climaxed.

Seeking to control his audience's timing, the ideal if exceptional preacher like Savonarola might admonish his audience not to cry out except at the end, when he unveiled the crucifix. Sometimes the preacher's control was total, the last word of the sermon coinciding with the audience's peak of religious energy; at other times, preempted by the spirit, he was forced to stop the sermon when he felt the emotional climax was in the hands of the

121. A particular case in U. Dorini (ed.), "Diario d'Incerto del 1529 e 1530 per l'Assedio di Firenze," *Rivista Storica degli Archivi Toscani* IV (1932), 147 (1530) (hereafter "Diario d'Incerto"). But this arrangement was very unusual.

122. For the "place of the men" and the "place of the women" in Santa Croce, see Richa, *Notizie*, I, 72 and G. di Pagolo Morelli, *Ricordi*, 137, 458. For the separation in Santa Maria Novella, "Chronica . . . S. M. Novellae," IX (1909), 200. For San Marco, Ps. Burlamacchi, 117, and especially R. Morçay, "La Cronaca

del Convento Fiorentino di San Marco," *ASI*, LXXI (1913), 13.

123. On one prohibition against laymen having chairs in church, see Trexler, *Synodal Law*, 66.

124. See the typical separations in pictures of the sermons of Bernardino, in Origo, *World of San Bernardino*, 12, 48. Also in the present work, Plates 2 and 22; see Plate 20 for iconization.

125. Savonarola, *Salmi*, I, 296.

audience.[126] At precisely this point the preacher raised up the crucifix, the host, an image, the monogrammed *IHS*, or whatever object was the center of devotion. The now united audience, full of remorse, love, and action, burst forth in one cry, gesturing toward the gleaming object. In exceptional cases, miracles accompanied this charged moment of human and divine contract. At other times, rhythmic movement changed the sermon inexorably and without premeditation into an immediate procession, which spilled out into the streets of the city. Ritual movement into the streets became an imperial and imperious demonstration that, through form, the freedom of nonform had been attained within form.[127]

To move the city, the whole triad of outside authority, social authority, and devotees had been necessary. Dramatic parts of the action themselves, preachers might bemoan this staging of hydraulic ceremonies, the whole complex and mutual building of power and communication through ritual. They might yearn for the days of the primitive church when rigid behavior without formal settings had been natural.[128] Their protests were no different than that ornate anticeremonialism Guazzo had spoken of: Ceremonies themselves, meant, "by a certain reflection," to make men behave correctly and honorably. The city exchanged only with great effort and ceremony.

Iconoclasm: Toward New Community

Worshiping sacred images, hosts, and relics articulated and affirmed social relations, and those who labored to achieve contract might well consider blasphemy and especially iconoclasm as crimes against society as well as God. Blasphemy offended the state, the government predictably wrote in a law of 1529, by "injuring or offending the present popular and free social arrangement."[129] The system of times, places, and objects around which society organized appropriate behavior was, it seems, threatened by iconoclasm.

Yet appearances, and our own ideological biases, deceive us as they did the Florentines. What was the constant change in expectations that the citizens had of Impruneta if not a form of mental iconoclasm? What was calling the Ladies of the Annunziata and Loreto "the biggest whores in Italy"

126. For example, Savonarola, *Amos e Zaccaria*, III, 157ff, where the orator in an incredible swell of verbal brilliance induced cries of *Viva Cristo!* and *Misericordia!* that forced him to stop. A case where the scribe noted that Savonarola's sermon ended perfectly, with the faithful crying *Misericordia!* is in *Amos e Zaccaria*, III, 285. Bernardino enouraged women to wail with him in his *Prediche* (Siena, 1427), 808. On injunctions not to cry out, see Savonarola, *Ezechiele*, II, 332.

127. When Bernardino raised his *IHS* on May 28,

1425, a woman was freed from possession, the crowd started crying *Jesu!* and the sermon was converted into a procession throughout the city of Siena; *Prediche* (Siena, 1425), II, 184. Authorities feared the possibility of such moving sermons ending in violence outside the church, perhaps against the Jews, as happened in Florence in 1488; Rossi, 238.

128. On such criticism of overceremonialization, see pages 472f, this volume.

129. *ASF, Prov.*, 208, f. 24v (June 26).

if not verbal assault? What was the repainting and movement of the images if not a physical one? Did the Florentine confraternities not annually berate, deface, torture, and otherwise publicly smash their individual martyr–patrons' images as they led them through the streets before communing with St. John on June 24?[130] Images were plastic, and the very process of preparing the exchange that was the essence of contract compromised the identity of the image. Nor is that the only problem with a narrow idea of iconoclasm. Florentines attacked the devil as an accepted, indeed integral, part of their social behavior, and unless we limit our definition of iconoclasm to attacks on what we perceive as "right order," and equate satanic images with "chaos" as did the Florentines, we shall have to accept attacks on any image as part of the exchange system by which Florentines continued to live together. Privately and publicly, they engaged in these two varieties of iconoclasm as a ritual for maintaining and transforming group or personal identities. Worshiping before a revered image creates life, but breaking one creates life as well.[131]

Private iconoclasm (Plate 4) against both Christian and satanic images marks the pages of the Florentine written and artistic traditions. In the former, violation of reciprocity was always the cause of iconoclasm, as the observance of mutual obligations was the basis of devotion. Thus the suave and amusing Piovano Arlotto told how he had decided to have one Santo Sano removed from the church wall, and instructed the master: "I want this one destroyed. Since I've been *piovano* here I have never seen a candle lit here. Nor have I ever realized a cent from it. Consequently, master, go ahead and destroy it."[132] The threat was no sooner uttered than a woman appeared before the saint with an *ex voto* for Sano's help during a plague. The offering was rich, and the woman was able to convince the *piovano* not to destroy the figure:

> When she left, the mason who was dismantling [the wall] said: "See how worthwhile it was to show your anger with him?" Said the *piovano:* "If I hadn't bared my teeth to this Santo Sano, he would never have understood me."

Piero di Cosimo de' Medici told another story of what might happen when relations with an image deteriorated. A shoemaker had asked his San

---

130. This is evident on reading any of the *sacre rappresentazioni* dealing with martyrdom. On Florentines' "tormented" saints, see *Le Opere di Giorgio Vasari*, ed. G. Milanesi, 9 vols. (Florence, 1973), III, 201 (hereafter Vasari–Milanesi). On a Greek's surprise in 1439 to see the citizens "crucifying a man like Christ," see Guasti, *Feste*, 191. On the decapitation of St. John performed at the Gate of Execution (where criminals were decapitated) on Aug. 29, 1451, ser Giusto, f. 65v. The images of the Virgin were defamed by Gentile Becchi, cathedral canon and mentor of Lorenzo the Magnificent; A. Rochon, *La Jeunesse de Laurent de Médicis (1449–1478)* (Paris, 1963), 35 (letter of 1471).

131. The destruction of Catholic images by Protestants certainly contributed to the latter's solidarity; J. Phillips, *The Reformation of Images: Destruction of Art in England, 1535–1660* (Berkeley, 1973), *passim;* N. Davis, *Society and Culture*, 186. The incorporation of satanic qualities into images of Christian saints is an iconoclasm of a completely different order. See the groundbreaking article on St. Anne (a Florentine patroness) by J. Wirth, "Sainte Anne est une Sorcière," *Bibliothèque d'Humanisme et Renaissance* XL (1978), 449–480.

132. Arlotto, *Motti*, 185f.

Giovanni whether his wife had cuckolded him. When the saint gave an unsatisfactory answer, the devotee screamed at him:

> May calamity overtake you! May God give you a bad Easter! You've never said other than evil. It was your evil tongue which caused Herod to have your head cut off. I know you haven't told me the truth about what I asked you. I've come here for a good twenty-five years or more to adore you, and I've never given you any difficulty. I promise you I'll never come back to you again.[133]

Thus broken contract could lead a devotee either to ignore the image—threatening it with oblivion—or actually to mutilate or destroy it. The latter procedure not only avenged the betrayal, but prevented the image–saint from repeating the betrayal. Desertion of one image was followed by a search for another object of worship, communication, and reverence; power was displaced rather than utterly destroyed. Arlotto told of a man who begged a Christ-Teaching-in-the-Temple to save his only son, who was sick. Despite the fact that the man had given the teaching Christ twenty-five years of loyalty without asking for a thing, the boy died. The enraged man appeared before the young Christ and yelled:

> You are a disgrace, nor do I ever want to come before you again. . . . If I had asked that big Crucified over there for this favor, I would have been better heard. I promise you that I will never again get mixed up with you or with children. For he who bothers with children, will again become a child.[134]

The iconoclasm so charmingly described in these stories originated in broken contracts, and ended with new ones. When it is remembered that images existed within social contexts, these stories take on social as well as religious meaning. Image stability even in the private sphere was important to society, because changing one's divine sponsor affected the patronal relations of society at large. A final story, this one from Franco Sacchetti, illustrates the social effects of individual iconoclasm.[135] Distraught by his gambling losses, a man stormed into a church in Ravenna and found the Crucified he blamed for his losses. It was surrounded by lit candles, evidence that large numbers of people framed their social relationships around this Christ. To the astonishment of other people in the church, the gambler seized the candles and, marching over to the tomb of the Florentine poet Dante, placed them in front of his ashes and said: "Take them, for you are more worthy than He!"

The gambler had moved the frame rather than attacked the image, but it came to the same thing; for by framing the body of Dante, he effectively forced others to kneel before it instead of before the Crucified. When his strange behavior brought him before the bishop, the gambler not only defended himself against the charge of heresy but argued that Dante was a better image for the devotees, and that he had done the right thing by bringing them to this image:

---

133. *Ibid.*, 40f.

134. *Ibid.*, 43.

135. The following is from *Trecentonovelle*, 269f.

I have always commended myself to the Crucified, and he never did me anything but harm. . . . Compare the writings of [Dante] and [Christ, and] you will judge those of Dante to be marvelous, above the nature of the human intellect, [but] the gospels to be coarse. If they have something of the high and marvelous about them, that's not so impressive, for he who sees everything, and has everything, shows in [these] writings a part of the all. But what is really imposing is that a little man like Dante, having not only not all, but not even any part of the all, has seen everything and written everything. And therefore it seems to me that he is more worthy of the lit [candles] than is [Christ].

Depersonalizing the Crucified, the gambler personalized the poet. Demonstrating to other devotees how he had been betrayed by the one image, he helped them to avoid the same mistake. The social significance of Florentine iconoclasm was that in questioning the productivity of an image it disturbed the frame of honors men paid that image, and thus threatened all the commitments that the candles represented.[136]

There were no altars to Satan and, if we reject the scuttlebutt about high- and low-placed devil worshipers, no retinues. Yet how necessary was his presence. To the faithful he was the force behind those who shifted from one ritual setting to another, the master of trickery and enemy of peace, the thirst for novelty. Nor was the devil mere nonorder: Satan was not the enemy of ritual, Bernardino of Siena warned his audience, for he had a cult equal in liturgical solemnity to God's.[137] He had to be represented, therefore, in order to be abused by all right-thinking Christians. Smashing the devil was thus like smashing one order of society, for since both sacred and diabolic images were sources of power, both activities regulated the social relations between men.

We may doubt that individual Florentines owned images of the devil that had obligations toward them; it is dubious if any inhabitant punished satanic images for nonreciprocal relations. Yet there can be no doubt that these same Florentines blamed the devil for their ill luck, and little doubt that their attacks on him were sometimes attacks on enemy factions whose social commitments they wished to compromise. In part, images of the devil were painted so that they could be attacked. Written sources have preserved evidence of individuals hitting and mocking paintings of the devil, and this practice can be documented in the paintings themselves.[138] The predella below Paolo Uccello's Corpus Christi altar at Urbino (the latter showing, interestingly enough, the Jewish desecration of the host) preserves the scratches that the faithful inflicted on the diabolic figures. Scratches are also evident on the devil in the Spanish Chapel at Santa Maria Novella in Florence, certainly inflicted with the same iconoclastic fervor as that shown at Urbino. Such examples of scratched paintings, comparable to the commissioned reworking of images mentioned earlier, can doubtless be documented on many other images; the subject has not been studied.[139] But as we now move to study public rather

136. On the threat iconoclasm posed to the families associated with images, see Phillips, *Reformation*, 72, 90f.

137. *Prediche* (Florence, 1424), I, 433–437.

138. One literary recollection is in Ps. Burlamacchi, 67.

139. I owe my examples to Samuel Edgerton, who kindly allowed me to read in draft his *Pictures and Punishment: Art and Criminal Punishment during the Florentine Renaissance* (Ithaca, 1985).

than private iconoclasm, we can examine such destruction of Satan as a common group activity.

The public attacked three types of images: those of the devil, those of bankrupts and traitors, and those of Christian deities. Iconoclasm against the first was perhaps the most common of the three. It took two forms. In the first, preachers organized processions on the devil's feast of Carnival in order to mock and "confuse" him. Be sure you are not in mortal sin, Bernardino told his listeners, and then "make fun of every hex, every evil, every incantation."[140] These processions in turn often led to a great city square for the most characteristic insult to the devil, the Burning of the Vanities. Here were all the artifacts of the devil, as they were identified by the preacher: the books, wigs, and cosmetics with which Florentines were said to worship the Prince of Darkness. There at the very top of the carefully arranged pyramid was the image of the devil himself, lord of all these objects. As the torch was lit, song broke out that "mocked Carnival."[141] Carnival cried;

> The boys are my death
> They have taken my glory. . . .
> Everyone has become a friar. . . .

The poet chronicled the victory of Lent that the insult to the devil had gained:

> Fourteen hundred and ninety-eight
> The twentieth day of February,
> Carnival raised his flag;
> He lost his reign the twenty-seventh day,
> Thanks be to God![142]

Through such actions the citizens expressed their repugnance for the novelty the devilish Carnival represented. Yet in these iconoclastic observances the solid citizens could delineate and identify social allegiances. Did the fine lady throw *her* cosmetics into the fire, as decorum dictated? Did the social dandy offer the devil *his* lascivious paintings? Did the youngster take part in the traditional Carnival rioting, or did he join this procession that insulted the devil in song?

Mocking devils was one type of official iconoclasm; a second such practice was to punish bankrupts and traitors by displaying insulting paintings of their persons. Those who violated commercial trust, those who broke their word to the *patria*, were perjurers who disturbed the principle of trust between men and were dealt with through a common iconoclastic procedure, the defamatory painting.[143]

140. *Prediche* (Florence, 1424), II, 169.

141. "In obrobrio di Carnasciale"; Parenti, in Schnitzer, *Quellen*, IV, 159ff (1497).

142. *Libro di Carnevale dei secoli XV e XVI*, ed. L. Man-zoni (Bologna, 1881), 58f, 74.

143. G. Masi, "La Pittura Infamante nella Legislazione e nella Vita del Comune Fiorentino (secc. XIII–XVI)," in *Studi di Diritto Commerciale in Onore di Cesare Vivante* II (Rome, 1931), 627–657.

These paintings were commissioned by the government either *ex officio* or on the petition of creditors, and placed in public places to be seen by the whole population. They showed the guilty persons hanging by the neck, or quartered, or being beaten, in other words being destroyed. *Cartelli* or rhymed captions at the foot of the picture identified the persons, and by their insulting content continued the destruction of reputation. These paintings were equivalent to the devil's fate at the Burning of the Vanities. Indeed, in them Satan was shown at the side of the perjurers; one traitor was shown in hell, whereas another hung upside down surrounded by devils. Such pictures were part of the Dantesque tradition of placing one's enemies in hell, but they were public rather than private defamations.[144]

Passersby doubtless swore at the figures, and perhaps threw things at them; I have not been able to prove the latter suspicion. In effect, the commune invited citizens to affirm their commitment to the social contract by blaspheming these persons. Paintings of communal heroes identified the city's friends; *pitture infamanti* denounced the common enemy. In short, they showed citizens to whom they should and should not do reverence.

When simulacra of such perjurers already existed at the time of the crime, there was no need to create an image showing their destruction. Vengeance could be wreaked directly on the existing representations. The life-size votive statues in the church of the Annunziata, which in 1502 were jokingly said to be "adored" as much as the Virgin whose *virtù* they framed, were a favorite target of contemporaries once their subjects fell out of favor.[145] Piero Soderini's figure was demolished in 1512 by Medicean henchmen, and in 1527 those of Lorenzo and Giuliano, and Giovanni and Giulio (Popes Leo and Clement) de' Medici were violently removed and ground to dust by excited republicans.[146] The "murder of the pope," as one contemporary in 1527 called the actions against the figures of the reigning Medici pontiff Clement VII in the Annunziata and in another Florentine church, carried a clear message to citizens. Not only was it a sign that, in Varchi's words, "having slaughtered him in wax, they would have all the more readily killed him in fact", but it was also a clear warning to pro-Mediceans in the city not to gather around any images of their patrons.[147]

Florentines took iconoclasm's effect upon ritual organization so much for granted that they never bothered to analyze the phenomenon, but simply described it in its political context. When in 1504 two sisters of the banished Giuliano de' Medici erected his wax votive statue in the Annunziata after he recovered from an illness, inhabitants certainly understood that the wax

---

144. *Ibid.*, 645. On obscene paintings of Savonarola, see Schnitzer, *Quellen*, IV, 193 (Parenti).

145. Warburg, *Gesammelte Schriften*, I, 349, for the 1502 statement.

146. On Soderini: Landucci, 330f. Significantly, the Medici arms were put in the place of Soderini's image. On 1527: Segni, *Storie*, I, 42f; Varchi, V, 13;

Cronaca di Lionardo di Lorenzo Morelli originale dal 1347 al 1520, in *Delizie*, XIX, 247 (hereafter L. Morelli), who adds that this was followed by an order to remove all Medicean *palle*, since these too had been an object of destruction, as in 1497; Landucci, 149.

147. Varchi, XI, 9; *Lettere di Gio. Batista Busini a Benedetto Varchi sugli Avvenimenti dell'Assedio di Firenze* (Pisa, 1822), 170 (hereafter Busini).

image created a stage for reordering social bonds around the Medici; in successfully pressuring the Servite friars to remove it, they destroyed that stage.[148] When in 1397 Carlo Malatesta ordered a statue of Virgil destroyed, his act immediately became a cause célèbre, creating identifiable groups of humanists and antihumanists.[149] In 1480 Pope Sixtus IV refused to make peace with the Florentines until they removed the defamatory paintings of the Pazzi. He said he was afraid that images of his friends and relatives were among them;[150] what he meant was that if they stayed in place, men could continue to defame him through his friends. Thus when Florentines described such iconoclasm, they were describing modifications in the social order because they were aware of the reciprocities embodied in the images. If Florentines resisted removing a defamatory painting of a condottiere who had betrayed the commune, it was because without such a painting other mercenaries would be faithless to the city.[151] So when Bernardo Segni pointed out to his readers that the Medicean images destroyed in 1527 had commemorated family "vows made to that most holy mother of God," he well knew that the same images expressed the reciprocities between men.[152]

Florentine governments and society, therefore, participated in the smashing of devils, and in iconoclasm against figures of the city's temporal enemies. A third and final type of image-breaking tolerated by society was the actual destruction of sacred images. I am speaking not of the vilification that the Florentines visited on the ancient statue or "idol" of Mars when the weather was bad, but of attacks on Christian images.[153] Rare, awful, and ominous, such acts were only undertaken when the commune was in desperate financial straits. Governments tried in every way to avoid such extremes, sequestering clerical monies, lands, and unconsecrated precious metals rather than *sacra*. Even when it became necessary to seize gold and silver with the mark of the saints on them, they distinguished between signs and images: In the crisis of the late 1490s Savonarola felt constrained to condone iconoclasm against crosses, but not against crucifixes.[154]

In only one case does the Florentine record show an image sacrificed to the commune's financial need. The Florentines had built a gold votive statue of the Baptist to reward his help in conquering Pisa in 1406. Later in the century, desperate for money to pay its mercenaries, the government melted down this image, and then later replaced it with an opulent painting on a standard. It showed the Pisan and Florentine *popoli* at the feet of the saint, and contained the motto: *Protector noster aspice*. According to Guasti, the purpose of this standard was to expiate the irreverent destruction of the gold statue.[155]

148. H. Butters, "Florentine Politics, 1502–1515," (diss. Oxford Univ., 1974), 80f, cites Parenti for this event.

149. E. Garin (ed.), *Il Pensiero Pedagogico dello Umanesimo* (Florence, 1958), 65, with complete references.

150. Masi, "Pittura Infamante," 648.

151. "Del dispingere Niccolò Piccinino ci maravigliamo esser richiesti. . . . Faccendolo, sarebbe di cat-

tivissimo esemplo, e dare materia a' capitani essere mancatori della loro fede, nè curare il loro onore"; *Commissioni . . . Albizzi*, III, 72, 94 (1425). Samuel Edgerton alerted me to this passage.

152. Segni, *Storie*, I, 42f.

153. For Mars, see page 70, this volume.

154. Savonarola, *Salmi*, I, 92f.

155. Guasti, *Feste*, 18.

Official iconoclasm against sacred images was rare, because it was dangerous. One Florentine government had built that statue of San Giovanni to
honor him and record his help; it had framed the Baptist's *virtù* with its
honor. Another government destroyed it. The insult touched not only the
saint, but the continuity of Florentine history; that is, the social relations that
history embodied. The value of the image and the value of the frame were
interrelated; destroying the former affected the latter. Thus, although melting
San Giovanni down enriched the commune, it simultaneously weakened the
government's reliability. This was why the iconoclasm had to be made good.

Everyday experience told men that when honorable frames were dishonored respect for images was weakened. Once the youthful opponents of Savonarola had convinced themselves that the friar was a wizard rather than a
holy man, it was easy for them to rip crosses from the hands of the friar's
followers and profane them. Christian though the crosses might seem, these
youth thought they were mandrakes of a diabolical friar.[156] After the prophet's
death, sacred objects associated with him and his friary were defaced; the
crown on a Virgin in San Marco was ripped off and paraded through the
streets on the head of a prostitute.[157] Defaming the frame always tended to
defame the image, and vice versa. It was in the full realization that images
and frames were so fused in civic perception that the commune protected the
world of sacred images in all but the most extreme cases of communal need.

Iconoclasm against sacred images had been the result of broken contracts
and part of the process of reconstructing social bonds. In 1498 assassins
carried the lifeless body of a former Standard Bearer of Justice to the church of
S. Procolo and unceremoniously dumped it on the floor, only to reconstruct
liturgically their own solidarity by breaking apart this whole relic:

> Men of the Ridolfi, Pitti, and Tornabuoni came together. . . . Jacopo Pitti stepped
> forward, and spit on [the corpse, and said]: "Valori, you won't govern us any more."
> And at that point Vincenzo Ridolfi cut off [Valori's] head with a bailing hook, and
> because of this others followed in wounding [the corpse]. Thus Francesco Valori was
> not safe from the fury of the *popolo*, [though he was protected] with the symbol of the
> Signoria.[158]

The transition past, men gathered in new community before the image that,
framed with the honors of the new community, sealed their pact. Once one
leader's murder had been avenged, his *familia* disinterred his body "and made
great lamentations and the [funeral] office, as if he had just died"; families
made peace with each other.[159] Those whose *pitture infamanti* stood in the city
insisted they be removed before they would kneel at the cleansed altar in
communion.[160] Those found guilty of causing the breach had been sacrificed

156. Ps. Burlamacchi, 135.

157. *Ibid.*, 164.

158. Parenti, in Schnitzer, *Quellen*, IV, 264.

159. For ceremonialized contracts of peace, see
Rubinstein, *Government*, 163; Compagni, II, 8; Becker,
Florence in Transition, I, 22; Pitti, *Memoir*, 106. The case

of the 1312 revenge killing of Corso Donati is in G.
Villani, IX, 12 and is analyzed by I. Del Lungo, "Vendetta," 388.

160. In addition to the case of Sixtus IV, Masi notes a
1302 case of Siena insisting a painting be removed;
"Pittura Infamante," 643; of the pope procuring re-

before the images they had defaced. Prelates lovingly washed, incensed, and purified the defamed images to make them ready for the new communion, while gifts mounted at their feet.[161] Finally, the new society of devotees knelt before the images to demonstrate the undiminished, indeed augmented, strength of their bonds to these images and to each other, acting as if there had never been social discord, as if the image was really the same as it had always been. Traumatic as the experience of discord had been, iconoclasm had contributed to revitalizing, perhaps transforming, human relationships.

The child had grown into a woman from the time, still young, her mother had first taken her to church to "learn to stand respectably and ornately, and to pray."[162] She had learned that this city had been organized so as to allow unequals to dine together, and that Holy Communion was but a metaphor of that immense undertaking. At first attracted by the glittering frames of the paintings and relics, she now sensed that they, and she the devotee, had no life apart from each other. And life, spirit, was the goal of this "built environment," for without it there could be no contract between unequal, or equal, inhabitants.

We imagine her, now grown, introducing Florence to a foreign visitor, and wanting to put its best face forward. Perhaps with some trepidation she leads her guest to see the defamatory paintings. She knows that some cities have forbidden such paintings, because they are an open admission that a city's merchants and citizens cannot be trusted: This city's inhabitants, they seem to say, will leave you in the lurch.[163] Florence, our guide must admit, obviously harbors many perjurers. Yet there is another side to the City of the Lilies, and our guide hastens her friend to see it. The thousands of votive statues that surround the great images of Florence provide overwhelming evidence of trust between citizens and credit with God; this *is* a city where contracts are kept. The visitor studies the history of travail and ultimate solidarity that each of these statues tells. One foreigner of the 1430s noted that the *ex votos* in the Annunziata portrayed the successful supplicant as he was at the historical moment he had made his promise to the Virgin.[164] These thousands of individual histories proved that the Virgin kept her promises and the Florentines theirs, for "it is certain," wrote the architect Filarete, "that no one would put up the image of the grace received if his prayers had not been answered."[165] Nor could the Florentines' trust in each other be doubted

---

moval of one of a bankrupt in 1425 (*ibid.*, 647); of paintings of Giangaleazzo Visconti being removed as part of a peace treaty in 1392 (*ibid.*, 645). And Jacopo Nardi noted that when in 1494 the Medici were expelled, all the *immagini de' rebelli* from 1434 and 1478 were canceled; *Istorie*, I, 16.

161. An instance of purification in Landucci, 233 (1501).

162. See page 91, this volume.

163. The 1390 Milanese information is in G. Giulini, *Memorie della Città di Milano* (Milan, 1770), pt. XI, 510.

I want to thank S. Edgerton for pointing this document out to me. In Florence the chronicler Stefani was resigned to the public display of a defamatory painting of the duke of Athens (1344), but unhappy, since it showed how gullible the Florentines had been in trusting the duke; rub. 608.

164. E. von Ivánka (ed.), *Europa im XV. Jahrhundert von Byzantinern Gesehen* (Graz, 1954), 165. My thanks to Creighton Gilbert for bringing this book to my attention.

165. *Treatise*, 322.

once one had seen such an array. Around the image, votive statues of the honorable leaders of the city stood fraternal guard, their honor vouching for the continuing *virtù* of the image whose power they framed, of the devotees whose piety they attracted. United, they gestured to Mary, electrifying the ritual setting. The Virgin, the city, lived.

Men could eat together because, our guide assured her friend, dishonor had been banished from Florence. "How is it," Piovano Arlotto asked a disrespectful devotee, "that you are not ashamed to come and put your cap and your lice onto the altar beside the chalice and to retch every morning in such a way I've often feared you would fill the chalice with something other than bread and wine?"

> The citizen went away in shame without saying another word. . . . The friars invited the Piovano to eat with them, and thanked him for what he had done to the citizen.[166]

These three chapters have introduced the reader to the problems of the city, to its basic cosmology, and to the fundamental elements of civil communication. Illegitimacy, lack of honor, and distrust, we have found, were basic problems inherent in the nature of the political order of Florence. Ritual, although obviously as broad in function as civic life itself, had as its central task the containment and solution of these problems.

Over the centuries, urban ritual justified itself with reference to a cosmology that placed the source of human and divine power outside the city: in the Christian heaven and at worthy courts, secular and ecclesiastical. What happened to the commune and its individual inhabitants was conceived as dependent on the will of these outside deities, kings, and popes. Yet these personages were perceived through images that the Florentines themselves created in order to manipulate. A paradoxical mentality was the result; it insisted on humility toward the true nobility and power of the extra-urban world, yet it infused outside objects brought into the city with the power and charisma necessary to individual and communal survival.

An unstable, tense, and conflict-laden population thus looked to its supreme sacred objects as living, vivacious incorporations of divine and human eros, and relied enormously upon their authority to preserve order: not the cold, bureaucratic order of the idol, but an order built upon caring images willing to facilitate communication between the social orders, and between individual groups. Around the holy things, the honored segments of the city identified ritual time and place for devotees whose devotion demonstrated the living power of the social order, as well as of the image itself. Images, relics, and hosts, always plastic, always full of the content of civil identities, functioned even in their destruction and desecration as sacred bridges tying and retying persons and commune to the sources of outside authority. Civil communication was, in short, ceremonial and sacrificial to the extent that it was successful. And the basis of communication between one

166. Arlotto, *Motti*, 38.

urban inhabitant and another, as between one human and his divine protector, was obligation and reciprocity. Identity of one was always infused with the identity of many.

It is true that the systematizers of ritual in this age easily imagined ritual as contributing to order and not to change. Yet in these same men's eyes the foundation of successful ritual was its volatile eros. A society that yearned for order could only verify its existence by the excited public commitment of devotees to holy things. Here in essence was the reason ritual in this unstable city played so large a role in transforming society as well as maintaining it. Because of both the spirit from which it sprang and the manipulative process of social ranking implicit in ritual communication, ritual was always a dialectic of social as well as religious energy. It remains for successive chapters to develop the evidence of living ritual in a living city.

STUDIES IN RITUAL COMMUNICATION

A few case-studies, of wise men, of conjurors, of witches . . . , stopping the movie . . . [for] a still of this victim within this or that context.*

*R*itual can be studied as a solution to social and cultural problems, as the basis of a cosmology, or as a communications system. But the ritual act is first and always an individual technique and experience. Only if we understand how the individual Florentine citizen worked through forms, and how he experienced such experiments can we finally understand the significance of the whole commune at work. To describe the persons in a chapel as mere pawns on a social chessboard or the members of a citywide procession as if they were only a crowd would be to understand nothing. The purpose of this part of the book is to introduce a few Florentines as individuals, so that we shall not lose them and their individuality in the crowd.

In these chapters we shall first study two individual relationships: the friendship between two citizens, Lapo Mazzei and Francesco Datini, and the spiritual relations between the merchant Giovanni Morelli and his deities. Then we shall probe small-group relations to understand the relation between individual and group identity: An examination of ritual in a nunnery and friary will be followed by a study of the ritual preparing for death, and of the place of the dying person in these group forms.

All these studies have a highly individual experience in common, and to a greater or lesser extent all were viewed by their actors as private rather than public or communal events. Yet the behavior of each subject, intimately personal as the back-

---

*E. P. Thompson, in *Midland History* I (1972), 51.

ground to that behavior might be, will be found to reflect the procedures and norms of his or her society. The street came inside in Florence, and the whole inspired its parts. But the private man marched into the streets and made the civic procession his own.

Chapter 4

The Friendship of Citizens

*The fact remains that I'm
a friend and not a friend.**

The desire for friendship, a durable fusing relationship between two microcosmically conceived male individuals, is pronounced within the Western tradition. In this conceptual pattern friendship is "true" only to the extent that coercion is absent between the parties, only when mutual utility is not fundamental to the relationship, only insofar as normal social conventions of human relationships have been discarded. Friendship is said to be spiritual and intentual in the extreme, pronouncedly individualistic, yet ultimately self-denying.[1]

Proponents of this concept of friendship despise the world and withdraw from it, and thus the undoubted intellectual and spiritual genius of the Western concept has been incapable of explaining the actual behavior of men in groups except by ascribing baseness to the *saeculum*. A thinker like Lorenzo Valla, who asserted that a relationship of man to God rooted in mutual

---

*Mazzei, I, 400.

1. P. Brunt provides an analysis of the fundamental Roman literature on friendship in his "*Amicitia* in the Late Roman Republic," in R. Seager (ed.), *The Crisis of the Roman Republic* (Cambridge, 1969), 199–218. The Christian and Renaissance conceptions are analyzed in A. Scaglione, *Nature and Love in the Late Middle Ages* (Berkeley, 1963), and A. Fiske, *Friends and Friendship* in the *Monastic Tradition* (Cuernavaca, 1970). An anthropologist looks at friendship in D. Jacobson, *Itinerant Townsmen: Friendship and Social Order in Urban Uganda* (Menlo Park, 1973). Paul Tillich provides a philosophical critique of a simplified view of friendship in *Love, Power, and Justice* (New York, 1954).

gratification reflected a high view of each, has remained a rarity. To this day, purist essays on friendship deny the social nature of amicable bonds. Modern biological sociologists take the extreme opposite view, denying or ignoring sentiment or intent as essential aspects of the relationship and deriving friendship exclusively from an environment controlled by social and biological paradigms.[2]

What follows disputes the usefulness of such a dichotomy. My analysis of a particular friendship of the early Italian Renaissance will establish, it is true, the great importance of social ritual, of utility, and of coercion to any civic relationship. But rather than arguing that sentiment was a secondary element in defining this relationship, I will insist that sentiment and society, internality and externality, content and form were in a dialectical relationship to each other. There was no sincerity without form and no form without sincerity. They were two parts of a larger unity that I intend to elucidate further: the nature of amicable relations in a civic *res.*

What was the character of this relationship between the Florentine notary Lapo Mazzei and the merchant of Prato Francesco di Marco Datini, which, spanning two decades, has left as its monument more than four hundred of Lapo's letters? What light does that link throw upon the political world in which these men operated, the city–republic of Florence? What role did sentiment and intention, custom and rhetoric play in creating and preserving social bonds in Renaissance Florence?

True to the purist tradition of friendship, scholars examining the friendship of these two men have painted it in classic terms.[3] The pious Mazzei, we are told, despised friendship based on utility, insisted on his individualistic liberty and equality as a prerequisite for relations, and in fact achieved and maintained this relation to his friend the merchant. Datini, though cantankerous and often self-serving, could in this view be generous to a fault, and deeply valued Mazzei for nonutilitarian, idealistic reasons. One writer, Christian Bec, has astutely pointed to the heavy formalistic element in the Mazzei correspondence, yet he like his predecessors has taken both the notary and the merchant at face value, conceiving the relationship as essentially purified of or transcending rhetorical elements.[4] In general, writers have not seriously considered the force of these men's very different occupations

2. The extremes of such views are reflected in L. Tiger, *Men in Groups* (New York, 1969). Tiger's book does have the merit, however, of emphasizing the peculiarly *male* nature of the Western view of friendship. Eibl-Eibesfeldt, *Love and Hate,* presents a balanced ethological view of the phenomenon of feeling and sensitivity. The major attempt, however, to provide a scientific theory of the relationship of feeling to form is in S. Langer, *Mind,* 2 vols. to date (Baltimore, 1967, 1972).

3. The letters of Mazzei are "the rare image of a disinterested friendship"; I. Origo, *Il Mercante di Prato. Francesco di Marco Datini* (Milan, 1958), xx. See

also E. Bensa, *Francesco di Marco da Prato, Notizie e Documenti sulla Mercatura Italiana del secolo XIV* (Milan, 1928), and the characterizations in C. Bec, *Les Marchands Ecrivains. Affaires et Humanisme à Florence. 1375–1434* (Paris, 1967), 113–130. Also A. Sapori, "Economia e Morale alla fine del Trecento," in his *Studi di Storia Economica,* 3 vols. (Florence, 1955–1967), I, 155–179. Finally Guasti's characterization: "Un altro amore di ser Lapo Mazzei era la pura amicizia"; Mazzei, *Lettere,* I, proemio, especially lxxvii (references to these letters in this chapter are limited to volume and page number).

4. Bec, *Marchands,* 122ff.

and social standings upon the relationship. They have failed to perceive that the rhetorical element in the letters was an attempt to bridge these differences and thus an essential part of the relationship, and they have pigeonholed the two men in the ethereal world of purist friendship. Doubtless, both Mazzei and Datini, living together in their heavenly garden, are today gratified by the effect of their rhetoric upon historians, even if the evidence will not bear such an interpretation. Modern historians, no less human than the objects of their studies, have confused the ideal these men strove for with the actual dynamics of the relationship. But with their hands if not in their hearts, Mazzei and Datini built and maintained their friendship upon utility, social position, and rhetoric, as well as upon feeling. To understand both the operative and ideal sides of their bond requires a knowledge of their persons and of the services each provided for the other.

Although Francesco Datini seems to have had some passing contact with the young Mazzei, the lasting association between the two started in 1390 when, by contemporary standards, both were old men or *vecchi*.[5] Datini was about fifty-five years old and Mazzei was forty. The difference in age was one of the main reasons the latter always referred to the former as "father." The fact that both men were at an age when one prepared for and, like the then past-fifty Datini, thought mostly of death, helped to blend the fraternity of a common destiny with the natural hierarchy dictated by age differential.[6]

The wives of both men outlived them. Francesco and Margherita Datini had no progeny to whom to pass their enormous wealth; only the husband's illegitimate daughter Ginevra mellowed what intimate life the couple had. Mazzei the notary, on the other hand, had eight or more children by his wife Tessa, and a substantial part of his time was occupied with seeing to their futures. Presumably, Tessa spent all her time rearing them, for the couple had no servants, a far cry from the wealthy Datinis, whose *familia* included many house servants as well as the merchant–husband's business employees.[7]

The financial conditions of the two men were worlds apart. Francesco "the rich" as he was called by some, had assets of more than 40,000, and a net worth approaching 25,000, florins.[8] Mazzei, though by no means indigent, was a financial pygmy by comparison. But both were "honest." Both, that is, were relieved of worry about bread for their tables or shelter for their bodies. Both possessed country houses, Mazzei's a simple *orto*, Datini's a substantial holding. Disparate as the two men were in their wealth, and different as was the regularity of their sources of income—Mazzei's regular income from official and semiofficial positions, Datini's the riskier income of the market— both men were of sufficient state to maintain that their relationship was not one of necessary dependence. Both were "free."

The two men were very different in the extent of their public activity. Mazzei lived in Florence. For his livelihood, of course, the notary depended

5. I, 171, 226.

6. On thinking mostly of death: I, 39.

7. I, 206.

8. I, 36, 430, 438.

on being regularly utilized by contractors—preferably by powerful ones like Datini, Niccolò Da Uzzano, and Guido Del Palagio—for notarizations, legal advice, and testaments. But he also drew upon official position. Throughout the two decades of the friendship, Mazzei was notary to the great Florentine hospital of Santa Maria Nuova. Because this public hospital was the mandatory final substitute heir to all Florentine estates, Mazzei's position brought him into contact not only with hundreds of testators and executors, but also with that much broader group of men who desired to buy what had passed to the hospital through testamental substitution. His bureaucratic fingers being in touch with a never-ending stream of valuable properties, Mazzei was a good man to know, and to the government a key administrator. His faithfulness in that office was recognized. Besides serving the commune as ambassador, Mazzei became the notary of a series of important short-term governmental bodies.[9] He came to know not only where land was to be found at good prices, but the inner workings of the government itself, especially the current state of communal finances and plans for taxation.

Datini was completely different. Born like Mazzei in the nearby town of Prato, he never willingly held governmental offices either in Prato, where he lived from 1383 after making his fortune in Avignon, or in Florence.[10] The merchant fought every attempt to involve him in the Florentine governmental and fiscal web. He accepted Florentine citizenship with distaste; it allowed him temporary tax relief.[11] He delayed selecting a house in the city, probably to benefit from a twilight role as semicitizen, semiforeigner.[12] He assiduously avoided coming to the city to defend his interests even when advised he could avoid higher taxes in that way.[13] His dislike of governmental office doubtless flowed from a belief that collegial governance made more enemies than friends, and he was fully aware that officeholding was associated with a willingness to lend to the government. Datini almost succeeded in completely avoiding political involvement. He was a late, great example of that European phenomenon of the merchant more needed by the city than needing the city. In his later years, for example, he moved to Bologna and refused to return to Florence until he received promises that he would be treated fairly.[14] How different from poor Mazzei, dependent on the city and its offices. It comes as no surprise to find that the notary was persistently patriotic, the merchant indifferent to that siren call.[15]

A friendship that lasted a score of years obviously rested upon respect and loyalty. But it is clear from the men's different conditions that utility played its role at inception. Mazzei would be the politically shy merchant's bridge to Florentine officialdom, furnishing advice and influence. The notary was to be Datini's "star who guides in [the commune's] unquiet sea."[16] Lapo probably first looked upon Datini as another rich Florentine whom he would advise and whose testament he would compose. From such relationships

9. I, lxix, 225, 318.

10. Origo, *Mercante*, 17, 36f.

11. I, 9, 35f, 48f, 56, 59, 61, 66.

12. I, 59, 66, 71f, 74.

13. I, 66f.

14. I, 384, 389.

15. I, 36, 176.

16. This is Guasti's characterization: I, xci.

sprang the security that Mazzei needed for himself and for his children when he died.[17] Datini, Del Palagio, Da Uzzano and others were expected to step in during any crisis and preserve the financial honor of their friend.[18] Private utility was the core of Datini's contribution, public usefulness that of Mazzei. In the short run Datini needed the notary more than the notary needed the merchant. In the long run the reverse was the case.

When in 1390 the two *vecchi* entered into close contact with each other, such practical considerations informed not only their actions, but their attitude toward and approach to the relationship. Perhaps they had been in continuous contact since 1387, but in September of 1390 a decisive step was taken with a formal proffering of friendship by the rich man to the honest scribbler.[19] The relationship did not grow slowly from acquaintance to friendship; acquaintance was transformed at this point by a quasi-formal contract into a qualitatively different bond, that of friendship. Establishing friendship by such formal instruments was a regular practice, encompassing obligations and understandings meant to be binding in part through being made public. Friendship was a social fact. In keeping with this fact, Datini's collection of Mazzei's letters starts with the establishment of the formal bond.

Francesco wrote to Mazzei in Florence at this time, "donating" his friendship and asking the notary to take the merchant for his friend. Lapo responded, "With all affection and love I accept being your younger brother and friend in every thing. And in me, such as I am, take that heartfelt liberty that you would take with yourself."[20]

The conditions Mazzei attached to the friendship were formally entered in these first letters. Though no change in the form of address was contemplated—each continued to address the other in the formal *voi*, even after Francesco became godfather to Lapo's child—Mazzei here for the first of many times insisted that his new friend eliminate from his letters all the rhetoric of *cortesia*, even if it proceeded from love: "I pray you from now on to treat me as suits a friend both in writing and face to face. And leave off those honors and praises I in no way merit."[21]

Furthermore, Mazzei promised to use Datini's possessions as if they were his own, a reciprocal rhetorical understanding.[22] Sealing the contract, the new friend immediately actuated the relationship by asking for something from Datini:

> Now that I've said what I have to say . . . I will begin to use [our] friendship. I enjoy solid simple foods, those which strengthen me for the tasks which I bear in rearing my family. If any salted anchovies come to Pisa this year, I would enjoy having a small barrel.[23]

17. I, 172f, also 325.

18. I, 35, 172f, 337. II, 240f. Mazzei once addressed Datini as *padre e rifugio mio*; II, 92.

19. Origo believes they had been close since about 1386–1387; *Mercante*, 36, 49, 171, but also Guasti in I, xli.

20. I, 6. A similar form is in a letter of the young doctor Sassoli to Datini, II, 363. Cf. also the proffer of friendship by Bartolo Pucci, II, 56f.

21. I, 5. See the similar statement to Datini's wife, II, 178.

22. I, 7. The further promise to have no secrets is at I, 5.

23. I, 7.

Mazzei also stood ready to obey Datini's every desire: "Your request I consider an order."[24] He was unworthy of Datini's friendship, and of no use to the merchant, he said. Thus he would obey the merchant if only to repay this undeserved trust.[25]

We may assume that Datini's letter proffering friendship was in the same vein. Discourse without flattery and an active, "used" friendship were to be the chief operating elements of these new ties. Not that feeling was secondary; in Mazzei's mind it was the key that opened the door to the change. From the beginning Datini wrote Mazzei how dearly he loved the notary, and Mazzei responded in kind, telling his powerful friend how his letters moved him to tèars, how often they stunned him into reflection. At night in fact Lapo placed Datini's letters, repeatedly read, on his nightstand among his "dear things."[26]

These were conventions dictated by the contract rather than, as the correspondents would have it, feelings making the contract necessary. Christian Bec in his examination of the rhetorical content of Mazzei's letters has hinted at the role convention played in generating emotions.[27] The ritualized emotions that, *from the beginning and without noticeable development*, flowed from these letters were intended to imprint the formal contract in the heart. Lapo did not read the letters of Jerome and Cicero for nothing. He knew, without of course saying so, that protestations against flattery were themselves flatteries—did he not say Datini's flatteries were undeserved? Like ritualized emotions, they were the building blocks of enduring bonds.

The active nature of Francesco's and Lapo's friendship is best examined in the services they provided each other. Those of the merchant for the notary were private or familial on the one side, social on the other. In the private sphere Datini provided Lapo with a series of alimentary services, often at the request of the latter but just as often spontaneously. If the notary's tooth craved anchovies, the merchant procured them for him.[28] He sent meat to Lapo's wife Tessa, grain to his mother.[29] Responding to Mazzei's request, Datini sent a mass of firewood to the family.[30] The letters are liberally sprinkled with information on such requests and gifts. Most common of all such *omaggi*, of course, were gifts of wine.[31] Lapo advised his friend on his preference, and Datini seems always to have met his friend's wishes. Although it is impossible in the present state of documentation to be sure, it seems that in the majority of cases Datini bequeathed these often substantial alimentations without cost to his friend: "If I were to count all the recompense I've had from you, at every step I've been doubly rewarded."[32]

A second area of private services encompasses aid in investments and loans. In one case Mazzei asked the influential Datini to procure him a loan of

24. I, 3, 15.
25. I, 4.
26. I, 4. Also I, 3, 11, 17, 116, 159, 242, 252.
27. Bec, *Marchands*, 120–126.
28. I, 7.
29. II, 87; I, 190.
30. I, 129.
31. I, 8, 148, 184, and *passim*.
32. I, 302. Datini refuses recompense: I, 184. On Mazzei's account entries in Datini's registers, I, 199.

100 florins by withdrawing the money from deposit in the wool gild, where it could be had at 8 to 10 percent. In this way he could avoid personally purchasing the loan on the open market, where interest was high and the transaction was taxed.[33] In another case he advised Datini of an investment possibility where grain could be bought low and later sold high. Fearful of the usurious nature of such activity, he urged Datini to buy some for him as well if the merchant decided to purchase.[34] Curiously, the letters contain no evidence that Mazzei invested in Datini's commercial enterprises, as did the doctor Lorenzo Sassoli, another of the merchant's favorites. This man gave Datini discretion over a sum of money, sure that his patron would bring about its fructification.[35]

Perhaps the most important of Datini's private services were his efforts in fostering three of Mazzei's children. By agreeing to be godfather to one, he ensured the child's protection and special attention when he came of age.[36] When it came time to marry a daughter, the notary turned naturally to his powerful friend. "I always thought that to marry [my daughter] I would sell my goods, or ask for help from two or three friends, and you first."[37] In the best style of the loyal friend with no secrets, Mazzei told Francesco that he had refused to complete the pact with the suitor until he had consulted with his "father" Datini, without whose advice he would have felt ill at ease.[38] In fact, however, Lapo went further, successfully using Datini's power and influence to move the young man to marry the girl at a lower dowry than desired. He would *not* meet the suitor's demands, he wrote Datini. Instead, the girl could wait two years and then lie about her age if necessary. If she became pregnant in the meantime, one of the suitor's relatives would intimidate him into marriage—at Mazzei's price.[39]

Could Datini be of use, his friend asked? Perhaps if the merchant wrote Meo the suitor a persuasive rather than threatening letter, the boy would be moved to marry for less. Insisting that Datini should not write if he did not want to, Mazzei nevertheless made it clear that such help was his due for all the aid he had freely rendered the other.[40] To minimize the effort Francesco had to expend on this business, the prospective father of the bride forwarded the merchant a draft of the letter that could be sent to the suitor under Francesco's signature.

This letter was sent to the suitor, and had the desired effect. Its threatening but persuasive conclusion: "You could not be his relative without being mine," as well as the promise that Datini's home would be the suitor's home, brought Meo to agree to marriage at the lower dowry.[41] The father-in-law was effusive in praising his friend the merchant: "You have given me a relative and son after my heart."[42] The formal involvement of Datini in the business ended in the convention that the friend was the source of the new tie.

33. I, 29.

34. I, 168.

35. II, 362.

36. I, 151.

37. I, 337.

38. I, 332.

39. I, 340.

40. I, 339.

41. I, 342, 354.

42. I, 365.

Datini's employment of Lapo's son Piero was quite as important to the notary. At the age of seven the boy went to live in Prato at the Datini *fondaco*, and his father was overjoyed that little Piero had another father. On Datini's advice Piero soon returned to school, and until 1403 he worked and attended school at the same time. In 1403 we find the eleven-year-old in the steady employ of Francesco at Valencia and Barcelona. Datini was in every sense an ideal patron to Piero. He read countless letters from the father urging him to take a special interest, and in fact seems to have done so, writing often to the boy in his capacity as substitute father. Datini took his duties as a foster parent seriously. Piero, like his sister Antonia and the infant godchild Francesco, named after the merchant, all served as instruments binding the two men together.[43]

A fourth and final area where Datini serviced the notary included those social actions that permitted Mazzei to play the patron himself. Mazzei was often approached by the poor: by a destitute woman who needed a loan, orphans, and the like.[44] Mazzei's relatives sometimes used his connection with Datini to supplement a simple existence: a "powerless friend and relative," the sons of a dead friend who had left his progeny in Lapo's trust—these and other types came to Lapo seeking alms.[45] Datini, who considered it his friend's duty and expertise to recommend "good alms" to him, regularly responded to Mazzei's passing-on of such requests.[46] Again, Mazzei forwarded to Datini a request from a gildsman to be excused from a nonattendance fine, for he had been sick at the time.[47] Mazzei's intercession also procured Datini's favorable treatment of supplicants' debts to him. Nofri d'Andrea Del Palagio expressed to his notary friend his eternal gratitude to Datini for the prorogation of a debt: "You could not believe without seeing," Lapo wrote the merchant, "the warm affection which Nofri has for you."[48]

It goes without saying that Nofri and all the others who benefited from the notary's tie to Datini were obligated to Mazzei as much as they were to Datini. After Mazzei shared a barrel of Datini's fine wine with the Florentine chancellor–humanist Salutati and the highly respected Guido Del Palagio, he wrote Francesco how much he had been honored by their enjoyment, implying that Datini was the source of Mazzei's status.[49] Francesco and Lapo both realized that social relationships required that the intermediary be constituted as a patron with the influence to oblige. This was after all the way divine aid was achieved. Lapo at one point had indicated that his old friend Guido Del Palagio had provided such status to him, had "given me my being."[50] Datini successfully competed with Guido in creating Lapo's patronal status, so that the notary could write him: "I am of you and Guido as much as I am . . . ."[51] The practice of creating value in the intermediary rather than

43. I, 215ff. On his age, I, 233; II, 16. More on the boy   47. II, 18f.
II, 243f, 262.   48. II, 34.

44. I, 42,45.   49. I, 8.

45. I, 9ff, 41f.   50. I, 12.

46. Read Mazzei's self-conception at I, 243.   51. I, 40.

dealing directly with clientage was, in fact, institutionalized, for in one case Datini's account books show that two barrels of wine intended as gifts for third parties were first given to Mazzei, to be distributed by him in Datini's name to the recipients.[52] As certainly as the secondary nature of the moon's light does not diminish its symbolic worth, so the notary's mediation brought him gifts of gratitude.[53]

We have imperceptibly entered the realm of Mazzei's services to Datini. Mazzei repeatedly intimated to his friend that services he received from Datini raised his own status. This status, in turn, enabled him to perform more effectively the tasks that his friend assigned to him. When Mazzei wrote, "You have honored me," to Datini, he meant, "I have increased your honor and influence."

The services that ser Lapo Mazzei performed for his rich outsider friend were overwhelmingly public or semipublic in nature. It is true that Mazzei sought to smooth relations between Datini and his wife Margherita, true that he took some slight interest in Francesco's illegitimate daughter Ginevra, true too that he encouraged Datini's employees to be loyal to their master, and played some role in looking after the financial and personal interests of these employees while they were on stints abroad.[54] Certainly Mazzei constantly urged Datini to write a testament that would make the best use of his wealth.[55] All these interpersonal involvements and their sincere motivations cannot be disputed. Yet even in seemingly domestic affairs such as these, the public well-being of his friend remained a central consideration.

Mazzei's profession was far more honorable than that of a merchant. (One potential client wrote Datini: "You certainly know that no gentleman who wants honor ought to be advanced by a merchant.") This was the key to his services, and to the friendship. Mazzei was a house intellectual, one whose dreary moralisms were tolerated by the merchant because they were part of the scribbler–client's role. This assessment will be substantiated in what follows. For now, it provides a justification to pass immediately to those services that dominated the correspondence: Lapo's efforts to widen Datini's circle of political allies, his constant advice to Francesco on which public stance to assume, and that most important service that was the impetus for the first two, Lapo's unceasing activity in attaining favorable tax and debt treatment for his friend. In comparison to the amount of space these tasks took up in the correspondence, the notary's purely private services, yes even his endless moral exhortations, pale almost to insignificance.

Networks of friendships were the building blocks of social discourse and of politics, and the notary approached his task of widening Datini's circle of allies with three guiding principles: First, independent of any immediate stimuli, Francesco should cultivate certain men of status; not only would they be politically valuable when need arose, but such associations would raise

52. I, 281.
53. I, 278.
54. Successively I, lxxxviii; II, 192, 217, 222.

55. For example, I, 210. See also Sapori, "Economia e Morale," 176–179.

Datini's stature. Second, when danger threatened Datini, he should cultivate and then retain new friends in a position to help him. Finally, Francesco should be alert to unsolicited help from powerful men and should seize the chance to obligate them to him. Like all his contemporaries, Mazzei believed that gifts and favors were the central means of gaining and maintaining these friendships.

Their formal relationship was still young when Mazzei advised Datini to seize the opportunity to befriend Guido Del Palagio, a highly respected Florentine who was close to Mazzei. In Lapo's characteristic words, Guido was a "good fish" to net. Datini followed the advice—perhaps he had be-friended Lapo in order to reach Del Palagio—and was soon making use of Guido's influence.[56] In subsequent years, Lapo divided his time between reminding his friend how fortunate he was that God had given him Guido as a friend and counselor and how much the merchant's status had risen through his friendship with Del Palagio, and regularly urging Datini to do what was necessary to maintain the friendship. The notary pushed Francesco to visit Guido, to write him, to "love and retain him."[57] He was often met with a selfish, often indifferent response, for the merchant, it seems, was more willing to take than to give. Datini was jealous of Mazzei's closeness to Del Palagio, and was not above accusing Mazzei of joining forces with Del Palagio to crosscut Datini's wishes. For Datini, Del Palagio was one of those who promised a lot but delivered little.[58]

When Guido died in 1399, Lapo advised Datini to continue his ties with the family, "for by serving it you have acquired it."[59] Recommending that he accede to a loan Nofri Del Palagio had requested, Mazzei told his friend: "One cannot predict the circumstances and needs which are bound to arise." It would be a shame to lose the friendship through neglect.[60] At that very moment, Lapo added, Nofri's nephew was a high government official. By lending to him, "it will appear [the family members] are obligated to you."[61]

But even while he encouraged continued ties to this esteemed family, Lapo urged Francesco to replace Guido with another high-standing Florentine, Niccolò Da Uzzano. Niccolò "is a man of energy and counsel, and is [a] good [man] and is powerful and loved. And I have always believed he fears God, and I have satisfied myself of this in the most secret things."[62] The notary had not composed Da Uzzano's testament for nothing.

Such friends were long term, chosen for their moral as well as political stature, and were consequently intended to bolster Datini's status through reputation as well as through power. Their type was found in every genera-tion of Florentine history, the purest examples of the honorific resources so crucial to society because so rare. Men like Del Palagio and Da Uzzano were

56. I, 26, 32f.

57. Successively I, 77, 118, 125, 66f, 79, 198, 136.

58. I, 23, 145, 217.

59. II, 48.

60. *Ibid.*

61. *Ibid.*

62. I, 257.

always pictured as above the storm: powerful but incorruptible, friends yet separate from the world of reciprocity. Vespasiano, in characterizing Lorenzo Ridolfi, incisively stated the ideal:

> He knew so well how to use his authority and position that he became everybody's friend. His authority was so great that no one could even venture to ask him to put his hand to any deed which was not just and honest.[63]

Another group of friends, however, was recruited in the midst of need and retained almost exclusively because of their political influence and office. Such a man was Francesco Federighi, whom Mazzei often recommended because of his proven political clout. Federighi was "no puny bird," Lapo assured his friend.[64] The relationship between Datini and Federighi started when the latter spoke out for the merchant to a tax commission after receiving a letter from Datini.[65] Thereafter the two remained eminently useful to each other. Federighi might be a rough-and-ready type and annoy many people, said Mazzei, but "any day it might happen that we have need of him."[66] "Believe me," repeated Mazzei, "one would like to have some friend in every post, and one time [helped] restores everything [given]."[67] Federighi was in fact so devoted to Datini that when he took over the office of bursar of the communal treasury, he wrote Datini asking if there was any way he could be of use.[68] Such a *padrone*, Lapo insisted, "will pull you away from many snares. And you see how many of these there are here. There are more snares than birds."[69]

Domenico Giugni was another friend of the political type, one who seems to have come to Francesco's aid spontaneously, without being asked, sure that Datini was worth his time. Richly rewarded, Giugni remained a powerful asset repeatedly flattered by the merchant and Mazzei. He became, in fact, "a new Guido" for Datini upon Del Palagio's death.[70] The list of such friends seems endless. The Torelli brothers, both jurists, entered Datini's web of clients by taking out a loan from him. By Francesco's positive decision in this matter, said Mazzei, he had "bound [the one brother] and obligated [the other]."[71]

When crisis or need arose, these friends were called upon to see Datini through, and it was usually Mazzei who directed the campaign that ensued. Datini often gave the word: Mazzei was to "use every friend" to protect his interests. Having prepared a plan of attack, the notary would then inform his friend Datini: "When it is time to deal with the tax, you will do what I say."[72]

63. Vespasiano, *Vite,* 405.

64. I, 278, further 45ff, 138.

65. I, 45–48.

66. I, 278, 314.

67. I, 316.

68. I, 281.

69. I, 173. Mazzei also called Domenico Giugni Datini's *padrone;* I, 347. These are the only cases where

Mazzei used the word *padrone,* and he never used the word *client.*

70. I, 335f, also 347.

71. I, 370. On Mazzei's encouragement to Datini to give gifts to the famous lawyer Antonio di Butrio, see I, 349, 358, 360.

72. I, 362, 380. Mazzei believed in preparing rather than waiting for the future; I, 67.

Mazzei prepared the onslaught by providing his friend with lists and assessments of those in office, his or Datini's ability to rely upon each, and in addition, lists of friends not in office who were close to the officials.[73] Thus in Datini's dispute with a painter, Mazzei was delighted that the impartial arbiter chosen to settle the dispute was at the same time a party to another dispute of which Mazzei was arbiter.[74] This Ambruogio could be "counted on as a friend," one who would even kill himself if Lapo asked him to.[75] In a tax threat of 1397 Lapo advised Francesco to approach Tommaso Rucellai because the latter's brother Francesco was in the tax diminution office. The two other officials in this office were, he added, not "out of your reach," for one was a friend of Guido Del Palagio; the other, a brother of a close associate of Mazzei.[76] Again, in 1399, Mazzei described five officials: one was his own "great friend," a few others were close to Francesco Federighi.[77] In 1401 he advised that Giugni was one of the Ventina tax commission, and described the others to Datini.[78] In the same year Mazzei had "friends among the new Signori, if necessary, and good ones. *Deo grazias.*"[79] So it went. One letter to Datini's office manager in Florence consisted only of such assessments: One Cristofano was deeply in debt, another was a relative, a third was a *pratico uomo*. Another was a high government official at Colle, but weak and obligated to others.[80]

Lapo did not advise Datini to seek out enemies directly and try to win them over; not being in the inner circle of citizens, Francesco did such things at his peril. An insider could take the direct approach. Thus the cardinal Cossa told Buonaccorso Pitti that he could not help Pitti as long as "a certain citizen" was against him, and advised him to approach this citizen indirectly: "Get someone to intercede for you, and you will surely be successful." But Pitti was enough of a patrician to go directly to the citizen:

> Then [Cossa] confided to me, under the seal of secrecy, that Niccolò da Uzzano was against me and that I should try and win him over. I spoke to Niccolò in messer Bartolomeo Popoleschi's presence, telling him what I heard. He replied that, being deeply obligated to messer Mariano, he had not refused to speak on his behalf. Moreover, he had been unaware of my interest in the matter, but now that he knew of it he would refrain from speaking for either party. He gave me his word to this effect in the presence of messer Bartolomeo.[81]

Unlike Pitti, Datini would have to work through intermediaries, and he could use this network of relations only if he knew what he was doing—how to handle these contacts, what posture to assume with each individual in any given situation, what he should not do and what he could not effect. In this Lapo was his sure guide. He attempted first to provide Francesco with a long-range positive image by having him do those things suited to his estate and age.[82] In 1409 he described the benefits to be gained by Datini's com-

73. I, 9ff, 35, 45–48, 66, 160, 179, 220, 386f, 389.

74. I, 15f.

75. I, 18f.

76. I, 172.

77. I, 220.

78. I, 349.

79. I, 360f.

80. II, 209f.

81. Niccolò then betrayed him; Pitti, *Memoir*, 85.

82. I, 286, 294, 321.

mending "to the Signoria or to someone who has a prior as a friend" a new government charitable initiative and by himself contributing 100 florins in alms. It would be particularly effective because Francesco had just been subject to a heavy tax. This would please his friends and shame his enemies. It would encourage other rich men to experiment with the virtue of piety. Datini's status in Florence would rise if he could develop a charitable image: "I mean that you would never again be manhandled [in taxes]."[83]

In the midst of crisis, Lapo had a particular set of guidelines. For example, he often urged Francesco to consult with his friends in and out of office on just what approach to take—as Mazzei had consulted Datini before settling on his daughter's marriage.[84] He recommended to Francesco that he not be at home when tax assessors visited his residence.[85] Yet he favored Datini's personal appearance before tax officials in Florence to appeal his case, though he was seldom successful in this admonition.[86] He advised Francesco at one point to picture himself as a Florentine citizen, yes, but one innocent of information and interest.[87] On another occasion he urged him to plead ignorance as to the value of his assets, though he realized that on all but the most technical plane Datini was well aware of his worth.[88] He often pushed Francesco to make much of the fact that he played host to all Florentines of any rank in his Prato palace.[89] Lapo insisted that Datini never be overbearing during crisis. In the midst of the 1400 plague he warned his friend not to press distracted Florentines to pay their debts.[90] In disputes over Datini's taxes, he urged, it was better for Datini to win a case in part and keep his influential friends, than to win everything in court and lose them, for both his age and estate required such mansuetude.[91]

Besides furnishing his friend with his own personal contacts, besides appearing in court as a proctor for Datini and advising Datini's other proctors or agents exactly how to behave there, the notary performed another service of inestimable value. He wrote Datini's letters addressed to governmental officials and other persons of note. Mazzei then submitted them to Datini, who seems normally to have sent them on without change. This practice is of great importance in understanding and evaluating the relationship of the two men, since it shows the notary at work assessing and evaluating, imputing to the friend, the friend's emotions. In these few pages I can only describe the highlights of this service.

In the classical tradition of house intellectuals writing other people's correspondence, Mazzei in Datini's letters to varied persons of weight had to integrate verisimilar emotions of the signatory into the broader framework of what emotions the circumstances and recipients called for. Not only did Mazzei provide the correct salutations and titles, differentiating between

83. II, 213. The same theme of charity and image is at I, 243.

84. I, 163, 169, 393.

85. I, 62.

86. I, 67.

87. I, 155, 293.

88. I, 411.

89. I, 288.

90. I, 248.

91. I, 320, also I, 294.

modalities of sentiment in the process, but in the body of the letter the apparently forthright emotions were those that Mazzei deemed right, or at best what he thought the recipient could accept as Datini's own.[92] The most striking evidence for this view is contained in the letter Datini sent to Mazzei's prospective son-in-law.[93] The draft of the letter sent to Datini—and sent on unchanged—included outrageous praise of Mazzei, the scribe thus imputing to the signatory the latter's own appreciation of him. The suitor read that Datini had more trust in Lapo than in most others, that he considered Mazzei's desires his own, that Lapo was not like most greedy notaries, and that the suitor could not be Mazzei's son without being Francesco's. All these words were Mazzei's. The notary urged his friend not to be bothered by the self-praise, "for this time I don't do it out of vanity." In other words, Mazzei took this incredible liberty because the circumstances and the recipient demanded this content.

In the drafts Lapo prepared of letters to tax officials and their friends, the notary put as much stress on the personal relations of Datini with the recipient as he did on tax problems at hand.[94] A central theme of many letters was Datini's desire to serve the recipient, in other words an offer to reward any service. Just as common was the humble statement that any help he received was most welcome, since Datini was useless to the official. Another usual sentence was to the effect that Datini was a simple man not to be compared to the recipient.[95] Expressions of love for the influential recipient were far from rare. To one Andrea di Ugo, Mazzei wrote for Datini that Datini's affection for Andrea was so great he could not express it.[96] To Niccolò Da Uzzano, Mazzei's words for Datini were, "According to what has been written me, you are among the masters of the tax. I remind you that I love you and bear you reverence."[97]

The seeming insincerity of such calculated expressions of love disturbed Mazzei and Datini as it does us. "Francesco, it is very dishonorable that a notary writes a letter in his own hand to someone, and signs the name of the sender without the sender saying one word."[98] Two elements of his duties could be troublesome, composing letters and actually writing them. For letters of lesser importance, Mazzei did not mind doing both. But when the recipients were politically important, Mazzei might recommend that the letter be in Datini's own hand, if not composed by him. Thus in a multiaddressed letter with personal variants, Mazzei furnished the letter full of insights into the tax matter in question and the personalities of the assessors, but urged Datini to write out each: "It honors you to write [yourself] and it makes it seem you are from Florence, and understand." To drive the point home to the

92. For extensive examples of the science of formal salutations, see I, 297, 372, 387, 389.

93. I, 341f.

94. For example, I, 48.

95. I, 48f, 98f. More on Datini's rhetoric 48ff, 75, 98f, 288, 386f, 393.

96. I, 75, also I, 387.

97. *Ibid.*

98. I, 91.

recipients, Mazzei had the letters end: "Niccolò [etc.], this [letter] is in my own hand."[99]

There were other reasons to have Mazzei's letters penned by someone else. Obviously the missive that Lapo composed for Datini to send to the notary's future son-in-law should not have been in Lapo's hand. Just as certainly, Lapo did not want actually to write the letter he had composed from Datini to Guido Del Palagio, since the latter was close to Lapo and would recognize the hand, then the style, and then the emotions.[100] Yet the practice was evidently so widespread that it could be the subject of mutual amusement. In one case when Mazzei conferred with Tommaso Soderini on how Datini could best approach the tax commission of which Soderini was a member, Soderini advised that Datini write to each member. Doubtless looking straight at Mazzei with a wry smile, he added, "I would do well to dictate them to him, and then he send them on." Lapo, who had already composed the letters, had to smile faintly at this jab.[101]

We have already seen that Mazzei was prepared to praise Datini's skills at correspondence lavishly, but in only one case did he actually insist that the merchant not only write but compose his own letter. Guido Del Palagio had, after all, made Datini his executor, and if Datini wanted to retain the family, the least he could do, thought Mazzei, was to write Nofri himself. It would be honorable, the friend insisted, for Datini to write "a few lines which appear to come from you."[102] But such advice was definitely not the rule. When Datini once furnished his friend with the draft of a letter he had composed for Rinaldo Gianfigliazzi, Mazzei praised it to the skies: "It is pure, and won't seem furnished word for word, and I treasure it for the honor it does you."[103] Having said this, he proceeded to rewrite the letter almost completely and return it to Datini.

What are we to make of these staged emotions composed by a man who professed to detest them and accepted by a merchant who treasured his friend's "true heart"? It could be argued that Mazzei and Datini felt that insincerity was necessary in the jungle of politics, but inappropriate for their own friendship.[104] Unfortunately the correspondence cannot bear this out, for although Mazzei did indeed have a dismal view of the outside world, he repeatedly vaunted the genuine feelings that Datini's friends had for the merchant, feelings that followed in the wake of just such letters and gifts. Furthermore, Mazzei's own protestations against Datini's flattery of him were ambiguous, being efficaciously ritualistic in their own right.

A better explanation has already been suggested: The formal proffer and acceptance of friendship dictated the expression of feelings and, to an extent greater than we would admit to today, the actual feelings themselves. Thus

99. I, 386f, also I, 352ff, 393.

100. Mazzei's reasons were so obvious that they did not need to be mentioned; I, 98f.

101. I, 393.

102. I, 364, also 360.

103. II, 35f, and see note.

104. On the world as a dark wood, and so on, see I, 30, 39.

Mazzei wrote Datini once that a dispute the merchant had with a painter could be settled if the painter would go to Datini and receive him as a father.[105] In another case, the notary urged Datini to beg his Pratese country-man Piero Rinaldeschi to accept Datini as a friend; this meant no more than that Datini wanted to associate himself to a representation that a Pratese citizen group headed by Rinaldeschi was making before the Florentine government.[106] In both cases, the creation of friendship went hand in hand with the settlement of disputes; the formal act preceded and caused the inner feelings.

But the clearest example of the practical simultaneity of communications and love is seen in a stupendous scene before the altar of the church of Santa Maria Nuova, where one Bartolo Pucci accepted Mazzei—representing Datini—as a friend after opposing him for months in court. Mazzei's report of the incident to Datini is worth repeating in full, because it shows so brilliantly how ritual activity between recent enemies was accompanied by warm expressions of undying love:

Francesco *mio.* In my view the meeting between Bartolo and me, sitting today in Santa Maria Nuova, that is in the closed church, was truly a gift of God. There I first of all asked as a favor that I speak for a half hour without Bartolo ever interjecting a word, [and] then I would be ready to listen to him till nightfall. I said to Bartolo: "Imagine that you were to go to the Six as a syndic or otherwise; the response which Francesco or I or Luca would make to you would be this. . . ." What I said to him came out so flowingly that it seemed God helped me to converse. I read him [our] whole pronouncement word for word. Then I told him how he disturbed you every day, for he was ruining your [contributions] to your charitable institution with this constant bickering involving thousands of florins, and further [how] Bartolo disturbed [Francesco] more with one request than Francesco's friends caused in a month. And in sum, [that] I had decided to ask a singular favor of him in this church, which was this: that is, that he dispose himself to *want me for his friend every day of his life starting today.* Then I spelled out to him the damages he would receive from bad debts, more than he thought, when we get a final response from Avignon, and how his hope in the Pisan profits was in vain, and how crazy it was to look into things long finished, or [into] the old account books of Boninsegna's bankruptcy which were in his creditor's hands, who had been dead for twenty years. And I can't describe to you the grace and force God gave me in person and tongue; as a villainous ingrate, I will never [truly] live up to it. And [I told him] that if he wanted me for a friend, he would be prepared to believe I had his honor at heart. And if the path of litigation pleased him more, he should not be deceived: I was of a mind that Luca and I would pursue him, facts at hand, every day of our lives at every court he would go to, [this] only in the defense of Francesco.

Having become red as fire, Bartolo responded to nothing if not to the [solicitations of] friendship: He had never done anything which would delight him more. *And he took my right hand, and spoke to me words so excessive and flattering I can't write them, all to establish this friendship, thanking me so much I can't describe it. Tears almost came to his eyes as he praised you with words; I was astounded. Then almost speechless, he stood up and drew me to the altar. And not seeing a missal, to my dismay he took a book from the lectern and swore before the majesty of God, making the sign of the cross on the book,* that neither he nor his brother *nor his relatives or friends* would ever offend Francesco or Luca or their possessions, nor ever prosecute them in or outside of court. *And he wanted not only my friendship but yours and Luca's, and [asked] that I take care of it.* He wants to cancel notarially the account of Pisa and Lucca since *as his friend—he called me such*—I had asked that he so cancel. Only in reference to the cloth of Avignon did he ask that he be harmed as little as possible if you win anything [at court], and in this I gave him that hope which seemed good to me before I had ended my talk. But he however had by then said: "I will never speak of it more than my friend wants" (that is, I, ser Lapo). And he said [he] was ready to submit his solemn oath at any time one wants to compromise [your differences] in me [as arbiter], if you want to commit yourself.

Well! Return to your peace, for God doesn't do these things if not for our good, even though he has no need of us. The weight is fallen to the ground, thanks be to God. Show this to Luca and not to others, if it pleases you. I got home at eight o'clock. [signed] Your ser Lapo. 16 December.[107]

It is neither surprising nor disappointing that ritual expressions of love came from formal circumstances, as they so impressively did in this case. The insincerity that the modern finds so objectionable is—to the extent it is any different from his own behavior—obnoxious because the traditional mode flowed from a different, more positive concept of the function of form. Form, the medieval man recognized, was creative. Ritual was a means of internalizing. Modern Western man is more liable to dispute the creativity of form while continuing to base his actions on its creativity.

Naive as Mazzei's combination of expressed disdain for ritual and assiduous use of its virtues may appear, we must somehow reckon with him as one man and not two. Consider for a moment his attitude toward gifts—not those to him, which we shall examine later, but those of Datini to either potential or proven friends. On the one hand Lapo seemed the perfect manager devoid of any true reticence about buying favors, much like the less pretentious Buonaccorso Pitti, who told how he "had tried . . . to enlist this cardinal as our patron and had presented him with a goblet of gilded silver which had cost me thirty-two florins."[108] Datini would soon see, Lapo wrote, whether his gift to an official had paid dividends.[109] Again, the notary assumed without question that a tax official had backed Datini in a commission meeting, for Datini after all had sent him wine.[110] In a letter Mazzei wrote for Datini to Federighi, Datini thought only God would repay Federighi for the aid he had furnished Datini, but he then turned around and sent him gifts, intimating that with more help more gifts would be forthcoming. It was simply part of Mazzei's duty to recommend gifts whenever a service was available or performed.[111]

Yet even in the area of gifts to others Mazzei was aware of the need for tact. Just as he sometimes warned his friend not to write directly to unfriendly

107. II, 56ff. (Emphasis added.)

108. Pitti, *Memoir,* 91.

109. I, 349f.

110. I, 27.

111. For example, I, 320. The letter to Federighi is at I, 281. Gifts for such purposes could even be de-

fended biblically. A mid-fourteenth-century merchant wrote, "Keep in mind that your generosity . . ., rather than justice or reason, will dispose him favorably toward you. Remember that authority which says: 'Gifts blind the eye of the wise, and alter the words of the just'"; G. Corti, "Consiglio sulla Mercatura di un Anonimo Fiorentino," *ASI,* CX (1952), 119. The biblical spot is Deut. 16:19.

officials, so he advised him not to send gifts directly. Suggesting to Datini that Federighi's services deserved a gift worth about two florins—perhaps some delicacy unavailable in Florence—he urged Datini to offer it so that it appeared to be not a payment for Federighi's tax help but rather a gift given "as a sign of love."[112] Datini should not send wine directly to members of another tax commission, Mazzei thought, but "as more appropriate," to someone with friends on the commission.[113] Personalistic as this system was, the posture had to be maintained that all gifts flowed from love, not contract, because otherwise the moral authority of the recipient would be compromised. Datini's friendship with Guido Del Palagio was still young when their mutual friend Mazzei warned Datini against sending Guido gifts for favors done. It was all right to present Guido with a mule, though he had plenty of them. But the merchant had to treasure Guido "with love and nothing else," for otherwise the upright man would never be his friend or be benevolent again.[114] Such remarks show that Mazzei was not just insisting on choosing the right time and place for presenting gifts. He recognized, I think, that a citizen network without gifts was impossible, and that achieving friendship within these networks, achieving love, would always require what the theologians called external works.

Having reviewed Mazzei's public services for his friend, and having seen the notary to be a shrewd professional consultant rather than the simple, piously sanctimonious true friend portrayed in earlier literature, I turn to an examination of the two men's conceptions of themselves, and especially Mazzei's view of his relation to Datini. Who was this broker between the world of power and the world of wealth, and how did he assess his relation to Datini? Only by confronting the world of action, just reviewed, with the world of sentiment and self-reflection about those actions, which we now enter, can we properly conclude anything about the nature of friendship in Renaissance Florence.

A persistent sentiment in Lapo's correspondence concerns the friends' common relation to God. In Mazzei's view, this was more significant than that of either man to his wife or anyone else, if not as important as the relations of the one friend to the other. They were pilgrims together, the notary wrote Francesco, two friends before God enlightened by him so that together they would be among the elect.[115] They would love each other till death, "in such a way that you comforting me and I you, we will go together to heaven and to the *patria* from whence we came. And up there in those eternal tabernacles will be our repose."[116]

Like a true friend, Lapo could not be in a holy place without thinking of Francesco. When he visited La Verna, he wrote Francesco that "I am often with you," and that "You have been in my mind many times, especially at that holy site."[117] When he was moved by a sermon, he wrote Datini, "I don't

112. I, 316, also 200.

113. I, 405.

114. I, 30, 45–48.

115. I, 8, 55, 72, 119. Datini went on an extramural

Bianchi pilgrimage without Mazzei, however; I, xcix–cv (1399).

116. I, 54.

117. I, 54.

know what it is but, as happened to me with [Guido Del Palagio] when he was alive, I can't be at a sermon without your being with me [in thought]."[118] In a similar vein, Mazzei furnished his friend with reports on preachers, on the latest cult, on worthwhile religious books. Lapo obviously projected the ideal of Christian brothers under God. But did the two friends actually practice their religion together? No. There is no evidence that they ever attended religious ceremonies together, prayed together, or knelt together.

Lapo attempted to translate his sentiments of spiritual brotherhood into practice in only one area; he sometimes urged that they contribute alms together. "I would gladly make one sum of his and mine," he wrote to a mutual friend.[119] To Datini himself Lapo wrote,

> I want to see you to make with you a devout company with a common treasury, where you put in a part of the money and I another, each according to his resources. And each year [we would] give it as alms.[120]

Yet behind this semblance of confraternal equality was inequality: "Take my littleness and put it alongside your grandness. And I want to contribute each year what you tax me."[121] In fact, even before God in sentiment the men were unequal, and Lapo had no expectation of standing in public alongside his friend as an equal. Unable like Guido Del Palagio to propose that he and Datini contribute an equal sum in a common act of charity, Mazzei was essentially telling Datini that he could heighten the merchant's honor by appearing in his train, so to speak, as a co-contributor.[122] The topos of the client contributing to the charity of the patron was common enough. Lapo, for example, wrote Datini once that one of the latter's employees might leave his wordly possessions to the orphanage that Francesco planned to build.[123] Obviously the two pilgrims, if they did get to heaven, have continued their differentiated roles into eternity.

The fact of the matter was that the two friends had no real relation before God; there is also no evidence the two ever actually donated alms in common. Certainly, Lapo spent whole letters chiding Datini like any preacher on the latter's faults: He should stop accumulating money and stop building, avoid usury, write a testament.[124] But these activities were conceived by Lapo as duties imposed upon him by God as part of his own position in the relationship with Datini, rather than being in any sense conceived as mutual activity: Datini did not spend any time serving Lapo's soul. If Mazzei did not preach to Datini, the notary apologized to the weary merchant, then God would whip him.[125] It was in short this client's duty to preach and, Lapo moaned at one moment in a sardonic jab at Datini, since Del Palagio had died, Mazzei had found no one ready to accept that preaching.[126]

118. I, 237.
119. I, 214.
120. I, 364.
121. I, 111.
122. Guido's proposal: I, 123.

123. I, 258.
124. I, 13, 193, and *passim.*
125. I, 210.
126. I, 299.

Lapo's feeling that both men stood as brothers before God corresponded to a singularly pessimistic view of the civic cosmos. Lapo and Francesco both saw the political world around them as a challenge to be conquered and made submissive. The notary's every action for his friend had as its goal Datini's victory over his foes. Through Lapo's expertise, "you have the advantage," he once wrote his friend.[127] Datini and Mazzei were in a sense alone sacred in the profane world, and Mazzei seems to have envisioned a different type of morality for his dealings with that world than he did for the friends' relationship with each other. Everyone was to be had for a price, for the world was a "dark forest" where friendship meant nothing more than "you and me, and I for you."[128] True friendship was especially difficult in this decadent age, almost impossible in certain places: Florence was the pharaoh's lair; the Roman court was worse; Avignon and French mores perhaps worst of all.[129] Lapo played on his friend's own moribund suspiciousness:

> Your best friends in whom you hoped harm you; those to whom you loaned money become your enemies; the goods given you are taken from you; further, your *patria* threatens you [with taxes]. And [Guido] who loved you most is dead. In your home she who ought to comfort you offends you; no need to speak of those outside [the home].[130]

With such a world view, it was easy for a man like Mazzei to feel morally superior. Sifting the correspondence to discover what Mazzei thought of himself and of Datini, the reader of these letters arrives at three sharply stated, but only slightly exaggerated conclusions. First, Mazzei regularly opined that he was the lesser man in terms of character; Datini was sagacious and a judge of character, whereas Mazzei was simple, ignorant of business, and overkind; Datini was strong yet charitable, Mazzei weak but ostentatious.[131] Second, considered on his own, Datini was not such a nice fellow. He was suspicious, moody, a complainer, greedy and an ingrate.[132] Third, Mazzei's self-contemplation showed him to be quite a pleasant and loving man. Useless and vain he claimed to be, but he was also completely selfless, poor but virtuous, the kind of man who when urged to do bad instinctively wanted all the more to do good; in short, a master of virtue who wanted to lead Francesco to a better life. And it was absolutely central to his own self-image that he was a free man, and at the same time a loving and willing servant.[133] He might not be Phintias to Francesco's Damon, Pyladis to Datini's Orestes, but neither was he some effeminate Sardanapalus who sought in friendship only gluttony and gain.[134] Among the "watered-down friends" of his day, he was among the best.[135] Constantly comparing Datini to

127. I, 19.

128. *Fondo bosco:* I, 39; II, 107, 194.

129. Successively II, 85; I, 327, 43, 135; II, 83.

130. II, 98.

131. I, 3, 7, 41, 44, 57.

132. I, 78, 274; II, 226f.

133. I, 3ff, 24, 54, 67, 80, 95, 130, 250, 300, 385.

134. I, 191.

135. *Ibid.,* 325, 326.

Christ, he assured his friend once that he would not be the first to desert him.[136] Indeed, he told one of Datini's factors that he, Lapo, was Datini's best and perhaps only friend in decadent Florence.[137]

These sometimes pitiable attempts to make the wish mother to the fact were addressed to a man surrounded by friends and associates who were all trying to prove the same disinterested love. To conquer his position, therefore, Lapo spent great effort in describing to his friend just what he had done for him and how. And such descriptions were accompanied by the running theme that Mazzei would know that Datini really cherished him as a true friend when the merchant stopped worrying about those problems Mazzei was dealing with, and left their resolution completely to the notary.[138] Let us look at the main themes of utility Mazzei regularly attempted to impress his friend with, a utility summarized by him in his phrase: "If you need [my] person, or my friends, or my things, I remind you I'm ready."[139]

Lapo had office. "My office is notary of the Grascia, which is quite useful at this time." Again, he assured Francesco that the latter had received a favor from the hospital of Santa Maria Nuova only because he, Lapo, was its notary.[140]

Lapo had friends. One of them, we have seen, would have killed himself if Lapo had asked him to. Another loved him like a son. Another was "of one spirit with [me]." A fourth owed everything to him. Still another would be counted as a friend, another was a friend "either in whole or in part." Mazzei was "very domestic" with another. And Lapo assured the merchant that he would cast off obligated friends if they did not back Lapo's solicitations for Datini.[141]

Lapo knew how government worked: "You will find that I know something of this city's regime. Truly, you can see that for yourself. I associate and come in contact with those who control the regime more than many of the notaries here."[142] Other notaries were ignorant of the means by which contract gabelles could be avoided, but Lapo put such expertise at Datini's command. Debtors were at a disadvantage with Datini because Lapo knew how to keep their cases out of court.[143] Over and over again he described to Datini the "subtle" means he used to guard the merchant's fortune and state. One example: He recommended that Datini procure a legal opinion from Bologna on his taxes. If it were favorable, the *consilium* could be given to Guido Del Palagio to be exploited. If not, there was no need to show it to their mutual friend: "I am seeking to be as subtle as possible."[144]

Such means were often behavioral manipulations, but perhaps the thing Mazzei stressed most to Datini was his technical ability to use words—did he

136. I, 63, 191, 214; II, 226.
137. II, 232.
138. I, 4, 17ff, 22, 47.
139. I, 149.
140. I, 318, 146.

141. Successively I, 35f, 179, 18f, 443, 172; II, 92. Also I, 316, 360, 369.
142. I, 64.
143. I, 19. Also I, 45, 219, 361.
144. I, 45–48. Also I, 169f, 380, 405.

not write his friend's important letters? "There is no embassy so displeasing that it cannot be made pleasurable with the form and mode of speech and with reverence and love."[145]

Lapo's self-praise and his constant insistence on how indispensable he was to Datini were required because those who denigrated his utility were often at Datini's ear. The friend constantly feared that Datini would decide his ability to manipulate the external world was overstated. "Lapo doesn't have it" (*Lapo non potè più*); that was what Mazzei feared Datini might decide.[146] And when Datini wavered, his friend could become shrill, writing the man of business that he *must not believe* that Lapo was *da poco*.[147]

So pressing was the notary's need to convince Datini that he sometimes forthrightly admitted that he would go to almost any lengths to please his mentor. In the abstract, Datini asked for favors from his friend only if Lapo thought they were honorable, only if Lapo would do them for himself. And Mazzei could assert that Datini had never asked him for anything dishonest.[148] The notary might insist on the right to say no, for partners helping each other in just *and* unjust matters "was not a friendship but a conspiracy."[149] Yet in the heat of everyday bargaining, Lapo meant it when he said that Datini's wish was his command. Representing the merchant before a governmental commission, he had "exaggerated both in truths and lies."[150] If Datini only knew how much his friend had endangered his own body and soul, he would trust him.[151] Just as he could recommend Federighi to Datini because the politico "would do anything" for Francesco, so Lapo tried to get Datini to see that "there is not a notary in Florence so determined to cover himself with florins that he would do what I am now doing [for you]."[152]

Malleable as Lapo's conscience might be, insistent as his and Francesco's protestations of pure love were, inherent tensions in the relationship placed strict limits on the progress of the ideal friendship that both sought. At the very beginning Lapo wrote as if that ideal had been achieved by the formal act of contract. During the long years of their association, Lapo could at times believe that the ideal existed. But the tensions were in fact constant and rooted. They may in fact have been the cement that over time made the pair inseparable.

For Mazzei the source of these conflicts was not in any way structural or unavoidable. Rather, it sprang from Datini's personal reaction to the notary's services. If, for example, the merchant in any way limited his friend's authority to handle Datini's affairs, Mazzei became despondent. When through an agent Datini actually canceled the effect of one of Mazzei's representations for him before the Signoria, Lapo was crushed: "The fact remains that I'm a

145. I, 377.

146. I, 40, 207.

147. I, 63.

148. I, 100, 172f; II, 90.

149. I, 37. Also I, 207.

150. I, 430. Also Origo, *Mercante*, 109.

151. I, 144.

152. I, 321. Also I, 279.

friend and not a friend."[153] If the merchant accused the notary of Santa Maria Nuova of himself profiting from a negotiation purportedly in Francesco's favor, Mazzei expressed outrage.[154] Datini blamed his friend for deceiving him, for being sectarian, for favoring Guido Del Palagio.[155] Whenever he thought Lapo had not been on his toes, Datini was ready to denounce his friend, and Lapo plaintively protested being dressed down.[156] Again and again the theme that Francesco was an ingrate crosses these pages. Some day the merchant would rue his ingratitude, Lapo thought, and see how little he had really known his true friend. The theme is recurrent; neither knew the other.[157]

The more numerous occasions when Datini rewarded Mazzei instead of complaining were just as likely to generate tension, for the notary lived in fear of sinking to the level of clientage, and said so. Certainly a substantial amount of Lapo's protests in this vein was rhetorical—Datini did observe half in jest that Mazzei would not visit or write him without a gift (*omaggio*)—but there was a definite element of justified discomfort; the notary's reputation with others was at stake.[158] When Del Palagio accused Mazzei of "kissing ass" (*lisciando la coda*), Lapo was not a little humiliated.[159] Mazzei pleaded with Datini not to send him gifts and then ask favors: "For the average person doesn't know [my] heart, and usually perceives things falsely. [They must not] think that I serve you or love you like some bricklayer who expects to be paid on Saturdays."[160] Datini might be surrounded by good-time friends, *amici mercadieri* or *amici pilucconi* who loved like merchants or beggars loved, flatterers who led one on and then could not produce, but Mazzei did not want to be one of them.[161] He would not be a salaried worker for Datini, but only a "servant from love."[162] Such friends did not genuflect before their masters, did not appear in a patron's account book under the rubric "Gifts scheduled for friends."[163] A sinner like Datini, who did not attend Mass very often, could hire someone else to pray for him; it was no part of a friend's task. He was a free man, Mazzei reiterated, and not obliged to anyone any more than he wanted to be.[164]

There had been a time when the young Mazzei had been in people's service, and then gifts had been his sustenance and enabled him to pay his debts. But that was no longer so.[165] Mazzei told Francesco how once as a young man he had been shamed by playing the client to a man of note:

I thought to sustain this friendship through external things rather than with internal spirit as I should have. . . . I often sent him small trifles. He repeatedly forbade me

153. I, 400.
154. I, 145.
155. I, 23, 144f.
156. I, 232, 234.
157. I, 74, 96, 145, 232ff; II, 226f.
158. I, 185.
159. I, 190.
160. II, 130.
161. I, 22, 191, 336, 339, II, 107, 194.
162. II, 58, 129.
163. I, 300; II, 25f.
164. I, 114; II, 25f, 152.
165. II, 25f.

to, but I thought he [only] said this out of politeness. Finally when he saw this didn't work, he began to send me now livery, now venison, now partridge. I became aware of my shame and of his displeasure, and I stopped and he stopped. Thus I am afraid this could happen to me [again].[166]

The merchant's gifts were constantly received under protest—but never returned, for that would have shamed the donor. A gift of wine, Mazzei asserted, compromised his liberty and violated his good will.[167] He did not like some of the wines Datini sent; he did not want partridges, and was too honest to sell them, as was the normal practice.[168] Why did Datini treat him above his station? If the merchant would send him coarse things of the type one would give a laborer, he would accept them.[169] Luxuries were not wasted on Lapo; they endangered the friendship. Mazzei instructed his friend on how to offer him gifts to avoid seeming overbearing.[170] He promised to ask for anything he needed, and warned Datini that unless the latter promised never to send another gift, their friendship would end: *e partiremo amicizia e comparatico*.[171]

With great skill Lapo made it impossible for posterity to decide how much of his protest was threat and how much was pretense. Convention dictated that he protest *and* that he accept gifts, yet certainly our notary had a problem. Perhaps the parameters of the problem are wrongly stated. Perhaps Lapo's annoyance at the gifts and even Francesco's acerbic criticisms of his friend were in fact interpreted and meant as expressions that they cared. That approach too was a recognized rhetorical device. One can only be sure that both men professed to understand the attainments and limits of their relationship as derived from their individual characters rather than from their social *personae*. But how important were the *public* persons, the *social* force, the constraints of setting?

Lapo of course recognized that he was the lesser of the two men as the world measured. Most often he gleefully accepted his position as an "obedient servant" of a *gran maestro*, thinking that

> it pleased God that because of the so good spirit you always have toward others, you should run across a little servant and friend full of every good intention toward you, in addition to the great men whom you have always had [as friends]. God watch over you.[172]

The faithful servant at times viewed Francesco as just one of a group of *maggiori* he served.[173] And in unguarded moments he wrote of himself not as part of a peculiar relationship, but as one member of Datini's entourage. He spoke to him of "We, your friends," to Datini's manager of "Our Father," and

166. I, 226.

167. I, 151; II, 48.

168. I, 325; II, 25f.

169. *Ibid.*

170. II, 129.

171. I, 43, 425; II, 25f, 58.

172. I, 66. Also I, 414.

173. For example, I, 249.

addressed letters to "Francesco, father of many."[174] Mazzei never sought to move from *voi* to *tu* in their correspondence. There are indications that both Datini and Del Palagio in personal conversation with Lapo addressed him as *tu*, but there is no hint that Mazzei reciprocated.[175] The notary probably preferred the more formal pronoun, for the *tu* that friends, colleagues, and equals like Del Palagio and Datini might use among themselves expressed dominion when addressed to a social inferior.

For all his willingness to accept the social difference between him and Datini, for all his professed confidence that love conquers all, however, Lapo bore uneasily the resentment, the sorrow, and even the shame of being unable to transcend the limits society placed upon such a friendship of unequals. He never blamed circumstances for these limits; like a true child of the classical Western view of friendship, he believed that one could not change the world.[176] His spite at these limitations was something more than a denunciation of Francesco's limitations, however; it was a small man's un-comprehending rage at an order he desired to but could not surmount.

This resentment surfaced in varied circumstances. Lapo might assert, for example, that he knew both Datini and his wife did not fault him for his lowly occupation of notary, but certainly it must have rankled when Margherita in jest called him a "little notary" (*notaiolo*) to his face.[177] Lapo might during the early years be "honored and flattered" when Datini visited him, as if a lord or friend were his guest. He might speak with equanimity about Datini's treating him as some lesser species: "I hear often of your great banquets [given for] men and women rich in the pomp of the world, and this is a lovely thing."[178] But the resentment showed years later when in 1407 he was apprised that Datini had elevated a foreign doctor into an instant intimate: "Wretched me, I've served you twenty years and I never could enjoy [even] goat-meat with my friends in your house and mine."[179] The fact was that Lapo rarely if ever talked of being in Datini's mansion at all, and felt thoroughly uneasy about being invited. He tended to dismiss out of hand Datini's assurances that Lapo could drop around anytime:

> An elderly neighbor has taught me that one ought not to go to visit a superior except when sent for. It would be enough to go when he wants you because, he said, you might go at a time when he had his mind on something else, and he would not want you. And I know your nature [,Francesco,] well enough.[180]
>
> Just once I would like you to invite me not in the Avignonese style, but in the style of the true friends of Florence—if there are such here. That is "I remind you, ser Lapo, that I am always glad to see you at lunch and dinner." And [if you acted sincerely] you would not make me flee by staging big feasts.[181]

174. I, 23; II, 47, 81, 217.

175. I, 23, 25, 135; II, 129.

176. II, 229.

177. I, 202; II, 187.

178. I, 31, 44.

179. II, 88.

180. II, 6.

181. II, 33. Datini always addressed Lapo as *ser*.

None of Datini's protestations of friendship could cancel out the effect of excluding Lapo from the company Datini's money could buy. No effort could convince Lapo that Francesco gave him gifts only *per segno d'amore*. The situation led him once to an uncharacteristic but indicative piece of sarcasm:

> I speak out of turn. It is my duty to act the lesser or true obedient [man], that is, accept as good and optimally done whatever the superior and father wants me to do, even if the things seems to me less than well arranged.[182]

Such was the sardonic, yet moving substance of their relation, of all relations of men of different strata seeking to love and be loved in a civic society of privilege and inequality. If we now try to analyze the relationship that we have studied, we are confronted with the inescapable truth that society provided the possibility and prescribed the limits of active men's friendships. Not only were the parties to this arrangement active men; their interactions were largely public, and the gratifications of their friendship were as well.

The notary had conceived his relation to the merchant in quite different terms: an atomistic union of equality beneath an altar used only by these two elect, one that blissfully ignored the chaos of an immoral surrounding world, a union in which gifts one to the other were never sold to the outside world and thus profaned. Yet in the moment the two communicated with each other through services and gifts, the value of these means of exchange proved to be derived from social and cultural rather than atomistic sources.

The giver protested that the recipient should assess not the market value of the gift, but the spirit in which it was given.[183] But this statement itself was a social value. It meant first that the donor accepted the principle of giving social values commensurate with services, but could not afford to do so. Furthermore, the admonition to consider intent did no more than urge the recipient to compare his intent to that of others; comparing intents is social science, not individual psychology. The donor realized that no procedure existed by which this could be done other than consideration of the previous history of the relation, and of all relations and exchanges the recipient had ever been a party to. Thus not only outsiders but also insiders could evaluate gifts only by social codes.

The identity and value of the means of exchange in this relationship being linked to the macrocosm and not to the amicable microcosm, the *personae* rather than some nebulous existential identity of the givers and receivers would themselves affect the value of the gifts transmitted. The *personae* were themselves an exchange value: "I give myself to you." How was one to interpret the meaning of such socially evaluated gifts without considering the foreordained status of the giver and receiver? How, in short, could the hierarchical and moral connotations of friendly exchange of goods and values not be central to the evaluation of the state of the friendship? The open

182. II, 48.   183. I, 14, 200.

contradiction of this and other friendships in a civic setting was that a microcosmic value relationship was to be activated, proven, and maintained by a macrocosmic code of exchange.

The inability to escape the social code permeates the correspondence. Lapo always explained that his endless services sprang from selfless love for Datini, and he railed when they were accepted otherwise. Yet the same boundless service provided by the rich Datini to his friend gnawed constantly, for Mazzei interpreted the merchant's gifts as disempowering instrumentalities, interpreted them, that is, as did society. Datini, on the other hand, probably saw Mazzei's gifts and services to him as client's services, and viewed *his* gifts as selfless offerings of thanks. Both considered their own status-identity, both interpreted the value of gifts with reference to their positions. What other options did they have? Words? Verbal expressive forms were recognizable only if they were presented as social codes. And those codes were strictly defined according to social position. There was a language of interrelation for every level of society. The language of friendship, alas, was also in its content foreign to the relationship, a property of society and not of the microcosmic friendship.

These limits to the fusion of character and *persona* were inherent in social living. Their peculiarly urban character was, as Mazzei constantly complained, that one man did not know the other. The partners of civil conversation, Guazzo realized, were not true friends but well-wishers (*benivoli*).[184] Each was buffeted by different interests and identities, each eminently cautious in baring his soul to the other, the insider to the outsider, the high to the low, the equals competing for precedence. Citizen friendship was a necessary (not a feigned) relationship of males who got along because of the fearful alternative so much a part of the urban identity: the city's potential for creation and destruction. Citizenship, more than merely a legal condition, was one's acceptance into the world of obligations, and Datini, who rarely held office, was every inch a citizen from this point of view.

The ritual of gifts and services, of language and mandatory epistolary salutations, appears in this light as a foundation of civil conversation, bringing together these diverse and fractured identities into amicable contact with each other. If the nature of the city and of social relationships in general set limits to closeness without an altar, drawing the line of mutual understanding at alliance, ritual provided the altar. Creating networks whose obligatory nature meant that someone like Lapo had to discard a friend if that friend would not be a friend to Francesco, ritual, whether bodily or verbal, provided a community of faith under the sponsorship of quasi-sacral leaders like Guido Del Palagio, who gave but did not receive, and shone in his own light without being obliged to others.

The manipulative genius of ritual at the interpersonal level has certainly been demonstrated in this chapter, but men's actions have not been severed

---

184. Guazzo, *De Civili Conversatione*, 258.

from their thoughts and feelings. It was not at all my intention to contrast ideal and real, but, quite the contrary, to reveal how rhetoric meant caring, and created it. In fact, the central finding of this examination has been that verbal gesture, gifts, services, and the like, the actual practice of communication, perceived so often as hypocritical, created strong bonds and internal feelings for others. Ritual action created internal states just as surely as, conversely, it could be the effect of internal states. Lapo and Francesco stayed together not lastly because of their rhetorical commitments. The very protestation against ritual, as Guazzo said, "tamed ambition," made men fitting diners at the common *mensa*. The same writer chided his antiritualistic partner:

> I don't know who is your perfect friend, but I know well that I have not yet found mine, with whom I can exercise that nude, simple, and frank liberty which you want to emphasize.[185]

Guazzo would have sympathized with, and understood perfectly that critic of the City of the Sun who found Campanella's utopia wanting:

> Among this race of men, friendship is worth nothing, since they have not the chance of conferring mutual benefits on one another.[186]

---

185. *Ibid.*, 257.

186. F. White (ed.), *Famous Utopias* (New York, 1955), 167.

Chapter 5

Father and Son

*The departure of dear sons from the joying view
of their most loving fathers.**

*Five out of six . . . sons want their father
to die so they can be free.†*

The *ricordanze* and personal letters that are so much a hallmark of the Florentine experience prove, if proof is needed, the unmistakable individuality of each author. Exposed to a wealth of common experiences such as birth, baptism, growth, marriage, sickness, aging, and death, each writer expressed his reaction to life from a unique cast of mind. Lapo Mazzei impresses us as a pious, slightly hypocritical man of warm naivete. Buonaccorso Pitti's memoirs reveal a rakishly confident, aristocratic, slightly superficial character. Who but the colorless, eminently bourgeois Goro Dati would have reacted to middle age as he did?

> I know that in this wretched life our sins expose us to many tribulations of soul and passions of the body, that without God's grace and mercy which strengthens our weakness, enlightens our mind and supports our will, we would perish daily. I also see that since my birth forty years ago, I have given little heed to God's commandments. Distrusting my own power to reform, but hoping to advance by degrees along the path of virtue, I resolve from this day forward to refrain from going to the shop or conducting business on solemn church holidays, or from permitting others to work for me or seek temporal gain on such days. Whenever I make exceptions in cases of

*A. Gherardi (ed.), *Statuti della Università e Studio Fiorentino* (Florence, 1881), 211.

†Sacchetti, *Trecentonovelle*, 290.

159

extreme necessity, I promise, on the following day, to distribute alms of one gold florin to God's poor. I have written this down so that I may remember my promise and be ashamed if I should chance to break it.[1]

And certainly the subject of this chapter, Giovanni di Pagolo di Bartolomeo Morelli, leaves an individual impression difficult to mistake. The personalities are so vivid—even Dati, in his colorlessness—that one is often tempted to lose oneself in that individual's image as one might in a Rembrandt portrait or in Our Lady of Impruneta, and ignore the equally significant common ground that these men shared.

The present chapter will delve deeply into the person of Giovanni Morelli, as it is revealed in the events surrounding the death of his oldest son Alberto in 1406. Although it will accord an important place to his unique character and responses to life, the purpose of this chapter is not biographical. Rather, the highly individual set of responses through which Giovanni, abandoned as an infant by both his father who died and his mother who remarried, came to terms with his abandonment by his son provides an outstanding vehicle for understanding *social* ritual. The main purpose of this chapter is to witness the formal world of the streets brought into the home and employed for eminently private ends. Marked as this record is by penetrating self-analysis, Morelli's unique laical description of solitary experience nevertheless shows all the qualities of creative public forms.

Usually Florentines acted out religion in public before the images and frames provided for them by the church, commune, and honorable men. Arlotto's and Sacchetti's characters all interacted with church images. Paolo da Certaldo advised his reader to see God in church, not at home. But Morelli in his unique experience prayed in the solitude of his bedroom, a ritual rarely reported and never enlarged upon elsewhere. I have made some sparse allusions to domestic ceremonialization: Dominici's recommendation that parents bring altar, paintings, and gestures into their home, Bernardino's instructions to women to frame their bedroom image as they would one in church. Savonarola too recommended the importation into the home of such public modalities as altars, candles, sex separation during prayer, avoidance of polluted areas like bedrooms, and the use of public times for private prayer.[2] Giovanni Morelli's record allows us to look into the soul of one merchant, and find his society at work in the bedroom. We shall see how he combined a highly formalized approach to achieve communion with his departed and beloved son with an indubitably genuine and even piercing individual spiritual impetus. Through understanding the way Morelli prayed to God and to his son, we shall better understand how he related to living men. By studying an exquisitely private grief and the manipulative methods with which Morelli dealt with that grief, we shall prepare ourselves to understand the feelings and sensibilities of an individual like Morelli when he left

1. Dati, *Memoir*, 124.

2. References for this domestic program are given on pages 352f, this volume.

his house to be swept up in the general processions that we shall later examine. It is here we can begin to understand that the city procession was no "mere" ceremony; that within it each man, in Savonarola's moving phrase, stood together with the crowd, was quiet, and thus was alone.[3]

The Morelli Ricordi

It was a tenacious, proud, and financially substantial twenty-two-year-old who set out in 1393 to record for "our children or our descendants" the past history of the Morelli clan.[4] This was a surprising undertaking, for the young man, of average height and complexion, genteelly delicate and of "consumate grace and gifts," was not married.[5] He was, however, madly in love with a girl he desperately wanted to marry. Perhaps passion led him to take up pen, and enabled him in these first pages to look back on his own checkered past with equanimity. For this *giovane*'s ascent had been marked by personal tragedy. He had never known his father, who died when Giovanni was little more than two. His mother too abandoned him, remarrying soon after her husband's death and leaving the children to be reared by her parents. When Giovanni was twelve his grandfather also died, and Giovanni found himself shunted about, and very reliant on his oldest sister Mea for comfort and solidarity. Alas, Mea too deserted him, dying in childbirth when Giovanni was sixteen. In 1393, despite all this personal difficulty, the future seemed sufficiently bright to permit the young orphan to re-create a firm and stable past for his clan. The entries written in these early years present his more distant ancestors in human but idealized terms, and have none of the endless remorse that mark Giovanni's later writing.

By 1402 Giovanni had progressed in his *ricordi* to the description of his father's generation. Much had changed for the now thirty-year-old man. He had married in 1396, but not the girl he loved. The latter had been denied him by her father. Instead Giovanni had taken a wife from the prominent but at the time politically suspect clan of the Alberti.[6] He had become the father of four children, and had been exposed to the heavy taxation of the last decade of the century, when the commune warred with Giangaleazzo Visconti. The loss of his sweetheart, the heavy taxes, the apparently utilitarian and loveless nature of his marriage, the fact that he was still politically unknown, and the financial difficulties he had experienced all help to explain the emergence at

3. *Salmi*, I, 297.

4. *Ricordi*, 85. Branca's introduction to the *Ricordi* is invaluable; 1–77; as is Bec, *Marchands*, 53–75. See also G. Brucker, "Giovanni Morelli's Florence," in Brucker (ed.), *People and Communities in the Western World* (Homewood, Ill., 1979), 219–255. Giovanni and his brother Morello were twenty-first in their quarter's tax lists in 1403, twenty-third in 1427; Martines, *Social*

World, 359, 366. I have translated many of the *ricordi* relevant to this chapter: "In Search of Father. The Experience of Abandonment in the Recollections of Giovanni di Pagolo Morelli," *History of Childhood Quarterly* III (1975), 225–252.

5. The self-characterization is in the *Ricordi*, 197.

6. *Ibid.*, 499f.

this point in the *ricordi* of those traits that will characterize the writing and the man for a lifetime: bitterness, pessimism, and distrust.

Giovanni's Father, Pagolo

Disillusioned with his life-experience, Giovanni took up the task of writing his father's biography. Pagolo—Giovanni never called him "my father"—emerges as his son's father. From the beginning, the reader is aware of just how central a role Pagolo and his wife Telda play in their son's own conception of self.

The boy who had eagerly transcribed the history of his more distant ancestors shuddered before writing about his father. He was ignorant, he wrote poorly; how could he hope to express the heights of his father's personality and accomplishments? Indeed, Giovanni feared that he might even diminish the honor due his father rather than increase it.[7] But he wrote.

As Giovanni saw it, Pagolo was a man who conquered perverse fortune and left his hapless son and the son's sons a record of bravery that could scarcely be matched. Pagolo had never seen his own father.[8] Giovanni sought to explain this by noting that his father had been (one of?) the youngest of many children, and that Pagolo's mother had died when the father was old. Putting these facts together, Giovanni decided that the father "cared little for this younger [child]" and "did not want the bother of taking care of" Pagolo. Thus Pagolo had been sent off to a wet nurse in the Mugello where he remained for ten to twelve years until "almost grown."[9] The theme of abandonment that permeates every page of Giovanni's own biography is central to that of his father. Yet there was something special, unequaled, about the sufferings and disadvantages of the father that kept Giovanni at a respectful distance from the paternal image: "Think what he must have been like, having stayed in the country all or most of the time: little better than a farm laborer!"[10]

The theme of his father's deprivation continued into the middle years of childhood. Giovanni's mother told him that her husband had bitter recollections of the years in the country. The nurse had been "the most bestial woman ever," who had "given him so many beatings that whenever he thought about it he was so enraged that if he had had her in hand he would have killed her."[11] The teachers Pagolo visited when he returned to the city assumed the same punitive role as the nurse, beating the boy so badly that Pagolo rebelled. He went from school to school seeking a teacher who promised not to thrash him, and left if the promise was broken.[12] Robbed of anyone who really cared, he was victimized by his older brothers, who

7. *Ibid.*, 143.

8. *Ibid.*, 144.

9. *Ibid.*, 144f.

10. *Ibid.*, 145.

11. *Ibid.*, 144.

12. *Ibid.*, 146f.

constantly tried to gain control of the boy's rightful share of his father's estate.[13]

Pagolo was more than equal to these terrible trials. "The abandoned youth" learned the three R's on his own. "Without father and in the hands of his older brothers," he was finally able to attain his part of the estate, aided only by "God and *ragione*." When the brothers died in 1363, Pagolo, though still a boy, buried them, collected their credits, made inventories, defended himself against their families, fought in the bishop's court against charges of usury, and, after all this, became the first member of the family to become eligible for the Signoria.[14] All this was done through "reason and care, not at all through force of money."[15]

Pagolo had obviously long since set about winning the friendship of others to protect him from his family. He won the love of God and of powerful men by serving, counseling, and remaining loyal to them. He sponsored their children at baptism. Thus in his trials he had "friends and not relatives" to defend him, and God on his side.[16] It was a remarkable achievement for this unknown father, and Giovanni wrote, "And you, consider and think what would give you the heart to continue, finding yourself in such a time and in such a series of events!"[17] This was the paragon of virtue who had sired Giovanni but left him, the image before which the awed son retreated, the heroic figure into whose shoes Giovanni urged his young boys to put themselves. The *ricordi* of course were written for his boys, and there is every reason to believe that the main beneficiary of this account was meant to be the five- to six-year-old firstborn, Alberto.[18]

Alberto learned next to nothing about his grandmother from the *ricordi*'s biographical information. Giovanni recorded that his mother Telda was thirteen when she married, and that she was very beautiful. She remarried when Pagolo died.[19] That was all—at this point. But Giovanni's deserter appears again, and her ghost is one of the main but least mentioned figures in Giovanni's life. Pagolo, on the contrary, is not a ghost. Giovanni had made him into a living force, and he remained so. His biography prefigured that of his son, though his son never explicitly noted the correspondence of their lives. The godly image and the unworthy devotee are kept apart.

Giovanni's Own Story

In July 1403 the now thirty-one-year-old Giovanni finished recording the history of the clan up to the present and began to describe himself. Judging by

---

13. *Ibid.*, 146ff.

14. *Ibid.*, 151f, 158f.

15. *Ibid.*, 155.

16. *Ibid.*, 149f.

17. *Ibid.*, 153.

18. "Perché iscrivo per sempro de' miei fanciulli e non per uomini"; *ibid.*, 284. On Alberto's reading abilities as a child, *ibid.*, 457.

19. *Ibid.*, 155, 203.

Giovanni's own thumbnail autobiography, he found one major difference between himself and his father, but one he did not expressly describe. The father had managed to develop a wide circle of friends and had become a major political figure in the commune. Giovanni at thirty-one had achieved none of this, and he was truly concerned that he would never attain to honor in the commune; a sense of failure pervades his autobiography. He had done everything possible to neutralize the baleful effects of his unfortunate marriage to the proscribed Alberti. He studiously avoided offending anyone, took the high Guelf stance of the regime in power, and opposed any attempt of artisans to attain political power, all to no avail. The classical inside outsider, he bruited it about that if he had "power or authority" he would deal with those who criticized the regime.[20] He yearned for the chance in political office to demonstrate just how faithful he wanted to be to the (anti-Alberti) commune and to its "good men and good merchants." Alas, it had not pleased God to give him a chance.[21]

There seems little doubt that the self-reflection that Giovanni had had to summon for his thumbnail autobiography was what caused him to desert his plan to take up a narration of communal history at this point, and instead to enter upon a detailed exposition of "the great injuries and persecutions which have happened to me."[22] The evidence of his potential life failure was so potent, so overwhelming, that like some tidal force, that background, its lessons, its terrible stunting effects upon his mental equilibrium had to be expressed. We owe these unique parts of his *ricordi* to chance, and to his sense of failure.

A defeated man of thirty-two takes up the task. His life, he writes, has till now been one displeasure after another. Things may, however, be different for his sons, and it is in the hope that his sons can avoid injury and achieve status through learning from their father that he starts his new task.[23] The catastrophes of his own life have been due, he states at the outset, either to fate, to the malice of others, or to his own stupidity.[24]

Giovanni's approach was of the greatest significance. He did not simply narrate his life step by step; rather, he posed a question: What were the injuries suffered by orphans in general, and Giovanni and his brothers and sisters in particular? And what could be done to counteract the effect of each? In other words, his new biography was to be seen through the prism of abandonment, thus continuing the approach taken in writing about his father. The moralisms and life-lessons he was about to pass on to his young sons were anchored within the desert harbor of abandonment.

With great force and feeling, the young father listed the injuries suffered by him and his three older brothers and sisters:

20. *Ibid.*, 195f.

21. *Ibid.*, 197.

22. The change of plans is evident in the *Ricordi*, 201f.

23. "E Idio, se voi sarete buoni, vi farà grazia; e dove noi per insino a qui abbiamo avute e abbiamo delle cose ci dispiacciono, voi sarete per avventura ristorati, ché sempre non vanno le cose a un modo, ma di continovo si mutano"; *ibid.*, 202.

24. *Ibid.*, 201.

1. They had lost their father when small.
2. They lost their mother through remarriage.
3. Their fate was in the hands of their father's testamentary executors who could not defend their estate though loyal and honest: "They cannot be compared to the father."
4. Within five years executors and children went through 5000 of the 20,000 florins in the estate.
5. Rather than earning money, the estate was declining daily.
6. The commune contributed to this, multiplying by six the tax load of the orphans and halving the interest it owed the estate.
7. "While children receive instruction and direction and status and good manners from their father, we remained without a head and without guidance." True, his "second father" and his wife treated them like their own children, "but they cannot be compared to the father."[25]

The damages deriving from these seven injuries were, in Giovanni's words, "neither imaginable nor recordable, but infinite." Yet some remedy was available "which would not leave the luckless orphan so nude and abandoned," and he turned to a series of simple recommendations intended for his sons.[26]

The immediate enemy and the key element of Giovanni's cautionary scheme for his sons was the figure of the mother of orphans. Caught in a male-dominated legal system that coerced her into abandoning her children if, for once in her life, she was to gain control of her dowry, either for the purpose of remarrying or to the end of endowing a secure widow's household, the mother was all too ready to desert her children and seize the only liquid asset that was indisputably her own. If a widow wanted to be a *persona*, in short, she had to leave her husband's house, and the children in it.[27] Her personal behavior if her husband should die was, therefore, uppermost in

25. That is, his maternal grandparents; *ibid.*, 202–206.
26. *Ibid.*, 205, 284.
27. The widow had to defend herself against her brothers once she had her dowry, however. Its size and thus her class were among the many considerations in the mother's decision, as was, of course, her closeness to the children and the availability of responsible relatives from one of the families to care for them. But the circumstance that a widowed mother could not have her dowry in hand as long as she lived under the same roof as, and thus was supported by, even the most juvenile oldest son and *his* estate, is an important discovery that demands further investigation. After having demonstrated that maternal abandonment after the death of a husband was an important social reality in Florence, Herlihy and Klapisch were perplexed: "Why did these young widows show such a propensity to abandon their babies?" *Toscans*, 558. Here is part of the answer. Giovanni Morelli's mother may have abandoned her

children in order to establish her *persona*, and Manno Petrucci made no bones of the fact that his mother left him because it was in her interest to do so, even if, since "we still had in hand the dowry of [our mother], it was in our [children's] interest to remain subject to her"; *ASF, Carte Strozziane*, II, 15, f. 64r, kindly brought to my attention by Elaine Rosenthal and Christiane Klapisch. Vespasiano da Bisticci, finally, presumed we would know that particular mothers acted in their own interest, for he records the following detail only in passing: "The young wife being left with four young children, and wishing to marry again, and to reclaim her large dowry, left [her husband's] house and her children with their [paternal] grandmother. . . . To repay the dowry [to the widow, the grandmother] had to assign almost all the income from the [dead husband's] estate, thus leaving an income of only five hundred florins for [the grandmother], the four grandchildren, and the nurse"; *Vite*, 561f (Alessandra de' Bardi).

Giovanni's mind, and it was in the light of her potential for destroying the children and their estate—no father could ever be so cruel!—that Morelli recommended to his sons a series of steps they could take to protect their sons from her.

The first recommendation was perhaps the most radical of all: Marry between the ages of twenty and twenty-four and "have children soon so you can rear them yourself." In this way, it is implied, you will not have to rely on your wife at all.[28] Like all men of his age, Giovanni Morelli vaunted the advantages of age and thought that children generated by grave adults would more likely be male, healthy, and long-lived, as had been the case in the good old days, when men had married at forty and lived long.[29] This makes it all the more remarkable that he would recommend marrying at such an early age. The young man and his young wife would simply have to act grave, and not fornicate wildly as young people do, in order to have good children.[30] Morelli apparently thought it more fruitful to take a chance on the character of children of very young parents, rather than on the stability of a mother once her husband had died. It is nothing short of startling that Giovanni felt the loss of his own father so greatly that he recommended such an early marriage age to his sons.

The second familial recommendation was that his sons, once fathers, realize that "in truth, there is no mother so degraded who is not better for the children than another woman," and take every testamentary precaution to ensure that their wives would not leave the children in the event of the father's death.[31] Important as this was, however, keeping mothers with the children was only the beginning. For with the father gone, the mother might allow her own family to ruin the estate and the upbringing of the children. Thus at all costs, he said, never allow your wife full authority over the children or estate; surround her with other executors *from your own family* who will keep an eye on her, and even force her to pay if she rears the children poorly.[32] Keep her, that is, but do not trust her: "If you know your wife to be of little wisdom, loving little, vain, lecherous, and a spendthrift . . . " It is monna Telda who haunts her defeated son's mind.[33]

Morelli passed on to his sons a view of the family very different from our own. He essentially considered his wife as the representative of another family and a merely instrumental figure in the male succession.[34] Thus his distrust of wives is almost equivalent to his distrust of the world outside the home, and he approached despair when he tried to recommend to his sons

28. G. di Pagolo Morelli, *Ricordi*, 206f, 211.

29. *Ibid.*, 110ff.

30. *Ibid.*, 211f.

31. *Ibid.*, 218, and generally 211–218.

32. "Però dico che in lei al tutto non t'affidi. . . . Lascia che ella con due o tre tuoi parenti possa fare"; *ibid.*, 216.

33. *Ibid.*, 217.

34. Branca considers Morelli's nuclear family as a refuge from an unreliable world. The *ricordi* do not support this vague and sentimental view. Morelli, for example, does not even record his wife's death; he says nothing positive about her, and not once does he evoke a scene of domestic warmth between husband and wife. A father, a son, and male ancestors do not a family make; cf. the introduction to the *Ricordi*, 28–30, 47f.

what testamentary provisions to make in case his wife should remarry. Who was to protect the children? Whether friend or relative, whether the father's or the mother's relatives, they were all dangerous: "Relatives and friends are 'outsiders' because when money or goods are in question, no person wants more your interest than his."[35] The dreary advice multiplied: "Test a friend a hundred times . . . before you trust him once."[36] "Have no faith."[37] Never trust a servant.[38] If someone says he is loyal, trust him less, and trust no one who spontaneously offers to serve you.[39]

> And thus be wise—I say this to you on the basis of three things which have already happened to me and damaged me: Never trust anyone. Make things clear, and especially with a relative or with a friend more than with outsiders, but with everyone. Notarize everything.[40]

What then was the shepherd to do for the eventuality that his wife would remarry and his lambs fall completely into the hands of the wolves?[41] Clearly the "least bad" remedy was to keep the mother. After that Morelli wavered, but basically he favored putting the financial management of the orphan in the hands of the communal office of orphans rather than in those of friends and relatives.[42]

The recommendations that I have outlined touched the sons' eventual behavior as married men. What follows examines the behavior of his sons in the world outside the home, and is aimed at providing the sons with guidelines on how they might proceed if he, father Giovanni, were to die.[43] The loss, Giovanni repeated, was a grave matter: "The advantages that the child receives if the father is alive are so great, in so many ways and in so many places, that they cannot be recounted."[44] This man who never knew a father who never knew *his* father re-evokes a father who might have been. Children receive from their father good lessons at every hour; he teaches them virtue; he counsels them in daily adversity. The father will tell his children the news of the city, things he has read in history books, his experiences in business and government, who has been a friend and who a family enemy. "And thus in many things recollected by the father, the son will find example and remember them well."[45] Giovanni seems to have decided to write down his social wisdom for fear he might never have the opportunity to advise his sons face to face when they matured.

The core of the social wisdom Giovanni wanted to pass on, however, was more than household philosophy, the easy generalities expected of older

---

35. "Istrani"; *ibid.*, 219.

36. *Ibid.*, 226f.

37. *Ibid.*, 227.

38. *Ibid.*, 232.

39. *Ibid.*, 227.

40. *Ibid.*, 243.

41. *Ibid.*, 219f.

42. "Per molte cagione è meglio il Comune che parente o amico"; *ibid.*, 222.

43. "Ché ciascuno e' ne vederebbe molto più di me"; *ibid.*, 284.

44. *Ibid.*, 269.

45. *Ibid.*, 267ff.

men; he wanted to teach a way of acting for sons involved in the outside world. This was the apex of what a live father could do face to face:

> He will make you expert in speaking to citizens, to officials, to rectors. In the embassies he commits to you he will instruct you in the tenor of words, the modes or courtesies which have to be given, the [modes of] entry in embassies according to who [is receiving the embassy]. . . . He will either charge you: "Do this, and bear yourself in such and such a way," or you will be with him, and will see his manner both of speaking and acting, and you will learn quite a bit.[46]

It was the most important thing this father could reduce to writing.

So here was the paradox: Morelli was about to instruct his sons on how to win friends through formal behavior, and at the same time was telling his six-year-old Alberto that the outside world was loveless: "If you are rich, be prepared to buy friends with your money if you can't have them otherwise."[47] Harsher: "Cash . . . is the best friend and the best relative there is."[48] Most utopic: "But above all, if you want to have friends and relatives, put yourself in a position where you don't need them."[49] Why, the reader of such dicta asks, should one bother with "the tenor of words, the modes or courtesies" of "embassies" if friends and relatives were "outsiders" who would never seek anything but their own interest? The paradox is real, and there is no full answer. Giovanni was as naive in his cynicism as Mazzei was in his idealism; like the notary, he had to deal with the real world and recommended a course of action aimed at establishing friendship, something his moralisms did not allow for. There is no solving this conflict; we can only try to understand it, first by examining the course of action he recommends.

Morelli divided his action program in two, dealing first with people who needed help from the Morellis, then with the sons themselves going to others. In dealing with those asking favors, the merchant spelled out for the sons the verbal codes they would encounter so that they could recognize them:

> If I only had two hundred florins I'd have the means to double them. I'd gladly give you half the earnings. . . . You can count on me: How could you believe I'd lie to you? I'd rather be quartered. . . . There are twenty people who would do this for me, but I don't want to give them this information nor this profit. On the other hand it makes me feel good to give you the break, a person I know.[50]

Those seeking monetary favors accompany their words, Morelli taught, with courtesies intended to weaken you. Some will give you gifts, some will invite you to dinner and otherwise bestow marks of honor on you, others will try to put you in a position where you are ashamed to say no.[51]

The Morellis had to meet these attempts to snare money with excuses, and Giovanni again spelled out the correct language:

46. *Ibid.*, 268.

47. *Ibid.*, 253.

48. *Ibid.*, 279.

49. *Ibid.*

50. *Ibid.*, 240f.

51. *Ibid.*, 241.

I've vowed [not to]. . . . I've taken an oath [*sacramento*]. . . . I'm bound to my brother not to obligate myself without his agreement. . . . I'm sorry, but I want to think about it. . . . Why is it necessary to offer me [your friend] all these guarantees; why didn't you just tell me your needs? You've given me doubts [about it] where I wouldn't have had any. . . . I want to think about it.[52]

The recommendations continue: Be suspicious of anyone offering services, and never trust anyone who does this with no apparent cause.[53]

When Morelli turned his attention to his boys seeking out contacts in the world, the tone was very different. True, the attitude was still one of great caution, bordering at certain times on a recommendation that one show no initiative at all:

Because in Florence there are depraved people who with evil and vicious [intentions] pass on malicious gossip and compromise you in new ways and with new snares. And because one can't know everyone, always say good of everyone, and don't agree with someone speaking bad of others. Either be quiet or say good.[54]

Yet this statement itself indicates that he differentiated between good and bad men, and sought trust through action. If the reason for never criticizing was that one could not know everyone in a city, and thus could not be sure unknowns would not maliciously carry criticism abroad, then it followed that if one did know persons, one could speak honestly because one could trust such persons. In fact the purpose of Morelli's action in society was to create bonds of trust and love through obligation.

Morelli phrased this aim as follows: The sons were to become "expert" in acquiring "friends and relatives whom you see love you and serve you and tenderly aid your status."[55] As if determined to highlight the conflict with his previous ideas, he charged his boys to "retain and preserve good friendship or, rather, increase it."[56] They must move men to "condescend" to friendship with them.[57] What the sons should be after was not mere utility, but love: "Love [all citizens] and bring them love," he urged the boys, and cause them to love you through the marks of tenderness you give them.[58] Thus in an unfriendly world, he urged a program of ritual forms with which one could protect oneself through winning affection. Basic pessimism yielded to a search for security through love.

Morelli distinguished four different groups in society that his sons should manipulate. First came boys their own age, the father repeatedly insisting that his sons cultivate peer relations of trust and mutual obligations from very early life.[59] Obviously he wanted Alberto and the others to seek out

---

52. *Ibid.*, 241f.

53. *Ibid.*, 227.

54. *Ibid.*, 276.

55. "Ancora sarai savio, acquistato gli amici e' parenti cioè quelli vedi ca t'amano e ti servano e sono teneri dello istato tuo"; *ibid.*, 277, also 262.

56. *Ibid.*, 277f.

57. "Quai pensi farlo condiscendere ad amicizia teco, eziandio che ti costi un poco"; *ibid.*, 274.

58. *Ibid.*, 236f, 274, 277.

59. Most pronounced *ibid.*, 257ff; also 260, 271. On the following, *ibid.*, 253f, 263f, 283.

da bene peers with *da bene* fathers, not only for immediate gain but because the boys when grown would have to coexist with their age cohort. Second came *da bene* neighbors, living preferably in the ward and at least in the quarter. Third in importance were powerful men of the same area associated with the party in city hall. Finally, the boys should cultivate one special man of the type of Guido Del Palagio, which we have previously called an honorific resource.

All these social types required a more or less standard pattern of behavior. First and most important, the orphan should make himself visible. To make friends one had to be in the streets, saying good things about those he wanted to approach but could not, in the hope the word would get back to the potential patron.[60] Preferably, one made oneself available "day and night" to these resources and offered one's services without being asked—the very thing that Giovanni saw as suspicious when done to him.[61] In the presence of such people the boys should use those courtesies and words that would please the group, the language of "embassies" taught by the father, and should always be "mannered and reverent."[62] Gifts were a part of such courtesy, but Morelli urged moderation; overdoing anything was "bestial." Giovanni was clearly referring to the behavior of "new men" who thought they could win through ostentation what they in fact lost through grossness.[63]

In addition to waiting upon men outside his home, the ambitious orphan should spend substantial time and money entertaining them in his own home. The home for Morelli was essentially a ritual setting. Honoring outsiders by inviting them in, the young man will often ask them to dinner, ply them with good wine—Morelli specified different types for different occasions—and will do this not only in his urban residence but at the rural villa.[64] The public calendar played a role in this whole scheme. Morelli mentioned the feasts of Santa Croce and Sant'Onofrio, most important in the quarter of Santa Croce, as particular days when one should publicize one's efforts to build and solidify ties.[65]

The details are endless, but the reader has seen enough to ask what exactly Giovanni was telling his sons to aim for. Seeing him use the same methods toward others that he suspects when they are used toward himself, we might think he sought only to instrumentalize the naivete of others. But there is no evidence for this point of view. Morelli obviously did not think the powerful men he sought to cultivate had attained their position through stupidity. We hear him characterize friends and relatives as outsiders, only to discover that he sought to institutionalize ties through *imparentarsi*, through relating to others by godparenthood, as if such spiritual relationships were successful in reducing the willingness of either partner to harm the other.[66]

---

60. "E se non puoi per la via del parentado, fattelo amico in dire bene di lui"; *ibid.*, 274.

61. *Ibid.*, 253, 277f.

62. *Ibid.*, 257, 268, 276.

63. *Ibid.*, 253, 262, 272.

64. *Ibid.*, 237, 253, 260, 276.

65. *Ibid.*, 261.

66. *Ibid.*, 253, 263, 274.

Finally we find him advising his sons to spend money on these bonds as if their maintenance was more important than wealth and as if some profit had to yield to a higher good. If a friend persists more than two or three times in soliciting a loan, Morelli said, it may be best to give it rather than lose the friend.[67] If you are having trouble collecting a debt from someone favorably disposed to you, write it off if it is small rather than antagonize him.[68] What, in the end, was Morelli reaching and searching for?

The abandoned thirty-two-year-old sought something above power, or, better, he sought friends whose power was not based on mere force. He viewed social activity as more than the instrumentalization of fools. We have only to look at the zenith of the social pyramid that Morelli wanted to manipulate, and see how and why he wanted to cultivate the "Del Palagio type":

> Again, exert yourself to associate and be domestic with one (or with more) excellent man [who is] sage and old and without vice. And watch his modes of operating in words, in counsel, in the way he orders his family and his things. Take the lead, imitate him, and thus follow him and try to make yourself like him. Keep him always present in your mind, and when you do something, mirror yourself in him. If you are to speak before a [government] office or in some authoritative place, keep this capable man in mind, take heart and frankness from him and follow his style. Having him always in mind, you will choose the right ways and will not fall into vileness of spirit, and you will be open and daring, since you will always be comforted by his image.[69]

Is this not the father whom Giovanni had lost? Was he not telling his sons that they could find in society an authoritative image, frame, and gestural code, and that the image was like a father? Certainly it is significant that the best of social bonds was with a man characterized not by power but by wisdom, age, and virtue, like Giovanni's father who, it will be remembered, won his way through "reason and care, not at all through force of money."[70] Giovanni believed that the best friend was a father, a charismatic head, as had Mazzei in recommending first Guido Del Palagio, and then Niccolò Da Uzzano. Apparently the imitation of such men's behavior was a normal pedagogic practice, for Giovanni Cavalcanti also sought out a father from the same motivations:

> And because I was not skilled in understanding how the business of the republic was administered, I completely disposed my spirit to carry in it some rule of governing

---

67. *Ibid.,* 239f.

68. "Acciò non ti perdessi i danari e l'amico"; *ibid.,* 238f.

69. "Ancora, t'ingegna d'avere usanza e dimestichezza con uno o con più valente uomo, savio e antico e sanza vizio, e quello ragguarda ne' modi suoi, nelle parole, ne' consigli, nell' ordine della famiglia sua e delle cose sue; da lui imprendi, da lui appara, e così seguita e t'ingegna di somigliarlo: abbilo sempre innanzi e nella tua mente, e quando fai una cosa ispecchiati in lui. Se di' parole a ufficio o luogo autentico, abbi questo valente uomo innanzi, piglia cuore e franchezza da lui e seguita lo stile suo; e avendo sempre innanzi, tu piglierai que' propi modi e non verrai in viltà d'animo e starai franco e ardito, però che sempre sarai confortato dalla sua immagine"; *ibid.,* 283.

70. See page 163, this volume.

myself. And, as the least fallible, I elected the rule and art of distinguished citizen Niccolò Da Uzzano, the most reputed or rather most sage of masters.[71]

Such quotes help us understand what Giovanni Morelli sought in the outside world, and further clarify the ritual textures by which he sought to achieve his goal. Like Peter Delfin staring at the death mask of Traversari, Giovanni sought to "participate"—we shall meet this word again—in his honorable resource as the only way to win over both that resource and the other Florentines who depended upon him for their own limited value in an ignoble commune. Perhaps social ritual started without sentiment existing toward the objects of one's action, but positive social communication could not be effected until one had through formal behavior participated in the life of that resource: "Tell a lie near the truth, in such a way that you are believed, and not found out as a liar." But ultimately, avoid lying about yourself "like fire."[72]

Let us summarize our view of Giovanni Morelli on the eve of his greatest tragedy. An abandoned son without political office who looked back on his life and found unmitigated disaster, he mourned himself as the inevitable product of orphanage, living in a world that from mother to hired help was without love. Only between the father and the son could the link of trust exist.

Yet Giovanni did for his sons what his father had not done for him; he gave them the means to find friends, lovers, even a father, in case they should lose him. He taught them a formal code of behavior that could create love for them, and thus gave them a chance to love and speak in a world where obligations and love were inseparable. It was as though, through the ritual he taught his sons, Giovanni Morelli was trying to reconstruct a love he had never known.

The Son's Death

Three years later Giovanni had added little of a personal nature to his previous *ricordi*, concentrating instead on communal history of the time since his father had died. Then in May 1406 the tragedy struck and the besieged father characteristically inserted his recollection of Alberto's sickness and death into a description of the heavy taxes he had paid during the war against Pisa:

> In the midst of these times, so dark and unpleasant for me because of the indecent and uncalled for taxes that I have and have always had, or a bit before—on Monday morning the nineteenth day of May 1406—my first child Alberto took sick with nose bleeding.[73]

71. G. Cavalcanti, *Istorie Fiorentine* (Milan, 1944), bk. II, ch. 1.

72. Morelli, *Ricordi*, 252f.

73. *Ibid.*, 455.

Morelli described the horrible siege of seventeen days before the boy died in great pain on June 5. The boy could not eat, never slept, and was constantly in pain: "There is no heart so hard," Morelli burst forth, "which would not have pitied him, seeing him in such pain."[74]

> He commended himself repeatedly to God and to His mother the Virgin Mary, had the *tavola* of the Lady brought, and embraced it with so many expressions of penitence and with so many prayers and vows, that no heart is so hard not to be moved to great pity to see him.

The boy commended himself to his mother and father and to all the relatives present, but nothing helped. "None of the great help and the many prayers and vows helped. God wanted his life to end!"[75]

The death of Alberto seemed a model of decorous tragedy: a courageous boy, a room full of sorrowing relatives, and penitence on Alberto's part for his own sins. Yet there was one thing missing, something that would emerge later as perhaps the most fateful part of the tragedy. No priest had been present; the nine-year-old boy had not died in a sacramental setting.

The father who had been obsessed with the loss of fathers by sons had now been deserted by his son. Unarticulated at first, this frightening thought—or its reverse, that perhaps Giovanni had deserted the boy—would come to dominate his mind. For the moment, his recollection of these sad days was more conventional and idealistic. The boy had been ill since birth, yet he had conquered all adversity. On his own he had wanted to go to the shop at age four. At six he knew the Psalter; at eight he knew his Latin grammar. Alberto could write letters to his relatives, compose things in Latin and read merchants' letters. In every way excellent, this youngster had had a fine memory and speech, and good looks; he was genteel and well-mannered, but had a boy's shyness and impishness.

No wonder, thought Morelli, that his loss was an inestimable sorrow not only to his father and mother, but to everyone in the neighborhood, relatives, schoolmates, and the servants. Morelli closed his account of Alberto's death with the information on his burial, and with the following prayer:

> That God has reposed his soul in paradise, and that it please Him to give [continued] life to the father, to the mother, to the brothers and sisters, if it is for the best of their souls. If not, God's will be done.[76]

In other words, Morelli hoped that God had had enough, and that the family and first of all he, Giovanni, would not prove to be vessels of death for which Alberto had been only an omen. Several months later, Giovanni would again fear that his son's death had been but a premonition of his own.

Immediately after the boy's death, family members took the necessary steps to ease the hurt. They left the house for a whole month (that is, until the

---

74. *Ibid.*, 456.

75. "Idio volle avesse fine la sua vita"; *ibid.*

76. *Ibid.*, 457f.

St. Gregory Masses had been finished), avoided the room where Alberto had died for the rest of the summer, and the father himself did not go into the room for six months in order to avoid pain. "From the day he left us we alienated ourselves from thinking about him as much as it was possible to do so, except in prayer."[77] As he would later explain, Giovanni believed that through avoidance procedures the time would soon come when he would be able to feel warmth in thinking about the son, and not pain only; that he would in a sense feel close to, in warm communication with, the dead son. Despite his hopes and precautions, it did not happen that way.

Against all expectations, the pain of the boy's death did not subside in subsequent months:

> I never would have thought that God's dividing my son from me . . . would have been and is to me such a grave knife. . . . I cannot, nor can even his mother, forget. Instead we continually have his image before our eyes, remember his ways, his conditions, words and acts, day and night, at lunch and dinner, inside and out, sleeping and awake, at the villa and in Florence.[78]

And here Giovanni dropped a key phrase: "We think he is holding a knife that is stabbing us in the heart."[79]

What could it be? Why was it that Alberto in death seemed to be haunting and persecuting his parents, and especially Giovanni, who prayed God "that this not be a cause of hurrying the hour of our death."[80] Where was the warmth of sweet remembrance rather than the pain of loss?

The Holy Spirit

As the first anniversary of the death of the son approached, the pain and torment of the father became almost unbearable: "It seemed to me my soul with my body was tormented by a thousand lance tips."[81] The anniversary arrived, and Giovanni decided to do everything he could to end the torment, to pray so hard and well and correctly for his son that the son would stop hurting him. Morelli stated the purpose of his ritual undertaking at the beginning: "And seeing that in this world I could never be at peace with him, but hoping to communicate to his blessed soul some refreshment or at least some memory of me, [his] afflicted and suffering father. . . ."[82] He wanted,

77. This was specifically done so as not to think about the boy: "in quello volontariamente ci specchiamo, ma è il contradio; ca dal dì si partì da noi chi siamo dal pensiero di lui istranati quanto è possibile"; *ibid.*, 459.

78. *Ibid.*, 458. Branca gives the word *coltello* ("knife") the sense of "pain." See the same word, n. 79.

79. "Che noi istiamo e' ci tiene un coltello che ci passa il cuore"; *ibid.*, 459.

80. *Ibid.*

81. *Ibid.*, 476.

82. "E veduto che di lui mai al mondo potea essere contento, isperando pure di fare sentire alla sua be-

to use words we encounter later in the spiritual experience, to create a condition where "a word [said] in memory of [Giovanni] would content [Alberto] and of [Alberto, Giovanni]."[83] Giovanni therefore was about to undertake a ritual regimen intended to lead to communication with his son's soul. It would aim at establishing a relationship with Alberto that would end the torment seemingly caused by the son, and permit instead sweet painless memories of the type Giovanni had awaited in vain since Alberto's death. In the coming drama, not the least actor would be the devil, who would insist such spiritualistic communication was impossible, that the soul was a mere shade, that there was no way that a feeling man could contact an unfeeling soul whose body was ashes:

> He wanted to prove to me that my operation and effort had been in vain; that the soul was nothing or just a bit of shade, which could feel neither good nor bad except in an impassive way; that it doesn't see or sense; that it is affected by neither heat nor cold nor by any passion nor by any delight.[84]

Correlating these quotes, which are the heart of the nature of Giovanni's project, establishes beyond doubt that the purpose of the ritual prayers and the subsequent vision we will learn of was to end the father's travail, to contact his son and communicate fully with him, and to win over as a friend a son who since his death had shown himself an avenger.

Giovanni's torment was heightened by the fear that he had brought it upon himself, perhaps had even been responsible for the son's death. Denouncing his own failure in caring for his son, the father would later write:

> And in the end, when he was sick unto death, you didn't recognize that he was going to die because you weren't prepared to let him put himself at peace with God [in confession], [for you believed] that since he was young he would be forgiven [his sins].[85]

Though the Italian text is difficult, the meaning is clear: Giovanni should have had the boy's confession heard "so that a word said in memory . . . would content . . ." both. To make the point forcefully: The father believed that Alberto's pious behavior on the eve of death had not been enough for a good death. His soul had yearned for a sacramental and ceremonial death, but Giovanni had held back. Because of this neglect, Alberto had haunted the father: a classical case of imperfectly ritualized death.[86]

nedetta anima alcun rifrigero o almeno ricordanza di me affritto e tribolato padre"; *ibid.*

83. For the text, see n. 85.

84. "Volea mostrare la mia fusse istata vana orazione e fatica indarno operata, e che l'anima fusse niente o un poco di fiato, che bene né male potea sentire se non come cosa impassibile, che non vede né sente né è da caldo o da freddo o da alcuna passione o da alcuno diletto oppressata"; *ibid.*, 492.

85. "E utimamente, malato a morte, non conoscesti dovea morire per non ti fare contento di farlo acconciare con Domenedio, come che picciolo e scusato fusse, e acciò che una parola in memoria di te l'anima sua e d'esso la tua dovesse contentare"; *ibid.*, 501f.

86. Morelli had certainly violated no ecclesiastical law, since fourteen years was the most commonly accepted latest age for first confession; see for example Bernardino, *Prediche* (Florence, 1425), V, 40f. On

With this background in mind, we turn now to the prayer ritual that Giovanni undertook, one that shows the same propitiative and manipulative characteristics as the rituals of friendship he had recommended to his sons years before.

Giovanni first described the chronological setting for this ritual: a time one year to the hour and point (*punto*, a term with astrological associations) when Alberto's soul left his body. In Morelli's words, this was the point at which he would "participate" to the maximum in the bitter recollection of his son's death.[87]

He described his dress: a nightgown with knees bare, nothing on his head, and around his neck a *coreggia* or halter, which was traditionally used as a sign of desperation by which people pleaded for commiseration.[88]

Finally Morelli described what would be the object of his prayers and the instrument of his release: "the figure of the crucified son of God, to which [Alberto] many times had commended his bodily health." It was a traditional painting, with Mary and John the Evangelist on the right and left of the cross.[89] Thus Giovanni set about his spiritual exercise at the exact time of death and with the same "cross" that Alberto had embraced, determined not to think about himself but only about his departed son. In the course of the event, we will find him constantly embracing and kissing the images of Christ, Mary, and the Evangelist in the same places as his son had.[90] Domestic as was the setting and as personal as was the goal, the form was strikingly similar to that used by a confraternity during its "correction" on Good Friday. Morelli's behavior derived from the outside world of the street and chapel.

To achieve his spiritualistic goal, Giovanni divided his behavior toward each of the three images of Christ, Mary, and the Evangelist into three distinct and repeated procedures. At first he stared fixedly at the image or at some part of it (for example, when looking at the Crucified he concentrated on the wounds) and reviewed in his mind the sorrow the image in question had undergone, and then his own faults. The second procedure was profuse crying, which was the desired outcome of the gazing and contemplation, and occurred when his "heart and all the senses [had] come to the highest tenderness."[91] Only when these two procedures had been effected could the third and final procedure follow: prayers to each of the images begging the salvation of Alberto's soul. This outline of an obviously highly stylized ritual (whose authoritative source remains a mystery) permits me to comment on some of the more interesting and significant elements of this drama. Let us look at these procedures one by one.

the topos of the dead child who haunts because he died without ever having confessed, see J. Penli-käinen, *The Nordic Dead Child Tradition* (Helsinki, 1968).

87. "Che quanto più t'avvicini al male o al bene più ne diventi partefice, così, avvicinandomi io, misero, isventurato, ai dì e ore crudeli"; *ibid.*, 475, also 479.

88. *Ibid.*, 477.

89. "La figura . . . alla quale esso molte volte la salute del corpo raccomandata nella sua infermità avea"; *ibid.*, 476. Note that Alberto had commended himself *to the figure*.

90. *Ibid.*, 487, 491.

91. *Ibid.*, 477.

The reflective or contemplative procedure, called by Morelli *immaginare*, was intended to "dispose my soul and body and all my sentiments with more fervor and love."[92] It consisted essentially in looking at the suffering of the image and blaming himself for that suffering. When looking at Christ, for example, he was "looking into myself at my sins, in which I saw that I had harshly offended the son of God."[93] When looking at Mary, he "considers that my sins were the reason of such affliction."[94] And when gazing at the Evangelist, he said, "I am sorry for my sins because my iniquities are placed upon your shoulders."[95] Morelli's guilt in such divine matters was but the other side of his guilt over Alberto's fate. Thus while gazing upon Mary, "and remembering the suffering of my son which I had caused, I began to be greatly ashamed, so much that I almost had to give up praying."[96]

A second immediate goal of the contemplative procedure was to induce in Giovanni a sense of participating in the agony of the figured deities, because only through doing this could he hope to attain his request. Thus to Mary:

> Make me a participant in your sorrow and in your affliction, so that with full justice, participating in your afflictions, I will merit receiving a pledge of as much happiness as your son repurchased for us on the wood of the cross.[97]

Giovanni thought the deity in question granted this participation, and he realized it would have to be substantial before he could approach the deity. Thus in describing this procedure before the Evangelist:

> And taking on to myself a part of the pain of his affliction, not as much as I ought but that part which through grace was conceded to me, I thus turned toward the devout saint with the eye and with the heart and prayed: "O devout and most loyal saint. . . ."[98]

Evidently, this was the same procedure Giovanni had recommended for cultivating potential friends in this world: Participate with them in their happiness and sorrows; take on their identities, and thus win them over.

The crying that followed was unremarkable except that it was outside his control; though he wanted to cry, tears came to him from without.

The third procedure, the prayers, had several interesting elements. They too were structured. First came certain standard prayers, for Christ psalms and lauds, for Mary the Salve Regina (preceded by the sign of the cross), and for the Evangelist a part of that saint's gospel.[99] Then came an unofficial prayer to each of the three, extemporaneous but of course highly rhetorical

92. *Ibid.*, 476.

93. *Ibid.*, 477.

94. *Ibid.*, 484.

95. *Ibid.*, 489.

96. "Ricordandomi del dolore che io avea portato del mio figliuolo, forte me cominciai a vergognare e di poco meno che io non mi levai dall'orazione"; *ibid.*, 485.

97. *Ibid.*, 486.

98. *Ibid.*, 488.

99. *Ibid.*, 478, 485, 487f.

and possibly recommended to him by some unknown person or book. These extemporaneous prayers in each case apologized for past sin, asked for the favor of receiving his request, and closed with the request itself: the salvation of the soul of his son Alberto, which, as in the prayer to Christ, he called for at the hour and point of his death. That is, he asked that Alberto be saved one year from his death, to the instant.[100] In praying to Mary and John, Morelli also assured them that he had full faith in their ability to get what they wanted from God.[101]

The pronounced liturgical nature of the prayer was especially evident in the procedure followed in addressing the Crucified. It was essentially a series of conjurations:

> "And since because of my sins I am not worthy of such a gift [as the beatification of Alberto's soul], my lord, I ask you for it by the merit of your most holy incarnation"; and at this point I said the gospel of the annunciation of the Virgin Mary. "Again I pray you, my Lord, . . . by the merit and infinite gift of your most sweet and suave birth"; then I said His holy gospel [of the Nativity]. "Again I ask you it by the merit of the worthy words and works of your most delectable apostle Magdalene, through which she merited the grace of the resurrection of Lazarus her brother"; [this] while saying His holy gospel [about Lazarus].[102]

This liturgical pattern continued through five further conjurations, a rhythmic, almost hypnotic chant aimed at saving Alberto's soul through flattering Christ's achievements, inducing Christ's liberality by pointing up his unparalleled wealth of merits. And the attentive reader has noticed that the conjuration of Mary Magdalene was to the point: Giovanni was asking essentially the same favor as the Magdalene received for Lazarus; he too wanted to be with a loved one: "I wish that [Alberto's] soul be content in eternal life as much as, if it were possible, I would desire to again have his body alive on earth."[103] Giovanni seems to have believed that his own suffering at Alberto's hands since the boy's death was evidence that the boy was not in heaven after all: that only someone not in paradise could have haunted him as Alberto had. No other interpretation can be placed upon his words to Christ:

> that you command [his soul], by your special favor, to present itself to the sight of Your Most Holy Majesty so that its wish, [so] desired by it as a final goal, will be satisfied.[104]

Three summary points emerge from this description of Giovanni's ritual procedure thus far. The first requires no elaboration; the success of the ritual would depend on Giovanni's ability through formal procedures to convert

---

100. "Io ti priego che in questora e in questo punto l'anima del mio figliuolo Alberto, la quale in questora, fa un anno, si partì . . .', per tuo ispeziale dono, le comandi che si rappresenti nel cospetto della tua santissima maestà acciò che essa sia contenta dell' utimo fine da lei disiderato"; *ibid.*, 479f.

101. *Ibid.*, 486f, 490.

102. *Ibid.*, 480f.

103. *Ibid.*, 483.

104. See n. 100.

himself from one internal attitude to another or, stated differently, on his ability to identify with the person he was trying to obligate.

Second, Giovanni's success would rest upon the authority of the image and frame he was worshiping. Specifically, Giovanni, though a private person praying to Mary in his room for a private end, conceived both himself the devotee and the Virgin to be encompassed within a Florentine frame:

> We faithful Christians living in the city of Florence believe ourselves through your special gift to be acceptable to your sight although unworthy. And this has been demonstrated to us by you, most sweet mother, in the many graces which you have conceded through your mercy to our unworthy city. I take comfort in these facts, I too have recourse to your benignity and to your clemency.[105]

Finally, success depended upon the authority of the source from which Giovanni took his procedures and, almost as important, on his own ability in the extemporaneous part of the procedure to say things well. Giovanni asked the deity to forgive his "raw speech." He apologized in speaking to the Evangelist: "I know that reading the gospel you have composed of the most holy works of Christ would be more useful than the ignorant speech of me, sinner."[106] Giovanni admitted to "raw speech" when speaking to the Virgin as well. And in addressing Christ, he started by asking the latter to "concede to your little servant and faithful Christian enough of your infinite grace that I can say those words in praise and reverence of you which merit reaching through to your sight."[107] Yet he ended by fearing that they had done more harm than good:

> My Lord, pardon my ignorance, which has not been favorable but rather bothersome to my prayer. That [ignorance] has not allowed me to stand before Your Majesty with that due reverence and with those appropriate words.[108]

Such remarks are highly significant, for they show again that Morelli in his room knew that there was a better form for a better emotion than he, an ignorant merchant, had at his disposal. He feared in fact that instead of his ignorance making his prayers appealing to Christ, such *rozzo parlare* would bother him. This had been Francesco da Barberino's point of view. The most private experience imaginable turns out to be viewed as only successful to the extent one can verbally gesture in a socially correct way.

In fact—and this is perhaps most fascinating of all—there is little doubt that Morelli, like more illustrious men, was himself recording all these prayers and inflections as exemplary procedures that had worked. Why else did he carefully transcribe each prayer and movement, if not to pass on to his descendants this successful experience?

The success of the ritual still remained to be gauged. Giovanni instinctively felt that his prayer had been heard and, apparently to repay their

105. *Ibid.*, 486f.

106. *Ibid.*, 490.

107. *Ibid.*, 478, also 486, and 490 (*ignorante parlare*).

108. *Ibid.*, 483.

condescension, he seized the *tavola* repeatedly and, as he had earlier, kissed each of the three figures to whom he had prayed, and then said the Te Deum. Feeling happy and of good hope (doubtless that he would no longer be haunted by Alberto), he dressed for bed, climbed in, made the sign of the cross, and got ready to sleep.[109]

We now enter the second part of this eventful and dramatic scene. Giovanni rolled endlessly in bed, not sleeping, tormented by the Prince of Darkness. The devil wanted to convince him that Alberto's soul was untouchable and that his efforts had been in vain, and urged him to think about his own life and its unhappiness. With great confidence, the mourning father decided he was capable of withstanding Satan.[110] He deserted his earlier decision to think only of Alberto and not of himself, and now permitted Satan to lay out before him the miserable story of his own life. Giovanni noted that in the moment he agreed to think about himself, all turmoil passed.[111] His first thought was this:

> I have never had one hour of perfect happiness, and that, if something seemed to have been so, that it was not true, but that [the seemingly good event] had been [intended] to give me more pain and more torment.[112]

The clarity of paranoia evaporated the clouds of ambiguity and doubt. Lying in bed tempted by the devil, Giovanni now reviewed his life again in much greater detail, reflections that he later entered in his *ricordi* as a history of tragedy. He had started life with "not a little disgrace in the world" because he was the lastborn and thus last-dowered surviving child of Pagolo.[113] Your father, Giovanni heard Satan say, having died in your third year, you were "abandoned by the cruel mother" in the fourth. You lost much of what was rightfully yours, which your father had earned with so much effort. In the same year you were sick. Thrust upon the world of shops and schools in your fifth year, you lived for years in inner turmoil and torment, what with having to submit to a schoolmaster who beat into you fear and trembling. In your sixth year the orphan's taxes were multiplied by six. In the seventh year you were sick again. The schoolmaster's thrashing continued in the eighth year, and in the ninth you had pox twice and almost died. In your tenth and eleventh years the schoolmaster continued with a discipline much severer than schoolchildren have to endure today. In the twelfth year your maternal grandfather or "second father" died, and you were moved to Friuli under the governance of your stepfather, away from the villa and into city life; in the process, you lost perhaps one-half your estate.

Besides the themes that Giovanni had already made his own in earlier

---

109. *Ibid.*, 491f.

110. "Parendomi conoscere chiaro era il Nimico per inducermi a peccato e a errore, e di ciò parendomi essere sicuro, preso confidanza di me, disposi volere seguire d'intendere quello che nell'animo mio o alla memoria era appresentato"; *ibid.*, 493f.

111. "E come i' fu' così disposto, tutti quelli affuscamenti si partirono"; *ibid.*, 494.

112. *Ibid.*, 494f.

113. *Ibid.*, 494–497 for this and the following.

writing about himself, certain new ones emerged here, under the impress of his son's death, which sharpen the picture of paranoia. The beatings of childhood—described as almost identical to those suffered by Giovanni's father Pagolo—are striking, as is the previously unmentioned reference to illness. A third new theme was that Giovanni never had a normal childhood: an illness in his seventh year, the devil reminded him, "robbed you of the delightful times of your childhood"; the schoolmaster's beatings in your eighth year were "displeasing to childhood liberty."[114] A reflection upon the twelfth year bears the same message:

> And if you think about it, when you were at the age most delightful to [human] nature, you were already worrying about your financial condition. And seeing and feeling it getting worse day by day, you mentally exerted yourself a lot. And wanting to exert yourself to repair [the damage to the estate], you were greatly tormented by not being able to, not knowing how to, and yet wanting to.[115]

The history of Giovanni Morelli continued. From fifteen to twenty years of age one "outrage" succeeded another. "Your oldest sister died on you," Giovanni mused, and you had to pay a dowry to marry another sister; the wars forced high taxes on you; you were "outraged" by relatives and neighbors.[116] And you were sick for one whole year. In short, "you became a nuisance to yourself, to him who governed you, and to whomever knew you."[117] You fell in love and were about to marry the girl when she was taken from you and given to another. At this point you didn't know whether you were coming or going.[118] Your twenty-first year was an "inferno." Taxes were so high you had to sell properties to pay them and moved from one section of the city to another trying to obtain lower tax assessments.

Now you are in your thirty-fifth year. You have lost your holdings in the public debt and lost other properties to evil relatives. You are without money and relatives, and without any honor in the commune; you have had no political office. You do not know of a way to attain any of these things, and you receive no comfort or help from anyone. Your wife for instance comes from a proscribed family, so she has done you little good. You have had over the years sixteen mortal illnesses.[119]

What seemed to you the "best thing that ever happened to you"? The birth of your son.

> This has turned on you, into the greatest sorrow and into the greatest torment you have ever had. You acquired a male [child] so that your heart could be thoroughly broken. He grew up smart and vivacious and healthy so that you would be more tormented with greater pain through his loss.[120]

114. *Ibid.*, 496.

115. *Ibid.*, 498.

116. "E ti morì la sirocchia maggiore e maritati"; *ibid.*, 499.

117. *Ibid.*

118. "E non conoscesti ti fu ventura"; *ibid.*

119. *Ibid.*, 499f.

120. "Tu l'avesti maschio per farti bene crepare il cuore; tu l'avesti intendente e visto e sano acciò che con più pena fussi della perdita tormentato"; *ibid.*, 501.

Who or what was this unnamed force that gave Giovanni a son and made him healthy "so that" (*acciò che*), Giovanni would be tormented, masked something bad as good "so that" (*per fare*) the torture would be worse? Giovanni did not say it was his father, or his son, or the deities; like Cambi, who listed the saints on whose day misfortune fell, he remained noncommital and avoided the unpleasant search for one central enemy, sometimes through the passive voice: "You were completely abandoned by a prosperous future."[121] Yet the projection so evident in such language could no longer restrain Giovanni's acknowledgment of guilt—perhaps prefigured in the coincidence of Giovanni's sixteen mortal illnesses with the sixteen days of Alberto's agony—and he immediately burst forth a dirge of self-accusation:

> You wanted the best for him, and you never gave of yourself and contented him. You didn't treat him as a son but as an outsider. You never wanted to allow him an hour of repose. You never once showed him a happy face. You never once kissed him so that he thought it affectionate. You exhausted him at school and through many, repeated, and harsh beatings.[122]

Then you denied him confession, the chance to be at peace with God, and so

> You saw him die in dark, harsh, and cruel torments, and you never saw him have one hour of repose in the sixteen days the sickness lasted. You have lost him, and will never again see him in the world. And as a memory of him you remain constantly in fear and in torment of [losing] the other [children].[123]

A nuisance to everyone including himself, the father, it seems, had visited on his son what the father's father, through abandonment, had visited on Giovanni. All three were united through their beatings, Pagolo's and Giovanni's administered by outsiders, Alberto's the work of his father. These similarities were not pointed out, but Giovanni was evidently aware of them. The temptation of the devil had led to the brink of desperation:

> Representing these and many other painful and evil things to myself and reflecting on them, [I was] not far removed from resorting to suicide in order to put an end to so many adversities.[124]

The denouement approached. Giovanni's new biography of simultaneous paranoia and guilt was, like everything in this remarkable night, part of a structured undertaking leading to a resolution of the father's torment. Now Giovanni turned again to the Crucified, compared his own suffering to that of Christ and found himself fortunate indeed; he considered that even among those of the world he was not alone, since all men were tormented in

---

121. *Ibid.*, 494.

122. *Ibid.*, 501.

123. The only intervening text between these two

quotes is that on confession, for which see n. 85.

124. "Di poco meno che per porre fine a tante avversità i' non corsi in disperazione"; *ibid.*, 502.

one way or the other. His spirit at peace after this torment, he fell asleep. The stage was now set for the final act of this great undertaking.

Giovanni had slept soundly and without dreams for an hour when his spirit stirred and he experienced a vision while still in slumber. Before describing it, he averred that it had been granted to him through the inspiration of God and several saints: the Baptist (both Giovanni's namesake and the patron of Florence), St. Anthony (a popular saint who had helped the Guelf families of Florence overthrow the regimes of the Ciompi period), St. Benedict (a saint who had aided the commune when Giovanni was little more than a year old), St. Francis (a favorite saint of Giovanni's urban quarter of Santa Croce), and St. Catherine of Alexandria, Morelli's own particular saint and the central figure in the vision that followed.[125] These were the deities who would, through the dream, prove to him that his prayers had been answered, that Alberto was in heaven, that the boy's death had not been the father's fault, and that Giovanni still had many years of peaceful life ahead of him.

The vision was divided into two parts, the time before Giovanni felt himself lose all his sensations, and the time after that. The first part started with Giovanni at his *contado* house of Settimello, plagued by the ineradicable image of Alberto. To get rid of it he decided to exercise by walking toward Monte Morello, a high point in the area that besides (incidentally?) bearing Giovanni's family name, was home to a group of hermits living together in familial love.

During the first part of the climb up the mountain, the father, though "wanting both with the eye and with thought and with every act to think about other things," could only envision Alberto's image, and especially his own failure in his relations with his son:

> . . . my reproachments of him, my menaces, my failure to make him feel at peace, my alienating myself from him, the fact that I had taken little or no pleasure in him, and had given him little pleasure in me.[126]

Tormented by these "cruel things," Giovanni increased his pace till he was fairly rushing toward the mountain. Slowly he lost track of time and way and goal, and finally lost all his sensations.

With this spiritualization came a flood not of recrimination, but of sweet memories of the child's birth and early years. He remembered the place, and the day and the hour, at which "he had been generated by me," and how happy he and his wife had been.[127] He recalled how he had felt the boy growing in the womb, awaited the birth with anticipation, and then took joy in the fact that the child was male and healthy. The boy grew "from good to better," and Giovanni and his wife took much pleasure in his words and his love for his parents. As he grew his ability to "speak in embassy," answer

---

125. *Ibid.*, 503. Morelli does not himself allude to these civic associations.

126. "I miei rimproveri contro a lui, le mie minacce, il mio poco contentarlo, il mio istranarmi da esso, l'avere

io preso poco o niente di consolazione in lui, o a lui poca o niente appresentatagli di me"; *ibid.*, 504.

127. *Ibid.*, 504f.

well, read and write twice as well as was expected of him, and pray, delighted all. The proud-father image of this section clashed with his own guilt at ignoring the boy, and moved him to sit down, now some two miles along the road, and weep while he recalled again the boy's tormented death.

At this point he considered for a half-hour going to the monastery of hermits on the mountain, thinking that he would find contentment and peace if he remained with them overnight. While he was weighing this option, a bird flew down from the mountain and sang beautiful melodies. But as Morelli approached it, the melodies became first somber, and finally horrible to hear.[128] Giovanni fled toward the mountain, wanting to know whence the bird had come. On the way he was assaulted by a sow, which covered him with filth, an experience so bad he decided on the spot never to eat pork again. Finally he saw in the twilight distance two almost starlike lights. Arriving at their source, he knelt and prayed for an explanation. Suddenly, "as if a veil had been lifted from my eyes," Morelli was surrounded by a brilliant light. It was his special saint, Catherine.

Morelli recognized her immediately, of course, because she was young, and very white, her eyes were full of splendor, and she held in her right hand a palm and in her left a wheel with which she had completely cut up the sow of lechery Giovanni had encountered. This was the standard iconography of Catherine who, unlike monna Telda, had resisted all suitors; Giovanni had seen her in church hundreds of times. Seeking some explanation as to why he had been granted such a beatific vision, he asked Catherine to "make me a participant" in her virtue so that he could understand. Immediately, one of the birds that were circling around singing beautiful songs flew up to Catherine as if it wanted to be held in her hand. The heavenly woman placed her hand on the bird, which immediately changed into an angel, a beautiful spirit who was none other than Alberto. The father had succeeded in contacting the soul of his son.

Overcome with excitement, Giovanni ran toward the spirit crying: "My son! My Alberto!" But there was a difference between body and soul, and Giovanni drew back when he realized one could not embrace pure spirit, even if he could see, hear, and speak with it. Instead, he listened to the words of Alberto, who had received permission to speak from Catherine:

> Father, be comforted, for your prayers have passed the heavens and been accepted in the sight of our lord God. As a sign of this you see me here to console you. Put yourself at peace and hope in divine providence, and this benign lord will satisfy whatever just and honest questions you have.[129]

Giovanni would not only have the comfort of knowing his son was in heaven, but would be able to learn something of his own role in his son's

128. Branca says the bird's description fits that of the medieval bestiaries, and thinks the bird figure throughout is Alberto; *ibid.*, 507, 512.

129. "Vi darà consolazione delle giuste e oneste vostre domande"; *ibid.*, 514.

death, and consequently something of his own future. The two had been related from the start. Here are the questions he asked of Alberto after he had thanked God and Catherine for seeing Alberto "in a place of eternal salvation of your soul":

> Son, tell me if I through my sins am the cause of your being removed from the world. And tell me if I will be consoled in the world by your brothers, or if I can hope to have more [sons]. I also ask you, hoping in the virtue of God and [assuming I do not] contravene his sacraments other than as I did after you left me, if I can hope He will grant me a good status in the world, both in possessions and in communal honors. Finally [I ask] if I will have tò leave this life young or old.[130]

Alberto smiled and partly resolved the anxieties that had brought Giovanni to the mountain. Giovanni had not been responsible for Alberto's death: "Father of my body . . . , it pleased God to call me to Him for the salvation of your soul and family. The mode and form [of my death] were bitter to everyone, [but] this was due to my sin."[131] Giovanni could hope to retain his sons: "If you pray God to watch over those you have acquired, they will remain kind to you." He could hope to increase his status: "You have already had and will yet have many graces, if you recognize their source. . . . And you can expect to receive more favors than your merits deserve." Finally, he could hope to live long: "I counsel you to exert yourself to depart old. This would be your salvation and that of your family, and would please God."

The vision was all but concluded. Alberto closed with perhaps the most calming words possible, and went his way:

> "Before the majesty [of God] I will always be favorable to your needs and [to those] of my faithful and earthly mother. . . ." Which words having been uttered, every vision vanished. And I awoke, completely afrighted and partly happy.[132]

Giovanni had found a patron, even a father, in his son.

Postscript

Giovanni did live long, dying in 1444 at the age of 72. He did gain honor, holding a series of political offices, including the highest office of Standard Bearer of Justice. But it is unclear if the man changed. Sometime around 1421 his second wife walked out on him, and Giovanni, forced by the government to pay her fifty-six and one-half florins a year, complained bitterly that "this

---

130. *Ibid.*, 515.

131. "Il modo e la forma è suta amara a tutti, e questo per lo nostro peccato"; *ibid.*, 516. The *nostro* probably refers to Alberto, but could refer to both Giovanni *and* Alberto, or impersonally to all humans.

132. "Dinanzi all quale Maestà sempre sarò favorevole ai vostri bisogni e della mia fedele e carnale madre. . . . Le quai parole dette, isparì ogni visione; ed io mi destai tutto ispaventato e 'n parte allegro"; *ibid.*

burden is killing me."[133] Doubtless, Giovanni Morelli was not an easy man to live with. Yet how tortured was his life. In the same year 1421 he again took up his pen to make a last entry in his book, the record of the death of his second-born son, Antoniotto. The short memoir notes that the boy had been "confessed, communed, and oiled"—as Alberto had not been. It tells us little about Giovanni's feelings about this new tragedy, but perhaps enough to allow the reader to guess whether the man had changed. The boy had been sent to a town west of Florence, where he fell sick:

> God did not want him to go there, or [did not like] my negligence, so that I suffered more. . . . Christ take his soul [into heaven]. Give [my other sons] a long and good life with male children and good Christian females, so that I am worthy not to see the death of the others. Let this please God who is the donor of every good and of every favor. Amen.[134]

133. "Monna Andrea mia donna partita da me delgli ani 6 e più, per sue chagio[ni], e per mezo dela Singnoria, cioè de' nostri Signori, feciono le desi l'ano fiorini 56 e 1/4, la quale graveza m'ucide"; this information is not from the *ricordi*, but from Giovanni's estate declaration of 1428 (*ASF, Catasto*, 72, f. 131v) and was generously passed on to me by Gene Brucker. Morelli had obviously been living without a wife all this time, but not without female ministration; he declared an illegitimate son Fruosino as a deduction, born Mar. 5, 1428.

134. "Non volle Idio v'andassi, o la mia nigrigenzia, per più mio dolore. . . . Cristo abbi l'anima e me faccia degno non vedere la morte degli altri, prestando loro vita lunga e buona, con figliuoli maschi e femmine buoni cristiani. E così piaccia a Dio donatore d'ogni bene e d'ogni grazia. Amen"; *ibid.*

Chapter 6

Brothers and Sisters

*Coming from persons of such great
religion, these prayers are more useful
than are two thousand horses.**

Sources usually need interpretation. The Mazzei–Datini
correspondence remains impenetrable unless analyzed, and the ritual activity
and vision of Giovanni Morelli make little sense without careful study. Other
texts, however, stand best alone; indeed, glossing can detract from their
meaning and power. This chapter offers the initiated reader such a selection,
with little gloss.

The documents excerpted here deal with small-group ritual, and represent a continuation of our search for common elements of formal behavior in
different civic settings. We have already witnessed two friends communicating with each other, and an individual talking with deities and a dead son;
now we enter the convent to watch religious persons manipulating each other
to extend their identity beyond the group. The community of friars and the
cloistered nuns we shall observe are not, however, microcosmic units creating
their own meaning and their own dynamics unaffected by the outside world.
They are social units; the citizens will be found peering into the friary to find
ideal form at work; and we will see the nuns acting to counter inside the evil
of the world outside.

The two sets of translations come from a later phase of our period, and

*Cited in Trexler, "Le Célibat," 1329.

refer at times to practices that cannot be documented earlier. But the ritual mechanisms at the base of these practices do reflect Florentine culture as a whole, not that of any particular instant of time. How these nuns and friars interacted is characteristic of earlier periods as well as of their own. The first set of documents demonstrates how Savonarola and his friars through ritual formats created fraternal life together in the years 1494–1498. Its anonymous author was a young man or boy who participated in the events he described.[1] The second set of records describes the formal activities of nuns' life in common. The setting is the mid-sixteenth-century Dominican nunnery of San Vincenzo in Prato, a house under the continuing influence of the martyred Savonarola. The selections are taken from fra Serafino Razzi's 1591 biography of the nunnery's star attraction, the mystic Caterina de' Ricci.[2] Both authors' words had hagiographic intent. Yet both of the settings they described have the unmistakable ring of truth.

San Marco

EVENING RECREATION AT THE FRIARY

While [the friars] sang psalms and hymns in the evening, [Savonarola] often had a [friar] come in the form of little Jesus.[3] He having sat down in the middle, [the friars] made a circle around him. Each [then] donated him his heart, or had someone else donate it for him. [Each] asked some favor for himself and for others, as for example that God would grant him that such and such a layman would come to the service of God in holy religion. Sometimes they got together an embassy to the Lord from among the [friars] present to ask for some favor or preparation for some upcoming feast.[4] And often they had the Virgin brought, calling her "our *mamma*." And here

1. On the position of the anonymous author, see the Introduction to Ps. Burlamacchi, ix–xi. The population of the friary ranged between 200 and 300. An age profile is not easily available, but there were many novices and young friars of fourteen, fifteen, and sixteen years of age. Perhaps one-half of the census was made up of teenagers, drawn into San Marco by the charisma of Savonarola. The integration of these adolescents into the life of the friary was one of the main purposes of the activities described here.

2. For Razzi, see Di Agresti's Introduction to Razzi, *Vita . . . Caterina de' Ricci*. The editor has compiled the entry and death age of the nuns of S. Vincenzo, showing, as I indicated earlier in this volume (Chapter 1, n. 84), that most girls were twelve to fifteen years of age when given their habits; G. Di Agresti, *S. Caterina de' Ricci. Cronache-Diplomatica-Lettere Varie* (Florence, 1969), lxxiv.

3. That is, dressed up as Jesus presumably looked. This passage is from Ps. Burlamacchi, 46. The practice of dressing clerks to look like biblical figures was

ancient and incorporated into the liturgy; for an old case in Florence, see Davidsohn, *Storia*, I, 1065. Generally on the practice see O. B. Hardison, Jr., *Christian Rite and Christian Drama in the Middle Ages* (Baltimore, 1965). Whether these theatrical elements of the liturgy had survived in fifteenth-century Florence is uncertain. Perhaps Savonarola's devotion was a monastic adaptation of the lay *sacre rappresentazioni* instead of a continuation of the liturgical tradition. A. D'Ancona, *Origini del Teatro Italiano*, 2 vols. (Turin, 1891), II, 157–162 takes the former view, seeing clerical *rappresentazioni* as decadent forms of a lay innovation.

4. "The Lord" means the exposed host or, less probably, an image of Christ. The interchangeableness of a live or inanimate representation of Christ is shown in the writer's easy passage from one to the other. The use of the "embassy" as a central educational method was noted in Chapter 5. It emerges here to teach ritual attitudes and gestures toward divine images. The mental link between embassy to a temporal and spiritual lord is evident in the text.

they would bestow many honorific titles on Him as a means of thanks, like "Sweet Jesus," or "Jesus Saint of Saints." The novices would repeat each, and then they would start with another [title]. They did the same for the Virgin Mary mother of God, saying: "Beautiful Virgin," "Gracious Virgin," "Virgin Mother of Mercy," and [then] each would yell the title.[5] And in this fashion they spent their time usefully, exercising their bodies.

THE EPIPHANY PROCESSION OF 1498

And in the year 1498 [Savonarola] held another procession within the octave of the Epiphany.[6] In it all the friars were dressed in sacred vestments: the acolytes in whitest surplices decorated with gold and silk; the subdeacons in tunicles; the deacons in dalmatics; and the priests in chasubles.[7] Just three of the latter [also wore] the most beautiful copes decorated with silk and gems and gold. They were first the servant of God fra Girolamo [Savonarola], second fra Francesco Salviati the prior of San Marco, third fra Domenico da Pescia prior of [San Domenico di] Fiesole. At the head of the procession came an acolyte dressed in a very beautiful surplice, and this was fra Jacopo Gucci.[8] He looked like an angel, who carried on a pole a most beautiful star. The whole multitude of friars followed him.

After these [friars] came those three with the silk copes, made up to look like the three Magi, and they sang in a high voice according to the mode of the psalm this verse: "Where is he who has been born king of the Jews?[9] For we have seen his star in the East." And the friars who were in front of them all responded in the same mode [with] this verse: "In Bethlehem of Judea, for so it is written by the prophet." And singing in this fashion, they searched for the [new]born little Jesus throughout the friary. When they came into the church they drew near the wall on one side and the other, half [on the side] as one stands when the Salve is sung after compline, but more spread apart so that they would be against the walls of the church. There they sang matins and did three stations, one in the lower part of the church, the women's part, one in the choir of the laymen, and the third in the choir of the friars.

And while they celebrated matins, certain young [friars] dressed up like angels went to the crib, took the little Jesus, put him on a prepared portable altar, and placed him in the middle of the lower church.[10] They said in chant: "This is the lord whom you [the Magi] sought, and the angel of the testament whom you wanted." And the

5. "The Virgin" means an image. Note the care in spelling out the titles that this authoritative group of holy men and boys used in addressing different deities; obviously, verbal gestures were here being recorded for subsequent use by persons who wanted to copy San Marco.

6. The text reads 1497, which is 1498 in the common calendar. The original text is in Ps. Burlamacchi, 117f.

7. The finery was in marked contrast to the friars' normal Mendicant habits. Obviously, they were dressed to seek out the newborn Christ Child, and one recalls Botticelli's *Adoration of the Magi*, in which one of the kings wears ecclesiastical garments.

8. Jacopo was the seventeen-year-old son of a Florentine merchant father and a Scotch mother, and was born in Scotland. As an only child he represented a particularly selfless paternal offering and may have been placed in front for this reason. At the time of the procession he was a novice; he made his

profession Mar. 12, 1498; *Biblioteca Laurenziana, fondo Biblioteca di San Marco*, cod. 370: *Chronica Conventus Sancti Marci de Florentia*, ff. 98r, 159r (hereafter *Chronica . . . S. Marci*); *Archivio del Convento di San Marco, Liber Vestitionum*, at the year 1496. I would like to thank the friary for access to its library and archive.

9. The liturgical search in the friary and the church for Jesus was ancient, but doubtless Savonarola's staging was affected by the rich tradition of Magian processions in Florence; see page 298, this volume.

10. It would be interesting to know whether the angels wore wings and whether the scene with the portable Christ Child from the crib resembled the paintings of the age; many of the scenes described here and subsequently in this chapter have a strong pictorial quality. On the question of the chronological relationship between developments in festivals and pictorial art, see G. Kernodle, *From Art to Theatre* (Chicago, 1944); Baxandall, *Painting*, 71–78.

friars responded: "My God, my God, is it you?" Then one of the three Magi took the little child Jesus and, beginning on one side with the friars who stood along the wall of the church, gave [him] to all [one at a time] to kiss the child's feet, singing that verse of the Canticle: "My delightful one clean and red, elected from the thousands." To which the friars responded: "My lord and my God."

When this was finished, everyone went to the second part of the church [and] arranged themselves as before, and sang the lauds, the portable altar with the little Jesus being in the center. The lauds finished, the second of the Magi took the child Jesus in his hands saying in chant: "Fasciculus myrrhe dilectus meus mihi, inter ubera mea commorabitur." And having entered the choir of the friars, he gave [little Jesus to each of the friars] to kiss his little hands. And having entered into the choir, the *Pretiosa* being terminated, the third of the Magi took the little Jesus in his hands, and [then] gave [him] to all of the friars to kiss His holy mouth, singing: "Obsculetur me obsculo oris sui."[11]

Then with torches lit and red crosses in hand, all the friars went to the refectory to dinner, and while they ate someone preached from the pulpit. Such was the fervor and joy of the friars in those days that their hearts burned for love of Jesus. And laymen, even some of [Savonarola's] enemies, ran to peek through cracks in the church doors, and seeing, came away filled with the same fervor.[12] The servant of · God fra Domenico da Pescia had the same thing done at Fiesole and, in a similar way, fra Antonio di Olandia, the prior of San Domenico di Prato, consoled his friars in his friary.[13] One used many other diverse means to ignite and inflame the hearts of the friars in love of Jesus, which for the sake of brevity I will omit. You may conclude this: that paradise was in these friaries, and [that] such spirit descended to earth that everyone burned in love, and the friars could say: "Blessed are the people who know joy."

San Vincenzo

A VISIT BY THE AUTHOR

After having confessed and communed, the sisters sing a solemn Mass of the Madonna. And in the evening they hold a devout procession through all the principal places of the monastery with the said Virgin, with lights and songs. And in the present year 1591 the writer of these narrations, fra Serafino Razzi master of holy theology and their confessor, was present in the church, outside however. With much spiritual content he heard and saw through the grate the said holy procession when it left and when it returned to the church. The aforesaid glorious Virgin [was] of natural and average height for a woman, richly dressed, [and] placed upon a certain litter. She was carried by four or more sisters, with an abundance of lights and the most devout songs and psalms, hymns and devout lauds in Italian.[14]

11. There is some confusion in the movements. Apparently the rite was divided into three parts executed by different kings, in each part one gift of gold, frankincense, or myrrh being bestowed, with first the feet, then the hands, and finally the lips of the image being kissed.

12. The enormous impact and the authority of the rites in S. Marco are mirrored in this detail. The urban friary not only fulfilled its role as a center for saving

grace complete in itself but informed the lay city what rites could be followed to purify it.

13. Here again is the phenomenon of exactly reproducing the ritual of one house in that of the other houses. We have already seen that the ritual of the city was ordered performed in the same fashion and at the same time in the cities of the dominion; see page 5, this volume.

14. Razzi, *Vita*, 35. Note that the terrible sack of Prato

DRESSING SISTER MARIA DA REGGIO

And it sometimes happened that when the sisters dressed her up on Good Friday as a widowed Virgin, and placed dead Jesus in her arms to represent the day's mystery, she, because of her noble and pious contemplation, fainted. [It was] the same manner that some believe had come over the glorious mother of God, Mary always Virgin, when her blessed son, dead, was taken down from the cross and put in her arms. One also tells how one day this sister Maria da Reggio had gone with her companion into the garden to pray to a large wooden cross that is placed in a certain part of [the garden], in memory of the passion of our Lord. Having arrived and prayed, she went into ecstasy of spirit with her eyes open. After some time her sense returned, and she told her companion how she had seen Jesus in the said cross, so full and covered with blood that it was heartbreaking to see him. And this semblance was impressed so fixedly in her heart, that she then painted him with her own hand; and afterward she and other persons painted so many similar crucifixes, that till the present day many are to be found.[15]

THE PROCESSION OF THE SUNDAY BEFORE
CARNIVAL AND LENT, 1549

The Sunday of Quinquagesima of the year 1549, the third of March, Sunday of Carnival, one wanted to hold a procession, as was customary in the nunnery, to placate God toward the sinners who are accustomed to offend Him so much during this time.[16] [Thus] the mother sister Caterina [de' Ricci] was asked by the father confessor and by the nuns to be willing to represent in her person our Lord in passion, when he carried the cross to Mount Calvary.[17] She who was always most obedient condescended and submitted to the wish, especially to [that of] the mother prioress. She was dressed in a red gown that reached to the feet, [which was] wrinkled at the top around the neck, and was tied with a green belt. The diadem was put on her, [as was] a suitable cross on her shoulders, and also a false beard on her chin: similar to that which it is thought and written was that of our Lord.[18] Dressed therefore in this

had occurred on the traditionally inauspicious feast of the decapitation of St. John, but that the feast was celebrated in this nunnery as a happy day. This indicates the highly corporate concept of divinity; what was bad for Prato was good for a nunnery within it. The phenomenon of dressing the statue of the Virgin must be seen in comparison to the dressing of sister Caterina referred to repeatedly in subsequent pages.

15. *Ibid.,* 47. The true-to-life theatrical impulse is particularly marked here: Mary looked just as she did at the time of the Passion; an image of the dead Christ is placed in her arms: the pictorial Pietà motif seems to have been exactly reproduced. The important fact that the nun is transformed so that she literally looks like Mary in action will be reencountered subsequently. Here the emphasis is upon her participating so much in Mary that she started to be like her. Later the emphasis will be upon the effect this transformation had on the observing nuns. Finally, the initial dressing of the nun was a first step leading to that transformation.

16. Savonarola had used this approach: countering

within the evil without; see page 473, this volume. The source for this procession is Razzi, *Vita,* 164f. Significantly, this and all the accounts translated subsequently were omitted from several of the manuscripts and printings of Razzi's *Vita.*

17. On the common performance of women in *sacre rappresentazioni* in the sixteenth century, see D'Ancona, *Origini,* I, 403ff.; II, 157–162. It must always be kept in mind that Caterina was a mystic and apparently fell into trances at the beginning of each such event. Thus the nuns chose from among themselves not only their most famous colleague, on whose charisma the material well-being of their house depended, but a woman who was otherworldly throughout the drama, directly in touch with the numinous.

18. Caterina's clothing corresponded to scores of contemporary paintings of Christ in passion; the use of Christ's beard makes for an exact replica. On her wearing Christ's hair, see page 194, this volume. It cannot be stressed enough that reproducing the pictorial scene was assumed to increase the power of Caterina to affect herself, the sisters, *and* God.

fashion and with a crown of thorns on her head, she entered the choir of the church, where all the sisters were congregated. She was between two angels, one of whom carried the column and sponge, [and] the other carried the lance and nails. Having posted herself then on the presbytery on the right side of the altar along with the two angels, the holy procession started, which was carried throughout the nunnery. Since the servant of God Caterina had gone into her usual ecstasy, it was majestic to see her thus walking along with the said cross on her shoulder, the sisters singing psalms with much fervor and spirit.[19]

[The nuns] having then returned to the church, the suffering Jesus stopped on the right side of the altar from whence he had departed.[20] With her face turned toward the sisters, she beckoned them, even though she was alienated from her senses, to come to kiss the cross she carried, in which was embedded a particle of the true cross.[21] The reverend prioress was the first, and after she had kissed the said cross, [Caterina–Jesus] put it on her shoulder and wanted her to embrace it with both hands. She did the same to all the other sisters, [therewith] signifying to one after the other that they had to carry their various crosses as Jesus had. And to one nun who seemed hesitant to take the said cross, she said: "Take it, daughter, for my cross is not heavy, but light and sweet." And to some others she said that they should take their hands out from beneath their scapulars and take it themselves. Then after all the sisters had adored the cross in this way, she turned to the reverend father confessor—who was permitted to be present at that time, and who carried the most holy sacrament in the aforesaid procession—[and] gave him the same cross to kiss. Then she placed it on his shoulder and wanted him to hug it tightly with both hands.[22] Finally [after] she herself had kissed, embraced, and hugged it with indescribable affection, [and] placed it upon her shoulder for a little while, she left the church with the two angels. And when she came onto a certain terrace that was close in to the church at that time, she awoke from the ecstasy she had been in during the whole time of the aforesaid procession.

And these were the diversions that the virgins of this nunnery engaged in at the very time when laypersons usually almost go mad and give themselves over totally to the search for excess, vanities, and sins—that is, they represented the mysteries of the passion of Christ. . . .[23]

THE PROCESSION OF THE FEAST OF THE ANNUNCIATION, 1549

On the twenty-fifth of March, the beginning of the year 1549 in Florence, the *madonna* prioress considered how greatly the sisters were spiritually excited toward divine love

19. Thus the image around which these nuns' spirits were raised above normal experience was one that, though eminently familiar to them as that of a sister, during the period of the common ritual was numinous and itself oblivious to its surroundings. The most powerful force in the nunnery was a creature of the lesser sisters who had dressed her, pointed her perambulations, and fed off her divine condition.

20. Here Razzi as later changes from the feminine to the masculine gender. The writer himself describing the event becomes a participant in the illusion.

21. This was done either to heighten its power, one suspects, or to eliminate any concern that the nuns were too much adoring a piece of wood.

22. It is interesting that the exposed body of Christ

carried by the nunnery's confessor seems to have taken a back seat, in terms of reverence paid, to Caterina–Jesus. But see page 193, this volume, for another type of behavior toward the host in one of these processions.

23. Razzi's concluding statement shows the double purpose of the procession, comparable to those of the processions in Savonarolan San Marco. First, the procession was a form of diversion intended as a substitute for the cloistered nuns who could not participate in the traditional joys of Mardi Gras. Second, this diversion became an effective foil to the sinfulness of secular events, and essentially neutralized God's ire. It did this by converting make-believe—itself a memorial pleasing to the divinities—into a participatory reality in which the nuns felt themselves sinners accompanying Christ to the cross.

when they saw mother sister Caterina, who was still in the flower of her years, dressed like a saint in processions.[24] [Therefore] she wanted [Caterina] to represent the Annunciate Virgin on this day. When it happened that she having been dressed very prettily in white, and sister Maria Maddalena degli Strozzi [having been dressed] to look like the archangel Gabriel, [Caterina–Mary] entered church in much majesty, accompanied by two angels and four archangels richly dressed and adorned, and by the holy procurators and advocates of the nunnery.

And the procession proceeded in this order: S. Caterina da Siena went in front with the crucifix between two angels who carried the lamps. Next came the sisters two by two. After them came S. Orsola and S. Agnese martyr side by side,[25] and after them came the archangel St. Gabriel very well dressed, bearing his lily in hand.[26] Then came the glorious Virgin Mary between two archangels who held up the sides of her rich silk mantle. And she held an open book in her hand, in which one read in large letters: "Thus the Virgin conceives." Lastly came the father confessor with the most holy sacrament between two other archangels with lamps.[27] In the instant the procession got under way in this order, the servant of God Caterina went into mental ecstasy. To the greatest consolation of all the sisters, she remained so the whole time the aforesaid procession lasted. For they saw her changed in a certain way, her face transformed into the grace and beauty one thought the Virgin had.[28]

The father [confessor] stopped at every station with the most holy sacrament and blessed the sisters with it. The Annunciate Virgin, she too, reverently adored it and then, having stood up, gave her benediction as well to the nuns.

When they then returned to church, and the father confessor had replaced the most holy sacrament in the ciborium, the Virgin sat down on a rich seat prepared [for her] on one side of the altar.[29] On the other side, the archangel Gabriel, after having paid her due reverence [through genuflecting], greeted her and spoke to her some of the stanzas apropos of the mystery.[30] The Virgin having herself spoken what pertained to her, she stood up. The sisters [then] brought her a little Jesus from the crib and she, taking Him and adoring Him with the highest humility and devotion, wept over Him while all the said saints and sisters knelt behind her.[31] Then raising herself up and standing between the saints [Orsola and Agnese] and the angels, she gave the said Jesus to the father confessor to kiss, and then to all the sisters. During the whole time she remained in ecstasy and her face was resplendent with a divinity I cannot express, which enraptured all hearts into love.[32]

24. Here the pedagogic goal of the processions is clear: Caterina insensate and transvested became a prime means of forming inner states. The source for this procession is Razzi, *Vita*, 165f.

25. That is, Sts. Ursula and Agnes as mentioned later: two of the patrons of the nunnery. Each of these characters was of course iconographically correct, bearing her traditional distinguishing sign.

26. It is noteworthy that the saints—as distinct from the angels—were all female in this nunnery presentation.

27. That is, the presence of God.

28. This is the clearest statement of the function of these processions. The sisters' "spiritual excitement" depended on Caterina's uninterrupted insensateness; she had to be the opposite of profane. As seen earlier, this condition was thought a precondition for her participating so much in a deity as to be transformed in her gestures. Now in this passage we find the nuns consoled when the face itself became

recognizably that of the Virgin they knew from paintings and literary traditions. On which, see Baxandall, *Painting,* 57f.

29. Apparently, the host had been carried naked in the procession.

30. That is, the gospel text of Luke on the Annunciation. It is fascinating that both in the Ps. Burlamacchi account of the Epiphany procession and Razzi's accounts of the Passion and Annunciation, there is little emphasis upon the historical re-creation taking place, and much more upon the staging action and the processional activities. Thus here Razzi does not say that Mary and Gabriel played out a historical moment, although we clearly have a pictorial re-creation of that scene, but speaks only of appropriate stanzas, leaving the reader to determine that it was here that the gospel scene was actually re-created.

31. Again the child-Jesus image from the crib is used dramatically. It is unclear whether the nuns cried for joy or, knowing the child's fate, in sorrow.

32. Most directly: It was Caterina's transfigured face

Happy servants of God and fortunate above many other nuns, who enjoyed for such a long time the sweet and holy company of this terrestrial angel [Caterina]! She brought them daily so many gifts, favors, fervor, and consolations, and she allowed them to pass this life, usually so tedious and bothersome, without any disgust, always occupied with similar holy exercises.

After all the sisters had kissed and adored Jesus, the archangel Gabriel said: "Jube domne benedicere," and they [then] sang a happy and devout compline.

THE NUNS ELECT THEIR PATRON SAINTS

A procession similar to this one was also held other years at the beginning of the year, at the Annunciation. It was the custom at this time for the sisters with much simplicity to put the procurators and the holy advocates of their nunnery to the vote. Usually they passed all of them with great favor, with all the votes being black [beans], which signify "yes" at Florence.

But it happened one year that when Jesus was put to the vote, a white bean was found in the bag, a contrary vote. It was believed that the good sister [Caterina] had confused her vote and given a white instead of a black [bean]. Or perhaps she did not want to accept Jesus as procurator and advocate of the nunnery for some other reason, as much as she like the others recognized Him and revered Him as patron and lord not only of their house, but of the whole world. But the nuns did not err in selecting Him procurator, for it is written of Him in the gospel: "The Lord of the vineyard said to his procurator: Call the laborers and pay them their wages." Matt. 20:8.[33]

THE PROCESSION OF THE FEAST OF ST. AGNES, 1553

On the twenty-first of January, 1553, the feast of S. Agnese virgin and martyr, the sisters who arranged the feast on that day wanted to give the whole nunnery some particular contentment of spirit. With the help of their father confessor and the mother prioress, they therefore arranged to hold a solemn procession in which, along with other saints and angels, the servant of God sister Caterina would take part, representing Jesus at the age of twelve years.

[Caterina] was then dressed by mother sister Maria Maddalena Nardi in a garment of red satin reaching halfway down the legs. She then put on her a lovely wig of real curly hair, which reached down beneath the ears, and on top a make-believe light royal crown. In her left hand she held an orb signifying the world, with a little cross on top, and in her right hand she carried a gilded scepter. On her feet she wore a pair of low leather sandals decorated with gold and silver, like those of the apostles.[34]

And the aforementioned mother sister Maria Nardi, [now] seventy years old, narrated to the writer of this life, master Serafino Razzi, how the mother sister

that reduced the nuns to a common spiritual state. The cadenced bestowal of an image-doll to each nun functioned of course to weld the nuns together as well, as each nun's identity poured into the image by the caressing. The phenomenon is similar to military flag ceremonies, where the flag becomes increasingly sacred as it moves through more and more hands, the hands handling the object ever more gingerly.

33. This remarkable document needs little comment; patron saints were obviously dependent upon the good will of their clients. Though stylized, the ritual preserved real meaning. The fact that the patrons

were apparently voted upon on a regular calendrical basis is even more striking; Razzi, *Vita*, 166f.

34. The pictorial quality of the figure is patent, as is the by now familiar attempt to match the dress to the age of the figure (long hair, but not the beard Caterina wore when she represented Christ in passion). Art historians will be able to state whether the accoutrements of the orb and scepter carried by the teaching Christ were already in the iconographic tradition, appeared subsequently, or represent an overlay upon the basic theme that is not represented pictorially. The source of the procession is Razzi, *Vita*, 172f.

Caterina while she was being dressed as Jesus went into ecstasy for a little while, so that it was easy to dress and arrange her as [Nardi] wanted. For [while in ecstasy] she did not object to anything, as she did at other times.[35]

In addition they dressed up mother sister Maria Maddalena Strozzi, [Caterina's] custodian, in the person of the Virgin, in red damask with a little brocade coat and a long veil over it, and a crown on her head. And they dressed mother sister Maria di Jacopo Cini up in the person of S. Agnese in white damask with a little brocade coat and a veil over it, with a diadem and a silk garland on her head.[36]

The aforementioned sisters having been dressed in this fashion, they came into church behind two angels. There the other sisters were gathered with the reverend father prior fra Taddeo Bartoli then prior of San Domenico, and the father confessor fra Francesco Dardinelli. Jesus stood in the middle, his mother on the right and S. Agnese on the left.[37]

And the Salve Regina having been sung after compline—which is said right after vespers—the procession got under way through the principal places of the nunnery, psalms and hymns being sung. And the countenance of the servant of God Caterina, as usual rapt in ecstasy, changed. A certain great majesty shone in her face that both frightened and contented the nuns.[38]

When she arrived at the dormitory, she said: "Here silence is observed"; at the refectory: "One should not complain about the food"; at the infirmary: "Here one exercises charity." At the work hall He turned to his mother and said: "Here they praise me and you."[39] Then they returned to church. The sisters prostrate on the ground begged mercy of Him, for it seemed to everyone that he had penetrated their inmost heart. Therefore he turned to them and told them he wanted them to ask him for pardon and mercy not as [might be done] in a feast or representation, but in truth, and with the whole heart.[40]

Then he sat down in the presbytery, and had his virgin mother sit on his right and S. Agnese on his left. And [Caterina–Jesus] remaining all the time in ecstasy, all the sisters went one by one to pay him respect, and he gave each of them a little painted Jesus that embraced a bullfinch.[41] [At the same time] he told [each of] them to follow him and his mother, commanding them for her, embraced each of them and sent them back to their place. The said painted Jesuses having been distributed and all the sisters genuflecting before Jesus, the glorious Virgin, even she, got up from her chair and, taking the crown from her head, prostrated herself on the ground before her son, commending the aforesaid sisters and the nunnery to him. But he immediately touched her with the scepter, almost like another Ahasuerus [raising] the

---

35. This is perfect evidence of Caterina's simultaneous power and helplessness. Her divine state made her helpless so that, through accepting the identity the nuns dressed her in, she could then empower them.

36. Again, a typical iconographic representation of the Virgin and Agnes.

37. Wanting to vivify the pictorial element of the scene, Razzi identifies the actors as those represented.

38. This final reference to the phenomenon of transformation adds the insight, absolutely typical of the Florentine attitude toward the sacred, of the *fascinans tremendum* reaction to what they have created. On this duality, see R. Otto, *The Idea of the Holy* (New York, 1958), 12–40.

39. This whole passage seems to represent the boy-

Christ teaching. Note the switch from the feminine to masculine gender.

40. This passage shows what was sought and had been achieved in the procession. The sisters begged mercy of the boy because, in effect, Caterina had successfully deceived them into acting as if they thought she was Christ. Or, truer to the document, Christ had so successfully made Caterina into himself that the nuns fell prostrate to the ground. The passage from representation to reality has been so successful that Caterina–Christ can call for the nuns' individual internal commitments. The external has led to the possibility of internal conversion.

41. These gifts remind the author of the little "holy cards" priests still distribute to Catholics after ceremonies. The gifts here were apparently not pictures but some type of rounded figures, perhaps of wax or terra-cotta.

beautiful Esther, and had her rise and, replacing the crown on her head, had her sit down. Nor did he fail to show similar signs of particular love to S. Agnese, keeping her at his side throughout the procession. She having for some time supported his left arm, with which he held up the world orb, with her right hand, he then wanted to support her, and did sustain her hand upon his left shoulder, saying to her as an allusion some words from the Canticle of Solomon.[42]

And they say further that when in climbing certain stairs one of the angels in front of her fell, she immediately extended her hand, supported him, and freed him from danger, even though she was in ecstasy. Finally, having brought much spiritual contentment to the sisters, she blessed them and dismissed them. Having left the church, she came out of ecstasy.

And such were the spiritual diversions of this house while this noble spouse of Christ [Caterina] lived among them. But we would be too prolix if we desired to recount all the processions the devout nuns made in her time, and [all] the mysterious visions she had.

---

42. The exquisite laws of precedence and ritual exchange remind one of Francesco da Barberino's teaching; Caterina–Christ's model etiquette is comparable to the "embassy" in the Savonarolan procession (page 188, this volume).

Chapter 7

Death and
the Life of Society

*I saw a new custom. . . . Behind a bier
on its way to the cemetery went a large
brigade singing, and then behind it . . .
went men and women wailing. And when it
was over, those who wailed paid those who sang!**

At this point we have examined three types of social and religious relationships. Through the Mazzei–Datini correspondence we probed the nature of the relationship between citizens. The experience of Giovanni Morelli permitted us to examine a private relationship of father and sons. Finally, the texts of ritual activities in San Marco and San Vincenzo showed us something of the nature of ritual activities in small groups. The manipulative patterns of the broad culture were common to all three private situations: In each case, the parties remained courteous with and formal to each other despite unquestionable human warmth; in all three, participating in another's experience—distanced though the other was—was found to be the beginning of communication.

The present chapter directs our attention to small-group activity in a lay setting. Continuing to focus upon individual experience, we will probe two aspects of death ritual: the spiritual preparations for death, exemplified in the story of Pietro Pagolo Boscoli (d. 1513), and, in the wake of that preparation, the attitude society showed toward those it had condemned as they went to their death, illustrated in the execution of fra Michele Berti da Calci (d. 1389).

Pietro Pagolo Boscoli was executed for conspiring against the lives of

*Sacchetti, *Trecentonovelle*, 234.

Giuliano, Lorenzo, and Giulio de' Medici. He died for what he did. Fra Michele, a member of the heretical friars called the Fraticelli, lost his life for what he believed *and* what he did; he maintained heretical teachings and refused to recant them. Though the occasions of both deaths were unusual, the death rituals were not. From these cases, we can learn a good deal about the way most individuals prepared for death, and about the role society usually played in death.

In this concluding chapter on private experience, we ask again what role ritual behavior played in maintaining and transforming Florentine society. In the ritual of death, the very notion of society is at stake; when society kills its members, it changes its identity in order to maintain that identity. In the case of the political heretic Boscoli, both he and society took pains to formalize his passing so as not to affect the identity of society. In the case of fra Michele, the reader will discover a society fearful of someone dying at odds with it. In both, the subtleties and drama of private behavior have Florentine society as an audience. This last chapter on private ritual is also an introduction to the public procession.

The Gethsemane of Pietro Pagolo Boscoli

When the Medici returned to Florence in 1512, they found a different political atmosphere than the one they had left in 1494. Mediceanism had lost much of the magic it had possessed in the days of Cosimo and Lorenzo the Magnificent, who as benevolent first citizens had increased the city's world stature while managing to avoid any outward disrespect for republican and oligarchic institutions. The republican rejuvenation of the Savonarolan and Soderinian periods had changed all that, and many citizens equated the family's authority with tyranny. Savonarola's sermons had led the way in bringing about this change in attitude, one nurtured as well by some literary circles in the city under the influence of Roman ideals of tyrannicide. When the grandson and the son of the Magnificent entered Florence in 1512, their lives were constantly in danger.[1]

A few months later, a conspiracy to kill three of the four leading members of the family was uncovered. Two of the men involved were sentenced to death by decapitation and were duly executed on February 23, 1513. One was the thirty-two-year-old Boscoli; the other was Agostino Capponi, age forty-three. The political facts of the conspiracy are irrelevant to our present theme, as is the heroic myth that grew up around the martyrs during and after the Last Republic.[2] Here we are interested only in their preparation for death, which started immediately after they were sentenced.

1. Commentaries on the period include R. von Albertini, *Das Florentinische Staatsbewusstsein im Übergang von der Republik zum Prinzipat* (Berne, 1955), 31–36, 77, 90; F. Gilbert, *Machiavelli and Guicciardini*.

2. On Nardi's use of the story, see *Istorie*, VI, 16. On Boscoli, see *Dizionario Biografico degli Italiani*, XIII, 219ff, and A. Verde, *Lo Studio Fiorentino 1473–1503. Ricerche e Documenti* III (Pistoia, 1977), 825.

Scarcely returned to his cell in the palace of the Bargello, young Boscoli was visited by Luca Della Robbia—a descendant of the famous artist of the same name. This twenty-eight-year-old humanist editor had come to help his friend Boscoli through the latter's impending passion, and to judge the quality of that friend's upcoming behavior: Pietro Pagolo wanted to die a Christian hero and Luca would measure his progress. Della Robbia remained with Boscoli throughout the night—eight hours in all—till the end came the following morning. Within a short time after Boscoli's death, Della Robbia wrote down everything he remembered, and the resulting *recitazione* is the source of our examination.[3] He considered Boscoli's last hours something of a model of both Christian and human behavior. Our task is to find the role that formal action in the area and group around Boscoli played in preparing him for a good death.

In the *Recitation*, the friend and author divided Boscoli's spiritual "management" into two parts.[4] In the first the author himself was the friendly manager, his reciprocated affection for Pietro Pagolo being the precondition for their common aim of preparing Boscoli for death. In the second part of the preparation, a professional manager of souls appeared. The Dominican fra Cipriano did not know Boscoli; he approached him with technical skills and general knowledge of human personality rather than as a friend. Both Luca and the friar would use authoritative means to prepare Boscoli, but the former was a dilettante; fra Cipriano, a professional. Both came away from the experience having taken Pietro Pagolo to their hearts, but Luca had gone there as a friend, whereas Cipriano developed love in the process of managing the doomed man's soul.[5]

Since the unifying theme of the whole drama was preparation for death, it is important to know from the start exactly what Boscoli thought this preparation did and did not involve. It did not require further reconciliation with death; Boscoli's humanistic training offered him models enough of that sort, and he admonished his managers not to waste time on that.[6] Nor did it involve faith: Pietro Pagolo believed as the church believed. Something else could not be taken for granted, however: "a perfect conformity of his will with that of God."[7] To achieve this conformity, the managers working with Boscoli had to dissolve a certain "hardness of heart" and move him toward a state of spiritual communion. This state, the phenomenal goal of management, was variously described as "abstracting myself completely into God," "conjoin[ing] my intellect with God's," becoming "completely spiritual," reaching a "certain sweetness," a "heat of spirit," in which "with affection and fervor" one was "in love with God."[8]

3. Luca Della Robbia, *La Morte di Pietro Paolo Boscoli,* ed. R. Bacchelli (Florence, 1943), 62, 81, for his motivations in going.

4. The word *management* appears twice: "Fra Cipriano, voi avete a maneggiare uno speculativo ingegno"; *ibid.,* 110. "Così giudicò il frate e gli altri che l'avean maneggiato"; *ibid.,* 142. The friar Cipriano was also said to be "pratico e da governo"; *ibid.,* 110.

5. Cipriano later told Della Robbia how much he had been affected by Boscoli; *ibid.,* 145f.

6. *Ibid.,* 121.

7. *Ibid.,* 64.

8. Consecutively: *ibid.,* 90, 132, 88, 91, 125, 124, 90.

Luca understood the goal and the visible signs of the condition Boscoli sought: "I follow you. You want to have a sweet affection for God with tears and sighs, and you want your intellect to spontaneously consent to the faith."[9] That is, Pietro Boscoli wanted to conjoin reason and belief in an aesthetic unity. He did not intellectually doubt any particular dogma, but he did want his body and soul to be one in experiencing the truth of Christ. Luca pointed out that although such self-abstraction was not necessary to salvation it could be obtained: "And then you will still obtain the tears, because you will be helped by confession, communion, indulgences, and by the prayers of those standing around."[10]

Thus Boscoli and his friend planned and staged an emotional state, which each person, place, and thing contributed to bring about. The single companion who was to be Boscoli's final guide, for example, was carefully chosen to be someone who would be appropriate for Boscoli's character and thus able to move him spiritually.[11] Until this confessor arrived, Luca assumed the role. Then the small group that was in the room was carefully instructed in its place in the ritual. These people were mostly members of the Florentine Confraternity of the Tempio, a group charged with helping condemned men through their last hours. Boscoli placed these professional managers back far enough from himself and Luca so they would not disturb him, and asked that instead of the normal loud chanting they busy themselves with prayers for his soul.[12] Finally, Boscoli thought of what was going on outside the prison during his preparations. He was assured that many were thinking and praying for him.[13]

Thus from the beginning Boscoli recognized that he would arrive at the abstract state he desired only through formal arrangements and methods. Some of his ideas on the subject were unusual. As he rejected the confraternal singing, so he at one point refused the *tavoluccia* (an image of the Passion usually held up close to the face of persons wanting to concentrate) on the grounds that he did not need it to attain his state.[14] (He later accepted such an image and a crucifix as prayer objects.)[15] The fundamental approach was clear: Through careful placement and then by artful procedures, Boscoli expected to manipulate his surroundings and to be manipulated by them. Two particular methods used by Luca deserve mention.

The first of these methods involved the use of Latin for prayer and for the biblical *exempla* Luca brought to Boscoli's attention. Only on the brink of death and after his confessor had left him did Boscoli pray in his native language. Luca called the Latin phrases he used the "formal words of Christ," leaving no doubt about Latin formulas' accepted place in affective and effective prayer.[16] First among these prayers were the Pater Noster and Salve Maria.

9. *Ibid.*, 82.

10. *Ibid.*, 83f.

11. *Ibid.*, 68, 73, 75.

12. *Ibid.*, 117.

13. *Ibid.*, 64, 76ff, 87, 120, 131.

14. *Ibid.*, 85.

15. *Ibid.*, 127, 139.

16. *Ibid.*, 86.

Luca's second method was to recall biblical stories, which he then interpreted for Boscoli. He thought such "figuring," as they called it, to be
particularly appropriate for the educated Boscoli, and the latter constantly
encouraged his friend to use this method: "Luca, when some pretty interpretation occurs to you, speak it out."[17] Della Robbia's protestation that "I
have no spirit, nor am I skilled in Holy Writ," was in vain, for Boscoli insisted
on his right to manage his own death: "This isn't the time for ceremonies. Do
what I tell you; say what God inspires you to."[18] The patient told the doctor
what to do to make him well. Throughout, Boscoli considered his friend an
instrument through which to tune his spirit. He sought no mere intellectual
comprehension or joy through these interpretations; rather, he sought to
develop his mind, fancy, and will into one:

> [God's] divinity I can understand, that is, believing in it and imagining it as far as it is
> possible for us to imagine such a thing, if one can so speak, since there is no word for
> it. But I believe well enough, and am satisfied enough when I think about it. But
> [God's] humanity does not represent itself as well to me, even though I believe it. You
> understand.[19]

Luca's efforts were not completely successful. Having progressed to the
point of reading the Passion of Christ to Boscoli, he found that Pietro Pagolo
remained unmoved by the oft-heard words of the evangelist. The condemned
man voiced his dissatisfaction:

> Oh, if I could cry some at the passion of my lord! Liquify, my hardened heart! Do you
> not know that I would do so willingly? Accompany me willingly. Luca, I am not in
> order: [the heart] remains hard. Will desire suffice?[20]

Despite all Luca's work, despite constant comparisons of Boscoli to
Christ in passion and to Savonarola before his execution, Boscoli remained
unsatisfied, unmoved by the suffering of others, unable to participate.[21] At
the least, however, the patient had stopped indulging himself in complaints
about having eaten too much—which dulled the spirit—had thought to worry
about his mother, and had much appreciated his friend's efforts.[22] That was
something after all.

Boscoli clearly needed a professional manager, and at this moment, fra
Cipriano arrived. Luca described his qualifications:

> Boscoli could not have had a person more suited [to him], for the said friar was quite
> experienced at confession, was learned, full of fervor, quite active, practiced in
> governing, very loving and civil.[23]

Before the friar went in to meet the man whom he would govern, Luca

---

17. *Ibid.*, 97.
18. *Ibid.*
19. *Ibid.*, 99.
20. *Ibid.*, 103.

21. *Ibid.*, 103, 107f.
22. *Ibid.*, 68f, 89, on eating too much.
23. *Ibid.*, 110.

wanted to apprise him of one thing. Boscoli had it in his head that he had been a good example to the Florentine *popolo* by conspiring against the Medici; he thought himself a Brutus who had at least tried to strike down a tyrant.[24] Luca feared that Boscoli might believe he had not sinned in conspiring. Since Thomas Aquinas had said such conspiracies were illicit, the friar had to make it clear to Boscoli that he had sinned: "Well, explain that to him, so that there is no chance of his deceiving himself."[25] In other words, Luca felt a responsibility to ensure that his friend recognize that, by attempting to destroy the city's order, he had sinned against the divine order. Luca may have thought that Boscoli's oft-repeated statement that he died willingly concealed an attitude of moral superiority over his executioners.[26] Boscoli had to recognize his sins against the civil order, accepting its supremacy, just as unquestioningly as he accepted the authority of the church. Luca seems to have been concerned lest his friend, no religious heretic, die a political outsider; that is, one still angered with the civil order. For him a voluntary death had to include a recognition of the righteousness of the society that killed one.

Luca brought fra Cipriano to Boscoli and introduced him: "Son of a *contadino* from Ponte a Sieve, but learned and good. God has sent him to you. Do not doubt that he will satisfy you."[27]

Boscoli's reception of the friar delighted Luca, who saw in his friend's courtesy a factor favorably predisposing the outcome of the professional's efforts:

> Fra Cipriano came into the presence of Boscoli, and was received with every reverence. Because, lying on a mattress with his feet fettered and [his hands] manacled, he got up part way as best he could. And with both hands he took off his hat. When fra Cipriano said: "God save you, dearest brother," he responded: "And [God] save you also, my father. You are welcome."[28]

It is stunning that a manager saw a good omen in Boscoli's flawless execution of greeting ritual, and just as noteworthy that the author spelled out the particulars of bodily and verbal gestures in this setting. Luca indeed contrasted the calm dignity with which Boscoli greeted Cipriano and proceeded to confess to him with the physical and mental agitation of the other condemned man, Agostino Capponi, with whom Luca spoke while Boscoli and the friar were executing the sacrament of confession: Capponi was convinced of his innocence, and this made him restless, loud, and generally discontent till the moment of his death.[29]

The friar's methods in managing Boscoli are only partly known, since the historian of the event rejoined the two only after confession was past. But thereafter the friar used two particular techniques. The first consisted in encouraging Boscoli to repeat certain Latin phrases over and over again. One

24. *Ibid.*, 72, 80.

25. *Ibid.*, 112.

26. *Ibid.* On dying voluntarily, *ibid.*, 76, 120, 131.

27. *Ibid.*, 113.

28. *Ibid.*

29. *Ibid.*, 114ff, 129f.

of these was a passage from the Pater Noster: "Forgive us our debts as we forgive our debtors," which Della Robbia records as having been repeated at least three different times.[30] Another was "Deus, in adiutorium meum intende; Domine, ad adiuvandum me festina." When this was first uttered, Cipriano reacted: "That's good. Say this verse with all your sentiment."[31] Then Boscoli repeated it, and, "animated by the friar," returned to it thrice.[32]

The Dominican confessor's second ritual technique consisted in first presenting to Boscoli three central thoughts he was to dwell on, and then regularly admonishing him to re-evoke them:

> So that you arm yourself, I want you to accompany yourself in this great passage with three women. The first is that I want you to believe what Jesus Christ and the holy mother church command. The second is that you have a vivid hope for the remission of your sins through the passion of Christ. The third is that I want you to do this death for the love of Christ and not for anyone else. . . . Then [Boscoli said]: "You say well. I have to have three things." And then, with other words, he repeated what the friar had told him.[33]

Boscoli subsequently rearticulated these three devices from memory.[34]

In all, then, the managers used four distinguishable methods. First, prayers and biblical passages in Latin were used as verbal "weapons." Second, these prayers and passages were repeated, in the belief their repetition would be efficacious. Third, and also through biblical passages, the sentiment of divine history was linked to Boscoli's condition. Finally, particular mnemonic moralisms were introduced into Boscoli's mind and constantly re-evoked.

The client had now reached the point that the professional manager thought propitious for the sacrament of communion and the indulgences of the Confraternity of the Tempio. Boscoli yearned for the "great strength" eating the body of Christ would give him and, in fact, it was the sight of the host that finally brought him to tears: "And he began to cry with such devotion and decorum that he seemed a little virgin."[35] Thus when Boscoli cried like a child of the opposite sex, it was evident that he had reached the desired state of purity and abstraction. Luca told how Pietro Pagolo took the host "not without tears," and received the indulgence.[36] He *was* fervent, Luca noted with gratification, saying that Pater Noster *con grand'affetto* and saying aloud the Magnificat and the Salve Regina together with his two companions.

The spirit did not last. The sinner reached the top of the mountain, but descended quickly, disappointed: "I am resolved to die, but I would like to abstract my self completely in God. But I cannot. I do not satisfy."[37]

The time approached when Pietro Pagolo would be led to his death, and yet there was no fulfillment. True, at moments he seemed to lose touch with

30. *Ibid.*, 109, 131, 134.

31. *Ibid.*, 125.

32. *Ibid.*, 132, 133, 138.

33. *Ibid.*, 122f.

34. *Ibid.*, 134, 140f, 143.

35. *Ibid.*, 129.

36. *Ibid.*, 130.

37. *Ibid.*, 132.

his surroundings, so that the friar had to ask: "Do you hear me?"[38] But nothing lasted:

> I have to have three things in this passage. I have to believe the faith; I have to have firm hope that God will pardon me; and the third is that I have to support this death for the love of Christ and not for others. All right, I do these things, but bring them often to my attention. My, how I want to transfer myself completely into God! But I cannot as I want to.[39]

Led from the room toward the place of execution in the judicial palace, his head already covered, Boscoli asked for more time, "for it did not seem to him that he had accomplished what he wanted."[40] Boscoli died strong in faith, hope, and charity. We know that because Luca Della Robbia took the trouble to examine his friend's face after the head was severed from the body. It preserved its decorum, a sure sign there had been no despair. But he died without having already entered his heaven.

Three central aspects of this scene summarize its relevance to the subject of this book. The first is the nature of a good death. We have noted Della Robbia's own emphasis on Boscoli's desire to transcend his surroundings and body, to become completely spiritual. Yet fulfilling this individualistic wish definitely depended on Boscoli's self-reckoning with the sociopolitical order. Agostino Capponi, for example, bragged of his innocence, and at the beginning Boscoli himself thought of himself as an exemplary Brutus. To Luca this was "fantasy." "No one is innocent," he pressed upon Capponi and, through the confessor, upon Boscoli.[41] Before one could hope to abstract oneself from the body politic, in short, one had to recognize that one had sinned against it. This was why Luca insisted that Boscoli understand he had sinned by participating in the conspiracy. For Luca and the confessor, feelings of moral superiority only caused the type of disquiet and agitation Capponi showed. The corollary to recognizing individual guilt toward society was to accept society's guiltlessness in the execution, that it was God who wanted Boscoli's death, and society bore no responsibility.[42] In Luca's view, Boscoli should go to the next life ascribing his death to the will of an extraterrestrial force, not to Florence or to the Medici. Though Luca never speculated how the city could be affected if Pietro Pagolo did not absolve society and condemn himself before leaving this life, we know from Giovanni Morelli what that effect could be: The spirit of the dead could haunt the living. Boscoli's repeated assurances to family and friends that he died voluntarily were essentially assurances that neither he nor his death would return to haunt Florence. By seeking, albeit in vain, to "abstract" himself, Boscoli validated the political order that had condemned him. A good death was one in which the commune's offering did not appear an offering to the victim. As Boscoli never

38. *Ibid.*, 133.

39. *Ibid.*, 134.

40. *Ibid.*, 142.

41. *Ibid.*, 115.

42. "Non si volta una foglia d'albero senza la volontà di Dio"; *ibid.*, 71.

questioned the faith, the stability of the ignoble commune's altars, so he never questioned the integrity of the political and social order. He had sinned in conspiring against it.

A second element that stands out in this drama is the conviction among all concerned that men needed other men when dying, and that there could be no good death alone. Boscoli pleaded several times not to be abandoned until it was all over.[43] What men offered was not only their love but the authoritative skills and pedagogy they brought; a good death in the city necessitated expert management done in love.

The third aspect is the phenomenon of participation—a word not used in the document—which was considered a crucial element in progressing toward the good death. Luca and fra Cipriano did not manipulate so that Boscoli could participate. A more complex process was at work: Boscoli himself worked upon his managers, and had to succeed in manipulating them if he himself was to be moved. The circuit is clear: Ordered to exercise his imagination by the client, the manager or governor suggested to the client that he think about the suffering of some divinity. Boscoli's moving repetition of the biblical words first had the effect of moving not him but the audience around him to tears. Luca twice recorded this phenomenon, and later added how moved Fra Cipriano had been during the confession.[44] This participation of the managers in the client in turn led to a heightening of the latter's spirit. In this condition, Boscoli could pray so powerfully that, in Luca's words, "it seemed he pulled all of heaven down to his aid."[45] Thus Pietro Pagolo had to move his managers in order to move or force (as Luca's words suggest) the deities. Throughout, mutual dependence and social authority reigned in the ritual of death, right down to that wonderful sign of spiritual progress: the courtesy with which Boscoli had welcomed his professional manager.

Fra Michele's Way of the Cross

The condemned had prepared himself; he now had to make his way through the streets of Florence—as Boscoli the patrician did not—to the place of public execution. On the way he will meet constituents and enemies and exchange words with them. He will die at the stake without society wanting him to. His death will be as unsettling for Florence as Boscoli's ritual was edifying and reassuring.

The bearer of this cross was fra Michele Berti of Calci near Pisa. He had come to Florence at the beginning of 1389 to minister to followers of the Fraticelli in Florence. The mission was dangerous, since from the beginning of the 1380s the authorities had been cracking down on these heretics.[46] Michele

43. *Ibid.*, 96, 135.

44. *Ibid.*, 94, 139.

45. *Ibid.*, 125.

46. J. Stephens, "Heresy in Medieval and Renaissance Florence," *Past and Present*, no. 54 (Feb. 1972), 37f.

stayed through the winter, however, and on Palm and Easter Sundays he carried out the normal liturgy of these feasts for his small flock in private. He was about to leave the city on the Tuesday after Easter when certain "daughters of Judas" betrayed him into the hands of the civil and ecclesiastical authorities. By Friday the eve of May Day he was dead, having been found guilty of obstinate heresy by the bishop and inquisitor and given over to the commune for burning. Throughout these days, an anonymous follower of the sect recorded the events, and was a personal witness to Michele's way of the cross. His story is the source for our examination.[47]

The trial was like many others. Accused of a series of doctrinal errors—that Christ had not been a king while he was on earth, that he had not owned anything while on earth, that Pope John XXII and the ecclesiastical hierarchy that had been appointed in his wake had become heretical because that pope had denied the poverty of Christ—the little friar had strenuously resisted all compromise, had constantly protested the notaries' and examiners' distortions of his words, and had sought death willingly as a martyr for Christ and the truth. All attempts to get Michele to recant failed, and it was a reluctant hierarchy that proceeded to the ceremony of degradation that ritually unmade his priesthood. The saint—so his biographer called him—came to this decisive consistory of degradation "dressed in every vestment from the first [given] when he made himself a [minor] clerk up through [that given] when he became a priest."[48] By the time he left, the "pharisees" had "taken from him one vestment after the other until only a *cioppa* he wore remained. Having shaved the tips of the fingers and chipped him (*trugiolatolo*), they shaved away his clerical tonsure."[49] Once handed over to the civil authority, Michele remained in prison for one day and two nights before taking his final walk. The story of fra Michele becomes of great value to the student of Florentine formal behavior and its cosmology at this point, from the final prison day till his death. Throughout these hours, the citizens of Florence tried to understand why Michele went willingly to his death. The exchanges on this question between the saint and his audience are extremely revealing of the Florentine mind and spirit.

In prison Michele was the object of unending ridicule by his fellow prisoners, who, though presumed guilty of having violated civil or criminal law, like Boscoli had absolutely no qualms about the authority of the church, its rites, and its beliefs. Some prisoners tormented the friar and insulted him because he did not want to believe in the pope.[50] Others reviled him because he would not take communion.[51] The prison experience was a foretaste of what was to come, for the prisoners were deeply discontented, perhaps frightened, by a man who not only did not believe as others did, but would

47. *Storia di fra Michele Minorita*, ed. F. Flora (Florence, 1946).

48. *Ibid.*, 46.

49. *Ibid.*, 48.

50. *Ibid.*, 50.

51. *Ibid.*, 51.

not do what others did. A citizen came to him in prison and asked him right out: "Oh fra Michele, why don't you do what others do?"[52] Another citizen said to him with some bewilderment: "I don't know what kind of a man you are. Why don't you believe that which others do?"[53] Their bewilderment could find only one exit. They decided that the friar had the devil.[54]

Those prisoners and visitors who were exposed to Michele before the last march were the first to reveal the true substance of the city's repulsion by and fascination with this heretic, and to clarify for us in what they thought Michele's uniqueness consisted. The little friar did not question the rights of the temporal regime in Florence or elsewhere, as did many Florentines. Instead he rejected the ecclesiastical hierarchy and consequently one ritual basis of this ignoble city's stability. The most disquieting heresy of Michele was that Christ was not a king while he was on earth. The evidence that the Florentines who participated in the coming drama were frightened because Michele threatened the ritual community of the *popolo* around the altar will become irresistible as the march unfolds.

Michele had been convicted of subverting the Florentine *popolo*. Having prepared himself for death by imagining that at the end of Justice Street his stake would be surrounded by St. Francis and two Fraticelli martyrs, he now went into the street to meet this subvertible people—or rather a portion of them, since it was a rainy May Day eve, and most people were indoors enjoying themselves.[55] At the start he assumed the posture he would never change: He would not really be an actor in the drama of bearing his cross at all. Rather, the audience would be the players, sending their words toward a barely responsive Michele who served mainly as a target of their own fears and curiosities. Michele was to be an image.

The mood of the crowd was unique, for all forms of popular justice were absent. No bystander spat on him, none seems to have waited with anticipation to see his skin boil, and after his death no one decimated his bodily remains. Instead the people first implored the saint to recant, then they ridiculed him, trying through irony and very mild cruelty to bring him down from his determination, and finally they remained puzzled. The artless author of this narrative describes a reflective, unusually troubled crowd.

What were its main concerns as perceived by our witness? Schematically, they can be divided in ascending order of importance between dogmatic, authoritarian, representative, and life concerns. In the first, bystanders objected to Michele's false dogma; in the second, they queried the saint on why he believed otherwise than did experts; in the third they asked whom Michele represented and stood for; in the last, they wondered why Michele would choose death even if he were right in his beliefs and attitudes.

The drama began, and it soon became evident that the crowd's dogmatic concerns were few:

---

52. *Ibid.*, 52.

53. *Ibid.*

54. *Ibid.*, 53.

55. *Ibid.*, 44f, 53, 71.

Stupid as you are, believe in the pope![56]

Oh, you say that we are neither baptized nor Christians.[57]

Oh, you don't believe in God![58]

Its concerns about authority were more substantial, indeed the dogmatic concerns prefigured them:

> You are a martyr of the devil. Do you think you know more than so many [theological] masters? Do you think that if master Luca knew that this [viewpoint] of yours was the truth, that he would want to lose his soul [by denying your belief]? You want to know more than him, and you can't gloss at all in comparison to him.[59]

Such concerns about intellectual authority mirrored those expressed during the trial. The examining theologians had ridiculed Michele: "Do you think you understand the scriptures better than so many masters like us?"[60] And in a significant enlargement of the field of authority, those same masters had asked "if he wanted to believe what so many masters and the whole *popolo* of Florence believed."[61] On the street as well, the crowd had called upon its own authority: "*Voce di popolo, voce di Dio!*" only to have Michele respond: "The voice of the *popolo* had Christ crucified, and had St. Peter killed."[62]

Such courageous responses as this made the crowd wonder if this man was in some way standing there for them, representing them and not the devil. Their questions in this vein were at once provocative and revealing:

Michele: I want to die for Christ.
Crowd: Oh, you do not die for Christ.[63]
Michele: Christ died for us.
Crowd: Oh, you are not Christ, and you don't have to die for us, you![64] You are not among the pagans![65]

Of uppermost importance, however, was the crowd's last major concern: trying to get Michele to live. Their entreaties ranged from simple demands he repent and live, to the most striking note of all, often repeated, that even if he were right, he should repent. "Don't wish to die!"[66] "Repent, repent, don't wish to die!"[67] With no little irony, the author described the martyr marching through the Mercato Nuovo, the new Florentine market, and being accosted by the merchants: "Repent, repent," and in the Piazza del Grano admonished by gamblers and loose women: "Repent, repent!"[68] "Do not wish to die,

56. *Ibid.*, 63.

57. *Ibid.*, 66.

58. *Ibid.*, 62f.

59. *Ibid.*, 66.

60. *Ibid.*, 32.

61. *Ibid.*, 30.

62. *Ibid.*, 66.

63. *Ibid.*, 68.

64. *Ibid.*, 68f.

65. *Ibid.*, 69.

66. *Ibid.*, 62.

67. *Ibid.*, 64.

68. *Ibid.*, 65.

dumb as you are."[69] "Recant, recant, don't wish to die."[70] As the procession rounded Santa Croce and approached the Place of Justice, the bystanders made a new appeal:

Even assuming that this is the truth, you don't want to die for it.

St. Peter [himself] recanted . . . ! You can do it too, for if St. Peter were here, he would recant!

Fra Francesco and fra Giovanni would not want you to die for this, and if they were here they would recant. Christ and many other saints fled death many times. Don't you want to do that which your leader fra Francesco da Camerino did? He recanted.[71]

And finally the forceful, elemental cry: "Escape with your life! Escape, escape!"[72]

Michele responded to all these exhortations with such calm and humility that his words were less retorts than cues to cadence the players' remarks. The crowd was not infuriated, but perplexed. Some had insecure, ready answers: He is possessed by the devil.[73] But clearly, the crowd did not feel the devil's presence, and could not understand the ritual setting. One said with evident astonishment: "He's going to his death happy!!"[74] One man ran alongside the saint conversing with him, trying at once to understand this strange man and to change him.[75] Someone called out to him: "You're not asking anyone to pray God for you!" Michele immediately disarmed him: "I ask all faithful catholic Christians to pray God for me."[76] The crowd could not understand such forceful passivity, and it was anguished by the implicit question of its own Christianity. Despite the danger, the friar's supporters in the crowd started to argue with others, so great was the mental confusion.[77] Then, one person cried out what can be one key to explaining this scene: "You are killing yourself!" Michele would not tolerate any such misunderstanding of what was happening; he would not allow the *popolo* to go away at peace as had Luca Della Robbia from Boscoli's execution, and he struck back: "I am not killing myself. Rather, they are killing me."[78]

Having prayed along the way to two different images of St. Francis that were held up to him, having said the Credo, the Te Deum, and the last words of Christ, the friar yielded himself without argument to the executioners.[79] His dead body thrown in a ditch, a group of the faithful rescued it. Preachers in the city were disquieted by the cadaver's disappearance, and from their pulpits they complained that the body should have been watched, "for they will canonize him, and will make him a saint."[80]

69. *Ibid.*, 65.
70. *Ibid.*, 68.
71. All *ibid.*, 69f.
72. *Ibid.*, 64.
73. *Ibid.*, 63, 67.
74. *Ibid.*, 64.
75. *Ibid.*, 65f.
76. *Ibid.*, 64.
77. *Ibid.*, 71.
78. *Ibid.*, 69.
79. *Ibid.*, 68, 70f, 74f.
80. *Ibid.*, 76.

The populace remained disquieted, some unsure that Michele had been a heretic in fact, others vaguely uneasy:

And while the people returned home, the majority thought wrong had been done. They could not have enough of speaking bad of the clergy. One said: "He is a martyr"; another, "He is a saint," another the contrary. And thus, there was more disquiet in Florence than ever before.[81]

We have witnessed another highly formalized action involving an individual, but this one has brought us to the brink of social behavior on the grand scale. Formalism was evident not only in the author's description of the procession's setting, which in the market and red-light districts permitted appropriate dramatic verbal exchanges between juxtaposed moral principles, nor was this theatrical formalism limited to the author's perception of the whole scene as a mirror of Christ's passion from the daughters of Judas through the judicial official effectively washing his hands of the friar, to the hours at which things occurred, to the removal and hiding of the body and, of course, the way of the cross itself. The societal audience, the actors themselves were made to feel uncomfortably aware that they were playing roles once played by Christ's tormentors, and despite themselves, they responded appropriately as the total form required.

Different from the normal funeral procession and from Boscoli's execution, Michele's formalized way of the cross transformed the relations between the actors; it proved that ritual was a transformational as well as sustaining phenomenon. Michele's action took on this character because the friar would not admit, to use the words of one of the actors, to killing himself. Unlike Boscoli, he did not internalize guilt, did not accept his crime as a sin, did not abstract himself into an outside deity. Instead he died for the truth at the hands of the audience of ritual actors. He insisted that the authorities, and the *vox populi*, were killing him.

Funerals serve to kill a person socially who has naturally died. The ritual of the last hours and subsequent exequies are meant to establish a commonality between the person dying and society. Each wants his death, each recognizes its necessity. In this way, the incalculability of nature is neutralized, and society can maintain its claim to sovereignty. In the good death, the dead person does not become an enemy; the society does not remain at the mercy of nature.

In the case of Boscoli's violent death by execution, it was very important that the victim accept his preordained fate as right for society and for him. But in fra Michele's case, society did not in fact want its victim to die; it was Michele himself who preferred death to doing and believing falsely. Society insisted that the friar accept certain practices and beliefs that were fundamental to social order, more fundamental in fact than those civil orders which Boscoli's conspiracy had attacked; Michele could not. Of the two

---

81. *Ibid.*, 75f.

requisites, practices were certainly more important than dogma. The crowd cared less for theology than it did about his accepting communion, less about internal convictions than external conformity. So Michele had to die, despite the fact that he was not a social criminal in the narrow sense, despite the fact that he was the type of clerk beloved by Florentines: poor, humble, and self-abnegatory. Society killed a good clerk without wanting to, and without Michele recognizing his guilt and society's right to kill him.

The viewers' disquiet was understandable. Michele did not die because he rejected a temporal regime or because he had violated temporal law. Nor did he die because of some abstract theological dogma. He died because he refused to kneel before the city altars; he challenged the sovereignty of those altars around which a *popolo* without a temporal sovereign developed a civic identity.

Michele challenged the meaningfulness of ritual formations. Yet even that crime was not decisive enough to put the executioners at peace with themselves. They insisted that Michele was not among pagans as Christ had been; but perhaps this was a repetition of the Crucifixion after all, and the Florentines were modern-day deicides. They insisted that everyone took communion at the civil altars, and thus could not be doing wrong; but perhaps they were all being instrumentalized by false priests. They said Michele claimed they had not been really baptized as members of the church; but were these actors really brothers in God—or in Satan? Michele's had been a bad death, an indecorous, discourteous happening. Rather than having welded men together in the face of an enemy, Michele's ritual procession had unsettled the city.

III

THE RITUAL OF
THE CLASSICAL COMMUNE

> *These are all accompanied by ritual and by prestations by whose means political rank within sub-groups, tribes, tribal confederations and nations is settled. But the remarkable thing about these tribes is the spirit of rivalry and antagonism which dominates all their activities.**

In the chronicles of Florentine history, contemporaries recorded seemingly endless, seemingly identical descriptions of scores upon scores of formal processions involving major parts of the population. These reports were made not by those who had nothing better to do but by businessmen who wanted to get the history of their days down on paper.

Over the two-hundred-year span of republican history for which we possess extensive sources, the ceremonial life of the commune was clearly a major preoccupation of Florentine governments, corporations, and individuals. The amount of money spent by families, confraternities, religious bodies, and governments is nothing short of astounding. The time that merchants and bureaucrats, common workers, and rulers expended in almost endless rounds of processions staggers the imagination. The cost to the productive process in the city was formidable; closing shops made poor men penniless and small merchants poor.

Why, then, did chroniclers think these events so crucial, and why did Florentines expend such energy in a formal behavior that moderns tend to dismiss as mere spectacle? The answer is that contemporaries believed that in these rites they witnessed the political process at work. Inhabitants participated to be part of that process. Rather

---

*Mauss, *Gift*, 4, describing the potlatch.

than being theater, the formal public life of this city articulated the changing order of things, and was part of that change.

At certain times of the year the Morellis and Mazzeis, the Datinis and the Boscolis of Florence, as well as the city's priests and workers and women and children, left their homes and neighborhoods to participate in this history. In the chapters to come we will examine what they did and why they did it, focusing on three general stimuli. First were the calendrical and unscheduled rituals of celebration during stable times. Then there were ceremonies intended for visiting foreign dignitaries. Finally there was a ritual of danger in which inhabitants, through formal congregations, sought to guard against threats to the political and social fabric of the city.

Chapter 8

The Ritual of Celebration

*At that time there were three hundred
authentic knights and many brigades of
knights and pages who every evening sat
down at table with many courtly men, gifting
many and various things on the main feasts.*
—G. Villani, 1283*

*The four potenze of plebs and workers
accustomed to hold an armeggeria on May Day
in very fine dress, gifted to them for the day. . . .*
—G. Cambi, 1533†

Goro Dati was euphoric when, around 1410, he described the feast of the patron John the Baptist. Having withstood the Milanese attempt to subvert its freedom in 1402, Florence had captured Pisa (1406). As the city rushed to become a sea power, booty from its small empire filled the city. There seemed no end to the possibilities and riches offered by its new position in Italy. For Dati, the feast of San Giovanni was no longer a territorial rite, a paltry local festival to satisfy local needs, but the finest celebration of the saint in the whole world, a proud announcement, one might add, that the *arrivistes* had arrived. The opening lines of his description seem to say that the days of internal and external insecurity were past, that the Florentines need do nothing but celebrate, and that the whole world and its wealth would come to the city:

> When springtime comes which delights the whole world, every Florentine begins thinking about celebrating a beautiful feast of San Giovanni, which is in midsummer. And right at the beginning each person provides for suitable clothes and adornments and jewels. Anyone having to offer wedding banquets or another *festa* waits until that time, so as to honor the feast. Two months beforehand they begin to make the *palio* and the clothes of servants and pennants and trumpets and the cloth *palii* that lands

*VII, 89.
†XXIII, 129.

commended to the commune give as *cens,* and *ceri* and other things they have to offer, and to invite people, and to gather things for the banquets, and to have the horses come from everywhere to run the Palio. You see the whole city involved in preparing for the feast and the spirits of the youth and women involved in such preparations. They do not omit, however, to do all those things that show happiness and spirits full of joy on the festive days preceding the feast, such as S. Zanobi, and for Ascension and Pentecost and Trinity Sunday and for the feast of Corpus Christi, [such as] dancing, singing, banqueting and jousts and other graceful games. For it appears that they have nothing else to do in those times lasting up to the vigil of San Giovanni.[1]

This is the stuff of romance to be sure: a city where private interests are so far submerged by love of the *buon comune* that families postpone their feasts till the day when the city and its main patron are honored; an urban time in which "everyone" works not to sell but to show; a scene where "everyone" consumes but no one buys. For all its romance, however, Dati's description does isolate two enduring dreams of this merchant city: communality over familial individuality, and sacrifice over contract. In the pure city of festival, Dati intimates, there are no needy. "Everyone" exchanges wealth without the need for formal contract, for everyone—the groundwork having been laid by the women and boys who prepared the feast—is united beneath the altar of the Baptist in sacrifice. Truly, such a city was a "paradise."[2]

The following pages study the public celebration, not by dismissing Dati's vision, but by enriching it with the reality of political process at work in public festivities. We shall find that the public feast was quintessentially private, that private festivities were very political. The festive life that Dati thought an affirmation of existing fact we shall see always bearing the seeds, even the fact, of transformation. Dati could confidently speak of the commune as something "which does not die," but these pages will continually document the Florentines' constant fear of its demise: The families that "honored the feast" had to have the feast to honor themselves. The great civic *festa* re-created the ever-fragile commonwealth.

Our examination proceeds in three parts. A historical sketch will show how the predominantly private and personal character of all festive life in the early history of celebrations made room for incipient public and governmental representations as well. Then we shall study the social and political character of private celebrations during the classical period of Florentine *feste* (1343–1480), with special attention to the feasts of Carnival and May Day. Finally, our attention will turn to the study of the great communal feast of St. John as it was celebrated after 1343.

When Knighthood Was in Flower

Originally, no substantive difference in tone or content distinguished the celebration of the feast of St. John (June 24) from that of any other feast.

1. Guasti, *Feste,* 4f.   2. *Ibid.,* 7, 15.

Florentine celebrations, whether on the nonecclesiastical feast of May Day or on the feast of the Baptist, vaunted neither public institutions nor officials, but honorable private men. Only haltingly did the communal celebration of St. John rise to challenge mere personal and familial representations, and the communal celebrations of a later time never lost elements of private grandeur, for the city never lost the need for family honor.

The earliest records of both the feast of St. John and May Day manifest this courtly and private rather than communal tone. Giovanni Villani told how the Rossi family and its neighbors across the river got together in 1283 because the Guelf city was in a good state this St. John's Day:

> a company and brigades of a thousand men or more, all dressed in white robes with a lord called "Of Love." This brigade did nothing other than occupy itself with games and amusements and dances of women and knights and other *popolani,* going through the area with trumpets and diverse instruments with joy and happiness, gathering together for meals, dinners and suppers.[3]

In the two months this "court" lasted, the brigade of "three hundred authentic knights" welcomed visiting gentlemen and buffoons from abroad, and offered them hospitality:

> No foreigner passed Florence of any name or standing, whom the said brigade did not compete to invite and accompany on horse through the city and outside as needed.[4]

Referring to the same events, Stefani added that similar brigades carried on their activities for two whole years on every feast day, not just in Oltrarno, but in all six parts of the city. He mentioned equestrian *armeggerie* as one of the games they engaged in.[5]

Thus a series of powerful private men gathered in "courts" around the city and festively enacted different knightly diversions on the feast of St. John. They were organized into brigades with different liveries headed by persons called *signori* or lords (also *messeri*). The narration implies that these courts were the focal points of noble pilgrimages, visitors being received hospitably at these several places in the city. Nowhere does Villani mention government as an element in these festivities. Instead the city was essentially transformed into many cities or courts, with movement back and forth between them.

The first description of May Day in Florence has exactly the same tone and content, but adds a few details to what was obviously an almost precommunal type of festivity:

> The city of Florence exalted itself greatly because of the victory [of Campaldino, 1289]. . . . And to show its happiness and good condition, every year on the calends

---

3. G. Villani, VII, 89. A. Pucci says the *signore* was called "the God of Love," and that on Easter and the other three *pasque* the *cittadini cari,* having "banished avarice," invited the *men possenti* to meals; *Centiloquio,* IV, 7.

4. G. Villani, VII, 89.

5. Stefani, rub. 160. As mentioned earlier, the city was only divided into quarters in the fourteenth century.

of May brigades and companies of genteel youth were formed. Dressed in new clothes, they constructed courts in several parts of the city covered with drapes and banners, and enclosures of wood. Similarly [companies and brigades] of women and young girls went through the city dancing in train and in pairs of women with [musical] instruments and with garlands of flowers on their heads, spending their time in games and enjoyments, in dinners and suppers.[6]

From this early courtly character of all spring and summer feasts, two fundamental trends developed over the next half-century, and they would shape the whole subsequent history of the Florentine republic. The first was the emergence of a public and communal celebration of the feast of the patron, St. John, which, though by no means eliminating elements of private, pseudofeudal celebration, increasingly emphasized the presence of the government, the *popolo*, and the artisans. The second was the increasing visibility of lower- and middle-class groups in May Day celebrations, a trend that would finally convert this day into a predominantly popular feast, and drive more pretentious groups back to Carnival in January and early February. In order to clarify both the history and social character of May Day and Carnival, let us look at these developments.

With the consolidation of a constitutionally anchored gild system in Florence during the 1280s, St. John's Day inevitably developed *popolani* manifestations to balance those of the so-called *grandi*. The result was a curious mixture of civic parade and feudal bluster. When Florentine cavalry reentered the city on July 24, 1289, after its triumph at Campaldino, the Florentines treated the event as a delayed celebration of their patron's feast. Villani first described how the clergy went out in procession to meet the knights. Then in the same breath he mentioned that gentlemen executed the demonstration of knightly skill called the *armeggeria*, and that the *popolo*, organized into gilds, marched under gild flags.[7]

The simultaneous celebration of two opposed principles of organization, the feudal and the civic, rendered such celebrations highly volatile; the pseudofeudal brigades were, after all, competitive enough in themselves. On May Day 1300, for instance, the by-then traditional dances of upper-class women were disrupted when two festive brigades of the competing families of the Cerchi and Donati collided with each other while watching their virgins and matrons dance.[8] Now, however, private brigades and public organizations collided as well. On St. John's vigil less than two months later, gild consuls marching in front of their organizations were attacked by a group of *grandi* who resented the increased prominence of civil organizations, and the demise of honorable men. The *grandi* too wanted to be part of the parade, and

6. G. Villani, VII, 132. In his later verse adaptation of Villani's chronicle, Antonio Pucci speaks of people "imitating every great baronage" in this 1290 May Day; *Centiloquio*, IV, 60. It is unclear if Florence's patricians were feigning the behavior of their northern European betters, or if popular groups (discussed later) were *contrafaciendo* their betters.

7. G. Villani, VII, 132. An earlier reference to this mixture can be found in Paolino Pieri's account of the cardinal Latino's entrance in 1280: "le insegne de le ventuna arti, et fecero cinquanta armeggiatori"; Paolino Pieri, 43.

8. G. Villani, VIII, 39; Stefani, rub. 217.

as they pummeled these representatives of the civic order, they screamed: "We are the ones who gained victory at Campaldino, and you have removed us from the offices and honors of the city!"[9] "The city" was no longer simply its magnates. This St. John's procession, and all those in the years to come, were fundamental statements about the nature of the political order. As such, they were challenges to the excluded groups.

The *popolani* families that had led the attack on the magnates and created the civic procession now sought to consolidate their position, not only against the magnates but against those minor gildsmen whose backing had been essential to the *popolo's* struggle. In December 1306 the government abolished the organization of the procession according to gilds, probably because in such a procession, the butcher gild was equal to the gild of the wool capitalists, bearing its own flag and marching on its own as did its betters.[10] Instead, the city's offertory procession was to be organized under the flags of the military companies of the city (*gonfaloni*), effectively putting the rich great gildsmen at the head of each division and destroying the processional solidarity of artisans, who were consequently banned from civic representations as artisans.

Since such a processional order represented the commune at arms rather than at work, it might be thought to have flattered the knights whose honor was war; clearly, the great *popolani* families wanted to ape the knights' feudal ethos if not their legal status. But just as surely the *grandi* received little solace, for the military organizations were *popolani* institutions designed to control the magnates. Organization according to gonfalons, and marching on foot to make a *popolano* offering, challenged not only the lower gilds' processional pretensions, but those of the *grandi* as well.

The victory of the *popolo* had led to a partial distinction between the public and private character of Florentine festivals. Yet the victory left problems behind. First, the impulses of honor and family, of all those ethological elements we label personal or feudal, had perforce to find other outlets. Second, the exclusionary processional politics of the great gildsmen meant that artisans would seek another place for themselves in processional and festive life. They would do this with almost natural right, for although the commune that the city showed to the world in the St. John's procession was not a commune at work, gild membership was the alpha and omega of political participation in the city. Work remained constitutionally if not processionally the identity of the city. The artisans were disadvantaged.

As a result of this exclusion, the regimes of the coming decades had to contend with an increasing visibility of artisan groups in festivities other than those of San Giovanni. These artisan festive groups developed a mode of celebration both aping and parodying the traditional festive modes of the old aristocracy and the pretensions of the great *popolani* families, the so-called patricians. These mock heroics of the artisans drove those with any preten-

9. Compagni, I, 21.   10. Davidsohn, *Storia*, IV, 463f.

sions to genuine honor away from the feast of May and back to Carnival. Let us trace this development.

The first substantive description of a festival in which lower-class elements presumably participated comes from May Day 1304. To revive old traditions of neighborhood competition, Villani tells us, the section of San Frediano erected on boats in the Arno a fantastic image of hell that featured fires, men dressed like devils and nude souls, and much screaming. Citizens watched from the sidelines, and marveled not only at the actors but at the fine scene.[11]

It may be of course that the participants were in fact not artisans or workmen at all, but rather the scions of important families, young blades out for a good time, seeking the attention of their elders. My suspicions to the contrary come from indisputable evidence of artisan festive groups in the 1330s and 1340s. In 1333 artisans in the Via Ghibellina—477 of them, according to Stefani—combined into a brigade and elected a signore who, presumably rich, paid for the yellow livery they wore. On May Day and after, this brigade marched through the streets of the city in festive gaiety. Then to celebrate the feast of S. Onofrio on June 11, another group of 520 artisans from the Corso de' Tintori—probably dyers—joined a brigade liveried in white and led by a signore. According to Villani, both these *signori* were called "kings," and did pretty much what their betters had traditionally done in May.[12]

Villani and Stefani reacted to these artisan celebrations like great gildsmen. Stefani blamed the artisans for undue pride and pretension, whereas Villani saw the hand of God in the fact that the flood of November 1333 hit the Via Ghibellina and Corso hardest.[13] It seemed to the finer people that chivalry and genteel joy were being perverted, that their holidays were being taken over by commoners, and that God was as displeased as they were.

The development of nonpatrician festive manifestations reached its denouement in 1343. In this year the duke of Athens, Walter of Brienne, enjoyed extraordinary authority in the city. Finding his support among the political class slipping, Brienne sought to replace that backing by recruiting followers from among the *popolo minuto*—petty shop-owners and workers not included within the gild system. For May Day 1343 he created six festive brigades from among *minuti* ranks, appointed their *signori* or *messeri*, and bore the expense of livery for each group. Like the aristocratic and artisan groups that had preceded them, these groups were based in different parts of the city, their *messeri* taking such high-flown names as Emperor and Paleologue. Two of the groups from different sides of the river were soon involved in altercations.[14] There can be little doubt that under the guise of the festival

11. G. Villani, VIII, 70. On the choreographers of this event, see F. Flamini, *La Lirica Toscana del Rinascimento anteriore ai Tempi del Magnifico* (Pisa, 1891), 196. Villani's source, Paolino Pieri, says the "company" of Borgo San Frediano put on the show, led by a *signore* called "Il Sezza d'Aprile" who invited people to come "nel Reame di San Friano"; Paolino Pieri, 78. The fullest description of the event is Pucci, *Centiloquio*, IV, 195ff, who says the brigade was *di giovani*.

12. G. Villani, X, 219; Pucci, *Centiloquio*, VI, 84f, copied by Stefani, rub. 495.

13. G. Villani, X, 219.

14. Stefani, rub. 566, 575; G. Villani, XII, 8.

Brienne had created a geographically based following to counter the power of the constitutional gonfalons.

Florentines of "honest" origins despised this demagoguery, but Brienne persisted. When it came time to plan the feast of St. John, the dictator ordered that the participants be organized under the flags of their gilds and not under those of their wards, as they had been since 1306. This bow in the direction of a work ethic was a direct slap at the *popolo*'s gonfalons, and seemed to make the wool-carder gild equal to the Calimala, and the large number of minor gilds superior to the few major ones. The citizens were annoyed beyond measure, said Stefani, for they "remembered the offering of the gonfalons and [now] saw the *gente minuta* and wool carders raised up."[15]

Brienne had recognized, indeed institutionalized, the rights of the artisans to festive organizations. Although he kept the civic character of St. John's distinct from the private character of other periods and feasts, he again represented the former as occupational in nature. Brienne was the first but not the last Florentine ruler to prove that social equality was more plausible under a lord than under the government of a merchant elite.

The inherent exclusivism of the Florentine political class, the citizens' incessant determination to separate themselves from their menial origins and pretend to an honor that burghers did not possess, is vividly apparent in an incident of the Brienne period glossed by Stefani. Citizens of quality were astounded to find that Brienne's courting of the *minuti* was more than demagoguery; this great noble's French courtiers and soldiery were in fact socially more at ease with Florentine artisans and workers than were the good families of Florence! Citizens were shocked, said Stefani, when these representatives of feudal Europe invited lower-class Florentines to go drinking with them. The latter had italianized the French word *compar* ("co-father" or "ally") as *ciompo*, Stefani tells us, so that when the French said to them, "*Compar*, let's go drinking," the Florentine artisans responded, "*Ciompo*, let's go drink. And thus they said: 'Ciompo, Ciompo' as if everyone was a *ciompo*, that is, *compare*."[16] Recalling the sharp limits of association in the friendship between Mazzei and Datini, we can appreciate how repugnant this *modo francesco* of easy fraternity was to citizens of solid estate like Stefani, who saw themselves being dragged down from whence they had come.

Brienne was driven out (Plate 17) by the patricians of Florence, but his tenure and its immediate aftermath were decisive for the future of the Florentine celebratory mode. First of all, May Day lost its upper-class texture. Stefani, writing in the 1380s, could say that May Day dances in the churches and squares were still customary.[17] But by the fifteenth century the switch of the "better" families to Mardi Gras had become clear. Carnival was by then the feast par excellence of private, pseudofeudal celebrations of honorable

---

15. Stefani, rub. 575. C. Paoli misunderstood what Brienne had done; "Della Signoria di Gualtieri Duca d'Atene in Firenze," *ASI*, n.s. Appendice (1862), 114f, 118.

16. Stefani, rub. 575, 795, also 564. Rodolico was

unable to come up with a better etymology for "Ciompi," that is, the wool proletariat of a generation later; *I Ciompi* (Florence, 1971), 102f.

17. Stefani, rub. 217.

families and individuals, and May Day had a more popular tone. Neither feast had sacred associations of note.[18]

A second result of these developments was that feasts from mid-May till the end of June took on a predominantly civic tone. On May 24 citizens honored their first bishop, Zanobi; on June 11 came the feast of the apostle Barnabas, who had given the city its great victory at Campaldino. And finally came the feast of the main patron. From a period of time that served predominantly to augment the honor of individuals, families, and brigades, the weeks before St. John's had evolved into a celebration of the whole city, focusing upon saints' days.

A third result was that for decades to come the *minuti* and generally the nongild inhabitants of the city did not figure as independent participants in these main religious festivities. The feasts from Zanobi to the Baptist belonged to the political class. The *minuti* brigades of Brienne were dissolved and the organization of the offerings on St. John's Day reverted to the wards or gonfalons, which increasingly were regarded as the watchdogs of the supremacy of the honest people over the lesser artisans. The disenfranchised *minuti* who watched the gonfalons make their offerings on St. John's 1394 remembered, for example, that only the previous October those same units had ridden through the city menacing the *minuti*, who had once again tried to organize themselves.[19] Indeed, St. John's 1394 featured a 700-man strong contingent of soldiers in an exhibition of military power.[20]

Finally, civic feasts from this time on were conceived as memories of victories not only over foreign powers, but over domestic enemies as well. Thus after the expulsion of Brienne on the feast of St. Anne in 1343, her day was made a perpetual holiday, with the express purpose of fixing in the memory of citizens the fact that the tyrant's expulsion had been achieved "by the grace of God and the good men." This was obviously a backhanded condemnation of the bad lower classes whom Brienne had courted.[21] The practice of converting victories over the lower classes into civic feasts continued. Shortly after the defeat of the radical Ciompi in 1378, St. Julian was similarly honored because his day witnessed their defeat.[22] The return to power of the patrician oligarchy in 1382 was planned on the feast of St. Sebastian and executed on that of St. Anthony, so both days were declared

---

18. The church's attempt to sacralize May Day did not work; Davidsohn, *Storia*, VII, 560f. At this point Davidsohn argues a quite different historical scenario for the presence of different classes in public affairs than the one hesitatingly put forth in this work. For the continuation of my scenario, see Chapter 11, this volume. A mid-sixteenth-century Florentine source characterized May Day and Carnival not in terms of class participation, as do I, but by what he understood to be the formal characteristics of the days: on May Day the women dressed up; during Carnival the men dressed as women dressed on May Day; A. Grazzini (Il Lasca), *Tutti i Trionfi, Charri, Masche-*

rate o Canti Carnascialeschi Andati per Firenze . . . (Florence, 1559), Dedication. See page 414, this volume.

19. Panciatichi, f. 174v.

20. *Ibid.*, f. 177v.

21. "So that [the memory] be fixed in the minds of citizens that on the day of St. Anne . . . the Florentine *popolo* was liberated from tyranny by the grace of God and the virtue of good [men]"; Richa, *Notizie*, I, 28.

22. *Tumulto dei Ciompi*, 91.

holidays, and we learn that the books of governmental bureaucrats were decorated with these saints' images to commemorate their aid to the better citizens.[23] In the fifteenth century a horse race run on the feast of one such antiplebeian saint was in fact listed as "for a victory" just as others were "for a victory" over foreign enemies.[24]

After the expulsion of Brienne the Florentine regimes had once and for all set the structure and tone of festivities from Carnival through June. The lower classes were to be carefully controlled, and banned from representation in civic feasts. Pseudofeudal celebrations that could compete with the government of the *popolani* were to be subordinated to the representation of the government and other urban corporations.

Yet such a regime could not represent itself honorably; it stood for nothing, neither a nobility of work nor one of arms. Here too Brienne was to have a fundamental impact. For if the Florentines rejected his flirtation with the lower classes, they learned a great deal from him on how to stage a truly princely celebration. We shall return to the enormous inflation of the St. John's celebration at a later point. For now it is enough to suggest that, having ejected the nobility from their own political order, the *popolo* all the more needed a noble self-representation. Their mentor was the French noble Walter of Brienne.

The century and a half from 1343 till about 1480 represents the classic period of Florentine republican celebrations. The time was past when feudal forms and ideals completely overshadowed the manifestations of civic ones. The days when Lorenzo the Magnificent and his successors would give birth to a new civic identity by impregnating these civic modes with Medicean family honor were still ahead. This central era—one in which the lower artisan classes had no festive identity—will be the focus of the remainder of this chapter.

This era comprised three regimes. The first stretched from the late 1340s until about 1380, a period when the Parte Guelfa's constant assertion of feudal ideals and claims was generally balanced by strong popular counterclaims. The period is poor in sources on festive life, but it is clear that the feast of St. John was increasing in importance and magnitude and that its public element predominated. The period from 1380 till the ascent of Cosimo de' Medici (1434) was important to the festive history of the republic both in its own creativity and in its implications for the future. The public mode of St. John's Day was thoroughly established, but the city was ruled by a conservative patriciate with all the pretensions of any honor elite. The essential identity of cultural goals between the regime per se and the Parte Guelfa meant that the strength of the public sector was often expressed not only in public representations of governmental bodies but also in feudal forms, especially those of the dance, the joust, and the *armeggeria*; private forms could be made into

23. Panciatichi, f. 146v. For the drawings in the account books, see *ASF, Prov.,* 141, ff. 43rv (Apr. 29, 1450).

24. And thus a victory over internal enemies; *ASF, Manoscritti,* 119 (*Cronica di Benedetto Dei [1400–1500]*), f. 38v (hereafter Dei, *Cronica*).

public ones. The final period spanned the lives of Cosimo and his son Piero de' Medici and the early years of Piero's son Lorenzo. It essentially continued the festive mode of the high Guelf period, but with a cautiously increased emphasis upon forms that flattered the leading family of Florence. The *signore* of the festive brigade became the de facto lord of Florence, and the Guelf public forms—a fusion of civic and feudal forms—were made private.

From the foregoing, three tensions emerge that form the axes about which the celebratory mode revolved. First came a chronological tension between a predominantly public celebratory mode around the feast of St. John (the procession of the whole clergy, of the governmental subdivisions of the city, of the government and bureaucratic offices), and a preponderantly feudal, personalistic, and private mode (jousts, dances, and *armeggerie*) most pronounced around Carnival.

Second, the corollary group tension between familial and public celebration persisted, even though the interdependence of the two modes was recognized. The fundamental Florentine political dynamic, in which the families of the city fed off the public charisma, and in which the public sector had charisma only through its ingestion of family honor, was nowhere more evident than in this period. When Dati said that the families waited till St. John's to "honor the feast," he meant not only that the families profited from the commune, but vice versa. Thus the commune itself had to adopt feudal festive forms in its celebrations if it was to prosper. By the same token, feudal forms at any time had public meanings.

A final tension is implicit in the previous two: the tension in the forms themselves. Jousts, *armeggerie*, and dances were associated in the Florentine perception with feudal northern Europe and with the kingdom of Naples; processions of clergy, government officials, and sections were associated with a civic mode. The former activities were aristocratically, familially, and individually oriented; the latter, publicly and popularly. For all that, Florentines wanted their city, if not their government, to be noble. It is this most fundamental of all citizen concerns, that the city generate legitimacy, honor, and trust through legitimate forms, that leads us to choose this tension between the forms of celebration themselves as the decisive approach to the understanding of this period.

The Persistence of Honor

Courtly love was the form and passion that suffused all the pseudofeudal activities of Florence centering around Carnival. Describing a round of such activities in 1459, an anonymous versifier spoke of a dance where the beautiful women seized in love the hearts of "the flower of the young men":

> There there were a thousand enamored visages
> Seized by Venus and by Cupid,
> Taken and bound in the snares of love.[25]

25. Ricordi . . . 1459, 23f.

He spoke of the joust, where young men, very lions in their ferocity, horrible in their visage, furious in arms, fought for the love of the lady:

> Boldly each bragged
> He would make a strike for the love of a dame.
> Armed from the head down to the soles of the foot
> Each set about acquiring fame.[26]

Finally he described the *armeggeria*, where the audience looked upon the brigade's *signore* and cried:

> I nest myself in your love,
> To you I commend myself, my signore.[27]

The common spirit of these three main sports of the pretentious Florentine explains why they were often performed consecutively (Plate 15). Thus the wine seller Bartolomeo Del Corazza concluded his accounts of two dances during Carnival 1419 and 1421:

> Then the dance having been concluded, they mounted their horses and held *armeggerie*. . . .[28]

> Then after giving the prize [for the dance], [the brigade] held jousts in the said piazza with long lances, without shields, with soldiers' helmets and armor.[29]

Of these three activities, the joust and the dance were competitive, the best participants receiving prizes; like most competitive games, they were performed within a specific area, and were fenced off from the surroundings. The *armeggeria*, on the contrary, was not competitive and to a certain extent was unrestrained, its primary purpose being the creation of an erotic and lovable male. Through the *armeggeria* the woman would see a man worthy of her love because of his authority over his brigade, his love for his fellows, and their love for him. She would decide that any *messere* who could command the love of such a band of expert horsemen commanded her love. We shall see that this sentimental game was political. The *armeggeria* performed for dame Florence.

THE BRIGADE AND THE *ARMEGGERIA*

In the days of the Cerchi and Donati both men and women formed brigades, but by the later fourteenth century women's festive groups were historical curiosities embalmed in the reveries of Boccaccio. The brigades of the fifteenth century were male, and they were required to be small from fear of conspiracy—twelve, the number of the apostles, was the maximum

26. *Ibid.*, 21.

27. *Ibid.*, 27.

28. Del Corazza, 277. The editor Corazzini misdated one of the dances.

29. *Ibid.*, 276.

number.[30] Generally speaking, the brigades we encounter seem to approximate this rule. Thus when the Parte Guelfa created four brigades for festive purposes in 1399, it limited the number of each to a dozen.[31] The private brigade *del Fiore* of 1416 had fourteen members, as did another brigade in 1421; still another in 1435 had seventeen members.[32]

Apostolic modesty was, however, only a surface phenomenon. When Villani talked about the 1283 Rossi brigade of hundreds of nobles he meant the whole company. To meet the requirements of the law, later Florentines simply identified the brigade with the few upper-class or rich friends who were the center of attention. The brigade of 1435 was said, for example, to be composed of members of the Della Luna family, the Medici, Pazzi, Panciatichi, Della Stufa, Portinari, Alberti, and so on, and a brigade of 1464 found scions of the Carnesecchi, Marsupini, Bartolini, Pucci, Vespucci, Altoviti, Boni, and Girolami families accompanying their Benci *signore*.[33] But each of these brigades had a large bevy of retainers and retinue, so that the total number involved could be quite substantial. In the Benci brigade of 1464 each of the nine members had nine other youth around his horse and thirty torchbearers. Adding the especially large retinue of the *messere*, the total number came to around 400 members.[34]

In theory the brigade that participated in the *armeggeria*, joust, and dance was a group of equals who elected a *messere* or *signore* to lead them during Carnival. But in fact the impetus for private brigades seems usually to have come from one person who was elected *signore* in exchange for a promise to feed and clothe his brothers, and generally underwrite the forthcoming activities. Consequently the Florentine private brigade closely followed the personalistic feudal model. Service was rewarded with protection, the group combining fraternity and hierarchy. In a ceremony modeled on the Florentine practice of giving a baton to its mercenary general, the new *signore* received a baton or some other symbol of authority from his friends.[35] From that point on, the brothers were considered a social unit, and this was expressed publicly by wearing a common livery—that of the family of the *signore*.

Before the brigade ever stepped into the street, therefore, it had accomplished a number of important socializing functions. First, it had brought youthful friends together into an obligatory relationship and helped to extend that relationship past the festive season.[36] Second, it involved the families of the youth in that relationship; indeed, diarists identified *armeggiatori* as the sons of certain citizens rather than by their Christian names.[37] Third, the brigade created a putative hierarchy of friends and families, for the *signore*'s

30. *Statuto . . . Capitano,* 309.

31. Ps. Minerbetti, 239; also in 1406, 354f.

32. Del Corazza, 255f, 276, 290.

33. *Ibid.,* 290 (1435); P. Gori, *Le Feste Fiorentine attraverso i secoli. Le Feste per San Giovanni* (Florence, 1926), 41.

34. *Ibid.,* 42ff.

35. *Ibid.,* 42.

36. One sees evidence of this solidarity in Francesco di Tommaso Giovanni's record that when a jouster was killed in 1428, he and the other participants "di tutto gli facemmo le spese e nutricammo i figli finchè furono grandi"; cited in Truffi, *Giostre,* 167.

37. See, for example, the list of 1459; Cambi, XX, 371 copying Pietrobuoni.

family paid out large sums and thus created credits with the families of the brothers. Finally, the brigade's members marked themselves off from outsiders by their livery.

The government no longer permitted noble brigades to divide Florence into little cities as in the thirteenth century. The brigades of the fifteenth century performed their feats on different days or at least at different times of the day, so as to diffuse the danger of confrontation.[38] But then, to accommodate family honor as well as to protect the citizenry from these heavily armed and ferociously screaming horsemen, the government warned citizens that the fault was theirs if they were accidentally hurt, for the horsemen would not be prosecuted:

> The magnificent and potent Signori etc. ban and notify that since they have notice through certain Florentine citizens that on the fourteenth day of the present [month] a mounted *armeggeria* is to be held in the city of Florence with, as they understand, a large concourse of riders, that if any accidental case occurs in which any person, of whatever status or condition he be, is injured or killed or trampled in any way by the said *armeggiatori* with the lances and their horses on the said day or the evening of [that] night in the city of Florence, no office or official of the commune of Florence will be competent, nor can form a process nor proceed against them in any way. For this has been solemnly deliberated and provided by the Signoria.[39]

Citizens retreated to their homes and looked out from the safety of their barred windows to see the spectacle; they witnessed an important part of the political process at work. First, they sought out the *signore*:

> *He for many reasons has great power*
> *Since his family can do much,*
> *Son of Piero and grandson of Cosimo.*
> *Thus these genteel [youth] made him* signore. . . .
> *Whence he wanted to show everyone*
> *That they were all subjected to one* signore.
> *Now that genuine youth moves*
> *Upon a horse marvelously ornate,*
> *Everyone watches what he does.* . . .
> *His dress surpasses easily that of*
> *All those of whom we've spoken,*
> *And well shows that he is* signore.[40]

Second, they asked how rich could the *signore* show his brigade to be. Could the brigade muster the panoply necessary to divide the festivities into two days, the first only for its parade (*mostra*), the second for another shorter parade and the actual "war"?[41] How many layers of livery would each brigade member be laden with? The audience watched closely as each rider ceremonially stripped off one layer after another in an act of charity—each

38. See page 233, this volume.

39. Gori, *Feste*, 41 (1464).

40. *Ricordi . . . 1459*, 30f. Note the patent attempt to

suggest that the *signore* (young Lorenzo) is lord of the commune as well.

41. For such a case, Del Corazza, 254 (1415).

layer given away—until he reached the minimum necessary to show his equestrian skill.[42] How richly were the horses appareled, and how often were their clothes and those of the pages changed during the festivities?[43]

Finally, how well would the *signore*'s men ride? The actual equestrian activity, so often completely neglected by the chroniclers in favor of the riches displayed, was simplicity itself:

> First, each rode standing up in the saddle with a golden dart in hand, as is customary in *armeggerie*. And then each rode with a golden battering lance, and they broke [them] at the foot of the window where the said dame was.[44]

Each rider broke the lance at a gallop, and if it could be said of each:

> And no one found fault with him
> Either in armeggiare or in his dress. . .[45]

the *signore* and his brigade were a success.

Armed with this information, the spectators judged such demonstrations within a political context. The actors were, after all, *sir di guerra*, armed men or boys who were making some type of claim upon their audience. They were rich, and they were capable of combat. Whose sect did these men follow? Was the family of the *messere* aligned with the regime, or was it opposed? What was the occasion? Was this family celebrating some fortunate private event, like the *armeggeria* staged by the Corsini in 1369 when Piero was made a cardinal, or that done in 1389 on the occasion of Maso degli Albizzi's knighting?[46] Or was the occasion a communal celebration that the family attached its honor to?

Spectators pondered such questions not as outsiders, but as an audience to which the brigade laid claim; a flawless display of family honor and riches attracted followers or at least approval. Ritual perfection was imperial, and that was the problem: The unity of brigades, their perfect execution of ritual forms under a *signore*, was meant to please the citizens, honor the families involved, but at the same time honor the commune that relied on family honor. Yet the ritual success of one brigade disturbed the precarious balance between family honors, and could thus trigger civil disturbances. The *armeg-*

42. The term used for such stripping was *stracciare; ibid.*, 243. "St[r]acciando e donando e tutta maniera di gente, donando e dando per amore"; *Diario d' Anonimo,* 464 (1386), and 456 (1384).

43. Various descriptions of horse and human dress are in Del Corazza, 242, 254f, 264, 281. Eve Borsook describes funeral effigies' clothes being changed in the sixteenth century, "Art and Politics," 38. Presumably the clothes on the large wax votive statues in SS. Annunziata were also ritually changed; Warburg, *Gesammelte Schriften,* 99.

44. Gori, *Feste,* 43 (1464). Boccaccio's description is much the same in his *Fiametta; Opere* (Milan, 1966),

1018–1021. Francesco da Barberino carefully distinguishes between the *armeggeria* and the joust; *Documenti,* I, 336f. Piponnier has noticed that descriptions of French equestrian activities are almost exclusively limited to the *cortège*, clothing, and so on, "as if they attach much more importance to formal aspects and aesthetics of the joust than to action, heroism, physical prowess"; *Costume et Vie Sociale. La Cour d'Anjou. XIVe–XVe siècles* (Paris, 1970), 61f.

45. *Ricordi . . . 1459,* 28.

46. G. Monaldi, *Diario,* in *Istorie Pistolesi e Diario del Monaldi (1340–1381)* (Florence, 1733), 434 (hereafter Monaldi); Naddo da Montecatini, 111.

geria was a test of the ability of a burgher commune to contain within itself both honor and civility.

Two distinct elements of political process were enacted in these streets, both of intense interest and importance to spectators. First, *armeggerie* tested the strength of the existing regime or alliance of families, and thus often had transparent competitive ends. Thus when in 1384 and again in 1386 the brigades of the Alberti and Castellani took to the streets on different days of the same week, the Florentine audience well knew that it was witnessing a political test between two great families, the latter identified with the regime, the former opposed to and threatened by it.[47] When in 1391 the Company of the Corso, which had its center in the piazza of the Alberti, rode haughtily through the streets of the city on the feast of S. Onofrio, beating and breaking their lances on the quintain, citizens regarded such sport as an Alberti attempt to maintain its status within a regime opposed to it.[48] Machiavelli, in describing the events of these years, perceived what the exhibitions were all about. Families had seized upon Charles of Durazzo's acquisition of Apulia and Florence's purchase of Arezzo as opportunities to display their individual power in the city:

> As great rejoicings were made in Florence on account of this acquisition as ever took place in any city for a real victory. They served to exhibit the public and private wealth of the people, many families endeavoring to vie with the state itself in displays of magnificence. The Alberti surpassed all others; the tournaments and exhibitions made by them were rather suitable for a sovereign prince than for any private individuals. These things increased the envy with which the family was regarded, and being joined with suspicions which the state entertained of Benedetto [degli Alberti] were the cause of his ruin.[49]

Thus the *armeggeria* always presented a warning and a challenge. If it were held by the Corsini when that family was identified with the regime, or by the Albizzi and Castellani when those families were so identified, such an exercise affirmed "the commune" and humiliated those families less identified with it. If, as was the case with the Alberti, these loud demonstrations of family valor were performed by endangered families, they were tests of those families' rights to the streets and as such called for responses from "the state," that is, the Albizzi and Castellani. No wonder that after the *armeggerie* of the 1380s, the commune sponsored a formal Mass of Peace attended by the families involved![50] In these *armeggerie* the political process was laid bare, its quintessentially familial tensions revealed; like the governmental priors drinking fraternal wine after their deliberations, the city proved through its Mass of Peace that honor and civility could be combined. It was to be

47. Panciatichi, f. 150v; Naddo da Montecatini, 73, 82.

48. Panciatichi, f. 161r. The celebration of S. Onofrio in the Piazza degli Alberti is again documented in Dei, *Cronica*, 38v (1472).

49. Machiavelli's analysis (*History*, 146) was influenced by Stefani's long but rambling description of the 1384 events mentioned earlier; rub. 995.

50. Panciatichi, f. 150v.

short-lived for, as Machiavelli explained, the Alberti had created an envy that they were unable to humble.

The second element of the political process in the *armeggeria* was the creation and affirmation of alliances between families. Here the emphasis was not upon challenge but contract, one family wooing the other in public so as to affirm its serious intent to be friends. Such ritual pacts were not spontaneous, but planned by two families so that the *armeggeria* became a type of public treaty-signing.

The complex layers of such festive diplomacy are partly visible in the Benci *armeggeria* of Carnival 1464 and in the events that preceded it. During the winter, citizens were preoccupied with the illness of Cosimo de' Medici. The city was filled with expectancy, for its future would be unsure when this city father passed away. Had not Palla Strozzi intimated that he would consider conspiring against the government only after Cosimo died? The latter's son Piero was sickly, his grandson Lorenzo a fifteen-year-old teenager at the University of Pisa. It was a period when all alliances were in flux, and the future of emigré families such as the Strozzi hung in the balance.

In a letter to Lorenzo in February, Filippo Corsini described how three youths had set out to have a good time during a rare Florentine snowstorm. They were Lottieri Neroni, Priore Pandolfini, and Bartolomeo Benci, all from families allied to the Medici. They marched down to the house of Marietta degli Strozzi to engage in a snowball fight with her. Yet this was no ordinary street-corner fight, but a choreographed scene complete with audience:

> What a spectacle, immortal Gods! For [the scene] was made decorous by dignity, by the lights of innumerable torches, by the clamor of trumpets, and by the sweetness of flutes. . . . What can I say about the excitement of those standing about, what of the applause of many of them?[51]

The girl answered with snowballs herself, and the joy of one of the males was unequaled when he "sprayed the face of the snow-white girl with snow."[52] What was this all about?

Marietta was the granddaughter of Palla Strozzi, who had been banished by the Medici in the 1430s and had died in 1451; her mother was Alessandra de' Bardi, who at this time was living in Bologna with other members of her husband's exiled family. Marietta was sixteen and nubile, a lovely girl of solid estate who, although at the moment politically disadvantaged because of her father Lorenzo's fate, would be an enormous asset in the political battle to come if the Strozzi were rehabilitated. The ponderables were roughly similar to those Giovanni Morelli's governors had faced before they decided to marry him to Caterina degli Alberti. Thus the snowball fight must have been either directly political, an outright attempt by the Medici and its supportive families to flatter the Strozzi, or indirectly political, the actions of up-and-coming youngsters of powerful families watched by their fathers.

51. I. Del Lungo, *La Donna Fiorentina del Buon Tempo*   52. *Ibid.*
Antico (Florence, 1906), 200f, 237f.

This alliance aspect of Florentine games is perfectly clear in the *armeggeria* that followed soon after the snowball fight. The main actors were Bartolomeo Benci and Marietta di Lorenzo degli Strozzi. The almost theatrical setting of the whole—Del Lungo called this *armeggeria* "a painting"—is evident at the very beginning of the anonymous account:

> Notice of a festival done on the night of Carnival for a dame . . . who was the daughter of Lorenzo di messer Palla degli Strozzi. The said festival was done by Bartolomeo Benci, playing the part of one enamored of the said dame . . . who desired to acquire more grace with the said dame.[53]

The theatrical use of the words *dama* and *chome innamorato* prepares us for the fact that the two never did marry, and that indeed some of Benci's partners in the brigade were already married.[54] Obviously something was involved besides "acquiring grace." The description of the *armeggeria* reveals that family politics were involved.

After the brigade of nine members had dutifully elected Benci its *messere* and had been his guests at a banquet, the enormous liveried party of perhaps 400 including torchbearers, musicians, pages, and the like proceeded to the Strozzi home, pulling behind them a contraption twenty yards tall showing the triumph of love. At the top of this *trionfo* stood a flaming, bleeding heart—perhaps the least complicated of Florentine symbolic efforts. But more central to our purposes is that two sets of arms covered the *trionfo*: that of the Benci, and the device of Lorenzo di Palla Strozzi.[55] This *armeggeria* was no simple excess of young blades, but a political statement of hope and potential: Marietta, though perhaps uninterested in Bartolomeo, might become a bridge to political alliance between the Strozzi and the Benci. The publicity of the act announced this potentiality to the populace.

This was not a spontaneous Benci offering to the Strozzi. In fact, the whole spectacle was superintended by four masters of ceremonies: two Benci, *and two Strozzi relatives of Marietta*, all four of whom rode together.[56] At the center of action for the ensuing manifestations of horsemanship stood the image of Marietta, worshiped by all those political fellows: "She showed herself [at a window] in the midst of four lit torches with such gracious dignity, that it would have sufficed for Lucrezia herself."[57]

One would have to know the immediate political background in order to understand the *armeggeria* fully. And, particularly, one would have to know under what guise the other eight young men of the brigade honored *their* "dames" after Marietta had been feasted.[58] Did the Benci–Strozzi *trionfo* go along to each other distaff window? Were the unions between the family of

53. Gori, *Feste*, 41; Del Lungo, *Donna*, 197.

54. *Ibid.*, 200.

55. Gori, *Feste*, 42.

56. Gori, *Feste*, 43. Vanni and Strozzo Strozzi were,

of course, from sections of the consortery that had chosen the Medici in 1434, and had not been banished; Rochon, *Jeunesse*, 568.

57. Gori, *Feste*, 43.

58. The sparse information is *ibid.*, 44.

each other youth and that of his "dame" demonstrably affirmed in the presence of the Benci–Strozzi arms? Our source is silent on this point; we cannot even be sure if the Benci's Medici patrons were behind the whole affair.

It would be easy to see these exercises as mere fantasy games of a feudal never-never land that had little to do with Florentine reality. But we have seen that this was certainly not the case. Conversely, these celebrations might be viewed as fronts for the articulation of alliances, the game and demonstrative aspects of the *armeggerie* being dismissed as merely external. But that would also be false. The right understanding of this Florentine sport recognizes the politics of the game, both the importance of such honorable forms to Florentine self-regard, and the importance of the bonding process. The central tension remains. To be acceptable, the *armeggeria* like the dance had to be done perfectly, according to the norms of the audience. But such perfection was irresistible, and if the honor of the brigades' families was augmented by an increased retinue, this gain endangered the balance of the whole.

The content of the *armeggeria*, as was said at the beginning, was feudal and personalistic, and it is from this point of view that we have studied it. But like the joust and dance, the *armeggeria* was subject to incursion by civil forces. Because it was associated with knightly honor, a commodity the ignoble government needed; because publicly sponsored *armeggerie* could defuse conspiratorial impulses; because communal funding of such noble demonstrations lightened the substantial financial burden carried by individual families; and because participation in publicly sponsored *armeggerie* would increase commitment to the commune (that is, to communal families) at the expense of commitment to private groups, the Florentine government in the later fourteenth century began to take certain *armeggerie* under its aegis. It was no accident that the Parte Guelfa was the entity charged with organizing these demonstrations, nor that public *armeggerie* occurred only in the period 1380–1434; the regime identified itself with an antipopular, quasi-feudal familial ideology.[59]

The difference between private and public *armeggerie* lay not in their content but in their effects. Since an essential purpose of the *armeggerie* was to demonstrate wealth, the commune and not a particular family was the beneficiary of public admiration to the extent that the commune bore expenses. In the Parte-sponsored *armeggeria* of 1386, for example, one chronicler noted that the horses were dressed first in white, and then at midday their costumes were changed to blue.[60] In the *armeggeria* staged by the Parte to celebrate the fall of Pisa in 1406, the government again took pains to stress its prodigious liberality; the warriors and their horses were publicly undressed in the public square, the heavy coats and drapes removed to reveal an equally sumptuous garment beneath. Chroniclers described each in great detail.[61] In

59. I have found such *armegerrie* only in 1386 and 1406.

60. Naddo da Montecatini, 82 (Feb. 9).

61. Ps. Minerbetti, 355; Del Corazza, 242ff.

every such event witnesses marveled at the livery that the commune provided.

A second difference: The public *armeggeria* was performed in the great public squares, and had the magistrates of the city as observers. Thus in the *armeggeria* of 1406, each squadron of twenty warriors first performed its equestrian feats in a space stretching from the Mercato Nuovo to the palace of the Parte, where each participant received a garland from the captains of the Parte. The squadron moved to the main square to break the mock "Saracen" or quintain, then went through the city *armeggiando*, to return in the evening to the main square to repeat its acrobatics.[62]

The most important difference between the private and public *armeggeria* was that the latter's brigade seems to have been chosen by the Parte or the government itself. Our information on this point is slim; we cannot be sure that the Parte did not simply order preexisting groups for a public festival. But we do know that from the moment they stepped into the streets the government controlled their organizational and festive activity. Thus in the 1406 festivities, the Parte "invited" sixty youth to *armeggiare*. It divided them into six squadrons or brigades of ten. Two performed on October twenty-sixth, two on the twenty-seventh, and two on the twenty-eighth. Each of the six was dressed in a special livery. And on each day, the two brigades were kept apart from each other.[63]

From such evidence it is fair to assume that to a greater extent than with private brigades, these Parte groups fostered the idea of communal rather than private sponsorship of bellicose activity, even though the "commune" was more a conglomerate of families than any objective entity. Moreover, to the extent that such youth groups became associated with the commune, they lost some of their familial identity and resembled a random collection of youths, an abstraction no longer unified by strict bonds of familial clientage. It is certainly significant that the chroniclers' descriptions of public *armeggerie* in 1386 and 1406 do not mention the proper name of a single participant, evidence that the commune ennobled itself at the expense of family solidarity.

THE JOUST

No equestrian activity was more associated with the feudal ethos than the joust. Here was the aristocratic sport par excellence, an individualistic demonstration of equestrian skill to win a lady. Yet at least from the early fourteenth century, the commune, acting like any feudal court, sponsored this sport and remained its prime supporter till the end of our period when, for a short time, the protocourtly Medici family used jousts as a means of honoring individuals like themselves. We must try to understand how the

62. *Ibid*. A description of the quintain (*saraceno*) tilted in the main piazza, and the location of the *Buca del* *Saraceno*, are given in Cambi, XXI, 117, 126, 160.
63. Del Corazza, 242ff.

joust, in content and ethos so uncivic, was, as opposed to the *armeggeria*, almost always sponsored by the city.

There was one practical explanation. A large city like Florence attracted professional jousters seeking challenges, and the government brought them in to provide entertainment. Throughout the period northern European and Italian knights dotted the roads of Tuscany, earning their livelihood from the stakes they won at their sport. Florence was an advantageous stopping point, for any inhabitant who could afford it could mount a horse and try his luck; the city did not legally limit riding to a particular class. Villani recalled a joust in 1329 in which such professionals took on any challenger willing to wager on himself, and again in 1377 a diarist recorded a planned joust in which "anyone" could test his skill for *Madonna Libertà*.[64]

The tension within the Florentine joust was evident enough: On the one side the joust had been "disenchanted," for theoretically anyone could participate. The reward was cash, given for merit and skill, not class. On the other side, however, the joust retained an aristocratic character because of its association with the horse and the lady. A *popolano* who defeated a visiting knight rose in the estimation of his fellows not only because of his skill, but because such skill demonstrated a right to social status.

It was certainly with this conflict in mind that the regime from 1382 to 1434 attempted to dampen competition by *popolani*. The Parte or the government would sponsor the jousts, and limit participation to honorable men who followed the regime.[65] There was no longer any question of persons "of any condition" participating, and whenever we find the names of those who entered the lists, they are almost invariably the sons of good families associated with the regime.[66] As with the *armeggeria* so with the joust: The commune in this period supplemented civic display with noble sport. But the joust was particularly suited for such civic incorporation, and was much more commonly sponsored than the *armeggeria*.

The most important reason why the joust was so regularly sponsored by the city had to do with the nature of the affair: The joust rewarded individual skill without necessarily fostering family charisma, as did the *armeggeria*. The challenger might, it is true, march to the list accompanied by a brigade of family members and associates; the parade of the joust was little different from that of the *armeggeria*. But once he entered a list like the one in Piazza Santa Croce (Plate 12), about 125 feet long and 60 feet wide, he could bring either shame or honor to his family.[67] Thus the communally sponsored joust was the main public performance in which individual skill could be demonstrated. This regime proved that the joust, the epitome of individualistic demonstration of *virtù*, was the best means for the commune to use to ensure

64. G. Villani, X, 131; *Diario d'Anonimo*, 325.

65. This trend was accompanied by a decline in the number of persons knighted by the commune; G. Salvemini, *La Dignità Cavalleresca nel Comune di Firenze e altri scritti* (Milan, 1972), 124f.

66. For example, Del Corazza, 255 (1415), 290 (1435); Cambi, XX, 172–176 (1428).

67. Del Corazza, 245. Further details on how Piazza S. Croce was outfitted for jousts are in Masi, 206 (1516).

its identity and equalize its youth beneath it; festive individualism was the best insurance the commune had against familial strength. In fact, individualism and governmental strength were two sides of the same coin.

THE DANCE

The dances of May Day had been the catalyst for the civil war in early fourteenth-century Florence. War and dance were still associated in the fifteenth century for, as we have seen, dances often immediately preceded the jousts or *armeggerie*. In the motions of the dance, men suggested to women an athletic eros that they proceeded to demonstrate in the war games.

During the period under examination, dances were most commonly sponsored by families, but the commune occasionally made use of their genteel aura to impress foreigners and satisfy the needs of its more ambitious citizens. To judge from the limited evidence, the social dance was at home in the individual *loggie* of the patrician families and was associated with the banquet. When it became a public event that left the family palace to delight the city as a whole, the banquet often went with it.

The best narrative source for the dance, as for the joust and *armeggeria*, is the diary of the Florentine wine seller Del Corazza, who described five different balls in the period from 1415 to 1435. Four of these were staged by nongovernmental brigades, and all four were during Carnival, as were most of the *armeggerie*.[68] Del Corazza describes the basic operating mode of the dance. A brigade procured the right to fence off a certain area, most commonly the marketplace;[69] it provided the sweets and drinks that were standard fare at each dance, and invited participation.[70] Perhaps dancing was usually limited to the brigade and an equal number of girls, but in at least one case, at the Carnival dance of 1415, the brigade played host to some six hundred women and a large number of men.[71]

These dances were competitive, with the brigade providing prizes. In one staged in 1419, the brigade chose some men to judge male dancing, and four women to judge female dancing.[72] These judges sat above the dance floor framed like any other authority. The scene around the fenced-off area represented a purified hierarchical structure within which socially prescribed dancing gestures were judged.[73]

To observers like Del Corazza the dance itself was unimportant; indeed his extensive descriptions of the events yield not one bit of information on the

68. Del Corazza, 254 (Feb. 10, 1415); 255f (Feb. 23, 1416); 276 (Feb. 2, 1419); 277 (Feb. 26, 1421). The public dance is *ibid.*, 290 (Nov. 13, 16, 1435), and its preparation is detailed by Francesco Giovanni, one of the four officials charged to arrange the *festa:* Giovanni–Carnesecchi, Oct. 1435.

69. Del Corazza, 254, 277.

70. *Ibid.*, 276f.

71. *Ibid.*, 254.

72. *Ibid.*, 276. Corazzini dates this 1420, but a check of the universal calendar shows it was 1419, before Ash Wednesday. Pietrobuoni says that the sixty *giovani* and the many girls who danced in 1459 were selected to participate because they were "the most apt at dancing"; copied by Cambi, XX, 369.

73. See the precise description of a 1454 signorial frame *ibid.*, 321.

types of dances performed.[74] What was important was the activity of the male brigade. Del Corazza detailed the setting for the dance, its area and the formal arrangement of judges, and he twice listed the winners of the female and male competitions.[75] But above all, he described the wondrous unison that the male brigade showed in its livery:

> And all fourteen youths of the brigade dressed in the same livery, that is in cloth the color of a peach blossom, which reached down to just below the knee; with blown-up sleeves, the left sleeve embroidered with pearls, that is, an arm that came out of a little cloud and threw flowers down the left arm. The shoes were of the same cloth, except that the left was half red, and a branch of flowers of pearl was woven into it.[76]

> This brigade was fourteen strong, and they dressed in lined crimson of squirrel skin tucked up on the outside more than half an arm, with a fantasy of pearls on the left arm, with big hoods fringed in white and red and green, and shoes devised with new white and red and green devices embroidered with pearls.[77]

> All dressed in green damask with a parrot of pearls on the right sleeve, with hoods of cloth edged in green and red, with green and red shoes embroidered in pearls. And then to *armeggiare* all were in a crimson doublet with stripped garlands of brass.[78]

This almost exclusive attention to male dancers is characteristic of Del Corazza and of other urban commentators on pseudofeudal activities. Both the women and the male youth were outside the political process, but the males were the political class of the future. Therefore, as in the joust and *armeggeria,* so in the dance citizens primarily recorded the activities of their males and not their females. They saw in such liveried uniformity the imaginative nonindividuality of the coming political generation. Here were sons dressed by a *signore* performing honorable games in unison and without rancor. Though in touch with females in the dance, they preserved decorum; it could be hoped that the same decorum would be preserved in the more virile politics of the *armeggeria,* and in their future adult lives.

If citizens viewed the dance within the context of male solidarity, however, they realized that the aristocratic ethos they aped, different from the civic ethos, placed as much importance upon female ritual as upon that of males. When noble visitors came to town, they were taken on a tour of the richest nunneries of the town, where the nuns performed their rituals for the admiring visitors. Women and girls served in a sense as the liminal bridges between different powers, serving to disarm visitors and permit communication between males. Del Corazza the wine seller might ignore the girls and women, but a city attempting to ennoble itself through the dance could not. Individual burghers might prefer to imagine women as static objects who kept their eyes down; governments knew that without girls and women, there was no dance.

It is no accident that one of the two extensive descriptions of Florentine women at dance in this period occurs in the one biography by Vespasiano da

74. An example of the intricacy of dances is provided by Baxandall, *Painting,* 79f.

75. Del Corazza, 276f.

76. *Ibid.,* 255f.

77. *Ibid.,* 276.

78. *Ibid.,* 277.

Bisticci written specifically to honor women, and not in one of his many lives of males; that this particular dance was staged to honor foreign dignitaries and was not a strictly domestic affair; and that this dance was sponsored by the commune, not by a private brigade or family.[79] By examining the relevant passages in this vita of Alessandra Bardi, we may again verify the tension in the content of honorable public displays; essentially familial and private in nature, they were made to contribute to the nobility of the commune itself.

Writing in the later part of the fifteenth century, Vespasiano remembered clearly the reason why the commune had sponsored this particular dance. He speaks of the noble train accompanying the emperor Sigismund on his Italian trip of 1431, and remarks:

> These gentlemen were also curious to see the city itself, which at this time was full of splendor and riches and famous throughout the world. They were received with the highest honor by the Signoria, and by all the citizens, who showed them all possible courtesy and, in order to entertain them and let them see the most accomplished and seemly ladies and the most goodly youths of the city, they determined to give a ball in the Piazza dei Signori.[80]

Vespasiano described how the event was organized and, in a few words, the course of the dance itself. The government invited "all the youth" of the city to assemble on a platform in the main piazza, dressed of course in livery and to the hilt (fur down to the shoes). The girls first danced for the imperial ambassadors, who were apparently ensconced above the platform, and then fetched the latter from their position of honor into the dance. Alessandra's behavior was excellent: "It was something everyone marveled at: Alessandra's dexterity, how she knew how to do everything well."[81]

But the writer's recollection of the general setting was much more acute than what he remembered of the dance per se. For Vespasiano, Alessandra's behavior in serving the ambassadors food and drink was the real essence of the ritual of social communication:

> Because of her dexterity it was ordained that Alessandra would take in her hands a tray full of sweets and carry them to the ambassadors, with a napkin of Reims linen on her shoulder. She took it and with immeasurable gentility placed it before [each] ambassador, each time making reverence with curtsies down to the floor, naturally and not affectedly, such that it appeared she had never done anything else. Her ways and habits greatly pleased the ambassadors and all those standing about. Having put down the sweets, she took the cups of wine and did the same. And she did everything such that it seemed she had always done them, and she did not seem reared by an inexpert woman but by a most prudent one, who had taught her every little thing, as one sees.[82]

This assessment reminds one of Giovanni Morelli's similar praise of his sister Bartolomea:

79. Vespasiano, *Vite*, 558–583.
80. *Ibid.*, 565.
81. *Ibid.*, 566.
82. *Ibid.*, 567.

> She knew how to sing and dance perfectly, and could have served a banquet of men
> or of women just as politely as any youth who was trained and experienced in
> marriage [banquets] and similar things.[83]

Alessandra's ritual contribution to Florence's diplomatic position continued:

> Then after the snack and some more dancing, the ambassadors stood up [to leave], for
> the hour was already late. They were accompanied by many citizens and to the side by
> those youths from the *festa*. And Alessandra . . . had put her hand under the right
> arm [of one ambassador], and another [girl] supported his left arm. . . . The ambas-
> sadors had been so greatly honored that one day seemed a thousand till they could
> return to Siena to tell the emperor everything, describing to him the so modest
> women they had seen, and especially Alessandra: her worthy habits, and her su-
> preme beauty.[84]

An anonymous description of the public dance of 1459 honoring the
visiting count of Milan is no less punctilious in its attention to ritual detail.[85]
So strong was the witness's awareness of contacts between the count and the
Florentines, in fact, that the dance seems merely an excuse for greeting or
contact courtesies. He tells us that Count Galeazzo Maria Sforza made
"worthy reverences and lovely bows" to the male dancers, and that "the
women stand up, doing reverence to [the count's] person, and bow almost
down to the floor" when the latter passed. When young girls invited the
count to dance, they too "made a bow down to the floor, with the most ornate
and prompt reverence." The young Sforza "danced without error," of course,
but our viewer was more interested in how the audience behaved during the
princely dance: Every time the count in dancing approached the stands, our
chronicler twice recorded, those in that section of the audience rose up.

> While the count danced with [the Florentine girls],
> Men and women, everyone, stood up and bowed
> As many times as he passed in front of them. . . .
> And everyone honored him worthily.
> They put him in the middle and danced with him,
> And as he passed everyone stood up.

The poet did not, in short, ignore the audience. Rather, he envisioned
the dance as a total scene, made up of those on the dance floor plus the
interacting people in the stands who danced to the prince's movements,
within the "circuit" of the fence. Let us imagine the stands surrounding the
square as undulating social groups:

> Three levels around with lovely seats,
> The one higher than the other, so that he sees
> Who sits down first and who later. . . ,

83. G. di Pagolo Morelli, *Ricordi*, 179.

84. Vespasiano, *Vite*, 567.

85. The Italian text of the following passages was

generously furnished me by Rab Hatfield. The passage is noted in his "Some Unknown Descriptions of
the Medici Palace in 1459," *Art Bulletin* LII (1970), 237,
n. 45.

Each row socially divided:

> *And it appears that one plans an order*
> > *That the first row, closest to the fence,*
> > *Was elected for the great and worthy [male] citizens.*
>
> *And the next, a little lower and parallel,*
> > *For the women who are not apt at dancing*
> > *Either because of age or obesity or widowhood.*
>
> *And the one in front was decorated solely*
> > *So that the women and girls who would be making the* festa
> > *All around [the area] would have a place to rest.*

This seating arrangement combined with the order of the floor to produce a total visual impression. There was beauty: the first row of dancing females so lovely that one could slake one's thirst "to see beautiful women and beautiful things, and well examine all their parts." There was social order, everyone seated "where his estate allowed him to sit." And there was divine order, for the women were like angels, their movements paradisiac. The author saw "angelic hierarchies" in this social ritual, and the total image of the count, the frame of Florentine dancers, and devotional stands blended into astronomic unity:

> *The whole appeared a heaven of lovely roseate circles,*
> > *In which the count represented the sun,*
> > *And the [Florentine] women and* garzoni *shining stars.*

From the meager information presently at our disposal, a social history of the Florentine dance appears far off. Some cautious evaluation of these public performances may, however, still be put forth. Their ethos was feudal, these original contacts with ladies being the spur to the military events that either preceded or followed them. In them, spectators witnessed and participated in correct forms: a common clothing for young males identifying them as allies of a *signore;* proper womanly behavior and proper execution of "embassies". "It is a marvelous thing," said another observer of the ball and banquet of 1459, "to see with what beautiful order everything proceeded."[86] The dance as a crystalline demonstration of correct personal relations both affirmed existing codes of body gestures and taught how citizens could live together like nobles at table. Around the dance whirled the joust and especially the *armeggeria,* which, though formalized, represented the violence that made the dance possible.

In the joust, dance, and *armeggeria,* we have seen the persistence of honor, of that feudal ethos that was the main source of dignity for families, individuals, and the commune itself. Each form was primarily associated with the private world of classes striving for honor and status, and each was characteristically performed during Carnival rather than on civic feasts like St.

86. Cambi, XX, 370.

John's. Yet these public activities of the familial sphere were made to contribute to the honor of the commune as well as to that of the family. Government did not try to divorce itself from family honor. Rather, Florentine regimes sought to be the biggest family of all so as to protect the families that made them up. By incorporating such feudal honors into the civic fabric, a talented regime could in fact solve the inherent tension of all noble sport. The ideal *armeggeria*, dance, or joust, we have seen, was judged good to the extent that it presented a perfect, unified ritual; yet by attracting retinue, such perfection diminished the status of less perfect ritual units. If the perfect regime developed the perfect noble and personalistic ritual, it could reduce families to subjection. But that development was not to be until the time of Lorenzo de' Medici. Deep into the fifteenth century, the noncharismatic representation of civil organization held sway. It is time to examine the classic civil feast.

The Feast of St. John and Other Friends

Dati may have slightly exaggerated when in the early 1400s he argued that the feast of St. John was unparalleled in the world. But his brave words would soon be fact. During the course of the century the festival's length, cost, and participation left visitors awed at the wealth of a body politic that could afford such expenditures.

This was as it was meant to be, for one of the main purposes of this event was to draw approval from other states, and thus add some luster to the city's tarnished burgher image. In this section, however, we will be primarily concerned with what this and other celebrations meant to the Florentines. As in describing the family celebrations of the Carnival season, now as the calendar reaches mid-June we attempt to understand the relevance of public celebration to the body political and social.

We emerge from a period of unconsecrated celebrations staged first on May Day and later during Carnival, and enter a sacred cycle of civil feasts dedicated to Zanobi, Barnabas, and finally to the Baptist himself. We leave behind a group of celebrations in which women and youth, groups outside the political body, had played a role, and enter one in which the participants are mostly mature males. We bid farewell to events of genteel splendor, which while binding together small groups of men had fostered competition between families and individuals, and enter the giant magnetic field of contract and sacrifice that was the feast of the Baptist.

Preparations for the great feast began months before. In the days just before its formal beginning, wagons bearing the cloth *palii* that would later be awarded to the winners of the horse races were pulled through the streets of the city *ad spectaculum populi*— to excite the populace for the coming events.[87]

87. An accident on June 17, 1467, crushed a boy when the *palio* overturned in the Prato ad Ognissanti;   M. Palmieri, *Historia Fiorentina*, ed. G. Scaramella, *RIS*, XXVI, pt. 1, 185.

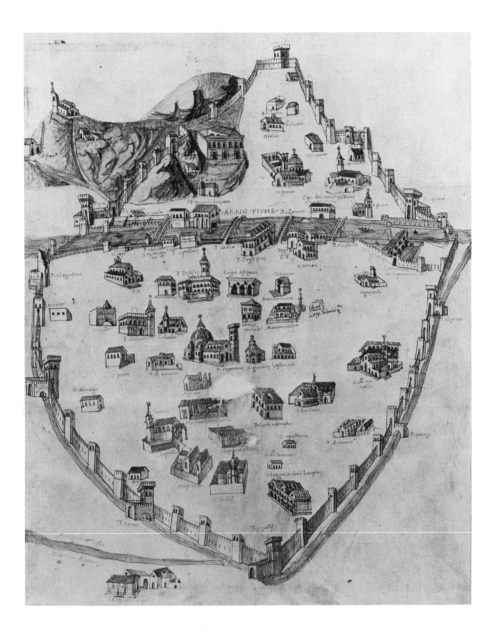

PLATE 9. Pietro del Massaio. *Iconographic Map of the City of Florence.* **c. 1471.**
Vatican Library, cat. 1.2.

241

PLATE 10. *An Offering to St. John the Baptist.* Attribution: Rossello di Jacopo Franchi. c. 1440.
Florence, Museo Nazionale del Bargello.

PLATE 11. *The Race of the Palio in the Streets of Florence* (at Piazza San Piero Maggiore). Anonymous. Attribution: Giovanni di Francesco Toscani. c. 1440.
The Cleveland Museum of Art, The Holden Collection.

PLATE 12. *A Joust in Piazza Santa Croce.* Attribution: Shop of Apollonio di Giovanni. c. 1470.

PLATE 13. *A Tournament in Piazza Santa Croce.* Attribution: Shop of Apollonio di Giovanni. c. 1470.

PLATE 14. *The Presentation of the Flag of Siena*.
Attribution: Vecchietta. Mid-fifteenth century.
Esztergom, Christian Museum.

PLATE 15. **Domenico Morone.** *Scenes at a Joust.* **Late fifteenth century.**
Reproduced by courtesy of the Trustees, National Gallery, London.

PLATE 16. *Corpus Christi Procession in Florence.* **Attribution: Attavante degli Attavanti. Early sixteenth century.**
Florence, Biblioteca Medicea Laurenziana; *Chorale* 4, c. 7v.

PLATE 17. *The Expulsion of the Duke of Athens from Florence.*
Attribution: Jacopo di Cione. c. 1343.
Florence, Palazzo Vecchio.

Workmen laid out, raised, and sewed the enormous canopy or "heaven," the cloth umbrella covering the whole Piazza di San Giovanni and the area where the wealth of the Florentines would be shown. As the vigil of the feast approached, the streets were cleaned, and along the solemn processional streets and horse race routes, the somber walls of buildings were covered with cloth; chairs and stands smothered in the same rich cloth were placed in the streets, transforming the face of the city.[88] On the morning of the first festive day the paltry shops of the small merchants were closed, unless these men had first paid a fine enabling them to stay open. In the churches Masses commenced throughout the day, in fulfillment of testamentary bequests— one small evidence of the concentration of contract on such a feast.

Overseeing the preparations were a group of *festaioli* appointed by the government.[89] They ensured that the citizens observed the shop regulations, and consulted with the ecclesiastical authorities so as to guarantee that the whole clergy would turn out. The honor of the commune in the eyes of the world rested in their hands, as did the task of creating a proper setting within which the city would compete and contract for the coming year. The *festaioli* were the ultimate tribunal determining festive order; their carelessness could cause a scandal that would insult God and man.

In the republican period the number of days taken up by the feast increased from two to ten, bringing with it a corresponding increase in participation.[90] Despite this magnification, the essential *journées*, the basic types of social representations, remained few in number and their functions constant. I shall now isolate the days and times when each of these elements crystallized.

THE DAY OF THE MERCHANT

> On the first day they ostentatiously show their things in the more frequented places of the city. For almost all the artisans and those with warehouses who do business in such places put whatever precious things they have outside if they have such things. . . for the greater honor of the city, and perhaps for greater profit.[91]

Jewels and rich cloths, fine glass and armor, reliquaries; all those "priceless" things characterized not by salability but by extravagant cost were put out for all to see on the first day of the *festa*. The government ordered these wares exhibited; it was a crime not to.[92] From the earliest reports of 1410 when the

88. Guasti, *Feste*, 5 (Dati).

89. The first time I find the word *festaioli* used is in ASF, *Prov.*, 143, ff. 221r–222r (Sept. 5, 1452). But the practice of appointing communal officials to superintend processions and celebrations is much older. Thus "four citizens deputed to order" a procession in early 1389; *ibid.*, 77, ff. 341r–342r (Mar. 18). By the early sixteenth century, the chroniclers normally listed the names of the *festaioli* for St. John; an example in Guasti, *Feste*, 29 (Cambi, 1514).

90. As early as 1407, debt safe-conducts for the feast extended from June 20 to June 30; ASF, *Prov.*, 96, ff. 23rv (Apr. 29). On the expansion of actual festive action, see subsequent pages.

91. The description is in G. Mancini, "Il bel S. Giovanni e le Feste Patronali di Firenze descritte nel 1475 da Piero Cennini," *Rivista d'Arte* VI (1909), 223. For earlier descriptions, see Guasti, *Feste*, 5, 10f. The motivation was noted by ser Guisto, f. 105r (1473).

92. Guasti, *Feste*, 25 (memorandum of 1513); for the date, see *ibid.*, 49f.

mostra was held on the morning of the twenty-third, just before the solemn procession, till those of the sixteenth century when it was pushed back to the twenty-first and even the twentieth, this demonstration of wealth remained the beginning of the citywide activity associated with the Baptist's birthday.

The "*mostra* of their riches," as another visitor characterized this activity, might seem no more than the proud ostentation of the *arriviste* so representative of Florence and other Italian cities.[93] Here was the prime manifestation of that joyous impulse that in another setting led one Florentine church to load all its silver *ex votos* on a wagon to show them off, and caused Piero de' Medici to chisel into the marble frame of his chapel the announcement that "the marble alone cost 4000 florins."[94]

Yet the *mostra* was more than lifeless complaisance; it was a statement of the city's changing social, financial, and spiritual relationships. To the foreigner a measure of resources, to the lower-class Florentine proof of the authority of the citizens, to the fellow citizens visiting each outdoor display a measure of others' financial standing or at least of their pretensions, the *mostra* also flattered and manipulated the patron, St. John. Florentines expected their saint to witness and revel in the citizens' success at bringing this global wealth under his aegis.[95] Depriving other cities deprived others' saints as well. The view that the patron was pleased by the augmentation of his clients' wealth was in fact so deeply rooted that the most elaborate gift to be offered him in the coming days came from the city's mint.[96]

Thus the straightforwardly materialistic fashion with which the Florentines always started St. John's birthday should not be juxtaposed to the presumably more spiritual offerings that were to follow. In fact, the *mostra* was the beginning of civil sacrifice, all the more so because the wealth was not hidden, but displayed communally. Walking along one of these thoroughfares where goods were displayed, the viewer might have thought himself before some altar filtered by images. One must imagine goods displayed in an iconic fashion in front of shops, this serialed representation creating the illusion of a world of wealth distinct from the dingy shops behind this brilliant exterior. The merchant in this fashion united his propertied face with his neighbor's to create a sense of personal value larger than and different from his own possessions. To enter the single shop, one had to cross through not a single gathering of goods, but in a sense one had to get behind the common icon of a street lined with wealth.

93. Guasti, *Feste*, 20 (1439). In describing the Palio of San Giovanni, an anonymous versifier before 1408 expressed the same simple love of riches:

> *Of Florence noble garden*
> *How well you show your treasure!*
> *That every day I am more enamored;*

ibid., 14.

94. For the silver wagon, Cambi, XXII, 44–49 (1514). For Piero de' Medici's pride, Gombrich, "Early Medici," 299.

95. "God requests and desires from man the accus-

tomed and triumphant ceremonies at every step and grade of the spiritual and temporal. Through both sacrifices and vows and solemn diversions and the adornments of his people, a delighted God becomes a placable friend and the benefactor of cities"; F. Altoviti, *In Defensione*, f. a–v recto (1497).

96. From an early point, special significance was attached to the mint's *cero*. In retrospect, Villani believed that when in 1340 it fell from its cart onto the stairs of city hall, this presaged the collapse of monetary values that followed; G. Villani, XI, 114.

The *mostra* of wares reflected in all its purity the broad tendency to iconize wealth on all appropriate forms. We have seen that the walls of buildings were transformed. But the same was done to women and children. A portion of Bellini's *Procession in Piazza San Marco* shows the iconized nature of the nonpolitical groups, a row of Venetian mothers and daughters looking little different than those in Dati's description of Florentine streets:

full of young women and girls dressed in silk and decorated with jewels and precious stones and pearls. . . .[97]

. . . from one end of the city to the other on that straight street full of flowers are all the women, and all the jewels and rich adornments of the city.[98]

Women were so many mannequins whom Florentine men fantasized not undressed, but as paste for cloth and jewels. Antonio Pucci in 1373 thought them queens but for the sumptuary laws:

> And I say that if Florentine women
> Could wear their jewels [in the city],
> Florence would have a thousand queens
> Crowned with silver and gold.[99]

During the feast of St. John's, men dressed their women to fit their fantasies, and the visitor witnessed, in one anonymous versifier's stunning description,

> . . . women
> Who seemed like columns,
> Ever more pretty from the Prato to San Piero
> In their haughty dress.
> That day I saw a thousand queens . . .
> You wouldn't have said they were persons.[100]

In the streets of the *mostra* one viewed, therefore, not only mere things, primary relics of their masters' wealth and power, but the human forms through which material could be converted into spirit. The process of urban transformation was already under way.

THE PROCESSION OF PURIFICATION

If the demonstration of material riches was always first, and was consequently pushed backward from St. John's Day, the solemn procession of the clergy tended to maintain its fixed date on the morning of the twenty-third. True, by the early sixteenth century three "ordinary" processions were staged on the three previous days, probably in each of the three quarters other than

97. Guasti, *Feste*, 5 (Dati).
98. *Ibid.*, 8 (Dati).

99. Pucci, *Centiloquio*, VI, 186.
100. Guasti, *Feste*, 14f.

San Giovanni.[101] But with two known exceptions, the solemn procession was held on the saint's vigil throughout the republic.[102]

In Dati's day, at the beginning of the fifteenth century, the procession of the clergy was held on the same morning as the *mostra*, and the chronicler witnessed both from the same sumptuary point of view:

> Then at the third hour a solemn procession of all the clerks, priests, monks, and friars goes through the city. And the number of religious orders is great, with so many relics of saints as to be almost infinite and moving. And this does not count the marvelous richness of their habits, nor the very rich robes they wear on their backs—as many as any place in the world: vestments of gold and of silk and of embroidered figures.[103]

At the head of the procession came members of the religious orders: cross in front, then pairs of males in their orders' robes, and in the place of honor at the rear of each order's contingent, a baldachin or "standard" with that order's most prized relic.[104] Some estimate of the size of such contingents will provide scale: In a 1391 procession not on the feast of the patron about 270 religious participated, roughly equivalent to a requirement of the early sixteenth century that six couples from each order participate in the ordinary processions.[105] Of the secular clergy, perhaps 110 might take part in such a lesser procession. In a 1390 procession the total was 112, composed of 52 clerks (young males in minor orders, equivalent to one clerk per parish), plus 60 prelates and rectors. But in the solemn procession of June 23 the whole male clergy was supposed to participate. In 1394 the clerical procession of San Giovanni consisted of 380 members (190 pairs) of religious orders, and 132 secular clergy.[106] The secular clergy, especially the canons of the cathedral, also bore their relics under baldachins.

With the movement of the procession from the cathedral, all the bells in the city started to ring and continued until the long procession returned to its starting point. Along the north side of the Baptistry the procession went west on the present Via de' Cerretani along the old north wall of the city, then followed that wall-route south on the Via de' Tornabuoni to the Ponte S. Trinita. Crossing into Oltrarno, the procession immediately turned east along the Borgo San Jacopo till it came to Santa Felicità and the Ponte Vecchio. Crossing back into center city, the crosses, images, relics, vestments and clergy went up the Via Por Santa Maria to Vaccherecia, where they turned into the Piazza della Signoria, to be reviewed by the government seated on the *ringhiera*. From there the procession turned down the Via de' Gondi to the Piazza San Firenze, and then north, this time along the east flank of the old walls on the present Via Proconsolo. It finally entered the cathedral area on

101. Guasti, *Feste*, 25f.

102. In 1473 the general procession was said to be "usually" held on the twenty-second; ser Guisto, f. 105r. Yet in 1516 it was moved from the "customary" twenty-third to the twenty-second because so many things were planned after it; Masi, 205.

103. Guasti, *Feste*, 5.

104. Further details *ibid.*, 27.

105. The requirements of 1513: *ibid.*, 26. The figures for the non–San Giovanni processions of the 1390s are in Panciatichi, ff. 159r, 161rv.

106. *Ibid.*, f. 177v.

the east, passed the Opera del Duomo, and circumambulated the cathedral on the north before reaching its point of departure.[107]

During its course, the procession had offered spectators wealth mixed with sacrality: interminable bell-ringing, liturgical song from participants, the ever-present trumpets announcing its coming, holy water, incense, and blessings. In itself, the procession of clergy did not seem to change much. According to the government's herald in 1476, ecclesiastical ceremony was much more stable than the secular.[108] Whence then its importance? Why then did the *festaioli* insist year after year that the clergy wear ever-richer clothing, "better than ever," and why did they demand that all the clergy take part with all their paraphernalia?[109] Why in fact did the sixteenth century add the ordinary processions to the solemn processions?

The explanation derives from the fact that until the mid-fifteenth century the procession had immediately succeeded the *mostra*, on the same morning. The procession took the goods of the *mostra* and transfigured them, so to speak. The *mostra* showed what the merchants had taken in; the procession showed what they had given out. The procession of the clergy must be understood as a demonstration of wealth like that of the *mostra*, but of wealth that had been given to God and thus purified. The procession, by showing the results of continuous charity and altruism, created the civil condition for the contracts that were the center of the day. Without trust, without sacrifice, there could be no contract.

THE DAY OF THE CITIZEN-SOLDIER

> *The great offering, which was that evening;*
> *From every gonfalon they came*
> *Two by two in turn.*
> *My, if you want to hear,*
> *Dear companion, listen to the method:*
> *For my eyes have never seen so much wax*
> *In torches.*
> *Not four, five, or six.*
> *But more than twenty thousand, if I'm not to lie,*
> *Came in order.*
> *For they were sixteen [gonfalons], each with its brigade.*
> *The festival has begun*
> *With so many games and people to enjoy*
> *That I think never again to see the like.*[110]

107. Though this route was more or less standard, some processions were broader in scope, moving more toward Santa Croce on the east, and because of the special devotion at the Servi and Observant Dominican churches, toward the north. See Plate 9 for the domestic processional routes.

108. R. Trexler (ed.), *The Libro Cerimoniale of the Florentine Republic by Francesco Filarete and Angelo Manfidi. Introduction and Text* (Geneva, 1978), 81.

109. "E meglio che il solito"; Guasti, *Feste*, 27 (1513).

110. *Ibid.*, 12 (anonymous).

Throughout the republic, the offerings of the wards or gonfalons were fixed on the evening of the twenty-third, as was the procession of the clergy in the morning. The women of the city lined the streets of each ward in their finery, and saw the section flag-bearer lead their masters on foot from each ward into the Piazza San Giovanni, there to make their torch-offerings to St. John. It was one of those civic duties no family could escape, unless one was willing to pay a fine. In the early fifteenth century the government passed two laws insisting that at least two males aged fifteen to sixty-five from each *domus* of Florentine citizens go to make their offerings in the procession of their gonfalon.[111] When the representatives of each family arrived at the gathering point, they were rearranged with the others, the "more worthy and the older" persons in front, the *garzoni* or younger youth in back.[112] Unfortunately, we do not know how precedence was arrived at, nor who had the last word in each gonfalon.

Looking back across the activities of the twenty-third, from the *mostra* in the morning through the ecclesiastical procession to the evening offering of the citizens gathered in their gonfalons, we see that the citizens of Florence approached their saint demonstrating two different, even opposed things. The citizen in his shop that morning expressed the joy of accumulation, but when he joined his gonfalon for the evening offering, his presence and behavior ascetically ordered in his civic section expressed virtues that were *not* the measure of accumulating, individualistic merchants, but rather military skill, liberality, and charity, the "natural" virtues of honorable men who looked askance at the greed of the merchant. By both demonstrating their wealth outside their shops and marching in their companies, citizens expressed different sides of the same self: accumulation and honor, individuality and family, financial expansion and civic place. By going public with its wealth, the ostentatious *mostra* celebrated a city where coercion and fear of disorder were unnecessary. The parades of the wards demonstrated brotherhood, yes, but directed against the audience of the nonrepresented. They demonstrated these different selves not only to the saint, but to foreign audiences, to themselves, and, not least important, to that domestic audience of the politically excluded.[113]

THE DAY OF THE MORAL LAYMAN

One thing more than any other made the Florentine feast of St. John world-famous: the inventive floats and other fantastic devices that delighted inhabitant and foreigner alike. Ever changing, ever more incredible to contemporary viewers, these contraptions combined the efforts of skilled artisans and writers, and thus have been of continuing interest to literary and art

111. *ASF, Prov.*, 95, ff. 43rv (May 12, 1406); *Statuta*, III, 298–301.

112. "E in ciascuno Gonfalone tutti i suoi cittadini a

due a due, andando innanzi i più antichi, e così seguendo insino a garzoni, riccamente vestiti"; Guasti, *Feste*, 5.

113. See page 222, this volume.

historians. Who made them, when and in what context did they first appear, and what was their domestic festive significance?

One source that has already been mentioned suggests that festive contraptions had a venerable antiquity in Florence: the record of the portrayal of hell done on the river Arno in 1304, itself said by Villani to have been a revival of older custom.[114] Yet this event, the only piece of data on festive representations until the end of the fourteenth century, was certainly not a direct antecedent of the festive apparatuses of the classical Florentine celebratory mode. It was an immobile representation, whereas the floats (*edifizi*) of the fifteenth century would be processional in character. The earlier representation was not directly biblical in inspiration, whereas those of the later period narrated the Bible. The 1304 show was put on by a section of the city, but the classical *edifizi* of St. John's would be prepared and presented by the lay confraternities of Florence. Finally, the former delighted a May Day audience, whereas the floats of the Renaissance would grace the feast of the patron. We must come much closer to the fifteenth century, in short, and deal with more immediate historical background to the great floats of that century; the evolution of festive machines during most of the preceding century seems lost to the historical record.

The immediate historical predecessors for these outdoor representations seem to have been confraternal representations done in church to augment divine cult. Thus in the later fourteenth century a confraternity housed in the Carmine across the Arno performed the story of the Ascension, and the inside of the church was fitted out with mechanical devices to feign these mysteries.[115] Perhaps at the same time the ancient liturgical ceremony of Epiphany, in which clerics imitated the search for the Christ Child, was being taken over or participated in by laymen.

But when did this theatrical impulse issue into the streets? We can only approach this question through ascertaining when confraternities themselves first took a substantial part in the celebratory life of the commune. Since earlier in the fourteenth century, the feast of St. John and most other saints' days had excluded any public demonstration by private groups. When did these confraternities appear?

We have seen that these private brotherhoods were ancient, generally citywide in membership, and included broader segments of society than any public body. Yet though they were undoubtedly an important part of Florentine corporate life, they do not seem to have participated in public manifestations until 1377, when they made fleeting appearances. Deprived by a papal interdict of their priests and divine cult in that year, the Florentines held what one chronicler called "secular processions" in which companies of flagellants bearing their relics, always the focal point of group cohesion, marched through the streets behind baldachins or standards beating them-

114. See page 220, this volume.

115. Sacchetti, *Trecentonovelle*, 160 (written in the 1390s). On the church stages, see M. Fabbri, E. Garbero Zorzi, and A. Petrioli Tofani, *Il Luogo Teatrale a Firenze* (Milan, 1975).

selves as propitiation for Florentine sins.[116] But after the end of this war with the papacy and the victory of the oligarchic regime over the Ciompi (1378–1382), there is no further evidence of lay confraternities participating in any public procession until the last decade of the century.

On the feast of the Epiphany in 1390, a group of laymen staged a long Journey of the Magi in the streets of Florence. The mid-point of their journey was the Baptistry of San Giovanni, where Herod conversed with them. Their goal was the church of San Marco, where the Christ Child was found and adored.[117] Whence had they come? A reference of 1434 to the place "where the Magi are" provides a clue both to the group's original home and to its founder. The house was outside the western Porta San Frediano, and had belonged to one Baldassare degli Ubriachi, now deceased. Since "Baldassare" had been the name of one of the three kings, one suspects that the group may have been patronized by this old Ghibelline family and particularly by Baldassare. It also suggests that the processional group moved from this western approach to the Baptistry, thence to Ubriachi's "chapel of the Three Kings" at Santa Maria Novella, and then to San Marco.[118]

From this point on, the appearance of Florentine confraternities in celebratory ritual increased, their presence finally becoming one of the most characteristic elements of the feast of St. John and other civic celebrations. Perhaps the determining impulse was the civic euphoria on surviving the Visconti threat (1402) and conquering Pisa (1406). In celebrating the latter event, twenty "companies with standards" marched in procession.[119] In 1426 the same diarist tells us that the "companies of flagellants" helped celebrate a new treaty, and in the following year, 1427, the same "companies of discipline" feasted a peace.[120] Obviously, companies that had been associated with crisis ritual like flagellation were being transformed into groups manifesting joy during the ritual of celebration.

These groups' mechanical contraptions and floats apparently first appeared outside in the early fifteenth century. The earlier Journey of the Magi does not seem to have made use of them; it was, after all, simply an outdoor liturgy and the representations seem to have been limited to the dress of the kings and their retinues. A long verse description of the feast of St. John written sometime before 1408 also makes no reference at all to any manufactured representations. This omission becomes all the more important because Dati, writing just a year or so after the copier of the verse description, gives us our first clear evidence that the confraternities were representing things, and were taking part in the St. John's celebration.[121] These two

116. Trexler, *Spiritual Power*, 130–133.

117. Hatfield, "Compagnia," 108.

118. "A' dì 22 di giugno [1434] Eugenio IV giunse al luogo dell'Abbate, cioè il luogo che fu di Baldassare Ubriachi, dove sono i Magi, sopra la porta a piè di Monte Oliveto, in su la strada fuori della Porta a San Friano"; Del Corazza, 284f. See also the note *ibid.*, for further information, and *ibid.*, 286, where another comtemporary speaks of the same place "a Monte Uliveto, overo al luogo di Recho Capponi in sulla strada." On this whole argument, see my article on Baldassare: "The Magi Enter Florence. The Ubriachi of Florence and Venice," *Studies in Medieval and Renaissance History*, n.s. I (1978), 152–157.

119. Del Corazza, 242.

120. *Ibid.*, 279.

121. Guasti, *Feste*, 9–17.

sources combined indicate that the appearance of the confraternities in the St. John's celebration and the appearance of floats and other mechanical devices both took place within a very few years.

Dati's description of the feast shows that these private groups were organizationally integrated with, and part of the identity of, the different orders and churches. They were in fact part of the ecclesiastical procession of the morning of the twenty-third:

> And with many companies of secular men, each of which goes before the order [of the church] where that company meets. There are [men] dressed as angels, and music and instruments of every type and marvelous songs, all presenting most beautiful representations of those saints and of those relics, to whom they do honor.[122]

Dati also indicates that representational activities were not limited to the confraternities, but were engaged in as well by the gonfalons or wards when they went to make their offerings. In front of most of the sixteen sections, he tells us, were "men with games of suitable enjoyment and beautiful representations."[123] Also, a law of 1415 forbade making pictures or signs or using base or undignified words, especially when the gonfalons went to make their offerings.[124] In 1465 these gonfalon spectacles were profane "pleasure wagons," certainly like the "triumphal wagon full of madmen" that the Florentines used in their feasts at mid-century.[125] These were persons on wagons doing amusing things, it seems, rather than floats. Despite intimations that the administrative sections of the city could have become the institutional bases of important theatrical representations, however, they did not. The future belonged to the private confraternities.

In Dati's time, these confraternities marched with the clergy of the churches they met in, and represented the latter's saints. Thus in 1439 a visitor who saw bearded early Christian hermits and St. Augustine probably witnessed the efforts of the confraternity that met in the church of the Hermits of St. Augustine (Santo Spirito), and the St. George he saw may have been the representation of a boys' club of the church of San Giorgio.[126] Even in the sixteenth century contemporaries could refer to such representations as those of the church rather than of its confraternity.[127] Still, the specifically theatrical impulse that they introduced slowly became separated from the procession of the twenty-third. Responding to the archbishop's demand that the floats be banned from the formal procession, the government in 1454 ordered that June twenty-second be given over entirely to the edifices of the companies. The groups themselves still took their places in the solemn procession of the twenty-third along with the religious orders, but without their floats.[128] This change is of great importance: In the previous half-century, lay

122. *Ibid.*, 5.

123. *Ibid.*

124. *ASF, Prov.*, 105, ff. 166r–167v (Oct. 23, 1415).

125. Strozzi, *Lettere*, 425; P. Bracciolini, *Opera* (Basel, 1538), I, 203 (*c.* 1452). M.-L. Minio-Paluello kindly referred me to Poggio.

126. Guasti, *Feste*, 20.

127. Cambi, XXII, 45.

128. R. Trexler (ed.), "The Episcopal Constitutions of Antoninus of Florence," *Quellen und Forschungen aus Italienischen Archiven und Bibliotheken* LIX (1979), 252. Guasti, *Feste*, 22f (Matteo Palmieri).

companies had become important parts of the communal organizations of salvation by taking part in the purificatory procession of the twenty-third. Yet, at the same time, their theatrical representations were coming to be viewed as distinct in themselves, and could be isolated from the purifying procession.

What was produced could now be separated from who produced it, because by midcentury the commune had adopted the widespread practice of presenting an integral cycle of biblical history. Thus in 1454 the edifices presented by the confraternities on the twenty-second started with an Archangel Michael float, followed by Lucifer Expelled, then Adam, Moses, and so on, into the fulfilling New Testament: the Annunciation, the Magi, the Resurrection (the Passion was omitted as unsuitable for the celebration), the Ascension, and so on.[129] As a result of this development the theatrical unity of the presentation became an identity apart from that of any particular company. The more important the adult confraternities became to the success of the whole festival, the less distinguishable the identity of any particular group became. But there was a still more profound effect of integrally representing the past, one related to the already mentioned imperial desire to reconstruct the bodies of saints of the holy past. By presenting the whole history of human salvation, the Florentine lay confraternities were, in a sense, creating an integral saving grace that was unrelated to the history of the commune itself. These effects added up to the beginning of a festive life whose representations were unrelated to the history of the commune.

THE DAY OF THE COMMUNE

To this point we have witnessed the merchants offering their accumulation to St. John, the clergy and later the companies purifying that accumulation, and the citizens ranked in military sections parading separately to the Baptistry to offer their candles. I have saved the representation of the whole commune till after that of its parts because, if the evidence has been read correctly, the commune was a relative latecomer to the ritual scene. Created to regulate the struggle between citizens and to govern the subject, its ritual development was inhibited by the determination of the citizens to prevent official charisma from replacing the personal charismas of the city's families.

For many years the main problem of communal government was that it had no real access to ritual honor. Though it is in the nature of a sovereign body to receive the submission of its subjects, the only subjects that government had in the city were those *senza governo* of some other entity, like widows and orphans, and this was a slim base upon which to build its ritual image. The military companies or gonfalons offered to the saint by themselves, and performed no act of obeisance to the communal government; the

129. The Jewish community did Moses, "a cavallo   e altri"; *ibid.* con assa' cavalleria de' principali del popolo d'Israel

members of the wards were, after all, the governors of the city, not its subjects.

Familial reticence about magnifying the governmental image had enduring impact upon ritual forms. For the length of the republic, when government did appear in the St. John's events, it did so as one of many other groups offering to the patron, rather than as the recipient of offerings from civil groups. It appeared twice, during the celebration, accompanied by a small retinue: just before the gonfalons made their offerings on the twenty-third, and on the twenty-fourth at the end of a series of other offerings to be mentioned shortly.[130] The magnification of the role of the government in festive activities was not the result, therefore, of any increased authority of the commune over citizens. Rather, it was due to the commune having found outside sources of ritual honor. The main access to ritual honor for the commune was to come not from within the city, but through empire: the expansion of the city into the *contado* and *distretto*. Empire provided honorable subjects who paid homage only to the government. In becoming a part of the ritual scene, extra-urban subjects tremendously fostered the ritual position of government.

Communal government emerged from its civic ritual isolation in three stages, the first of which came in 1343, when the Signoria first found subjects worthy of its pretensions. The way was shown not by a duly elected burgher government, but by Walter of Brienne, duke of Athens, who exercised almost royal authority. It was a representative of feudal Europe who would show the Florentines how to celebrate their (still small) dominion with due nobility.

Before Brienne, subject communes brought annual offerings or tribute to the city each St. John's morning and, after showing them in the square outside city hall, offered them to the saint in the Baptistry. These *cens* sometimes were food offerings or wax torches (*cerotti*), but in some twenty cases took the form of *ceri*—gaily painted cardboard, wood, and wax candles. They were imposing and colorful enough—too folksy for later tastes—ingeniously hollow on the inside so that different parts moved, and each was borne upon a festive cart.[131] But they were few and not particularly dignified or ostentatious. Brienne changed all that, and Villani's eyewitness account is worth citing in full as evidence of the wonder the duke's innovations induced in these burghers:

> On the morning of the feast, besides the usual *ceri* from the approximately twenty strongholds of the commune, he received more than twenty-five cloths or *palii* gilded in gold, and hunting dogs, and hawks, and goshawks as homage from Arezzo, Pistoia, Volterra, San Gimignano, Colle, from all the counts of Guidi, from Mangona and Cerbaia, from Monte Carelli, Pontormo, from the Ubertini and the Pazzi of Valdarno, and from every little baron and count roundabouts, and from the Ubaldini. Together with the offering of the *ceri*, this was a noble thing and feast. And all the *ceri*

130. *Ibid.*

131. "E ceri . . . sono vituperio di tale festività"; Guasti, *Feste*, 27f (memorandum of 1513). Vasari also

mentions how *goffi* they were thought to be; cited *ibid.*, 62. The *ceri*, long and narrow, are quite distinct from the later *edifizi*, which had narrative themes.

and *palii* and the other tributes were gathered together in the Piazza Santa Croce, then one after the other went to the Palace where the duke was, and then they offered them at San Giovanni. He added to the other side of the [cloth] *palio* [of San Giovanni] of crimson samite cloth a trim of gray squirrel skin as long as the pole. It was very rich to see. And he made a very rich and noble feast, the first and last he was to hold, because of his evil actions.[132]

Villani's combined admiration and regret is almost tangible. If only he had not tyrannized the "good men" of Florence, the chronicler seems to say, Brienne could have ennobled the commune by more festivals of this type. Here again was that fundamental Florentine desire to be noble, but without the disadvantages of formal nobility. The lessons offered by Brienne were not ignored; after he was expelled, Florence kept this new munificence of *palii* until the end of the republic. Part of the solution to the ignobility of the government was to represent itself to foreign subjects as a powerful feudal lord whom those subjects—including landed members of the nobility— served as retinue. Each succeeding June twenty-fourth, the Piazza della Signoria filled with the ever-increasing tributes and especially *palii* of foreign communes and vassals; all then marched to the Baptistry for the solemn offering to the saint (Plate 10). In 1514, a deathblow was given to the tradi- tional *ceri*; their quaint form had finally become too much for the roman- ized Florentines. They were publicly burned *per magnificenza* and later replaced by more dignified forms.[133]

An important first step had been taken in 1343. The commune of Florence emerged with a ritual identity rooted in the subjection of the dominion. A second step was taken in the early fifteenth century, when new precedence arrangements and a new public rhetoric that heightened the position of the Signoria came into vogue. Gene Brucker documents this impulse to "exalt the majesty of the supreme executive" publicly by citing a decree of 1420 that forbade the foreign judicial officials of the commune (*podestà*, captain, and executor) to sit on the same level as the priors in the Palace or loggia.[134] This is the first known case where the *podestà*, heretofore the most honored figure in the commune, took a lesser place. Brucker shows further how new forms of address exalted the Signoria, like this proclamation of Lorenzo Ridolfi in 1428: "As only one God should be adored, so you, lord priors, are to be venerated above all citizens, and those who turn their eyes to others are worshipping false idols and are to be condemned.[135]

Rather than such changes representing a strengthening of the Signoria's authority over the great families, Brucker says, they illustrate a desperate attempt of a factionalized ruling class to maintain a semblance of its sovereign authority; by exalting the government, citizens attacked factions.[136] In ritual terms, this means that the families, realizing that their honor was nothing

132. G. Villani, XI, 10. Subsequently about a hun- dred *palii* and some thirty *ceri* were offered.

133. Guasti, *Feste*, 49f (Cambi); Landucci, 345.

134. *Civic World*, 308.

135. *Ibid.*, 308f.

136. *Ibid.*, 309f.

without governmental virtue, attempted to maintain the communal image. In the process, another modest step had been taken toward objectifying the government as a ritual identity.

The third stage, like the first, was mediated by the Florentines' exposure to the etiquette of the European nobility. When Martin V came to Florence in 1419, he presented the Signoria with a papal rose, and Pope Eugenius IV added a noble sword and biretta during his visit in the 1430s; both had the effect of magnifying the position of the priors in the eyes of citizens.[137] But the visit of the emperor Frederick III, the first imperial visit in centuries, was by far the most important in its influence on the Signoria's image. Frederick entered the city on January 31 and left on February 6, 1452. Proceeding to Rome for his coronation, he returned north in late April and stayed in Florence again May 5–7, leaving the peninsula itself in June. Throughout his stay in Florence he was greeted by an unequaled display of Florentine talent, wealth, and curiosity. Our best source for these events emphasizes how the Florentines took every chance they had to catch a glimpse of the emperor, surrounded as he was by all the trappings of nobility, "many trumpets and pipers and horns and falcons and goshawks and dogs for every type of wild animal, as is proper for such a lord."[138]

The impression made by the imperial visit certainly influenced the Florentines' proximate decision to raise their own sovereign still higher. Late in 1453 and early in 1454 the following changes were made in the Signoria's ceremonial ambient: the Signoria received 1000 florins to spend on tapestries, cloth, doormen, and table silver in the Palace (the previous silver perhaps having been given, as was customary, to the recent imperial visitor).[139] Also in the Palace, the courtyard was cleared of the unsightly makeshift offices of five governmental bodies; they were moved elsewhere so that, in the chronicler's words, the courtyard would be "freer, more spacious, and lovelier." Outside the Palace, markets that had traditionally been held in the Piazza on five different days of the year were assigned to other squares in the city; obviously, the Piazza was being purified of mercantile associations. Then the Signoria's processional ritual was changed in two respects. First, the mace-bearers who accompanied the Signoria in public were fitted out with rich silver maces whose inspiration was recognizably aristocratic. They were made "after the fashion of the Roman curia," said Sozomeno, and Pietrobuoni spoke of the new maces as *alla cortigiana*.[140] Second, the processional position of the Standard Bearer of Justice was made more honorable. Traditionally he had walked on the right of the *podestà*, with the first among the priors on the left. Now the Standard Bearer, who by 1433 was addressed with such portentious titles as "Father of the Republic," took center place, the *podestà* moving

137. Gori, *Feste*, 158.

138. Pietrobuoni, copied by Cambi, XX, 293f.

139. Examples of "tutti gli arienti della mensa del palagio" being given visitors are in L. Morelli, 176, 185. The changes of 1453 and 1454 are described in

Sozomeni Pistoriensis Presbyteri Chronicon Universale, ed. G. Zaccagnini, *RIS*, XVI, pt. 1, 49 (hereafter Sozomeno), and in Pietrobuoni copied by Cambi, XX, 320–323.

140. *Loc. cit.*

to his right and the executor marching on his left; the Standard Bearer of Justice had now definitely replaced the *podestà* at the center of sovereign representations.[141] From a representation in which the leading foreign official, a noble, had stood at the center flanked by two Florentine officials, the image of Florentine dignity now showed the highest Florentine official flanked by two noble foreign officials.

This trend toward increased magnificence continued during the following decade. On the eve of St. John's in 1454, the retinue that accompanied the Signoria for the offering at the Baptistry was enlarged through the requirement that the whole domestic governmental bureaucracy go with the Signoria and the gilds.[142] In 1456 the old office of *sindicus et referendarius* added the sobriquet "Herald of the Signoria," a designation unmistakably feudal in inspiration.[143] In 1458 the priors changed their names from *priori dell'arte* to *priori di libertà*, thus divesting themselves of the last traces of their origins in the world of work.[144] Through the same law the Standard Bearer took on still more ritual pomp. The bimonthly investment ceremony was modified so that instead of the *podestà* giving the pennant to the new Standard Bearer, the old *gonfaloniere* gave it directly to his successor. Finally, in 1465 the days on which the Signoria entered office were declared work and debt holidays, so that on those days, in the law's words, citizens and inhabitants could honorably accompany the government.[145]

Thus through obeisance of *contado* and *distretto* subjects and the retinue of the bureaucracy, through the development of quasi-princely rhetoric, and through modifications in its ritual space and movements, the mid-fifteenth-century government of Florence appeared very different in its St. John's offering than it had a century before. Despite all these changes, however, the caution of the families of Florence continued to prevail. The government still remained only one among many offerants to St. John, and despite these more pompous arrangements, no one made offerings to the Signoria. Only in the grand ducal sixteenth century, and then only in the words of a foreign observer, does one encounter the idea that these tributes were offered not to the saint, but to the government.[146]

The offerings to St. John on the morning of the twenty-fourth formed, consequently, a summary representation of Florentine institutions and values from which none was excepted, not even the government. To achieve an overview of these offerings, I shall list their order in 1454: first the Parte Guelfa, then the *palii*, *ceri*, and *cerotti* of the dominion's subjects; the offering of the Florentine mint; offerings of prisoners freed by the government; offer-

141. *Ibid.* The *gonfaloniere's* title is in Cavalcanti, *Istorie*, IX, 5.

142. All "intrinsic" officials were involved because it was necessary "to show more honor to the feast and saint"; *ASF, Prov.*, 145, ff. 75v–76v (June 6, 1454).

143. Trexler, *Libro*, 43f.

144. Cambi, XX, 367f.

145. *ASF, Prov.*, 155, ff. 243v–244v (Mar. 11. 1464/ 1465).

146. Montaigne speaks of subjects offering to the grand duke; cited in F. Bernard, *Les Fêtes Célèbres de l'Antiquité, du Moyen Age et des Temps Modernes* (Paris, 1878), 263f.

ings of the jockeys who were to ride in the horse race that afternoon; the offering of the *palio* of San Giovanni—the reward of the winning jockey; and finally the offering of the Signoria.[147] These offerings translate into the following categories of representations: the urban gentility (Parte), the subjects (*palii*, etc.), the Florentine powers of accumulation (the mint), Florentine charity and liberality toward captured foreigners and domestic criminals (the prisoners),[148] those who wished to control the outcome of equestrian battles (jockeys), the prize for such victory and symbolically all battles the commune had ever won (the *palio* of San Giovanni), and, finally, the whole commune (the Signoria).

Two of these offerings deserve further comment. The first offering, that of the Parte Guelfa, consisted of a cavalcade of all those noble men of the city associated with it. A statute of the Parte of 1335 insisted that each "knight, page, and noble" in Florence had to offer with the Parte captains, each carrying a candle of at least one-half-pound wax; anyone not in Florence at the time had to provide a substitute.[149] But the procession of the Parte also included all honorable foreigners in Florence at the time: in Dati's words, all foreign knights, lords, and ambassadors. Consequently the first offering presented to the saint not only Florentine nobility, but nobility *tout court*. It represented a pan-European family of nobles and nobility that transcended local citizenship and loyalties. Through such a representation, burgher Florence tied itself to that distinguished corporation.[150]

The offering of the mint or *zecca* is noteworthy because of its narcissistic character. The Florentine gold florin had a representation of the Baptist on one side. Thus when the elaborate *cero* of the mint, replete with coins painted on a figure of St. John at the top of a group of accompanying saints and angels, came before the altar of the Baptist accompanied by some four hundred candle-bearing members of the Calimala gild and that of the changers (Cambio), the Florentines were in substance offering to the patron the wealth these international bankers and merchants had earned through exchanging with others the representation of their saint on the florin.[151] Similar to the practice of the Roman *aurum coronarium*, offering the mint's *cero* to the patron was more than a trade of honor for wealth. It was St. John's gift to himself,

147. Dati's varies slightly from that of Palmieri; cf. Guasti, *Feste*, 6f, 23.

148. The offering of prisoners probably derived from the older custom of releasing captives of war; G. Masi, "Schiavi, Servi, e Manomessi nel Comune Fiorentino," *Il Marzocco* XXVIII, no. 6 (Feb. 11, 1923), 4. The fact that those who bore the *ceri* of submission were called *figli* hints that they too were (still?) thought of as hostages; Guasti, *Feste*, 49 (Cambi).

149. F. Bonaini (ed.), "Statuto della Parte Guelfa di Firenze compilato nel MCCCXXXV," *ASI*, n.s. *Appendice* (1857), 21.

150. Because representatives of various foreign powers were present in this segment, its parade certainly saw struggles for precedence; see page 327, this volume.

151. For a description of the sixteenth-century *cero* of the mint, Guasti, *Feste*, 62 (Vasari). For the previous century see Dati *ibid.*, 7, and Mancini, "Bel S. Giovanni," 225. The mid-sixteenth-century painting by Stradino in the Palazzo della Signoria is the only extant painting of this *cero*. Deities covered with coins and paper money can still be encountered in the Italian south and in some Italian sections of New York; the latter are represented in the F. Coppola film *Godfather: Part II*.

the best possible expression of Florentine ability to exchange under his aegis, to contract under his protection.[152]

THE DAY OF THE PALIO

After the heat of the day had passed on the afternoon of the twenty-fourth, the citizens and inhabitants of Florence lined the route across the city on which the main horse race of the Florentine calendar was run. To the delight of the crowd, the *palio* of San Giovanni, which was to be the goal and reward of the winner (Plate 11), was solemnly paraded from the starting point (*mosse*) in the meadow near Ognissanti to the finish line at San Piero Maggiore.[153] The nervous horses were then guided by their jockeys, both of which were distinguished by their livery indicating provenience, into the starting positions. For many, everything that had gone before was but a preparation for the Palio, as the race was called. Within minutes the whole festival would be crisply consummated.

It is regrettable that we know so little about the inner workings of the Florentine Palio, for as Dundes and Falassi have shown in their work on the modern Sienese Palio, an Italian horse race is as susceptible to precise analysis as Clifford Geertz's Balinese cockfight. Certainly there was betting; certainly liens of dependence were created around the race. But we simply do not have the information even to speculate on the sociology of the Florentine Palio.[154]

It can be said with some confidence, however, that the Florentine Palio of this period had none of the neighborhood associations that Siena's would develop. Neighborhoods do not seem to have sponsored either the horses or the jockeys, who came from all over to compete for the rich prize. The Florentine Luca Landucci bragged that his brother Gostanzo together with the latter's mount Draghetto had won twenty *palii* from 1481 till 1485, winning not only in Florence (the *palii* of S. Reparata and S. Vittore), but at Siena, Prato, and Arezzo. Rich men owned famous horses, like Lorenzo de' Medici's Lucciola, which were ridden by hired jockeys.[155] But neither rider nor horse in the Florentine Palio seems to have had any relation to the city's corporations.

Most of the *palii* held in Florence during the year commemorated victories that the commune had won over its enemies.[156] The race itself was, as

152. On the Roman coin offerings, see Ladner, "Gesture of Prayer," 251.

153. Guasti, *Feste*, 15 (anonymous).

154. A. Dundes and A. Falassi, *La Terra in Piazza* (Berkeley, 1975); C. Geertz, *The Interpretation of Cultures* (New York, 1973), 412–453. On the Sienese Palio S. Silverman. "On the Uses of History in Anthropology: The *Palio* of Siena," *American Ethnologist* VI (1979), 413–436. Abundant notes on Florentine horse races are contained in BNF, II. I. 153 (*Carte Palagi*), which I have not carefully scrutinized. In addition to Dati's description, the only substantive chronicular details

of the Florentine Palio I encountered are in Pietrobuoni, f. 171r, a description of the *mosse* or starting point elicited because of a scandal (omitted in Cambi's copy of Pietrobuoni). Winners of various *palii* are reported by several writers, especially by ser Giusto.

155. Landucci, 50.

156. Cambi says this was the purpose of the races; XXII, 237. The *palio* instituted for the fall of Pisa (1406), however, was later converted to a joust because the latter was "more genteel," and because the youth could better show their prowess; Truffi, *Giostre*, 137 (citing a versifier of around 1420). Note that the *palii* instituted to celebrate the anniversaries of S.

noted, derived from cavalry exercises; it converted into a wagering sport the typical insult ritual of racing that contemporaries held around beleaguered cities. Indeed, the prizes for some races were none other than the cloth *palii* that conquered communes or lords had offered to the commune as tribute the same morning.[157] In this fashion, the morning theme of subjection continued in the horse race that afternoon.

SURROUNDING DAYS AND EVENTS

Embedded in political functionalism, the basic elements of the San Giovanni *festa* that have been reviewed were slowly embellished with feudal games and various theatrical elements. Each addition served a purpose, each responded to a felt need. If originally the feast had been limited to the period of the vigil and the birthday, it extended further back and forward in time. Jousts and *armeggerie* came to be expected during these days, though they were never institutionalized. Tournaments—mock battles—and wild-animal fights or "hunts" surfaced on occasion, used "for magnificence" by *festaioli* determined to awe foreigners (Plate 13).[158] Masks became widely used in different events, as did bonfires, buffoons, and other elements of festive nonsense. There will be more to say of these additions. But now we must turn to the analysis of the basic feast; we have seen the display, now we shall look at the feast as political action.

The World of Contract

On the evening of the vigil of St. John's, 1366, the bishop of Florence, Piero Corsini, left his palace and proceeded to the church of San Giovanni to celebrate vespers accompanied by members of the three *vicedomini* families of the see of Florence, as was their annual duty. The party arrived in the church, whereupon one member of the Tosinghi and of the Bisdomini families formally approached the bishop and asked his license "to depart from him and go to offer along with those of the Parte and beneath the banner of the Parte, leaving behind with him other members of the said consorteries."[159]

One year later, the *vicedomini* arrived late at the episcopal palace to accompany the bishop, and found that the bishop had gone on to the Baptis-

---

Reparata and S. Barnabà were foot races originally, the former between *homines; Statuto . . . Podestà,* 436f. For the first indication of public races involving boys and girls (1475), see page 394, this volume.

157. The *palio* offered by Arezzo, for example, was the prize in the race of S. Lò; Landucci, 257.

158. I have found "tournaments" ("that is, a representation of a mounted battle,"; Palmieri, *Historia,*

189) mentioned on May 12, 1392 (Ps. Minerbetti, 158), on three consecutive days after San Giovanni 1470 (Palmieri, *Historia,* 189), and in 1516 (Masi, 207, with an extensive description). Wild-animal *caccie* were held Oct., 1439 (ser Giusto, f. 36r), Apr. 29, 1459 (Cambi, XX, 370), and not again until but often after 1513; Landucci, 340.

159. *AAF, Benefizio . . . Tani,* ff. 69v–71v.

try without them. On the following day, when everyone was in the bishop's palace again to accompany him to Mass, Bishop Corsini said to these guardians, and the notary transcribed:

> I know that I am not required to give you the insignia and can do without this, since you did not come yesterday evening to vespers as you were required to do. Nevertheless I want to be benign with you and, while not prejudicing episcopal rights, I intend to give them to you.[160]

In these two brief examples of what occurred all over Florence during the days of the Baptist, we find the central meaning of Florentine solemn celebrations: settings for the articulation, demonstration, and re formation through conflict of the manifold contracts binding male citizens to each other, and subjects to citizens. St. John's feast day, clearly the most important of such contracting occasions, forced individual citizens to enact multiple contracts in sequence. Thus in 1366 the two families first publicly manifested their allegiance to the bishop and then went to demonstrate their equally public allegiance to the Parte. The following year the same families failed to appear before the bishop, demonstrating by their absence that other obligations took precedence to those they owed their prelate. Deprived of his right to retinue, the bishop publicly notarized the fact that the guardians had failed in their duty, and that his willingness to renew the families' access to the insignia sprang from liberality rather than obligation, for the guardians had broken the contract that might have obligated the prelate. Women, children and nongildsmen lined the streets to watch the processions of their men from one contract scene to the other, and found themselves bound into the contracts through their governors. A society regenerates itself. The men imagined that they alone gave birth to the commune, and resurrected it.

In everyday life religious times, spaces and objects played a role in the organization of society that is unimaginable today. The very activity of the marketplace required a technique or ritual of interpersonal relations.[161] Merchants swore by the milk of the Virgin or of their own mothers if they wanted to sell their product. Contracts of small import included the "penny of God," a means by which traders essentially invoked religious sanctions to prove their sincerity.[162] The tritest matters were notarized. Hundreds of commercial contracts foresaw excommunication if a contract was violated; all were ritual securities involving spiritual sanctions.[163] In these everyday negotiations people used hosts, relics, Bibles, and altars as solemnizing forces, imposing malediction upon themselves while constantly aware that perjury was a sin as well as a crime. Social relations were suffused with consecrated behavior.

160. *Ibid.*

161. See the analysis of the marketplace in Hall, *Silent Language*, 106f, 127ff. An excellent study of ritual marketing in Greece is J. Campbell, "Two Case Studies of Marketing and Patronage in Greece," in J.-G. Peristiany (ed.), *Contributions to Mediterranean Sociology* (Paris, 1968), 143–188.

162. On the penny, see G. Paoli, *Mercato, Scritta, e Danaro di Dio* (Florence, 1895).

163. On excommunication in contract, see Trexler, "Florence by the Grace," 124f.

In a society where incalculability was the rule rather than the exception and where contracts were difficult to enforce, it is not surprising that contractors sought out those times that would best bear witness to their pact, times at which not only many earthly witnesses were about, but when particular divine figures were active and thus able to serve as guarantors of earthly contracts. The medieval calendar was a kaleidoscope of times identified by their bonding function, times that derived their force from the divine sanction of the saints who "controlled" the day. One did not simply observe the anniversary of a contract, but chose a particular day to start with, the day of a saint both partners would be bound to. Simple partners to a business contract, the living tying themselves to the dead, government binding itself to particular divine patrons, confraternities and parishioners rekindling their liens to each other and to their saints, the individual renewing his tie to his name-saint—all such relations were demonstrated in public on those particular days just as the Tosinghi and Bisdomini publicly demonstrated their different ties on St. John's Day. For such ritual enactments were not merely symbolic; they did not merely stand for the contract in question. They *were* the essence of contract, the thing itself. If partners to a contract were not seen in public recognizing liens—if the episcopal *guardiani* failed to accompany the bishop—these liens were considered void and lapsed in fact if not in memory.

St. John's Day was a giant magnet for the rearticulation of contract because the setting was most coercive. The civic deity was the greatest of the saints (the only one besides Mary who had been born saved) and consequently the best possible arbiter and witness of contract.[164] Beyond this, his feast was the occasion for the demonstration of the power and purity of the whole community, and thus contracts sealed on that day had, in some sense, the approbation of saint and commune.[165] The actions of the clergy and the laity purified not just the churches of Florence, but the city as a whole. Florentines made these days into the most solemn of the year, and thus the actions on those days became most binding. If, as one preacher said, marriages would not last six months without the sacramental solemnities, Florentines obviously thought they would last longer if performed on June 24. This is part of what is behind Dati's remark that pending marital links were postponed until St. John's "to honor the feast."[166]

In the traditional agrarian feast of St. John the emphasis had been upon the *comparatico* or spiritual relations ritually achieved between humans and the plants that fed them.[167] The city of Florence's celebration reflected this agrarian source in some weak fashion, for after the morning offerings of the twenty-fourth, families repaired to their houses for marriages and banquets. Food was the instrument around which social bonds were affirmed:

164. Dati, *Istoria*, 127.

165. "And that the Deity might appear to participate in what had been done, public processions were made and solemn services performed to thank him"; Machiavelli, *History*, 313.

166. Giordano da Rivalto–Moreni, *Prediche*, sermon 50. Dati's statement is examined in my "Setting," 137.

167. Lanternari, "Politica Culturale," 82–88.

These things and offerings having been made, men and women returned home to eat. And as I have said, throughout the city on this day marriages and great banquets are held with so many fires, sounds and songs and dances, *feste* and joy and ornament, that this city seems a paradise.[168]

In the urban feast, the emphasis remained on human relations in contract, performed under the aegis of the Christian saint and his government. There were few agrarian motifs.[169]

Three basic types of social contracts may be isolated from the hundreds of liens established on this day. First came fraternal contracts, in which groups of so-called *amici* came together and offered to the patron. The military companies or confraternities serve as good examples. The Baptist functioned in these cases as a "mutual friend" or arbiter who regulated disputes within the fraternity, a patron who through serving as a common object of worship sealed the brothers in equality or, in Robertson-Smith's terms, in the mutual guilt of the sinner.[170] These relations of equality were also expressed through a fraternal meal or *pietanza*, which commonly followed such offerings.

Hierarchical contract, the domination mode of union between honorable subjects and ruler, is best illustrated in the ceremonial offerings of the subject groups of the Florentine dominion. The commune of Florence established precedence among these subjects, ranking each according to the antiquity of their submission and their honor. In that order, each subject brought his tribute into the Piazza, and in the same order each proceeded to the Baptistry to present his tribute to the saint.

Thus the fraternal offering essentially regulated social relations between the governing merchants of Florence, whereas the offerings made by subjects maintained domination or inequality between representative groups. The cement of the fraternal and hierarchical contracts was provided by a third type of contract that ritually made brothers of unequals. Charity, perfect charity, "showing intrinsic love by extrinsic operation," was a crucial ingredient in any formal presentation to a saint, a ritualized exchange between two disparate groups enacted before the saint to make merit for the superior one.

The oldest such charitable festive practice was to release selected prisoners on a regular basis.[171] A second such practice was to feed a group of selected poor for a specified period of time around the feast.[172] In both cases, the inferiors were purified through washing, dressed in rich clothes, and otherwise identified as clients of the patronal commune; then they were

168. Guasti, *Feste*, 7 (Dati).

169. Lanternari notes two further agrarian elements in the Florentine *festa*: The fireworks were preserved, and the florin itself showed the saint standing upon leafy branches and a tree trunk; Lanternari, "Politica Culturale," 67. But to my knowledge no contemporary description of the Florentine festival hints at such agrarian motifs.

170. E. Leach summarizes the different theories of sacrifice in his "Structures of Symbolism," in La Fon-

taine, *Interpretation of Ritual*, 266f.

171. The practice was "old" at the end of the thirteenth century; ASF, *Prov.*, 4, f. 45r (July 21, 1294).

172. On the occasion of a victory in 1440, the commune instituted the practice of dressing up twenty poor males for a certain period of time; *ibid.*, 131, ff. 126r–127r (July 9, 1440); *ibid.*, 157, ff. 63v–65v (June 13, 1466). A related practice was testamentarily ordering a group of poor to be dressed in white for a funeral; an example in Del Corazza, 267.

marched to the saint's altar. The exact roles of prisoners and commune in the offering were not clear to contemporaries. Communal laws say that the prisoners were offered to the saint by the commune, a variation on that theme being that the Signoria, by liberating prisoners, "made a gift to God of [the prisoners' grave] guilt and costs."[173] Yet a fifteenth-century chronicler says that when taken to the altar, the richly dressed poor offered the patron commune to the saints.[174] In either case, it is clear that an identity was established between the donor and the sacrifice; charity to the powerless purified power.[175] The most evident recipient of such caritative offerings was the clergy itself, a purified body that the politicians offered to the saint. In effect, the clergy's rich clothing proved the charitable conversion of worldly Florence.[176] If in the hierarchical mode St. John served as a patronal friend of the commune, approving its right to dominate others for him, in the charitable mode of offering he was the lord and Florence's charitable citizens the subjects, the saint being disarmed by the ritual fraternity that unequals acted out before his eyes.

Thus the commune's celebration of its saints showed the equality of the "fathers" of society within the offerings of the fraternities and gonfalons, the political domination by the commune of foreign subjects, and, through a ritual distribution of property, the fraternity of citizens with nonpolitical inhabitants of the city such as prisoners, the poor, the clergy, and hospitals. Each type of contract linked groups and individuals with one another and publicly affirmed their particular interrelationships by using a sacred figure— in this case St. John—as their security. The subject could believe that the lords of Florence would not violate his status and terms of subjection if the commune recognized them in public; the politically excluded saw represented before their eyes the duty of the government to govern and feed them; citizens and inhabitants saw in the ascetically ordered wards the political class's willingness to restrain its violence and arrange within itself the rules of precedence. Everyday communal anxieties gave place to confidence in an established order; from distrust came trust, from dishonor the honor of mutually recognized and sacralized relationships. The females who had given birth to all these contracting males witnessed the generative power of males in groups, and from a society ruled by patronal networks came an expression of solidarity built around sacred symbols and governmental forms. In the successful feast of the patron many of the problems associated with Florentine social relationships could be ameliorated.

Viewing the feast of St. John as an enormous contractual setting does

---

173. "Deo et beato Johani offerantur"; *ASF, Prov.*, 3, f. 45r (July 21, 1294). "Donando ad Dio lor cholpe grave' e spese"; F. Luiso, *Firenze in Festa per la Consecrazione di Santa Maria del Fiore* (Lucca, 1904), 16. This means that the government absorbed the prisoners' past jail costs, which prisoners normally paid before they could be released, and paid the debts of prisoners as well.

174. Pietrobuoni, f. 165r.

175. Leach, *loc. cit.* This corresponds to the sacrifice theory of H. Hubert and M. Mauss, *Sacrifice: Its Nature and Function* (Chicago, 1964).

176. For the development of this idea, see page 359, this volume.

not, of course, presume that Florentines unthinkingly took to the streets to publicize their loyalties. They did so when their own position was honored by that lien, and tried to avoid it when it was not so honored, or when it was not necessary. Commitments of any type were dangerous, and participation in the *festa* was perhaps as often coerced as voluntary; the commune insisted that certain groups present themselves publicly, and private groups like confraternities also required their members' presence. Indeed, a primary purpose of any procession was to measure and assess the commitments of men to groups. In the small confraternal procession around the cloister of a Florentine church, the group's notary and captain stood raised on a dais in the center and marked off attendance.[177] On St. John's Day, the government's notaries checked off those of the dominion's subjects whose tributes appeared in the piazza and at church, and then specifically warned those who had not appeared to do so immediately.[178] When in the early fifteenth century citizens were not assiduous enough in attending their gonfalon's offerings, the commune ordered them to do so.[179] The commune took the same attitude toward recalcitrant churchmen; if they would not attend, the commune would cease to give them alms.[180] The Parte too took attendance, and imposed fines on nonparticipants.[181] Many persons were coerced into taking part; the public setting of the offerings was an excellent forum in which to measure commitment.

Nor does viewing St. John's as a day of contract suggest that the offerings made to the saint and the gifts exchanged among hundreds of contractors were indelible signs of friendship. When Gostanzo Landucci won the Palio of S. Lò one year in the early 1480s, he did not take the *palio* home and mount it on the wall as a trophy of his equestrian skill. He sold it back to the Aretines—who had given it to the commune as tribute—for forty florins, and won it again in a later horse race in Arezzo.[182] The countless *palii* received by the Baptist each year hung in the church for that year as signs of submission,[183] but they were then either auctioned or used as altar cloths (*pallia*).[184] The alienation of gifts was repugnant to some—we recall that Lapo Mazzei said he did not like to sell his "as everyone else did." But in the context of St. John's Day this was a perfectly legitimate practice between citizens, and between them and their saint. These were civil relations, said Guazzo, not amicable ones. The function of gifts or tribute was to demonstrate the extent of one's regard. Once it had been presented, once the quality

177. *Libro degli Ordinamenti della Compagnia di S. Maria del Carmine scritto nel 1280*, ed. G. Piccini (Bologna, 1867), 39ff.

178. *Statuta*, III, 298ff. On human and animal ritual as "public counting devices" (cf. the expression "Stand up and be counted"), see Rappaport, "Sacred," 26; Dawkins, *Selfish Gene*, 123, with a summary of V. Wynne-Edward's theory of epideictic behavior.

179. ASF, *Prov.*, 95, ff. 43rv (May 12, 1406).

180. ASF, *Prov.*, 145, ff. 86v–87r (June 19, 1454).

181. Bonaini, "Statuto," 21.

182. Landucci, 50. Landucci identified the first *palio* won by Gostanzo as that of S. Vittore rather than S. Lò, but the latter's *palio* was provided by the Aretines, not the former's.

183. Guasti, *Feste*, 18f.

184. "E de' Palii fassene paramenti e palii da altari; e parte de' detti Palii si vendono allo 'ncanto"; Guasti, *Feste*, 7 (Dati).

of the relationship had been witnessed by third parties, the gift could be alienated. Thus the medium by which values were exchanged between men and with their saints was alienable once removed from the context of the contract. Only in that ritual was the medium sacred.

Finally, this contractual setting was not provided for reasons of religion and civil coherence only. The festival of St. John was a way of raising money both for individual merchants, who profited from holidays (for example, by making the *palii*), and for the commune, which through monies gathered during *feste* covered the cost of charitable donations and funded communal maintenance of the temples. During the festive period the government permitted anyone with debts in the city and most of those Florentines banished from the city to enter, see the feast, and procure the spiritual benefits without the danger of being seized by the commune or by his creditor—for a price. Civic officials were sent to the gates to collect a tax and issue chits affording such protection from creditors.[185] Within the city, Florentine law forbade most shops to open, since that would offend the honor of the city's saint— unless the owners paid what amounted to a tax. Small shopkeepers complained bitterly about such licenses, but bought them anyway.[186]

The offerings themselves were a source of wealth. On the morning of June 24, 1366, the bishop went to San Giovanni to say Mass. Upon entering the church he posted his familiars and nuncios

> to guard the altar in order to receive [each] offering that comes to the said altar. All the custodians who had been at the said altar for the *operai* of the said church step aside, [for the bishop rightfully received all offerings to the altar] from the beginning of the bishop's office up till the said Mass. . . . [Many] came to offer certain *palii* of cloth and of muslin, namely the *palio* that Count Roberto sent on this day, the *palio* that . . . sent, the *palio* that . . . sent, and many others, ten in all.
>
> Then those of the Florentine mint came to offer. But before they proceed, they ask the said lord bishop to permit the offering that they bear to belong to the *opera* of S. Giovanni. . . . [He answers:] "I consent that the said oblation is received for it by the priest, but I do not want this offering, from wherever it comes, to be given at the altar, but over there, separately, down in the choir, to be received by a priest for the said commune and *opera* and *operai*."[187]

Obviously, both the bishop and the *opera* had a financial interest in procuring as many offerings as possible, and thus an interest in extravagant participation in such offerings.[188] Indeed, whenever we find the Florentines being admonished to perform their offerings, it is the Calimala gild's *opera* of S. Giovanni that is behind it. These lords of the Baptistry fabric were the ones who complained in 1406 that citizens were not making their offerings with their gonfalons, and it was the same *operai* who in 1454 persuaded the

185. "Cives missi ad portas"; Guasti, *Feste,* 51 (1516). The *festaioli* for San Giovanni 1514 "collected a lot of money from the aforenamed exiles and debtors, and also from the aforenamed artisans"; Masi, 141f.

186. Masi, 141f (1514) gives a breakdown of the cost

of the *bulletini*.

187. AAF, *Benefizio . . . Tani,* ff. 69v–71v.

188. The *opera* also resisted having to disburse some of the offerings it received; Landucci, 257.

government to have all the intrinsic officials of the commune parade on the twenty-fourth and make an offering.[189] The motivation was obviously to increase the *opera*'s income. It was the *opera* that sold the gifts after they were received, and thus raised money to maintain and augment the fabric of the church and the services within it.

Thus coercion was sometimes used to foster participation, offerings were quickly converted to cash, and the festival was a means of raising money. How could St. John be pleased by such evidence of unwilling, apparently routinized, participation? How can one maintain that Florentines and subjects offered to the saint with heartfelt commitment? The problem for the commune and all groups that contracted on this day was evident. Without ritual commitments in public, the city and its parts feared anarchy; people had to be forced to join in procession. But a procession or offering or contract without emotional commitment risked the ire and retribution of God and the saints, who knew men's hearts. On the one side a commune not generating life through ritual would soon lose its identity; on the other, men recognized that public hypocrisy was socially and religiously debilitating. How could contracts be solidified when sincerity was partially lacking?

The answer is that ritual in and of itself "put men at peace."[190] Forced to participate, a citizen angry with his place or position came to terms with them within the solemn setting provided by his fellows. Ritual transformed anger and individuality into friendship and community. Participation forced unity upon participants by committing them to the public show of solidarity with their contracting group or person and with the saint. They then spent the next year living up to the public actions they had been forced to take. Just as form generated such inner states in private relationships, so it did in public ritual.

The World of Competition

The Florentine people,
Who were subtle interpreters of appearance. . . .[191]

The chroniclers recording the Florentine celebration always delighted in its order, its completeness, and above all, its lack of "scandal." They tended to view order not only as the norm for celebrations, but as their very meaning. Yet these same men also realized that these celebrations were a stage for competition as well as contract. They did not like to talk about struggle within civic forms any more than moderns do, but their faithful recording of what happened shows that contract being necessarily public, competition was rarely absent from the scene. For most political Florentines realized what only a few were ready to admit: that the Florentine political order was inherently discordant; that, moreover, it was even in the interest of the public good to nourish discord in certain places.[192] The ritual of celebration was one of those

189. *ASF, Prov.*, 95, ff. 43rv (May 12, 1406); *ibid.*, 145, ff. 75v–76v (June 6, 1454).

190. For the motivations for ritual, see page 113, this volume.

191. Machiavelli, *History*, 383.

192. Some scholars continue to deprecate violence within ritual, as did contemporaries, without seeing its functional centrality, as did contemporaries. See

social processes where men struggled with each other in the very act of binding themselves together.

This competitive drama in which men and groups tried to outdo each other not only mirrored real disparities within the citizenry but actually generated power for a city that lacked coercive and charismatic authority apart from the meager honor of its families. Mere parade emptied of the passion for place would have been superficial and unappealing to the saint. Ritual as a competitive *process* gave the Florentine commune and its citizens much of the pride both had in the city's public life.

Ritual forms are often thought to have one function: uniting the social body by providing psychological calm. In this view, when civil division emanates from ritual, it has failed. The Florentines shared this view, but they also understood that public ritual was so central to communal life that its failure had to be risked. For only when ritual actors accompanied consensual images like St. John and the commune, within an approved spatial and chronological setting or frame, could those actors create personality, identity, civil life. Communal and citizen personality did not result from mere doing; one had to insert oneself into a framework of personal and material values or be placed there by some more powerful individual or group.

Ritual was a demonstration of being but also the stage of becoming, the very working out of personal and civil order and structure. It is this combination of ritual required for showing a given order, and ritual manipulated by participants to increase their own personality by augmenting that of the social order, that characterizes self-governing urban society in preabsolutistic Europe. Medieval urban ritual avoided routinization because ritual celebration was the formalized presentation of violence as well as fraternity. The miracle of celebration was that a feast like St. John's permitted the contained release of energy. Ritual behavior was the door to spontaneity as well as spontaneity's memory.

The evidence for such competition is especially sparse on St. John's Day. We recall the actual attack on the gild consuls in 1300, but to our knowledge such violence against officials, though often planned, was never actually repeated on any subsequent feast of the patron.[193] The law forbidding vile signs or words when the companies went to make their offerings on St. John's Day (1415) may hint at tension in the ranks of the gonfalons.[194] There is some evidence of struggle for place in the ecclesiastical procession for the Baptist: For example, in 1454 the friars of St. Anthony absented themselves from the patron's procession because a reordering of precedence in the procession had endangered their status. Participating under those conditions, the brothers explained to a punitive Signoria, would have diminished the order's honor.[195] In processions on feasts other than that of the Baptist we find further evi-

J. Heers, *Fêtes, Jeux, et Joutes dans les Sociétés d'Occident à la fin du Moyen Age* (Montreal, 1971). Savonarola condemned those who cited the views of earlier Florentines that one ought to nourish discord in certain places for the good of the commonwealth; *Aggeo*, 244.

193. See pages 218f, this volume. A typical plot to seize the Palace when the priors were outside for the festivities is in Stefani, rub. 792 (1378).

194. See page 255, this volume.

195. *ASF, Prov.*, 146, ff. 87v–88r (Apr. 29, 1455).

dence of this exquisite concern with honor and place. Thus in 1515 and again in 1518 the canons of the cathedral of Florence attempted to improve their position and caused the communal master of ceremonies no end of headache.[196] And in 1522 the same official took note

> that the rector of the university wanting to come to honor the feast [of Corpus Christi] asked [permission] to precede the *podestà* of Florence. And neither the Signoria nor any of the chancellors would concede this. He did not come to honor the said *festa*. I record this for another time, etc.[197]

It is not difficult to surmise why the evidence for scandalous disorders of this type is so slim. First, the sources that might tell us how Florentines established the precedence of the "worthier and older" (Dati), especially in the gonfalons, have not surfaced. Second, chroniclers did not dwell on struggles for precedence because they thought them to be undignified. We do learn that from the late fourteenth to the mid-fifteenth century a squabble between the cathedral canons and the Dominicans of Santa Maria Novella over the correct route of the Corpus Christi procession (Plate 16) split the citizenry into warring camps.[198] In 1385, the bishop of Florence (of the Acciaiuoli family), bearing the head of S. Zanobi (of the Girolami family) in a procession, fell into a precedence dispute with those bearing Our Lady of Impruneta (of the Buondelmonte family), and this disagreement ended in the Lady of Impruneta being insulted and the bishop of Florence being forced to flee the procession and seek shelter in a nearby house.[199] Such examples could be multiplied, but they give us no sense of the normal tension of St. John's Day, no feeling that such use of the procession to heighten and diminish honor was not aberrant.

If we recall what the fundamental dynamic of public behavior was, however, we may use a source that aptly illustrates the hypertense competition of even the most stable of feasts. Processional competition comprised a struggle for place near consensually valid images: relics, hosts, visiting dignitaries. These images themselves competed for place, and the audience viewed the resulting order of the images in procession as the hierarchy of grace with which such consensual authorities looked upon co-citizens. Of all these charismatic sources, the most important were civil sources of authority such as Our Lady of Impruneta, the head of S. Zanobi, the Annunziata (*not* carried in procession), and other such religious symbols. Without a king, Florentines competed for relics and images, defining their civil position through them. On the other hand, limited by the prerequisites for civil order, they regularly

---

196. Trexler, *Libro*, 120, 128.

197. *Ibid.*, 130.

198. To "remove divisions among citizens," two societies called companies of the Corpus Christi, one meeting in the cathedral and the other in Santa Maria Novella, were suppressed as far as it was possible for

a communal law to do so; *ASF, Prov.*, 80, ff. 69r–70r (Aug. 7, 1391). In the mid-fifteenth century letters to the college of cardinals from the Signoria describe the continuing debate and division between citizens; Morçay, *St. Antonin*, 457f; Trexler, "Magi Enter Florence," 155f.

199. Panciatichi, f. 150r (June 11, 1385).

attempted to traditionalize precedence in the access to the images. Ritualization of the violence that had originally attended the competition resulted.

The documentation of the ceremonial first entry of the bishop of Florence to his see transmits this sense of competition better than any other source. The bishop was a sacred figure, and he was a Florentine. Thus persons competed for his presence in the same way they did for the host, the image, and the altar of St. John.

From the moment the bishop entered the city his way was marked by danger to his own status and to that of those who served or hosted him. He was a charismatic figure, and spontaneous liberality was expected from him; yet every movement he made in the civic ambience threatened to freeze this liberality into duty. "Scandal" was constantly near the surface as lesser men, realizing the power of precedence, tried to establish a right to share the bishop's charisma. Thus when he dismounted his horse at San Piero Maggiore, where he would spend his first night in the city, the bishop had the *right* to give his horse, spurs, and saddle to anyone he pleased, but was *expected* to present them to families and religious who had traditionally received them and had what contemporaries called "preeminence" in the matter. Fights over these objects were common.[200] When the bishop entered the same church and exchanged gifts with the abbess who was its prelate, another challenge to order emerged. If the abbess did not notarially affirm on the spot that she understood her hospitality to imply no episcopal right over the nunnery and church, she endangered her immunities. If she took such a step, however, she insulted the episcopal honor. Since his three episcopal families accompanied the bishop into the nunnery and the church, the abbess also risked compromising the "liberty" of her parish's families to them. In 1358 these problems required notarizations:

> We pray you in the name of the abbess that you admonish these your notaries not to notarize anything that could submit this nunnery to anyone, and especially to these *vicedomini* who are here . . . and caused scandals.[201]

After a particularly violent encounter many years later, the commune had to step in, permitting the abbess to notarize on the spot in her name and in the name of the parish's *popolani* that the episcopal families' presence at table in the nunnery on that day "gave them no rights, jurisdictions, or preeminence in the same church of San Piero."[202]

When the bishop left San Piero's the following day to take possession of his see, his notarizations continued. At every step, the prelate insisted that he chose freely to be aided by one person rather than another, and that no right was established. Meanwhile the cathedral canons and *vicedomini* themselves

200. The "preeminences" (Landucci, 288) of receiving the spurs of the bishop's horse belonged in the fifteenth century to the Strozzi; Strozzi, *Lettere*, 168, 174f. Arguments over the objects took place in 1358; *ibid.*, 175; AAF, *Benefizio . . . Tani*, f. 33r. They occurred again in 1370; Strozzi, *Lettere*, 175, and in other entrances.

201. AAF, *Benefizio . . . Tani*, f. 34r (1358).

202. ASF, *Manoscritti*, 167 (extract of a law of Jan. 23, 1385/1386).

notarized, so as to defend and enlarge their rights vis-à-vis the bishop and each other. When the bishop had entered the cathedral and approached his ceremonial chair, for example, the provost of the chapter attempted to help him sit down. Immediately the latter called out: "You are witness that I, in the name of the chapter of Florence, put the lord bishop in the chair. You, ser Tino notary, make a record of it for me!" The bishop responded in an instant: "I announce that I enter in this chair by myself as its lord, and through no one else's hand. You, Lorenzo notary, make a record of it for me!"[203] From the time the bishop entered the city until the time he finally ended the long ceremony, the scene around this consensually powerful figure was one of careful vigilance to find a formal fault that left room for new rights to be established, constant notarial activity, and, not uncommonly, outright violence. The ceremony around such figures was an experiment in social mobility through form. I further suggest that the ritual of celebration as a whole, including the feast of St. John's, was viewed by the initiate with just such apprehension and elation. Bystanders at public demonstrations watched and remarked changes great and small. In 1458 they quickly noticed that the Standard Bearer of Justice took a place in the midst of the priors and not his customary place on the right. This was a sign of Luca Pitti's incredible power, they realized.[204] How could a man like Donato Velluti fail to notice substantial shifts of others' positioning when he could describe his own shift of behavior toward the duke of Athens as follows?

> I sweetly began to distance myself from him, in part but not completely. I asked him
> for nothing, nor did I go to see him except on feast days to hear Mass [with him], and
> also on occasional feasts to render him reverence, leaving right afterward.[205]

The Florentines were indeed, as Machiavelli said, subtle interpreters of appearances.

The successful *mostra* of St. John's, the parade of the gonfalons, the ecclesiastical procession, and the various offerings of the twenty-fourth; the *palii* of that afternoon and the various jousts, *armeggerie*, dances, wild-animal fights, and tournaments that were occasionally added—all demonstrated with a thousand refinements the position of men within the governing class and the state of their alliances, and re-formed all or many of them.

The World of Work and the World of Celebration

In the long period between the expulsion of Brienne, when the lower classes were excluded from the celebration of St. John, and the rise of Lorenzo de' Medici, opportunities for demonstration during communal feasts were

203. *AAF, Benefizio . . . Tani,* f. 34v (1358).

204. Machiavelli, *History,* 313.

205. *Cronica Domestica di Messer Donato Velluti,* eds. I. Del Lungo and G. Volpi (Florence, 1914), 163 (hereafter Velluti).

rigorously limited to members of the citizen class who had reached maturity. Sons of powerful families marched in the gonfalons, but they represented their families. The *villani* who bore some floats of St. John on their shoulders came from nonrepresented segments of Florentine society, but they were doubtless disguised to represent not themselves but the confraternity or its benefactor. There is no evidence of corporate activity by noncitizen groups on St. John's, and very little on the feast of May Day.[206] Indeed, the feast of the patron was as much a celebration of victory over the plebs of the city as it was a celebration of the city's general honor. Solemnity had to be the monopoly of the "good men," both to avoid profanation—the nonrepresented made fools of themselves when they tried to ape the ritual of their betters—and to preserve the social order.[207]

Preserving the social order meant seizing every opportunity to vaunt the honor of mature political males. Thus every significant victory, both internal and external, caused the government to ordain that that victory be remembered every year with suitable processions, offerings, and closing of shops. Preserving the social order also required ever-new communal contracts with the churches of these saints who had brought victory. This filled the calendar with dozens of obligations to different churches, days when communal officials or their surrogate gild consuls had to march in procession to the church, hear Mass, and offer candles.

These overburdened calendars commemorating military prowess and socioreligious contracts were thought necessary whether they were good or bad for business. Without enduring communal recognition of God's mercy, the commune would be harmed by the divinities. Yet they did conflict with much business life; they were meant to honor one particular group within Florentine society and were easily resented by those lesser workingmen who had no festive outlet and suffered from these festive interruptions.

Thus the commune was constantly faced with two diametrically opposed tasks. It had to generate and maintain life on the one hand through ritual, on the other through work. The result was predictable. Cycles in which ritual obligations continued to mount were followed by laws reducing obligations, in turn followed by a new swelling of obligations. In the late fourteenth century the Mercanzia or merchants' court cut back on the obligations of its officials to offer candles and wax to different churches.[208] But in 1414, and

206. There was a great deal of governmental activity regulating companies during the 1380s and 1390s, some of which was possibly directed against such groups. In 1388 flagellant confraternities were regulated: ASF, Prov., 77, ff. 215r–216r (Dec. 2). The Corpus Christi companies were dissolved in 1391; see n. 198, this chapter. In April 1393 two brigades organizing mass fistfights were suppressed; it is interesting that they were located in the same areas in town where the Corpus Christi societies were; Panciatichi, f. 172r. And in August of the same year the government forbade organizations in the dominion *faccendo*

il messere, that is, brigades led by substantial persons; ASF, Prov., 81, ff. 211 rv (Aug. 22).

207. On the inappropriateness of lower-class solemnity, see Della Casa, *Galateo*, 35, 45.

208. ASF, Prov., 83, ff. 286v–287v (Feb. 12, 1394/1395). A much earlier attempt of this type at Siena has been well studied by A. Vauchez, "La Commune de Sienne, les Ordres Mendiants et le Culte des Saints. Histoire et Enseignements d'une Crise," *Mélanges de l'Ecole Française de Rome. Moyen Age, Temps Modernes* LXXXIX (1977) 757–767.

again in 1417, the communal law stepped in and pared the offerings intervening governments had established. God did not want immolations from those
in need, the law of 1417 intoned. Times were hard for artisans, and what they
did earn should belong to their families for sustenance rather than to anyone
else.[209]

Despite the law of 1417, scores of offerings were either reestablished or
newly instituted in subsequent years. In 1437 it was made more difficult to
establish new offerings, but the accumulation was continued.[210] In 1460
another fundamental law cut back the fifty-five offerings to thirty-five because
the gilds were being impoverished and the time of their members consumed
by the constant rituals.[211] In 1474 the commune again attempted the impossible, this time addressing itself to the holidays on which all shops had to close.
There were many feasts observed with closed shops in Florence, the law
noted, that were not prescribed by mother church. True, the law went on,
every saint deserved veneration, but people had to be able to sustain themselves. When heads of families could not do so they cursed, and God obviously did not want that type of offering.[212]

Till the end of the republic, various regimes experimented with means to
soften the hardships incurred by artisans and workers during festivals.
Preachers encouraged the rich to be especially charitable to these unfortu-
nates on such days.[213] Governments were told to cut back on the gabelles
levied on occupations harmfully affected by ritual activities.[214] Moved by the
complaints of shopkeepers with as many as ten children to support, the
government might waive the fines they had incurred by working on feast
days.[215] And the government tried to limit shop closings to those parts of
days when ritual activities were under way.

But the cycle that replenished ritual life was too necessary to be cut back
definitively for mere economic reasons. There were those in fact who maintained that feasts were good for the workingman because charity took center
stage during feasts: The more public demonstrations there were, the more
alms for the destitute and the more work for poor artisans; an enemy of
holidays was an enemy of the poor artisan.[216] Yet this was not a credible
reason for maintaining this agenda, for the Florentines realized that more
trades suffered from the feast than benefited from it.

A law of 1460 limiting celebrations points up the problem.[217] Cutting
back on many other feasts, it nevertheless insisted that the celebration of

209. *Ibid.*, 102, ff. 148r–149r (Jan. 21, 1413/1414); *ibid.*, 107, ff. 154r–155r (Aug. 28, 1417).

210. *Ibid.*, 128, ff. 148v–149r (Aug. 28, 1437). The first waiving of the 1417 law came only months after its passage, and added no fewer than five; *ibid.*, 107, ff. 277rv (Feb. 9, 1417/1418).

211. *Ibid.*, 152, ff. 242r–243v (Sept. 14, 1460).

212. *Ibid.*, 164, ff. 288r–289r (Feb. 25, 1473/1474).

213. Savonarola, *Amos e Zaccaria*, III, 234.

214. *Ibid.*; *Ruth e Michea*, I, 66.

215. *ASF, Prov.*, 159, ff. 96v–97r (July 16, 1468).

216. A *festaiolo* in 1514, for example, recommended destroying the *ceri* and building other things "be-cause it will allow many poor men to earn some money"; Guasti, *Feste*, 28. Francesco Altoviti charged that Savonarola was against the poor, who could earn wages during festivals; *In Defensione*, 8r. But Savona-rola, on being blamed for famine, countered: "I had processions held to find alms for you"; *Ruth e Michea*, II, 123.

217. *ASF, Prov.*, 152, ff. 242r–243v (Sept. 14, 1460).

August 11 continue to be celebrated, for on that day only two years before the regime had been saved with the help of God. To have canceled that feast would have meant not only humiliating the regime that had benefited from God's grace, but disdaining the aid itself and thus weakening the regime. Multiplied a hundredfold, the calendar rich in offerings, in contracts, in solemnity, and in caritative processions was as necessary to stability for many different civil groups as this August 11 was to the Medici regime. Ritual rich in virile affirmation was born, sustained, and then perhaps subjected to economy. St. John's Day endured, a perpetual symbol of all the masculinity, history, and dominion any regime could muster. To survive, the republican order had to maintain that ritual order, and its vitality. For if ritual were to generate life, it had always to embody it.

In the ritual of celebration that we have examined, we have continually seen the importance of the street and the piazza. Here was the place of contract, the arena of competition, the space in which the civic form was shaped, challenged, and reshaped. Forced from it, Florentines were deprived of dignity and honor, of the means to manifest and thus solidify their bonds. Giovanni Morelli had wisely spent much time teaching his sons how to relate to their peers in public and relatively little teaching them domestic lore. Alienation and powerlessness were the lot of one imprisoned in the home, whereas identity and the chance for better status could be found only in public.

Seizing these streets from the "courts" and "castles" of the genteel families, early fourteenth-century governments built for the future. By creating a soon traditional and magnified ritual of civic demonstration, they inseparably linked the civic and not the private mode with celebrations held "so that the deity might appear to participate in what had been done."[218] Driven from beneath the sacred canopy, the genteel modes of celebration did not wither. They maintained their own vitality on Carnival and at other times of the year, for this was necessary to family and individual honor. Indeed, communal celebration itself needed the aura of honor, and in the later part of this century the joust, dance, and occasional *armeggeria* made their way back into the feast of St. John, if always in a subordinate position and sponsored by the government. Neither honor nor civility could long exist without the other.

All feasts reflected male domination of society and showed the liens and conflicts that defined a male political order. But though Carnival recognized the meliorative importance of women, youth, and even lower-class males as images permitting communication between families and groups of families, St. John's assigned these liminal groups to the audience, as devotees of the political process and order. In these festivities, it seemed that the city had been generated by male lineages married to each other and to the commune, and not by sexual copulation and daily work.[219] Visitors to the patron's *festa* in

218. See page 265, this volume.
219. On these different concepts of generation, see Munn's *Walbiri Iconography*. It goes without saying that observers of the San Giovanni activities constantly referred to the "virile" men who exchanged with each other.

this period marveled at a commune that could work endlessly at ritual at the expense of the shop, whose political males seemed able to generate life without women and without workers, a commune that with seeming ease produced genius and imagination from a seedbed of grave governors. Over it all stood the image, altar, and spirit of St. John the Baptist, the virginal male prophet of Christ and Christianity.

Under the aegis of the Baptist, the male community of citizens demonstrated its strength to these liminal groups and to the dubious world of feudal Europe. More important, it publicly ordered and reordered the interrelations between its members so as to solidify its commune for the coming year. The frame of the commune within which these festivities were performed, the image and altar of the saint before which they unfolded, the presence of governed devotees, all provided the coercion to complete this re-formation of the commune without open violence. We recall how Giovanni Morelli expected more from the Virgin because she was devoted to the community as a whole. Like Mary, the Baptist was a consensually valid image that had to be on good terms with the whole community to benefit the individual. Such relations required not only a dignified, nonviolent ritual, but one still infused with spirit. Different from the limited contractual and competitive setting of Carnival, San Giovanni's ability to bind citizens and advance them could only be utilized if men consensually recognized and offered to the saint, and subjects and governed unquestioningly recognized and vaunted the legitimacy of the male political order.

The commune "did not die" because this order created its life and maintained its continuity in ritual: The commune always "honored the feast." The ritual of celebration could often seem more necessary than work itself. The commune also "did not die" because its ritual gave life to its image abroad. Without a domestic ritual for foreign eyes, the commune of Florence could have as little communicated with the foreign world as, without it, citizens and inhabitants could have communicated with each other. It is to diplomatic ritual that we now turn our attention.

Chapter **9**

The Ritual of Foreign Relations

*The city was free and governed by the popolo.
Nonetheless it could not do without the great
citizens for now, since [it was] these men who
were intimate with the lords of Italy.**

*Preaching in Santa Reparata, [the friar] conjured the
emperor [in Pisa] . . . , and with great fervor extended his hand
and arm toward Pisa, and commanded the emperor to leave.†*

*An immense ambition and vainglory induced [Lorenzo
de' Medici] to never say "no" to any foreigner, no matter
if even of the lowest quality, as long as he believed
he would speak well of him.‡*

A festively bedecked but tawdry skiff adrift among princely galleons, the republic of Florence faced serious disadvantages in negotiating with foreign potentates. The ignobility of its citizenry, the governmental instability that resulted from short terms of office, the very diversity of the urban population all contributed to the distrust with which honorable foreigners viewed commitments made by this city of usurers, sodomites, and handworkers. "The Florentines and Venetians," said Pope Pius II, "consider an oath sacred to the extent it is useful to maintain it."[1] Florentines recognized, even shared, this distrust. Many accepted the axiom that honor was credit, that kings told the truth when less noble men might not. In 1414 a Florentine counselor felt it necessary to lecture his colleagues that "it is not true what others have said, namely that a promise of any prince can be trusted."[2] The chronicler Stefani protested against a duplicitous king, angrily stating that one should be able to expect the truth from kings.[3] "Everyone must keep

---

*Parenti, in Schnitzer, *Quellen*, IV, 41.

†Ps. Burlamacchi, 113.

‡Rinuccini, cxlviii.

1. *I Commentari*, ed. G. Bernetti, 5 vols. (Siena, 1972–1976), IV, 7.

2. Brucker, *Civic World*, 382.

3. Stefani, rub. 656.

faith, and especially princes," said the humanist Poggio Bracciolini. Like the foreigner, these Florentines expected less rectitude from mere Tuscan burghers.[4] The Florentines could not be trusted, among other reasons, because they had no prince. In Florence one could not answer *sub verbo regis*.

Foreign princes asked: Was the city maintaining its alliances, and could it? Did the evidence suggest, for example, that the government's commitment though genuine was hollow, because the regime could not command adhesion by citizens and subjects? On the answers to such questions rested the security not only of the Florentine regime, but of the thousands of Florentine merchants living abroad, from small shopkeepers to the very pilots of foreign ships of state, who suffered at the hands of foreigners when diplomatic relations were troubled. How could the city reassure foreigners? The Florentine government might verbally affirm its citizens' loyalty and friendship, its subjects' submission to the citizenry, and ambassadors might pass on such assurances to their sovereigns. But in the end the most trustworthy evidence of the state of diplomatic relations was the behavior of the inhabitants of Florence. "He was honorably accompanied to the audience by many Florentines," a Venetian wrote home in describing the reception his city's ambassador received on the Arno, "and *thus* they promise not to enter an accord with the Spaniards."[5] Through seemingly casual behavior the city showed commitments or antagonisms, whether it wanted to communicate them to foreigners or not.

Aware of the diplomatic importance foreigners attached to citizens' everyday behavior, Florentine governments could act in two ways to protect the city. They could simply prevent foreign agents from viewing urban differences. The king of Naples must not be allowed to see, said one counselor in 1409, "that he has a Florentine faction which opposes the alliance as too dangerous." If the Milanese ambassadors remained in Florence, opined another advisor in 1422, they would surely become aware of fights in the city; he suggested they be sent out of Florence at once.[6] But such recommendations had no lasting utility precisely because civil comportment had to be seen by foreigners if the city was to be trusted. The second course was really the only lasting solution. If foreigners had to see Florence, they must see a united city. The city's behavior had to be formalized.

Public behavior, either on the feast of St. John or in the wake of some important foreign event, became a primary instrument of Florentine diplomatic communication. Yet was a processional unity of diverse civil forces possible? Could the city express a unified message to a targeted foreigner? The competitive and contractual drama of the civil procession was watched not

4. Poggio specifically condemned princes, not private persons or republics, for duplicity; D. Wilcox, *The Development of Florentine Humanist Historiography in the Fifteenth Century* (Cambridge, Mass., 1969), 142f.

5. "Scrive, a l'audientia a dì 30 [Feb. 1527] fo acompagnà honoratamente da molti fiorentini; sichè pro-

metteno non far accordo con ispani"; *I Diarii di Marino Sanuto*, eds. R. Fulin et al., 58 vols. (Venice, 1879–1903), XLIV, 13 (hereafter Sanuto). This whole report is an outstanding example of a foreigner's measurement of Florentine sincerity.

6. Brucker, *Civic World*, 232, 440.

only by inhabitants but by the agents of foreign powers. Mobilizing a success-ful procession to honor a foreign power was a political and social achieve-ment, the best possible evidence of diplomatic credibility. By expressing the unity of the personalities of the city, it disarmed foreigners, embracing them yet distancing them. That was the message of the perfect San Giovanni:

> *For all their mutual strife,*
> *United for the good of the commune,*
> *And death to whomever would challenge them.*[7]

In this chapter we will study public diplomacy in order to discover its types, purposes, and relations to civil problems. Concentrating on the period of classical communal ritual up till about 1480, we will first examine noncon-tact ritual, the procedures used in the city to influence foreigners who were not present. We will then turn to contact diplomacy, first studying the forms of Florentine embassies abroad. Embassies were the preferred method of conducting negotiations during much of the fourteenth century, for the Florentines had deep reservations about welcoming foreign lords into their own city. In the early fifteenth century, however, these hesitations yielded to a policy that aggressively sought the princely presence, and we shall next study the ceremonies used in these welcomes, which played such an impor-tant part in the total ritual effort of the fifteenth-century city.

A Renaissance city in search of honor welcomed, but warily watched, its betters. We must watch and listen to the Florentines quite as carefully. Our task is to participate in that aural subtlety that allowed Florentines to hear one set of bells ringing more convincingly than another, that visual subtlety that measured how far the cap was raised in salute.[8] If we can develop this skill, we shall not only be able to interpret the diplomatic significance of such acts as could contemporaries, we shall sense why diplomatic ritual was such an integral part of international relations, and discard in the diplomatic realms as we have in other areas of civil life the useless notion of the polarity of form and meaning.

Ritual at a Distance

In the summer of 1399, after Ladislaus of Hungary had driven Louis of Anjou from Naples, the Signoria of Florence spent two weeks discussing what should be done to celebrate their ally's good fortune. Throughout these meetings, one member of the government resisted the majority wish to celebrate the king's victory publicly. Buonaccorso Pitti pointed out to his colleagues that Florence was still allied with the king of France; honoring Ladislaus, he believed, would insult France and endanger Florentine mer-

7. Guasti, *Feste*, 17 (1407–1409).   8. See pages 288f, 318, this volume.

chants in that kingdom. Pitti preferred ritual silence in the city. Why not send an embassy to Naples, he suggested, congratulate the victor in this less public fashion, and line his hands with florins? "Bring him our encouragement and a secret gift of up to 10,000 florins, which ought to please him more than the 6000 florins I estimate we would spend on public holidays."[9] Pitti's argument fell flat. In the end, the defeated politician records, "the holiday was held with ringing of the palace bells and three days of jousting, bonfires, and tournaments."[10]

Why in the collective wisdom of the Signoria did silence seem inadvisable? Certainly everyone understood that such celebrations were dangerous because third parties might feel insulted. Something as routine as honoring a new pope could be interpreted by another power as an insult, for insulting one power by celebrating another was common diplomatic practice.[11] Florence rarely courted such antagonisms, and to celebrate the defeat or misfortune of an enemy was almost unheard of.[12] Obviously, all of Pitti's colleagues weighed the options of silence or celebration carefully before deciding on the latter.

Occasionally the commune chose silence. Just fifteen years before Pitti's defeat in council, the Florentines abruptly canceled a victory celebration of their own military forces when they learned that the duke of Anjou had died. The reason was that the government did not want it to appear that the festivities celebrated the death of the duke;[13] by remaining silent, Florence communicated to France its respect for the dead duke. During the war with the papacy in 1376–1378 the regime decided to observe the papal interdict of divine services because Florentine propaganda required the commune to appear an obedient daughter of the church. To have done otherwise would have given foreign lords the pretext to attack Florentine merchants in their lands. Another interdict was observed in 1511 because Louis XII of France would have viewed a resumption of divine services as evidence that the Florentines had come to an understanding with the Francophobe pope.[14]

Doing nothing, in short, communicated a political position just as surely as did public celebration. Given the option between silence and public action, therefore, the Florentines almost always chose the latter, for they believed that they could better control what they were saying through ceremonial activity than without it. One may imagine the arguments that prevailed over Buonaccorso Pitti: The king, so it may have been argued, would think a 6000-florin public celebration worth more to him than 10,000 florins given in secret. The commune desperately needed Ladislaus' goodwill, and it was only normal courtesy to celebrate an ally's good fortune. Would the latter not be offended by a secret gift, the priors may have asked themselves, and think

---

9. Pitti, *Memoir*, 62.

10. *Ibid.*

11. "Fece loro onore eccessivo, a fine d'offendere altri"; Vespasiano, *Vite*, 363 (Donato Acciaiuoli).

12. Florence did celebrate the revolt of the cities of

the Papal States in 1375–1376; *Diario d'Anonimo*, 304ff.

13. "E perchè non si potesse dire si fusse fatta per rendere gratia a dio della morte sua"; Panciatichi, f. 148r.

14. Trexler, *Spiritual Power*, 118, 181.

the Florentines too ashamed or fearful to give it in public? "Men are thought to lack either desire or power," a counselor would warn his colleagues in an almost identical debate half a century later, "and shame to the city would result."[15] Would the king not decide that the Florentines considered it more important to save a few of their lowly merchants in France than to honor a prince in public? Might Ladislaus not conclude that without a public celebration and the commitment it entailed, Florence could not be trusted? And would not Florence then be in greater danger from Ladislaus than otherwise? This was probably the thinking that defeated Pitti. A need to associate itself with noble achievements, in the eyes of both foreigners and citizens, moved the typical government to act publicly.

The most common occasions for ritual activity in the diplomatic realm were international events that directly or indirectly affected the city. Treaties that the commune signed with foreign powers were of direct bearing, whereas elections of popes, princely coronations, marriages and births in noble families, peace treaties between foreign powers, and, occasionally, victories of one foreigner over another were of less immediate import but also required a ritual statement.

Both types of events stimulated a common, highly formalized set of actions within Florence. The official notification of the event triggered this formal response. By July 26, 1381, for example, the commune knew that Carlo of Durazzo had in fact entered Naples, but it was only the official notification of September 10 that brought about public celebration.[16] Commonly, the formal program started with the arrival of a courier bearing the news. Treated as a personification of the prince he served, the runner was crowned with laurel at the gate, marched toward city hall to the triumphant accompaniment of trumpets and citizens, where he handed over the notice and received rich gifts from the lords of Florence.[17] Then the government ordered the ceremonial response to proceed.

"Ritual spontaneity" came first. Fireworks, blazing candles, and bonfires lit the city, demonstrating the popular mood of goodwill and joy. These exhibitions may be called ritualized because they seem generally fixed in form, were often paid for by the commune, and were conceived as part of a total package of expression. Guileless exuberance was the emotion communicated by this night of happiness, as if every Florentine poured into the streets unable to contain his or her elation.[18] Whatever the cause of celebration, Florentines acted, in Machiavelli's words, "as if they had won something themselves," an insight that is the key to understanding the nature of the communication. The Florentines wanted the foreign celebrant to identify Florentine emotions with his own and, consequently, his polity with the city's.[19] This spontaneous festive act found its literary expression in the

15. *ASF, CP*, 55, ff. 103v–104r (1459).

16. *Diario d'Anonimo*, 430.

17. On these gifts, see Trexler, *Libro*, 97 seq.

18. See, for example, Ps. Minerbetti, 8, and the *Diario d'Anonimo* for the months Dec. 1375–Apr. 1376.

19. Machiavelli, *History*, 146; Masi, 251.

congratulatory letters sent in the following days, in which the government assured the foreigner that "everyone" was beside himself with joy at the happy turn of events, and had publicly demonstrated that joy.[20]

The second communication to the foreigner was solemn commitment, expressed through thanks offered the deities. Treaties in fact could require that their public reading be combined with a solemn procession of the populace.[21] At least a solemn Mass and at most a three-day series of solemn processions led by priests and followed by laity, sometimes in their military orders, formally committed the city to the exuberance expressed the evening before. The miraculous *tavola* of Impruneta might be brought to the city, and the commune's most treasured relics unveiled for public view, an unsurpassed method of flattering the object of the celebration.[22] Communication between two earthly powers benefited from communication with the celestial powers whom both professed.

Combative adhesion was the final element of such celebrations. War games, jousts, and armed parades staged by the dignitaries of the city and their sons demonstrated the strength to aid as well as intimidate an ally; they showed, in short, the sovereign submissiveness of the city.[23] In the midst of such activity, the honorable members of Florentine society might publicly remove their outer clothing and ostentatiously give it to the poor. This not only demonstrated the joy of the foreign prince's Florentine friends, but gave living proof of the unity of the city's rich and poor in celebrating his fortune.[24] For a city involved in public charity, it was thought, was a city at one with itself, and the prince could flatter himself to think that his fortune was what had caused the unity of his ally.

From the courier's welcome to the final event, contemporaries viewed such pomp as parts of a ritual whole: "And then the feast was completed which the priors wanted carried out for the above coronation of Hungary received by King Charles."[25] Official letters describing the ceremonies were dispatched, and agents of the celebrated power penned their own assessments of the pageant's sincerity and cost, as well as an estimate of how unified the populace had been in paying this honor.[26] It was these foreign

20. A characteristic expression of this type is found in the instruction from Florence to its ambassador in P. Kendall and V. Ilardi (eds.), *Dispatches with Related Documents of Milanese Ambassadors in France and Burgundy, 1450–1483*, 2 vols. (Athens, Ohio, 1970–1971), I, 3ff. The Ten says that the ambassador has been sent to the French king because the latter could not be present to witness the citizens' joy.

21. Rinuccini paraphrased paragraph 12 of the Peace of Lodi (1454): "Item che la presente lega e confederazione si debba pubblicare solennemente, fatta la dischiarazione con solennità e procissioni consciente, e simili cose"; Rinuccini, lxxxiv. A firsthand description of the events is in Pietrobuoni, f. 168v, and a similar event in 1428 is also described *ibid.*, f. 122r.

22. After reporting the 1452 league between France,

Milan, and Florence, Pietrobuoni said that Impruneta was brought in "per memoria della soppradetta legha a conservatione"; Pietrobuoni, f. 157r. Cambi, in copying Pietrobuoni, changed this to "because they considered it such a good thing, they had the *tavola* . . . brought to us with worthy processions"; Cambi, XXI, 290.

23. For example, Ps. Minerbetti, 8, 158f, 239, 355.

24. *Diario d'Anonimo*, 464. Another form of charity used to celebrate good news was the suspension of debts; ser Giusto, f. 135v (1480).

25. Ps. Minerbetti, 8 (1386).

26. See the fine example referred to earlier in Sanuto, XLIV, 11ff. Cf. Commynes' assessment of the treaty the French king made with the Florentines during his

lords who finally decided whether, in the words of the Florentine sources, the celebration, far from simply memorializing a noteworthy event as if it deserved recognition independent of the relations between Florence and the other power, had actually "preserved and augmented" the happiness and good fortune of the foreign party or the treaty; whether, that is, the celebration had favorably affected the state of foreign relations.[27]

A myriad of other forms of ritual commitment surrounded this celebratory core. A Florentine alliance with foreign states might first be possible, for example, only after the commune of Florence had as godfather sponsored the newborn child of the potential princely ally, as when in 1390 Maso degli Albizzi traveled to Milan and lifted a Visconti child from the font. "This having been done," says our source, "[Visconti] made a league with us."[28] Ritual time and space in the city was partly shaped by these alliances. The establishment of the feast of St. Louis of Anjou in 1388 remained throughout the republic a ritual reminder of the alliance with France.[29] If a Florentine devotion to the patron of another city already existed, it could be magnified. Thus the Venetian alliance with Florence in 1425 was first celebrated with the traditional three days of procession, but then in 1427 St. Mark was more enduringly honored. The commune ordered the silk gild to refurbish and enlarge the decrepit Sylvestrine church of San Marco with a view to augmenting divine services. In the words of the enabling legislation, this would express the commune's gratification at its alliance with Venice, a city whose constitution was similar to Florence's. Increasing the cult in San Marco, the law continued, would foster the fame of the Venetians through the honor it would do their patron, St. Mark.[30]

The countless celebrations whose course we have synthesized were the standard means of ritual diplomacy at a distance. Yet they were clearly more and less than they seemed. Diplomacy was as complex at the public level as were negotiations between single diplomats; the network of domestic and foreign alliances and antagonisms, the fears of the Florentines at the successes of allies, all mitigated against straightforward ritual expression. Committed to public expression, the commune by the nature of its multiple political

visit to the city in 1494: "I believe they made it willingly. They gave the king 120,000 ducats . . . , and they lent the king all their palaces . . . , and they changed their arms . . . [to] the kind the king wears"; *The Memoirs of Philippe de Commynes*, ed. S. Kinser, 2 vols. (Columbia, S. Carolina, 1969–1973), II, 471.

27. Ps. Minerbetti, 8; Pietrobuoni, f. 157r.

28. G. di Pagolo Morelli, *Ricordi*, 331. In 1327 the commune was godfather to the son of the duke of Calabria; G. Villani, X, 22.

29. *ASF, Prov.*, 77, ff. 124r–125r. Ps. Minerbetti, 50f, 83 gives the background. An older example of consciously honoring the dead for diplomatic purposes is

in a chancery letter to the Pavian government in 1258 during a Pavian threat to Florentine merchants. Florence, the letter states, had always revered the memory of two Florentine bishops who came from Pavia; B. Quilici, "La Chiesa di Firenze dal Governo del 'Primo Popolo' alla Restaurazione Guelfa," *ASI*, CXXVII (1969), 332.

30. "Domini . . . cupientes Sancti Marci quem . . . patronum defensorem illustrissimum venetorum dominii veneratur et habet fraterno quidem amore unitate confederatione parique studio libertatis et vivendi modo florentino generali convientus atque conforme ecclesiam . . . recipere incrementa"; *ASF, Prov.*, 117, ff. 254rv (Aug. 7). I would like to thank Samuel Cohn for checking this text.

commitments was forced to equivocate. It did so either by calculated insincerity in its ritual expressions, or by highly artistic ambiguity.

Black could be painted white; celebrations could be totally insincere. It might seem, said Giovanni Cambi about one such diplomatic communication,

> that the city was festive and in good state, but in fact it was like those who masquerade in silk and gold and appear rich and powerful, yet when the mask and the garment come off, they are the same persons they were before.[31]

But for all the duplicity of which the Florentines were capable, one fact must be constantly recalled: Forms created sincerity by committing their authors. When in 1494 the French king Charles VIII entered Florence on his way to claim the crown of Naples, he behaved not at all like the beloved ally he was said to be. Not only did the city narrowly escape sacking; Charles condoned the revolt of Pisa, even if he did promise to ensure that the city eventually returned to the Florentine fold. Despite these facts or because of them, Florentines behaved like the most overjoyed of allies when Naples fell to the French king in February 1495. They lit up the city "spontaneously," and ordered three days of processions ostensibly "in memory of such an acquisition."[32] In fact, however, the purpose of these celebrations was to disarm Charles, to dissuade him from harming Florence on his return north, and, most important, to encourage him to return Pisa. In fact, almost everyone in Florence was thoroughly frightened by Charles's victory. In Guicciardini's words,

> all the bells were rung as though it were a feast, and there were great demonstrations of happiness over this news, though as a matter of fact everyone was sick at heart. Our dependence on the king and the fact that our fortresses were in his hands made this display necessary.[33]

Despite the transparent duplicity of such expressions of joy, obvious to Charles no less than to the Florentines, the king was not remiss in recognizing Florence's celebrations. From Naples he wrote to the government that he deeply appreciated the Florentines' public celebration of his conquest.[34] Why? Was this verbal courtesy as insincere as the original motivation of the celebration? Not at all. Charles doubtless understood that half the value of such a victory was its celebration by other powers, and thus the Florentine celebration had a propagandistic value independent of its motivation. Charles could be grateful for the celebration for a second reason: The public demonstration in Florence bound its citizens to him in a fashion no mere gift could have done. The celebrations not only showed dependence, they increased it.

31. Cambi, XXII, 2.

32. Landucci, 101.

33. Guicciardini, *History of Florence*, 108; see also Rinuccini, clix. Cf. the pompous exequy the Florentines accorded Carlo da Calabria in 1328 "as a courtesy" to King Robert of Naples, though the city was happy to see Carlo die; Pucci, *Centiloquio*, V, 326.

34. Landucci, 102.

Insincerity was in a sense converted to sincerity through ritual. The very fact of the demonstration made Florence's reliance upon France still greater.

Another type of insincere ritual aimed to accomplish the exact opposite of what the ritual seemed to foster. We have already noted potential French fears in 1384 that under the cover of celebrating their own victory, the Florentines might be celebrating the death of the duke of Anjou. There is reason to believe that rituals intended to hurt foreigners were part and parcel of Florence's ritual treasure. Florentines commissioned Masses for the Dead for those who were living—a practice prohibited by European synodal law, which nonetheless recognized its efficacy.[35] One Florentine burgher hated the Visconti so much that he wished a Mass for the Dead be offered in the presence of visiting Milanese ambassadors instead of the Mass of Peace the envoys thought they were sharing with the Florentines. The burgher did not leave his purpose in doubt: Such a ritual should be performed "so that the [Milanese] tyrant would soon die."[36] The episcopal vicar-general of Siena, Sigismondo Tizio, used the trappings of the Mass to accomplish similar ends against Siena's enemies.[37] Such uses of ritual forms were not, of course, meant to trick God, who certainly knew who was alive and who was dead; God was rather constrained by forms to favor the Florentines. These forms were insincere toward earthly principals, who as in the example of the Milanese ambassadors cited earlier, could actually contribute to the demise of their principals by effectively praying for his death.

The most common response to complex diplomatic relations was neither silence nor deceit, but ambiguity: carefully constructed, artful celebrations designed to maintain and augment friendships without estranging others. Florentines sought to achieve in public forms the same level of representational sophistication expected of their diplomats, who were instructed in particular behavioral postures before going on their missions. To be "virile . . . , not timid or craven," to maintain a "strong and virile posture," were straightforward enough charges.[38] But other recommendations were more difficult: One embassy was to show neither fear nor timidity, but was to avoid bravado; an embassy to Genoa was to proceed "not basely but with grandeur, yet not arrogantly."[39] Such recommendations were made with the diplomatic situation in mind, and could thus result in extremely delicate, if not indecipherable, recommendations, like that of the counselors in 1382 seeking to balance two contending powers:

35. Florentine synodal law does not mention this practice, but many other synods do. For Prague in 1349, see C. von Hefele, *Conciliengeschichte* VI (Freiburg, 1890), 687.

36. "Piaccia all'altissimo idio che sia suta la detta messa per suo rinovale chome si fa a' morti, et che tosto manchi il tiranno"; Pietrobuoni, f. 125v. A contemporary *evocatio* of St. Ambrose is in Richa, *Notizie,* V, 17.

37. J. Burckhardt, *The Civilization of the Renaissance in Italy,* 2 vols. (New York, 1958), II, 483, who believed that Tizio used a particular set of authoritative gestures to the same end.

38. Brucker, *Civic World,* 449 (1423); 228 (1408); cf: "Hoc ita magnanimiter, quod nullus timor ostendatur"; *Diario d'Anonimo,* 448 (1383).

39. Brucker, *Civic World,* 441 (1422); 226 (1407).

Reply to the ambassador of King Charles so that he will not break off relations completely, and also so that the duke of Anjou will not be provoked to anger. The ambassadors should understand the commune's intentions by intuition rather than by words.[40]

Public celebrations brought such artistry from the audience into the streets, challenging the foreigner's sophistication in comprehending public commitment. In 1392, for example, Florence signed a peace treaty with Giangaleazzo of Milan, which Florentines viewed skeptically. This doubt was reflected in the ritual ostensibly celebrating the treaty, for Dati tells us that Masses and offices were said in honor of God, but that other celebrations were suppressed.[41] When Pope Julius II conquered Bologna in 1512 and ended French power in the Papal States, the Florentine government responded to the pope's request for a victory celebration with caution, for it was determined not to alienate its French ally. The government decided that the archbishop of Florence and the clergy could hold a procession and thus fulfill the minimum requirements of the papacy. But it forbade the laity to take part individually or in confraternities, and ordered that no bells be rung so as "not to embarrass our [French] confederates."[42] Citizens like Cambi read what they thought was the truth behind a skillful veneer. He thought the government had decided not to "show any sign of happiness, but rather it showed displeasure."[43] Foreign agents obviously had no easy time interpreting the nonverbal behavior that was being "shown." Like the Florentine ambassador who distinguished between the honors paid him on embassy and the "contrary intent in the hearts of citizens," and the Florentine counselors who saw the ruse behind the Pisans "walking with bowed head," so foreign reporters had to dissect the body of the celebration and determine its actual meaning.[44] Their task, difficult enough if one could assume that the government controlled celebratory modes, was enormously complicated by government's factual inability to say what it wanted. Florence was not a court where all representation could be orchestrated but a commonwealth where competition between interests was rarely absent from any public show. When in 1521 the Medici pope took Milan from the French, the government decided to do nothing, for it feared for the safety of Florentine merchants in France if a celebration were ordered. But, Cambi tells us, "those citizens who did not have possessions in France thought it would serve them well to have fireworks, *so that one could see the Florentines at one with the pope.*"[45] This group of citizens was also able to effect the (tardy) ringing of the Palace bells in celebration of the pope's victory. But how vociferously did they ring? In a similar case in 1523, diplomats had to be as skillful as were the Florentines in noting that the cathedral bells sounded more loudly and insistently than those of the Palace, and

40. *Ibid.*, 103.

41. Dati, *Istoria*, 35; see however the different report of Ps. Minerbetti, 158.

42. A. Renaudet, *Le Concile Gallican de Pise—Milan. Documents Florentins* (Paris, 1922), 680.

43. Cambi, XXI, 298.

44. On the ambassador, see Salviati, 177 (1398); for the Pisans, Brucker, *Civic World*, 212.

45. My italics; Cambi, XXII, 188. This shows how independent Florentines could still be of the Medici.

recognize, in the relative calm of the latter, governmental unhappiness at the event in question.[46] Foreign agents had to understand the political divisions in the city and judge the extent to which ritual diplomacy at a distance was a communication with the outside world, and how much of it was intra-urban communication.

The domestic content of ostensibly diplomatic communications could be so profound as to convert the foreign party into an instrument of domestic expression. To avoid being deceived, princely informers had to recognize the ignoble Florentines' peculiar need for a charismatic foreign personage around whom to order and clarify their civil relations. Stefani describes at great length how Charles of Durazzo played this role in the 1380s. The king had so much become the object around which domestic alliances were clarified that *Viva lo re Carlo!* had become a standard greeting among citizens, and one who did not use it was considered "not a friend of the public good of Florence." The news that Charles had been crowned king of Hungary was followed by celebrations that brought this private infighting to the city streets. Though the festivities were ordered by the commune, the great families used the figure of Durazzo to push their own politics, producing a scale of celebration (twice what would have been done if the Florentines had taken Pisa, said Stefani) completely out of proportion to the event.[47]

The foreign prince was crucial, therefore, but at times a mere golden calf for a domestic political dance. Stefani told how after Charles's death his supporters insisted he was still alive, whereas his denigrators maintained he had died long ago.[48] The citizens were commenting on their own identities, and the foreign agent who did not perceive that the identity of Florentines was ineluctibly linked to that of foreign princes could only end by deceiving his prince. As the Florentine commune attempted to conceal these domestic complexities, informers had to uncover them.

From the Florentine point of view, the ritual of diplomacy at a distance had every chance of success if done according to the best form and with strong intent. Spectacular successes could be verified by coincidences in time. Goro Dati, for example, noted with obvious satisfaction that the decline of Visconti rule in Milan coincided to the hour in 1403 with the first act of Florence's celebration of the feast of San Giovanni.[49] At the end of the century, chroniclers pointed out that the decision to bring Our Lady of Impruneta into Florence, and her actual entry, coincided with two catastrophes suffered by imperial forces in Livorno.[50] Neither of these reports suggested that God had decided to answer Florence's prayers; it was simply intimated that the city's forms had been effective. Nor are our sources free of the implication that God killed Florence's foreign enemies. Perhaps it was a faultlessly executed Mass for the Dead that, in Giovanni Morelli's striking language, led John the Baptist to "permit" Giangaleazzo Visconti to die in 1402.[51] In the view that Florentine saints harmed foreign enemies, in the

46. *Ibid.*, XXII, 240.

47. Stefani, rub. 995.

48. *Ibid.*

49. Dati, *Istoria*, 77.

50. Trexler, "Setting," 135.

51. G. di Pagolo Morelli, *Ricordi*, 399.

belief that Florence by manipulating the Mass could itself do such harm, we trace that confidence in civic cosmology and forms that permitted fra Domenico da Pescia to conjure enemies away from Florence by occult force.

The diplomatic ritual we have just examined was all accomplished outside the vision of the principals for whom it was intended, and without the participation of their agents. This type of ceremony had the distinct advantage of keeping friends and enemies at a distance. Once the commune sent ambassadors to princely courts, the commune, embodied in its embassy, ceased to be a separate entity. A Florentine embassy fell within the centripetal field of a charismatic power, and suffered from its inferior position in the diplomatic corps. On embassy, Florence's identity suffered from its own burgher nature.

If on the contrary Florence invited foreign princes to visit the city, it ran the serious risk of endangering the domestic status quo. Once princes' images participated in the civil ceremonies that honored them, they could violently restructure the ritual organization of the city. Clearly, a few hundred or thousand florins expended on ceremonies honoring a distant prince had many advantages over direct contact with superior honorific powers.

Ritual at a distance, however, was impractical and dangerous if done in isolation. International relations required that ceremony be meshed with an intimate exchange of views possible only in direct communications. Just as important, courtesy required that Florence, like other powers, personally go to congratulate or commiserate with princes after some significant event: The honor of a prince was directly related to the diplomatic retinue he could command into his presence. Princes did not hesitate to inform other powers when their presence was expected. In 1310 Henry of Luxemburg not only requested that Florence arrange civil celebrations of his pending coronation in Rome, but from his residence in Lausanne asked the Signoria to send an embassy there to congratulate him.[52] Furthermore, any prince traveling through Tuscany might expect a welcome in Florence, and failure to extend such an invitation was a breach of hospitality. Finally, dangerous to the public order as a princely visit might be, it could be necessary to that domestic order as well. A successful foreign policy, therefore, one that preserved and augmented the city's honor and strength, required Florentine governments to combine ritual at a distance with the ritual of visitation.

The Ritual of Visitation

EMBASSIES ABROAD

Until the second quarter of the fifteenth century, the commune of Florence preferred to send embassies abroad rather than welcome principals to

52. G. Villani, VIII, 120; IX, 7.

the city. Diplomatic insult abroad was less dangerous than the threat of social disorder at home.

Embassies to foreign powers were public events, and not withheld from the citizens' view. The ambassadors' formal departure, their every action abroad, and their reception back into Florence were all subject to close scrutiny by inhabitants, for they saw their embassies as a purified image of the city's highest honor and deepest aspirations, drawn together to encounter the foreign world of nobility. Chroniclers' reports reflect the heroic efforts the city took to neutralize its social inferiority abroad, and to present an image of noble behavior at home.

The embassy thus epitomized the right way for Florentines to act in their own intra-urban relations; ambassadors were the educators of the commune. From the time of Francesco da Barberino, the jargon of international diplomacy was the language of interpersonal relations between Florentines, the word *embassy* for example being used to designate one Florentine carrying a message to another across the street or piazza. Giovanni Morelli's boys were trained in "embassies" to neighbors, girls in "embassies" to dancing partners; nuns watched the skill with which their sisters carried out "embassies" to altars and statues, fraternities sent "embassies" to each other and so forth.[53] Preachers delivered sermons to packed houses in the cathedral on "those qualities necessary for one who is to be an ambassador or legate."[54] Examining the attention contemporaries accorded the diplomatic embassy abroad will leave little doubt of the strict relation between civic identity and form on the one hand and ambassadorial activities on the other.

The successful embassy first required that the ambassadors or orators be of higher social quality than the citizenry as a whole. Even if the Signoria itself had been permitted to go on embassy, its social level would normally not have sufficed. Expertise was vital, of course, but the skill of the statesman and lawyer had to be combined with the best name and title, one uncontaminated with merchandising: "It is sensible and redounds more to our honor," said one counselor in 1399, "for us to have a knight and lawyer there, rather than a lawyer and merchant."[55] At one time it had been common to send only members of the Parte Guelfa on important embassies; indeed the Parte, guardian of that which was best in Florentine society, had in the old days sent its own embassies to foreign courts. And throughout the republic, the ideal diplomat was the type of man who could barely suffer the egalitarian mores of the city. Donato Acciaiuoli had a real advantage as ambassador to the pope, said Vespasiano da Bisticci, since he came from a noble Florentine house.[56] Agnolo Acciaiuoli at the court of Milan had the edge over Venetian ambassadors because although the latter were "very ceremonious," their ceremonies were forced; Agnolo in contrast "had been reared since childhood in the

---

53. See pages 170, 188, this volume.

54. *Cronic[a] di Giovanni di Iacopo . . . Morelli*, in *Delizie*, XIX, 126f (1435) (hereafter G. di Jacopo Morelli, *Cronica*); see also E. Santini, *Firenze e i suoi 'Oratori' nel*

Quattrocento (Milan, 1922), 127.

55. Martines, *Lawyers*, 320.

56. Vespasiano, *Vite*, 358.

courts of lords," and was so practiced as to be natural.[57] Confirming Vespasiano's assessment, Rinuccini characterized Agnolo as "a man of great skill whose manners allowed him to consort easily with lords, more at home in courts than in a *popolare* and civil way of life."[58] So much in demand was this honor elite that in 1465 the commune had difficulty gathering enough of its members together to welcome a visitor because, as one reporter noted, most of those "capable of riding" were away from the city either on embassies or in provincial offices.[59] To alleviate this problem, the fifteenth-century commune often sent "youth ambassadors" from the best families along with elders.[60] Noble *and* young, they could be doubly effective in disarming the foreigner. Historically, then, two groups politically suspect within the city were considered ideal for representing the commune abroad.

The Departure

Once the ambassadorial entourage had been selected and ordered to depart, it often marched through the streets of Florence. The departure was formal, and the party stopped for the night shortly after leaving the city. In this civic procession, citizens could decide for themselves how reputably the regime intended to represent the community, both in the ambassadors' social quality and in their dress and accompaniment.

Giovanni Villani was in the streets to see an embassy depart for the Hungarian court in 1347. It was a time of intense antimagnate feeling, and our politician–historian expressed disappointment that the regime had picked ambassadors of inferior quality because it feared that *grandi* included in the embassy might betray the regime to the king. Certainly the embassy was "solemn" enough:

> Each of the said ambassadors was dressed at communal expense in scarlet robe thrice trimmed with squirrel. And each of the said ambassadors took with him two or three servants dressed in two colors per ambassador. Two knights of the court went with them. Thus there were more than a hundred horses, and beasts with loads. One can't remember such a rich and honorable embassy leaving Florence in our lifetime.[61]

But clothes alone did not make the ambassador. Having praised the outlay, Villani joined other communal sages in criticizing the government for excluding the *grandi*. Three nobles should have been included among the ambassadors, Villani thought. Not only did their exclusion further alienate the *grandi* from the regime, but it harmed the mission itself. For what else could the king of Hungary do on seeing the low social quality of the embassy but wonder (*ammirare*)?[62]

57. *Ibid.*, 378f.

58. Rinuccini, civ.

59. Strozzi, *Lettere*, 399.

60. On this institution, G. Vedovato, *Note sul Diritto Diplomatico della Repubblica Fiorentina* (Florence, 1946),

14 seq., and for the late texts of the laws on youth ambassadors, 67 seq.

61. G. Villani, XII, 108. The *cavalieri di corte* were communal buffoons, not "real" knights; Flamini, *Lirica Toscana*, 193 seq., and Trexler, *Libro*, 34f.

62. "Diedono materia a' grandi e a' nobili di sdegnare

Florentines were clearly more at ease when men of better social quality were chosen, and citizens could then give themselves over to incredulous descriptions of ambassadorial opulence without the nagging suspicion that the ambassadors were, after all, not much better than themselves in social standing. The departure of Piero Pazzi for an embassy to France in 1461 left a deep impression on Vespasiano da Bisticci:

> I can say that in my day no ambassador ever left Florence with such pomp as did messer Piero. His own person and those of the servants and boys [were] covered with infinite garments and jewels, and [there were] as many beautiful horses as could be found. I believe no one could have done more in all things than he did, to such an extent that the government, informed of this fact, wanted them to ride about the city so that the *popolo* could see such pomp as had never been seen.[63]

The concern for quality and riches was inextinguishable. For two months in 1493 before the embassy departed to congratulate Pope Alexander VI on his election, an army of tailors, coat-makers, and embroiderers worked on the richest garments for ambassador Piero di Lorenzo de' Medici and his youthful company. Piero wore a necklace said to be worth 200,000 florins and, *per magnificenza*, publicly took it off and put it on the necks of pages who were already loaded down with jewels.[64]

No one doubted the city's impressive ability to make money and spend it—no inferiority complex there. One correspondent in 1404 reeled off the incredible resources of the commune: some thirteen million florins spent for Tuscan liberty in sixteen years, ordinary revenues spent entirely on military ventures, extraordinary income generated through some sixty forced loans in three years: "There is not a king or province in the world that could have done the same."[65] The city's problem was not wealth, but the burghers' social inferiority and the usurious means through which the wealth had been earned.

Florentines traveling abroad did not have a reputation for niggardliness, but for throwing their wealth around like the *arriviste*:

> Florentines [when they go] outside Florence are like persons who have their bladder full and haven't dared piss because they were [at home]. But once they leave there they flood a wide path with the urine their prick emits.[66]

As the embassy entered the court, it acted to counter this profane image.

At Court

To purify communal wealth and origins, Florentines on embassy encased themselves in princely raiment. Then, as if that clothing were soiled by the

essendo ischiusi degli onori del comune in sì fatta cosa, e d'avere piuttosto riotte e discordie cittadinesche, e al signore fare ammirare"; G. Villani, XII, 108.

63. Vespasiano, *Vite*, 397.

64. Masi, 19f.

65. Brucker, *Civic World*, 197f.

66. P. Aretino, *I Ragionamenti*, ed. A. Foschini (Milan, 1960), 345f.

ignobility within, they changed clothes constantly, and made that fact known. An admiring Vespasiano da Bisticci tells us that Piero Pazzi "traveled in such state that every day he would change his sumptuous attire once or twice, and all his attendants would do the same." As at home with *armeggiatori* and horses, the Florentines on embassy to Alexander VI, said Masi, changed their clothes at every possible opportunity, so that they were never seen with the same vestments on two different days.[67] What on the surface seems little more than vulgar ostentation was in effect a form of purification in the presence of one's superiors or judges.

Displays of grandeur at court served the practical goal of equalizing the Florentines with their hosts and with the diplomatic corps. But they also strengthened the regime at home. Florentines recording their ambassadors' court activity reflect this fact when they proudly state, "Never had an embassy of Florence or any other power displayed such richness of garments and jewels," and "One speaks of nothing else in Rome but this ornateness," or even that their emissaries "shamed all the other ambassadors of the other powers."[68] Yet Florentine regimes benefited, in the citizens' minds, not through demonstrations of superiority but through avoiding shame. Such diary reactions to ambassadorial success were really expressions of relief that Florence had, as Masi once put it, "not been shamed by the embassies of other powers."[69] It was this that was uppermost in the minds of contemporaries. Gianozzo Mannetti ensured his place in Florentine history not least by refusing to be preceded by a Genoese embassy when he was ambassador in Naples.[70] Reports on these embassies are tinged with defensive concern, and expressions of easy confidence were completely absent.

Ambassadors normally communicated information of this type to their principals, for it helped states judge relations between powers. But the presence of diplomatic protocol in Florentine chronicles and diaries to an extent apparently unparalleled in other political settings suggests that in Florence, such details filled historical, and not merely informational, purposes. In their defensive fashion, the city's chroniclers show that diplomatic history was in part a search for survival through honor. Nowhere is this more pronounced than in chroniclers' accounts of the fashion in which their emissaries were brought into the presence of princes. No chronicler in a self-confident polity would have imitated Matteo Villani in recording that when Florence's emissaries entered the imperial court in 1355, the emperor's barons raised their hats to them.[71] Only a citizen thirsty for honor would have mentioned that after the ambassadors had thrown themselves at the feet of the august presence (the normal Florentine method of doing reverence to princes abroad), the emperor would not let them kiss his feet.[72] With obvious gratification, Villani recorded that Charles IV took their hands and placed the

67. Vespasiano, *Vite*, 397; Masi, 20.

68. Rossi, XXIII, 280; Masi, 20.

69. *Ibid.*, 129.

70. Vespasiano, *Vite*, 472.

71. M. Villani, IV, 53.

72. *Ibid.*, and on kowtowing, Pitti, *Memoir*, 58, 63.

ambassadors at his side, going so far as to kiss them on the mouth, a definite sign of intimate friendship and mutuality.[73]

This same sense of indebtedness to nobles who ceremonially equalized the Florentines continues in fifteenth-century sources. Emissaries still reported ceremonial information, of course; the chancellor of a 1461 embassy to the French court, for example, noted with satisfaction that the king honored the Florentines by his gait and by the movement of his cap.[74] Chroniclers, on the other hand, passed the same information on to posterity as historical proof of Florentine identity. Though writing almost half a century after the event, Vespasiano still thought it important to note Pope Nicholas' etiquette toward a Florentine embassy of midcentury: The pontiff received the Tuscans in public consistory, an honor, Vespasiano pointed out, "usually reserved for emperors and kings."[75] The contemporary Pietrobuoni recorded the unprecedented reception of Florentine ambassadors at Milan in 1450 with the same gratification. Exceeding previous practice, the duke's brother had met them five miles south of Parma, and at five miles from Milan Francesco Sforza himself had greeted them with embraces and kisses: "And never since Florence has been on the map, never did an embassy go out for [the Florentines] with such magnificence and such honor paid to it."[76] It scarcely mattered to Pietrobuoni that Sforza had won the ducal dignity for his family only weeks before, or that Florentine money had financed the condottiere's instant rise to hereditary office. The legitimating function of a princely office was more important to the Florentines than the history of that office. In a princely world, Florentines had to be received by betters if their embassies were to win honor for the city. They had, in a sense, to create dukes so they could then compete with them.

The ability of Florentine bankers to subvent royal and princely pretenders had another distinct advantage: It diminished the chances that Florentine embassies would be humiliated when at the courts of such personages. There is little doubt that such insults were common enough. The method was well known. Although welcoming the Florentine ambassadors with acceptable demeanor, the prince went out of his way to greet munificently and give readier audience to ambassadors from other powers.[77] When these and still worse insults became the subject of discussion among communal counselors, they were denounced with paroxysms of rage and hurt pride; the "shame, humiliation, and disgrace" that counselors suffered when communal ambassadors were detained against their wills, or received so

---

73. M. Villani, IV, 53.

74. See the extensive description of greeting ritual in Santini, *Oratori*, 187f.

75. "E dove per antica consuetudine si dava udienza in concistoro publico a' re e agl'imperadori, la dette a' Fiorentini in publico concistoro"; Vespasiano, *Vite*, 477.

76. "Et mai dapoi che Firenze fu posta, mai andò

fuori imbascieria per loro che tanta magnificentia et tanto honore fusse loro fatto"; Pietrobuoni, f. 152v. For the Sforza pragmatic on the reception of ambassadors, see A. Maspes, "Prammatica pel Ricevimento degli Ambasciatori inviati alla Corte di Galeazzo Maria Sforza, Duca di Milano (1468-10 Dicembre)," *Archivo Storico Lombardo*, ser. 2, XVII (1890), 146–151.

77. Vespasiano, *Vite*, 350, 363, 378f.

inhospitably that they felt "like Jews," sometimes led to calls for war.[78] But the normal procedure was to conceal the disgrace, so that it did not become general knowledge and thus did not enter the historical record. In one particularly colorful case of popular retribution for an insult, some 800 Florentine youths were said to have walled up the entrance of the Milanese ambassador's residence in Florence. Yet we know of this event not from the chroniclers of Florentines, who concealed such dishonorable behavior as well as the diplomatic affront at its source, but from a foreign reporter.[79]

The Return Home

Writing for posterity, Florentine chroniclers ignored such insults and stressed the positive. Their accounts of embassies usually conclude with a list of those knighted while on embassy, and the details of the ambassadors' formal reception back into the city *con grande onore*. In 1461 Piero Pazzi had left the city on embassy with enormous ostentation; Vespasiano did not fail to describe his equally pretentious return:

> All the men of condition in the city came to meet him. It seemed that the whole city rejoiced during his entry. . . . Entering Florence with the greatest honor, [he found] all the streets and windows full of people who awaited his entry. He entered with his servants dressed in completely new clothes, with silk coats, and sleeves and caps embroidered with pearls of the greatest value.[80]

Like other ambassadors, Piero had consorted with princes; returning to the city, he was treated like one. Yet the embassy had cost Piero dearly, and the commune had not reimbursed his ostentation. When his father's will was probated, it was found that Piero had inherited much less than had been expected, primarily because of the expenditures he had made on the embassy of 1461. Vespasiano approvingly noted that an appreciative government answered Piero's request for redress, and repaid all his ambassadorial expenses. Piero had spent this money in splendor and liberality, the commune reasoned, and that deserved recognition.[81]

These remarks on the Florentine embassy show how citizens were fascinated and concerned with its details, and how the structures of the embassy were related to the domestic sense of hierarchical forms. Once considered in context, Florentine embassies jump to life as part of a specific civil and political experience, all the more linked to that experience because, in an age before mass communications and stable indicators of national prestige, embassies alone could personify the dignity and power of the commune to both the Florentines and other states. Florentine ambassadorial ceremony was no mere mechanism to keep parties from each others' throats in a "barely

78. Brucker, *Civic World*, 112f, 246, 460. A case where arms were taken up is in *Diario d'Anonimo*, 466.

79. The Venetian Sanuto is cited by D. Queller, *The Office of Ambassador in the Middle Ages* (Princeton, 1967), 184.

80. Vespasiano, *Vite*, 397f. Also Marco Parenti's epistolary description in Strozzi, *Lettere*, 261. See for other reentries *Diario d'Anonimo*, 452; Masi, 129f; Rinuccini, liii.

81. Vespasiano, *Vite*, 398.

civilized age"; [82] rather, it was the language of the peoples abroad, a political action demonstrating pretensions and hopes, reflecting the texture of the represented society.

VISITS FROM FOREIGN PRINCES

If this rich domestic texture is plainly visible in embassies to foreign powers, it is of course most visible in those cases when foreign princes came to Florence. The state visit to the Tuscan city brought into play all the contradictory elements making up civil identity. Now the prince provided a charismatic force, an objective image around which all Florentines could form and articulate their political and social bonds; yet, important as he was, the visiting ruler marched in a Florentine procession as part of the city. The city and its individual personages took this opportunity to flaunt their *virtù*—at the feet of a prince. The city celebrated its ability to attract such honorable persons, yet in doing so it admitted how central the visitor was to its own identity.

The history of princely visits to Florence may be divided into four periods. The first stretched from the late thirteenth to about the middle of the fourteenth century, and was characterized by frequent visits of Guelf dignitaries to the city. Gene Brucker has listed some of the more important ones: Pope Gregory X and King Charles of Naples in 1273, the brother of Philip the Fair in 1301, Robert of Naples in 1310, Charles of Calabria in 1326. [83] To this list should be added the important papal legations: the cardinals Latino, Acquasparta, Prato, and Orsini all received festive receptions during this period, which may be said to end with the entrance of the duke of Athens in 1342.

During this era Florence was allied with the papacy and the Guelf house of Anjou; in domestic affairs, the period was dominated by struggles between magnates, and between them and the *popolo*. Thus it is not surprising that both the Anjou and the cardinal legates came to the city mainly as domestic peacemakers, two of their number as long-term *signori* charged by the city with reconstructing an irremediably divided burgher community. [84] No matter how violently at odds with each other in domestic politics, citizens thought they could unite around a Guelf authority that most citizens supported in international affairs.

These early charismatic visitors, then, provided consensually valid images around which a base, trustless citizenry could realign itself. When a visitor neared the city, warring elements welcomed him in processional

82. "An insulation of elaborate ceremony helped to protect the fragile thread of civilized intercourse against the violence and brutality still prevalent in European society" and "An exaggerated politeness stemmed from an underlying crudity"; Queller, *Office*, 184. On the function of diplomatic ceremony see the astute remarks of A. M. Bettanini, "Note di Cerimoniale Diplomatico," in *Studi dedicati alla* *Memoria di Pier Paolo Zanzucchi dalla Facoltà di Giurisprudenza* (*della Università Cattolica del Sacro Cuore; Pubblicazioni*, ser. 7: *Scienze Giuridiche* XIV) (Milan, 1927), 360f, 364.

83. Brucker, *Civic World*, 297.

84. These were Carlo of Calabria (1326) and Walter of Brienne (1342).

order, a public celebration they could not have staged without his presence.[85] Entering their midst, the prince reformed the civil order: The legate or Angevin prince chose a group of young women through whose marriages the warring families of the city were united. Public kisses of peace between male heads of families, oaths sworn upon sacred books and stones, and other formal exchanges were the first communication between the parts of the new order, which was sealed by the threat of eternal damnation for the "close friend" who would break the bond.[86] In welcoming these Guelf princes, the commune certainly demonstrated that same "sense of vulnerability" that Brucker sees as characteristic of later periods.[87] The foreigners were more the last resorts of a desperately divided political body than guests of a confident host city.

The second period stretched from the mid-fourteenth century until 1420; few visitors came during this time. The Guelf alliance slowly crumbled, Naples being ruled not by martial males speaking for a united kingdom, but first by an ineffectual queen and later by contending Angevin claimants for the crown. The authority of the papacy during this same period was in continual decline. By the time of the Great Schism (1378–1417), ecclesiastical authority in Florence as elsewhere was at rock bottom. Faced with contention between their former allies, the Florentines had to rely on their own resources to settle civil disputes. There were of course historical and institutional reasons for this long period without foreign guests: Carlo of Calabria and Walter of Brienne had taught the Florentines how dangerous foreign peacemakers could be. Furthermore, certain new public institutions encouraged limited autochthony, the funded public debt (begun 1345), itself originally reliant for its solvency upon papal credibility, being the most important institution making Florentines reliant on Florence. But the basic reason for the scarcity of foreign visitors during this period was the absence of a united papacy or Guelf secular authority recognized by the majority of citizens.

The third period may be called the Age of the Magi. The aristocratic ethos of this period of Florentine history had as one of its main cultural artifacts the spectacular processions of the Three Kings, which were staged by a Company of the Magi from 1390 until 1469.[88] This festive period roughly corresponds to that in which foreign rulers were most welcome in the city, the reception of real kings as against play Magi beginning with the entry of Pope Martin V in 1419. Rab Hatfield's view that "the sensibility of Florentines in matters of pageantry was changing" around 1470 may be compared to the reception of real princes: By the 1480s the city welcomed fewer foreign dignitaries, and put more and more effort into receiving the Medici. This was the fourth and last period of visits during the republic.[89]

---

85. Examples in G. Villani, VII, 56 (the cardinal Latino, 1278); VIII, 49 (Charles Valois, 1301).

86. Examples *loc. cit.*, and VII, 42 (Pope Gregory, 1273). Typical was the statement of Compagni: On Charles Valois' visit in 1301, "everyone showed oneself a friend to everyone else"; II, 9.

87. Brucker, *Civic World*, 297. Paolino Pieri witnessed the city's vulnerability in 1301 and 1303; 67ff, 73.

88. Hatfield, "Compagnia," 108, 118.

89. *Ibid.*, 119.

Domestic and foreign conditions clearly influenced the number, circumstance, and forms of such visits. Trust, honor, and civility, the fundamental and enduring problems of civil life, were always at stake, producing a dynamic ceremonial life that has left lively witness among Florentine writers and diarists keenly aware of these problems when princes and prelates came to their city. In describing the visits of the princes at each stage I shall emphasize the politics that whirled about the princes, politics brought to life by the words of concerned contemporaries.

The Decision to Admit

At no time during the republic did a foreign dignitary enter Florence without the approval of the government. Nor did the government act before consulting its advisors as to the advantages and disadvantages of the visit, whether it was dangerous to domestic security, or how high a diplomatic price refusing the request entailed.[90] If the government decided to welcome the visitor, it then dispatched representatives to him who would negotiate the exact course the visit should take, in this way hoping to ensure that the visit would redound to the honor of both visitor and host.[91] If admission was refused, proper steps were taken to save the commune's honor and defend the city, if that became necessary.[92]

Gene Brucker has found early fifteenth-century communal counselors to have been preoccupied with three major disadvantages of princely visits.[93] First, a visit might seriously complicate relations with third powers. Occasionally this argument was decisive, as in 1352 when the government forbade four Angevin princes to enter on the grounds that the Signoria did not wish to anger King Louis of Hungary.[94] During the Great Schism the commune refused popes from different obediences the right to visit the city.[95] Generally speaking, however, this argument was not persuasive. An astute ceremonial arrangement could usually obviate any real danger of alienating third parties as well as the visitor himself: A defamatory painting of a visitor's ancestor could be covered so as not to annoy the guest;[96] the great tarp of fleurs-de-lis might be hung before the arrival of an imperial visitor "for greater honor," and thus honor France, but could then be removed before the emperor entered, to avoid offending him.[97] When during the Great Schism Florence admitted ambassadors of the Avignonese obedience though itself loyal to the Roman papacy, the Signoria asked the Frenchmen not to enter churches

90. A 1301 example of such a consultation in Paolino Pieri, 67ff, followed by G. Villani, VIII, 49.

91. In 1459 the herald went out to meet Galeazzo Maria Visconti, "a sominabstrare l'ordine della cerimonia e pompa della entrata a llui commessa"; Trexler, *Libro*, 75.

92. For example, when Henry of Luxemburg was alienated in 1310; G. Villani, IX, 7; Rinuccini, ix (1312).

93. Brucker, *Civic World*, 298.

94. Brucker, *Politics and Society*, 145.

95. Communal counselors refused attempts to invite Gregory XII of the Roman, Benedict XIII of the Avignonese, Alexander V and John XXIII of the Pisan obediences to the city; Brucker, *Civil World*, 296–299.

96. Panciatichi, f. 178ra (1394).

97. "Per maggiore honore furono poste le tende di San Giovanni, ma perchè erano dipinti a gigli, furono levate avanti che entrasse"; ASF, *Manoscritti*, 167, s.p. (*Ceremoniale della repubblica estratto . . .*).

during divine services.[98] Legal opinions were obtained before the ambassadors could speak in council,[99] and the size of the council hearing them was limited. All this was done with a view to making the visit seem less than official, thus avoiding diplomatic complications with Rome.[100] Other cases where the argument of alienation of third powers was decisive could probably be found. But this danger was perhaps the least pressing of communal concerns.

A much more imposing argument, and one with good historical precedent, was that the visitor might seize power. The Angevin Charles of Calabria had entered in 1326 as a friend, but had used his stay for an attempt at full power.[101] For many Florentines, the experience with Walter of Brienne, duke of Athens, in 1342–1343 was decisive. Given wide-ranging powers as a peacemaker (*paciere*), he had used them to weaken the Florentine political class.[102] Throughout the second half of the fourteenth century Florentine politicos constantly warned their fellows on the basis of this experience: Florence could do without the help of lords of other states.[103] Such admonitions were necessary. In 1363 and again in 1364, for example, Malatesta condottieres invited into the city to receive the baton of military command tried to extend those soldierly rights to civil authority, creating a crisis atmosphere in which citizens thought themselves about to fall under new tyrannies. "Never pick as captain of war," Filippo Vallani warned after narrating one such case, "someone who is a tyrant of some notable state."[104]

If the Florentines feared traditional friends such as the Malatesta and the French, it is not surprising that apprehensions of "Ghibelline" German princes long withstood evidence that the emperors lacked the power to conquer the city. In 1310–1311 Henry of Luxemburg posed a real threat, but later imperial visitors provoked anxieties out of all proportion to their real power. Thus the commune refused to admit Charles IV in 1355, Rupert in 1401, (though he was allied to the city), Sigismund in 1412, 1413, and 1432.[105] Only in 1452 was this long tradition broken, when the emperor-elect Frederick III visited the city with the greatest pomp.[106]

Besides "Ghibellines" and latter-day Guelf princes, Florentine citizens with high offices in foreign realms also might be barred from the city as threats to urban tranquility. As citizens they had rights to civil office, but as foreign dignitaries they shared in the charisma of the prince they served. The result was a charismatic citizen, an irresistible attraction to that citizen's

98. *Diario d'Anonimo*, 474.

99. Ps. Minerbetti, 46f.

100. Panciatichi, f. 154v.

101. G. Villani, X, 2, 110.

102. *Ibid.*, XI, 1 seq.

103. One counselor in 1363 said firmly "that one should keep in mind the time of the duke of Athens"; F. Villani, XI, 69. And in the same year the chronicler "thought of the time of the duke of Athens, and how

he made himself *signore*"; ibid., 73.

104. *Ibid.*, also 96. The fact that a condottiere made a *cerca* or "recruiting perambulation" through the city after receiving the baton (see the extensions on the front endpaper) added to the danger of bestowing the baton; Del Corazza, 283 (1431); Trexler, *Libro Cerimoniale*, 96 (1485).

105. Brucker, *Politics and Society*, 163; *Civic World*, 299f; Vespasiano, *Vite*, 565, 567.

106. See pages 310f, this volume.

friends and clients in Florence, and thus a danger to the republic at large. When in 1355 the Grand Seneschal of Naples Nichola Acciaiuoli entered Florence with a magnificiently wasteful retinue, many citizens were uneasy.[107] Acciaiuoli was the natural head of the Florentine contingent at Naples, which included some of the most potent patrician families of Florence. Attracting these and other friends and neighbors, he offered an endless series of banquets where the young men of his court flattered the young women of Florence, and thus their citizen-fathers. Yet Acciaiuoli was a candidate for the Signoria; his name would have been lifted from the bag at any time.[108] Those citizens who condemned the luxury and effeminacy of his court must have suspected the motives behind the Seneschal's grandeur. In a subsequent visit in December 1360 those suspicions came to the fore.[109] Now his name was the last in the electoral bags before a new scrutiny was done; had he not come to the city knowing he had to be appointed to the Signoria of January–February 1361? Would this great noble not use office as a springboard to tyranny? When information from foreign allies confirmed the existence of a conspiracy in the city, the suspicions toward this great citizen became so strong that he was forced to leave the city to alleviate them. The city government promptly passed a law that, while effectively preventing Acciaiuoli from attaining the priorate, also regulated the basic problem of the charismatic citizen: No Florentine who was the lord of cities or fortresses, no Florentine holding hereditary office elsewhere, could hold the office of prior.[110] The citizen of rank might still enter the city, but the city was not receptive.

When Florence refused to welcome such dignitaries, or limited the military retinue of those it did permit into the city, the foreigner might readily conclude that the city did not trust them. Just as Jacopo Nardi interpreted the emperor's unwillingness to stay in Genoa overnight in 1496 as a sign that "he trusts [the Genoese] little," so, inversely, princes judged Florentines who refused them entry.[111] When in the late 1340s the commune forbade the husband of the Neapolitan queen to enter Florence, Matteo Villani referred to the "suspicion and shame this imposed upon [foreign] friends."[112] Writing to its agents in 1409 after refusing entry to another Angevin prince, the government sought to counter the obvious insult: "This isn't because we don't trust him, but because it is not our custom to receive such princes in our cities."[113]

The third reason cited by counselors opposed to visitors was related to the danger of a foreign coup; it was feared that scandals or disorders might break out among the populace. Foreigners could usurp power in the city, after all, only with the connivance of part of the Florentine population. Florence's identity was so fundamentally shaped by its links to charismatic

107. M. Villani, IV, 91.

108. *Ibid.*; Brucker, *Politics and Society*, 147, n. 182.

109. M. Villani, X, 22, 23.

110. *Ibid.*, X, 23; Brucker, *Politics and Society*, 147,

n. 182.

111. Nardi, II, 19.

112. M. Villani, IV, 43.

113. Brucker, *Civic World*, 299, n. 239.

foreigners that their entries provided the impetus for potentially violent realignments of ritual order around such images of virtue. Let us look more closely at this decisive relation between princely visits and domestic turmoil.

To begin with, since the government's decision to permit an entry announced its favorable attitude toward the visitor, this could weaken its authority among that part of the citizenry that opposed the admission. Such opposition might amount to nothing more than murmuring and complaints. Matteo Villani, for example, criticized the "indiscreet action" of the Signoria in banning Louis of Taranto and a group of Angevin princes from even entering the *contado* of Florence, since these persons were from a family allied to the commune and should have received honor. Villani was not convinced that the counselors who had blocked the visit actually believed their stated reasons for doing so; just a few years before, in 1355, the Signoria had welcomed with "superabundant honor" not only a Ghibelline, not only a tyrant under church excommunication, but a traditional enemy of the commune:

> Sometimes [the commune] cannot be blamed for honoring an enemy. But it appears a most detestable thing to impose suspicion and to shame faithful friends rather than to give them their due honor. For the mad ignorance of the inconstant regime of our city [,however,] it was thought all right to do this this time.[114]

The chronicler Stefani reacted similarly when a cardinal of the Roman obedience came into the city a generation later, and departed without due attention being given him:

> When one makes a big thing of one cardinal and treats the others badly or does not honor them, it then appears that he who is not honored does not consider this an honor but a shame. In this way one creates enemies.[115]

Mere murmuring could turn to citizen action, and become the civil tinder fueling the prince's potential for creating scandal. In such circumstances, a foreign lord's very presence in the surrounding countryside might be enough to spark political realignments. When Henry of Luxemburg approached the city in 1311, some Florentines who were angry with the government's refusal to welcome the emperor went out to the imperial camp. Paying him court while provisioning his army, they assured Henry that most residents of their city differed with the government and desired his presence within the walls.[116] When Charles IV approached Florence in 1355, the government had to soften its proscriptive legislation against the city's magnates in order to prevent them from betraying the city to the emperor.[117] And in 1413 the Signoria had serious difficulties with its citizenry because of the presence of

114. M. Villani, IV, 43; a similar condemnation is in G. Villani, XII, 116.

115. The Signoria feared offending the French king if it honored the Urbanite cardinal; Stefani, rub. 990.

116. Rinuccini, ix. The pro-imperial actions of the family of the Asini were never forgotten; *Tumulto dei Ciompi*, 87.

117. Brucker, *Politics and Society*, 153 seq.

Pope John XXIII in Tuscany. It instructed its emissary in Siena to urge the pope to bypass Florence: "If he says that he would like to visit our city, then inform him that for good and sufficient reasons, and to avoid any scandal, His Holiness should decide not to come here."[118] Instead of entering the city, John set up quarters in the suburbs of Florence, whereupon scores of Florentine benefice seekers left the city to court the pope. So dangerous and extensive was the traffic that the Signoria took steps—not successful—to stop it.[119] Here then are three cases in which the Florentine government had to modify established domestic policies because of a nearby princely presence. The loyalties drawing Florentines to these presences were both financial and honorific; either could endanger the security of the city itself.

In striking fashion, Brucker has shown how the question of admitting foreign dignitaries came to a head in communal councils during the early fifteenth century.[120] The constant fear of a coup de main, the threat of "movement" within the populace itself, and the concern that receptions would complicate relations with third principals, resounded in city councils. Occasionally other preoccupations were expressed: that the cost to the commune exceeded the visit's value, or that the presence of a large court might cause a grain shortage in the city.[121]

Countering these fears was a group of politicos who were increasingly sanguine about the ability of the regime to tolerate and control visits. They pointed out the advantages of foreign visits: The commune increased its honor when dignitaries were hosted, and merchants and artisans made money by provisioning them. "Not since 1381 has our regime been more stable than it is now," cried Cristofano Spini during one such debate in 1408, "and there is nothing to fear."[122] "*Utilitas et gloria,*" "*utilitas civium . . . et multa beneficia*": money, honors, and glory awaited those not fearful of visitors, other counselors asserted.[123]

During the 1420s, Florentines faced with a depressed economy found profit a persuasive argument indeed. Visits would stimulate trade and increase gabelle revenues; welcoming dignitaries was a form of charity, since their presence would give work to the poor.[124] The commune should seize "anything that would contribute to our [financial] advantage," said one counselor. One should "investigate every possibility for gaining these florins," said another, for "florins are the means by which we preserve our liberty."[125] Such sentiments obviously reflected practical concerns about the Florentine balance of payments and about unemployment.[126]

But more was sought than mere material profit. A dream of empire motivated some counselors. Far from foreigners being kept at arm's length and the commune deprived of their honor, they could be attracted into the

118. Brucker, *Civic World*, 372.

119. *Ibid.*, 364.

120. *Ibid.*, 295 seq.

121. For example, *ibid.*, 297.

122. *Ibid.*, 300.

123. *Ibid.*, 298.

124. *Ibid.*, 425; Martines, *Lawyers and Statecraft*, 297.

125. Brucker, *Civic World*, 425.

126. On this concern, see Molho, *Public Finances*, 134f.

city and disarmed by the magnificent receptions accorded them. It was not only the communal economy that could be saved by touring courts; the idea was afloat that communal honor and glory could consume the rest of the world, once that world was in their midst! That was the unspoken utopic vision that was slowly being formulated in the 1420s.[127]

In February 1419 Pope Martin V entered Florence on his way from Constance to Rome, the first pope to visit the city in almost a century and a half. Some citizens who had opposed his entry found their fears well founded. When during Martin's stay the government welcomed envoys from Bologna, which had broken with the church, the pope interdicted Florence. Disturbed city counselors recognized in this action that once a superior power was in their city, it could neutralize the city's sovereignty by exercising its own: "It should be noted," a chronicler of a later papal visitor would say, "that the church and the Holy Father can hold court and sentence in Florence."[128] Martin's hosts were angered: "We live in freedom," one of them said, "and neither the pope nor any cardinal should be the supreme lord of our city."[129] The pope wanted the Bolognese expelled, said another, but that would be tantamount to surrendering Florentine liberty.[130] The upshot of the affair was unedifying. The word was spread about that the envoys had left the city on their own, but this fooled no one. The Bolognese had obviously come to the city to obtain Florentine recognition of their liberty. Their withdrawal, if not actually urged by an embarrassed Signoria, was at least evidence that Florence was not in a position to recognize that liberty.[131] Once again the presence of a great prince, this time within the city itself, had forced the Florentine government to veer away from its intended policies.

Despite such difficulties, however, the commune and its pontifical guest maintained relations. One counselor believed that contacts with the church had actually been improved, even though the commune had refused to further the pope's reconquest of the Papal States.[132] Another found that a "minimum of scandal" had resulted, and a third counselor later said that the stay had turned out to be good for business.[133] A Medici with properties in the public brothels told tax officials that "when the court of the pope is here [these properties] are rented . . . , but when the pope is not here they are not rented, for they are in a bad area."[134] Remarks of this type show that attitudes had changed, that Martin's visit was, as Brucker had argued, a turning point

127. Florentine arrogance during this period is often highlighted by Brucker. Note, for example, Lorenzo Ridolfi's warning: "We have 145 lances, and we want to govern the world"; *Civic World*, 437. The shame underlying such statements is explicit in Cavalcanti's long account of Florence's military humiliation at the hands of a woman field marshal surrounded by a female staff; *Istorie*, III, 10.

128. "È da notare che lla chiesa e 'l santo padre può in Firenze far fare giustizia e ragione"; Pietrobuoni, f. 136r (1435).

129. Brucker, *Civic World*, 424.

130. *Ibid.*

131. The pope suspended the interdict for four days; the envoys left in two; Pietrobuoni, f. 101v.

132. Brucker, *Civic World*, 425.

133. *Ibid.*

134. ASF, Catasto, 625, f. 355r (1442).

in Florentine attitudes toward visits. In the decades that followed they became ever more frequent.

What explains this sudden and profound change from the commune's policy of excluding princes to one of welcoming them? The fact that Martin's visit passed without major disorders certainly contributed to the commune's readiness to admit foreigners in the future.[135] Clearly the demonstrated material strength of the aristocratic regime played some role, and the enlightened leadership of intelligent men in moving reticent followers away from a conservative past may, as Brucker has argued, have had its influence.[136] Experience and confidence all contributed to the change.

But a full explanation for such a massive change must transcend immediate political considerations, and incorporate the two overwhelming impressions that the visit of Martin V made on those Florentine witnesses recording their feelings. The simple fact of the countless papal ceremonials stunned these writers. Florentines visited the ceremonies assiduously, transcribed the minute actions of participants in the greatest detail, and expressed repeated gratification for the numerous consecrations of their churches, hospitals, and other public and private buildings by the pope and his cardinals.[137] Like nothing else in the city's memory, the sacred presence indelibly impressed upon citizens the value of a ritual head of undoubted authority in a city of artisans and merchants. The pope was so politically weak that street urchins taunted him with insulting songs.[138] But in terms of fulfilling a precedence-ordering function before the eyes of the citizenry, and in terms of honoring Florence, the pontifical visitor was a revelation.

Second, Florentines found their leading men treated, if not equally, at least honorably. Traditionally the visit had been dangerous because there was no charismatic source within the city equal to the noble visitor. Now the elements of such an elite were being forged. Political leaders such as Maso degli Albizzi and Niccolò Da Uzzano and moral leaders such as Guido Del Palagio were emerging as a charismatic center, claiming a level of respect previously reserved for princes and imperial knights.[139] Some Florentines might be repulsed by the comparison of their leaders to Roman heroes, but this playful yet serious packaging of honor represented the wave of the future, one that eventuated in the princely charisma of the Medici at the end of the fifteenth century.[140] The process of magnifying the formal authority of the Signoria was another aspect of a general trend: the creation of a representational sovereignty, not necessarily coextensive with material

---

135. Brucker, *Civic World*, 425.

136. Brucker's view is that enlightened men of the elite convinced their more fearful inferiors that the visits were not dangerous; cf. *ibid.*, 295. Yet he gives much evidence that other members of the elite, presumably also enlightened, were opposed to visits.

137. See, for example, Pietrobuoni, ff. 101v, 102r; Del Corazza, 256–276. An unpublished account is in *ASF, Carte Strozziane*, II, 10 (*Ricordanze di Cambio di Tano Petrucci, 1408–1426*), ff. 48v–49r, brought to my attention by Christiane Klapisch.

138. The famous "Papa Martino non vale un lupino."

139. See in general Brucker, *Civic World*, ch. V.

140. Brucker sees the preparation for Medici charisma in the elitism of figures like Maso degli Albizzi. The Standard Bearer of Justice was now called "Father of the Republic"; see pages 259f, this volume.

strength, that could deal on equal terms with feudal and papal Europe. The sight of such civic leaders integrated into the court around Martin V encouraged the citizens to seek more visitors of rank and honor in the future. The city was feeling its way toward generating a charisma of its own, one that could attract the outside and, without the application of crude force, regulate the inside.

The decision to admit had been reached. *Festaioli* were appointed to organize the ceremonies of entry, and the Signoria's ceremonial agent journeyed out of the city to negotiate with his like numbers in the camp of the visitor; together they arranged the details of ritual communication that would be central to the visit. Streets were cleaned, and the final arrangements made for lodging the guests. The noble presence entered Florentine territory; the hosts awaited it, their priests armed with the censers that fumigated and neutralized the approaching prince.

Through the Gates

From the time the dignitaries had entered their territory, Florentine observers watched and listened, patching together rumor and eyewitness into an anxious overview of the coming events: How would their government welcome the visitors, and how would the visitors react to the commune? As Machiavelli knew, Florentines were no mean judges of reality and appearance. They realized that there was a different procedure for receiving persons of different quality and office, and judged the receptions on that basis. They knew as well that certain key points in the period of visitation were especially laden with information, and concentrated their attention on them. The first such point was that moment when the Florentine welcoming party marched through the streets on its way to meet the visitor at some point in the suburbs. With what resources did the city plan to meet the visitor? How would these merchants about to host their betters first "pay him court" (*corteggiare*)?[141]

Throughout its history the republic used two basic units to welcome dignitaries outside the city: citizens on foot and equestrians. The former reflected the city's burgher nature; the latter asserted the city's quality. In the early period this coupling was referred to as "citizens and *armeggiatori*."[142] Citizens carried out the baldachin that they would hold above the visitor; the horsemen, attached to the Parte Guelfa in these early days and called as late as 1386 the *armeggiatori della Parte Guelfa*, bore banners and were charged with placing themselves around the visitor's horse so as to lead him to the city.[143]

141. Instances of Florence (and its *cavalieri di corte*) "courting" visitors with "courtiers": Compagni, III, 32 (1310); Trexler, *Libro*, 77f. On "giovani atti a corteggiare," Cambi, XXI, 39. It goes without saying that the commune did not lavishly welcome dignitaries of mere republics, with the occasional exception of lordly Venice.

142. For example, Paolino Pieri, 43, 78; Compagni, II,

9; G. Villani, VII, 56; VIII, 49; M. Villani, V, 23; VII, 100. For details of such groups, see Compagni, I, 20.

143. Describing the entrance of the cardinal Latino in 1280, Paolino Pieri (90), speaks of the baldachin (*palio*) "sopra capo . . . ad modo d'Imperadore o di Papa." The baldachin was only then coming into use; when Charles d'Anjou entered in 1284, he refused it. For these interesting descriptions, see *ibid.*, 43, 46. The

By the early fifteenth century, however, chroniclers spoke of "citizens and youths," the term *armeggiatori* no longer being used in this context.[144] These *giovani* were mounted as had been the *armeggiatori*, so that the basic duality of foot and mount was preserved.

The main criteria used by Florentine observers to judge the city's welcoming party were the size of the group, its quality, and the distance the party traveled to meet the guest. The number involved could be small, and in some cases as few as eighteen youths were involved. Or it could be enormous, three hundred young horsemen or more taking part.[145] Several factors affected size. There might be a political intention of communicating extraordinary or minimal regard for the visitor. The quality of the visitor also definitely played a role. Florentines scrambled to be near a great prince or prelate in order to heighten their own positions, but they were not so anxious to contribute to the welcome of a mere ambassador. Cambi told how some three hundred citizens went up to Fiesole to welcome the young cardinal Medici in 1492: "And one didn't have to plead with them [to do it] as one has to when they have to go to meet some ambassadors for the public."[146] Again, so many honorable men might be away from the city on official business that it was difficult to give a proper welcome: In 1465 "all those fit to ride" were not enough, since so many were away on other tasks.[147] Size could also be affected by the reception a visitor had received at previous stops on his trip: In 1354 Florence heaped honor on the cardinal Albornoz in order to exceed the honor the Milanese had just paid him.[148] Finally, size was affected by the extent of the visitor's contingent. A sense of competition marked these visits, a desire to appear neither ostentatious nor ignominious in the presence of nobility.

Quality was as important as size, and the communal government, which never sent its own officials outside the city to welcome guests, nonetheless used all its persuasive powers to move honorable men and youth to do so "spontaneously." Though loath to report less honorable welcoming committees, observers never omitted mention of a group whose quality honored the city. They report at different times that "the most important *popolani*" went to welcome visitors, "the great citizens," or *i principali*.[149] The youth were "the most genteel" or "the most polished in the land."[150] When the greatest lords came, the chroniclers memorialized the welcoming committee with still greater flourish: The emperor was greeted in 1452 by "the most noble . . .

1386 *armeggiatori della Parte* were used to welcome festively a messenger bringing good news. As part of this welcome, they "broke the lance"; *Diario d'Anonimo*, 464. One might assume from this that these *armeggiatori* also performed military games when a foreign dignitary came to town, though our sources never say this.

144. *Giovani* first enters the vocabulary of the entrance in Del Corazza, 256 seq.

145. Trexler, *Libro*, 119 (1515); *ibid.*, 71.

146. Cambi, XXI, 63.

147. Strozzi, *Lettere*, 399.

148. M. Villani, III, 84. A century later the same motivation: "Ne inferiores sint aliis Italie principibus qui filium ducis cum honore magno susceperunt"; *ASF, CP*, 55, f. 103 v (1459).

149. M. Villani, V, 23; VII, 100; Trexler, *Libro*, 82.

150. *Ibid.*, 74f; Del Corazza, 257.

citizenry in the city";[151] in 1515 Pope Leo was met by sixty *giovani*, all liveried sons of officeholding citizens (*statuali*) between eighteen and twenty-four years of age, perhaps chosen pro rata by the nine members of the Signoria, as they were at other times.[152]

Visitors normally met their hosts in the immediate suburbs, at points that depended on their office as well as on the direction from which they approached. The welcoming party for Pope Eugenius IV in 1434 and that for Leo X in 1515 met the pontiffs at two different points because they approached the city from different directions. But after leaving those points, and before entering by different gates, they both stopped at the nunnery of Monticelli, Leo doing so because his predecessor had done so;[153] though a Medici, he was pope and obeyed the laws of that office. For the welcoming party to travel any significant distance from the city was a signal honor, carefully recorded by chroniclers. In 1460 the Florentine party went three miles out to greet the marquis of Mantua, and in 1471 it traveled eight miles to meet the duke of Milan.[154] When in 1452 citizens and youths went all the way to Scarperia, some twenty miles north of Florence, citizens noted this fact as an important honor paid the German emperor.[155]

Citizens and youths met princes and noble vassals. While trumpeters and fifers rested after saluting the city's guests, Florence's ceremonialists advised their counterparts of the state of the city's preparedness.[156] Perhaps the visitors wished to wait till Sunday, when a greater welcome could be arranged by a city released from work?[157] Or the visitor might insist that a public holiday be declared. If the visitor had to enter quickly and be about his business, the city would "do what it could" in a short period, even if not fully prepared.[158] The ceremonial chiefs then reviewed the myriad of precedence-related details that would confront the parties once inside the city. A king on pilgrimage to Rome might limit the commune's welcome to that due a penitent, if royal, visitor.[159] A prince in mourning would have other requirements.[160] A balance had to be struck when princes required a humble image: No prince entered without evidence of his estate, but the symbols of mourning and penitence had to be inserted into the royal pageant. Then came specific questions of gesture, curtsies, and the like; every step, action, and stage had to be prearranged so as to avoid embarrassment.

The parties took their positions and started the procession toward the gate. Peasants and citizens might stand by the roadside to receive a blessing

151. Cambi, XX, 279, introducing this language while copying Pietrobuoni, f. 154v.

152. Masi, 164; Trexler, *Libro*, 119.

153. The papal master of ceremonies noted the Eugenian precedent; D. Moreni (ed.), *De Ingressu sum. Pont. Leonis X Florentiam Descriptio Paridis de Grassis* . . . (Florence, 1793), 3.

154. Trexler, *Libro*, 78, 85.

155. Pietrobuoni, f. 154v.

156. On these negotiations, see Moreni, *De Ingressu*, 3 seq.

157. The emperor, for example, entered on Sunday; Trexler, *Libro*, 72. The duke of Urbino by entering on Sunday could be accompanied by many citizens; *ibid.*, 94 (1482). Pope Leo waited outside the city three days so preparations could be completed; Masi, 163.

158. Trexler, *Libro*, 83.

159. *Ibid.*, 90 (visit of King Christian of Norway).

160. *Ibid.*, 83 (visit of Don Federigo of Naples, 1465).

or the coins visitors threw "for magnificence."[161] Actual scenic elements might be set in place along the suburban route. In the one republican case of which we know, the religious orders of the city each put up an altar along the suburban road, on which they piled their most treasured relics. As Pope Leo passed each altar gleaming with its precious metals, the friars around each altar broke into litany.[162] The city was about to welcome its guest.

Under the gate or in an *anteporta* built for the purpose and furnished with grandstands, city officials awaited the guest. Minor officials came to the gate to meet most visitors, high governmental groups came to meet more important guests, and the Signoria itself appeared at the gate to welcome popes, emperors, and kings. Host met guest in the context of a "capitulation," a formal ceremony in which the visitor swore before notaries to respect the freedom of the city.[163] A member of the communal chancery delivered the welcoming speech, and the guest or his orator reciprocated.[164] The forms of address with which visitors were addressed followed standard practice, of course, one Florentine ceremonial text listing twenty-three address forms for personages from the pope to a knight, and seven more for different types of ambassadors.[165] Gifts were exchanged, one guest for example offering a sum of money to buy the release of debt prisoners.[166] Now those Florentines who had remained in the city inserted themselves into the processional order. Perhaps the visitor approached the city under the baldachin of the Parte; as the actual entry began, the republic's baldachin was raised above him.[167]

So detailed are the accounts of entries that one can imagine citizens scribbling notes as the cortège passed. One of the first things that commanded their attention was the condition of the gate itself. For the entry of Martin V in 1419, one chronicler recorded, its lattice was completely removed, a gesture that "had never before been done [anywhere] for popes or emperors."[168] Later diarists repeatedly looked at the gate for information. When Eugenius IV came in 1434 the gate of San Frediano was "completely open," by which the chronicler meant that some part of it had been leveled; that too "had never happened before."[169] When two cardinals entered in 1451, Florentines recorded that the gate was completely opened, as it was again for the queen of Cyprus and for René of Anjou, "for more magnificence and honor."[170] In 1494 Charles VIII of France found all the hinges removed

161. A bishop threw coins when Martin V entered in 1419; Pietrobuoni, f. 98v. The same happened when Eugenius entered in 1434; Traversari, *Hoedoeporicon*, 136f. So did Leo X in 1515; Moreni, *De Ingressu*, 3f.

162. *Ibid.*, 7f; Masi, 164.

163. The word is used by Del Corazza, 285, 297.

164. For example, Trexler, *Libro*, 90, for Christian of Norway (1474). Apparently the welcoming speech at the gate was extensive only when pope or king entered; otherwise the oration seems to have been held in the piazza where the Signoria awaited the majority of visitors.

165. *BNF*, Cl. XXV, cod. 348, ff. 1v–2r (fragment from the late fifteenth or early sixteenth century).

166. Emperor Frederick III, 1452; Pietrobuoni, f. 155v. More on the custom of releasing prisoners in Moreni, *De Ingressu*, 12f (1515).

167. How the different baldachins were used and positioned is best described in Trexler, *Libro*, 75ff (entry Pius II), and *ibid.*, 123 (Leo X). See the front endpaper for common routes followed by visitors.

168. Pietrobuoni, f. 98v; Cambi, XX, 142.

169. Pietrobuoni, f. 132r.

170. Trexler, *Libro*, 73 (1451), 82 (1461), 90 (1442).

from the gate, the sluice or lattice removed, and in general "everything wide open."[171] Again in 1515 a chronicler conscious of the information contained in the ritual of the gate noted that for Pope Leo's entry, *"per magnificienzia,* the Signoria of Florence had the gate torn down, that is, the gate of the *anteporta,* and had the lattice removed from the gate."[172]

This celebratory destruction did not stop with the gates, but extended along the subsequent processional route. The overhanging sections of houses were sometimes ripped down, for example.[173] Chroniclers explained this destruction by the desire for Florentine magnificence, but other motivations were also involved. House overhangs were surely destroyed to avoid damaging the honor of guests, whose flags might otherwise have to be lowered.[174] The ostentatious destruction of parts of the gates served still another purpose: It was a substitute for giving the keys of the city to a visitor. Ripping down the gate showed the voluntary, "spontaneous" magnanimity of the host; giving the keys of the city to a visitor, on the other hand, was a statement of subservience that the Florentines never made. The Sienese might give their city's keys "and all other insignia of jurisdiction" to the emperor in 1432, "calling their city his city," as reported by a condescending Matteo Palmieri; the Florentines did not.[175] In 1515 the papal master of ceremonies demanded that the city bestow its keys upon Pope Leo; even the moribund republic of this late date refused. The government told the papal ceremonialist that its practice had always been to rip down the gate for popes, but never to give its keys.[176] Thus the destruction or lowering of gates, seemingly an act of magnanimous obsequiousness, was in fact a defense of sovereignty. The government having maintained its dignity, the procession entered the city streets. The people, having waited so long, stood in awe of their betters.

> The most serene emperor had in his company many dukes and marquises and counts and knights and squires, for one said he had brought the flower of the barons of Germany. It was something to see for they were beautiful men adorned with vestments covered with gold and silver and pearls and precious stones, with a great quantity of lovely necklaces of gold and pearls and jewels of great value. There was one among the others that the emperor wore that was worth more than the value of everyone in a well-off city. And the majority of the said barons and knights [and] squires wore long hair down to their shoulders, white and combed so that it appeared threads of gold. Almost the whole of the majority wore garlands of pearls on their heads. And all were well armed with the most beautiful and rich armor one ever saw,

171. Masi, 25. Details of this entry, with routes, are in E. Borsook, "Decor in Florence for the Entry of Charles VIII of France," *Mitteilungen des Kunsthistorischen Institutes in Florenz* XII (1961–1962), 106–122, 217.

172. *Ibid.,* 163.

173. *Ibid.,* 166.

174. On such a humiliation in 1362, see M. Villani, XI, 3. On the *sportelli,* see G. Fanelli, *Firenze Architettura e Città,* 2 vols. (Florence, 1973), I, 150ff.

175. "Et sic se Senas recepit, ibique a Senensibus amice susceptum ei claves portarum et prima sellas et omnia iuridicionis insignia concessere, suam esse urbem dictitantes"; Palmieri, *Historia,* 138.

176. The papal ceremonialist recorded, "Vexillifer et Priores remanserunt in sua vanitate . . . et fecerunt insuper ordinari, quod vexillifer nullus claves civitatis offerret papae, sicut alii magistratus [aliarum civitatum] consueverunt, et hoc quia ipsi florentini portam ad terram deiecerunt, et patefecerunt in totum"; Moreni, *De Ingressu,* 6f.

with so much gold and silver table and altar silver and other magnificences that it would be impossible to recount. And the number of horses was . . . , the men so well accoutered, the horses so beautiful and large that it would be difficult to be able to assemble as many in [the whole of] Italy. And [the retinue] was so rich, so well accoutered that one said it was true that they were worth several hundreds of thousands of florins of cash in gold. And [the emperor] had with the said company great numbers of falcons, beavers, a magnificent number of hunting dogs and other animals for pleasure. . . . And in the said company he had a large quantity of noble trumpeters and fifers and every type of sound, and many heralds and *jongleurs* and buffoons, as one expects with a barony of this type.[177]

In passages of this type, Florentine observers of such entries gave naive expression to all those inadequacies they felt in their own lives. The Germans were richer than the Italians, courts were wealthier than cities, these foreigners had blond hair, and their hunting animals fittingly decorated a superior social caste. Yet these same anxieties made our observers all the more astute in watching how their city related to the noble world; they witnessed the tension and competition that often lurked beneath the surface serenity. In 1459, for example, Pope Pius II tried by different means to have the Signoria carry his litter, the first time a pope had attempted to enter Florence in this fashion. Despite evidence that the Florentines relented and bore the litter while ostentatiously showing their dislike at doing so, the Florentine herald recording the dispute insisted in the official communal Book of Ceremonies that the Signoria had not borne the litter, and subsequent ceremonial masters in the sixteenth century followed this view.[178] The contemporary herald, in fact, seems to have believed that to retaliate for the Florentine refusal the pope surrounded himself with his feudatories and a host of mercenary soldiers armed with crossbows. Instead of the ecclesiastics being near the pope as was expected, the herald said, the pope was in the midst of a retinue "which is expected from a tyrant who fears his surroundings," who "lives in fear."[179] How could such behavior fail "to strike the spirit with no little indignation"?[180] Later in the procession the Signoria was openly disgraced:

The day was rainy, and many times I saw our sublime Signoria, dressed with grave vestments as is the custom of our highest magistracy, thrown and forced into the mud because the supreme pontiff was accompanied and surrounded . . . by armed satellites. They were a bothersome and proud lot without any regard [for others]. The servants of our supreme Signori—mace-bearer or commanders or others—mattered [just as] little to them.[181]

177. Pietrobuoni, f. 158r (1452).

178. Trexler, *Libro*, 75; ASF, *Manoscritti*, 167, "D", s.p. (early sixteenth century). The refusal of the Florentines entered the *Motti* tradition: The Signoria told the pope who requested they bear his litter "come era stato portato da' Sanesi," that their gowns were too long, that is, that they might fall; *Facezie e Motti dei secoli XV e XVI inediti*, ed. G.P. (Bologna, 1874), 78f. But a contemporary Milanese source says

they (unwillingly) did bear part of the litter; *Archivio di Stato, Milano, Potenze Sovrane*, 1461 (Galeazzo Maria Sforza to Francesco Sforza, Apr. 25, 1459), kindly furnished me by Rab Hatfield from research he is doing on the 1459 receptions.

179. Trexler, *Libro*, 76.

180. *Ibid.*

181. *Ibid.*

Again in 1515 observers noticed the competition. Changes had taken place since the entry of Pius II, for now the Signoria bore the papal litter without protest; that much of the old sense of sovereignty yielded to the demands of honoring Leo X, a papal native son. But the honor the Signoria was willing to pay a Medici did not extend to Rome per se: Despite determined efforts by the papal master of ceremonies, the government refused to treat the cardinalate as its equal or superior.[182] The Florentine Signori barely raised their caps as the cardinals marched past; they dropped their eyes rather than raise them in recognition; they refused to stand. This same tension manifested itself throughout the visit.[183]

Such lifting of eyes, caps, and person was something that could not be concealed from the city at large, yet the masters of ceremonies, rather than the chroniclers and diarists of Florence, are the source of these embarrassing details. The chroniclers almost uniformly neglected such negative news, and accentuated the positive, such as the perfect order, and the enormous opulence, of the procession. Diarists and historians repeatedly chronicled each element in the procession: the number of flags, candles, musicians, and persons; their names and titles; the distances between them; the names and numbers of floats, *spiritelli*, and other "machines." Time after time the procession was found to be *bella, bellissima, perfetta*. What were the reasons for this almost uniformly positive attitude toward the entrance procession? Why did the contemporary historian record the entry with incredible detail? Why then did his continuer in copying him omit some of these details, as if they were unimportant, but record those entries of his own time with the same amount of detail as his predecessor?[184] The answer to all these questions seems to be that the description of the event was intended to serve the same morally affirmative functions in the future as the entrance itself did in the present. We may reflect on these common functions as the long procession moves from the gate to the center city, the next point of critical contact between principals.

First, citizens saw and chroniclers described a civic cosmos fused with the social cosmos of the entrant. In everyday life national differences might seem paramount, but in the entry procession these differences were seemingly overcome. Visiting *giovani* marched in conjunction with Florentine *giovani*; the servants of the visitors and those of city officials walked together; the lords of burgher Florence associated with princes from beyond the walls.[185] True,

182. Moreni, *De Ingressu*, 6f and seq.

183. *Ibid.*

184. For example, when Cambi used Pietrobuoni as his main source for the fifteenth century, he occasionally omitted the latter's extensive descriptions of ceremonies, but Cambi's eyewitness accounts of the later period are replete with such descriptions. See how Poggio justifies his long description of the entry of the emperor into Rome in 1433: *Two Renaissance Book Hunters. The Letters of Poggius Bracciolini to Nicolaus de Niccolis*, ed. P. Walter Goodhart Gordan (New York, 1974), 176–181.

185. "Segui di questo hordine tutta la famiglia de' cittadini innanzi apresso quella de' pretori della nostra città, susseguente la famiglia del nobilissimo conte Galeazmaria, apresso e tronbetti, dipoi e giovani della nostra città con gli scudieri del conte, dipoi e pifferi e l'araldo con 'l principe e nostri pretori, e dipoi e cavaglieri con gl'altri externi honorati, e conseguendo tutti gl'altri con tutto l'altro numero de' nostri splendidissimi cittadini, tutti onorati sicondo le dignità e tempi dell'ordine del principe"; Trexler, *Libro*, 75. The Milanese report was more modest, speaking only of "la famiglia dele zentilhomini fiorentini et nostri mescolati insieme"; *Archivio di Stato, Mantova, Gonzaga,*

Florentine women do not seem to have accompanied the distaff entourage of visiting female dignitaries. They might be recorded in absentia, one letter writer finding the women of a visiting female dignitary pretty, but not comparable to the women of Florence,[186] but they were not fit matter for processional integration, nor for chroniclers' reports. Yet the procession did present a panoply of social complementarity between male groups, which helped downplay national divisions. For a base city-state on the make, nothing could give a greater sense of well-being than a procession that seemed to mute male national differences, bringing Florentine males up to the social level of their European cohorts.

Second, such processions and reports advertised Florence's strength and dignity to the world. When "gentility itself," as one Florentine letter writer enthusiastically labeled such a visitor, entered the city, it proved that Florence was worthy, for no foreign prince would enter if he feared being insulted by a mediocre reception.[187] The Florentine chronicler who listed every noble who entered, consequently, was telling the world that all these good men had been suitably "courted," not defamed, by the city.

Giovanni Villani's report of the entry of Charles of Calabria on July 30, 1326, illustrates this type of thinking: It lists by name twenty-three dukes, counts, and knights who entered with Charles and his wife.[188] But these dignitaries, Villani assures us, were only the most illustrious of a brilliant entourage of some nineteen hundred nobles. Two hundred of these were Knights of the Golden Spur, and some fifteen hundred beasts of burden made up the baggage train of the entry procession. The moral of such numbers and quality was clear. The chronicler meant to say that this event, and his record of it, were the best possible advertisement for the city:

> Take note of the great enterprise of the Florentines. They had suffered so many afflictions and losses in persons and property that they had practically collapsed. Yet less than a year later through their effort and money they could get such a lord to come to Florence with such a chivalry and baronage, and the legate of the pope to boot. This was considered really outstanding by all Italians and, wherever one knew of it, by the whole world.[189]

Third, the noble entry was a school for burghers whose lessons the chronicle passed on to future generations. Noble foreigners taught Florentines how to act. Gentility itself, virile yet courteous in its contours, was expected in visitors of any age, for nobles were born with manners. When Don Federigo of Naples came to Florence in 1465, his mere thirteen years did not prevent him from fulfilling all the Florentines' expectations. In mourning

1099 (Firenze), fasc. 77 (Apr. 17, 1459, letter of Niccolò de' Carissimi to Francesco Sforza), furnished me by Rab Hatfield.

186. Strozzi, *Lettere*, 424 (visit of Ippolita Sforza, 1465).

187. "Pareva la gentilezza"; *ibid.*

188. G. Villani, X, 1. Lists of such entrants are com-

mon; another example in Strozzi, *Lettere*, 399; Rinuccini, lxxvi–lxxvii; Pietruboni, ff. 154v–155r.

189. ". . . in meno d'uno anno col loro studio e danari feciono venire in Firenze uno sì fatto signore, e con tanta cavalleria e baronia, e il legato del papa, che fu tenuta grande cosa da tutti gl'Italiani, e dove si seppe per l'universo mondo"; G. Villani, X, 1.

for his mother, he wore black. Marco Parenti wrote a friend that "he showed *virtù* above his age, as is to be expected from royal persons, who are expected to be ahead of others in presence and *virtù*"[190] The don's skill was natural, and after the boy left the city Parenti wrote that "for a child he was full of good repartee. And one can see it is not memorized."[191]

Such behavior was an example for each corporation in the city. Florentine youths learned their manners through associating with foreign youths, servants learned from servants, and so forth. The visiting entourage was a continuing challenge to Florentine counterparts, and the greater the effort of the guest, the greater that of the host. When Galeazzo Maria, duke of Milan, entered the city in 1471, he brought with him an entourage so impressive as to stagger the Florentine herald:

> I would not know how to nor could I narrate all the things in particular. . . . The quantity of his baggage trains, his servants and all the accompaniment of his princes and barons so richly dressed, that the least dignified were dressed in rich brocades. . . . It seemed to me something more splendid than anything else in our city. . . . *Our people exerted themselves in imitating his retinue.*[192]

The moral and emulative function of the entry and its record is nowhere more apparent than in those rare cases when chroniclers blamed visitors for setting a bad example, and used their own record to warn by example. Thus when the Grand Seneschal of Naples came to town in 1355, Matteo Villani could not hide his displeasure. He described the accompanying "youth dressed in strange and queer garments . . . with marvelous gowns of gold and silver, of precious stones and pearls." The Seneschal held continuous banquets and insisted that Florence's young women be there morning and night for these morally dubious affairs:

> These effeminacies weakened his reputation in the *patria*. When the citizens considered [the circumstances of the times, they thought] these made manifest that they called for virtuous and virile things, and not the lewd softness of women. We think that the bad example of his lord [the king of Naples] and the vanity that moved him to solicit the benevolence of the youth and the vain barons and knights who were with him made him forget his accustomed *virtù* and the fortitude of his spirit. . . . This time, he brought to mind . . . the detestable life of Sardanapalus.[193]

The same profound expectation of finding a moral life in the noble foreigner informed the work of Machiavelli. He too described the entry of Galeazzo Maria in 1471, and like the contemporary herald pointed out the emulative efforts expended in welcoming the duke "with all the pomp and respect due so great a prince, and one so intimately connected with the Florentine people."[194] It was at all costs necessary not to appear "mediocre" in

190. Strozzi, *Lettere*, 400.

191. *Ibid.*, 402.

192. Trexler, *Libro*, 85 (my italics).

193. M. Villani, IV, 91.

194. Machiavelli, *History*, 345.

such a presence.[195] Yet for the great sixteenth-century moralist this very emulation of the Sforza prince proved the city's undoing. Florence's youth were already dissipated by peace and spent their time on gambling and women; that much was not the duke's fault. Yet Sforza's own behavior, Machiavelli felt, was the worst possible example for the city's already jaded youth. Though the duke and his wife had ostensibly come to Florence to fulfill a vow to Santissima Annunziata, they and their party ate meat during this Lenten time "without respect for either God or His church." Such "unprecedented exhibitions," the moralist continued, only worsened the city's youth:

> Their manners derived additional encouragement from the followers of the duke of Milan. . . . If therefore the duke found the city full of courtly delicacies, and customs unsuitable to well-regulated conduct, he left it in a much worse state. Afterwards the good citizens thought it necessary to restrain these improprieties and made a law to put a stop to extravagance in dress, feasts, and funerals.[196]

Thus as the visiting cortège wound its way from the gates into center city, Florentines gained their first impressions of the tense unity before them. They reveled in the integrated orders of society, complimented themselves on the honor this brought the city, and recorded it for future generations. They watched how "society" behaved and learned from their betters, generally but not always looking away from what did not fit the expected picture. These visitors gave life to the city, transforming its humble image with the virtue of nobility. Florence's self-identity grew as nobles impregnated the city with virile gentility.

At the Ringhiera

For all but the pope, the emperor, or the king, the welcome at the gate was only the prelude to the true center of the ceremony in the main public square. The Signoria of Florence greeted only the greatest dignitaries at the gate; it awaited most visitors on the *ringhiera* or platform in front of the Palazzo della Signoria.[197] In this encounter observers gathered the most direct impressions of the relations between their city and the foreigner.

The focus of attention was upon the motions of the visitor and the Signoria in relation to two geographical locations within the Piazza. First was the famous Loggia dei Lanzi to the left of the Signoria as they faced the visitor entering the Piazza from Vaccherrecia: How far down along this loggia would the visitor ride before dismounting? Second was the *ringhiera* itself: After the Signoria rose from its seats, how far along that platform toward the steps

195. The fear of *mediocrità* was expressed by Filarete in his ceremonial book: Trexler, *Libro,* 76.

196. Machiavelli, *History,* 345.

197. Only in 1377 is there a record of the Signori greeting the latter elsewhere than at the *ringhiera:* The cardinal of Ravenna met the priors at the newly completed Loggia dei Lanzi (*Diario d'Anonimo,* 446) where classically knights, judges, and doctors would gather; Panciatichi, ff. 177rv. Pope, emperor, or king on entering the city went directly to a church to worship at a Florentine altar, and then to his domicile.

leading down from the Palace entrance would the Signoria proceed? Finally, where precisely would the parties meet? Synchronic behavior was expected. The visitor would dismount and the Signoria would rise from its seats on the *ringhiera* "at the same time"; the meeting of the two parties should take place at a predetermined point without either party being forced to halt and wait for the other.[198]

The farther away from the *ringhiera* the visitor dismounted, the more courteous he was to his host. Thus when the duke and duchess of Milan rode into the Piazza in 1471, they dismounted at the far end of the loggia, "perhaps eighty yards" away, the citizen-diplomat Rinuccini noted with characteristic attention to such detail.[199] Most entrants, however, dismounted somewhere along the loggia. When in 1485 Niccolò Orsini entered the square to receive the baton, he is recorded as dismounting halfway down the loggia, as had Galeazzo Maria Sforza in 1459.[200] Some visitors rode almost to the Palace end of the loggia before dismounting, however, and by 1515 Lorenzo di Piero de' Medici, because of his predominant position in the city, could ride past the loggia to the very bottom steps of the Palace.[201] Generally speaking, to go past the loggia on horse was an insult.

The Signoria, in the meantime, had risen and started along the *ringhiera* to greet the visitor. Normally, the master of ceremonies tells us, the priors came one-half to two-thirds of the way along it to welcome new captains of military forces. To come to the very end as it did in 1515, was, as the ceremonialist reminds us, "to honor [the captain] more."[202] The papal legate was paid the greatest honor: By the early sixteenth century the Signoria came to the end of the *ringhiera,* descended the steps, and marched out into the Piazza to kneelers prepared for them. For most other princes, the Signoria came to the end of the *ringhiera* and thus to the Palace steps, or actually went to the bottom of the steps.[203]

Witnesses to these precontact maneuvers watched and recorded the details of this diplomatic dance with great care, eager to report as "most pleasing to the *popolo*" some "demonstration of great friendship" by a visitor.[204] Yet when something went awry, citizens showed concern and even outrage as they tried to understand what was happening in political and ceremonial terms. In April 1465 the young Don Federigo of Naples entered the Piazza and rode straight up to the *ringhiera* without dismounting! Writing

---

198. "A un tempo pervenono al piano della porta . . ."; Trexler, *Libro,* 75. "La Signoria si mosse dal luogho dove sedeano. E lui a uno medesimo tempo smontò da cavallo . . . , e a uno termine di tempo arivarono a grado della porta"; *ibid.,* 95.

199. Rinuccini, cxv. An example of a visitor dismounting at the beginning of the *loggia* is in Trexler, *Libro,* 83.

200. *Ibid.,* 96, 75.

201. *Ibid.,* 118. Lorenzo followed the ritual of mercenary captains entering the city, he being the first

Florentine to take the *bastone.*

202. *Ibid.* On how far down the *ringhiera* the Signoria came, *ibid.,* 96, 116.

203. *Ibid.,* 120, 83, 94f; Rinuccini, cxv.

204. "Entrano i signori in su la ringhiera per favellare al Duca così a cavallo. E il Duca ismontò da cavallo e i signori scesono sino a presso alle scalee del piano innanzi alla porta, e quivi si parlono insieme. . . . Fu dimostrazione di grande amicizia, e fu molto accetto al popolo"; ser Giusto, f. 89r (visit of duke of Milan, 1467).

to an associate, the merchant Giovanni Bonsi explained what had been agreed upon among the parties, and what had happened:

> The agreement had been reached that the Signoria would come to the *ringhiera;* and that when the lord would reach the beginning of the *ringhiera,* he would dismount; and that the Signoria would rise and would come toward him up the middle of the *ringhiera.* This did not happen at their meeting. He came on horse right up to the Lion and in front of the Signoria. They stood up from their seats and talked together [with Federigo], as one does with a cardinal or legate.[205]

Marco Parenti tried to understand the special conditions that might have caused this scandal:

> He visited the Signoria at the *ringhiera* without dismounting, as the very person of the king [of Naples] would do. This was a bit too much. But it was done this way so as not to make any distinction between him and the duke of Calabria [Jean d'Anjou], who was received in this way when he came to Florence for the war of King Alfonso. But [the latter] was the firstborn of the king, while this one is not firstborn. There's quite a difference, because the firstborn is scheduled naturally to become king, and thus participates in royal honors, the secondborn not.[206]

Just how enraged Florentine citizens could become with visitors who violated hospitality in this setting is shown in Rinuccini's record of the 1484 visit of the duke of Calabria, when the visitor did not even go to the *ringhiera* where the Signoria awaited him!

> He did not go to visit the Signoria at the Palace when he entered, although the Signoria had dressed up and placed itself ceremonially to receive him, and had gathered many citizens as its retinue. This was reputed a very insolent thing, especially since he himself once before had gone to the *ringhiera* to visit the Signoria. [Despite this behavior], and despite what he had done to the city five years ago, all his costs were paid everywhere in our territory, to our great ignominy, by an ordinance considered bad and vituperous by the whole city.[207]

Such attention to detail in private letters and in *ricordanze* gives us some idea of the perceptiveness with which Florentines watched proceedings.

Now the parties met and exchanged greetings. In welcoming a legate, the Signoria was expected to genuflect as its "reverence." Greeting the count of Milan in 1459, each of the priors, "one by one, very reverently, touched [the count's] hand while almost on the ground, [then] kissed and embraced the said count."[208] In addition, after the middle of the fifteenth century the priors

205. Strozzi, *Lettere,* 402. It is again characteristic that this merchant was interested in and aware of the arrangements. Details of the order on the *ringhiera* are in Trexler, *Libro,* 116, 118, and 129f, showing the Standard Bearer sitting in the midst of the priors. Originally he had sat on the priors' right, but Luca Pitti, when Standard Bearer in 1453, changed this, and Machiavelli cited his act as evidence of Pitti's

power in the city; *History,* 313; also Cambi, XX, 321.

206. "Che fu tenuto da molti troppo"; Strozzi, *Lettere,* 399.

207. Rinuccini, cxl, is effectively arguing that the government controlled by the "tyrant" Lorenzo did not defend the city's honor.

208. "La riverentia de' magnifici Signori fu ingi-

tipped their hats when hats were tipped to them. Vespasiano da Bisticci, in reporting this change from the "strange custom" of not doing so, praised Donato Acciaiuoli for introducing this courtesy when he was Standard Bearer of Justice.[209] Visitors were closely watched and their own reverences recorded. Thus the notary Naddo da Montecatini, writing in the 1370s and 1380s, noted that one visitor "raised his hat and nothing else," and that another particularly friendly visitor "when he made his reverence lifted his hat from his head, as well as a little bit of his scapular."[210] Rinuccini noted that in 1471 the duke and duchess of Milan "touched the hand" of each of the priors, and then formed a circle with the government, thus combining a manifestation of Florentine inferiority with a subsequent gesture of equality.[211] When foreign nobles made some "great, great sign" of reverence to the Signoria, Florentines were ecstatic.[212]

The meeting at the *ringhiera* was finished. If the entrance and the salutation there had proceeded with an "increase of reputation" for the Florentine government through the gentility and courtesy of the visitor, observers led by the herald described it as having unfolded with "the greatest humanity and benignity."[213] If the first day of this drama had been of uncertain issue, citizens all the more keenly awaited the events of the next day.

Visitations

The first day's activities ended with the visitor being accompanied to his quarters by the same group of citizens that had welcomed him. There were four categories of residences. First, the so-called Hall of the Pope in the Dominican friary of Santa Maria Novella hosted popes, an emperor, and many other important princes and dignitaries during the fifteenth century. Second came the hostels, the customary residences of diplomatic visitors through the period. The hostel Alla Corona near the cloister of San Lorenzo was most identified with the diplomatic service, and its name was almost a code word for the residence of ambassadors.[214] Ecclesiastical visitors usually stayed at friaries or monasteries associated with their own orders. Finally,

nocchiarsi come di costume quando arrivarono alla presentia del legato"; Trexler, *Libro*, 117; the Signoria's humble bowing is in the Mantuan letter cited in n. 185.

209. Vespasiano, *Vite*, 364.

210. Naddo da Montecatini, 29f.

211. Rinuccini, cxv. An extensive handshaking description is in ser Guisto, ff. 95v–96r (1471).

212. Trexler, *Libro*, 117 (1498).

213. *Ibid.*, 84. On the theme of increasing reputation through visits, see Brucker, *Civic World*, 298. An ambassador's extensive description and evaluation of

the ceremony at the *ringhiera* is in R. Magnani, *Relazioni Private tra la Corte Sforzesca di Milano e Casa Medici. 1450–1500.* (Milan, 1910), 29f.

214. One hostel Alla Corona adjoined the cloister of San Lorenzo, and was fitted out with rooms called "the Imperial Room," "the Room of the Duke," and so on; Trexler, *Libro*, 95, for references. In 1413 a counselor demanded that government business be kept secret, "ut que consuluntur non sint prius nota in hospicio Corone quam in loco presenti"; Brucker, *Civic World*, 358, n. 188. More on the Alla Corona in *Diario d'Anonimo*, 352. Another such hostel was Alla Campana in the Borgo San Lorenzo; Trexler, *Libro*, 82, and a third was Al Leone; *Diario d'Anonimo*, 418, 477.

visitors were often the guests of private persons, staying with the Pazzis, Vespuccis, Tornabuonis, and, later in the fifteenth century, with the Medicis. The commune paid room and board for all substantial visitors and, in the case of quartering in private residences, reimbursed the host.

In this fashion several private residences in Florence became settings for public ritual. For on the following morning and often on the third morning as well, representatives of the city appeared at the doors of these palaces or at the other residences to accompany the city's guests through the day's activities. When the Signoria itself honored a visitor in this way, it came suitably retinued, usually with the citizen group that met the visitor at the gate, sometimes with members of important executive committees of the government like the Ten or members of the Council of Seventy-Two.[215] Customarily, the Signoria visited in residence those visitors whom it had met at the gate the previous day, that is, emperors, popes, and royal persons; papal legates, though they were not met at the gate, were also visited in quarters by the Signoria.[216] Flexibility was possible, and the Signoria could visit some lesser dignitary it particularly wanted to honor. When in 1462 the Signoria visited a group of French ambassadors staying in Santa Maria Novella, the Florentine herald did not know why his masters had indulged "such variety."[217] But when in February 1495 the government visited the cardinal Colonna, the communal ceremonialist had a concrete explanation. The Signoria, he said, acted

> beyond the customary (since he was not a legate), [and] with quite a number of citizens, more than fifty. This was because of the events of the Pisan rebellion [against us]. He was the principal secretary of the said king [of France], and it had been decided this would be a good idea.[218]

Like the *ringhiera* and Loggia dei Lanzi the previous day, the stairs of the visitor's domicile were critical points of formal contact between the two powers. Visiting the greatest dignitaries, the Signoria had to execute the etiquette of this ritual of the stairs perfectly, followed on the third morning by the citizen group that again appeared at these steps to accompany these great princes to the Palace for a visit there. The ritual of the stairs was also important to lesser visiting personages, who on the morning of their second day in Florence were met there by the citizen group for their visit to the Palace.

The stairs were critical locations for measuring the relations between powers. The question that preoccupied the government, chroniclers, and other citizens was this: Where between the base of the stairs leading to the quarters, and the quarters themselves, would the visitor choose to meet the

215. Trexler, *Libro*, 97.

216. The *modo e costume de' legati* is detailed *ibid.*, 80f.

217. "Questa tanta varietà da quegl'altri a me a cche

fine non è nota, nè ancora ricercarla m'è comesso"; *ibid.*, 82.

218. ". . . chè così s'era consultato essere bene, ecc."; *ibid.*, 116.

group of citizens? What had to be avoided at all cost was the impression that these citizens were like "anxious familiars seeking their prince."[219]

To prevent such embarrassment, the government in the latter part of the fifteenth century prescribed citizen behavior. To accompany the ambassadors of popes, emperors, and kings, the citizen group was to mount the steps if the ambassadors did not come out to meet them; they were to go to the foot of the steps to meet ambassadors of dukes and other princes; they went only within the door of the residences housing visiting Sienese and Lucchese ambassadors. To fetch princes themselves, however, citizens were to follow the lead of the visitor, even if this meant going all the way into their actual living quarters.[220]

Unfortunately for the government that tried to standardize this ceremony, the citizen groups often had minds of their own, and a personal interest in paying greater homage to visitors than was their due. The citizens who greeted the ten Venetian orators who stopped at Florence on their way to Rome to congratulate the new pope went right up to the last of their private rooms, a clear violation of decorum.[221] In another case citizens went up the stairs and into the bedroom of two other orators, and in a third instance they mounted half the steps when they should have waited at the bottom.[222] The ceremonialist Filarete protested these excesses in the communal Book of Ceremonies, noting that one such violation led to others, for citizens cited previous excesses as precedents for their own.[223] But since the government often chose as escorts for guests those Florentines who knew them well, there was almost irresistible pressure on citizens to go out of their way to honor those who were in effect their own foreign patrons.[224]

Unable to control their own citizens at times, Florentine regimes were at the mercy of princely guests. The requirement that citizens ascend the steps as each prince demanded recognized the obvious fact that these princes could not be regulated. Instead the commune relied on the gentility of the visitor, his willingness to avoid arrogance, his desire to treat the inferior Florentines with kindness. The ceremonialist Filarete was generally satisfied with princely behavior in his lifetime; temporal lords had always come out of their rooms to meet their escort.[225] "In his humanity" the marquis of Mantua had always come forward, sometimes to the head of the stairs, sometimes even descend-

219. When Filarete described the insulting procession of Pius II in 1459, he thus characterized the stair ritual: "Al montare delle scale, vidi l'empito del popolo e e nostri Signori montare su per quelle non come nostro sommo magistrato ma come famigli affannati cercare loro principe"; *ibid.*, 76.

220. *Ibid.*, 92.

221. *Ibid.*, 92f.

222. *Ibid.*

223. "Fu chi ne mormorò assai, pertanto ne fo nata. . . . E benchè io lo vietassi, pure fu chi me ne biasimò. . . . E credo con quello fusse in gran parte

caggione di questo mio peso, parmi quand'io ho vietata e ricordata una così fatta usanza, essere scusato. E medesimamente a questo ultimo oratore quale a ccasa e Corbinelli, non potrei tanto dire che parte di quelli che per esso accompagnare furono mandati non si montasse gran parte delle scale. E così continuo veggio variare e nostri usi. Fu chi mi rispose che così era fatto a nostri a Vinegia, ecc."; *ibid.*, 93.

224. Including princes who were godparents for citizens; examples in Vespasiano, *Vite*, 342, 399.

225. Trexler, *Libro*, 92. For the exemplary graciousness of the future Nicolas V on the stairs, see Vespasiano, *Vite*, 36.

ing all the steps to meet his Florentine accompaniment.[226] Federigo of Montefeltro, duke of Urbino, and other gracious princes did the same.[227]

Unpleasantness did occur with lesser visitors, and was quickly recorded by contemporaries. In 1464, for example, the herald on duty at the residence notified the ten Venetian ambassadors of the impending arrival of their citizen escort, yet when this group arrived the ambassadors were still not dressed. As a result the citizens not only went all the way up the steps to the rooms, but then had to wait around until "it suited [the ambassadors]," something that annoyed the hosts.[228] In the following year Florentines thought another insult was visited on them when Don Federigo, the adolescent who had not dismounted to greet the Signoria, paid so much honor to foreign visitors in his quarters as to offend his hosts. The correspondent Marco Parenti wrote his friend that during the boy's stay a Venetian ambassador came to Federigo's quarters:

> And when [the ambassador] left, [the don] accompanied him back to the steps of his room. When our citizens came to visit him representing the Signoria, he did nothing, not [even] leaving his bedroom. There are those who murmured about this, but I don't know why it happened. [The government] could not have spent more magnificently or more liberally on the [guests].[229]

Once the guests had met the visitors and exchanged greetings, the whole party organized itself, trumpets in front, for the procession to the Palace of the Signoria. The attention of observers now shifted to the priors.

The Signoria awaited the arrival of the guest within the Palace, the chair of the Standard Bearer of Justice left vacant if he were absent.[230] How should they greet their guest? The communal herald instructed the government on the psychology and politics of greeting one type of visitor, the socially inferior ambassador, as distinct from princes and nobles:

> When someone not a subject [of Florence] comes to speak to the Signoria, either for himself or as ambassador, and he has to sit down with the Signoria, but is not of such a quality [that the Signoria can] walk out to him, it is nice if the Signoria starts to stand, more or less according to the quality of the man, [in order] to seat him. [And it is decent if] with humility and sympathy the Signoria shows him a happy face, shows him tenderness in [shaking] hands, and pleasant words so as to domesticate him and give him courage in speaking. These kindnesses often please foreigners, as much [as are useful to the Signoria] the gratified reports they give [their masters] of their embassy.[231]

226. "Le persone proprie de' principi temporali che intendono visitare e nostri excelsi Signori per e tempi miei si sono sempre fatti incontra a nostri cittadini per loro mandati, come el nobilissimo principe illustrissimo marchese di Mantua, chè essendo lui alloggiato a Santa Maria Novella sempre s'è fatto per sua humanità incontra a nostri cittadini talvolta tutte le scale, e talvolta al principio della smontata"; Trexler, *Libro*, 92.

227. *Ibid.*

228. "E benchè per me si facesse loro nota la venuta di cittadini, ancora alla giunta de' mandati ne restava alcuni a mettersi le palandre. Che si fecino aspettare tanto che si parono"; *ibid.*

229. Strozzi, *Lettere*, 401.

230. *BNF*, Cl. XXV, cod. 348, f. 2v (late fifteenth-century ceremonial fragment).

231. *Ibid.*, ff. 2rv.

Having briefed the Signoria on their comportment, the herald recorded each step of the subsequent formal proceedings: on what exact spot the parties met, where and how they sat down, and where they took leave of each other. Different grades of persons were met at different distances from the Udienza, the domestic residence of the Signoria being no less informed by such hierarchical spatial arrangements than any other palace in town.[232] The reception in the Palace might continue with the visitor being shown the Palace's holy of holies, the chapel of St. Bernard in which were kept historic parchments, precious relics, a famous copy of the Justinian Pandects, an equally renowned Greek New Testament, and an assortment of precious stones.[233] Just as in his subsequent visits around the city the guest would search out the city's other relics, so in a Palace chapel aglow with tapers, the communal lords unveiled to honored guests the Signoria's treasures to be touched, prayed to, and marveled at.

This basic Palace welcome was refined and developed in the fifteenth century. One change was that the priors now doffed their caps on greeting visitors at the Palace. What seems such a minor point did not appear so to Vespasiano da Bisticci, who made this innovation by Donato Acciaiuoli major evidence of his hero's accomplishments. Before Donato, the biographer tells us, Florence was a rather gauche city, but Donato, "a man practiced in courtesy," changed that when he was in office:

> He had ordained that when the ambassador of the king [of Naples] or of the duke of Milan came, the herald was to come to the Signoria's room to tell him. Then he would leave the room and go up to the exit of the little hall, and take [the ambassador] by the hand, and doff his cap, and lead him back to his room. Then after he had spoken to him, he accompanied him back to the place where they had met, and there doffed his cap and said goodbye. This is the way things are done by men experienced in the way things are done at the courts of princes.[234]

A second change in the ritual of visits of the Palace was that the Signoria was now permitted to leave the Palace, welcome visitors in the streets, and accompany them back to the Palace. The point at which the parties met became still another valuative element in judging relations, another point at which the citizens could learn "how things are done at the courts of princes." In 1465, we are told by the communal herald, the priors went to the Mercato Nuovo to meet a papal legate.[235] On another occasion they went all the way to Piazza San Giovanni to meet the duke of Milan, and the following day went to the Canto degli Stampatori to meet him.[236] In these greetings Donato Acciaiuoli was again in the forefront, publicly instructing his fellow citizens in

232. For example, Trexler, *Libro*, 78–81.

233. In 1465, for example, a legate visiting the Signoria, "dopo le molte congratulationi e riferite gratie della sua grandissima humanità e benignità, ancora a miei tempi più non usata, gli furono mostre le Pandette"; *ibid.*, 81.

234. Vespasiano, *Vite*, 364.

235. Trexler, *Libro*, 81 (1471). Another observer viewed the same street greeting as "a mutual demonstration of great love. God maintain it!"; ser Giusto, ff. 95v–96r.

236. Trexler, *Libro*, 85.

gentility. A political culture determined to be accepted by its betters welcomed, and recorded, their leader's example. As Standard Bearer, Donato in 1474 led the priors out to meet the king of Norway on his way to the Palace, and in recording the scene, the communal herald perfectly reflects this Florentine sense that decorum could disarm the most princely of personages:

> When our excellent Signori heard that the most serene prince wanted to visit them, our high magistrates went out to meet him, up to the [Canto de'] Tornaquinci, with quite a number of the principal [persons] of the city. When the noble prince saw them, he dismounted from his horse, and they encountered each other [on foot] at the door of Francesco Sassetti's house. Together they came back to the Palace. Having sat a while in the Udienza, they came into the Saletta [of the Palace] with much good cheer. This prince dined with the majority of his retinue [in the Palace]. Our excellent Signoria kept him company up to the first gallery. Everything happened with much benignity. And then he was reaccompanied by our excellent Signori up to the door [of the Palace] where, having mounted his horse, he went to see the lions and other things of the city he desired to see.[237]

The Gift

The commune's presentation of gifts to the visitor was the penultimate act of the ritual of visitation. Those great lords whom the Signoria visited in their quarters on the second day received their gifts either before the Signoria arrived or immediately after it left to return to the Palace;[238] the majority of foreign visitors, however, found their gifts awaiting them at their residence on returning from their visit to the city hall.

Each visiting dignitary could expect a certain amount to be spent on him, for the Florentine chancery followed European custom in bestowing gifts according to rank. An ambassador of the pope was expected to receive more than one from Siena, a king more than a duke. Theoretically, status relations were stable, and the size of gifts could be regulated by laws, of which the Florentine ordinance of 1473 is typical.[239] Practically, however, all attempts to regulate gift giving according to rank were problematical. It was impossible to draw up a table of gifts that did not reflect past gift-giving practices and thus an antirational, historical contextuality. Nor were legally established limits on gifts impractical only because one had to act within a specific political context in giving any gift. There was a basic psychopolitical factor to contend with: The purpose of the gift being first to express the love of the commune, recipients naturally compared their gifts to what their official predecessors had received and what other states' dignitaries were given.[240] In an official

---

237. *Ibid.*, 90.

238. *BNF*, Cl. XXV, cod. 348, f. 2v.

239. The administrative ordinance "circa limitare e disporre delle spese et apparecchi et presenti et doni che s'usano fare dal popolo di Firenze . . ." is in *ASF, Deliberazioni dei Signori, Speciale Autorità,* 34, ff. 131v–132v (Dec. 17, 1473); the ordinance was issued by authority of a law of Oct. 26 by the Cento. The communal Camera dell'Arme supervised execution

of these laws (*BNF*, Cl. XXV, cod. 348, f. 1r) and, perhaps starting in 1506, listed the legal limits on page one of its *massaio's* annual journal; *ASF, Camera del Comune, Giornali del Massaio della Camera dell'Arme,* 17 and following. The Camera dell'Arme controlled payments for all feasts and welcomes.

240. Pius II compared his welcome unfavorably to that accorded Galeazzo Maria Sforza in 1459; *Commentari*, II, 31.

gift, recipients sought personal identity. How could the commune express affection if its gift was of the same value as one previously given the same person, the same as one given to that person's predecessor in office, or inferior to one given an official equal from another state? In a traditional society with limited methods of communicating power and affection, neither rationalistic conceptions of hierarchical order nor concern for the cost of such gifts could restrain the tendency toward larger gifts. The commune of Florence recognized these realities by retaining the right to supersede the statutory limits it had set on gifts.[241] At the same time, it attempted to individuate the gift through its *varietà* and workmanship while staying within the legal expense limits on materials for gifts. It used art.

Although all possible items, from horses and fine cloth to paintings, cameos, and strange animals, were presented to visitors at their quarters, the core diplomatic gift was food—various sweets, wines, and staples—set in a frame of rich and artistic bowls, cups, and jars of precious metal that were also kept by the visitors.[242] The idea was that the visitor would use these vessels and food to eat together with his entourage. Thus the specific setting in which a visitor might best "recognize the mode of the affectionate love of the city of Florence" was at table with his own retinue, not with his hosts. Away from the Florentines and among his fellow nobles at table the emperor Frederick, in the Florentine herald's words, could be

> almost stupefied at the number of delicacies, the quantity of poultry, the enormous amount of food caught at the hunt, the great mass of *ferma* meat, the number of both white and red wines, the abundance of grain. It was such as to not appear provision for just a group of people, but for the most imperial of princes or for a populous region.[243]

The gift clearly had the purpose of identifying Florence as a city of wealth and charity, and the Florentine practice of gifting "all the silver of the table of the Palace" to distinguished visitors shows the utopic aspect of such giving quite clearly: Like the potlatch, stripping one's own table for a visitor increased rather than destroyed the *persona* of the giver.[244] But the ritual of gift giving involved a complex process of exchange that implicated the total political context and thus the persons involved in the web of exchange. First, the gifts that the Florentines gave their guest were identified as being themselves gifts to the Signoria: Pietrobuoni explained, for example, that the city's gifts to the emperor in 1452 were themselves presents to the government from its dependent and allied cities, towns, and fortresses.[245] Then, these gifts having been passed on to the visitor, the latter distributed them forthwith to his retinue. The foodstuff was his property, but his retinue immediately ate it;

---

241. It was foreseen, for example, in the ordinance noted earlier.

242. See, for example, Trexler, *Libro*, 77, 84, 89. The Panciatichi chronicler regularly records the gifts given visitors, as does Giovanni di Jacopo Morelli, often with the monetary values.

243. Trexler, *Libro*, 72.

244. Two consecutive cases of presenting a visitor with "all the silver of the table of the Palace" are in L. Morelli, 176, 185. On identity and the gift, see Mauss, *Gift*.

245. Pietrobuoni, f. 155v.

the basins and cups could also be distributed among his fellow nobles. This third transfer of property was often consecutive to the second, the dignitary receiving them from the Florentines and immediately distributing them to associates.[246] Alternately, a dignitary could await a subsequent ritual setting elsewhere, and then give the Florentine presents to another prince as his gift.[247]

Viewing the gift in this total dynamic context, we see that it was more than a static objective statement about the resources and emotions of the Florentines who, in one chronicler's words, "forced themselves to demonstrate the happiness felt through exterior acts."[248] The Florentines' gift was an instrument that, within a formal context, heightened resources and emotions. By entering the city, the prince had made it more honorable: "The honor belongs not to the honored, but to those who honor," one counselor explained to his colleagues in encouraging them to outdo themselves.[249] Thus when Florence presented its gift, the city not only stated the value it attached to the recipient, but in effect returned to the recipient "a small token" of what the latter had already given Florence. When the prince, whose own identity was embodied in the gifts others gave him ("One should keep in mind," the Florentine herald told the Signoria, "that the pope and the emperor and the [Neapolitan] king and the cardinals honor themselves when gifted") then gave those gifts to his entourage or to other princes, he honored the city that gave him both the wherewithal, and the formal setting, within which to demonstrate his own liberality.[250] The Signoria stripped its own table, in short, to facilitate relations between noble persons; it profited, and its identity was heightened, each time that noble exchange ensued.

The ceremony over, gifts could be and were sold. We recall that jockeys sold the *palii* they won in horse races back to the commune;[251] doubtless Florence like Venice sold diplomatic gifts at auction or otherwise alienated them, and it would not be surprising to find visiting princes selling their gifts back to the commune shortly after the ritual.[252] This practice in no way proves

---

246. Agnolo Acciaiuoli for the commune gave the emperor a silver bowl with 14,000 florins in it, "which were accepted with pleasure. Then Sigismund spread the coins on the table and gave them by handfuls to his courtiers till not one remained"; Vespasiano, *Vite,* 321. Cf. this Maori explanation: "Suppose you have some particular object, *taonga,* and you give it to me; you give it to me without a price. We do not bargain over it. Now I give this thing to a third person who after a time decides to give me something in repayment for it (*utu*), and he makes me a present of something (*taonga*). Now this *taonga* I received from him is the spirit (*hau*) of the *taonga* I received from you and which I passed on to him"; Mauss, *Gift,* 9.

247. I have not been able to document such a difficult case. But this is certainly one fashion in which Florentine art works given as diplomatic gifts found their way into the most varied state collections. For a case of royalty asking that Lorenzo de' Medici give to

her a gift Lorenzo had received from the Turk, see page 460, this volume.

248. Giuliano de' Ricci, *Cronaca (1532–1606)* (Milan, 1972), 217.

249. "Honorem enim esse non honorati, sed honorantis . . . "; ASF, CP, 55, f. 103v.

250. "Debbesi havere a mente che il papa et lo imperatore et il re et i chardinali s'onorano di presenti, o si provede delle spese condecentemente o a sadisfacienzia"; BNF, Cl. XXV, cod. 348, f. 1r. An alternate system of exchanging accreting values may be viewed in the *palii* of 1514: A marquis wins the race "almost as a tribute." He then gifts both the *palio* and the horse to a Medici. That *palio* is then bestowed on the winner of the next race; Sanuto, XVIII, 314 seq.

251. On this resale, see page 268, this volume.

252. I have been able to document the auction of

either insincerity or a modern objectification of human relations.[253] Gifts had meaning within a ritual of exchange, where their aesthetic and material value ideally induced sincerity and subjectivity, and thus facilitated diplomatic contacts. Governments spent such money and skill in order to convince the ruler of their love; Florentine writers stated the monetary value of the commune's gift to witness their city's affection. Once that communication of regard was past, the gift like any relic could be preserved or alienated. But in the ritual of presenting the gift, the status of the city had been raised, and that was what counted.

Seeing the Lions and Other Notable Things

Their official tasks completed, visitors to Florence like the king of Norway commonly toured the city, examining the buildings, relics, lions, and nunneries of which they had heard or which their hosts recommended to them.[254] Such tours could not be undertaken at leisure; to do that, such dignitaries had to come to the city disguised, for they were at all times surrounded by protocol, their slightest movement watched for signs of approval or disapproval.[255] The guided tour of the city, in short, tended to become one further field of communication in which a distinguished visitor maintained a role, and in which communal reporters found important information.

This tendency to reduce leisure-time touring to formal proportions was nowhere more evident than in the elevation of the feast of St. John into a spectacular festival intended in part for visiting European nobility. The horse race, the parade of floats, the procession of citizens and clergy, the exhibition of wares, as well as the wild-animal shows, jousts, and marriages associated with this feast attracted hundreds of dignitaries in the fifteenth century. Visitors tried to time their arrivals to coincide with the feast; the commune postponed parts of the feast to accommodate visitors' itineraries.[256] The feast of St. John became an affair of state with diplomatic profit or loss at stake. Knowing that the spectacle "gave admiration to foreigners," chroniclers could complain bitterly when the city was "shamed" by a second-rate festival.[257] So much was the festival a matter of citizen pride that the very

tribute *palii* at Florence, (page 268, this volume), but not of diplomatic gifts. For public auctions of these gifts at Venice, see D. Queller, *Early Venetian Legislation on Ambassadors* (Geneva, 1966), 42.

253. Queller thinks it was "stingy" for the Venetians to auction these gifts: "One can approve of the principle that the gift should go to the state . . . , but public auction strikes a discordant note in the ceremony of diplomatic relations"; *ibid.* Although this author obviously expected personalistic commitments to be more important than impersonalistic profits, another author imagines that Europe had long since laid aside the "gift economy" for an (impersonal) "profit economy"; L. Little, *Religious Poverty and the Profit Economy in Medieval Europe* (Ithaca, 1978), 1–34. On the subject of reciprocities in international gifting, see the important work of W. Dillon,

Gifts and Nations (The Hague, 1968), and for a theory of gifting in a modern tribal culture, see E. Schwimmer, *Exchange in the Social Structure of the Orokaiva* (London, 1973).

254. On Christian's tour, see page 323. For visitors' tours during the Council of Florence (1439), see D'Ancona, *Origini*, I, 246–253.

255. An example of dignitaries in Florence disguised is in Masi, 144; Landucci, 346 (1514).

256. Trexler, "Setting," 140. One visiting dignitary agreed to the postponement of the Palio until her arrival, but not to the offering to St. John, "per non irritare S. Johanni con loro [fiorentini] et contra noi"; Magnani, *Relazioni*, 29f.

257. Guasti, *Feste*, 27; Rossi, XXIII, 243f.

animals taking part in a festive *caccia* (hunt) could be taken to task: "The lion hunt vituperated us, for a bull chased them all into the stalls like sheep."[258] Conversely, guests could be accused of indifference to the city's best efforts. "We think," said one letter writer to a fellow Florentine, "that [the visitors] cared little and had less esteem for our festival and our things."[259]

Generally speaking, however, it was not the Florentine "things" that complicated visitors' attendance at Florentine festivals, but the inherent problem of precedence and protocol; not what was going on at center stage, but the seating order in the stands. When Alfonso, duke of Calabria, was in Florence for the celebration of the Baptist, for example, "a dispute arose as to how one should arrange to have him see our feast."[260] Some time before, our source tells us, the Anjou pretender to Alfonso's title had been in the city for the same feast, making it as difficult now to honor Alfonso without offending the pretender as it had been then to honor Jean d'Anjou without offending the Aragonese. The government decided to duplicate the earlier protocol, hoping thus to avoid all possible misunderstanding between Florence and its guest:

> because earlier when the most illustrious prince duke Giovanni was here for the same celebration, one had decided to prepare for the prince a place separate from that of our Signoria at the spectacle: to avoid every perturbation [arising] from imperfect ceremonies, to preserve the dignity of our high magistrates and the dignity of the most illustrious prince the son of King René and, similarly, the duke of Calabria.[261]

In other words, when Jean d'Anjou attended the festival in 1454 no way could be found for the Frenchman and the Signoria to watch the procession of floats together without injuring their honor and that of the Aragonese claimants, so the two principals were separated. The Signoria now planned to repeat this procedure with Alfonso. But when the latter heard of this plan, he was determined to outdo himself in princely courtesy by flattering the inferior Signoria:

> When the most illustrious prince Alfonso heard this, with great humanity he [said] that he would [rather] be together with our excellent Signoria at the feast in order to well demonstrate every possible benignity and love toward our republic.[262]

Alfonso's determination to publicize a friendship and courtesy superior to his Angevin competition continued at the offering of the Signoria the morning of June 24, for now he insisted on going with the government to make the offering. This gave rise to another difficulty:

258. Strozzi, *Lettere*, 433. The lion was the official animal of Florence, so its retreat had ominous overtones.

259. *Ibid.*

260. Trexler, *Libro*, 83f (uncertain date). A century later the grand duke could afford to exclude foreigners from his banquets so as to avoid creating precedence-related battles; S. Berner, "Florentine Society in the Late Sixteenth and Early Seventeenth Centuries," *Studies in the Renaissance* XVIII (1971), 71 (quote misunderstood by author).

261. Trexler, *Libro*, 83f.

262. *Ibid.*, 84.

For since the ambassador of the king his father was [also] there, another dispute arose among the first men of the city over the procedure to follow in going to the offering. In summary, since there had been no previous consultation on this, the mode of sitting on the *ringhiera* [before going to the offering] was [as follows]. . . .[263]

How easily Florence could damage her own relations, not only with the visitor, but with those who were absent, not only in direct diplomatic contexts, but at the very games. Yet how necessary did such visits seem to a city like Florence. For in the visit the city heightened its *utilità*, its *onore*, its identity.

Profit

When the luminaries had gone and city life assumed its normal course, the balance sheet had to be drawn: Had this enormous expenditure of time, money, and anxiety been worthwhile? Was the city better for having hosted these noble guests?

Visitors almost always expressed general pleasure at their reception. Eleanor of Aragon, for example, wrote in 1473 that the Florentines "have shown themselves to have been very pleased by our stay here."[264] One has little trouble finding Florentine contemporaries thinking money "well spent, if [a visitor's] friendship can be acquired," or cases where the Florentine intention of "increasing benevolence in many parts through honoring those [who come here] from many parts" was fulfilled. Pietrobuoni, for example, told how the son of the king of Navarre had prevented the Valencians from sacking the Florentine colony there because he had been so honored during his visit to Florence, "which was money well spent."[265] But it is difficult to judge the objective results of particular visits, and unimportant to our theme. It is central, however, to learn of the more categorical recollections of the city that the Florentines wanted their visitors to take with them. The answer to this question is available in the writing of the communal heralds, who recorded for posterity what they believed had impressed the visitors.

There can be no doubt that the nobility of their city was most on the heralds' minds, as it had been paramount in the minds of those who had approved the expenditures. "Our predecessors," one counselor had argued in fostering such pomps in 1459, "have always placed honor before utility";[266] the communal heralds reflected this desperate desire to have visitors leave knowing the city was more honorable than they had thought when they

263. *Ibid.* The offering was an institutional means for representing the visiting dignitary as a part of the political fabric of Florence. I can document it only during the period of Medicean ascendancy: A Cibo visiting in 1488 chose to offer with a particular *gonfalone* or ward of the city; Fabroni, *Laurentii*, II, 386ff. The analogous practice in Venice was to invite a visitor to vote on particular issues in the Grand Council; Fabroni, *Laurentii*, II, 226f. Compare these practices to the "domesticating" rituals used by lords, page 426, this volume.

264. Cited in D'Ancona, *Origini*, I, 273f. Note also the Florentine herald's record that in 1467 the young duke of Milan called Piero di Cosimo de' Medici his "father" during his visit; Trexler, *Libro*, 83.

265. "Ex diversis partibus, ex quorum honoratione benevolentia augebitur civitati multis ex locis"; ASF, CP, 55, ff. 103v–104r (1459); Pietrobuoni, f. 158v (1452); ser Giusto, f. 66r (1452).

266. "Semper enim maiores nostros honores utilitati preposuisse"; ASF, CP, 55, ff. 103v–104r (1459).

arrived. The concern is everywhere in the *libro cerimoniale* that these heralds wrote for the government. When the emperor Frederick entered in 1452, he immediately recognized, one wrote, "with how much love and benignity and happiness of spirit he . . . was received."[267] Entering the richly caparisoned cathedral, Francesco Filarete continued, the emperor was able to isolate the specific reasons why he and his barons were "very happy and not without amazement":

> Not without great stupor of spirit he considered the nobility of the men who had come to meet him, then the reception of His Majesty outside the gate, the spectacle of our most noble *popolo*, the beauty of the decoration of our excellent temple, the benignity and humanity of our high magistracy, the noble urbanity of our citizens.[268]

The theme of nobility was insistent. When Pius II attended a dance during his stay in Florence, the visitors were moved to believe, said Filarete, that they were in an aristocratic paradise:

> I will not relate the noble pomp and the quantity of rich and most ornate garments with rare devices and embroideries of both men and women. They certainly appeared to every single person rather an angelic than terrestrial thing with such a quantity of pearls and most noble jewels. What was most amazing to the foreigners was the quantity of noble women, the order and magnificence of the youth, the mode of dancing and feasting done with every type of gentility and civil joy.[269]

A second striking memory that the ceremonialist found etched in the memories of visitors was the city's ability to turn night into day. When during the emperor's stay two cardinal legates arrived at night, they noted that despite the hour the Signoria awaited them on the *ringhiera* in a city ablaze with light:

> Not without wonder the ecclesiastical princes saw the great number of our *popolo* who with such patience and devotion awaited them at such an hour and without any armed guard. [They were] accompanied by a mass of citizens and with a quantity of lights in candlesticks which turned the obscurity of nocturnal shadows into the clearest solar light. All the streets were full of people and lights wherever they passed, [and] our principal square, lit by many bonfires, was jammed with people bearing torches.[270]

Finally, and most striking of all, the ceremonialist believed that visitors such as these legates were incredulous at the lack of arms: "at such an hour and without any armed guard." The emperor, he tells us, was stunned by such "noble urbanity,"

> . . . to see such an ornate and free *popolo* all dressed in civil [not military] costume, without any anxiety at all, without any martial guard or arms of war.[271]
> I was given to understand that the whole imperial court was not without much

---

267. Trexler, *Libro*, 71. In my edition of this book, I failed to indicate its location: *ASF, Carte di Corredo*, 61.

268. Trexler, *Libro*, 72.

269. *Ibid.*, 77.

270. *Ibid.*, 73.

271. *Ibid.*, 72.

wonder that among the many honors accorded them and the other pomps and nobilities of our city was this: that they did not see one man wearing a sword. To them this was something very beautiful.[272]

We recall how upset the same Filarete was when Pius insisted on entering in 1459 surrounded with mercenaries, "like a tyrant." Now we can more clearly understand this resentment. It was not only that Pius should have acted like a priest, not a soldier. By his behavior he stated that he did not trust the ignoble Florentines; he seemed to say that the best way to preserve order was through monarchy and monarchical arms. The communal herald, on the contrary, believed visitors found that Florence, a burgher town said to be without martial abilities, needed no barracks of soldiers to maintain order. The receptions of visitors brought together a mass of citizens and inhabitants with no danger of insurrection, he seems to state. It was possible, Filarete implies, for men to live together in "noble urbanity," without arms or a prince; mutual trust was possible among traders. The Florentine dream of living together with honor seemed realized in these noble receptions, when unarmed citizens kneeling before a superior lord turned night into day.

And the princes left, "content with the highest sweetness," "content and satisfied. . . ."[273]

> . . . and all the princes ecclesiastical as well as temporal both noble and private who were present at the event became acquainted with the honor and valor of our nation and city, from which all departed happy and content and full of love.[274]

272. *Ibid.*, 73.
273. *Ibid.*, 72ff.
274. *Ibid.*, 78.

Chapter **10**

The Ritual of Crisis

How this city is to be governed . . . [by] liberating this popolo and this city from such confusion.*

And the Ciompi issued a decree that any person found wearing the [bourgeois] cloak could be killed without [fear of] penalty or banishment. Whence the people in the Piazza and throughout Florence, all of them, stripped their cloaks off their backs for fear of being killed: We could wear the same clothes they did.†

A decree was issued that for the rest of the month, all inhabitants, craftsmen as well as citizens, could wear the [bourgeois] cloak, and that from August 1 everyone had to [dress without the bourgeois cloak and] carry arms. . . . And anyone who didn't carry them could be plundered and held suspect of our way of life‡

The feast of Florence's saint is over; the city's inhabitants know their rulers' just order, and are filled with the pride of those who light the darkness. The visitor has departed, and Florentines idolatrously worship themselves in the brilliance of another's authority. And then disaster strikes. It may come from within, a crisis of political and social origins involving struggles in the political elite or with the vast disenfranchised base of society. Or the crisis may come from external sources: a military threat, earthquakes, winds, drought, flood, or plague. Internal and external danger may concatenate, suggesting to the Florentines that divine displeasure, and no mere natural force, explains their dilemma.

The city knows what must be done, and it first marshals its expressive agents to communicate with itself, with the foreigner, and with the divine forces that threaten its well-being, through traditional processional forms that have proven their efficacy and given the community its identity. If these

*Parenti in Schnitzer, *Quellen*, IV, 251; Tommaso Ginori *ibid.*, I, 102 (1498).

†*Diario d'Anonimo*, 367 (1378).

‡"Diario d'Incerto del 1529 e 1530 per l'Assedio di Firenze," 151 (July 29, 1530). See also *ibid.*, 152 (Aug. 1, 1530).

331

efforts prove unavailing, the government consults with its religious specialists and modifies its traditional propitiative forms in favor of rational ones
urged by experts who fit the cure to the particular disease. Still plagued by a
wrathful cosmos, the endangered city turns to frankly experimental forms
recommended by charismatic religious figures.

In this process, old assumptions about correct social place and station
are challenged; the traditional organization of society in ritual proves
faulty at best, dangerous at worst. The social groups within the given processional order are shuffled and reordered, and new faces and groups appear.
Crisis ritual depicts the organizing mind of the community at work, experimenting with orders to discover the right one.

Reorganization is powered by a search for values and feelings that, in the
contemporary view, have been lost, crushed by the formalism of good times.[1]
In stable times, Florentine men and women led a public life full of the tension
between order and value, between system and growth. Grave sexless males
and purified fruitless money dominated public forms. That social order perceived as purely formal and oppressive in the sight of the punishing judge
now had to be reinfused with elements of growth, with women and children,
and before all with love, charity, and the redistribution of property.

But how could the premodern city in crisis blend the order necessary to
civil life with the values necessary to growth? Clearly all formal behavior in
the most settled times was laden with challenge and competition, a constant
re-formation and reaffirmation of existing order. But that ritual competition
had been waged by the dominant males of society among themselves, beneath the sacred canopy. Major crises, however, brought the hegemony of
males and their regimes into question. Their rule and authority had been
based first on their demonstrated control over the governed and second on
the shared conviction that the political order spoke for God. Now it seemed
that the mature males had to show their humanity and shed all symbols of
station. It seemed further that alone these authorities could not speak of God,
and had to rely to a greater extent on those very liminal groups in secular
society whose subjection was the mark of traditional authority. There was
great danger in trying to bring fraternity and love into the traditional political
and social order.

This chapter examines the organizational and emotional forces at work in
the classic behavior of crisis. The period of inquiry is roughly the same as that
for the classic ritual of celebration and diplomacy, ending on the eve of the
new crisis ritual of the Savonarolan republic. Here as in the previous two
chapters, however, I shall occasionally utilize material of the later period
when it is evident that the behavior in question is a continuation of the classic
response.

---

1. The view that past forms crushed content is particularly marked at such times, as for example in the
comment on Florence's sterile past by Savonarola,
Giobbe, II, 243.

The Continuing Crisis

Normality and *abnormality, system* and *transition, continuity* and *crisis* are terms that have no meaning apart from the political system in which they are found. They mean one thing in a kingdom, another in a republic. In the former, the occasional interregnum with all its uncertainty might be quickly overcome, the cry "The king is dead, long live the king" then reaffirming the belief that the normal condition of men and kingdoms is stability, that reality is objective and structured, and that the hereditary bearers of power are suitable and appropriate to any time.

It was different in the Renaissance republic. Florence's government was composed of commoners serving for short terms. Neither the individual politician nor members of his family could hold consecutive terms of office. The purpose of government was to limit the accumulation of power and authority by charismatic private elements. Florentine government was not, therefore, constitutionally suited or appropriate to the need of a particular time; rather, it was a calculated creation that faced conditions of calm or crisis devoid of both the special abilities required by the times and the "natural" authority ascribed to feudal heads of state. It had power, but lacked authority; there was no king's touch in the republic.[2]

We can now see another significant implication of these oft-repeated facts, for at every step individual Florentine governments seemed out of step with the legitimate authorities of the cosmos. Not only had the names of the persons of government been pulled by fortune from a bag, but the times at which these elections took place, as well as the bimonthly entrances into office, occurred on certain numbered days of the month, days unrelated to the qualitative times of the liturgical calendar. Doing something or avoiding something on a particular saint's day was significant; entering office on the first of the month was merely reasonable.[3]

Florentine civic time was consequently *sine specie aeternitatis,* and the personages of government were qualitatively appropriate neither to the sacred time of the liturgical calendar nor to the teleology of inexplicable events. In its everyday stable existence the commune featured impermanence and cosmic meaninglessness. The ritual of government in such endless flux was no expression of constancy, but a working attempt to bring an

2. I have earlier described the attempt made through special commissions (*balìe*) to provide continuous *potestas* in extraordinary circumstances; in the fifteenth century these *balìe* themselves became standard features of government. But they never did have the same *auctoritas* as the basic constitutional institutions to go with their power; on the *balìe*, see Rubinstein, *Government.*

3. When some particular date of civic constitutional

activity repeatedly brought bad luck, the commune sought a safe date. Thus when the Signorie for September–October of both 1433 and 1434 proved themselves troublemakers, officials attributed this to the date both had been drawn for office: August 29, the inauspicious feast of the decapitation of St. John. The government changed election day to August 28. "That has been the practice ever since," writes Guicciardini, "except for a few years in the time of Savonarola"; *History of Florence,* 4.

ever-changing local reality to terms with the outside world of gods, princes, and natural forces. In Florence the normal ritual of government was a crisis ritual attempting to legitimate the city's human and cosmic relationships.

Examining the rituals of election shows that the normal assumption of power was a significant passage rather than a mere tradition in an order "that cannot die."[4] Consider the process through which citizens passed before being selected for office. Florentine governmental offices were filled by scrutiny. Every five years, special panels of eminent citizens reviewed the qualifications for office of all potentially political residents. The names of those who passed these scrutinies were then placed in bags, and whenever a particular office had to be filled, chits were lifted from the bags by lot.

Thus even by law the very identity of the political community was revised pentannually. In fact, however, that identity changed much more often, for the threat of disorder often necessitated a new scrutiny before the old one expired. The inherent willfulness of the scrutiny, in which some citizens excluded other citizens from political rights, was immeasurably emphasized when disorders forced a premature redefinition of community.[5]

The period of scrutiny was consequently one of central importance to the commune (Brucker notes the quasi-sacred awe with which contemporaries invested it), but of no significance to the liturgical calendar that dictated sacred times.[6] How was legitimacy to be generated in such circumstances of cosmic meaninglessness and willful personalism? The task was attacked first by linking the scrutiny mechanism to consensually accepted sacred images, whose power was at the disposal of the commune if correctly manipulated, and then by linking it to astrological time. In 1385, for example, the times at which the commissions executed the different steps of the scrutiny were determined by a clerical astrologer hired by the commune.[7] Then the willful and competitive scrutiners were transformed into spiritual brothers: In 1393 these creators of the new communal identity immediately upon sealing the bags sang the Te Deum and then exchanged confections and fine wines, in one contemporary's words, "in the charity of togetherness" (*insieme carità*).[8] Finally a retinue was created for the new regime by a public procession that committed the participants and viewers to the government or, as the chroniclers regularly described the motivation, brought the city to peace. Thus in 1382 when priors took office after a scrutiny had purged the bags of supporters of the previous broad regime, the government ordered a clerical procession to put the city at peace. A high government official having been assassinated only days before, the new executive filled the city with mercenary troops before the commitment–peace procession unfolded.[9] These postscrutiny pro-

---

4. On rites of enthronement as rites of passage, see Van Gennep, *Rites of Passage*, 110–115. The quote is Dati's, *Istorie*, 69.

5. The scrutiny also served to bring into politics youth who had reached officeholding age since the previous scrutiny.

6. Brucker, *Civic World*, 354.

7. Panciatichi, f. 150r; Naddo da Montecatini, 78f.

8. Panciatichi, f. 176r. An eyewitness account of a scrutiny in 1378 gives further details; *Tumulto dei Ciompi*, 78f.

9. Panciatichi, f. 143v.

cessions were also keyed to significant astrological time; in 1385 the same astrologer who had timed the scrutiny timed the procession that followed its completion.[10]

This triple mechanism of choosing astrologically favorable times and consensually valid images to usher in the scrutiny, surrounding the scrutiny process itself with ritually fraternal behavior, and finally creating commitment through retinue processions applied not only to scrutinies, but to any actions that had the effect of redefining the identity of the community. In 1387, for example, a law that restricted officeholding to a more limited group was followed by a peace procession to assuage the unrest generated by this unusual action. One can easily imagine that here too, astrological timing and acts of fraternal charity between the lawmakers also took place.[11]

The fact that Florentine intercalaries recurred at least every five years is only one mark of the highly volatile and ever-changing nature of constitutional order in the republic. Until the late Middle Ages, for example, the municipal law itself was subject to semiannual revision (*riformagione*).[12] The system of drawing by lot from the bags to determine officers provides further emphasis in this regard. If through ritual the results of the scrutiny could be legitimized despite the emotional and turbulent history of the regime's origins, the subsequent lotteries to determine which persons would lead the commune for a specific time made it most difficult to maintain the patina of legitimacy. With the communal executive changing every two months, hardly a week passed without names being drawn for this or that office, without names being announced, without the assumption of some office, the separate ceremony of swearing to do one's best, and the return of previous magistrates to private life.

The Florentines were eminently aware of the pedestrian nature of such procedures, and wished that political realities had permitted the adoption of the Venetian model, so much more stable and dignified. The distinguished lawyer Lorenzo Ridolfi, who with his broad international experience certainly knew what he was talking about, said in one debate over a new scrutiny in 1413 that the Florentines were the laughingstock of their neighbors because "they were always holding elections."[13] If Florentines could feel so mortified during a scrutiny, how much more undignified must it have seemed each two months, with friars rummaging about in bags to find names that might fit the manifold formal requirements of office (*divieti*), but none of the needs of the time, and none of the social qualities most states thought natural for those in authority.

The random qualities of the persons who assumed communal executive office explain in good part the substantial ritual mechanisms used after the lot drawing to make the inappropriate appropriate and to define authority by

10. *Ibid.*, f. 150r.

11. *Ibid.*, f. 153v.

12. By 1322 the statutes of the Capitano were three

years; Davidsohn, *Storia*, V, 132.

13. The scrutiny in question was the captaincy of the Parte Guelfa; Brucker, *Civic World*, 314.

generating retinue for the new officers. Shops were closed so that the Signoria could enter office honorably; that is, accompanied by all the citizens. After the new Signoria had attended a solemn Mass and heard a sermon, the nine men marched in procession the few blocks down to the main public square, where they took the formal oath of office in public view. At different points in this procession, they distributed alms to the poor and thereby became brothers while attracting the poor to their following.[14] Here, as in the scrutiny period, ritual created rather than simply maintained legitimacy by appeals to divine powers outside sacred time, through fraternity, and through the creation of retinue. In periods of particular tension, the elaborateness of this office-taking ritual was increased. Thus in 1377 the inaugurations were extraordinarily pompous, obviously to intimidate the regime's opponents, not into silence but into participation in the general joy.[15]

Internal Crisis

The normal ritual of government thus reflected a preoccupation with legitimation. It did not so much express established authority as attempt to create a particular officer's own right to exist. It is not surprising, consequently, that when Florence was faced with genuine internal crises, the commune's actions and attitudes were typical of governmental passages as a whole. To illustrate this point, we shall examine first the ritual of major constitutional crises, then the ritual used when governments survived outside threats by the political class, and finally the behavior of social revolt.

Following the expulsion of the Medici in 1494, the revived republic guided by the Dominican Savonarola undertook a major governmental reorganization. The central necessity during this period of uncertainty was to ensure that God inspired the founding fathers of the new regime. From the pulpit the friar recommended not only a procession but a series of participatory rituals clearly intended to accomplish these goals. Every deliberation of the councils was to be preceded by prayer, and the purist preacher urged the lawmakers to avoid the astrological consultations that were so deeply rooted in governmental practice.[16] Private citizens were told to fast for three days.

14. More on this process in my "Setting," 126f, 132f.

15. The citizens might also be ordered to accompany their new lords (*Diario d'Anonimo*, 309–313; 1378), whereas neighbors and family normally accompanied each member when he entered and left office: "Perchè Lionardo mio suocero usciva la mattina de' Signori, io pregai molti cittadini del quartiere che venassono a farli compagnia al tornare a casa. E così ci vennero assai a farli honore. Accatai sei pezzi d'asse per ponere su le panche, come è usanza"; ser Giusto,

f. 70r (1456). A famous case where the accompaniment home of a Standard Bearer forced to leave office was so enormous as to constitute a rebuff to those responsible was that of Niccolò Capponi, in 1529; Segni, *Storie*, 151f; Varchi, VIII, 25.

16. The Florentines probably believed that their prophet would know the right days better than any astrologer; Savonarola, *Aggeo*, 134. See also n. 3, this chapter, in which the same Dominican apparently persuaded the Florentines to disregard their notion that S. Giovanni Decollato's feast was inauspicious.

The friar probably had in mind fasting's purgative value for the spirit, and asserted that through the citizen's fast God might be moved to illuminate the constitutionalists.[17]

This same theme of spiritually vitalizing the government as a prerequisite for appropriate, significant action reemerged in 1502, when for the first time the head of government, the Standard Bearer of Justice, was elected for life rather than for two months. This was a decisive move toward more honorable continuity in government. On September 21, the venerated image of Impruneta came to the city in procession so that, in the chronicler's words, God would give the governors the grace to elect someone *apt* to lead the disturbed city in the path of God.[18] Another witness to the same event defended this radical departure from constitutional tradition by explaining that these *cose nuove* were necessary for the peace and concord of a troubled *popolo*. Fearful that God might not approve the action, the same writer viewed the procession of the twenty-first, replete with the type of ritual charity already seen in scrutiny ritual, as a means of getting the new order off to a good start.[19]

The same fundamental ritual procedures of first converting actors from profane to spiritual personalities, then making these politicians brothers through common prayer, and finally staging a procession, were used after aborted conspiracies and when illegitimate governments were toppled. In 1340, for example, the discovery and suppression of a massive conspiracy on the feast of All Saints was followed by a procession: "Because of our city's liberation from danger, the commune held a great procession and offering to St. John on November 26, and ordered that every year on All Saints the said offering be made."[20] The story was much the same after the collapse of the Dietisalvi conspiracy in 1466, when, in Machiavelli's words, "it was ordered that the citizens should go in solemn procession to thank God for the preservation of the government and the reunion of the city."[21] In 1522, the uncovering of the Alamanni conspiracy was followed by a procession that "prayed God for those who govern the city, and asked that He guard us in the future."[22] The expulsion of the Medici and the restoration of the republic in 1527 had as a sequel a procession thanking God for restoring liberty.[23] Machiavelli at one point provided a suitably realistic but forthrightly religious explanation for all such ritual procedures after constitutional crises, speaking of a procession held so that "the Deity might appear to participate in what had been done . . . [and] to thank Him for the recovery of the government."[24] Ritual, the author of *The Prince* often intimated in his writ-

17. *Ibid.*, 144.

18. My italics; Landucci, 250; Rinuccini, clxviii. For an instance of a procession to inspire the government on whether to change foreign allies, see Landucci, 193 (1499). More on the concept of *spirare* in my "Setting," 143, n. 39.

19. Zafarana, "Per la Storia Religiosa," 1113.

20. "Un grande processione offerta a San Giovanni . . . "; G. Villani, XI, 119. Villani's word usage allows a reading of either "to St. John" or at St. John's."

21. Machiavelli, *History*, 332.

22. Cambi, XXII, 204.

23. *Ibid.*, 328f.

24. Machiavelli, *History*, 313.

338   *The Ritual of the Classical Commune*

ings, could be for Florence, as it had been for Rome, a central tool of a noncharismatic political order in affirming the validity of each new identity.[25]

Florentine regimes doubtless used the ritual activities of internal crisis to seek confirmation from the divinities, but just as surely the procession was meant to provide a psychological surety that everything was in order. Processions and other ritual activities in crisis were undertaken, in the words of different actors and chroniclers, to "liberate this *popolo* and this city from such confusion," to "get rid of confusion through the greatest order," and to calm "discordant spirits."[26] In effect, laymen were asked or forced to participate in processions to prove that the city was united. But was it? The fact that retinue for any procession had to come from the citizenry meant that a procession might, in another contemporary's phrase, "lead to something other than prayer."[27] Especially during periods of internal crisis, the procession was an activity used to create order, yet the potential harbinger of disorder.

The dangers of processions in times of disorder were legion. "Undisciplined youth" acting on their own or at the urging of the politician fathers might disguise themselves as women or priests and scandalize participants and observers.[28] Participation by men who had bloodied their hands in the disorders might further irritate God against the city.[29] Opponents of the regime might be infuriated by the sight of that regime praying to God, and its hypocrisy could seem outright sacrilege.[30] The Signoria or other processional groups might be attacked in the street and insulted.[31] The Signoria's presence in the procession might be used as an occasion to exclude the government from the Palace and manage a coup—processions attended by the Signoria were even encouraged by conspirators with that in mind.[32] Almost as bad, the proper accompaniment to "honor the procession" might fail to materialize, and the spectacle of a dishonored government participating in a ceremony without a dignified retinue might highlight the weakness of governmental authority and communal solidarity as much as any misfired political

25. For these views, see page 529, this volume. Also J. Preuss, "Machiavelli's Functional Analysis of Religion: Context and Object," *Journal of the History of Ideas* XL (1979), 171–190.

26. Schnitzer, *Quellen*, I, 102; IV, 251; Nardi, *Istorie*, II, 1.

27. Schnitzer, *Quellen*, IV, 248 (Parenti).

28. An example in Savonarola, *Ruth e Michea*, I, 269.

29. The terrible storm on Corpus Christi 1522 may have been caused by the archbishop's impurity. He had ordered an execution that morning, then proceeded to carry the host in procession; Cambi, XXII, 206f.

30. Cambi denounced the hated Medici regime in 1527 for holding processions while Florence was threatened by foreign troops. They were not held for the *popolo*, he said, but so that God would overlook that regime's own faults. Our Lady of Impruneta was brought to the city in these circumstances, Cambi

continued, to liberate these functionaries and not the city from danger; Cambi, XXII, 296. In 1529 the anti-popular Filippo de' Nerli said that although the Signoria might join in processions ascetically, they were not humble toward the citizens but persecuted them every day; F. Nerli, *Commentari dei Fatti Civili occorsi dentro la Città di Firenze dall'Anno 1215 al 1537*, 2 vols. (Trieste, 1859), vol. II, p. 136 (hereafter Nerli).

31. As in the early fourteenth century; Compagni, I, 21.

32. For example, Stefani, rub. 792 (1378). Some later examples: A friar tried to entice the Signoria to SS. Annunziata with the idea its return to the Palace would be barred; Nerli, II, 45. In 1522 a conspiracy was hatched to kill the Medici archbishop while he carried the host in procession and end his effective rule of the city; Masi, 257. In 1527 the republicans tried to use the clamor of a procession to exclude the philo-Medicean government from the Palace; Varchi, IV, 2, 3.

act.[33] Emboldened by evidence of such weakness, malcontents might announce their intention to attain power through the very imagery of the procession; in one case, a painting of the pregnant Virgin borne in a procession was interpreted by contemporaries in just this fashion.[34] And the greatest danger of all was that the procession could turn into an uprising of the repressed lower class, operating on its own or instrumentalized by powerful citizens.

The attempt to liberate the populace from anxiety through processional order thus presented a significant risk. This risk was certainly rooted in the inequities of the social order, which divided rich and poor, old and young, males and females, and in-families and out-families. But the very potential of the procession itself must be considered. It was the procession, after all, the populace's ordered enthusiasm, that could win commitment to the regime, and it was the procession that could convince the godheads that the populace enthusiastically and genuinely solicited or welcomed God's gift of order. The enthusiasm of a procession determined its terrestrial and celestial effectiveness, and processions had to be so constructed to include this necessary ingredient. The procession of crisis was therefore more than a potential stage for instigating disorders. It was itself powerful, and the inherent rather than accidental nature of processional danger can be best understood by examining the famous Palm Sunday procession of 1496.

Conceived by Savonarola as an opportunity to put people's minds at peace, this procession had been carefully planned by both friar and government to ensure its emotional success.[35] No one was disappointed. The participants sang lauds as they went, grown men burst into tears as they found themselves swept up in an almost dancelike saintliness, each tearfully loving the other in a craze of fraternity.[36] Yet the very paradisiac quality of the procession and especially the unbelievable piety shown by the grown men of Florence provided one of the tensest moments of this regime. Moved by their fraternity and oneness, by the sound of continuously ringing bells and angelic lauds, convinced that divinity itself had infused them with such spirit, the participants, even the grown men, started to cry *Viva Cristo!*[37]

The danger was evident, for any *Viva!* except at well-defined times and places sounded like a signal for uprising and was strictly forbidden. Perfect fraternity had indeed been achieved through processional solidarity. Yet in the wake of the procession, the same political leaders who had encouraged the procession now seriously questioned a fraternity that led to forgetting one's place. In the procession, enraptured mature males gripped by holy

---

33. A spectacular example of 1377 is in Trexler, *Spiritual Power*, 147–154.

34. Schnitzer, *Quellen*, IV, 220f (Parenti). In the same period the Signoria forbade a procession in Oltrarno that it suspected was a pretext to provoke attacks on Savonarolans; *ibid.*, 169.

35. Savonarola, *Amos e Zaccaria*, III, 71, 123, 139, 152f.

More on this procession in Trexler, "Adolescence," 251, 262.

36. In fact, two years later the Dominican staged an actual religious dance in the Piazza San Marco around a statue of Christ crucified in which the same grave males participated; Ps. Burlamacchi, 134.

37. Savonarola, *Amos e Zaccaria*, III, 160.

madness had put aside their gravity. Could a republic long survive such
ecstasy?[38] Was going out of one's mind (*impazzare*) really the logical conclusion of brotherhood, as Savonarola argued? Secular men did some ridiculous
things during the profane Carnival, the preacher noted, so was it any wonder
that, possessed by love of God, they should act as they had in the Palm
Sunday procession? But the government rejected such arguments; such
shouts were all but forbidden in future processions.

The optimal procession for uniting the wills of the commune proved a
great danger to order. Too much spiritual value endangered material relationships. That was the nub of the problem of processions: They were absolutely necessary for social order yet endangered it, for the procession *was* a
social order. There could be no talk over the long run of suppressing processions, for then the government was seen to be weak and thought to care only
for itself and not for the public good, which could not be protected without
processional offerings to God.[39]

Thus a fundamentally contradictory attitude was at work. The government feared public gatherings during crisis and often suppressed them, yet
turned about and generated processions in the same circumstances to marshal and channel emotional excitement. "Troubled spirits" motivated both
cancellation and generation.[40] A procession might be canceled for fear that
disrespect would be shown to a holy image, yet at another time an image
might be carried in procession for the precise purpose of calming passions
and bringing the population to a uniformly devotional attitude.[41] A horse race
might be postponed because of the fear of crowds gathering, but in one
instance horse races were staged for the specific purpose of relaxing a tense
population.[42]

The threat of spiritual enthusiasm to established authority was not limited to Florence, of course. Yet when combined with the dangers inherent
in the Florentine political and social order, the risks seemed immeasurably
greater. Internal turmoil in the principality rarely threatened the principles of
political and social order, but how vulnerable were these principles in a
burgher republic!

The third type of internal crisis, the social revolt, emphasizes that vulnerability, and helps clarify the role of formal behavior in Florentine society.
From the point of view of behavior, this type of crisis differs in two ways from
other types of internal crisis. In the social revolt, subject groups normally
excluded from politics and the procession formed processional units and
demanded a right to the public forum, thus breaking the normal processional
monopoly of the *communitas florentina*. In the social revolt as well, the proces-

38. On this and the following, *ibid.*, 160f, 183, 206.

39. Cambi, XXI, 237; XXIII, 12f.

40. A *locus classicus* on the fear of crowds is in Filarete, *Treatise*, 41f.

41. On postponements to avoid being irreverent to
saintly patrons, see Trexler, "Setting," 140, and on

refusing to postpone to avoid irreverence, see page
326, this volume. On the power of images to calm
the populace, see Trexler, "Image," 16.

42. "Per sospetto" and to avoid crowds the government canceled a horse race in 1502; Landucci, 244. To
resuscitate the *popolo*, horse races were held in 1497;
ibid., 152.

sion reached its apex as political force. If it was always a form of politics in the republic city, during a social insurrection the procession was most purely politics' content; heaven and earth, to recall Hegel's dictum, became one.[43]

Two major factors inhibit the study of the social revolt in Florence. First, the wool workers' (Ciompi) revolt of summer 1378 was the only major *movimento* of subjects (*sottoposti*) in the city's history.[44] Second, during most of that summer the city was forced to observe an ecclesiastical interdict, which helps to explain why institutional religion played a minimal part as an expressive agent or as an identifying center.[45] A third peculiar factor of the Ciompi revolt, however, adds a silver lining: Our sources give us more information on lower-class behavior at this point than at any other time before the sixteenth century.

THE EXCLUDED

The future of the salaried male day laborers of Florence was the question that dominated all minds during the course of the Ciompi revolt, which lasted from June 20 through September 1, 1378, and continued in aftershocks into the mid-1380s.[46] Despite decades of sporadic labor unrest and several fruitless conspiracies before this time, the *sottoposti* in early 1378 still had no rights to political or religious organization, and thus no processional identity. These urban poor might be the *popolo di Dio*, but they were not part of the *popolo di Firenze*.[47] Yet in 1378 they seized these rights and that civic identity. How did they use formal expression to achieve such goals?

One formal element contributing to this victory was the Ciompi's ability to meet and plan. Usually held in the immediate wake of street actions, the meetings of Ronco and Belletri, of Camaldoli, Santa Maria Novella, and

43. See Introduction, this volume.

44. On the revolt, see the various works of N. Rodolico, including *I Ciompi* (Florence, 1971); V. Rutenburg, *Popolo e Movimenti Popolari nell'Italia del '300 e '400* (Bologna, 1971), and the following three works by G. Brucker: "The Ciompi Revolution," in Rubinstein, *Florentine Studies*, 314–356; "The Florentine *Popolo Minuto* and Its Political Role, 1340–1450," in L. Martines (ed.), *Violence and Civil Disorders in Italian Cities, 1200–1500* (Berkeley, 1972), 155–183; *Civic World*, 14–59.

45. Mass was first reassumed on Aug. 5; Trexler, *Spiritual Power*, 157. However, excommunicated Florentines were not readmitted to the church until late October; *Diario d'Anonimo*, 388. The first clerical procession in months was held on Oct. 25; *ibid*. Although institutional religion was not prominent during the summer, religious motifs were: The revolt was blamed on the previous war with the church; certain Ciompi called themselves the *popolo di Dio*; the rule of the Ciompi was compared to the forty-day Passion of Christ (*Tumulto dei Ciompi*, 58); miracles

were registered (*ibid.*, 78); a prophet was active (*ibid.*, 119); the end of the Ciompi threat was attributed to the prayers of the good people of Florence (*ibid.*), as was the calming effect of the Dominicans upon the Ciompi during late August, which was credited with preventing something worse.

46. This formulation recognizes the fundamentally class rather than political nature of the revolt (Brucker), but admits Brucker's demonstration that the institutional implementation of the Ciompi programs fell to supporters of some wealth and status. Criticisms of Brucker's views on the independent political force of the Ciompi are in A. Molho, "Cosimo de' Medici: *Pater Patriae* or *Padrino?*" *Stanford Italian Review* (Spring, 1979), 9–18, and especially in S. Cohn, "Rivolte Popolari e Classi Sociali nella Toscana del Rinascimento," *Studi Storici* XX (1979), 747–758.

47. The distinction was formally recognized in August; Stefani, rub. 801. There may be a link between the *minuti*'s patron St. Gabriel (i.e., the messenger of God) and this name.

Sant'Ambrogio are important to the formal history of this period not because of what little we know of their content, but because of the impact they had on the propertied classes. These meetings proceeded with forms of solidarity that could be the basis for a social overturn. Though antagonistic chroniclers occasionally amused themselves with stories about the disorder at such meetings of the *minuti,* they and the government generally reacted to them as they did to any conspiracy. Far from being chaotic, Ciompi meetings were believed to be tightly organized and possessed of the spiritual solidarity of a sworn community.[48] Far from a takeover leading to chaos, the victory of the Ciompi would, authorities and chroniclers seemed to believe, lead to a new ritual and a new order: Ciompi meetings began the claim to legitimacy.

Another formal element contributed to this claim: the nonverbal and verbal communications systems established between different neighborhoods of *minuti,* which passed on information about impending processional presentations. Three such systems may be mentioned. First were the church bells. When the bells in a church of S. Ambrogio were rung, for example, they could pass information to the area of Belletri west of the Via S. Gallo, whose churches then rang it on to the Oltrarno churches of San Frediano and Camaldoli, and from there upriver to S. Niccolò.[49] Second were torches, also used to relay information from the church towers.[50] And third were verbal greetings, used by the Ciompi to identify its supporters just as certainly as they were used by government agents.[51] In addition, the many oaths that the insurrectionaries, both in private meetings and in the public square, took from friends and former enemies had their effect; they clarified moral allegiances and struck fear in those who heard of these bonds or witnessed them.[52] None of these means of communication was peculiar to the Ciompi, but the latter's ability to establish a communication's space and a language in the city impressed opponents and contributed to the emerging public identity of the insurgents.

At the very root of the Ciompi's ability to go public was possession of a banner. The flag was the most important image of group solidarity in the

48. For example, note the liturgical cadence a communal official used to describe the meeting of "ribaldi e gente minuta e di vile condizione" at Ronco in July: "Quivi con grandi sagramenti e leghe si legorono insieme e bacioronsi in bocca d'essere alla morte e alla vita l'uno coll'altro e difendersi contro a chi li volessi offendere; e dierono ordine d'andare a tutti e loro pari, per li luoghi e contrade dove dimoravano, a dare il sagramento e ricevere promessioni"; *Tumulto dei Ciompi,* 19. Two typical examples of ridicule of disorderly Ciompi conventicles are in Stefani, rubs. 800, 802. An example of scorn at *minuti* disorders is in an anonymous chronicler's dismissal of the *minuti* government because none of its members knew Latin: *Tumulto dei Ciompi,* 121.

49. Bell sequences are *ibid.,* 22, 141.

50. Torch messages were part of a conspiracy to be

hatched on Good Friday, 1379; *Diario d'Anonimo,* 394.

51. An indication that government prescribed what cries could be used by inhabitants is in Brucker, *Civic World,* 51, n. 169 (Dec. 1378). For the use of such cries as greetings distinguishing friends from foes, see page 289, this volume. In Sept. 1378 militiamen encountered two Ciompi: "Di che fu detto loro diciessono: 'Viva il populo e l'arti'; ed e' ciò non volendo dire, ma il contrario, sì gli uccisono amendue"; *Tumulto dei Ciompi,* 120.

52. See the quote in n. 48. The chronicler most interested in the oaths and most concerned that they be observed is the one writer who was a supporter of the Ciompi; *Tumulto dei Ciompi,* 75, 79f, 86; more on oaths of the *minuti* in Brucker, "Florentine *Popolo Minuto,*" 179.

summer of 1378, and it became the prerequisite of procession in a city whose hosts, relics, and images were eerily unseen and unheard. At first the *minuti* co-opted the flag of the furriers' gild and the communal Libertà banner, both of which they surreptitiously obtained.[53] Then in July they seized the most important flag in the city, the Standard of Justice. "And with that flag in hand," a horrified communal official wrote, "they did the greatest damage."[54] Observers wrote as if people were mere adjuncts of banners throughout the summer. "All the flags [were] in the Piazza, with the people under them."[55]

Moving from co-optation of traditional banners to the establishment of their own identity, the Ciompi on July 20 bared their own device, which from then until the 1380s would unsettle the *popolo* of Florence: the banner of the archangel Gabriel, armed with sword and cross. Hanging from the house in Camaldoli, Oltrarno, where it was reverently guarded when not in use, it proved the existence of a new ritual space.[56] Along with the Standard of Justice, it was probably the same flag of the angel that all the established gilds followed to the church of S. Barnaba on July 21, and probably with it in hand these gildsmen took their oaths of loyalty to the Ciompi.[57] Kissed in reverence by patrician supporters of the Ciompi in the Piazza dei Signori, the flag of the angel manifested in public the secret *sacramento* or oath that bound the dispossessed together.[58] And as we shall see, once that flag was confiscated, little solidarity was possible.

For all the importance of these elements of identity and legitimacy, they were not decisive in forming the Ciompi. That role was reserved for the procession itself: the power to march, and the ability to do so in a disciplined form with retinue. Uprisings in Florence almost always started their public life with a few activists stepping into a square, raising a flag and a rallying cry, then waiting to see if others would fall in behind them. The famous Ciompi meetings came after, not before, processional actions, to justify past acts through thought of future actions: "Fearing that they would sooner or later be punished and castigated for the things they had done, great numbers of them

53. *Tumulto dei Ciompi*, 15, 107, 129. A cautious reading of the sources, which are ambiguous, suggests that the Ciompi's use of different flags corresponded to different stages in their own self-consciousness, not that they had a clear consciousness of separate solidarity throughout the summer. They seem to have thought of themselves first as (new) gildsmen opposed to the military structures of the city and to the wool gild to which they had previously been subject, then as a separate corporation, and finally, after their fall, as publicly if not emotionally allied to the Parte Guelfa and to its flag as a condition of their resurgence. The present evidence does not, however, allow any certainty on this question.

54. *Ibid.*, 24. Cf. this passage: "Di che quando si vide pe' buoni uomini e per gli artefici, che i gonfalonieri non andavano alla difesa dei signori, così come era ordinato, allora, chi per paura e chi per amore, seguitava il popolo minuto e il gonfalone [di giustizia] nominato di sopra, e andavagli dietro seguitandogli; perchè ciascuno dubitava del furore; *ibid.*, 25.

55. *Ibid.*, 120 (Sept. 1).

56. On Camaldoli's house, *ibid.*, 122. The flag of the Ciompi is described *ibid.*, 77, and Gabriel is named as the angel *ibid.*, 121. Stefani says that the flag went back to the period of Walter of Brienne as a symbol of the wool *sottoposti*; rub. 795, 566. He alone says that the flag was unfurled on July 20; other chroniclers do not mention it until the events of late August.

57. *Tumulto dei Ciompi*, 27; Stefani, rub. 795.

58. Prisoners released by the Ciompi on Aug. 28 kissed the angel on the flag as part of their oath to support the *minuti*; Stefani, rub. 801.

came together and met."[59] The processional action was the heart of Ciompi identity and legitimacy.

That identity was expressed in different forms. It might be the ability of arson squads to march to the homes of particular opponents and, with perfect corporate discipline, hurt things not persons, torch one house but not the next, burn but not steal.[60] Contemporaries commented on the solemnity with which the *minuti* could send emissaries, and their ability calculatedly to insult governmental officials.[61] Certainly the parade of 1000 crossbowmen on July 28, organized by *lo stato del popolo minuto*, impressed witnesses.[62] The petition of the Ciompi on August 27 was clearly irresistible, in part because it was put forward at the end of a long march throughout the city in which the *minuti* showed their coercive unity.[63] Within a processional context they too could pompously knight supporters like Luca Da Panzano, and the Ciompi's rejection of Panzano's attempt to introduce a flag other than that of the angel into their ranks at the end of August demonstrated, in the same processional context, just how self-conscious the Ciompi were of their public self.[64] Moreover, when on August 31 the *minuti* marched proudly into the public square of the city for their decisive test of strength, they were so impressive as to win that most improbable of all accolades, the praise of an enemy of these *gente di basso mano*: "The *popolo minuto* came [into the Piazza] with their retinue of wool carders under the banner of the angel. And it was truly a large and handsome brigade, in good order." It was the physical presence of the Ciompi in the streets, in order, and in command of formal modes of communication, that gave life to the symbolic world about them.[65]

59. *Tumulto dei Ciompi*, 19, explaining the meeting of Ronco. The assembly at Belletri also followed street action; *ibid.*, 26.

60. *Ibid.*, 108, 130, 141f; Stefani, rub. 792, thought this precision was either a miracle, or showed the arsonists were under the tight rein of certain *grassi* or "fat cats."

61. One writer says that the Ciompi priors were dressed improperly; *Tumulto dei Ciompi*, 41. A later writer says that the Ciompi's petition to the Palace on Aug. 28 was criticized by the government "che le cose non si dimandavano in quel modo, nè era onore alla signoria concederle per forza; e che' eglino medesimi davano contro a loro guastando quel che avevono fatto, e volevano torre la reputazione al governo che si avevono acquistato." The Ciompi returned in embassy, says the writer, "solennemente," but the petition was presented "con' grande arroganzia"; *ibid.*, 38. More on the Ciompi being "senza riverenzia alcuna" *ibid.*, 119, and on them receiving reverence from the priors, *Diario d' Anonimo*, 368. On the reception by the Ciompi of the priors at Santa Maria Novella, Stefani, rub. 802, and 803 for the ritual secrets of Michele di Lando's success. A further formal ability of the Ciompi noted by Stefani was their potential for building barricades to divide the city scientifically;

ibid., rub. 804. More on barricades in *Tumulto dei Ciompi*, 17.

62. *Ibid.*, 77, 115; *Diario d'Anonimo*, 371. It is important that the forty-eight flags made for these crossbowmen "to strengthen the *popolo minuto*" showed the four quarter symbols of the city (twelve each), and *not* the symbols of the sixteen military companies, which were anti-Ciompi.

63. "A dì 27 d'agosto il popolo minuto si raunò co' loro armi e fornimento et andorono pella ciptà, e, capitando al palagio de' nostri signori, ivi feciono resistencia et dierono una loro petizione"; *Tumulto dei Ciompi*, 151.

64. This ceremony was all the more important because Panzano renounced the knighthood given him by the *popolo di Firenze* and then accepted it given by the *popolo minuto*; *Diario d'Anonimo*, 376. This clearly shows the outsider status of the Ciompi, as does the other distinction between them as the *popolo di Dio*, a name Stefani says Panzano bestowed on them, and the citizens as the *popolo di Firenze*; Stefani, rub. 801, 802. But see also N. Rodolico, *La Democrazia Fiorentina nel suo Tramonto* (Bologna, 1905), 442. For the Ciompi rejection of the Parte flag, Stefani, rub. 801, also *Tumulto dei Ciompi*, 80, 153.

65. "E in buona fe' grande et bella brigata et bene in

RECONSTRUCTING THE COMMUNE

The government of Florence may be said to have lost its authority through three fundamental changes in ritual procedures. First, representational civil identity had been changed. The sixteen military companies no longer represented the city; they had been replaced by the gilds, which dominated public representations of urban corporateness as they had at the time of Walter of Brienne.[66] Florence seemed defined by occupational rather than military forces, the lowest occupational ranks thus gaining a parity impossible under military organization. Second, the Palace had lost all semblance of separateness; Lady Florence could not choose to be alone. Stefani, for example, bemoaned the fact that whereas before the revolt it was unusual for three citizens to eat with the Signoria in any one week, now three or four hundred swarmed around this queen.[67] The third change followed from the second. Government may be said to exist where a ruler may give flags to corporations and reclaim them at will; that ritual of exchange was broken in summer 1378.[68] Reconstructing the commune, therefore, meant much more than simply repressing gatherings and meetings, divesting inhabitants of arms, and so forth;[69] a government that feared procession was no government at all. The commune had to reassert the representational force of the military sections of the city, demonstrate the separateness of the Palace, and reassume its ritual links with the city. It did so with no final victory in sight, for Florence was a republic. The struggle to regain Palace authority in the fall of 1378 was only an accelerated variant on the eternal struggle between the center and the city that created it and lived off it.

A beginning was made on August 31, the dramatic day on which the

punto"; *ibid.*, 152. "Bene in punto" includes the sense of order *and* richness. Nanni Bonifazii, who wrote this letter, served a lord but did not bother giving the names of *minuti* because of their low social station. One writer saw a direct relation between the absence of procession to support the Signoria and the growth of the Ciompi order; *ibid.*, 23. Stefani said that a *movimento* of 1382 would have been successful if the bakers "si fussero armati, e venuti in piazza con ordine . . . ," but that "con poco ordine entrarono in piazza, saltabeccando in qua e là, e' furono subito rotti"; rub. 905. For the fear the Ciompi would be officially granted "useful days" to burn, see *Tumulto dei Ciompi*, 131, an interesting fact relevant to the conception of time.

66. The *gonfalonieri* of the military sections had failed to respond to the Signoria on July 20, and were discredited. The victory of the *arti* or *popolo* over the military was symbolically demonstrated by their capture of the Palace of the Podestà, symbol of the *commune* (the *camera del comune* was kept there), the flags of the *arti* being flown from its windows and towers; *ibid.*, 75, 112. One of the first acts of the revolutionary government was to demand all the flags of the mili-

tary companies, which were brought to the Palace on July 22 or 23; *Tumulto dei Ciompi*, 113; *Diario d'Anonimo*, 369. When the standard bearers of these companies were then changed to a predominantly *minuti* group, the flags were given back to the sixteen new *gonfalonieri* on July 25. Our best source was present, and was gratified to learn that the flags of all the government divisions had "the same signs [on them] as before"; *ibid.*, 370; *Tumulto dei Ciompi*, 114.

67. Stefani, rub. 885. On Michele di Lando's awareness of his need to separate himself from his Ciompi supporters from the beginning, see *Tumulto dei Ciompi*, 57.

68. When, that is, the *gonfaloni delle compagnie* refused to come to the aid of the Palace on July 20, when the *arti* refused to yield their flags, when flags were forcibly taken from government buildings, and so on.

69. All of which the government tried to do in early September; *ibid.*, 86. One interesting provision ran as follows: "Che niuno dipintore non ne dovesse dipingere a niuno uomo, nè cittadino, nè forestiero, nè di che stato o conditione si fusse, a pena della vita per ciascuno che fusse trovato"; *ibid.*, 85 (referring to flags *c.* Sept. 25).

government faced down the Ciompi. In order to destroy the solidarity of the Ciompi, it required all the gilds, massed in the Piazza, to give over their flags to the Palace; once this was done, said the bann, each person was to stand beneath the flag of his military company and none other.[70] Understanding that obedience to this demand would destroy their occupational identity, the Ciompi quibbled, then refused: "If we have nothing, to what would we rally?" they asked. And, "We would then be without a symbol. . . . Give us another flag. . . . Give us the old flag [of the Standard Bearer of Justice]."[71] When this was denied, and the Ciompi remained obdurate, they were attacked by other gildsmen and the flag was taken from them and into the Palace. Divested of their public solidarity, the Ciompi soon watched their flag thrown from that Palace to a clamoring crowd in the Piazza, which cut it into three pieces and proceeded to jump on it.[72] Iconoclasm is never practiced against impotent idols. In the wake of this violent reaction, the very house in which the flag had been housed and guarded was burned to the ground, one of only two *minuti* properties torched in these hectic days.[73] The Palace won this important victory, but the struggle over the civil identity of Florence would continue for decades.

Then on September 10 another step was taken. In a ceremonial setting, the leaders of the remaining gilds came to the Palace and received the flags given the government on the last day of August. This not only insulted the Ciompi, whose gild had been dismantled, but expressed confidence in ritual reciprocity between Palace and city.[74] Flags could only be given by the Palace if there was some certainty that they could be reclaimed: "All flags," one communal counselor urged on this same day, "should be brought to the Palace [if] bestowed by others than the *popolo e comune di Firenze*. And harsh laws should be passed that no one can or dare erect flags other than [those of] the commune."[75]

Overconfidence soon led to a setback when the government tried to stage the long-postponed feast of St. John. On October 1 it announced that on the seventeenth and eighteenth the feast would proceed with all the trimmings. Yet when the time approached to make good, the city was in such a dangerous state that no palio was run, although the government had specifically announced that it would be. The offerings of the military companies were omitted, and there was no procession. Instead tribute was quickly collected from the subject communes and lords, and other events carried through "quite hurriedly," said one contemporary, "because of fear of disturbances . . . , [and] to suppress every gathering."[76] Government limped along to recovery for several years.

---

70. *Ibid.*, 82, 152.

71. *Ibid.*, 82; *Diario d'Anonimo*, 378.

72. *Tumulto dei Ciompi*, 83, 120f.

73. *Ibid.*, 122.

74. One diarist specified it was an insult to the Ciompi; *Diario d'Anonimo*, 384. On the Nativity of Mary, Sept. 8, many citizens had gone to Prato to see the Belt of Mary, the first significant religious action mentioned in this period, and one that brought some lightening to tension; *Tumulto dei Ciompi*, 122.

75. *Diario d'Anonimo*, 384, n. 2.

76. *Tumulto dei Ciompi*, 148, also 85; *Diario d'Anonimo*,

The Ciompi revolt was certainly rooted in material causes and fed by economic interests: Were shop boys to control industrialists, Stefani asked, production minimums to replace maximums as official city policy?[77] Our brief analysis has studied the formal mechanisms through which the shop boys created an identity and legitimacy, and those through which government ultimately destroyed it. We have found that the procession *was* politics in the summer of 1378, as always in Florentine life, and that as in any internal crisis, it served to redefine and reaffirm civic identities. Yet in the social revolt the definition of the *communitas florentina* itself had been placed in question: Were male outsiders, the hands and arms of the Florentine economy, to enter the community? The answer at this point was clearly negative. But the question would surface a century later.

External Threat

The vendettas of God become evident after he has long waited and tolerated [us] more.[78]

All the evils that Sulla committed in Rome in ten years Marius revenged in a few days. Do you believe that the justice of God is less than the world's, one for one?[79]

Because of Florence's bad government, my spirit is much disturbed and expects worse in the future. I see that neither signs in the heavens, nor the pestilence of flooding, nor plague, nor famine seems to cause the citizens to fear God. Nor do they recognize their defects and sins, but instead they have completely abandoned holy charity, human and civil. They run the republic with great avarice, like a crooked business or tyranny. Whence I am deathly afraid of the judgment of God.[80]

Such was the tenor of the chroniclers' pronouncements when the hand of God lay upon Florence. Who could protest, in a city full of individual sin, in a polity of unworthy, greedy businessmen? For some Florentines any outside military or natural threat was evidence of God's anger at the city; for others, such disasters might at first be explained by natural causes. But when two or more external threats concatenated, most Florentines quickly convinced themselves that the hand of the Almighty was present, for sympathetic *télé* could not be accidental.[81] Viewing the significance of such threats egocentri-

---

387; Naddo da Montecatini, 26. The first procession mentioned is that celebrating the final peace with the church, on Oct. 25; *Diario d'Anonimo*, 387. The following day a bann ordered all citizens to go, one quarter at a time, to Santo Spirito to be absolved of the excommunications imposed during the war with the church; *ibid.*, 388. A very large funeral service with the whole clergy in attendance took place in December; *Tumulto dei Ciompi*, 89.

77. Rub. 804, 812, 887.

78. Compagni, III, 38. More on the concept of God's vendetta in Giordano da Rivalto–Moreni, *Prediche*, sermon 45, where the saints battle with God to pre-

vent him acting. Also G. di Pagolo Morelli, *Ricordi*, 437, where God sends a great plague.

79. Compagni, II, 1.

80. "Ma al tutto hanno abbandonata la santa carità umana e civile, e solo a baratteria e tirannia con grande avarizia regono la repubblica. Onde mi fa temere forte del giudicio d'Iddio"; G. Villani, XI, 118.

81. Typical is the 1542 report of Segni, after listing a group of disasters, that "stimavano i popoli che tanti segni disusati e rari non fussono venuti a caso, e che e' dovessono significar qualche gran rovina"; *Storie*, 630f.

cally, Florentines quickly traced the ultimate source of the evil to their own sins, which had become intolerable to God the Father. It was always God the Father who punished.

The distinguishing quality of external threats was their opacity of intent. It was not easy to determine quickly whether God's hand was present, and, if so, what particular aspect of Florentine life needed correction. Enter the clergy. From the time danger threatened until the trial was past, Florentine regimes relied heavily upon the urban religious both to determine the true cause of the disorder and, in a typical formulation, to "see if they could find some way one could placate the ire of God against the city and [its] citizens."[82]

Florentine politicans and chroniclers did not readily admit that they had sought out the priests; it was unseemly for virile males to admit impotence and consult virginal clerks, and opened them to the charge that they had spent their time arranging processions instead of practical actions to meet the crisis. Dino Compagni told how he and the other priors in 1301 had followed the recommendation of a holy man and held a procession to calm passions in the city, but had been ridiculed: "Many made fun of us, saying that it was better to heat the irons."[83] Such sterile machismo explains why chroniclers sometimes reported government-sponsored crisis processions with a note of condescension, saying that they were held "to please the clergy" or "on the recommendation of the bishop."[84] For all that, the number of times that the government went to the religious specialists is impressive, though the cases known to us must represent only a fraction. The Signoria doubtless sought out the bishop in 1340 when a comet and a great plague were followed by an enormous hailstorm that covered the city like a large snowfall.[85] In 1399 the bishop was consulted when a crowd of Bianchi descended upon the city.[86] In 1448 the archbishop Antonino responded to a communal request that he help end the plague.[87] In 1499 the Signoria, on the advice of the clergy, decided to observe the feast of the Holy Cross after a series of Standard Bearers had died inexplicably.[88] And in 1530 the government appointed a commission of the clergy to determine why God was angry with Florence and how he could be placated.[89] These samples, chosen at half-century intervals, show that Florentine governments regularly relied upon religious specialists. Omens that might portend future disaster, such as blood-sweating statues and church roofs that caved in, and many other events stimulated the authorities to consult with the clerks.

Generally speaking, these consultants were not members of the ceremo-

82. Varchi, XI, 54.

83. "Seguitammo il suo consiglio; e molti ci schernirono, dicendo che meglio era arrotare i ferri"; Compagni, II, 13.

84. G. Villani, XI, 114 (1340). A fascinating discussion of this charge of obeying *i preti* is in Busini, 107.

85. G. Villani, XI, 114.

86. Ps. Minerbetti, 240ff.

87. *ASF, Prov.*, 139, ff. 125r–126r.

88. Cambi, XXII, 128–131.

89. Varchi, XI, 54.

nial clergy, the honorable prelates and dignitaries who would carry relics or wear brilliant chasubles in the subsequent placative procession. Nor were they members of the cural clergy, those lower-class priests and friars who did the day-to-day work of the ministry. True, bishops were often consulted, but mainly because they were responsible for coordinating the ecclesiastical response. Those most commonly making their opinions felt in the Palace were rather seers or prophets: wandering hermits like the fra Benedetto whom Dino Compagni listened to; holy nuns like Catherine of Siena (1377), suor Maddalena (fl. 1497), and suor Domenica (1528); even an occasional visionary laywoman, usually a widow and thus thought of as a quasi-religious person.[90] Such a person was always of undoubted repute, "with a reputation as a good woman who has always behaved perfectly, a virgin in body and mind, as her confessor testified," for without such credentials she would get no hearing.[91] Personal more than official charisma was the essential qualification. A commune faced with an external disaster it did not understand tended to reach beyond its normal cultic resources to find a secret known only to those liminal personalities outside the official world.[92] In the structural sense all clergy were liminal. But grave external crises showed that only individual religious persons characterized by insight rather than by membership in a distinct social group could pierce the divine mind and determine the correct response.

Usually, these holy men or women first advised the authorities if in fact the disaster was a divine warning or naturally produced, for this would determine the actions of the commune. As one might expect, the clergy in every case we know of urged religious ritual; no case of disaster on record was explained as purely natural.[93] Consultants normally explained that God was

90. The Parte Guelfa played host to Catherine of Siena many times, trying to use her *quasi come profetessa* to foster its politics; Stefani, rub. 773. On Maddalena, see Schnitzer, *Quellen*, IV, 173f; Landucci, 146; P. Villari, *La Storia di Girolamo Savonarola e de' suoi Tempi*, 2 vols. (Florence, 1926), II, cxcvi, clxxvii; Savonarola, *Ezechiele*, I, 305ff. On a *pinzochera* at Santa Maria Novella, see R. Ridolfi, *Studi Savonaroliani* (Florence, 1935), 262. On suor Domenica, see Busini, 46f; Varchi, XI, 105 (1528–1530). Laywomen visionaries active during the Savonarolan period included not only Rucellai, but Vaggia Bisdomini and Bartolomea Gianfigliazzi; Villari, *Savonarola*, II, cxcii. It is most instructive that the Signoria trying to defame Savonarola in 1498 forged a confession from the friar in which he admitted using some of the ideas of the lay *donne* mentioned here, and then stopped seeing the women because he did not want them to claim the ideas were theirs; *ibid*. The chroniclers rarely state directly that the Signoria called in prophets and interpreters of signs, as Compagni does say and as we know it did with Savonarola and Benedetto da Foiano (1529–1530). Note, however, one prior reportedly trying to win over his fellows to a policy by referring

to Camilla Rucellai's dicta; *ibid.*, clxiv, f. On the concourse of men of state to hear what Maddalena had to say, see Schnitzer, *Quellen*, IV, 175. Segni reports that the Signoria in 1530 had hope for the future because of the predictions of the preachers; *Storie*, 263. Ambassadors of the republic visited the simple layman Pieruccio during the same period; Busini, 29f, 46f. On the clerics who came to the Palace in April 1495 to disprove Savonarola's claims of prophetic insight, see Ps. Burlamacchi, 78ff; Schnitzer, *Quellen*, IV, 37; Savonarola, *Giobbe*, II, 310, 433.

91. Schnitzer, *Quellen*, IV, 174 (Parenti).

92. On the use of nonrepresentative liminal forces, see M. Douglas, *Purity and Danger. An Analysis of Concepts of Pollution and Taboo* (London, 1970), 120, 124; Crocker, "Ritual," 61ff.

93. It might, however, take repeated omens before the government convinced itself that God was behind them; Cambi, XXII, 128–131. For a debate on the causes of the flood of 1333, see G. Villani, XI, 2, who tells us most Florentines believed it was caused by avarice, usury, women's dress, drunkenness, and gluttony.

angry with Florentine sins, sometimes specifying the particular delicts. These might be private or structural, their eradication requiring only individual correction or executive action touching general society. From the beginning Savonarola emphasized that homosexuality was responsible for weakening the city, and throughout these years the Officers of the Night assiduously prosecuted those guilty of this crime.[94] In 1528, again, taverns were closed by law because the government had been convinced that the sins committed in them angered God.[95] And in 1530 an official commission of clerks explained to the government that Florentine misfortunes like the siege to which the city was then subject were due to God's ire at Savonarola's execution in 1498.[96] Another favorite explanation was the sumptuousness of dress in the city, and laws against such ostentation were passed in the midst of crisis.[97]

The reports of the religious specialists on the causes of crises went beyond specifics, however, and centered upon the very core sins of an urban order: Usury, leading to a lack of compassion, ended in personal and divine relations without charity. Charity diverted the poor from scandal, furor, and rebellion, Giovanni Villani intoned in commenting on events of the late 1320s.[98] It erased sins, said Archbishop Antonino in the mid-fifteenth century, but also averted tumults and clamor by the famished plebs.[99] Charity was the prerequisite for a stable social order for Savonarola as well: The only way citizens could hope to travel to their villas and repose in leisure was through continual charity while in the city.[100]

Charity's departure was externality's entrance. It was not that formal behavior and elaborate ceremonies were condemnable in themselves, nor that by some inevitable process of routinization Florentines lost the intent that had originally motivated their charity. Indeed preachers stressed that formally executed and public charity was necessary.[101] Yet the demon of idolatry always seduced citizens into mistaking the form for the substance, into following the external law of the Jews rather than the internal law of Christ.[102] The results were "beautiful and respectable ceremonies" without, in Cinozzi's words, "any charity and love of God and neighbor," or in the words so beloved of Savonarola, leaves without fruit, works without enamorative *virtù*.[103]

94. On Savonarola's emphasis, Ridolfi, *Studi*, 262f. The increased activity of the Florentine vice officials was discovered by my former student Thomas Compton in his examination of *ASF, Ufficiali della Notte*.

95. *ASF, Prov.*, 207, ff. 1r–2r (Apr. 7).

96. Varchi, XI, 54.

97. See, for example, n. 93, for the case in 1333, and the immediate sumptuary laws in *ASF, Prov.*, 26, f. 55v (Sept. 24, 1333); *ibid.*, ff. 147v–148r (Aug. 25, 1334). In 1459 the Signoria, in passing a sumptuary law, referred to a popular tract making the rounds that said all citizens agreed that women's sumptuous dress had to be stopped to avoid an imminent calamity; *ASF, Prov.*, 150, ff. 65v–67r; 71r–72r (July 3 and

31). Recall that just three months earlier the sumptuary laws had been waived for the entrance of Pope Pius II; see page 76, this volume.

98. G. Villani, X, 121 (1328–1330).

99. Antoninus, *Chronica . . .*, 3 vols. (Lyon, 1543), bk. XII, ch. 16, sec. 2.

100. I have lost the reference to this Savonarolan inducement.

101. See the explanations offered by Giordano da Rivalto–Moreni, *Prediche*, I, 165.

102. Savonarola, *Giobbe*, I, 381.

103. Villari and Casanova, *Scelta*, 3; Savonarola, *Salmi*, I, 49, 296; *Ezechiele*, II, 168.

If charity's absence was the cause of disaster, a great swell of fraternity was the first step in softening God's anger. Florentine history provided many examples proving that God could be won over. In 1333, Florentines read in Villani's chronicle, charity as well as prayers had rescued the city.[104] God wanted charity, and not just thanks, the same chronicler admonished his readers, but the charity worked only when its emotional sincerity was represented in perfect form.[105] Alms protected a city better than walls, the preacher Bernardino told his audience.[106] The plague might already be in the city, but worse could be avoided through charity, the city fathers told the citizens.[107] In 1453 the government provided alms to the Dominicans because "alms extinguish sin, and often while in the greatest danger our city has been subvented and preserved through the said alms and pious works."[108] From November 1494, when Charles VIII's French army threatened to sack the city on its way to Naples, until June 1495 when he returned north past Florence, citizens persisted in alms as one powerful way of avoiding the French fury; few doubted that these alms had combined with fasting and communion to avert disaster.[109]

The commune often led the way in exemplifying charity. When processions failed to halt earth tremors in 1453, the government ordered £1000 to be distributed to the poor so they would pray God to lift the travail from the better off.[110] Ten years later it spent £140 on the feast of St. Martin in the hope that the saint would help stop a threatened pest.[111] A century later the neighboring commune of Prato automatically responded to the threat of natural disaster with substantial alms to its clergy and other poor.[112] Florentines knew that a commune, just like a sick man, could be saved by charity. Charity, said the archbishop Antonino in the mid-fifteenth century, fully redeemed a city's sins.[113] Speaking of a sick man, the matron Alessandra degli Strozzi perfectly reflected the contemporary attitude toward the city's charity as well: "He gave much money for God, and extracted the prisoners from the prisons. And he did so much that he received the grace of recovery."[114]

Individuals followed the government's lead and the advice of preachers Crises were the right time to vow a gift to a saint, the gift to be given once the saint ended the danger to the city; they were also judicious times to make

104. G. Villani, XI, 2.

105. "Quelli che reggeano il comune per conforto de' religiosi per mostrare alcuna pietà, ordinarono che si traesse certi sbanditi di bando, pagando al comune una certa gabella, e che i beni de rubelli, ch'erano in comune, fossono renduti alle vedove e a' pupilli, a cui succedeano; ma non fu perfetta la grazia e la misericordia che dovesse piacere, perocchè si doveano restituire il prezzo che prima gli aveano, per certi ordini, fatti ricomperare dal comune alle dette vedove e pupilli, e non si fece; onde non ristettono a tanto le nostre pestilenze, che per lo nostro peccato ne seguirono assai appresso"; G. Villani, XI, 114 (1340).

106. Bernardino of Siena, *Prediche* (Siena, 1427), 961.

107. *ASF, Prov.*, 139, ff. 125r–126r (Oct. 3, 1448).

108. *ASF, Prov.*, 144, ff. 32rv (Aug. 17).

109. Schnitzer, *Delfin*, 336ff.

110. Pietrobuoni, f. 165r.

111. *ASF, Prov.*, 154, ff. 227v–228v (Nov. 8, 1463).

112. Di Agresti, *S. Caterina de' Ricci. Cronache . . . ,* xlix, 114ff.

113. Antonius, *Chronica*, bk. XII, ch. 16, sec. 2.

114. Strozzi, *Lettere*, 326 (1464).

one's peace with one's terrestrial enemies, and forgive debts and obligations.[115] In the Savonarolan period—the one time in Florentine republican history when we find a mass response of this kind sufficiently documented—the results of homiletic exhortation were impressive. In December 1494 different collections were held in the main churches for the "shamed poor" of the city and *contado*. Do not come to the altar empty-handed, the friar admonished in the midst of divine services. Convinced that the welfare of the city depended on citizens giving, he insisted that all who had unjustly taken usurious interest return it, including that owed to the biggest victim of all, the commune.[116] The results were again impressive. Streaming to the bishop's palace, Florentines returned some 40,000 ducats and received absolution.[117]

The success of these exhortations could be considerable, even though Florentine property owners feared that the constant pressure for philanthropy, and the demands for restitution, represented a de facto attack on obligations. Most were willing to accept the fact that the crisis had arisen because of an unjust distribution of property in the city. But it was one thing for an exemplary commune to forgive debts to it and allow bankrupts back into the city, and quite another for the government and friendly preachers to argue that the city's charity would be "imperfect" if citizens did not return their usurious interest to the robbed commune, especially when it was suggested that the government had a moral duty to force the citizens to do so. The stratagem was almost as old as the public debt itself.[118] The endless pressure of the religious specialists upon citizens to restitute or forgive the claims they had on other citizens or inhabitants was no more reassuring to creditors. Thus Savonarola and the citizens had to sail between the Scylla of either doing nothing or giving charity to persons they did not know and to whom they had no obligation (which would be imperfect charity annoying to God), and the Charybdis of endangering the principle of contract. Responding from the pulpit to fears of this type, the Dominican emphasized that he did not favor communal or individual default, but did wish to save the city. And his success in this navigation astounded contemporaries. Ideal charity, like the ideal procession, threatened the foundations upon which society was built.

Holy men and women had explained the causes of the crisis to the government and people, and urged countless acts of public and private charity as a first step in meeting that threat. Now they recommended prayers, both for the organized religious and for the laity. Preachers specified the content of the latter's prayers. Here, as so often typical of traditional practice,

---

115. Buonaccorso Pitti tells how the Bianchi pilgrims—warning of the dire vengeance of God—brought about "many reconciliations between citizens"; *Memoir*, 62.

116. This and most of the following are based on Savonarola, *Aggeo*, 256, 338f, 355; *Ruth e Michea*, II, 69.

117. Filipepi gives this figure; Villari and Casanova, *Scelta*, 477. The ritual setting of the restitutions is referred to in Landucci, 96.

118. For its use in the fourteenth century, see Trexler, "Florence by the Grace," 150 seq.

Savonarola recommended that literate Florentines read the ecclesiastical office, and the illiterate might either listen to or say a given number of Hail Marys and Our Fathers. Morning prayers were best, said Bernardino of Siena, the devil being more active in the evening, and Latin prayers were clearly superior to those in the common language. Prayers said within social structures such as the family were better than individual prayers, the idea being that unified prayer was hard for the deity to resist: "Let us gather together for our *virtù* is small. United it has great force."[119]

The ritual response moved toward its most public phase, the sermons and procession. Florentines stepped carefully, watching for signs that their procedures were acceptable to God. They knew from their own history, for example, that to turn back crisis one should first pray to God the Father, and only then to the Virgin. Some had read in the writings of Matteo Villani that in 1354 God the Father without the Virgin "did not work," and in 1435 the Virgin without previous prayers to God the Father proved just as fruitless.[120] In now choosing the images and relics that would be carried in the procession, the religious specialists and the government used similar care. Talismans that had lost their previous efficacy in processions were quietly ignored; for example, the miraculous relic at Sant' Ambrogio that in 1340 had failed to halt a concatenation of natural disasters never again appeared in processions.[121] Other objects were unsuitable for use in crisis; the sacred host, for instance, was apparently never borne during external crises. The central object of worship during crisis from the mid-fourteenth century forward was the Lady of Impruneta, but even she had to be brought into the city sparingly and carefully revered, the tabus on her handling being strictly observed. She was most often propitiated during drought, one chronicler tells us; another source suggested that her beneficial effects on the weather might be felt either in field or town.[122] Florence was her favorite object of pilgrimage, however, for her devotees were there. Occasionally other Virgins accompanied her, and they were joined by relics, "all the relics of the saints of Florence and the *contado*," one chronicler exaggerated.[123] Relics of San Giovanni Gualberti were especially popular, as was the head of San Zanobi, the arm of St. Philip, and the unsurpassed cache from the Carthusian house of the Certosa, home of the most rigorous religious group in the area.[124]

Once the public response to the situation had been determined and cleared with the government, it was explained to the faithful in sermons. The preachers detailed the gathering places, clothing, order, and times, and exhorted the populace to show the devotion and charity that were the precon-

119. For references to this material on recommended prayers, see pages 99f, this volume. Savonarola's *congreghiamoci* is in *Ruth e Michea*, I, 404f.

120. See my "Image," 13f, 21, for the appropriate texts.

121. For its last use, see G. Villani, XI, 114.

122. A *pratica* of May 9 (*sic*) considered the bad harvest weather: "Pensassimo se fusse da fare venir la tavola della Impruneta, o farla andare supra li monti"; Roth, *Last Republic*, 153; the usual use of the Lady is stated by Varchi, XII, 61.

123. Naddo da Montecatini, 64 (1383).

124. *Ibid.*, 98f (1388), 106f (1389). See also M. Villani, IV, 7 (1354).

dition of success. The preprocessional sermon had the dual and paradoxical purpose of calming and spiritualizing the devotees in an atmosphere heavy
with the sense of great impending happenings. The sermon itself was also
part of the unfolding patterned behavior, preachers and audience manipulating each other in an undulating flow of emotions aimed at spiritualizing the
community and each individual.[125] On the eve of the ultimate expression of
communal repentance, great preachers like Giordano da Rivalto, Bernardino
of Siena and of Feltre, and Savonarola could well make their audiences
believe that the church was full of angels far outnumbering the devils.[126] On
the following day, these angels would drive the devils from the air of the city.

THE CRISIS PROCESSION

How different was the procession of crisis from the communal celebration! And how frequent! Far from an occasional insertion into a calendar of
stability, it was an almost regular occurrence. In those periods when chroniclers of Florentine affairs allow us to tabulate them, we find that, excluding the
calendrical processions of propitiation on the rogation days and during Holy
Week, crisis processions were held an average of once a year, and often two
or even three processional cycles of this type were held in the course of one
year.[127]

The procession might be limited to a single day, but in many crises
experts recommended a three-day penitential march similar to those on the
rogation days. Fifteenth-century devotees were at other times urged to participate in processions held in three of the quarters of the city on three
successive days, followed by a general crisis procession of the whole city in
the quarter of San Giovanni. In one case propitiative processions lasted a
novena; in another they went on for a week; and in still another case, they
were held each Sunday during Lent. The options were many and depended
on the meaning of the crisis as interpreted by the religious specialists. What
follows here is a summary of the general procession, the only type for which
we possess extensive documentation.

The evening before the culminating Florentine procession of crisis, the
confraternity and canons of the *pieve* of Santa Maria of Impruneta set out for
Florence bearing their precious Lady, suitably veiled and protected.[128] They

125. On this mutual manipulation, see pages 117f,
this volume.

126. Telling the faithful how many angels or demons
were in a church commented, of course, on the emotional state of the crowd; see, for example, Bernardino of Siena, *Prediche* (Florence, 1424), I, 212; II, 160;
Savonarola, *Aggeo*, 214, 244; *Giobbe*, I, 258.

127. A few examples from the pre-Savonarolan
period: plague and concatenation in 1340, G. Villani,
XI, 114; plague in 1347, *ibid.*, XII, 84; wind and rain in
1347, *ibid.*, XII, 91; plague in 1390, Panciatichi, f. 160r,
and again in 1391, ASF, *Missive*, 22, f. 139v; earth

tremors in 1414, Del Corazza, 254; imminent
danger of plague in 1417, ASF, *Prov.*, 107, ff. 103r–
104r; earth tremors in 1453, Pietrobuoni, f. 165r.
Many of these actually comprised several processions. For a list of the processions during the siege of
Florence in 1529–1530, see ch. 13, this volume. The
figure of one per year results from a tabulation of
those in the anonymous Panciatichi chronicle.

128. The following is a general picture gleaned from
specifics. The picture, of course, varied from time to
time. On the confraternity, see ASF, *Prov.*, 60, ff.
30v–31r (June 8, 1372); *ibid.*, 107, ff. 110r–111r (June

marched to candlelight, attracting lay suburbanites who joined behind the procession. As the solemn cortège moved down the Impruneta road, other individuals and groups of *contadini* also made their several ways toward the city so as to arrive before dawn, when Our Lady could be expected to reach the gate of San Piero Gattolino.[129]

Early in the morning Florentines prepared for the day's crucial activities. Perhaps they fasted or prayed at home as recommended by their preachers. Shops were closed, of course, so that when they left home they might go instead to the church housing their favorite saint, asking blessings for the ceremonies about to unfold. In the later republic, it was common for many to go to the Servite church of the Annunziata before a procession, perhaps vowing to gift the Virgin there if the procession were a success—we do not know how the Lady of the Annunziata reacted to her colleague from Impruneta.[130] At given moments the sacred image of the Annunziata might be unveiled to those assembled, and this would unfailingly release a flood of tears, cries of *Misericordia*! so shattering and attractive to others in the street that the Lady sometimes had to be reveiled to calm the people.[131] Devotees seeking to prepare for the procession could not do better than to put themselves at the mercy of this (immobile) Lady before her peripatetic relation arrived from Impruneta.

At the break of dawn the streets were alive with anticipation. From the area of the cathedral came a procession of canons, chaplains, and altar boys bearing their great relics, and from other sections of the city other groups of clergy and some penitential confraternities also headed to the gate to welcome Impruneta, each group carrying its own relics and perhaps an important image.[132] From the distance, communal trumpeters announced the approach of the Lady and her retinue, a sight that could be truly impressive. In one such arrival in 1487, Tribaldo de' Rossi found the procession four miles long before it reached the gate, there to be joined by the Florentines.[133] The sun had risen, and the Lady entered the city.

Now accompanied as well by the Florentine clergy and often by some of the city's confraternities, the Lady proceeded down the main street toward the Ponte Vecchio until she arrived in the piazza of San Felice. Installed in a distinguished place, she watched as the whole procession of ecclesiastical and confraternal elements marched before her.[134] At times the Signoria was there,

28, 1417). In 1487 the procession left Impruneta at the Ave Maria, and arrived at Florence at dawn; Rossi, 236. In 1499 this was "customary"; Rinuccini, clxiii.

129. On the normal tendency of *contadini* to come to Florence during crisis for religious purposes, see Segni, *Storie*, 630f. The commune heightened this by ordering all companies within a certain area around the city to come; see, for example, Rossi, 237, 294f. The anonymous chronicler in 1377 noted the "molta compagnia del paese"; *Diario d'Anonimo*, 341.

130. See, for example, Segni, *Storie*, 630f (1542).

131. The passage in Segni, *loc. cit.*, suggests that in

the sixteenth century the Lady of the Annunziata was an important image for dealing with natural disasters. For information on her incredible power over contemporaries, see Landucci, 281, 287; Masi, 173; Varchi, IV, 4; Dorini, "Ragguagli," 61f; "Storia . . . Carnesecchi," 108.

132. S. Zanobi normally accompanied the Virgin and he was brought to the gate by the cathedral clergy.

133. Rossi, 286f.

134. The most extensive description of the procession at S. Felice is in Francesco Filarete; Trexler, *Libro*, 128f (1522).

suitably dressed in penitentially simple clothing, perhaps arrayed on either side of the Virgin. At crucial points in the ceremony at S. Felice, Mary was first undressed, then re-dressed with gifts formally presented to her, and finally the veil was lifted from her face. She now saw her city.[135]

From this point her itinerary varied.[136] But wherever she went in the city during this day (and she did insist on being out of the city by evening) her miraculous effects upon individual dispositions and savage heavens made themselves felt.[137] At every step of the way those who lined the streets joined in after she had passed, so that by the time she had completed her itinerary, *tutta la città* followed in her wake. The idea was that devotees in their neighborhoods, attracted by the charisma of their clergy and icons, would be irresistibly drawn into and converted by the procession.

Not uncommonly, the Lady of Impruneta visited the Piazza della Signoria toward the end of her stay and there became the center of an enormous outdoor service in that spectacular setting. The anonymous Panciatichi chronicler describes a stupendous altar with retable that held all the relics and images, and all the singers and performers during a 1390 procession against the plague:

> They put [the *tavola* of Santa Maria of Impruneta] in the Piazza of the Signori on the *ringhiera*. They had made a very large platform and on it stood the clerks, the lord priors, and their colleagues. And [they had made] another above it, where *messer* the bishop stood to sing Mass. [And there were] several other very ornate platforms still higher up. There stood the multitude of relics that [, being elevated,] every one in the Piazza could see. And there was a platform for the orphans and for the cantors. And the bishop preached during the Mass.[138]

At such grand penitential events those thousands who had accompanied the Lady jammed the square so tightly that in 1432 women and children fainted.[139] In 1389 Naddo da Montecatini described a scene of this type, adding the fact that the windows of the surrounding houses were full of people:

> The office was beautiful, large, and honorable. Truly in the Piazza and among the [surrounding] houses hearing the office there were some 25,000 Christians or more, between young and grown, males and females, devoutly praying Our Lady to

135. For the dressing, see Rinuccini, clxiii; Landucci, 199 (1499). The first account I find of ritual gifts being given her while in Florence is in 1467; L. Morelli, 183. After that they seem to have been a normal part of the ceremonies.

136. Perhaps the most common route took her to the cathedral, then along the Via Tornabuoni across the Ponte S. Trinita and back to S. Felice. An unusually extensive itinerary may be found in Rossi, 237 (1487).

137. The story of the Lady's insistence on being out of town by nightfall (Varchi, X, 37) is described in my "Image," along with other details of her visits.

138. "E posesi i sulla piaza de signiori, e quivi i sulla ringhiera, fatto un grandissimo palcho dove stetono e cherici, e signiori priori e loro cholegi, e uno palchc più alto dove stette messer lo veschovo a cantare la messa, e più palchi più alti molti adorni dove stette la moltitudine delle reliquie che ogni uno di sulla piazza le potea vedere, e uno palcho per gli orphani e pe' cantori, e predichò messer lo veschovo fra la messa"; Panciatichi, f. 160r. See the diagram based on this description in ch. 2, n. 15, this volume. The first mention I find of such stands is in *Diario d' Anonimo*, 341 (1377: "bello palchetto").

139. Palmieri, *Historia*, 136f.

gracefully pray her son Jesus Christ that he mercifully in his piety guard this city from every danger, and that he send peace, concord, abundance, and good to all Christians, and especially to this city and its *contado*, subject areas, and *distretto*. And may it please Christ that this be. Amen.[140]

It was not unusual for chroniclers like Naddo to be swept from reportage to such personal invocation. The scene at the end of a great procession, with the whole city packed in the Piazza, was enough to move many scribes. The sense of wonderment at the amazing effects of the procession informs many accounts. Thus in 1377 when the commune observed a papal interdict and its clergy refused to take part in services, the laity held what one chronicler called "secular processions," which were highly charged with these qualities. Stefani thought a "compunction had seized all the citizens," so that

every day . . . processions with relics and hymns were followed by the whole population. Every company beat themselves, including children down to ten years of age. There were certainly more than 5000 flagellants at processions and more than 20,000 people followed the procession.[141]

Reporting on the same processions, an anonymous diarist described banners and *tavole*, crucifixes and standards, the flagellation, the weeping, and the lauds, ending his report with the familiar individual invocation:

They begged almighty God to put in the heart of the Holy Father the pope a will to open his heart to sinners, to send to him and to us holy peace here and in the whole world so that we together with him will stand in the grace of Our Lord *messere Domeneddio*. Regard not our defects and sins, since one ought to do His will, and at our end lead us to His holy kingdom. Amen.[142]

To the humanist Matteo Palmieri in 1432, the popular pressure for procession, and the effect of the latter, seemed little less than incredible:

Since the plebs was burdened with a great scarcity of food and the imminent dangers of war, it was decided to placate God through supplications, [through] the operation of prayers. Therefore all religious [persons] were ordered to process through the city for ten days and to intercede for the salvation of the city, and similarly the whole *popolo* was to follow, and the days were indicated. These began on May 30, and at first some of course were remiss. But later, on the third day, when victory [over the Sienese] had transpired, so much faith was placed in such purgations and supplications that numbers grew daily. And by the ninth day opinions were so strong that someone who didn't follow the jubilant people's procession with various hymns and psalms was as good as shamed.[143]

When Our Lady of Impruneta entered, the crowds were enormous, and Palmieri was struck with wonder at what this could mean:

140. Naddo da Montecatini, 107.

141. On these processions, see my *Spiritual Power*, 131.

142. *Ibid.*, 132.

143. "Adeo opinio creverat, ut fere rubesceret, qui non sequeretur populo . . . "; Palmieri, *Historia*, 136f.

The whole city was there, and the line of religious [people] stretched [from the Piazza della Signoria] back to the church of [S]. Felice: men first, then women crying aloud together for the help of the Virgin with almost wondrous fervor. And when finally the *popolo* had processed through the city and the Ponte de Santa Trinita and returned to the Piazza dei Signori, it was such a multitude that every space was densely packed, so that many children and women were breathless from the density and could not stand erect. I have made note of all this because rarely are such concourses of supplication effected by our *popolo*, and especially by men. It is believed this must certainly presage something.[144]

Clearly, such emotional outbursts were spontaneous, even if in many cases the government encouraged such excitement. If it did not organize the procession, the populace took the matter in hand itself. On the day of solstice 1543 there was an earthquake at Scarperia, and in the same instant lightning struck the Palazzo della Signoria and the cupola of the *duomo*. The historian Bernardo Segni agreed with the popular feeling that this simultaneity was not accidental, and reported the efforts of the populace to avoid future disaster:

These prodigies were purged in Florence by many vows and many public processions of all the *popolo* of the dominion, who flowed to the Annunziata, women and men, youth and old mixed together: not because of any public command, but driven by their own consciences.[145]

I have sketched both the course of crisis processions and the palpable impact they had upon participants and chroniclers. Now it is necessary to examine the form of the processional city, for here more than anywhere else the immediate cause of the emotional reaction to these events must be sought.

First of all, the classical procession of remorse was ideally a demonstration without terrestrial witnesses. The repeated statements of the earliest chroniclers that "the whole city" was involved in the procession was not mere exaggeration; in later periods, we find preachers and governments forbidding men, women, and boys to watch the procession from the sidelines; they were either to join in or go inside, and close both windows and doors.[146] Not only did such attempts at totality appease the divinities, but they helped avoid the cancer of idolatry by concentrating all attention and activity upon the gods and not upon the participants.

Second, the city preparing for processions insisted that the sexes be rigidly separated.[147] Florentines approaching their churches might encounter guards directing each sex to separate entrances, and on entering the church

144. "Hec ideo annotavi, quia raro a nostro populo et maxime ab hominibus hos suppliciorum concursus efficiuntur, et nunc certo creditur aliquid presagire"; *ibid.* Palmieri seems to be suggesting that the men marched in procession (and were moved by the spirit to do so) with political aims.

145. Segni, *Storie*, 630f.

146. Landucci, 90f (1494); Savonarola, *Ruth e Michea*,

I, 269f (no women standing in the streets like whores; if one cannot take part, s/he should stay inside); Masi, 230–233 (1518). For the normal practice of leaning out windows during processions, see Naddo da Montecatini, 106f (1389); Schnitzer, *Quellen*, IV, 159ff (1497).

147. See, for example, *ibid.*, 26f; Nardi, I, 47; Landucci, 92ff (all 1494); Savonarola, *Salmi*, I, 305; *Ruth e Michea*, II, 321.

find the traditional sexual divisions of the church absolutely enforced.[148] Just as laxness in maintaining distinct sexual roles and dress might be the cause of the crisis, its solution, the preacher could tell his audience, lay in processionally manifesting sexual clarity to the divinities. Women would be as prominent in the ritual of external crisis as they were mute in internal crisis and in the ritual of celebration. Each sex had a role to play in resolving the crisis, and only once in the republican era were women excluded both from sermons and processions during a crisis.[149] But they would play this crucial role clearly marked off and separate from men.

A third characteristic of the crisis procession was the glaring emphasis on the distinction between clergy and laity. The former led the procession dressed in their richest possible vestments and bearing their accumulated treasures of relics and images, many of which were framed by coats of arms and other symbols of social authority. The clergy in crisis was not expected to humiliate itself in procession; rather, it was to vaunt its wealth.[150] Yet behind this opulent clergy came a laity divested of symbols of wealth and secular station. Gone were the rich clothing and the political divisions of the celebratory processions. The only lay corporate division in the crisis processions was between penitential confraternities, and they too wore penitential cloth. The city would represent its laity to the divinity not as a political order glorying in that order, but as socially if not sexually indistinct brothers and sisters. "All kinds of people," said the chroniclers, joined the procession.[151]

The clergy in front fulfilled several roles. First, they carried the sacred talismans, cross in front, which were the best hope, the greatest value, of a commune in travail. Second, sinful worldings used the clergy as an innocent body of powerless men to disarm a wrathful God, and the precedence of the younger clergy before the older reflected this intention. Third, these innocents appeared covered with the wealth of the Florentines. They were the embodiment of the eleemosynary munificence of the mature males. It was the ordered and honorable retinue these clergy provided for the sacred talismans that was meant to move the deity, rather than the individual qualities, prayers, or actions of these clergy.

Much the same can be said of certain lay individuals who were sometimes placed between the clergy and the laity proper: prisoners or indigents, by definition excluded from the social body, who were washed, dressed in rich clothes, and otherwise identified as clients of the laity, and marched to

---

148. "Diario d'Incerto," 147 (1530).

149. *Ibid.*, 148; Varchi, XI, 67. Women and boys were sometimes excluded from sermons during stress because they were thought less intelligent; Nardi, I, 47; Ps. Burlamacchi, 109f. And in 1497 women were excluded from the fire trial of Savonarola so there would be no scandal by this frivolous and ignorant sex; Schnitzer, *Quellen*, IV, 257f.

150. Specifically stating the clergy was richly attired in the 1414 anti-earth tremor procession is Del Cor-

azza, 254. In the wake of the rich ceremonial clergy the friars marched in their simple frocks.

151. "Dietro al cero andorno tutti gli uomini, cioè il popolo e ciptadini, e plebei tutti mescholati insieme"; Cambi, XXII, 140 (1518 anti-Turkish procession). In 1495 the whole *popolo*, poor and rich, noble and ignoble, followed the procession; Schnitzer, *Quellen*, IV, 62f (Parenti). In 1542 at the Annunziata, women and men, youth and old, were mixed together, presumably not during procession, but in church; Segni, *Storie*, 630f.

the altar to be offered to God or, in another contemporary view, to offer the commune to him.[152] The clergy in front was the city's institutionalized liminal body; the nameless prisoners or poor dressed by this same laity could also mediate the burghers with the godhead.

The role of the male laity that followed was to represent charity in action. This was done first by confounding the traditional forms of the city, and presenting to the deity a socially indistinct male body, "with everyone mixed together,"[153] betters associating equally and indiscriminately with lesser men. And it was done through action: In one fourteenth-century case "everyone" in a procession flagellated, equally guilty before the punishing God.[154] In others, lay *confratri* circulated through the lay orders with collection plates showing this charity in action; the alms collected in the procession might then be carried to the Lady of the Annunziata so she could see the results of processional fraternity.[155] Thus the static moral virtue of the clergy in front was followed by a sacred representation of moral action behind, these good works showing the fraternal solidarity of all mature males.

Women brought up the rear of the procession, in Palmieri's liturgical cadence "clamoring as one for the Virgin's aid with almost wondrous fervor" ("conclamantes auxilium Virginis fervore fere mirabili").[156] While nuns stayed inside and prayed, lay women marched in prayer. They were an essential part of the crisis procession, in 1399 required along with their children to take part in the novena processions of the Bianchi although men had the option of doing so or not,[157] their humility in flagellating with their children in 1377 taken by male contemporaries as evidence of the spiritual zeal of the whole citizenry.[158] Their classical role in the crisis procession, however, was not creative but indicative. As in the funeral procession their vocal mourning was intended to point to the deceased, so in the crisis procession they called the divinities' attention to the *pietas* of their husbands' work and charity.[159] In back, farthest from the *sacra*, their passionate dirge forced God to witness what went before: the charitable action of Florentine men, and the results of that action as seen on the backs and in the hands of the clergy. Demonstrating neither the quasi-iconic stature of the clergy, nor the dramatic participation of their men, women played an instrumental role in propitiating God toward a polis that was not theirs.

152. The former view is clear in 1436 when the Florentines donated a group of prisoners to Eugenius IV, who then offered them to God and freed them; G. Manetti, "Oratio . . . de saecularibus et pontificalibus pompis in consecratione basilicae florentinae habitis," in *Umanesimo e Esoterismo* (Padua, 1960), 318. For the latter view, see Pietrobuoni, f. 165r.

153. See n. 151, this chapter.

154. Trexler, *Spiritual Power*, 130–135 (1377). I have been unable to confirm flagellation in public crisis processions after this date.

155. This was the procedure followed by Savonarola; *Aggeo*, 169; Schnitzer, *Delfin*, 348. Some opposed it for the implicit pride of such procedures: "Elemosynae in omnium oculis mendicate, tubis canentibus, contra edictum tamen Salvatoris per urbem delatae"; *ibid.*, 393, 395.

156. Palmieri, *Historia*, 136f.

157. Ps. Minerbetti, 241f.

158. Trexler, *Spiritual Power*, 131.

159. On such use of women at funerals, see G. Manzi, *Discorso di G. M. sopra gli Spettacoli, le Feste, ed il Lusso degl'Italiani nel secolo XIV* (Rome, 1818), 75f. One of many cases in Florence is in Ps. Minerbetti, 183.

It is time to summarize, briefly, this interpretation of the classical procession of external crisis. Male and female religious specialists characterized by their insight rather than by their corporate order explained the cause of the crisis and offered prescriptions for its solution. Yet the procession in the public glare of God's eyes featured a ceremonial and institutionalized rather than charismatic and individualistic clergy, bearing consensually valid images that had previously proven their ability to perform miracles without disturbing social equilibrium. In the midst of material want, this front segment moved in procession covered with wealth. The mature males followed, pushing before them (hiding behind, so to speak) their miraculous talismans and their richly attired clergy. Their mien was humble, their clothing simple. Yet they themselves were not passive breast-beaters, but participants in a theater of fraternal exchange. Their institutionalized charitable instincts were embodied in the opulent clergy and talismans they had funded; their spontaneous charity was mirrored in their own classlessness; their social authority was proved by their crying women. In happier times women were mannequins used to celebrate their husbands' wealth; now women's pious wailing for the commune of their men proved the existence of sexual order in a processional society where all men were equal. The mature males ultimately put more faith in the ability of their images, clergy, and charity to sway God than in the spiritual force of their women and children.

Infection

In normal times and during most crises, mature males dominated ritual space. Women were present in domestic celebrations, but as sacred dolls for their husbands' wealth; in crisis, they normally only called attention to their husbands' placatory charity. Youth had no role in processional life during this classical period. Children were seldom mentioned, and had no clear processional role as yet.[160] The male subjects of the city, unseen in celebration, either exploded onto the streets in social revolt or, during the external crisis, mixed with the political males as objects of ritual charity. In many traditional societies, the deeper and more obscure the crisis and its origins, the more the marginal social groups assumed central representational roles in solving it. Urban Florence seems to have defied that law in the classical period, and to have relied mostly on its political laymen, and on the "mobile identity" of its male clergy, to resolve crisis.[161] The command of this laity and clergy over the representational center of Florentine processional life is one of the most impressive phenomena of this city.

Yet in one type of disaster, this ruling strata of Florentine society seized

160. For their development see ch. 11, this volume.   161. This concept is explained on page 3, this volume.

the first opportunity to desert home, work, and community. Stefani described their behavior during plague, and the prospects it opened up:

> In the same year [1383] and month of July there was a plot in the city of Florence hatched by the *minuti*. They estimated that the plague . . . was heavy in the city of Florence, and many citizens had fled, [and] believed that their moment had come. . . . The said plot was discovered. . . . In the [next] year many laws were passed that no citizens could leave because of the said plague. For they feared that the *minuti* would not leave, and would rise, and the malcontents would unite with them. . . . [But] it was still impossible to keep [the citizens in the city] . . . , for it is always so that large and powerful beasts jump and break fences.[162]

Plague was at first an external danger. Inhabitants heard of its location, judged its projectile, and undertook ritual processions to divert God's wrath. It became an internal danger once it entered the city, infecting personal relations, poisoning class contacts, making suspect even the relations between the government and the city. Just as this outside threat became an internal terror, so the outsiders who inhabited the city could become the only insiders if the citizens chose to leave. To study formal responses to plague is to understand at a deeper level the Florentines' attitude toward margins and edges, and to grasp the concealed despair in the face of a phenomenon that ultimately defied comprehension.

The advent of plague caused men to ask why it had struck and how it could be countered. They first studied the profiles of victims to determine the sociology of plague, then attempted to interpret the divine meaning behind those results. Florentines developed distinctions between the effects of plague upon different ages, for example. Stefani noted in 1383 that "many good men died, but [the plague] was found more among the young and children than among men and women of mature age."[163] Landucci in 1497 reported the opposite results of plague watching: The elderly of both sexes were dying, as well as male heads of families, but young boys and women of childbearing age were surviving. For Landucci the message was clear: God wanted the world to continue.[164]

Florentines also distinguished between the impact of plague upon different social classes. When Alessandra degli Strozzi in the mid-fifteenth century found the plague in the poor areas of the city, she thought it a sign that the "good people" of Florence could still be saved.[165] Writing more than half a century later, Giovanni Cambi interpreted the presence of the plague among the poor as a divine warning that the honest bourgeoisie had to congregate and demonstrate together, not flee. If the solid citizens left the city, or if the government of Florence forbade such expiatory gatherings, Cambi thought,

162. Stefani, rub. 954–956. The same thinking lay behind a patrician conspiracy in 1457; ser Giusto, f. 71v.

163. Stefani, rub. 955.

164. Landucci, 155, 158.

165. Strozzi, *Lettere*, 281, 314. Sociological estimates of the 1400 plague effects are in Mazzei, I, 248f; II, 348. In 1437: "Ci fa danno, ma in giente di bassa mano, fanciulli et fanciulle il più forte . . . ; la terra è molta vota di gente da bene"; cited in Molho, "Cosimo," 10, n. 9.

God would see that the good people also rejected him and did not heed his warning. Punishment followed: Plague spread into the "honest classes."[166]

This sociology of plague rested on certain attitudes toward social order. First, the marginal groups in society became bellwethers of the fate of the political class, and of its familes. Citizens were uncertain if the lower class was susceptible to plague or possessed some cunning immunity to it, preserving its solidarity while citizens broke and ran; they were unsure as well if plague struck the plebs because of their own lowly sins, or as an ominous prelude to the meek inheriting the earth if "good men" did not reform. But in any interpretation, all social groups and classes became interlocking parts of the whole in conceptualizing the meaning of plague. Second, this science of plague watching and interpretation presumed that there were effective procedures available for dealing with plague. These might involve direct contacts between affected and unaffected groups of the population,[167] or they might, as Cambi suggested, involve those not infected coming together apart from the afflicted. But in any case, plague was a reason for solidarity, not individualism. Third and most fundamental, these commentators clung to the basic precept of urban society, that the demonstration and articulation of social bonds were necessary and efficacious means by which to maintain and create community; ritual created life.

Governments during plague certainly accepted the basic idea of solidarity, encouraging their supporting classes not to leave the city by marketing variations on that great countermyth of the propertied:

> [The poor] would run through the city, robbing, killing, and driving out all the rich and good men. [They would] take their goods, and wall up and barricade the mouths of the streets, and reduce the city to a small circumference. . . . And in this small circle [they would] become strong with these goods, then sell the city to the highest bidder, then leave with these goods for Siena, and there remain and live with their riches.[168]

The myth implied that the *sottoposti* had some hidden strength unknown to the rich. Yet those same governments did not generally favor congregations or gatherings in the city during plague, and followed the lead of the doctors in strictly limiting rights of association. The governmental program accepted a wide-ranging calcification of familial, business, and governmental ties.

These prescriptions were not easy to accept, and from the beginning of the great plagues in the mid-fourteenth century until the end of the republic and beyond, governments and citizens alternated between enforcement of hygienic regulations and recourse to processional solidarities. In 1340 Villani found the city "completely full of lamentation and pain, and one was doing nothing but burying the dead." To counter the danger of infection, and as Villani said to get the population back to work, the government ordained that people leave the churches as soon as they had delivered bodies there.[169] Yet

166. Cambi, XXII, 219–222, 236ff; XXIII, 13.
167. On citizens bringing food to the poor *morbati* in 1400, see Mazzei, I, 243.
168. This primal fear is in Stefani, rub. 804, in the context not of plague, but of the Ciompi plots.
169. G. Villani, XI, 114.

when the scourge continued, the pressure to go in procession could become irresistible. In 1340, in 1383, again in 1457, and later, Florentines went in procession despite, and in the midst of, the danger of plague.[170] The crisis procession not only demonstrated a unity of will that God could not ignore, but provided the opportunity of intra- or interclass fraternity between privileged and underprivileged that was one important way of placating God. Suppressing processions eliminated that possibility, as did the citizens' flight from the city. Until the end of the period, many believed the absence of processional solidarity to be the cause rather than the result of plague. How ineradicable was the faith in solidarity's victory over death. At the beginning of the great plagues, Giovanni Boccaccio spoke of those who countered the "cruelty of heaven" with "humble supplications which devout persons made to God both in planned processions and in other guises."[171] And at the end of the republic Giovanni Cambi still protested the victory of social alienation over solidarity, of physical salvation over religious fraternity:

> This seemed a great abomination, for in tempestuous times one customarily turns to God, but we have made ourselves suspicious of the feasts of God and of the saints. . . . For we chose to first make human rather than divine provisions.[172]

Cambi's sentiments fell on deaf ears; many of those who could, fled. They had internalized, even if they could not utter the lesson of a crisis where gods and saints were dangerous to one's health and the faithful's processional efforts only worsened the crisis.[173] The clergy not only proved powerless, but in cloister died like flies. Lay liminal groups had as yet no creative function in crisis, and the city did not yet think of its caritative institutions as places where spiritual infection might overcome the physical infection in the streets.[174] No phenomenon contributed more to individualism than plague, none isolated the conflict between community and salvation so clearly.

Yet what meaning did an individual have apart from his bonds, what identity distinct from the forms of dominance and fraternity in which he lived, what means of expression other than the language of his body and mouth, what growth in a theater without audience? Cambi's outcries against civic authorities who seemed intent on ruining the city by forbidding ritual gatherings flew in the teeth of hygienic consequences. His moving cry for faith in God before faith in man expressed as nothing else could the inherent conflict of all urban existence, which crisis ritual did its best to meliorate: a local cosmology in an inexorable universe of scientific law, a belief in action crossed by the awful vision of powerlessness.

170. In 1340, the commune had originally tried to avoid contact in churches, but held a procession when the scourge continued; *ibid*. In 1383 a procession was held in the midst of plague; Naddo da Montecatini, 64f. In 1457 a procession was held after unsuccessful attempts at isolation; Pietrobuoni, f. 175r.

171. Boccaccio, *Opere*, 14, 19.

172. Cambi, XXI, 237; XXIII, 12f.

173. Naddo constructs his sequence of reportage of events in 1383 in such a way as to communicate to the reader his own despair; Naddo da Montecatini, 62–66.

174. On these later developments, see ch. 11, this volume.

PART **IV**

THE RITUAL REVOLUTION

. . . for theirs is the kingdom, power,
and glory.

Public ritual was a means through which Florentines attempted *to resolve the central problems of the city's political and social order: trust, honor, and credit at home and abroad. This was no less true in the later republic, when the resolution of these inherent conflicts could no longer be avoided, when the salvation of Florence as an independent political entity was constantly at stake. Now large national entities both Italian and ultramontane pressed upon Florence with enormous resources. These neofeudal states were forthrightly aristocratic and authoritarian in both political and artistic cultures; to them Florence's determination to maintain its republican order seemed parochial, archaic, and self-destructive. "It is a pity so beautiful a woman [as Florence] has no husband," one prelate commented in the mid-fifteenth century.*

"Yes, but she has a paramour," the interlocutor responded, referring to the Medici.[1] *Ultimately, the republic would have to develop an incontrovertibly charismatic center, and to do that Florence would have to use the representational resources of all its inhabitants, not just those of its citizens. Yet while transforming its center, the commune would have to leave intact the honor of the families that had always fed the weak center of the past. The problems of the Florentine* respubblica *were not different; only the formal behavioral solutions were. The final part of this work studies these new approaches.*

1. Pope Pius II, *I Commentari*, ed. G. Bernetti, 5 vols. (Siena, 1972–76), bk. II, ch. 28.

Two dominant phenomena of ritual life in the later republic command our continual attention in these chapters. First, this period witnessed the formation of institutions of laymen who did not hold political office, groups that had the specific task of contributing to the salvation of the city; through their processional incorporation into the civil identity during this period, the definition of the communitas florentina was changed. The process was slow, and in Chapter 11 we examine only the building phase before 1494, when these adult-supported institutions had salvational powers attributed to them but had not yet assumed the full representational roles in processional life that would formally incorporate them into the community. In this period, the marginal population became personnes morales; we shall study the foundations of boys', youths', and plebs' salvation groups.

Would these outsider groups become salvation itself, or the salvational retinue for a single charismatic savior? The struggle for the political and moral center of Florentine life was the second dominant phenomenon of formal life in the later republic, its essential content being the transformations of this center through the successive incorporations of outsider groups. In the first period of the processional revolution, examined in Chapter 12, Lorenzo the Magnificent (d. 1492) embodied the charismatic center that the Florentines had always sought fascinans tremendum, but in his wake the prophet Savonarola (d. 1498) transformed that center through placing young boys at the heart of the city's political and processional identity. In the second period (Chapter 13), Pope Leo X (d. 1521) and his nephew Pope Clement VII (d. 1534), Giovanni and Giulio de' Medici, constructed a center abroad, but during the Last Republic (1527–1530), young men entered the domestic processional center for the first time, and transformed it.

By the 1530s, the lower classes and even women, last of the liminal groups of Florentine society, showed signs of processional centrism. A new concept of Florentine community had evolved. Marginal groups so long scorned by the republic now played their role in the protoabsolutistic state of the Medici grand dukes. The city had its honor, credit, and trust at home and abroad. Its families had their honor without politics.

Chapter 11

The New Ritual Groups

*Like someone who cuts off his testicles to show his disdain for his wife, everyone has [acted] to show his disdain for the noble and ancient popolani.**

In the fifteenth century, a beleaguered gerontocracy of judicious fathers condemned, as had their ancestors, the common faults of all those groups that were excluded from government. Boys (*fanciulli*), youth or young men (*giovani*), and the plebs had all this in common with women: They lacked the gravity, the dispassionate reason, and the controlled sexuality that were the necessary moral qualities of governors. Each of these excluded groups was different, of course, and one could see it in their public actions.[1] Boys made any order impossible if left to their own devices. Their violent rock, fist, and truncheon fights during Carnival and springtime, their habit of dismembering the bodies of executed criminals, and other such gang actions all seemed to subvert the existing public order without substituting another. The *giovani* were different; they mocked the order of society consciously, and their constant interference in the political affairs of their fathers harbored the danger of a political overturn, another order. The plebs, finally, loved to play their betters, and this habit of social inversion could mean that they aimed not at generational but at social revolution. Still, the commonality of all these

---

*G. Cavalcanti, *Istorie*, III, 2 (1427).

1. The following is examined more fully in my "De la Ville à la Cour. La Deraison à Florence durant la Republique et le Grand Duché," in J. Le Goff and J.-C. Schmitt (eds.), *Le Charivari. Actes de la Table Ronde organisée par le Centre Nationale de Recherche Scientifique et l'Ecole des Hautes Etudes* (Paris, 1981).

groups was more readily perceptible to the political class than were their differences. When a foreigner wanted to insult this city of traders, he could say nothing more humiliating than that the city had a "government of boys," "of youths," or "of the meanest sort." It all came to the same thing: the belief that Florence wore a petticoat under its manly cloak.

Yet in the fifteenth century, each of these three groups developed institutions that were sanctioned by the grave lords of Florence and later played a role in the processional life of the city: confraternities of male children and adolescents; baronies and finally a militia of *giovani;* and the *potenze* ("powers") of the plebs. This chapter examines the pre- and early history of these institutions. It is to be sure a story of co-optation, of a gerontocratic class taking these groups into its procession. Yet it is also a tale of forced absorption and transformation, for the *communitas florentina* found it could not do without the processional presence of these outsiders. Once the procession included them, Florence was no longer the same.

Children and Adolescents

Before there were boys' institutions in Florence, there were "children," a vague, amorphous mass of youngsters who, upon being baptized, started out as innocents and ended up as "beasts." "Women and children" appeared in processions much as had Andromache with her offspring at the walls of Troy, calling the gods' attention to their masters, warning them that progeny would succumb if the masters died. Scarcely on their feet, however, Florentine brats appeared in the streets, beating balls against nunnery walls, burning mannequins of old women, stoning passersby, and mocking visitors: fitter victims of Herod, said one dour versifier, than the helpless Innocents whose murder had ruined that king's reputation. If only, the poet intoned, Herod would now put a stop to those

> . . . *bothersome and vain songs*
> *of those who never go down the street quietly.*
> *Thus the cruel Herod could return,*
> *but [this time] to kill those from four to twelve years,*
> *once he hears them, and only if he does.*
> *Certainly if that were done he would not be so*
> *much scorned as praised by the celestial choirs.*
> *For they displease everyone alive . . . .*[2]

2. Franco Sacchetti, *Opere,* ed. A. Chiari (Bari, 1938), I, 111. As part of their Magi theater the Florentines did reenact the Slaughter of the (baptized) Innocents, imitation infants being ripped away from mothers and wet nurses and cut to pieces by "soldiers"; cited in Hatfield, "Compagnia," 144 (1390). Since the concept of innocence will be important in the following chapters, note that Italian preachers told the faithful that infantile innocence started when through baptism the child became a member of the Christian community. For it was at that point (and not shortly after conception, as was a common theological opinion), that the child received a soul. I could not prove that point in my "Infanticide in Florence: New Sources

Orphans evoked less murderous sentiments. They were truly unfortunate, truly outside the familial organization of Florence, and along with widows formed the two lay social groups to whom Christian charity was due. Brought together in publicly supported institutions, orphans and foundlings were first among the liminal lay groups of Florence to assume a formal public role in the salvational work of city ritual. We sense this new role-awareness in the earliest extant Florentine painting of a group of orphans, dating from 1386.[3] In the fresco, overjoyed parents rush to the loggia of the Confraternity of the Misericordia to reclaim their little ones, while other children, guarded by the grave and dignified confreres, sit disconsolately by waiting for parents who do not appear. Our suspicions that groups of orphans had become important to the city's spiritual health are confirmed by the fact that, almost contemporary with this painting, orphans (foundlings?) appeared on the *ringhiera* of the Palace at the culmination of a crisis procession in 1390.[4] Part of a scenic platform of cantors and relics surrounding the sacrifice of the Mass, they looked down at a piazza full of adults who, in their devotion to the Mass, seemed to be doing them reverence as well. These orphans probably came from the foundling home of the Scala, rather than having been gathered at random.[5] If not in processions, at least as framed innocents, a body of institutionally subvented children had entered the Florentine representational universe.

The appearance of such interned children in the procession itself was first recorded on April 20, 1422, the day on which the first Florentine galley departed for Alexandria. To foster the success of this signal event in Florence's emergence as a sea power, the commune staged the last of three processions on this day. Along with "all the relics and orders of friars and priests with crosses" went "all the *fanciulli* of the Scala and of the shops and schools of Florence."[6] The former were the orphans and foundlings of the Scala, the same institution that had probably furnished the "orphans" in 1390.[7] It was the first time, and the last, in which interns of the city's welfare institutions, that is the *spedali* of the sick, poor, and foundlings, are

and First Results," *History of Childhood Quarterly* I (1973), 98–116. See now the unambiguous text: "Gli innocenti. Non di quegli che sono affogati ne' privai o uccisi in corpo per forza di medicine che non ànno l'anima, non s'intende per loro, ma per quegli ch'ànno l'anima pel santo battesimo; quegli sono gl'innocenti"; Bernardino of Siena, *Prediche* (Florence, 1425), IV, 412. Viewing innocence as a communal if marginal condition—but not as an outsider's—Italians understood how in 1506 the Signoria of Florence could order an infant "monster" starved to death; Sanuto, VI, 390, with a copy of a contemporary representation of the child.

3. Trexler, "Foundlings," 261; H. Saalman, *The Bigallo. The Oratory and Residence of the Compagnia del Bigallo e della Misericordia in Florence* (New York, 1969), pl. 6.

4. See page 356, this volume.

5. The foundlings of the Scala appeared in a later procession; see below, this page, where they are often called "orphans," the two words often being confused in the Florentine usage. The only other foundling or orphan home in Florence at the time was at the hospital of San Gallo; Trexler, "Foundlings," 261. On the latter home see also G. Pinto, "Il Personale, le Balie, i Salariati dell'Ospedale di S. Gallo di Firenze negli anni 1395–1406. Note per la Storia del Salariato nelle Città Medievali," *Ricerche Storiche* IV (1974), 113–168.

6. Pietrobuoni, f. 106v.

7. The only other possibility would be the boys' club that met at the Scala, but it did not move there until the 1430s; G. Monti, *Le Confraternite Medievali dell'Alta e Media Italia*, 2 vols. (Venice, 1927), I. 183.

documented as taking part in Florence's processions.[8] The same decisive fact is true of the remarkable presence of Florence's shop boys and schoolboys in this procession: Never before or later do Florence's chroniclers mention them as corporately participating in the city's processional life. Clearly, Florence in these years was groping for a proper way to present its children to God. It had made the decision to do so, but had not yet found the right form.

This form already existed, its processional value waiting to be discovered. The boys' clubs of Florence would become the classic Florentine institution for representing the young people of the city.[9] The first Florentine confraternity specifically for *fanciulli* was the Company of the Archangel Raphael or of the Nativity, which had been founded by a pious goldsmith in 1410. Obviously fulfilling some powerful urban needs, this club had grown by 1435 to some hundred members, and in other parts of the city additional boys' groups followed the lead of the Nativity and founded their own confraternities. By 1442 this new associative form had become so popular that the pope, residing in Florence at the time, decided that the clubs had to be regulated if needless proliferation was to be avoided and if the fervor of the boys, who had taken to starting their own clubs without the guidance of elders, was to be kept in tow. By papal brief of this year, Eugenius IV recognized the existence of four such groups, whose four adult custodians along with two of the city's most prestigious prelates would have to approve the institution of any further groups. The pope's expectations were clear: The custodians of the existing clubs would not be eager to share their status with others, and the clubs would thus remain limited in number. This did not happen; the youthful confraternities continued to multiply. In 1454 three new clubs were authorized to take part in processions along with the four established ones, and subsequent years witnessed still more institutions. On the eve of their explosion onto the political and processional stage in the later 1490s, about ten such companies existed.[10]

At the same time, the clubs had subdivided according to age. Originally, the boys' confraternities all resembled the Company of San Giovanni Vangelista in accepting adolescents between thirteen and twenty-four years of age. As early as 1442, however, the Nativity decided that it was best that the older and younger adolescents be completely separate. From that point on it planned to convoke the boys up to nineteen years of age in the confraternity's existing house on the western edge of the city; the older adolescents, how-

8. This was very different from other cities, for instance Rome, where institutionalized poor, nuns, and the like were regularly used in processions to incite charity; see, for example, G. Martin, *Roma Sancta* (Rome, 1969), 85, for the foundlings of Santo Spirito.

9. The information on these clubs is more fully documented in my "Adolescence."

10. They are overviewed *ibid.*, 207ff, 264. A subsequently discovered club was founded after the Medici were expelled and just as Savonarola was becoming preoccupied with boys' activities. The approximately fifty-member *societas puerorum et adolescentium*, meeting in the Oltrarno church of S. Jacopo Sopr'Arno with its governor Giovanni di Francesco de' Caponsacchi, had their group approved on Apr. 12, 1495, by the episcopal vicar on the authority of a papal brief; *AAF, Beneficiali*, "G", ser Francesco di Valsivigno (1490–1518), ff. 63r–66v.

ever, "too old to be among boys, too young to be among mature men," were to be sent to a deserted nunnery on Florence's east side to form "what might be called a middle school of virtue."[11] The city fathers had not only interned their children on Sundays and feast days in pious confraternities, but they had now started to subdivide adolescents according to their capabilities and psychosocial characters.

No sketch of the emergence of these new clubs would be complete without mentioning the church schools (*scuole*) that blossomed at the same time. According to Richa, a master of Latin and song was already instructing a school of twelve clerks at the church of San Piero Maggiore at the beginning of the fifteenth century.[12] This ecclesiastical institution took on a different magnitude, however, when in 1436 Pope Eugenius IV instituted a school for boys in the newly consecrated cathedral of Florence.[13] Children were to be recruited from the dioceses of Florence and Fiesole; they could enter at ten years of age, and had to exit at twenty-five. Not wishing to be outdone, Cosimo de' Medici in 1458 endowed a school of twelve young clerks in his parish church of San Lorenzo.[14] By 1478 there was also such a school at the church of Sant'Ambrogio.[15] These clerical schools were certainly different from the lay confraternities of the *fanciulli*. When these young clerks attended meetings they pursued a specific scholarly curriculum. They helped with liturgical duties during divine services and received beneficial incomes; their schools were forthrightly intended to produce future priests. Yet in other ways they resembled their lay counterparts. Both types recruited from the same age group, the Scuola Eugeniana requiring entrance between the ages of ten and fifteen, the charter boys of San Lorenzo ranging in fact from ten through sixteen years of age with a median of thirteen and one-half,[16] patterns congruent with what we know of the lay groups. Furthermore, Florentine fathers converted the clerical schools to their own ends, matriculating their sons in these schools and thus permitting them to take minor orders, but withdrawing them at the age they were expected to proceed to major orders. Many wanted their boys to receive the stipend, instruction, and discipline, but they did not want them to take up the clerical career. The prime social fact in

11. "Adolescentes dicte societatis postquam decimumnovum aut vicesimum annum sue etatis attingunt veluti pro ipsa etate operum adolescentiorum dignius aliquid exposcere videantur, et ad illos quos in ipsa quasi media etate ad hunc constitutos ad cetum virorum ac maiorum natu in via dei se districtius exercentium absolute transire non convenit, quique velut maiores pueris inter pueros et viris ac provectis minores inter viros locari congrue posse non videtur in media quasi virtutum scola per aliquod temporis spatium nutriri opus existat, cum ubi maius est periculum ibi cautius sit agendum. Et si locum haberent ubi iuvenes huiusmodi etatis medie convenire possent, ipsi qui de prefata et aliis societatibus puerorum qui sunt in dicta civitate optimum et laudabilem finem facere consueverunt in societatem

iuvenum huiusmodi se reciperent, et in altissimi servitio vitam suam continuarent, ac magna exinde iuventutis pericula evaderent"; *ASF, Dipl., Patrimonio Ecclesiastico*, June 22, 1442.

12. Richa, *Notizie*, I, 144.

13. See my "Adolescence," 215–218; on Eugenius' similar activity in north Italy, see A. Spagnolo, *Le Scuole di Accolitali in Verona* (Verona, 1904).

14. The first two business registers of this *scuola* have survived in the *Archivio di San Lorenzo (ASL)*, *Biblioteca Laurenziana*, provisional nos. 2381, 2461 (1459–1519).

15. Cianfogni–Moreni, *Memorie*, II, 57 (1478).

16. See the list in *ASL*, 2381, f. 3v.

question is the organization and development in Florence of institutions for boys; the young clerks' clerical schools were definitely part of that phenomenon. The prime political fact was the decision to represent the city's boys to God in the form of boys' clubs, and the young clerks immediately became part of that representational form. No later than 1442, these cathedral boys, and the four basic lay confraternities, were participating in processions dressed in white.[17] A new representational form had been born.

There must have been compelling reasons for such an important departure in Florentine associative and representational life, reasons that may be discovered in the condition of general Florentine society before the clubs, and in the positive effects these clubs were subsequently seen to have on that society. To understand these reasons, therefore, we must first know something of the conditions of their foundations, then the nature of their activities, and finally the reactions of adults. Together, these approaches should furnish us with the information necessary to comprehend the representational needs they fulfilled for the citizens and inhabitants of Florence.

The boys' confraternities of Florence were started by adults and matured in the womb of their fathers' associations.[18] Bringing one's children to meetings of adult confraternities was an old practice for Florentine fathers, but never, before the fifteenth century, had they encouraged these boys to band together within the adult groups. This was the decisive departure of these years. In the fifteenth century, the boys emerged from the associations of their fathers with a separate, if not completely distinct, corporate identity. Lay groups like the Purification remained under the "protection and care" of men's groups but, like the Vangelista, they met together with their adult custodian in their own hall, elected their own officers, wrote their own statutes, and were episcopally approved as independent bodies.[19] Most important, they had their own distinct spirituality.

The early years of the boys' Company of S. Antonio da Padova reflect this paternal heritage, emerging separateness, and spiritual distinctiveness. The founder of the group, like that of the Nativity, was a pious citizen, one Mariotto di Piero Montanelli, who in a long declaration of 1445 explained the history of his support. He had spent £150 in alms, he said,

> in the Company of St. Jerome, in [the church of] S. Giorgio where many devout persons meet on Saturday nights and other nights of the year. And similarly a large number of *fanciulli* meet in the said company on Sundays during the day and on other feasts of the year, during the day. . . . And as has been said, the company that meets at night (titled under the name of . . . St. Jerome), and the company or rather school of *fanciulli* that meets during the day on Sundays and other feasts (titled under name of the blessed Annunciation and of St. Anthony of Padua) [have received] several sums and quantities of money, about £150, and they appear in a book in which the company of night keeps its accounts.[20]

17. Trexler, "Adolescence," 208.

18. *Ibid.*, 212f.

19. *Ibid.*, 211ff.

20. *ASF, Dipl., Badia Fiorentina*, Dec. 21, 1445.

Montanelli had given these alms for one purpose: to "subsidize the boys" so that they could "form themselves in the said place or in any other place where the said company [of S. Girolamo] would go or move."[21] The donor obviously believed that institutionally, the two groups should be dependent on each other. The money was legally given to the night company of adults, whose "devout persons" would thus continue to influence the boys' group; but, on the other hand, if the men wanted the gift they would not move from their present quarters without the approval of the custodian of the boys' group.[22] Spiritually, however, the men depended on the boys. In this one case at least, the material welfare and geographical locus of the men depended on the spiritual force of the boys, who had attracted Montanelli's alms and "devotion."

In founding his boys' club in the 1440s, Montanelli had doubtless been inspired by the demonstrated success of the four established groups; he wanted, he said, to have in his quarter of Santo Spirito a boys' confraternity like those in the other three quarters.[23] What were the activities of these clubs he so admired, those which made him and many other Florentine adults open their purse strings? Let us examine what went on in these youthful companies of discipline, as they were called, which could make of street "beasts" the innocent lambs of the true Christian community.[24]

Certainly the majority of the boys' time in their clubs was taken up by their internal activities, the covenantal "practices of the old law" that they followed during their regular Sunday meetings.[25] Prayers, public confessions of faults, the "external cult" of lauds, the ritual admission of new members, and the like were the staple activities that structured such meetings. These practices were almost identical to those of the adult companies of discipline.[26] The fathers in certain clubs flagellated as part of their regular meetings; the boys apparently did not. The boys used a ritual for excluding members who had reached the maximum age, whereas adult groups needed no such form. But otherwise, the boys' clubs were in their normal internal activities little

21. "Le dette ispese avevo fatte pe' detti fancugli in presenza di più persone, chè lla mia devozione era per fare simile chonpagnia nello quartiere di Santo Ispirito. . . . E dette ispese avevo fatto solamente per chontenprazione e sosidio di detti fancugli. . . . Mi prometerono che' . . . detti fancugli si chonstruerebono in detto luogo overo in qualunque altro luogo dove andasse o schanbiasse la detta chonpagnia, nolla chavando del quartiere di Santo Ispirito"; *ibid.*

22. "Intendo ispendere per chotenprazione, aiuto, sosidio, favore, e mantenimento di detti fancugli e schuola che si raghuna di dì in detto luogo, e voglio e dichiaro che per quello ò speso o spendessi in detta chonpagnia [di S. Girolamo], i detti fancugli abino quella ragone che se propriamente essi di loro proprio ispeso avesono. Perchè chome è detto, a loro istanza

l'ò ne fatto e farò, e per quanto ò speso o spendessi, voglio e dichiaro che se s'avesse a baratare o tramutare alltro luogo, non chavandolo di detto quartiere che' detti di note, nollo posino fare nè pigliare alchuno partito sanza ispresa licenzia dell guardiano di detti fancugli che per lo quegli tenpi fussi"; *ibid.*

23. See n. 21.

24. Details on this subject in my "Adolescence," 219–231; the boys' clubs are called "discipline [i.e., flagellation] companies" by Matteo Palmieri (1454) and subsequent sources; Guasti, *Feste*, 22.

25. On this distinction, see Trexler, "Adolescence," 219.

26. On which see Weissman, "Community and Piety."

men's clubs, miniatures preparing the boys for the serious abnegations of adulthood.

Still, boys found it difficult to concentrate on the hard spiritual work expected of adults unless their discipline was mixed with activities more fitting to their age. To relieve the tedium, a Pistoian boys' confraternity of the early sixteenth century elected a *messere*—just as other boys did in Carnival groups—who supervised his brigade in dignified physical diversions like games of ball.[27] There is no reason to believe that the earlier Florentine groups did otherwise. These physical activities were viewed as concessions to the weakness of the young rather than as creative activities in themselves, and the goals of these internal activities were no different from the spiritual fervor expected of the men's confraternities.

Delivering orations was the second activity of the clubs, an activity borrowed from the procedural baggage of the older groups. Although still an internal activity, it drew attention from outside the clubs. Thus sixteen-year-old Giovanni Nesi (b. 1456) delivered an oration to the boys' group of S. Niccolò del Ceppo; he addressed the boys of S. Antonio da Padova at eighteen years of age, those of the Nativity sometime between the ages of nineteen and twenty-two.[28] His orations were all in Latin, a language many of the boys could not understand, but this did not detract from the edification offered the boys by such fine examples of precocious maturity. Latin awed rather than bored, and besides, a dignified bearing and suitable gestures as much as words marked the successful speaker, and they could be grasped by all. Here is the reaction to a sermon delivered to the Pistoian confraternity by a young boy, standing before a scaled-down rostrum and addressing his brothers:

> [He] explained the meaning of the words "company," "fraternity," and "purity," and to what end [the company] had been instituted and many other things, exhorting purity of conscience and right, honest, and virtuous living in these early years [of life]. He pronounced the said sermon not with artificial gestures, but with ones taught by God, [and] with such grace that he reduced many of the bystanders to tears and to great devotion.[29]

The third activity of the boys involved dramatic presentations, highly innovative manifestations of the new role of the young in Florentine representational life, and significant as a focus of parents' new understanding of their children. The boys' confraternities moved onto the stages already established by adult groups, and charged them with a new force, and a new message. The confraternities' first theatrical performances seem to have been in fixed locations, either indoors or in the vicinity of churches, and it is in the

27. "Adolescence," 219; on Carnival activities of *fanciulli*, see my "De la Ville à la Cour."

28. Possibly Nesi had moved to the older division of the Nativity after reaching the age of nineteen years, as shown on pages 370f, this volume. On these sermons, see my "Adolescence," 220.

29. On the importance of formal perfection and the repression of originality in the humanist schools, see *ibid.*, 238–245. The Italian word *compagnia* is equivalent to the English word *confraternity*. The special meaning of the Florentine word *fraternità* is referred to in notes 176 and 179, this chapter.

church of San Pancrazio that the boys performed the first known confraternal miracle play (*sacra rappresentazione*): the Birth of Christ, done by the Natività before Pope Eugenius in the mid-1430s.[30] The other boys' clubs followed. It is difficult to prove which of them did particular plays in the rich Florentine literature of *sacre rappresentazioni*, but that they did perform many of them there can be no doubt. Several of the plays started with apologies of infelicities because "we are only *fanciulli*," and still others had youthful personages as their dramatis personae.[31] The boys Confraternity of S. Bernardino may have been the group to perform the *Last Judgment* with Blessed Bernardino as one of the characters, and the boys of S. Antonio probably performed *Abramo ed Isac* in the Cistercian church of S. Maria Maddalena in 1449.[32] The clerical boys' schools were not to be left out, and they can be associated with particular plays. Thus in 1476 the Scuola Eugeniana was ready to perform a play called *Licinia* in the church of Ognissanti, and had to compete with other groups for Lorenzo de' Medici's attention. The school of S. Lorenzo did Plautus' *Menaechmi* in 1488, just at the time when other clerical youth, from the religious orders, entered the competition. In 1491 a group of young monks performed the *Judgment of Solomon* in the monastery of the Angeli with the future Leo X (Medici) in the audience, and in the following year another play, this one on a Florentine historical subject, was done by the same group before that illustrious visitor.[33] In 1491, finally, Lorenzo de' Medici himself allowed one of his own works, the *rappresentazione* of SS. Giovanni e Paolo, to be performed by the Vangelista, one of the original adolescent confraternities of the city.

Within the previous sixty years, consequently, the boys' repertoire had expanded from miracle plays to classical theater; they presented not only ancient stories but civic history; leading politicians as well as humbler literary craftsmen were their authors. These plays included all the basic elements of theater: a script, a musical score, scenery, and various degrees of dramatic action. Most significant for our interests, all the parts were played by *fanciulli*: not only those of the saint, the obedient son Isaac, father Abraham, and the Queen of Heaven, but also the lost son, the devil, the greedy man, the Virgin who fears Joseph will find her with the handsome angel Gabriel, the infanticide, the whore.[34] The youngsters imitated all the bad as well as all the good; they were Everyman.

The boys were doing more than staging their shows in fixed locations, however. By midcentury they had taken to the streets, preceding their pres-

---

30. Monti, *Confraternite*, I, 183. On church stage settings, see Fabbri, *Luogo Teatrale*.

31. Details in my "Adolescence," 227f.

32. In the early 1470s, the *festa* of *Abraham, Saul, and Sarah* was associated with the church of S. Giorgio, where this boys' group met; Dei, *Cronica*, f. 38v (1472). There is some evidence that the clubs took their theater from one church to another even in these early years, but only a careful study of the

sources will clarify how close the identification was between place, *rappresentazione*, and institution.

33. See the description of these two plays given by Schnitzer, *Delfin*, 84f.

34. "Adolescence," 232. The Camaldolan general Delfin thought it was better for secular people to play these parts than monks, and that perhaps it was better to read certain biblical stories rather than play them; Schnitzer, *Delfin*, 85.

entations on the feast of San Giovanni with long processions showing their personnel and scenery to the crowds that lined the streets. On June 22, 1454, groups of boys on foot led off the parade of *edifizi* or floats.[35] The Scuola Eugeniana came first, followed by thirty members of the Company of the Vangelista and the Company of S. Antonio dressed as angels in white. Then came the first float, which showed the archangel Michael, with God the Father above him in a cloud. This *edifizio* was followed by two more confraternities of thirty angels in white, those of the Nativity or Archangel Raphael and of the Purification. The parade ended in the Piazza della Signoria, where the boys of the *edifizio* of S. Michele were the first to stage an actual performance. Palmieri's account of the performance allows us to imagine how the boys on foot were related to the float of S. Michele. The latter, he says, "did the representation of the angelic battle, when Lucifer with his damned angels was chased from heaven." Is it not probable that the float—perhaps itself produced by the Vangelista, one of whose patron saints was Michael— was the center around which two contending groups of damned and loyal angels battled? Here in effect was a boys' game reminiscent of the many gang fights with which the city was all too familiar. But this one was a sponsored spectacle under civil auspices with beautiful discipline. All there was of good and evil could be performed by *fanciulli*, all the tensions of real life could be reflected in the San Giovanni ceremonies as they had been in the past: then only by men, now by boys, to console adults.

The boys' fourth activity was their processional participation. These new confraternities had had their processional itinerary prepared for them by earlier associative forms, as we have seen: first by their apparently noninstitutional appearance in crisis processions twice during the later fourteenth century, then by boys' presence as angels within adult confraternities in a San Giovanni procession of *c.* 1410,[36] and finally by their first institutional appearance in 1422, when orphans, shop boys, and schoolboys marched by corporation. A generation later, the new clubs of boys were established parts of the processional scene, as Pope Eugenius indicated in his brief of 1442.[37] Now on June 22, 1454, we find the clubs involved in processionally linked dramatic presentations, and on the following day seven of them are participating in the formal procession of San Giovanni.[38] Again in 1455 boys, unidentified by institution, took part in a procession, this one imploring God's help in an upcoming crusade against the Turks: "Singing and psalmodizing with great melody," according to two different sources, "boys and

35. The following is based on Matteo Palmieri's account, in Guasti, *Feste*, 20–23. The specific text for the first boys reads: "A dì 22. Nel principio mosse la Croce di Santa Maria del Fiore, con tutti i loro cherici fanciulli, e rieto a loro sei cantori. Secondo, le Compagnie di Iacopo cimatore e Nofri calzolaio, con circa trenta fanciulli vestiti di bianco e angioletti. Terzo, Edifizio di San Michele Agnolo; al quale soprastava Iddio Padre in una nuvola; e in Piazza, al dirimpetto a' Signori, fecero rappresentazione della battaglia Angelica, quando Lucifero fu co' sua agnoli maladetti cacciato di cielo. Quarto, la Compagnia di ser Antonio e Piero di Mariano, con circa trenta fanciulli vestiti di bianco e agnoletti"; *ibid.*, 21.

36. Dati says that the "compagnie d'uomini secolari" dressed as angels; it is possible these were *fanciulli*; *ibid.*, 5.

37. See page 372, this volume.

38. Palmieri in Guasti, *Feste*, 22f.

girls [went] first [before the others], then at the end the women, quite a few dressed in white, that is, a blouse over their clothes, and a red cross on their breast."[39] From this year until 1492, however, nothing more is heard of boys or their clubs' participation in processions. It was unusual then as it had been earlier for chroniclers to mention childish activities, unknown for social commentators to give them their sustained attention. Like their internal activities, their orations and drama, the adolescents' processions were like an underground river running beneath Florentine society whose full scope went unrecognized by adults. Few could have imagined that here were the makings of a ritual revolution.

Yet if the narratives are largely silent, other sources are less so. Adults watched children and adolescents act. They saw their bodily movements trained in the confraternal setting, heard what the young said in their orations and plays, and occasionally expressed their amusement or surprise. By studying the fragmentary adult response to children's acting, and by listening to the children themselves, we can hope to approach the reasons for this major new force in Florentine society.

At the beginning of the fifteenth century, children performed at home, if they did at all, for Florentines believed that the home was the correct stage and that parents were the best pedagogues. Just as Jesus had come to earth only after the race had been weaned of primordial behavioral grossness, only when the peoples had classified the difference between clean and unclean, reverence and irreverence,[40] so children had to learn these body behaviors before they could learn spiritual cleanliness. In the early 1400s the Dominican Giovanni Dominici painted a charming picture of how children learned spiritual values through physical motions in the theater of the family:

> The first regulation is to have pictures of saintly children or young virgins in the home, in which your child, still in swaddling clothes, may take delight and thereby may be gladdened by acts and signs pleasing to childhood. . . . Make of such pictures a sort of temple in the house. . . . Make a little altar or two in the house, dedicated to the Savior whose feast is every Sunday. You may have three or four different colored vestments, and he and the other children may be sacristans, showing them on all feasts how they should variously adorn this chapel. . . . They may . . . have in place the little bell and run to ring it at all hours as is done in the church. They may be dressed in surplices as acolytes, sing as well as they know how, play at saying Mass, and be brought to the church sometimes and shown how real priests do it, that they may imitate them. Teach them to preach after they have heard preaching several times in the church . . . , you and the family remaining seated while they speak from above, not laughing but commending and rewarding them when they have imitated the spiritual office. Pardon them punishment due when they take refuge at the altar and, kneeling down, ask as a favor from Jesus that you will not strike them, so that they may early accustom themselves to have recourse to the True God in their troubles and demand grace from Him who alone can give it.[41]

39. Respectively Francesco di Tommaso Giovanni, and Pietrobuoni, cited in my "Adolescence," 222f.

40. Giordano da Rivalto does not refer this specifically to children, but his analysis of the predominance of form over content is of enormous importance, and directly applicable to what Florentines thought the progression of their children was; see Giordano da Pisa, *Quaresimale*, 212–215.

41. Dominici, *Education*, 34f, 42.

Florentines liked to be told that their ancestors had always reared children in this family fashion. By taking behavioral forms from the public forum, parents had trained their children in the motions, sounds, and clothing of that forum they would one day enter. Yet how different was reality in the early fifteenth century, how inadequate the family seemed to moralists in Florence and around Europe. It was not that parents, kin, and servants could not furnish fit theaters for rearing youngsters, but that they did not. In the Florentine context, political, generative, and religious realities stood in the way.

The political problem of the family had two aspects relative to our inquiry. First, the freewheeling family politics that had so long characterized Florentine social and representational life threatened to become a thing of the past with the emergence of a narrow group of dominant political families. Prepared by the building of a political elite at the beginning of the fifteenth century, the process came to a head after 1434, when the Medici not only succeeded in making other patricians' family honor depend on Medicean approval, but gradually restricted these families' rights to manifest their honor publicly.[42] The boys' confraternities, therefore, could serve not only as a forum for individual family adolescents, but also as a theater that kept these multiple family honors before the public.

The boys' confraternities became all the more important in this regard because the Medici sought to hinder familial solidarity by barring the entrance of young adults (*giovani*) from political families into confraternities, one of the arenas in which they had traditionally formed future family and political ties. The groundwork had been laid by the previous regime, which had dropped the age at which young people were identified as future members of the officeholding class so precipitately that it was common for children to be so identified.[43] Now the Medici restricted the right of members of such families to belong to confraternities, including those young people of twenty-four, or even twenty years of age, many years below the minimum age for actually holding office.[44] The boys' confraternities were the presumed beneficiaries of this situation. If young men could not belong to confraternities, it was all the more important to have adolescent groups that would build those solidarities before it was too late. The benefits of the clubs extended to the nonpolitical families. To the extent that patrician families were excluded from adult confraternities, the humbler families took their place, and the heads of the latter could then place their sons in the boys' confraternities they protected.

The generative problem of the Florentine family was no less serious than

42. On this development, see page 410, this volume.

43. On the system of *vedere e sedere*, see page 392, this volume.

44. The twenty-four-year-old limit was imposed in *ASF, Prov.*, 134, ff. 208v–209r (Feb. 19, 1443/1444); this law was revoked on the urging of the archbishop on Apr. 5, 1452; *ibid.*, 143, ff. 32v–33v. But the law was reintroduced on June 19, 1455, and the age reduced to twenty years; *ibid.*, 146, ff. 147r–148r. See also Rubinstein, *Government*, 118, which wrongly states that the law barred membership for the following five years. Actually, the law barred anyone over the minimum age found in a confraternity from political office for five years each time so found.

its political decline. Many men were marrying late or not at all. Tabulations made by David Herlihy show, for example, that in 1427 only one-quarter of 4456 young males between eighteen and thirty-two years of age were married. The average age of men who married in 1427–1428 was thirty-four, and in the previous twelve months the average age of males fathering children was 39.75 years.[45] The effects of this phenomenon upon children were predictable. With the father dead before his children reached adolescence, young widowed mothers increasingly put their daughters in nunneries and either abandoned those who remained by remarrying, as had Giovanni Morelli's mother, or continued rearing their sons past the age when the latter were expected to come under the authority of their fathers. Not only was the fear of family extinction a vivid reality in these times,[46] the sons of those who did marry became feminized by continued exposure to their mothers, it was said, *and* by the homosexual courting they encountered in the streets from older males. Unwilling or unable to marry, the latter avoided fathering either through anal intercourse with female prostitutes, or by trafficking with these male adolescents, who quickly became prostitutes.[47] It was not a pretty picture.

The city's concern with what was perceived as a great wave of homosexuality informs all our sources in the early fifteenth century. The popular poetry of the time lambasts and twits the practice in verse after verse.[48] Trying to explain to their audiences why the Florentine population had dropped so precipitously since 1400, preachers ascribed the decline to "sodomy."[49] Government was concerned about the perceived link between homosexuality and low fertility, even if the former was something the grave fathers of Florence normally did not like to talk about. When in 1415 certain clergymen launched the attack by writing treatises or broadsides that specifically condemned the Florentine addiction to the crime, there were those who complained to the government, as there always were when the city's masculinity or that of its families was attacked. Yet so seriously was the threat taken that when the communal counselors were presented with this protest they recommended that the clerks be publicly commended rather than silenced.[50] In 1421 government itself seized the helm, trying unsuccessfully to pass a law that would have barred from office any male over thirty who had not married.[51] During these years it beefed up the authority of the recently established Office of

45. Herlihy, "Vieillir," 1340f, 1344, 1346.

46. See Masi's concern on page 11, this volume.

47. The problem is examined in more detail by Herlihy, *loc. cit.*, and in my "Adolescence," 235–238. A rich source for Florentine contraceptive methods is ASF, *Ufficiali dell'Onestà*, 2 (Condannazioni, 1421–1523).

48. See the examples in D. Guerri, *La Corrente Popolare nel Rinascimento; Berte, Burle, e Baie nella Firenze del Brunellesco e del Burchiello* (Florence, 1931); also A. Lanza (ed.), *Lirici Toscani del '400* (Rome, 1973), 569ff.

49. Bernardino da Siena, *Prediche* (Florence, 1424), II, 22 seq., 47. In the Florentine vocabulary, at least, sodomy included homo- and heterosexual anal intercourse, but unless otherwise specified it was understood as the former.

50. Communal *consulte* cited by G. Brucker (ed.), *The Society of Renaissance Florence. A Documentary Study* (New York, 1971), 201.

51. Pietrobuoni, f. 105r, who details the long, bitter attempt to pass this law.

Decorum (*Onestà*) to protect and recruit foreign prostitutes, in part to turn young men away from homosexuality.[52] So petrified were the priors by biblical evidence of what happened to cities like Sodom and Gomorrah that in 1432 they established a special Office of the Night to suppress the "vice which cannot be named."[53] And in 1433 the regime restricted the richness of women's clothing because although women were "created to replenish this free city," their expensive clothing was dissuading young men from marrying.[54]

The remarkable activism of Florentine governments in legislating morality in these years must be seen against a backdrop of incessant preaching on the subject by the Mendicant friars, the most prominent of whom was the Franciscan Bernardino of Siena. On the invitation of the government, Bernardino brought all his medical, social, and moral knowledge to bear in an attempt to stop the "disappearance of the race." Italy, he said, shaped like a womb, was the mother of sodomy; Tuscany had the lowest population in the world; Florence made the biblical sin cities seem only half bad.[55] Contraception and abortion certainly limited population too, the moralist admitted, but they stank less in God's face than sodomy and should not be spoken of—a curious inversion of traditional ranking.[56] Sodomy could be talked about. Its practitioners stank. This polluted the air, and thus caused the plague from which Florence was suffering.[57] Women dressed like whores and masked themselves in cosmetics to keep their husbands away from other men, but this had the opposite effect, for the means they used to whiten their teeth gave them insufferably bad breath.[58] Wives only added to the homosexual stink of their husbands. How could one doubt that this was a sin? Were those people serious who argued that Christ had not condemned homosexuality, citing the biblical verse "There are eunuchs who castrate themselves to achieve the kingdom of heaven" as a defense of sodomy?[59] Could one doubt that homosexuality was on the increase?[60]

Bernardino gave full vent to his rage when he assessed the condition of the families from which homosexuals came and the political factions the latter created. Once infected by it, the young could not desert sodomy until they were past thirty-two years of age.[61] Those fourteen to twenty-five years of age had to be watched so they did not become the active homosexual partners of

---

52. This was the justification given for the establishment of the Onestà in 1403; Trexler, "Prostitution." Plans to build two new brothels, which were never realized, were funded in *ASF, Prov.*, 105, ff. 248r–249r (Dec. 23, 1415). The charge of the *Ufficiali dell'Onestà* "conducendo et conduci faciendo feminas et meretrices ad civitatem florentinam" is mentioned in that office's deliberations of Oct. 5, 1436; *ASF, Misc. Repub.*, 33, f. 13v.

53. *ASF, Prov.*, 123, ff. 31v–36v (Apr. 12).

54. Law translated by Brucker, *Society*, 181.

55. These comments found respectively in his *Pre-*

diche (Siena, 1427), 899; (Florence, 1424), II, 22 seq., 46.

56. *Ibid.* (Siena, 1427), 908f.

57. *Ibid.* (Florence, 1425), IV, 274f.

58. *Ibid.* (Florence, 1424), II, 141; *ibid.* (Florence, 1425), IV, 116.

59. The sodomites' study of the Bible is referred to *ibid.* (Florence, 1424), II, 143; (Siena, 1427), 410.

60. On the increase, *ibid.* (Florence, 1425), IV, 116.

61. *Ibid.* (Florence, 1424), II, 35.

passive eight- to fifteen-year-olds. Why did children fall victim to this curse? Because they did not go to confession or communion, because their parents trivialized children's homosexuality as "what children do," because, in short, parents *did not care*.[62] Children become homosexuals, Bernardino glared at his audience with chilling insight, "only because of the coldness of paternal caring."[63] Parents taught children manners at the age of four or six, but abandoned them at ten or fourteen.[64] According to Bernardino, parents actively encouraged children to be homosexual, sending them out "too polished" in the hopes that their availability would win them the good graces of powerful patrons and thus, ultimately, offices. Such patrons took good care of them, to be sure: If a homosexual was arrested, said Bernardino, "doctors" (*medici*) "run to medicate the evil." As Cannarozzi has argued, this was an unmistakable attack on the Medici for protecting their homosexual clientage.[65] Why would homosexuals be allowed to participate in politics? Bernardino wanted to know. Was it not self-evident that their sexual passions were the opposite of the gravity necessary to good counselors?[66] Yet the fact was, he told his Florentine listeners, that political factions were insolubly held together by homosexual allegiances.[67]

Fire was the answer, Bernardino insisted in his Lenten cycle at Santa Croce in April 1424. Starting on Saturday, April 1, he preached each day on the following subjects: sinful women, games, blasphemy, judging others, women blind to sin, sodomy, sodomy again, sodomy a third time; then on Sunday April 9 he preached on all these sins of *luxuria*, all these sins that were so inevitably linked to boys' and young men's sexual torts.[68] All week he had built up his audiences for an entertainment he had planned. Now culminating his sermon by returning to the sins of sodomites and those who procured their release from prison, he yelled: "To the fire! They are all sodomites! And you are in mortal sin if you seek to help [the sodomites]!" He could go no further. The masses of people in the church and in the Piazza di Santa Croce, including great numbers of *fanciulli* and *garzoni*, gathered around an enormous pile of dice, wigs, and the like laid on the *capannuccio* or scaffold in the square, like tinsel on a Christmas tree, demanded that the preacher come into the square and start this first Florentine Burning of the Vanities.[69] There is no doubt that this bonfire had one great central sin to expiate, one central figure to torch: the homosexual who was sissifying Florence.

What an incredible indictment Bernardino made in these Florentine sermons of 1424 and 1425 of the city's familial, and political, order. Fathers were

62. *Ibid.* (Florence, 1425), V, 44, 42.

63. "Tutto per freddezza di carità paterna"; *ibid.* (Florence, 1424), II, 41.

64. *Ibid.*

65. On polish, *ibid.* (Florence, 1425), IV, 185, and the similar condemnation of fathers facilitating sodomy in Giordano da Rivalto–Moreni, *Prediche*, I, 230 (1303). On the Medici, Bernardino da Siena, *Prediche* (Florence, 1425), IV, 118.

66. *Ibid.* (Florence, 1425), IV, 273.

67. "È una usanza tra voi di parte, o guelfa o ghibellina; mai la lascerete se non quando il diavolo ve ne porterà. Chi vi dicesse non fare giurare gli ufici per parte una, nol faresti per l'usanza"; *ibid.* (Florence, 1425), IV, 116.

68. *Ibid.* (Florence, 1424), sermons 25–33.

69. *Ibid.*, II, 87.

sodomites, mothers masturbated at home.[70] Parents turned their boys into girls, so intent were they to have honors and offices for them, so powerless, one surmises, to effect this otherwise. Society seemed more capable of love than the family. Yet what a horrendous vision Bernardino had regarding the way politics worked. He might cry out to a Sienese audience: "Oh boys, if you want to exterminate your city and your *patria*, be sodomites!"[71] He could use the carrot in Florence, telling its citizens that they were so susceptible to the sin because they were so intellectually vibrant.[72] But at bottom, he had come to believe, Florentine factions were held together by boys: The love of boys was what bound the men of Florence together! This was bad, it was unnatural, the preacher was sure. Yet the observer hearing this sermon at a distance of five and a half centuries is less interested in the moral than in the cultural force of the message: The same fathers who were beginning in these years to patronize adolescent confraternities were being told by their preacher, willy-nilly, that Florentine politics was more than the gravity of ignoble men. The charisma of young boys held men together.

There can be little doubt that the adolescent confraternities were meant in part to be an answer to this threat, even though their statutes never seem to have mentioned the "vice." Probably, since the boys themselves were to be involved in drawing up their basic law, it was thought that mentioning the sin would encourage it. But the adult confraternities of the fifteenth century highlighted homosexuality in their statutes, making it one of the first grounds for immediate expulsion.[73] It would be excessive to argue that the adult and adolescent confraternal explosion in the fifteenth century represented a concerted institutional attack on homosexuality. But one can say that it did represent one decentralized approach to a civic problem that men felt had to be corrected. "A well-behaved youth is of the highest importance to the commonweal," the pedagogue Vergerio wrote at the time.[74] The preachers, the government, even the troubled parents of Florence agreed. Perhaps the confraternities could dress up the boys without effeminizing them. Perhaps they could play girls, be socialized, without becoming them.

Both the political and the generative problems of the Florentine family were intricately related to a third problem, a questioning of the religious function of both the clergy and the adult political community as ritual saviors of the city. The clergy was in a crisis of authority and morality in the early fifteenth century. Riddled by the Great Schism and increasingly under the control of the secular government because of the weakness of Rome, the local clergy had lost credibility. Its monasteries and friaries were notoriously weak both in numbers and holiness. So victimized was the secular clergy by papal and communal taxation that many churches were without priests, and the

70. (Siena, 1427), 902.

71. *Ibid.*, 281.

72. *Ibid.* (Florence, 1424), II, 64.

73. Although I have found mention of homosexuality

rare in fourteenth-century confraternal statutes, it is very common in the fifteenth-century confraternal rubric *de vita honesta*.

74. E. Garin, *L'Educazione Umanistica in Italia* (Bari, 1949), 61.

priests argued among themselves for the available benefices.[75] It was a depressing sight for laymen; the traditional role of the clergy and especially the religious clergy as an institution for ritually passing Florence through crisis was no longer unequivocal. Yet we must not copy contemporaries in over-emphasizing clerical immorality as a direct cause of this crisis of salvational functionality. The clergy had always been accused of moral decay in Florence; furthermore, the protective function of the Florentine clergy was, as I have argued, only moral through ritual expression. To some degree, the contemporary attack on clerical decline only echoed the ritual crisis of the adult male laity. How could God take seriously the procession of men whose families seemed more and more the toys of a few great families; of fathers whose boys were girls; of a Signoria that might not truly represent the fulcrum of authority and power in the commune? Could God take pleasure in, and thus reprieve, a play structure, one that had lost that magic ambivalence of expression and transformation that was the essence of the Florentine public representation?

The boys' confraternities offered hope to both clergy and laity. They could replenish the clergy, and as early as 1435 the Camaldolan general Traversari pointed out that well-trained clergy emerged from the confraternal ranks. One such group actually kept a book listing those members who had graduated to the religious life.[76] They could also reinvigorate their fathers' commune. The same Traversari added,

> [If the boys] decide to remain laymen, they retain the taste for supernal grace which they received in their tender years. To whatever magistracies of the city they are elected, they cultivate justice before all else.[77]

Fathers could ask for nothing more. The family theater that Giovanni Dominici had favored at the beginning of the century had proven a chimera, and Leon Batista Alberti's domestic dream, where grave young men worshiped at the feet of their fathers, had equally little future.[78] The family was out; fathers now put their hopes in social institutions, and were amazed.

Adults first noticed the skills of children as actors in adult spectacles, and found the former better actors. A chronicler observing young pages in a procession of 1428 spoke of youth bedecked with rich clothing through which shone "their angelic faces."[79] He described the adult Company of the Magi's three-year-old Francesco d'Andreuccio de' Ricasoli playing Christ in festival, and was astounded at the child's skill. The boy held a goldfinch in one hand, while "with the other he did things so spontaneously natural that a man of

---

75. See the constitutions of the Florentine clergy that were drawn up in response to this financial and leadership crisis, in my *Synodal Law*, 349–371; the crisis is also referred to by A. Molho, "The Brancacci Chapel: Studies in Its Iconography and History," *Journal of the Warburg and Courtauld Institutes* XL (1977), 64ff.

76. This was the boys' confraternity of S. Brigida; *ASF, Comp. Rel. Sopp.*, B XII 35. The first entered in 1425, and each successive one gives his occupation

before entering, the order entered, and the dates of entering and profession. Traversari is quoted in my "Adolescence," 209.

77. *Ibid.*, 210.

78. I have studied humanistic behavioral ideals *ibid.*, 238 seq.

79. Cited by Hatfield, "Compagnia," 146.

forty could not have done them better."[80] We see here amazement that one could dress up the young without obliterating their angelic purity; that "little angels" could be taught to simulate "natural behavior" artfully by careful indoctrination. Their behavior was not merely inspired by God.[81] Contemporaries were coming to believe that children could learn without being contaminated by the world, that this was the perfect age of spontaneity fused with learning.

It was soon clear that children could do more than imitate a grave Child Jesus. They could perfectly mime their elders, preserve all of the traditional political, generational, and religious configurations for which those fathers stood, all while in a state of innocence. Describing another Magi procession in 1468, Giovanni Caroli told how sons imitated fathers in public:

> They had so carved their faces and countenances in masks that they might scarcely be distinguishable from the real [fathers]. And their very sons had put on their clothes, which they then used, and they had learned all of their gestures, copying each and every one of their actions and habits in an admirable way. It was truly lovely for the real citizens who had convened at the public buildings to look upon their very selves feigned with as much beauty and processional pomp as the regal magnificence and the most ample senate of the city, which they would proudly conduct before them.[82]

It was an amazing feat, this procession in which the manly young, indistinct in gesture and clothing from their politician fathers, conducted the latter to the goal of the Three Kings. This was a promise for the future: The fathers' retinue would one day take the fathers' places, and be precisely the same in their physical and moral idiosyncrasies. Clearly, there was nothing to fear from the boys. If in the past they had been a distraction to their fathers and the city, now they would save them: "Not to confuse, but to save their seniors."[83]

What some boys were doing in adult confraternities others were accomplishing in their own adolescent confraternities. In the cloisters, piazzas, and churches of the city, adolescent groups worshiped age, ritually miming a familial ideal. Rossi pointed out long ago how markedly Old Testamental and Evangelical the surviving Florentine plays were, with their heavy emphasis on social and familial order.[84] By studying their parts in these plays, said a pedagogue who had authored one for his boys, the boys were admonished to "develop those foundations of the life of adolescents from which exactly the cult of God is formed."[85] Presenting their plays to their elders, they distilled lessons their fathers and mothers heard all too gladly. Isaac, boy that he was,

80. *Ibid.*

81. See, for example, the characterization of the Pistoian boys cited on page 374, this volume.

82. Cited in Hatfield, "Compagnia," 116; see also the interpretation of the passage by N. Davis, "Some Tasks and Themes in the Study of Popular Religion," in *Pursuit of Holiness*, 322.

83. This was the effect of the Pistoian boys, cited in my "Adolescence," 248.

84. *Ibid.*, 227.

85. *Ibid.*, 230.

submitted himself to his father Abraham and to God with all the mature deliberation of a grown man:

> *How ignorant, blind, proud, and mad is he*
> *Who searches for happiness outside of God!*
> *What is more bestial than to be a boy*
> *Of the world, and of the demon, full of wickedness!*[86]

A prostrate Ismael and Agar pleaded for God's forgiveness:

> *Lord, by whom we have been created,*
> *Without whom nothing would exist,*
> *And if we merit being expelled*
> *And to lack a bit of water,*
> *By your grace we are now liberated.*
> *Thus praise and glory always be to you.*
> *Here we stand, Lord, until it pleases you;*
> *For without you is war, with you complete peace.*

Upon which another boy threw himself at the feet of his terrestrial father, in front of all those fathers in the audience, and said:

> *O my dear father,*
> *I am an Ismael:*
> *And as that [Ismael] from God,*
> *I from you ask pardon;*
> *And if I am of such condition*
> *That I merit being expelled,*
> *Give me, if it pleases you,*
> *Water and bread, as to him.*[87]

How far this was from the behavior of those "boys of the world" that one little saint had condemned, who spent their time torturing animals, insulting their elders, ridiculing prostitutes in the brothels, and raising mayhem with tiny children. How much more serious was this activity than the gambling, jousting, tourneying, horse racing, hunting, birding, singing, dancing, and *armeggerie* their older brothers consumed their time with.[88] Confraternal boys, trained in the verbal and bodily gestures of Everyman, performed purified representations of the gerontocratic ideals of Florentine society.

Yet in these confraternal plays there was a message subtler than the affirmation of the status quo, one that called upon elders to be like their children, and pointed to children's institutions more than to individual boys as exemplary. We have already seen this revolutionary pedagogy heralded in the chronicler's wonder that three-year-olds could act as well as forty-year-

86. Original text *ibid.*, 227.
87. Text *ibid.*, 227f.
88. All these bad activities are contained in a list of prohibitions written into a projected set of *capitoli* for a boys' confraternity; *Bibl. Laurenziana, Acquisti e Doni*, 336, ff. 9v–12v (c. 1435–1447).

olds. It was but a step to the view that there was something wrong and shameful with adults as a group if they could not do as well as boys as a group. Thus Baldassare Castiglione wrote to a friend in the early sixteenth century after an adolescents' performance in Urbino:

> One of the comedies was composed by a *fanciullo* [and] recited by *fanciulli*. Perhaps they made the elders ashamed; they certainly performed miraculously. It was an incredible novelty to see little old men a palm high use [such] gravity, [such] severe gestures, [so well] copied.[89]

In Florence, a still more decisive step was long afoot. *We* are the ritual actors, the confraternal children told their fathers, you are but the audience! Starting their plays, the boys called their elders in the audience to order, as one day they would call society itself to order:

> *Be devout and don't make any noise:*
> *We do the work, you get the pleasure!*[90]

The beginnings of the idea that boys could change men had been revolutionary enough: Correctly trained in the confraternity, Traversari had told the pope in 1435, individual adolescents would bring their behavior into their parents' home and contribute to its betterment.[91] By now things had gone much further. Groups rather than individuals were becoming "a *universal* example for fathers and sons," as one later edition of the play *Abramo e Agar* said.[92] Society itself, the gerontocratic yet vulnerable order of Florentine fathers, was being admonished to imitate the ritual performances of its young. In the early sixteenth century, Pistoian boys of the Purità carried banners reading, "From the mouth of children," and "Theirs is the kingdom of heaven."[93] Their plays were "spiritual successes," said the group's friar corrector: "[The boys] gave the *popolo* quite an example and edification by marching in procession so composed and devoutly. Certainly example is more moving than speaking."[94]

The fifteenth-century boys' groups had laid the groundwork for two decisive transformations. First, the fathers had developed a social institution that might maintain gerontocratic social institutions while developing adolescent genius. Never before had the reverence for age and sexless gravity been so scrupulously and publicly manifested as in the dramatic action of fifteenth-century Florence. Yet as the fathers watched their children orate, march in procession, and act, they wept as Florentines had always wept at the processions of their fathers and clergy: "With such grace [that they] reduced many of the bystanders to tears and devotion."[95] As the century approached its end, Florentines increasingly looked to the "grace" of their young to deter-

89. Text in my "Adolescence," 247.

90. *Ibid.*, 231.

91. *Ibid.*, 210.

92. *Ibid.*, 228.

93. *Ibid.*, 248.

94. *Ibid.*, 249.

95. *Ibid.*, 220.

mine the future of the city. Thus by corporate segregation from public life, biologically mature adolescents could be indoctrinated to act out the ideal and even the seamy daily life of their elders without losing their innocence. The future would have all the gestures of the elders, but it would be a new age of gravity. The groups were manipulated to reach that end. If boys had always been prettified at home so that they looked like priests or women, now those youthful energies were institutionally harnessed in much the same way that society authenticated its more traditional ritual objects: through silken clothes, angels' robes, and other accoutrements designed to preserve the "shining brilliance" of powerful ritual objects, while neutralizing the erotic anarchy in the adolescent breast. They were in a sense pure object: Compared by pedagogues to horses, plants, and clay, the boys of the ideal confraternity responded to directions in much the same way as the festive machines of the Florentines, which, their movable parts concealed, could be made to behave "more naturally than nature."[96]

Still, these children were their fathers' sons, and in their unmechanical naturalness they could evoke the protective smile of God. Here was the second transformation: Acting out the biblical stories, visualizing for their elders the meaning of fraternity, they were slowly becoming a new fetish of a deeply religious society, a salvational instrument that could either supplement or supplant both their fathers' and the clergy's ritual position in the city. The essential new aspect of this realignment of sacrality was that the new cult object was a purer and more direct reflection of societal values and personages—a direct affirmation of the present, but at the same time a generational guarantee of the future. On the eve of the rise of Savonarola, adolescent confraternities, inspired by the adolescence of Lorenzo de' Medici, whom we have yet to study, were making the boys of Florence a part of the ritual identity of the city. More: It could even seem that they were the actors, the unchaste fathers their audience. As in the best drama, the play controlled the actors and the weeping audience.

Giovani

While adolescents worshiped weeping fathers in worthy temples, older brothers reveled outside, and many fathers liked it that way: "They say the *giovani* should not discuss public affairs, but pursue their sexual needs."[97] Young men were capable of maximum sexual activity, yet were still considered too young and dangerous for political community; such might be a facile characterization of the youth of fifteenth-century Florence. It will not do. In the Last Republic of Florence (1527–1530), these *giovani* emerged as a major force in the city and were absorbed, as their younger brothers had been

---

96. *Ibid.*, 246f enlarges this concept of mechanistic manipulation.

97. "Sfogare i loro piaceri corporei"; *Opere Politiche e Letterarie di Donato Giannotti*, I (Florence, 1850), 230.

in the Savonarolan period, into the politics and representational life of the Florentine commune. They too were part of the ritual revolution of these two generations of Florentine history, and the roots of that revolution must be sought in the fifteenth century.

Who were the *giovani*? Most simply, they were that age group, married or single, between the adolescents and the elderly or *vecchi*. Seen from another angle, *giovanezza* was that time of life on both sides of the "complete" age (*perfetta età*) of thirty years; it was the period in which the young approached the pinnacle of their physical and mental powers, and receded from it while still potent.[98] Those *giovani* over thirty were called *uomini fatti;* those under, *garzoni*.[99] The age at which adolescence ended and *giovanezza* started was a matter of dispute, but one interesting fact is apparent: Youth came *after* adulthood in the Florentine vocabulary. Cavalcanti characterized a jouster as "tender of age, such that our laws would sooner call him an adult than a youth. . . . Yet his hits did not seem at all those of an adult; rather, they were more deadly than those of hardened knights."[100] An adult, in Florentine usage, was a boy who had reached the age of discretion, and could be legally emancipated;[101] he was an adolescent. In the Florentine sources, we find people called adolescents up until the age of twenty-eight.[102] But generally speaking, the most common age of division was about twenty-four years, when sons had been emancipated, when men could become priests, when adolescents left their confraternities and switched from the white of adolescence and childhood to the green of youth.[103]

But youth was more than an age. It was a particular state of mind, spirit, and physique that, like nobility, both fascinated and terrified the ignoble elders. Perhaps the most common category of youthful specificity was sexual. The *giovane* had left behind the incoherent and diffuse eroticism of adolescence, and was now capable of directing his energies. He could make sex count.[104] Yet the calculation of the *giovane* was governed not by social restraints, but by his lustful goal. The clever, sagacious *giovani* driven by ferocious desires, whom we know from Florentine popular literature, haunted the elderly husbands of Florence, who knew these young blades would inherit their wives. They haunted the moralists, for they were the ones who solicited virgin adolescent boys.

The *gioventù* was also without religion or piety. The worst of them were

---

98. Aristotle's "perfect age" of thirty is referred to by Savonarola, *Ezechiele*, I, 143.

99. "Essendo egli ancora giovane, sebbene uomo fatto . . . "; Filippo Sassetti in *Francesco Ferruccio e la Guerra di Firenze del 1529–1530. Raccolta di Scritti e Documenti Rari pubblicati per cura del Comitato per le Onoranze a Francesco Ferrucci* (Florence, 1889), 63; "Garzoni da 18 in 30 anni"; Schnitzer, *Quellen*, IV, 159ff (Piero Parenti).

100. "Tenero d'età, tanto che le nostre leggi piuttosto adulto che giovane il chiamavano . . . nè mica parevano i suoi colpi d'adulto, anzi portavano molto

più che quelli degl'indurati cavalieri"; Cavalcanti, *Istorie*, VII, 14.

101. For ages of emancipation of the Corsini family, see Herlihy and Klapisch, *Toscans*, 575.

102. M. Palmieri, cited in Garin, *Educazione*, 114.

103. This change of color was made ritually when boys left the adolescent confraternities; *BNF*, Cl. XXXI, cod. 11, ff. 6v–7r (Company of S. Giovanni Vangelista).

104. See the characterization by a Sienese woman who should have known, in Herlihy, "Vieillir," 1347.

not simply high-spirited, Donato Giannotti would say; they were toughs (*bravi*) who "threaten bar keepers, dismember [statues of] saints, and break pots and plates."[105] Calculated ridicule was their stock in trade. To the modern, ridicule appears part of a total ritual system, but to contemporaries it did not. *Giovani* had absolutely no religious identity in society; the innocence of childhood was gone, but the gravity of age had not yet arrived. This absence of religious identity is confirmed by a ritual fact: The Florentine clergy, the mature laity of both sexes, and the children all appeared in the streets in times of crisis and were mentioned as imploring God for the salvation of the city. Not until the Last Republic can one find a single indication of the *giovani*, identified as such, marching in crisis.[106] No such thing as "*giovani* religiosity" was imaginable during the Florentine republic.

A last characteristic of youth was their liberality or, in pejorative terms, their social irresponsibility:

> They are in fact by nature splendid and liberal, because they have not yet experienced need, and have not yet earned with their own efforts the riches in which they swim. Someone who puts together property with his own sweat does not usually squander it.[107]

Here again, a psychological characteristic of youth had immediate social implications, this time touching the distribution of property. Youth were egalitarian, the humanist pedagogue Vergerio meant to say, but the world was not. Youth squandered fortunes, but Jews gathered them in.[108] In a thousand variations the figure of the penurious youth crossed the Florentine stage. We have seen that government in 1421 threatened to withold office from youth if they would not marry and thus assume responsibility. When that failed, it instituted an investment fund in 1425 for youth, in part to encourage marriage; it was no more successful.[109] A thousand youth, less pious than Giovanni Morelli, wandered through their twenties dissipating the estates left them by deceased fathers. Others whose fathers still lived pressed their fathers to emancipate them so that they could go on spending, or so many fathers understood their sons' motivations. The fathers, fearful that they themselves would be abandoned, refused:

> A man wants to have sons. But five times out of six they become his enemies, desiring their father's death so that they can be free . . . abandoning those for whom they should [be willing to] die a thousand deaths.[110]

105. Words of D. Giannotti, cited in *Francesco Ferruccio*, 289f.

106. The more standard mention of the *giovani* in a period of crisis was the astounded observation that "even *giovani*" were entering religious life; see, for example, my *Spiritual Power*, 131f (1377).

107. Vergerio's text is in my "Adolescence," 240.

108. On the relation between Jewish money lenders and spendthrift *giovani*, see my "Charity and the Defense of Urban Elites in the Italian Communes," in F. Jaher (ed.), *The Rich, the Well Born, and the Powerful* (Urbana, 1973), 80, 84.

109. *ASF, Prov.*, 114, ff. 117r–118r (*mons puellorum*); *ibid.*, ff. 156r–157r (Feb. 23, 1424/1425; *mons invenum*); also Molho, *Florentine Public Finances*, 138ff; J. Kirshner, *Pursuing Honor While Avoiding Sin. The Monte delle Doti of Florence* (Milan, 1978), examines only the girls' dowries.

110. F. Sacchetti, *Trecentonovelle*, 51, 290, sentiments

Liberality, religious indifference, and a calculating virility; these were the qualities that made up the image that Florentine elders had of their youth. To what use could they be put in the business world, in arms, letters, and government? Advising Florentine fathers considering careers for their sons in the early 1430s, Leon Battista Alberti gave what he thought was the city's attitude toward the first three career options:

> Our city does not take kindly to one of its own who gains too much reputation at arms. . . . Nor does our city praise men of letters much. Rather, it attends to and desires profits and riches.[111]

Many Florentine young men went into business, of course, but we do not know at what age they assumed decision-making positions. Even thirteen-year-olds might be named the heads of industrial firms, but such boys obviously made no decisions.[112] Sacchetti's warnings to his fellow fathers not to emancipate their boys might in fact indicate that in Florence, as in Venice, many sons were hindered from full involvement in business activity until well advanced in age.[113] Obviously, the fire and impulse of youth were not attractive qualities to the cautious, even dour Florentine businessman of the fifteenth century.

There was of course a strong feeling among many Florentines like Alberti that a business career was something less than honorable. Instead, fine young men might choose letters. Yet here as well Alberti indicates that the city was less than supportive, even if, as Martines has shown, it did heap honors on established scholars who worked for the commune.[114] Nor was Alberti's opinion isolated; in the coming years the view that young Florentines had to leave home to pursue excellence became something of a truism.[115]

That was certainly the case for those interested in a military career. The city was indeed unhappy when its boys took up arms, despite the fact that the psychological character attributed to youth sounded like a prescription for a military career. The fathers of Florence hired foreign mercenaries to do their fighting, not because of cost-effectiveness, but because they feared their youth would turn arms inward against the regime. The absence of a citizen army reflected a fear of youth, as Machiavelli would realize: Why should Sacchetti's son "die a thousand deaths" for his father when he had no *patria* to sacrifice for?[116] Unlike feudal Europe, which through its knightly institutions could profit from the passionate genius of youth, Florence could not. The youth lost, but the city paid as well. For how could a society that had so little use for

identical to those of Paolo da Certaldo, *Libro*, 242. Note that this fear of abandonment complemented the sons' fear that their fathers would die, and thus abandon them.

111. Alberti, *Libri della Famiglia*, 49.

112. R. De Roover says it was a common practice to list minors as head of commercial firms; *Rise and Decline*, 42. See also Herlihy and Klapisch, *Toscans*, 575.

113. On Venice, see J. Easton Law, "Age Qualifications and the Venetian Constitution: The Case of the Capello Family," *Papers of the British School at Rome* XXXIX (1971), 135.

114. Martines, *Social World*, 244–252.

115. On which see page 526, this volume.

116. Also page 520, this volume.

the idealism, liberality, and ferocity of youth be anything but pedestrian? Writing in the wake of the disastrous defeat of Zagonara in 1425, Poggio Bracciolini mirrored the opinion not only of the Roman diplomatic community where he was employed, but of many Florentines as well. The city had lost this battle because the government cared only for "graft and profit." It might have lost bravely, but instead did so with "disgrace and dishonor and extreme shame," so that the city was "a laughingstock and an object of contempt to all nations."[117]

The fourth possible occupation of young men, politics, was the least available to them, for, as Florentines and Europeans in general asserted, youth lacked the gravity necessary for membership in the active political community. Stated in simplest constitutional terms, Florentine law excluded those less than twenty-nine or thirty years old from significant office, and in order to bestow on certain offices "more authoritative majesty," as Machiavelli said, the law required thirty-five, forty, or even forty-five years of age.[118] Thus the law gave young men in their twenties good reason to "despair" of ever fully entering the halls of government.

Yet the complexity of Florentine practice refined this gerontocratic legal foundation, and made room for considerations of family, regime, and class. In fact, each patrician father and every regime had a solid family interest in seeing their sons in office as early as possible. Fathers of the middle and lower gilds, however, had no such interest, and they were the most determined opponents of youth's entry into government: Since these gilds had a right to only a minuscule proportion of offices, the larger the pool, the fewer the fathers who would ever actually win office.[119] As a group, all political fathers might fear the possibility of their sons combining under one great political patron and betraying the *patria*; patricide could be political as well as familial.[120] Yet the arithmetic of government office caused lesser fathers to eschew their sons' political ambitions.

Thus the patrician pillars of society could be found pleading a youth's case to hoary lower gildsmen: Liberalizing the entry of youth into government, they said, would benefit the whole political class, for this would prevent youthful despair.[121] The youth themselves may have been no less bitter than the lower gild fathers were suspicious, for their fathers did not

117. Bracciolini's complaints mentioned only the problem of corrupt politicians, not that of youth; Bracciolini and Niccoli, *Letters*, 90. But exactly the same characterization of government as a problem of elders, and the *giovani* as victims, is found later; see page 520, this volume.

118. Machiavelli, *History*, 152. An institutional study on age requirements in Florentine government is badly needed; for now, see Rubinstein, *Government*, 115, 118f, 124, 147f, 190, 220. Comparisons to the Venetian system may be had through Law, "Age Qualification"; D. Chambers, *The Imperial Age of Venice* (London, 1970), 82ff; Pullan, *Rich and Poor*, 116, 122f.

But see the fundamental article by S. Chojnacki, "Political Adulthood in Fifteenth-Century Venice," *American Historical Review* XCI (1986), 791–810.

119. This important point of class-specific attitudes toward youth, rooted in institutional arrangements, emerges from the communal debates of 1466; G. Pampaloni, "Nuovi Tentativi di Riforme alla Costituzione Fiorentina visti attraverso le Consulte," *ASI*, CXX (1962), especially 542.

120. Treason as patricide: *ASF, Prov.*, 31, ff. 11v–13v (Sept. 5, 1341).

121. Pampaloni, "Nuovi Tentativi," 542.

consider what the youth could do for the *patria*, but what individual young men could do for their family, their sect, their class. This was nothing new. These complex political interests bereft of an interest in the *gioventù* as such are already apparent in Filippo Villani's report of political conditions in 1363:

> Many youths not past adolescence found themselves in office through the efforts of their fathers in the regime. And it happened that when one did a scrutiny in those times, three out of four were not older than twenty years. Thus those in diapers were being scrutinized.[122]

Adult resentments of this type came to be abundant in the fifteenth century, when the oligarchic regime of the early years perfected a new system that allowed youngsters to be "seen" (*veduto*) or examined for office when they were in fact very young, even if they could not be "placed" (*seduto*) in office until a later age. The system worked to the advantage of youth, it seemed. For each time a young person was seen but was still not old enough to be placed, he accumulated a greater right to be placed in office once he reached the minimum age of thirty; the odds were that he would immediately accede to an office at thirty years.[123]

Thus Buonaccorso Pitti's unexceptional declamation of the early fifteenth century that "two sorts of citizens, youths and upstarts, have managed to worm their way into government by taking advantage of [the *vecchi*'s dissentions]" ushered in a whole generation of outrage that youth would "take advantage" of their fathers' disunity and inherit the earth.[124] In Venice an old doge was declaiming against bellicose youth; in Florence Bernardino of Siena railed against "young angelic" rulers.[125] As they worried about their own youth, Florentine chroniclers nervously reported a youthful conspiracy at Venice, a 1433 plot of *giovani* to "give each other their votes and [thus] get themselves elected instead of others."[126] There was a successful coup in a Florentine monastery where *giovani* monks drove out the *vecchi*, and a plot "among the bestial youth" to seize the communal election boxes and burn them so as to force a new scrutiny, and yet another conspiracy of "certain Florentine *giovani*" with the Milanese ambassadors to betray the city.[127] The Florentine contemporary Giovanni Cavalcanti wanted to forgive elders who did not understand the danger, but it was difficult for him. Rinaldo degli

122. F. Villani, XI, 65.

123. Rubinstein, *Government*, 64f.

124. Pitti, *Memoir*, 74 (1402).

125. Doge Mocenigo's warning against the "young" Francesco Foscari is noted in Baron, *Crisis*, 391f; on the *giovangeli*, Bernardino of Siena, *Prediche* (Florence, 1424), I, 202f.

126. "In questi dì si trovò a Vinegia, che circa di 40 giovani s'erano giurati insieme darsi le electioni tra loro, e le ballotte, et non ad altri. Privorongli degli ufici, et condannorongli et chi in prigione, et chi bandeggiorono"; G. di Jacopo Morelli, *Cronica*, 108.

127. On the contemporary coup at S. Salvi, see P. Puccinelli, *Istoria dell'Eroiche Attioni d'Ugo il Grande . . . . con la Cronica dell'Abbadia di Firenze* (Milan, 1664), 122. The victor was the *giovane* Bernardo Morelli, on whom see ASF, *Dipl., Badia Fiorentina*, July 6, 1463. The bestial youth's plan of 1433 is mentioned by G. Cavalcanti, *Istorie*, IX, 1. The 1435 plot with the Milanese is recorded by G. di Jacopo Morelli, *Cronica*, 132. On these years, see D. Kent, *Rise of the Medici*. These events are so chronologically concentrated in Venice and Florence as to make one suspect some contact between the *giovani* of both cities, though the sources do not so hint.

Albizzi loved his country, Cavalcanti believed, but why did he not more firmly disavow "the new and raw *giovani* of the government"?[128] "Many youth had recently entered government," he wrote, "and if some elders remained in it, they did not want to."[129]

Modern Florentine historians have paid little attention to this preoccupation with the youth in the early fifteenth century, but the historians of the early sixteenth century did understand. Machiavelli, for example, explained the Albizzi regime's loss of reputation by the fact that it had admitted "abject men, both *giovani* and newcomers, those not interested in mature deliberation."[130] His younger contemporary Donato Giannotti elaborated this view, showing that that regime's system of "showing and placing," intended to foster its sons, led to Medicean tyranny once that one family controlled the scrutiny process. Grandfather or father groveled before the Medici in the interest of their *giovani:*

> If he had sons, even if they were in diapers, he maneuvered to have them extracted so that, even if they could not be *seduti,* they would at least be *veduti* for the magistracies. This law consequently gave the [Medici] tyrants a golden opportunity to buy men and gain them as clients. Besides, it was totally absurd and ridiculous to hear someone in diapers nominated to the College or the Twelve or the Signoria.[131]

Destined to explode during the Last Republic, the problem of youth in the fifteenth century required a series of expedients to prevent the youth from despairing, as was commonly said, in order to control the threat of conspiracy among that segment of the population where calculated sagacity combined with ferocious eros. This goal was pursued in the ritual spheres of government, confraternities, and festive life.

The most effective co-optative step any government could take to aid youth was to allow them into the political community before age, a step that Venice had taken long before.[132] Three practices of the Medicean period deserve mention in this regard. The first was to ensure scrutinies every five years as required by law, so that youth of the proper age would be promptly eligible for office. The second practice was to permit a deceased magistrate's electoral rights to devolve upon his son even if the latter were below the minimum age. A twenty-five-year-old son, for example, might replace his father in a council with a base age of twenty-eight.[133] The third practice involved permitting a select group of young men useful to the Medici to be appointed to a position by decree regardless of age.[134] The government did

128. Cavalcanti, *Istorie,* II, 22.

129. *Ibid.*

130. Machiavelli, *History,* 262.

131. Giannotti, *Opere,* 113f.

132. The Venetian procedure for admission into the Maggior Consiglio kept the age requirement at twenty-five, but admitted a certain number of twenty-year-olds by lot; Chojnacki, "Coming of Age." The reticence of the Florentines to adopt such a procedure until the time of Savonarola is the strongest possible evidence of the threat *giovani* were thought to be in Florence. Even then the passions were heated, as in an interesting *consulta* quoted by S. Bertelli, "Constitutional Reforms in Renaissance Florence," *Journal of Medieval and Renaissance Studies* III (1973), 161f.

133. As shown in Rubinstein, *Government,* 148f.

134. *Ibid.,* 220f.

not go beyond these limited steps to foster actual participation in the political process. It did take two further steps that made some youth observers or instruments in the governmental process. Thus in 1465 several counselors urged that young men be permitted to state in council the opinions of their fathers' groups on various questions "so that they learn by heart and are instructed in governance." We learn from the same record that the older men spoke before the younger in council, and that it was good form for the young to rubber-stamp the opinions of their elders.[135] Still another observer role was created in the diplomatic field. Apparently not required until 1498, the practice of *giovani* accompanying ambassadors on embassies can be documented as early as 1418, when twenty-one-year-old Filippo di Cino Rinuccini, "wearing so many vestments and so many pearls," accompanied a formal embassy to the pope.[136]

Public festivals offered a broad realm for youth's occupation, and *giovani* formed a very important part of the commune's increasingly opulent displays. Groups of youth were charged with serving at banquets. Filippo Rinuccini recalled that in 1415 at the age of eighteen he and his cohorts "governed one of the tables" at a banquet offered for new knights.[137] They were of the age group that actually performed the jousts, *armeggerie*, and dances that were such important additions to the basic festival of San Giovanni. But the increased participation of the *giovani* must be carefully understood. First, it had no convincing pedagogic or preparative function. The humanist Guarino Veronese might praise the equestrian games he saw in Florence because they gave adolescents hope and a chance to prove themselves, and a contemporary versifier might praise the institution of a joust on the feast of St. Dionysius because it trained the youth in *prodezza* or prowess, but prowess and proof of what?[138] They would never be able to use those skills in the city. Second, the youth were important as the sons of their fathers, rather than as individuals. When recording their participation in jousts, young men might list their colleagues by name, for this was a quasi-legal fashion of recalling the bonds established in youth. But the chronicles of the age list individual jousters only as "the sons of" their fathers.[139] The youth were not important as an age group integral to the ceremonial representation of the commune.

135. G. Pampaloni, "Fermenti di Riforme Democratiche nella Firenze Medicea del Quattrocento," *ASI*, CXIX (1961), 247f, and 261f, where these concessions are meant to "stimulate virtue"; also his "Nuovi Tentativi," 526, and 534–536 for protests against elders being scrutinized by *giovani*.

136. Rinuccini, lv. According to the Herlihy and Klapisch Catasto printout in the *ASF*, Filippo was born in 1397.

137. Rinuccini, liv.

138. The letter attributed to Guarino, written to the chancellor Fortini, is in Truffi, *Giostre*, 77f. A horse race had originally been instituted to celebrate S.

Dionisio, but this was changed to a joust: "Il più bel fatto non s'ordinò mai, perchè c'è poche giostre e palii assai"; *ibid.*, 139. A further official athletic event was a foot race involving *garzoni* and *fanciulle*, first documented on the feast of Mary Magdalene, July 22, 1475. The *podestà* celebrated it in his palace, "come è di usanza, per tutti che si truovano in officio in quel dì. E per maggior festa, egli fece correre da garzoni uno stocco bello per dono al primo. E fece correre da fanciulle femine un altro donno di braccia 6 di panno pannazzo"; ser Giusto, f. 113v.

139. One may compare the *ricordanze* of Francesco di Tommaso Giovanni, which does the former, with the *priorista* Pietrobuoni, which does the latter.

There is no evidence that the activities of the *giovani* were thought to be accomplishing the same moral ends as those of adolescents. We have found that the institutionalization of adolescent energies was the cutting edge of a new view of their communal identity. This was not so for the *giovani;* the city fathers remained extremely suspicious of institutions for *giovani.*

Societies of youth had been very popular during the early thirteenth century, and nowhere more in Tuscany than in Florence.[140] But along with neighborhood groups and societies of women, they had disappeared, mourned by Boccaccio in an age when the commune insisted on repressing them.[141] At the beginning of the fifteenth century, such *societates iuvenum* again made a brief appearance: a confraternity of S. Matteo meeting in the church of Santo Spirito (1396), one of S. Michele in the Servite church (1420), the "certain societies of youth" who were said to carry communal torches in the feast of San Giovanni (1419). All are evidence that at the same time adolescent confraternities were getting off the ground, confraternities specifically for youth made the same attempt.[142] Much remains to be learned about this subject, but it does seem that the future did not confirm whatever hope men like Traversari might have had that a confraternal system for *giovani* would develop. After these grouped references, there are no substantial indications of youth confraternities for the rest of the fifteenth century, no known references to confraternities that had a maximum age other than those for adolescents. Generally speaking, those young men leaving the latter entered adult confraternities if they entered at all. There was simply too much fear of the young building groups of their own.

This extreme caution of Florentine elders can best be seen by comparing the longevity of youth groups that were formed to stage jousts, *armeggerie,* and dances with the functionally similar Venetian companies of the Socks (*della Calza*). We know some of the Florentine names: the groups called *della Galea* (1415), *della Sfera* (1416), and *del Fiore* (1419) staged *armeggerie.*[143] Francesco di Tommaso Giovanni was one of the nine members of the brigade of the Parrot in 1421, and his brother jousted for the Squires of Fortune in 1430.[144] Not one of these groups had any longevity; they disappeared after the events for which they had been formed, or so we must conclude from the fact that not one group is mentioned twice in the literature or gives any other sign of continued existence. The Venetian groups started at about this time, and had a continuous existence thereafter.[145] The contrast with Florence could not have been more glaring.

140. Boncompagno da Signo spoke of the *societates iuvenum* in his "Cedrus," in L. Rockinger (ed.), *Briefsteller und Formelbücher des Eilften bis Vierzehnten Jahrhunderts* I (Munich, 1863), 122. For more information on these early groups, see R. Davidsohn, *Firenze ai Tempi di Dante* (Florence, 1929), 517f.

141. Boccaccio, *Decameron*, VI, 9.

142. Respectively ASF, *Prov.*, 85, ff. 247r–248r (Dec. 8); ASF, *Not. Antecos.*, S 672 (Nov. 20); ASF, *Prov.*,

109, ff. 49v–50r (June 12).

143. Del Corazza, 254f.

144. Francesco di Tommaso Giovanni, cited in Giovanni–Carnesecchi, Feb. 1420/1421 and Jan. 29, 1429/1430.

145. On which see L. Venturi, "Le Compagnie della Calza (secc. XV–XVI)," *Nuovo Archivio Veneto* (*Archivio Veneto*, ser. 3, XVI–XVII) (1908–1909), 161–221, 140–233.

The Medici period brought not alleviation of the youths' inability to organize, but the contrary. Their organization for secular festivities remained ephemeral, and their right to belong to adult confraternities was now attacked. The easy move that Donato Acciaiuoli had been able to make from the adolescent group of the Nativity to the adult night company of S. Girolamo became a thing of the past when, in 1444, the government closed the doors of confraternities to *giovani* twenty-four years or older who had been examined (*veduti*) for political office, an age that was reduced to twenty in 1455.[146] Excluded from political office until twenty-nine or thirty years of age, future officeholders now found it difficult even to associate with their elders in confraternities. Savonarola was right when he later wrote that the "tyrant" prohibited congregations for fear of conspiracy against him. These laws did have the theoretical effect of forbidding all access to confraternities by the whole political class, old and young.[147] But their most important feature at this point is that their elders' fear of conspiracy affected the lives of young men long before they had reached the legal age for office.

By their political and confraternal policies, the fifteenth-century Medici fairly forced the young men of Florence into their own entourage; gleaming youth now hung around the Medici palace as once they had around Walter of Brienne. For more than a century republican pluralism had restrained Florentine families from building their own youthful—or plebeian—retinues in their neighborhoods, and had inhibited them from too recklessly fostering their sons' admission to government. Now the Medici followed the lead of the earlier "tyrant." Developing a true cult of youth, Cosimo and his successors showered the brilliant young men who came to pay their daily reverence with political favors and private honors, then sent them back to their neighborhoods to spread, and organize, the good word. The Medici rose to power on a ground-swell of class, age, neighborhood, and occupational particularism. As it pertains to youth, this thesis may be documented by three important sources from the years around 1471. They suggest that youth had a part in a thoroughgoing centralization and rationalization of the Florentine confraternal system, which created in effect a new, integrated geography of festive groups in the city, one that subverted the republican geography of Florence.

On August 25, 1471, a great festival honoring St. Bartholomew the apostle was held in the Piazza Santa Croce. This "very beautiful" event, we are told by a contemporary, included "a great cavalcade with two kings, one white and one black."[148] A document of 1489 furnishes us with further information on this event of 1471: The festival had included an account of the saint's miracles and martyrdom performed by a "society of the apostle San

146. On Acciaiuoli, see my "Adolescence," 210; the laws are cited in n. 44, this chapter.

147. Savonarola, *Trattato*, in *Aggeo*, 459. In addition to the evidence presented by Rubinstein, *Government*, 119, on the Florentines using these confraternities for political purposes, see Bernardino of Siena, *Prediche*

(Florence, 1424), II, 80, speaking of the "secret companies" through which "you help each other, rightly or wrongly, to get office."

148. Ser Giusto, cited in Hatfield, "Compagnia," 120; also L. Morelli, 188.

Bartolomeo" that met in the dormitories of the friars of Santa Croce and was composed of "many citizens, all still young." When performed in 1489 for the first time since 1471, the *festa* received the same kind of governmental subvention that the earlier one had obtained.[149]

This festival will prove to be of great interest to our inquiry for two reasons. First, we now know who these young men were who performed the 1471 *festa*, and what their institutional form was. On June 23, 1471, five of the six *spectabiles viri*, citizens of Florence, who were the *operarii opere festivitatis Sancti Bartholomei*, and thirty-one other Florentine citizens identified as "men and persons of the said *opera* of S. Bartolomeo," appointed a syndic to collect the money that the government had promised the *opera* to stage the upcoming feast. This document is the first to emerge in fifteenth-century Florentine theatrical history that lists the names of those who staged a particular theatrical event.[150] Who were these men?

The *opera* of S. Bartolomeo was overwhelmingly composed of established Florentines; almost all have family names, and none is listed by occupation. It was therefore easy to determine their ages by comparison with the government's *Book of Ages*, and to ascertain that this was, generally speaking, a group of youth. Of the thirty-six names, the ages of twenty-two were established, and they range from a low of fourteen (the next oldest being seventeen) to a high of fifty years (the next youngest being thirty-nine).[151] The mean age was twenty-seven and one-half; the group thus spanned the officeholding and nonofficeholding years. Using the same *Book of Ages*, I was able to determine where twenty-two members lived. Twenty of them came from families of the quarter of Santa Croce, as did several other individuals whom I could not locate in the *Book of Ages*, but whose families were established in that quarter. Still more interesting, eighteen of the twenty persons of the quarter of Santa Croce came from two contiguous wards or gonfalons.[152] Something very much out of keeping with the previous associative history of the city emerges. Florentine confraternities of the classical period of ritual had drawn their membership, as I have stressed, from across the city, as part of the commune's determined attempt to repress particularisms and family conspiracies. This festival, on the contrary, was staged by a group with a pronounced neighborhood character. A group of *giovani* from a neighborhood staged a festival, with the backing of the government. Still, the peculiar

149. *ASF, Prov.*, 180, ff. 26v–27r (May 27).

150. *ASF, Not. Antecos.*, L 139 (1470–1476), f. 51r (June 23, 1471).

151. Compiled from *ASF, Tratte*, 443 bis. The fifty-year-old was Matteo di Zanobi de' Cocchi (*Tratte:* di Cocco Donati); the presence of an elder in this group may be compared to the position of Doffo Spini in the company of the Compagnacci during the Savonarolan period; see page 478, this volume. Such a man may be the patron of the company, and it is at least possible he played the part of one of the kings in the festival.

152. The two members who seem to be from the quarter of Santa Maria Novella rather than Santa Croce are Jacopo di Alessio di Benedetto, the youngest member, and Lorenzo di Francesco di Filippo Lapaccini. Giovanni di Sandro Falconi probably lived in the quarter of Santo Spirito. The two wards in Santa Croce where members' residences seem to have been concentrated are Leon Nero and Bue. All this information has only approximate value, since I have used only the Herlihy and Klapisch printout of 1427 to locate the concentrations of families in particular areas.

character of this group must be kept in mind: This was an *opera* for a particular celebration, and the 1471 procuration document does not say that this *opera* was part of, or charged by, the Confraternity of S. Bartolomeo, however probable that may be. The most we can say is that here in Santa Croce, neighborhood concentrations of youth were being subvented by the commune for festive purposes. The fashion in which this group related to the Confraternity of S. Bartolomeo and how these *veduti* young men could organize given the existing law remain obscure. I suspect that the peculiar term *opera festivitatis*, indicating a short-term organization to perform one feast, was used to avoid the legal prohibitions against *compagnie* of *veduti*.

The emergence of neighborhood youth as festive units in the later fifteenth century can be studied in a second document roughly contemporary to that of S. Bartolomeo. In a poem probably written in the late 1460s, Giovanni Frescobaldi describes a game of *palla di Calcio* he had seen in the Piazza Santo Spirito, the first such description we possess.[153] Jammed into the piazza, a host of spectators of every social class watched a competition between two different sections of the city:

> And there were fifteen of this quarter
> of Santo Spirito, of equal skill,
> Strong as bulls and light of foot,
> Who want to make their fame prevail.
> On the other team were as many squires
> Hoping to attain honor;
> They are called the Players of the Meadow
> And are so disciplined at Calcio.

Who were the players, and what was the configuration of the neighborhoods they represented? Frescobaldi called them *garzoni*, and guessed that they ranged from twenty to twenty-four years of age. He named all thirty players, but many only by nicknames and only twelve by family. These are all of the first rank; here was a group of late adolescent *veduti*, we surmise, doing battle with each other. One group, we see, was identified as representing the Oltrarno quarter of Santo Spirito; the other came from Citrarno, specifically the meadow or *prato* on the western edge of the city in the quarter of Santa Maria Novella. Was this a neighborhood competition? The spectators certainly thought so, for when the Santo Spirito group finally won the match, and its two trumpeters blared out victory, "every lowly low-life [of Santo Spirito] was proud as a rooster" when the victors were crowned.[154] Yet the players themselves may not in all cases have come from the sections of town they represented. It appears that some of the youngsters were from families that

153. Printed in Lanza, *Lirici Toscani*, 601–607. An almost contemporary source refers to the *festa* "della palla grossa al Prato e a Santo Spirito"; Dei, *Cronica*, f. 38v. This would seem to refer to the same game, but see L. Artusi and S. Gabbrielli, *Feste e Giochi a Firenze* (Florence, 1976), 71. In the early sixteenth century the Prato was the customary place for the game of Calcio; Masi, 85.

154. "Ogn'infimo vil rizza la cresta"; Lanza, *Lirici Toscani*, 607.

lived on the other side of the Arno from the quarter on whose team they played; furthermore, members of the Sapiti family played on both teams.[155]

The significance of this document is many-layered. It is our first document referring to communally acceptable, neighborhood festive competition since the early fourteenth century.[156] As far as I have been able to determine, it contains the very first expression of neighborhood pride at competitive victory. Although it shows that *giovani* or late adolescents were the sources of that pride, it may transpire that they did not necessarily live in the areas they fought for. A pride in neighborhod ritual and festive activity was being stimulated, I suggest, that did not necessarily correspond to the residences of those furnishing that pride. Finally, this document hints that the competing teams were thought of as parts of play kingdoms: Frescobaldi calls the young men squires (*scudieri*), and notes that the victors were crowned.

Before pursuing this point, I should summarize the evidence of *giovani* formal activities in the fifteenth century. The *giovani* of Florence did not develop stable institutional identities during the fifteenth century, as did their younger brothers. They played an important role in communal festivities, but under the aegis of their fathers. They were feared, yet the representation of their honor, bravery, and liberality was important to this ignoble community of fathers. Toward the end of the century limited evidence of a new festive role as bearers of neighborhood pride starts to emerge. Yet through all this, *giovani* participation in government remained constitutionally difficult, and the youth flocked to the court of the Medici to obtain from these protoprinces what they could not obtain from their fathers. In this still private setting, yet to be examined, they would learn the behavioral language of supplication, and would study both the bravado and the sweet courtesy of noble youth at a center that worshiped youth. For at that center was the young, dazzling Lorenzo, and the brilliance of youth could blind the most astute observers. "Lorenzo was young," wrote Philippe de Commynes of the lord of the Via Larga in 1478, "and he was governed by young men."[157]

Plebs

The plebs of Florence is the third liminal group that began to assume a distinctive role in communal representation during the fifteenth century. Its support also came to be solicited by the traditional political center of the Florentine procession. Yet how different from the adolescents and *giovani* were these wage laborers, handworkers, and petty merchants and masters, how circumscribed could be the progress of the politically excluded (*non-*

155. Matteo Bardi fought for the Prato, for example, as did Ulivieri Sapiti, whose kin Antonio was on the other side. The same caution applies to these assumptions of family locations as mentioned in n.152.

156. For the earlier evidence, see page 220, this volume.

157. Commynes, *Memoirs*, II, 393.

statuali) toward the center.[158] For the plebs was a class, not a generation, and the pretensions of its members to the center were revolutionary in implication, totally unlike the evolutionary thrust of the hopeful younger generation. Despite the dangers inherent in co-opting their revolutionary potential, however, these descendants of the Ciompi stepped onto the communal stage of the later fifteenth century in their own, clearly identified "plebeian" groups called *potenze* ("powers").[159] It was an astounding change. During most of the republic the lower classes had had no institutions, let alone ones they could publicly demonstrate. Now *potenze di plebi* marched in the street and celebrated their neighborhoods, their occupations, their own solidarity, and their lords. They called themselves baronies, and their leaders were kings, counts, dukes, and emperors. They organized the city into festive kingdoms, and in the sixteenth century dared their workaday employers to challenge the borders of these new constructs. What was the source of this amazing transformation? When did the *potenze* first show their regal organization?

The stones of Florence provide a clue. One of the *potenze* had its center in the Piazza Sant'Ambrogio. There in the Red City, as that area was called, are several vestiges of the Gran Monarchia that once held playful sway in these parts. Set in and wrapped around the masonry on one corner of the church itself is a stone boundary marker reading "Città Rossa" on both sides, and another inscription reading "Gran Monarcha Giovanni. MDLXXVII" on both sides. Across the piazza is a confraternal hall with another such possession marker wrapped around its corner reading "Pauperorum societatis Sancti Micaelis delle Paci," and set in the same wall is a stone medallion enclosing a shield in which is set a chalice with an emerging Christ. The medallion is inscribed "MCCCCLXXIII."[160] Realizing that societies of the poor, though not unknown in the earlier history of Florence, assume a particular importance during the second half of the fifteenth century, the student senses that he has been led back toward the origins of this neighborhood's organizations for the poor. Leaving the Monarchy of the Red City, he enters the neighboring Signoria of Monteloro, and at its center finds another stone marker wrapped around the corner masonry. This one reads "Timor Domini. 1473."

158. This tripartite division of the marginal groupings of Florence follows contemporary terminology and conceptualization. I do not imply that the adolescents or *giovani* groups were all upper class; their membership was mixed and depended on the individual group. Nor do I suggest that everyone called a plebeian was actually poor, or a handworker; the term *plebs* in the later fifteenth century can refer to anyone who was not a *statuale*, that is, did not have access to political office, and the percentage of *nonstatuali* seems to have increased during the fifteenth century as heredity increasingly became a condition of political status. Thus the plebs contained substantial, perhaps even rich, men. Still, the distinction Florentines made between the *statuali* and the plebs during this period meant more than a political distinction. It was an economic distinction, the plebs being thought to have its real strength in the mass of handworkers at the base of society.

159. The first unquestionable use of the word *potenza* for a specific type of group is very late, in Masi, 237 (1517). But as we shall see, these groups existed by other names long before. Perhaps a sonnet of Francesco degli Alberti (1401–1479) uses it in this institutional sense: The Magi send their custodian of flags to another monarchy and offer to it "le lor potenzie e i regni"; Lanza, *Lirici Toscani,* 122f.

160. The inscription of the Gran Monarcha reads as follows:

$$\text{G.}^{a} \quad \text{M.}^{ca} \quad \text{G.}^{i}$$

Previous students merely transcribed "A. CA. T. G. M. G.," and not surprisingly could make no sense of the inscription; *L'Illustratore Fiorentino. Calendario per l'Anno 1838* (Florence, 1837), 55, with bibliography.

Could it be pure chance to find two inscriptions of the same year in two neighborhoods known later for their *potenze*? Written documents suggest otherwise. All signs point to the early 1470s as the time when the future *potenze* first delimited their kingdoms and placed boundary markers with the permission of the Florentine government. Other signs indicate that in those early kingdoms the *giovani* of Florence played a part with the plebs who would later dominate them. We recall the crowning of the *giovani* victors at Calcio, and the fact that the young men of S. Bartolomeo were concentrated in discrete neighborhoods in 1471. Let us return now to the latter celebration and examine a third important document, which will give us further clues on how *giovani* and plebs in these years were parties to the implicit recognition and citywide organization of the *potenze* of Florence.

"In the year of the flood of waters 5110," the Three Magi wrote a fantastic courtly letter to the "princes" of the College of S. Bartolomeo; the "Magi" was the confraternity or Company of the Magi, identified with Medici patronage, the College none other than the group that put on the feast in Piazza Santa Croce in August 1471. Discovered and published by Rab Hatfield, this letter was almost certainly written in this year about the coming event.[161]

The Three Kings (Gaspar, Balthazar, and Melchior) wrote their letter "in the eastern parts, in those regions that border on the equinoxial parts," and sent it to the "Italic parts of the splendid city of Florence." More exactly, from "the Thrones of our Dominations," the kings addressed their loyal "deputated Principalities" in general, and specifically the "princes, governors, and protectors of the *università dedichata al santo collegio* which was named after the apostle Bartholomew," and met in these "Italic" parts. They could not attend the latter's feast, the Magi wrote these "Signori Inlustri," but they wanted those of S. Bartolomeo to know that they approved of it. So they sent this letter by their servant Sheba the Tall and promised to send a formal embassy to these "princes."[162]

The allusive hyperbole of this fascinating missive can be partly pierced. The normal feast of the Magi in these years featured a great mounted embassy of the Magi to Herod; the Magi were telling those of Piazza Santa Croce that they would send a similar embassy. The character of the festival of San Bartolomeo was equally equestrian and triumphal in nature, as we have seen. As the legend went, King Polemio sent his legates with gifts to the apostle, and the latter was subsequently martyred by that king's brother, King Astiage

---

161. Hatfield ingeniously established a date of 1466–1468; my reason for dating it 1471 is deductive: If the 1471 festival was not repeated until 1489 (see page 397, this volume), it is questionable that it would have been performed only three to five years before 1471. The previous performances I can find recorded were in 1452; ser Giusto, f. 68r, and in 1459; Dei, *Cronica*, f. 23r. For the text of the letter, Hatfield, "Compagnia," 148.

162. "Guaspar, Baldassar et Melchior, etc. Per la grazia dello altissimo Idio nelle parti d'oriente a' leali principati diputati, etc. A' divotissimi et inlustri principi, ghovernatori et protettori della excellentissima università dedichata al santo collegio che sotto il glorioso nome dello apostolo Bartolomeo nelle parti italiche nella splendida ciptà di Firenze si conducie. Salutei in Christi. . . . Apresso a' troni delle nostre dominationi, l'opere vostre sono acciette. . . . Onde noi mandiamo Sabam Alto fante propio portatore delle presenti. . . . Data nelle parti orientali apresso alle regioni chon le parti d'equinozio chonfinanti"; *ibid.* The tall people of Seba were commonly confused with ancient Sheba (*Saba*).

of Media; the Persian Magi were in effect saying that the Magi cavalcade would not be able to meet that of its vassal princes on the day of the feast. Instead the Magi sent their servant Sheba the Tall; the Shebans, as we shall see, were also subject to the Magi. Effectively, the Three Kings sent to Kings Polemio and Astiage at Santa Croce a Sheban cavalcade—the same group, perhaps, that in other Florentine festivals escorted the queen of Sheba on her visit to King Solomon.[163]

Here is a clear indication that the city was divided into noble kingdoms whose principals and legates visited each other with great mounted cavalcades, and evidence as well that these kingdoms were hierarchically ordered. Not only do the letter's references to thrones, dominations, and principalities play on the angelic *Celestial Hierarchies* of Dionysius Areopagitus (references to powers [*potenze*] conspicuously absent) or merely reflect the hegemonies the Magi legend attributed to the Three Kings at this time.[164] The letter also shows a very practical submission of the S. Bartolomeo group, and of other Florentine neighborhood groups, to the Medicean Magi.

The outlines of this urban festive hierarchy are unmistakably present in the letter where the Three Kings explain why they could not attend the St. Bartholomew festival: They were involved, they said, in the ongoing business of "transforming *our* kingdoms, especially Egypt, Ethiopia and Nubia, Arabia, Sheba, India, both the Medias, and Armenia."[165] Where were these kingdoms? Along what streets and streams did the Magi, and thus the Medici, draw boundaries? Where was Sheba, from whence a queen went to visit Solomon (1 Kings 10:1–13)? Where was Egypt, where Joseph son of Jacob placed in a chariot by the pharaoh "ruled over all the land" (Gen. 41:41–42) and Hermes Trismegistus had been king?[166] Was Arabia, "all of whose land was red" not the Città Rossa of S. Ambrogio, India perhaps the area around the church of that land's apostle St. Thomas in the Mercato Vecchio?[167] Since

163. Written sources have not yet yielded confirmation of a procession showing the queen going to Solomon, as she is shown on several Florentine marriage chests (*cassoni*). But it is a safe assumption that such processions or *trionfi* did take place, since the *cassoni* paintings show Solomon's palace in relation to actual Florentine geography; see, for example, P. Schubring, *Cassoni*, 2 vols. (Leipzig, 1923), II, pls. 193, 196, 197. The *rappresentazione* of S. Bartolomeo of 1471 may have had as its text the one printed by C. Molinari, "La Rappresentazione di S. Bartolomeo," *Annuali della Scuola Normale Superiore di Pisa*, ser. 2, XXIX (1960), 257–283, as well of course as the *Life* of the saint in Jacopo da Varagine, *Leggenda Aurea* (Florence, 1952), 538–545, and various New Testamental Apocrypha. Continuity with the Magi story is provided by the fact that Bartolomeo's assassin Astiage was a Persian or Median king, as the Magi were traditionally thought to have been.

164. The shifting location of the Magi's presumed realms in the fourteenth and fifteenth centuries is studied by A. M. di Nola in her edition of John of

Hildesheim, *La Storia dei Re Magi* (Florence, 1966), 40–51.

165. My italics. "Noi ci troviamo ochupati a transformare i nostri regni—et maximamente Egiptto, Ethiopia e Nubia, Arabia, Sabea, India, Madia e ll'una e ll'altra, e 'Rmenia—per tanto è impossibile assentarci"; Hatfield, "Compagnia," 148.

166. The possible relation of these realms to Roman subject kingdoms is suggested by the reference to two kingdoms of Media, a Roman administrative division. It is also possible that more could be found about this list by examination of the rich Hermetic literature of the time. Further research on the subject of the Florentine Magi would also investigate the role that the Council of Florence (1439) played in encouraging the creation of such play kingdoms, and recall the still older interest in Persian kings and Eastern exotica, as in F. Sacchetti, *Opere*, 10, 111, 220ff.

167. On red Arabia, see Di Nola, *Storia*, 244. On S. Tommaso, see L. Passerini, *Modi di Dire Proverbiali*

Florentine documents almost always list different areas of the city according to a fixed order of quarters (S. Spirito, S. Croce, S. Maria Novella, S. Giovanni), the Magi may have listed their kingdoms in that order as well; the locations suggested do seem to fit that order. But we cannot be sure, since the classical sixteenth-century *potenze* did not preserve these biblical names.

The last of the kingdoms mentioned by the Magi, however, was less biblical, and did survive in the sixteenth century. All doubts that the fanciful geography of this 1471 letter corresponded to a real urban geography are set to rest by the fact that the Magi's Kingdom of Armenia must be the well-known land of the king of the Millstone (*Re della Macine*), which met in the church of the Armenian monks in the Medicean parish of San Lorenzo.[168] The king of this discretely plebeian group is first mentioned in the 1486 statutes of the Confraternity of the Resurrection as a well-established figure whose plebeian barony made *edifizi* or floats that it used on the feast of San Giovanni.[169] In the light of other evidence now at our disposal, the combination of Resurrection and floats in this earliest document in the institutional history of plebeian theater in Florence cannot be fortuitous. This must be the same "company of Armenians" that performed the *rappresentazione* of the *Resurrection* for the emperor Frederick III in early 1452.[170] It probably is the company that presented that play in the San Giovanni feast of 1454, and may even be the group that staged the *Resurrection* at the Council of Florence in 1439.[171] Thus, although the Magi letter of 1471 contains the earliest evidence of a planned festive geography in the city, at least one of the kingdoms in that festive city had a deeper antiquity.

It would be wrong to follow the lead of earlier students of the festive *potenze* and imagine that groups like the Macine had an institutional continuity stretching back to Walter of Brienne and beyond, for there is no present evidence of such a paternity. We would be just as errant to assume, as have these students, that the system of popular festive groups and that of the religious confraternities were separate and distinct from each other.[172] The

(Rome, 1875), n. 766, and note that under a painting of the saint (attributed to Uccello) that stood on S. Tommaso's main door was the inscription "India tibi cessit"; Richa, *Notizie*, VII, 232.

168. The importance of this kingdom to the early theatrical history of Florence was assumed by C. Singleton, "The Literature of Pageantry in Florence during the Renaissance" (diss. Univ. of California, Berkeley, 1931), 82–89; see also I. Del Badia, "La Compagnia della Gazza," *Miscellanea Fiorentina di Erudizione e Storia* II (1902), 97, 107.

169. The social character is clear from the fact that the company excluded *statuali* from membership: *ASF, Capitoli, Comp. Rel. Sopp.*, 100, f. 16v. On the floats, see subsequent pages.

170. The existence of the *rappresentazione* was discovered in a ceremonial fragment of the early sixteenth century; *ASF, Manoscritti*, 167; its association with this company was established in the cameral records

of the emperor's visit: "A Bartolomeo d'Antonio horafo"; *ASF, Camera del Comune, Onoranze*, 51, f. 47v (Jan. 31, 1451/1452); "Alla chonpagnia degli Ormini perchè feciono la festa del sipolchro a Santa Liperata inanzi allo 'nperadore"; *ibid.*, f. 48r; "E a dì 6 di febraio . . . alla chonpagnia del sipolchro per fare la festa della risuresione . . . "; *ibid.*, f. 57r.

171. The presence of the Resurrection *edifizio* in 1454 is mentioned by Matteo Palmieri, cited in Guasti, *Feste*, 22; the 1439 Resurrection is documented *ibid.*, 19. According to Benedetto Dei, "gli Ermini" presented an *edifizio* in 1459; Dei, *Cronica*, f. 23r, probably the same Resurrection. In the late fifteenth and early sixteenth centuries, this *edifizio* was generally known as "il monumento, cioè la Ressurrezione di Cristo"; Rossi, 271 (1491) (where mistranscribed "muvimento"); Guasti, *Feste*, 26.

172. This seems to be the assumption of all students, and I. Del Badia is not unusual; *Le Signorie o le Potenze Festeggianti del Contado Fiorentino* (Florence, 1876).

mid-fifteenth century seems in fact to have been a point of departure for the festive groups, and their appearance, we shall see, was closely linked to striking modifications in the structure of the religious confraternities; both neighborhood and occupational confraternities of plebeians were winning acceptance from the government of Florence. Here it becomes necessary to document and explain the incorporation of such groups in the years of this turning point in mid-century. Then we can study the context of the Medicean "transformation" of the early 1470s, and return to the massive festive appearance of these popular groups during the late 1480s.

There can be no doubt that the 1440s marked a turning point in the history of Florentine confraternities. The five-year period 1445–1450 witnessed the incorporation of occupational and neighborhood confraternities with little precedent in the city's history. Among the former groups, that of the poor scissors and knife makers may be mentioned. This *societas S. Lei* was appointing syndics in 1449, and its activities were superintended by the gild of the smiths, which supported these *sottoposti* because they formed the incorporated poor of the gild's shops.[173] It is an arrangement that will become classic: A gild made up of members of the political class allows its subordinates to organize a confraternity, supervises their activities, even supports the "corporation of the goods of the poor" by taxing gild members.[174] Surprisingly, there is evidence that not only the politically harmless scissors makers were incorporating in these years, but so were subjects of the wool gild, specifically the purgers, carders, and weavers who had played such a prominent role in the Ciompi revolt seventy years earlier.[175] At the same time, older hospitals of the disenfranchised, whose history and nature still escape the historian's full understanding, were beginning to act like confraternities. Thus midcentury dyers of the hospital of S. Nofri gained from the lords of the wool gild the right to assess a tax on all goods dyed by the master dyers.[176]

173. "Universitas membrorum . . . coltellinariorum, coltellariorum, et forficiariorum, qui vulgariter dicuntur *il menbro de' beni de' poveri* . . . ; omnes artificies artis fabrorum civitatis Florentie et de dictis menbris bonorum pauperum"; ASF, *Not. Antecos.*, T 278 (1434–1455), May 26, 1449; July 28 and Nov. 3, 1455.

174. A. Doren stressed that the classical Florentine gild had very little caritative or religious character; *Arti*, II, 194, and he did not mention such "menbra" of goods of the poor.

175. In 1435 the pope conceded the captains and deacons of the (German) wool weavers the right to decorate their new chapel in the church of the Carmine; ASF, *Dipl., Carmine*, Oct. 21. A. Doren, *Deutsche Handwerker und Handwerkerbruderschaften im Mittelalterlischen Italien* (Berlin, 1903), 132ff. Ten years later another group of German weavers began a second confraternity; M. Battistini, *La Confrérie de Sainte-Barbe des Flamands à Florence. Documents relatif aux Tisserands et aux Tapissiers* (Brussels, 1931). The 1451/

1452 *capitoli* of the company of S. Andrea de' Purgatori, meeting in Borgo La Croce, are in ASF, *Capitoli, Comp. Rel. Sopp.*, 870; see also *ibid.*, 843, the *capitoli* of 1515, with references to the earlier episcopal approval.

176. ASF, *Arte della Lana*, 197, f. 67r (Mar. 27, 1452). This hospital of S. Nofri was built sometime after 1339, when the commune furnished land to the *societas* of the same name to build a hospital; ASF, *Prov.*, 29, ff. 56v–57r (Oct. 7). This hospital was called "de' Tintori." Other hospitals of this type were S. Giovanni de' Portatori and S. Lò de' Maniscalchi, fourteenth-century foundations that are recorded in the 1427 Catasto and continued to exist throughout the fifteenth century. These hospitals seem to have offered possibilities for group solidarity. On Mar. 16, 1382, those who wanted to reconstitute the two Ciompi gilds met in S. Nofri; Panciatichi, f. 145r. But the whole question of the relation between these older occupational hospitals, often associated with the word *Misericordia*, and later confraternal develop-

These stunning signs of occupational corporations of *sottoposti* are matched by evidence that the disenfranchised were incorporating in their neighborhoods. The parish of S. Ambrogio alone offers two such cases, first the poor society of S. Maria delle Paci, whose inscription we read in that church's piazza, and second the plebeian confraternity of S. Maria della Neve.[177] Were these groups all new, or were some only now incorporating? The 1447 statutes of the latter confraternity suggest the latter. According to this group's fundamental law, members of the confraternity were to visit each home in the parish of S. Ambrogio every March to solicit money for the group's annual pilgrimage to Impruneta. To stimulate this charity, the confraternity was to show each resident the *cero* or painted wax edifice that would be given to Our Lady in May.[178] Such a specific mandate in a purportedly new company gives one pause for reflection: Is it not probable that this group was already engaged in these artistic, perhaps theatrical, visitational, and processional activities before it incorporated and thus gained the episcopal sanction? Might not this alleged earlier fraternity, as I shall call it, and thus the new confraternity be in some way comparable to the Macine, which was also a neighborhood fraternity doing theater? My suspicions that the S. Ambrogio group was in fact similar to the Kingdom of the Millstone, indeed related to its own parish's Grand Monarchy of the Red City, are not laid to rest by the confraternal statutes. Twice in their text the new confreres pay homage to their titulary "alma et diva *imperadrice*" of the Snow.[179] The wording may not be casual. The group that Walter of Brienne had created in this neighborhood in 1343 had been called "the Empire."[180] It would seem then that in the 1440s,

---

ments, remains to be resolved. It is hoped that the research of John Henderson, Jeffrey Newton, and Ronald Weissman will clarify this and other confraternal questions. I offer four facts, some of which qualify the broad lines of development I have sketched. First, collecting money for self-help was seen as a legal means of illegally raising funds for insurrection; Rodolico, *Popolo Minuto*, 102f (1345). Second, these hospitals could be festive organizations at least in part: In 1427, the hospital of "S. Nofri de' Tintori" noted that it "fa l'anno la festa di S. Nofri e 'l palio, che vi si spende £150 e più"; ASF, *Catasto*, 185, f. 628rv. On the feast of S. Nofri, see page 220, this volume. Third, these small hospitals were often incorporated groups (*compagnie* or *societates*) recognized by the commune, such as the "societas hospitalis S. Johannis Baptiste de via S. Gallo de Florentia"; ASF, *Dipl., Patr. Eccl.*, Jan. 19, 1331/1332. Fourth, some hospitals were *not* run by incorporated companies, as in the 1427 Catasto, where the scribe changed the word *compagnia* to "La *fraternità* dell'Asunzione di nostra donna . . . raghuna nell'ospedale di S. Piero Novello de' Ridolfi"; ASF, *Catasto*, 185, f. 755r. A fraternity was apparently different from a confraternity. Obviously, the complex structure of voluntary associations in Florence still requires a great deal of work.

177. The former's *capitoli* were approved by the bishop on Oct. 1, 1445; ASF, *Not. Antecos.*, M 347 (1426–1450), no. 212, the latter's on July 22, 1447; ASF, *Capitoli, Comp. Rel. Sopp.*, 606, f. 51r. Note also that the purgers' confraternity met in the parish of S. Ambrogio, in the Borgo La Croce; see n. 175.

178. "Un bello cero di cera gialla et non biancha . . . et con detto ciero si vadi pel popolo di S. Ambrosio dentro et di fora, achattando"; ASF, *Capitoli, Comp. Rel. Sopp.*, 606, ff. 40rv.

179. *Ibid.*, ff. 12r, 37r. I use the word *fraternity* as an associative type preceding confraternal incorporation not because the distinction is absolutely clear in the sources, but because, as in the case cited (n. 176) and in other cases, a fraternity was apparently viewed as something less formal than a confraternity. Note its usage to characterize a spontaneous unincorporated self-help group as in Rodolico, *Popolo Minuto*, 102f (1345), and the usage in these 1587 statutes of the Company of the Assunta: "la quale fu già fraternità di standardo; ma perchè gli huomini di detta compagnia aspiravano a vita più perfetta . . . che non più di standardo, ma compagnia di disciplina esser dovesse"; ASF, *Capitoli, Comp. Rel. Sopp.*, 494. On the Standards, see n. 200.

180. In 1343 the Città Rossa had a "Signore detto Imperadore"; G. Villani, XII, 8.

a preexisting festive fraternity, possibly already led by an emperor, finally succeeded in incorporating. From that point on, the confraternity of the Snow Empress maintained a continuous existence.

The hypothesis that some of the new neighborhood confraternities of this period derived from festive organizations is plausible in the light of the past history of festive groups in Florence and the festive situation of the 1440s; it is documented by later sources. Banding together for festive purposes in a "mock kingdom" (*reame di beffa*) was an old practice in Florence, as we have seen.[181] Yet these groups were ephemeral, both because they were politically dangerous and because in those old days the festive needs of the commune had been less substantial. With the explosion of festive activity in the early fifteenth century, and especially with the incorporation into the San Giovanni festival of floats and other machines, some type of continuity of festive groupings was required. Children's confraternities provided some continuity; the traditional cross-city adult confraternities provided more; unincorporated festive kingdoms, now maintaining some type of continuous existence, seem to have furnished still further continuity before they incorporated into neighborhood confraternities. Nowhere is this development clearer than in the case of the Kingdom of the Millstone.

After the confreres of the Resurrection started their company in 1485, they commissioned an Armenian friar to draw up statutes.[182] Their stated purpose was mutual assistance; like most other confraternities in Florence, the Standard Company of the Resurrection was intended to provide its poor, sick, and deceased members with financial assistance from dues and from the income derived from testamentary bequests made to the company. A confraternity was the only associative form in the city that could be relied on for such help, for it was an officially incorporated body that could sue and be sued in communal and episcopal courts to enforce bequests. Thus any group of men who desired to go beyond the immediate purpose of their association, such as festive activities, and provide for future needs had to form a confraternity and write statutes that were acceptable to the archbishop as well as to the commune.[183] This was to prove particularly difficult for the confreres of the Resurrection, for as their statutes clearly imply, the group's previous and continuing purpose was festive in nature, and included activities not only on the feast of San Giovanni but during carnivals, a fact that would obviously trouble any ecclesiastic called on to approve the statutes.[184] "The founders

181. See page 220, this volume. For the term *reame di beffa*, see *Prediche Inedite del beato Giordano da Rivalto dell'Ordine de' Predicatori, recitate in Firenze dal 1302 al 1305*, ed. E. Narducci (Bologna, 1867), 96 (hereafter Giordano da Rivalto–Narducci, *Prediche*).

182. In the statutes, the compiler is identified as Jacopo de' Martignoni da Firenze; ASF, *Capitoli, Comp. Rel. Sopp.*, 100, f. 28r. But this is probably the Basilian fra Jacopo Martignani da Milano who was prior of the church at the time; S. Orlandi (ed.), *"Necrologio" di S. Maria Novella*, 2 vols. (Florence, 1955), II, 337f. Perhaps

the prohibition of the company against priestly members required this misidentification.

183. Throughout, I use the word *confraternity* to refer to what the Florentines called a *compagnia* or *societas*, that is, a corporation. I do this to avoid confusion of the "company" with, for example, business companies.

184. "E per quello anno che sarà re, ogni festa che sarà appartenente al re debba farla fuori del luogho della conpagnia, dove a llui parrà. E non sia tenuta la conpagnia a niuna sua faccienda, nè ancora gli uomini

[*edificatori*] of this holy and devout company," the brothers admitted, "recognize that it is derived from the King of the Millstone."[185]

In fact, the statutes of the Company of the Resurrection are little more than an attempt to incorporate a fraternity whose activity was more festive than pious. The barons–confreres tried their best to mesh the regal with the confraternal form so as to make it acceptable to the ecclesiastical authorities. They argued that it was only fitting that the King of the Millstone should be honored by the company, for that was no more than to honor the company's origins. Yet when in 1486 the group sent its statutes to the episcopal palace for approval, the vicar could see how hollow that claim was. In fact, the King of the Millstone would be elected each year by the members of the confraternity, and the business of the barony would be carried out at the same time and place as that of the confraternity.[186] Most important, the episcopal vicar reading the statutes' rubric "Of the King" could see that, despite affirmations to the contrary, the finances of the two groups were inextricably mixed:

> We desire that when in the future the feast of San Giovanni includes *edifizi*, the kings then in office can and ought to undertake to make *edifizi* for this company, and not for others or for himself. And all profits that he makes should and will be the company's; if [the *edifizi*] are harmed by fire or other misfortune, then the company is indebted [to him]. And any king violating the aforesaid about *edifizi* is deposed and stricken de facto, and a new king shall be installed. And the company [cannot] give or loan anything pertaining to the *edifizi* when others are made, unless a four-fifths vote of black beans is gained in the body of the company; they cannot be conceded to anyone. And the captains who would go against this incur a penalty of ten soldi each.[187]

Thus the Resurrection might make the motions of distinguishing between the (carnival) *feste del Re* and its pious celebration of Easter. It might disavow the

siano abrigati a seguire le feste del re, se none come a lloro parrà"; *ASF, Capitoli, Comp. Rel. Sopp.*, 100, f. 9r. Although no specific indication of what these *feste* were is given, they must have been feasts of the Carnival season, that is, from New Year's to the eve of Lent, or of May.

185. "*Regi faciemus honorem et regnabit cum fraternitate sua.* Vuol dire: Faremo honore al re e regnerà colla sua conpagnia e fraternità. Avendo considerato gli edificatori di questa sancta e divota conpagnia, che essendo derivata dal Re di Macina . . . "; *ibid.*, f. 8v. Note the association in this biblical text between a king and a fraternity; were the groups referred to as fraternities the ancestors of the royal *potenze*?

186. For details, see *ibid.*, ff. 8v–9r ("El re si faccia in questo modo, cioè . . . "). Also: "E [el re] vada a sedere senplicemente come gli altri della conpagnia. E mentre che e capitani saranno a sedere, non possa ragionare di sue feste nella conpagnia. Ma ogni volta che saranno levatisi da sedere, allora possa ragionare e notificare alla baronia quella festa o quelle feste o colletioni o altre cose volesse fare appartenente alla cosuetudine del re"; *ibid.*, f. 9v.

187. "E vogliamo el re, che per li tenpi saranno quando si farà festa di Sancto Giovanni, facciendosi edifici, possa e debba pigliare a fare edifici per la conpagnia, e non per altri nè sopra di se. E ogni ghadagno che se ne facesse sia e essere debba della conpagnia, e così se per disgratia di fuoco o d'altro vi fussi perdita, la conpagnia ne sia tenuta. E qualunche re controfacesse a quanto è detto disopra d'edifici sia disposto, eraso di fatto, e faccesi nuovo re. E lla conpagnia dare nè prestare alcuna cosa apartenente a 'difici quando gli facessi altri, se non si vince in corpo di conpagnia per quarto quinti delle fave nere, non si possino concedere a persona alcuna. E' capitani che contra a cciò facessino, cagino in pena di soldi diece per uno"; *ibid.* This is the first such reference known to companies' procedures in making *edifizi*. See, however, the precious reference of the artist Neri di Bicci to two *edifizi* made by Giuliano da Maiano for the 1461 San Giovani, and to the three whales or dolphins and the signs of the four evangelists Neri worked on; *Le Ricordanze*, ed. B. Santi (Pisa, 1976), 163f. And note also the references to "cierti [quattro] bronzi per un charro che fè Antonio Manetti" for the San Giovanni of 1454; *Ricordanze* of Maso di Bartolommeo, to be published by Harriet Caplow, who generously furnished me with this document.

costs the barony incurred when it brought gifts in pilgrimage to Impruneta or Fiesole.[188] The fact was that the confraternity was only a kingdom—on its knees. This was unacceptable to the episcopal curia. Proceeding as would his successors, the vicar refused to accept the rubric "Of the King," which incorporated carnivals into the confraternity.[189] What seemed implied in the statutes of the parish confraternity of Our Lady of the Snow is here explicit: Fraternal groups called into existence and perpetuated by the demands of public ritual forms are the source of at least some neighborhood confraternities. These corporations first appeared in the 1440s; the process of incorporation continued in subsequent decades.

The reasons for this flurry of neighborhood and occupational foundations in the 1440s may be more specific than the demands of public ritual. A fundamental law of 1444 seems to have encouraged such foundations (the already mentioned ordinance that effectively forbade members of the political class to belong to the confraternities). This adoption of the Venetian custom of reserving confraternities for the disenfranchised classes was subject to exceptions, of course, and just as certainly the law did not preclude short-term festive brigades of *veduti*.[190] But it did open the doors of existing confraternities to a virtual takeover by the disenfranchised, and, given the ritual needs of the commune, encouraged the incorporation of new companies of *sottoposti*, which often took occupational or neighborhood forms. Clearly, the commune and its leading family believed the neighborhood and occupational groups were now more useful than they were dangerous. The process by which that new consciousness emerged has yet to be discovered in the Florentine sources, but it is already clear that this development presaged a ritual revolution.

A second cluster of events associated with the emergence of the plebs of Florence as a representational force dates to the early 1470s. Fresh from his pompous joust and marriage in the late 1460s, after his father's death in 1469,

---

188. "E ancora quando detto re volesse fare alcuno dono o alla Inpruneta o a Fiesole o altrove, non vogliamo che la conpagnia nè sia nè possa essere obrigata in cosa alcuna, ma faccino el re colla baronia di loro borsa"; *ASF, Capitoli, Comp. Rel. Sopp.*, 100, f. 9r. For such pilgrimages, cf. those of S. Maria della Neve, mentioned on page 405, this volume. Obviously, such pilgrimages were not necessarily thought of as completely religious in nature. Just as obviously, a clear relation exists between such kings carrying gifts to Impruneta, and the cult of the Magi.

189. "Excipimus tamen quintum capitulum. . . . Nullo modo confirmamus nec approbamus"; *ibid.*, f. 28r. Almost precisely the same thing happened in 1582 when the "charitativa fraternità della sanctissima Sancta Lucia et popolo" of that parish in the communal meadow (*prato*) sought archiepiscopal approval of its statutes. The index of statutes it prepared *before* writing them included a rubric XV entitled: "Del ciero di Santa Maria Improneta e dell'imperadore capo di paese." But turning to the relevant text page, one finds that rubric entitled: "Del ciero di S. Maria Improneta." The rest of that last page of statutes is left empty, with slash lines drawn through the empty space, and the episcopal approval follows only on the following page. That empty space had definitely been left for the section on the *Imperatore del Prato*, but had been left blank when it became certain the bishop would not approve it. Otherwise, the bishop's approval would have followed on the same page, for the bishop always wrote his approval immediately after the concluding rubric, on the same page, to prevent forgery; *ASF, Comp. Rel. Sopp.*, 1769. Despite this purposeful omission, information on the emperor *did* stay in other rubrics, for example, rubs. 1, 11. The reader notes that for the third time a royal fraternity was associated with pilgrimages to Impruneta.

190. For Venice, see Pullan, *Rich and Poor*.

and following the fantastic reception of the count of Milan in early 1471, the young Lorenzo de' Medici had "transformed his kingdoms" instead of attending the feast of S. Bartolomeo in August of that year. In October the festive fraternity and later *potenza* of Monteloro incorporated as a standard company—perhaps in connection with the Lorenzan organization—and in 1473 posted its stone boundary marker, certainly so connected.[191] But in the meantime the young ruler had received a clear admonition from one of his mentors: "Act grave if you want to be taken seriously by foreign rulers."[192] The boy reacted swiftly, and the years after 1471 witnessed a change both in Lorenzo's attitude toward festive life and in the communal law on festivities. A 1472 letter of Luigi Pulci to the young Magnificent, now more a *giovane* than an adolescent, gives the first evidence that Lorenzo had withdrawn his support from the festival of San Giovanni: "I am a little amazed that you have diminished this *festa* as much as you have. You are after all a citizen and fond of the *patria*, of which the Baptist is protector, and we ought to honor him."[193]

Despite such admonitions, the mind of the young master promptly became the law of Florence, and in 1473, the commune radically reduced its expenditures for the feast of San Giovanni.[194] Yet this law was only the beginning of a whole reorientation of communal ritual procedures. Another law of the same time ruthlessly prescribed the clothing and expenses Florentines could incur for funerals.[195] A third law was almost without parallel in the history of sumptuary legislation in Florence. It entered the individual Florentine home and prescribed the foods one could serve, the plates food could be served on, and the expense one could incur any time one invited a guest to dinner.[196]

The impact of such legislation has not yet been studied, but the intention was clear. Far from being a moralistic response to the excesses of Sforza's visit in 1471, as Machiavelli believed, these laws represented an attack on the right of the good families of Florence to demonstrate their honor. Lorenzo's critic Alamanno Rinuccini said as much: "[Lorenzo] eliminated all those things that

191. For the boundary marker, see page 400, this volume. The statutes of 1471 of this "compagnia di stendardo dell'Assunta" are referred to in the extant *capitoli* of 1578; ASF, *Capitoli, Comp. Rel. Sopp.*, 811. The term *standard company* is explained in n. 200.

192. The letters of Gentile Becchi are in Rochon, *Jeunesse*, 128, n. 346 (Jan. 29 and Feb. 14, 1471).

193. *Lettere di Luigi Pulci a Lorenzo il Magnifico e ad altri*, ed. S. Bongi (Lucca, 1886), 111.

194. Expenditures on the banquet for the Signoria on this day were halved, and those to the *festaioli* were more than halved; ASF, *Prov.*, 164, ff. 6v–8r (Mar. 24, 1472/1473).

195. ASF, *Deliberazioni della Signoria. Speciale Autorità*, 34, ff. 126v–128v (Apr. 27, 1473). Ostentation at baptisms was also regulated; ASF, *Prov.*, 164, ff. 38rv

(Apr. 21, 1473).

196. Recognizing the complexity of the legislation, the communal councils gave the Signoria authority to regulate by its own authority "conviviis tam publicis quam privatis, et tam inter affines et seu cognatos quam inter amicos et seu extraneos"; *ibid.*, ff. 8r–9r (s.d., but soon after Mar. 24, 1472/1473). That regulation by the Signoria is then recorded in the *Deliberazioni, loc. cit.*, ff. 129r–131r (Apr. 27, 1473). Laws of this type continued. One of 1475 fined tailors making prohibited clothes; ASF, *Prov.*, 166, ff. 178rv (Dec. 20), and one of 1477 re-regulated gambling; *ibid.*, 168, ff. 6v–7r (Apr. 15). Most of these laws were of a type well known in Florence; it is their conjunction at this time and the unprecedentedly intrusive private banquet law of 1473 that betray their special significance. For a 1330 law of this latter type, see G. Villani, X, 153.

had traditionally won support and reputation for the citizens, like marriage feasts and dances, *feste*, ornate dress. He damned them all, both by example and by words."[197] Here was no mere attack on domestic ostentation, but a comprehensive attempt to limit family honor in the home *and* in the public square. Funerals were public affairs. Marriages were commonly held in conjunction with public feasts. A palace banquet was the prelude or postscript to public show. The law reducing communal expenditures for the feast of the patron simply sealed the package.

Driven from the confraternities in 1444, the fine people of Florence had lost the right to feast together in confraternal halls. By the laws of 1473, they could no longer indulge their friends and allies in their own homes. The effect upon the great civic feasts was predictable. If in the San Giovanni celebration of 1454 we have every reason to believe that plebeian festive groups like the Kingdom of the Millstone were already providing some of the floats, the scions of the patrician families of Florence probably still provided the cavalcades that accompanied some of these theatrical machines: The *giovani da bene* were the people who were fit to ride, and the law of 1444 had not prohibited short-lived brigades. The evanescent companies of *armeggiatori* that Francesco Giovanni had joined could still rise for the particular occasion, as did the brigade of Bartolomeo Benci in 1464 and the *opera* of the *giovani* of San Bartolomeo in 1471.[198] But what group of *giovani* would dress up for such activity if they could not dine together at their *signore*'s table? The laws of 1473 removed the incentive for young men to band together in cavalcades; if the feast of San Giovanni was to have cavalcades to accompany its children's and plebeians' floats, they would have to be plebeian horsemen, who could dine from alms.[199]

For most of the sixteenth century, Florentine chroniclers distinguished two types of *potenze* or companies of standard, as they were called interchangeably: the five precedentially superior equestrian groups like the Grand Monarchy of the Red City and the Captaincy of Monteloro, and the approximately nine footgroups like the Kingdom of the Millstone.[200] At the begin-

197. Rinuccini, cxlviii. Note that the same author originally thought these laws were to a good end; *ibid.*, cxxi. Machiavelli's superficial view of the laws is recorded on page 315, this volume.

198. See pages 230f, 395f, this volume.

199. I am speaking strictly of communally sponsored festivities. There is every reason to believe that the *giovani* now sought to gather around the Medici table—which was, of course, increasingly exempt from the law in fact. For these developments, see page 519, this volume.

200. I plan to do a separate article on the history of these groups. For now, see the subsequent quote of Giannotti (1528), and of Masi, 237 (1518), distinguishing between the one and the other type. The five mounted *potenze* remained constant. The number of lesser *potenze* did vary, but nine or ten of these foot

potenze are mentioned both in the Antonio da San Gallo record of the 1545 San Giovanni (quoted by M. Plaisance, "La Politique Culturelle de Côme Ier et les Fêtes annuelles à Florence de 1541 à 1550," in J. Jacquot and E. Konigson (eds.), *Les Fêtes de la Renaissance*, 3 vols. [Paris, 1956–1975], III, 150f), and in accounts of the 1577 festivities by Bastiano Arditi (*Diario di Firenze e di altre Parti della Cristianità [1574–1579]*, ed. R. Cantagalli [Florence, 1970], 160f) and Giuliano de' Ricci (215–229). Thus when Varchi in the mid-sixteenth century mentioned fourteen companies of standard, "which are for entertainment more than anything else" (*Storia*, IX, 36), he was referring to the *potenze* by their other name. The name standard company entered the official vocabulary in the later fifteenth century, when the government in prohibiting confraternal activities, replaced the earlier qualification; "companies of lauds or discipline,

ning of this century, however, only the latter were called *potenze*; the mounted groups were called *compagnie di armeggiatori*.[201] In the foregoing analysis of the festive plebs in formation, I believe that I have pinpointed the origins of this distinction: The footed plebs were primarily involved in making *edifizi*, whereas the mounted plebs, profiting from the sumptuary laws of the 1470s, became responsible for cavalcades.

Yet the plebs' hour had not yet come. The vision of Florence as a city of workers, not seen in Florence since the Ciompi parades of 1378, was long withheld by Lorenzo's reticence to seem juvenile, and then by his fear of public show after the Pazzi conspiracy of 1478. From that year until 1488, no *edifizi* or cavalcades participated in San Giovanni observances.[202] When in that year the Resurrection's Kingdom of the Millstone once more rolled its *monumento* through the streets of the city, the last of the three periods of the fifteenth-century plebs had begun.[203]

August 26, 1488, is an important date in the history of Florentine working-class organization, for on that day the government for the first time approved an association of Florentine wool beaters (*battilani*).[204] This was not the first occupational corporation of *sottoposti*; as we have seen, both the company of the wool purgers and carders, and the scissors makers' company of San Leo, had been active since midcentury.[205] Nor was the new company of Santa Maria degli Angeli dei Battilani the first company of *sottoposti* approved by a major industrial gild, for the silk weavers had organized with gild approval in midcentury, and by 1481 this "element" of the silk gild had built its own hospital.[206] Still, the recognition of the *battilani* had particular importance. These men descended from the Ciompi, and their group may have been the first *sottoposti* confraternity actually to be recognized by that conservative bellwether of Florentine industrial organization, the wool gild.

When the *provisori* of this new company appeared before the wool consuls to seek their approval of the new institution, they cited no precedent for their action, only the justness of their cause, which was to care for their poor

either day or night," with "Compagnia così di disciplina come di stendardo, così di nocte come di dì"; *ASF, Otto di Guardia*, 222, f. 14v (Jan. 7, 1501/1502). The word *standard* referred to the identifying flag these groups flew during processions, as well as to their predominantly festive character, which, as we see, could have developed from their lauds.

201. See Giannotti's quote on page 413, this volume, and also Cambi, XXII, 249f, using the same terminology.

202. See page 451, this volume.

203. It was because no *edifizi* were being used in the festivities of San Giovanni at the time that the Macine phrased their *capitolo* as they did; see n. 187.

204. I could find no gild approval of the earlier company of the purgers and carders mentioned on page 404, this volume. For the *battilani's* "Capitulorum nove societatis S. Marie Angelorum confirmatio, et

retentio d. 4 pro libra battilanis," see *ASF, Arte della Lana*, 54, f. 148v. The *capitoli* themselves may be extant, but I could not find them; they were abstracted without reference by L. Passerini, *Storia*, 108.

205. See page 404, this volume.

206. On the company in 1455, Hatfield, "Compagnia," 138. On the hospital: "Constructus . . . superioribus annis . . . hospitalis misericordie textorum et filatoriorum civitatis Florentie et membrorum sirici"; *ASL*, provisional n. 1179 (July 3, 1481); in 1482 this "hospitale dirimpetto a San Marco Nuovo detto della Misericordia, ch'è della compania de' Tessitori," paid tribute to the church of San Lorenzo; *ibid.*, provisional n. 1930¹, ff. 40v–41v. If Del Migliore is right, the weavers' company can be traced still further back to a 1417 notice of the company in San Marco "del Ceppo dei Tessitori"; cited in Monti, *Confraternite*, I, 184. Another early approval of a (foreigners') confraternal statute is in Doren, *Deutsche Handwerker*, 141 (1440).

colleagues. It was for this end that the wool consuls and other "good men" had written confraternal statutes for the *battilani,* and it was to put their subjects' piety on a firm financial basis that the consuls, in approving these statutes, also levied a tax on the gild members themselves. With the aid provided by their lords and through their own contributions, the *battilani* soon had their confraternity under way. Within the year they had bought real estate and built a hospital of mercy and piety much like that of the silk weavers, and for the next century and a half the *battilani* of Florence preserved a distinct corporate identity as a hospital, religious brotherhood, and festive *potenza.*[207] The wool trimmers (*cimatori*) of the city soon followed the example of the *battilani,* winning approval of their own confraternity in 1494 by citing the precedent of the *battilani* and the purgers. Again, the wool consuls were enthusiastic in their support. Not only did such confraternities help their members, the consuls said, but the gild itself was honored, for each year these *sottoposti* confraternities made a public gift of tribute to their "patrons."[208] The wool lords praised themselves for being both charitable and religious in fostering these new institutions; they were at the least innovative.

What explains this extraordinary departure from the repressive associative policies of the past? What were the political realities that had, in a few years at the end of the fifteenth century, necessitated the organization of some of the most feared subjects of the Florentine industrial gilds? A series of coincidences between these institutional developments and Medicean political activity may be part of the answer. It may be mere chance that the silk weavers built their hospital the month after a plot against Lorenzo's life in 1481, and perhaps it was equally fortuitous that the wool trimmers' confraternity was authorized during the crisis of Piero de' Medici's authority in late 1494.[209] But such associations between the Medici and the cloth proletariat seem more substantial once we learn that many of the new foundations were located in the environs of the Medici palace. The silk weavers and the wool beaters met in the family parish of San Lorenzo, and on the feast of its titulary they paid public tribute to the church along with the barons of the Millstone, the confraternity of the servants of the Palazzo della Signoria, and several other important confraternities.[210] These occupational confraternities seem, therefore, to have been part of a family policy. They were instruments of Medici political power in the neighborhood, which, I suspect, were incorporated when the family needed their backing. As in the chess games still

207. On the *Re de' Batti* in 1588, see *Il Malmantile Racquistato di Perlone Zipoli* (i.e., L. Lippi), I (Florence, 1788), 221. In 1577 the *potenze,* whether neighborhood or occupational in focus, were considered made up of such artisans: "le potenze, cioè tintori e battilani et altri"; *Diario Fiorentino di Agostino Lapini dal 252 al 1596* (Florence, 1900), 195. For the land purchases and construction of their hospital, see *ASF, Dipl., Battilani di Firenze,* June 14, 1489.

208. "Approbatio capitolorum societatis cimatorum . . . come fu facto vedere di quelli de' purgatori e de' battilani"; *ASF, Arte della Lana,* 54, f. 166r (Aug. 26).

209. On the 1481 plot, see Rinuccini, cxxxiv–cxxxv.

210. Respectively *ASL,* provisional n. 1930[1], ff. 40v–41v (1482); 1933[2], f. 31v (1493); *ibid.,* f. 32v (1493); 1930[1], ff. 40v–41v (1482). Further evidence that the Medici party had support among the *infimi* is a statement that in 1469 family friends formed a conspiracy against its opponents, "among the butchers"; Lorenzo de' Medici, *Lettere,* I, 52.

played with living pawns and kings in Italian festive squares, the Medici were checkmating the republic by massing pawns in their own neighborhood, and in others as well.[211] In 1489 we find Lorenzo fostering his reputation among the wool weavers of Oltrarno by lending the King of Camaldoli plates and service for his barony's upcoming celebration of May Day. The paraphernalia bore the Medici arms and would thus advertise the patron's charity.[212] Donato Giannotti, writing in the early sixteenth century, would have understood perfectly:

> The standards, both the companies of *armeggiatori* and the *potenze* . . . are all things that decrease the reputation of the public [weal] and increase that of private persons. And if someone would examine their origin, he would find that they are used by tyrants, who introduce such *feste* to entertain the plebs, so that they can keep the republic oppressed by [the plebs] . . . , with whom they are popular.[213]

But if Giannotti was right in believing that the Medici fostered these plebeian groups to subvert constitutional authority, he was wrong in limiting their significance to the political sphere. The *potenze* transcended politics, for they remained active in Florence during two periods of Medicean exile from the city. They were obviously useful to the whole socioeconomic class that ran Florence and its gilds, not merely to any one political faction. Here was a way in which a city without any central office for disbursing welfare to its industrial poor could minister to those needs, and occupational self-help confraternities were but one example of the atomistic mutual aid characteristic of later republican history.[214] At the same time, *sottoposti* confraternities must have seemed an acceptable risk to the gild lords. By organizing these groups on the Venetian model so as to replicate the authority of the workplace in the confraternity (masters on top and workers on the bottom), the gilds might hope to gain the advantages of such groups without their subversive disadvantages.[215]

211. It would not be surprising to find patricians using the *potenze* in living chess matches, as festive groups are still used in the north Italian town of Marostica.

212. "A Domenico di Benedetto tocatore per il re di Camaldoli, due bacini con l'arme di casa, due nappi con l'arme di casa e de' Rucellai, dodici tazze pulite, ecc . . . "; copied by C. Carnesecchi from the Medici papers in *ASF, Acquisti e Doni*, 292. The reference is the earliest known to a King of Camaldoli, whose weavers subsequently remained one of the important *potenze* of the city.

213. "Tutti li stendardi, e compagnie delli armeggiatori e potenzie, saria da levare via; chè sono tutte cose che tolgono riputazione al publico, ed acresconla a' privati: e chi ricierchèrà la loro origine, troverrà che elle sono uscite da' Tiranni, i quali introducono simil feste per intrattenere la plebe, acciò che con quella tenghino opressata la Repubblica. E per questa cagione tutti li spettacoli, che si fanno nella città per rallegrare gli uomini, sarìa bene si facessino con ordine publico: acciò che i privati non ne acquistassino grado apresso il vulgo"; G. Sanesi (ed.), "Un Discorso Sconosciuto di Donato Giannotti intorno alla Milizia," *ASI*, ser. 5, VIII (1891), 25 (hereafter Giannotti, "Discorso"). The "tyrants" were the Medici.

214. They are also examples of the larger atomization of social life as a whole. On the charitable situation, see my "Charity." In her "On the Uses of History," Silverman has discovered the same phenomenon at the same time in Siena: "There was an inverse relationship between the strength of sub-communal localized divisions and that of the commune itself."

215. For the Venetian divisions, see Pullan, *Rich and Poor*, 72. Perhaps the most detailed description of the replication of gild discipline in a confraternity is in the *pizzicagnuoli* statutes of 1509; *Bibl. Riccardiana*, ms. Moreni, 54.

The new confraternities were necessary rather than desirable, for as the example of the wool trimmers' group would make clear, any type of workers' association remained dangerous. Not long after the trimmers' confraternity was approved in 1494, the brothers started to use their right of assembly for economic rather than religious purposes, and in 1508 were discovered conspiring to fix prices and strike. The wool gild quickly suppressed its subject corporation and seized its statute book. The trimmers were permitted to reincorporate only in 1510, after the masters of the trade blamed the past sedition on the company's *garzoni* and workers (*lavoranti*), and assured the wool consuls of their future obedience.[216] At all times in Florentine history, corporations of *sottoposti* were dangerous, for the social system itself was exploitative to the core. Yielding the meeting hall or the street to the working people of Florence might solve certain problems within the ruling class, and even express the self-confidence of its regime. But such organizations tested that authority as well. Once on the festive stage, the subjects could produce a subversive new commune of a Medicean stamp, or a workers' commune.

The organization of *sottoposti* confraternities was the first important plebeian social phenomenon of the later fifteenth century; the character of festive life during the same period, and the role of workers in these celebrations, made up the second. In these years Carnival became a festive occasion equal in importance to San Giovanni. The plebs played a far greater part in festive life than they had earlier, and in their representations, the plebs, like the children, represented Everyman, the world of honor, and the world of work. A fundamental realignment of the commune's festive identity was building, and the *potenze* of Florence were to be centrally involved in the change.

Perhaps the upgrading of Carnival was the most significant festive fact of these years. Previous Carnival celebrations in Florence had been the province of ephemeral groups of patrician *giovani* holding *armeggerie* and jousts to honor ladies; of *fanciulli* throwing rocks and lighting bonfires; of occasional groups of artisans dressing up like their betters. During those days, one mid-sixteenth-century historian of Carnival said, men had acted like women.[217] Government had generally kept its distance from this "feast of the devil" while carefully suppressing any citywide organization of Carnival activities. Lorenzo was instrumental in changing that, giving Carnival the stamp of approval that his forebears had bestowed on that other raucous feast "when every knot came unbound," the Magian feast of the Epiphany.[218]

216. "Si sono ragunati . . . alle taverne . . . et quivi hanno facti conspiratione contro alla decta arte et a' lanaiuoli d'epsa, di mutare pregi a' lanaiuoli et merchatanti. E più tosto una buona parte di loro si sono voluti stare che lavorare, in vergogna di decta arte"; ASF, *Arte della Lana*, 55, f. 57v (Mar. 12, 1508); *ibid.*, f. 72r (Aug. 21, 1510). In 1443, the young German weavers' confraternity had also struck, and its members had left the city; Doren, *Deutsche Handwerker*, 143.

217. "Prima gli uomini di quei tempi usavano il carneval immascherandosi contraffare le madonne,

solite andare per lo calendimaggio; e così travestiti ad uso di donne e di fanciulli cantavano canzoni a ballo. . . . Il Magnifico . . . pensò di variare . . . e il primo canto o mascherata che si cantasse in questa guisa fu d'uomini che vendevano berriquocholi e confortini"; Il Lasca, cited in D'Ancona, *Origini*, I, 255.

218. Burchiello, *Sonetti*, 229:

> *Tu nascesti la notte di Befana,*
> *Quando ogni legata si snoda*

On earlier Carnival celebrations, see my "De la Ville a

Now festive groups like the new Company of the Star provided a continuing institutional base for elaborate Carnival celebrations involving the whole city rather than single neighborhoods.[219] If in the old days it was not unknown for the poor and young to mock the institutions of the rich on Carnival, the *potenze* of Florence now represented that world of honor and nobility with a certain theatrical seriousness, an ultimate irony if one likes, which was directed and encouraged by the Medici. If working-class persons had appeared in earlier Carnivals, they did so now by celebrating their own occupations instead of ridiculing the notion of work. Florentine Carnival now presented the world of nobility *and* the world of work. Carnival festival under Lorenzo represented those two male forces that had for so long waged an unequal ritual struggle: the vile world of handwork now celebrated by its practitioners, and the noble world of honor now performed by the plebs, for tips.

This new festive world of the plebs, where handwork and chivalry had equal rights to gratuities, suffuses the earliest printed edition of Carnival songs (*canti carnascialeschi*), at present almost our only source for the study of Carnival in these years.[220] Here are small merchants and peddlers, wool workers and tailors, prisoners and mule drivers, made up as foreigners or Florentines, pretending to sell their goods to their female audiences by demonstrating the details of their craft.[221] The workaday lives of groups of humble artisans are represented to the Florentines as worthy of their recognition and support. The traditional European idea that employment was charity was alive and well in such a scheme, but the formal presentation of handwork as a positive social phenomenon performed by groups that were a recognized part of the community was unprecedented in the history of Florence.[222]

Yet woven through this riot of artisan floats and carts were other representations of a diplomatic and military nature. Mock brigades of foot soldiers marched through the Carnival streets pretending they were returning from pilgrimage, or displaced from their leaders, or in disarray after defeat, and begged the hospitality of the good people of Florence.[223] There were ambas-

la Cour." Further early indications of governmental support for Carnival-type festivals are as follows: in 1463 the Signoria sent its musicians to serenade the "messer del Corso de' Tintori" created for Carnival; ASF, *Acquisti e Doni*, 292, with reference to the Strozzi *spoglio* Cl. V, no. 87. "Fu Berlingaccio. Spesi soldi tre che gli diedi al Signore di Carnasciale de' famigli de' Signori"; ser Giusto, f. 107v (Feb. 17, 1473/1474).

219. The company is documented between 1490 and 1492, its name perhaps stemming from the "star" Venus, whom Florentines were encouraged to follow in the "Song of the Seven Planets" which the company staged on Carnival, 1490; M. Martelli, *Studi Laurenziani* (Florence, 1965), 39; the text of the song, attributed to Lorenzo, is in *Opere di Lorenzo de' Medici*, ed. A. Simioni, 2 vols. (Bari, 1939), II, 251. A relationship to Lorenzo's Company of the Magi is improbable because of the latter's devotional character at that time.

220. Textually reprinted by S. Ferrari (ed.), "Canzone per Andare in Maschera per Carnasciale facte da più Persone," *Biblioteca di Letteratura Popolare Italiana* I (1882), 5–62, but more accessible in the first hundred pages of Singleton, *Canti*. This edition and a proximate one are usually dated in the late 1480s, but actually date no earlier than 1492; see the song of that year on page 416, this volume.

221. Almost all these occupational demonstrations have a double meaning. The performers sold their products and their sexuality simultaneously.

222. A total view of Florence as a city of workers does not emerge, however, until the 1547 "*Canto* of the 100 Occupations"; G. Biagi (ed.), "Per la Cronica di Firenze nel secolo XVI," *Rivista delle Biblioteche e degli Archivi* XVII (1906), 80.

223. Several such early songs are in Singleton, *Canti*, 43, 68, 75, 100f, 119, 123f, 128, 183.

sadorial cavalcades as well, said to have come to honor Florence and bring it news from foreign kings, as this company did in 1492:

> *The lord of this company*
> *has been sent here to Florence*
> *with such great magnificence*
> *by the King of Spain,*
> *visiting the presence of the illustrious Emperor. . . .*
> *We have recently acquired*
> *the Kingdom of Granada.*[224]

These festive groups were none other than the *potenze*, the areas from which they were said to come corresponding in some cases to particular Florentine neighborhoods. In the preceding song, for example, we find the Emperor of the Meadow (*del Prato*), chief of the Florentine *potenze*, on the reviewing stand receiving these subject visitors.[225] In another song we perhaps find the mounted *potenza* of Nespola identifying itself and its street even while disguised as quite another party:

> *Long live, long live the* potenza
> *of this divine, vibrant Florence!*
> *This our* Gran Signore
> *of Ghinea and of the* Granvia
> *has come with fervor*
> *to join your retinue. . . .*
> *Riding is our occupation*
> *and we prefer a horse without saddle.*
> *For when we joust*
> *it is more agile and less sweaty.*
> *And if his back is bowed,*
> *he withstands the [jouster's] hit better.*
> *On our lances*
> *we show [the flags of] our* potenza.[226]

Not only the mounted *potenze* left occasional hints of their identity in their songs; so did the humbler footed ones. The "Song of the Millstone," for example, clearly identifies the Kingdom of Armenia or of the Millstone, as did its flag; like the lords of the *Granvia*, the Millstone and other such groups carried identifying banners.[227] But for every song that allows one to speculate

224. *Ibid.*, 75f; news of the conquest arrived in Florence on Jan. 5, 1492; Landucci, 62.

225. This is the only candidate for a festive emperor, and my view is shared by Singleton, "Literature," 151; the earliest known documentary reference to this *imperatore* is in 1511, when the Signori allowed their servants to serve him on the feast of May Day; Gori, *Festa*, 305.

226. This is one possible reading of "Con le nostre lance grosse, Dimonstrían nostra potenza," with the normal double entendre; Singleton, *Canti*, 43. There seem two candidates for the mounted *potenza* of Granvia: the Via Maggio Oltrarno, and the Via Larga near the Medici palace. Since the latter area did not have a mounted *potenza* in the sixteenth century, but the Via Maggio did (the Nespola), I suggest the latter is the group identified in the song. However, the Nespola is not documentarily verifiable until 1532; Cambi, XXIII, 117. The Gran Signore might be the Saraceno or target of an *armeggeria* rather than a jouster.

227. On the Macine emblem shown on a 1506 edition of its song, see Singleton, "Literature," 82, 89.

on the group that performed it, there are scores that do not. The "Song of the Used Iron Dealers" and other occupational ditties may have been sung by the occupational confraternities of Florence, but which ones? Who were the Monsir of the Orange, and the Gran Signore of Morea, India, and Syria?[228] Were the five squadrons of horse that accompanied the *trionfo* of Aemilius Paulus in the San Giovanni celebration of 1491 the five mounted *potenze* of Florence?[229] Since there were usually nine footed *potenze* through much of the sixteenth century, we may suspect that the fourteen bonfires on the Carnival battlefield of Florence in 1499 belonged to five mounted and nine footed *potenze*, and these same groups may also have manned the fourteen triumphal stage sets erected for Pope Leo X in 1515.[230]

These suggestions may or may not have merit, but it is clear that the *potenze* of occupational and neighborhood confraternities had moved from the margins toward the center of the festive stage, gently mocking nobility while preaching the dignity of work. The enfeebled patriciate that had so long kept its distance from work, plebs, and tyrants watched and cheered the gospel of social peace that these intimidating groups preached for Lorenzo:

> Monteloro, Apple, Red City, and Empire
> have warred together a long time,
> with the desire
> to drive one and the other from their states;
> each has consumed
> fame, time, and money.
>   Whoever can learn, learn!
> We are [now] united and we all cry for peace.
> Today we pass our time
> In feasting [and] armeggerie, with instruments and songs.[231]

The Carnival joke was on the republic, as Giannotti and Rinuccini well knew. Republicans might scorn such *cose di fanciulli, di giovani, di gente da bassa mano*, but the Medici used the new corporations of the fifteenth century to their own ends. Florentine children and *potenze* now played Everyman in confraternities that would soon command the processional center of Florence. In their own way both the adolescent confraternities and the plebeian *potenze* had mimicked the impotence of the old political culture, and in this they were at one with the less organized *giovani*. On the eve of Lorenzo's death in April

---

228. Singleton suggests that the Monsir of the Orange was paraded by the *potenza* of Mela; *ibid.*, 153. Along with the mounted *potenza* of Monteloro, this mounted *potenza* is first documented in 1501; Cambi, XXI, 159f.

229. Rossi, 271. The *trionfi* themselves were prepared by the Company of the Star.

230. 1499: Cambi, XXI, 136f. 1515: Landucci, 353–359.

231. "Canzona degli Amatori di Pace," by Giovanfrancesco Del Bianco; Singleton, *Canti*, 231. Singleton was able to date Del Bianco's work before 1510; "Literature," 207. It is possible however that the song, which notably does not list the Nespola mounted *potenza*, was written as early as the 1490s. It may also have been written in 1513, in conjunction with the *trionfi* of Discord, War, Fear, and Peace made to celebrate Leo X's papal election; see page 496, this volume.

1492 the center of Florentine festive life was in danger of being overrun by Lorenzo and his plebs, children, and *giovani*. The city was under siege from thunderbolts, visions, and prognoses of disaster, yet our preacher could think of nothing better to counter the ire of God than a procession of boys. With the pathos so typical of a declining political patriciate, a correspondent wrote: "You see what we have come to."[232]

232. Ridolfi, *Studi Savonaroliani*, 263.

Chapter 12

The Charismatic Center:
Innocence and Martyrdom

*Each of you needs to be reborn into
men without blemishes.**

*[The child cardinal] has not so
much ennobled his own house, as
the whole city.†*

*Fra Girolamo had three last wishes. . . .
The second [was] that he not be condemned
to die at the hands of the children of
Florence, among whom he had
had such a following.‡*

In the wings of the Florentine procession, outsiders circled the traditional center. Its competing parts welcomed the retinue of the young, of the neighborhoods, and of occupations, for they strengthened the center's own diminishing authority. In that center, an increasingly atomized governmental structure allowed individual offices as well as the Signoria to develop a ritual identity. Florentine families competed for its control, putting forward atomic individuals to represent the whole family. Chroniclers soon reported on such bureaucratic and familial individuality. Giusto d'Anghiari's 1477 report that the office of the Monte, by itself, was dowering nubile girls in pompous cathedral ceremonies, his unprecedented announcement in 1475 that a son had been born to a citizen, and his repeated approval of citizen Lorenzo de' Medici's "charitable" sale of grain to the city's poor at below-market prices, all point to one important development.[1] For the first time

*Cavalcanti, *Istorie*, III, 2 (1427).

†Landucci, 65, speaking of Cardinal Giovanni de' Medici (1492).

‡"Non sia sententiato a morir a le man di puti di Fiorenza, di la qual havia avuto tanto sequito"; Sanuto, I, 947 (1498).

1. Ser Giusto, ff. 119r, 114r (birth of Giovanni de' Medici), 107r, 108r, 111r, 112r (1473–1475). Outsid- ers', and rare Florentines', weddings, deaths, and burials were occasionally reported before this;

since Walter of Brienne, the ritual times, places, and objects of the city were being shaped around individuals.

The crisis of communal structures heralded the birth of a new sense of time. As the fiction of the commune "that does not die" evaporated, the biographies of the persons who dominated affairs became a part of communal history, and those of the Medici, who emerged triumphant in the competition for the center, came to be equated with the fate of the collectivity.[2] Popularly before and officially after his death, Cosimo was named *pater patriae*, and his return from exile in 1434 sounded like God the Father's creation of the world in the retelling.[3] Lorenzo the Magnificent, son of Piero the son of Cosimo, was akin to a divine son. His childhood, near martyrdom, and death, and the limbo of family exile after 1494 appeared to be the preconditions for the resurrection of the family after its return from exile in 1512.[4] The Medicean popes of the sixteenth century, in turn, were looked upon as holy spirits who, by bestowing immortality on the city, brought to a happy end the republican search for unquestioned credit, honor and trust. For these were princes who would not die, for a city that might fear no end.

This chapter first analyzes Medicean behavioral structures between 1434 and 1494, starting with Cosimo's foundations for the new manger, the boy-king Lorenzo's assumption of the center, and his relations with the new ritual forces on the margins of Florentine society. Without pausing, the chapter studies formal behavior in the Savonarolan and Soderinian period, from the expulsion of the Medici in 1494 until their return in 1512. Historians usually break their narratives of Florentine affairs in 1494, in part because the stern friar Savonarola seems so antithetical to the mercurial Lorenzo. We shall see, however, that the period of the prophet and the first Standard Bearer for Life brought to fruition behavioral patterns that had been initiated under the Medici, and also laid the foundations for the Florence of Popes Leo and Clement.[5]

On his accession to influence in 1494, Savonarola faced a choice. He could return to the old republican salvational model, which would have required the reformation and reinstallation of the clergy as an exemplary ritual force. Or he might adopt the younger lay generations as the salvation of Florence, an approach that had made headway in the Medicean age and had

Giovanni's birth seems to have been the first birth of a citizen's child, other than in one's own family, recorded in Florentine literary sources.

2. The immortal commune was mentioned on page 334, this volume.

3. Before, Feo Belcari called him this; Lanza, *Lirici Toscani*, 227; the official proclamation after his death is in *ASF, Prov.*, 155, f. 261v. See also A. Brown, "The Humanistic Portrait of Cosimo de' Medici, Pater Patriae," *Journal of the Warburg and Courtauld Institutes* XXIV (1961), 186–221; Molho, "Cosimo," 7f, 32. Note that by 1427, and thus before the Medici came to power, it was convention to call the (two-month)

Standard Bearer of Justice the "Father of the Republic"; Cavalcanti, *Istorie*, IX, 5. For the development of the simile between Medici and divine history, see later, and also R. Trexler with M. Lewis, "Two Captains and Three Kings. New Light on the Medici Chapel," *Studies in Medieval and Renaissance History*, n.s. IV (1981), 91–177.

4. On Lorenzo the Martyr, see my "Lorenzo de' Medici and Savonarola, Martyrs for Florence," *Renaissance Quarterly* XXXI (1978), 293–308.

5. A review of the bibliography on Savonarola's relation to Florentine history is in D. Weinstein, *Savonarola and Florence* (Princeton, 1970), 1–25.

as its most brilliant success the figure of Lorenzo himself. After an abortive attempt to reform the clergy, Savonarola chose to rely upon the charisma of the younger generation, as well a prophet of the New Age might, and to downplay the moribund rituals of the fathers and their clergy, as Lorenzo had done earlier.[6] A cult of youth linked the Magnificent and the prophets. Lorenzo had fostered the children's confraternities, and ruled as a boy; Savonarola placed the boys at the processional center, and was their charismatic inspiration. Further similarities between the two men abound. Lorenzo relied on the approbation of foreign princes for his authority in the city; Savonarola, on his direct link to God and the Virgin. In different fashions both men were martyrs, their varied fates little different from the fate of the city itself. Savonarola was a man of the spirit, and was thereby linked to the succeeding Medicean popes.

Thus the Lorenzan charismatic center passed unbroken to his successors: Savonarola, Soderini, Leo, and Clement. Patterns of formal behavior in and around that center had been initiated that no Florentine political revolt could alter. The need for a leader of the Florentines, who was yet immeasurably distinct from them, remained. Political innocents formed the retinue, proclaiming the glory of martyred leaders.

The Father

From the time of Cosimo's expulsion from Florence in 1433 until the election of Pope Leo X in 1513, the respect that foreigners paid the Medici was the most important single ingredient of the family's influence over fellow citizens. In the former year, Cosimo was the richest man in Florence; he could determine who was hired to command Florentine armies; his banks loaned money to many European monarchs.[7] Cosimo's political and financial credit at home and abroad ranked alongside that of any Italian noble. Yet only after his expulsion did the banker learn that the respect he commanded abroad could withstand statelessness. Severed from the *patria*, the exile retained great personal authority wherever he went. Cosimo's own description of this period illustrates how new that phenomenon was. With evident surprise he told how in 1433 he had passed over Pistoian mountain roads into exile and found them lined with rustics who publicly vowed to help him, honoring him, he said, "as if an ambassador, not an exile."[8] When he reached his new residence in Venice, Cosimo again measured his authority in terms of the honors paid him. Usually, he said, one lost one's friends with fortune, but, "scarcely to be believed," the Venetian nobility received him superbly, "as if an ambassador, not an exile."[9] Other Florentines drew another lesson from the facts

6. See my "Adolescence." On Lorenzo's neglect of the feast of S. Giovanni, see further below.

7. Molho, *Florentine Public Finances*, 188f.

8. A. Fabroni, *Magni Cosmi Medicei Vita*, 2 vols. (Pisa, 1788–1789), II, 99f.

9. "Ricevuto non come confinato, ma come

Cosimo had reported with such surprise. They concluded that if one were rejected by Florence but accepted by Venice, one's reputation in Florence could only increase, because Venice was better than Florence:

> I would say that Venice is more magnificent, because of its power and the gentility of its governors, than any other power in Italy. If [Cosimo] was honored by [Venice] and banished by a lesser [city], he is the more magnificent, for those who honor him are more noble and more powerful.[10]

Just as noble Venice had welcomed Cosimo when he was exiled, so the fine Este family of Ferrara accompanied him to the gates of Florence when he returned, and Pope Eugenius IV lent his authority to Cosimo's position by allowing the latter to hold the papal bridle.[11] Throughout the subsequent history of Florence, the Medici took to heart the teaching of the father: The whole of Italy had to be part of any ritual space the Medici hoped to create around the family manger. As Cosimo would say, his descendants had to "domesticate" themselves with the rulers of the various princely houses, for it was these kingdoms, duchies, and marches, as well as the peasant villages of the Pistoian mountains, that "gave reputation" to the Medici in Florence.[12]

The ceremonial honors paid Cosimo abroad were the more important because they could not be paid him at home. Florence's classical system of ritual times, spaces, and objects resisted the building of individual reputation through pomps, and Cosimo learned he could only compete within that system, not overturn it. He did not, as sycophantic historians have often wanted to believe, return to Florence from exile in triumph "like the Romans," but entered quietly.[13] Once in the city, he made one impulsive attempt to amend the ritual calendar by establishing the feast of St. Thomas as an implicit day of communal rejoicing for his return. But as one counselor quickly pointed out, Cosimo's return was a private matter, and Florentine feasts were designed to celebrate public victories and procure future grace for the whole body politic, and not for a single part.[14] The feast of St. Thomas never assumed any communal importance, and Cosimo learned from the

ambasciadore. . . . Fu cosa da non credere, essendo cacciato di casa, trovare tanto onore, perchè si suol perdere gli amici colla fortuna"; *ibid.* See also D. Kent, "I Medici in Esilio: una Vittoria di Famiglia ed una Disfatta Personale," *ASI*, CXXXII (1976), 3–63, who emphasizes the problems for another branch of the consortery brought on by the exile.

10. Cavalcanti, *Istorie*, IX, 27, and *ibid.*, ch. 22 for more of Cavalcanti's views on the exile.

11. Fabroni, *Cosmi, loc. cit.*; G. Cavalcanti, *Della Carcere, dell'Ingiusto Esilio e del Trionfal Ritorno di Cosimo, Padre della Patria*, ed. D. Moreni (Florence, 1821), 244. On Eugenius and Cosimo, G. Holmes, "How the Medici Became the Pope's Bankers," in Rubinstein, *Florentine Studies*, 379.

12. On Lorenzo "domesticating" himself at Cosimo's

behest, see Rochon, *Jeunesse*, 103, n. 46. On the Sforza "giving reputation" to the Medici, see, for example, B. Buser, *Die Beziehungen der Mediceer zu Frankreich während der Jahre 1434–1494* . . . (Leipzig, 1879), 423, and *ibid.*, 433, where Luca Pitti said the dependence on Milan was so great Florence could not send ambassadors when and where it chose (1464–1465).

13. Cosimo describes it in his *ricordi*, cited in Fabroni, *Cosmi*, II, 103. Moreni's Roman return of Cosimo was fantasized in his editorial notes to Cavalcanti, *Carcere*, 261.

14. The festive institution was done while Cosimo was Standard Bearer of Justice in early 1435; *ASF, Prov.*, 125, ff. 210v–211r (Feb. 17, 1434/1435); Del Migliore, *Firenze*, 485ff; Dorini, "Culto," 20f.

episode. Once again late in life the *pater patriae* lent his name to a similar undertaking, a feast established in 1458 to celebrate the family's victory over internal enemies.[15] But generally speaking, Cosimo avoided the formal personalization of the official calendar, and sought to create significant familial times through more subtle means.

One such means was to build chapels in honor of Sts. Cosmas and Damian in several major churches of the city, ensure that divine services were said in them, especially on those saints' feast, yet resist the temptation to make the feast an official communal celebration.[16] Something like a broad private feast seems to have been the result, one that provided citizens, all those who were now naming their sons *Cosimo*, and at least one confraternity of adolescents the opportunity to honor the family on the birthday of its leader. In this way the Medici could measure their status annually without Cosimo incurring the charge that he was impinging on the public identity.[17]

Another means through which Cosimo created significant Medicean times was by patronizing established communal festivities so lavishly that their communal character was overlaid, and confused with, a Medicean quality. The feast of San Giovanni stubbornly retained its communal character, but the tactic was wondrously successful when Cosimo adopted the feast of the Epiphany and the visits of foreign dignitaries to these ends.[18] We have seen that the visits of real lords, dating from 1419, and the play hospitality offered the Magi on the Epiphany, starting in 1390 and lasting till about 1470, were two festive styles that served the function of legitimating the city through royal visits. They could also legitimate Cosimo.

The festival of the Magi became closely associated with the Medici soon after Cosimo's return. On the feast of the Epiphany the great man took part in the Magi's journey, wearing a gold gown one year, walking in rich fur in another. Medicean *festaioli* laid out the processional route for a Confraternity of the Magi that was little more than a family *brigata*.[19] We do not know if these festivities represented Cosimo and his descendants as the very Magi, as did several *Adorations of the Magi* painted during the fifteenth century, but

15. This *festa* was all the more arrogant because for the first time in Florentine history no particular saint was associated to the Medicean success; see pages 276f, this volume.

16. There is no census of these saints' altars in Florence, but all indications are that they were established in many places. The one in Santa Croce had the obligation of a Mass each week in memory of Cosimo's contributions to the Franciscans; *ASF, Dipl.*, *S. Croce*, Jan. 31, 1456/1457. That at San Marco housed the boys' Confraternity of the Purificazione; Morçay, *St. Antonin*, doc. 71. Cosimo's 1429 endowment for the celebration of his saints' feast in the Baptistry is in G. Vasari, *Le Vite de' più Eccelenti Pittori, Scultori e Architettori*, ed. K. Frey, I (Munich, 1911), 342, reg. 80. On the clientele's early celebration, see Rochon, *Jeunesse*, 334; R. Marcel, *Marsile Ficin (1433–1499)*

(Paris, 1958), 445. The feast was also celebrated in different parts of Europe by "domestici e famigliari, e . . . compagni delle loro ragioni di traffichi e botteghe"; Biagi, "Per la Cronica," 73 (retrospective written *c.* 1532). During the first Medici exile, its celebration in Rome by Cardinal Giovanni de' Medici was an occasion for supporters and antagonists to measure Medicean strength, *Misc. Fior.* I, 93 (letter of Oct. 1, 1504). Several extant paintings of the saints were done for still other chapels.

17. For example, Giovanni Rucellai says his family named his grandson Cosimo after Medici; *Zibaldone*, 35.

18. On the communal qualities of which, see pages 298 seq., this volume.

19. Hatfield, "Compagnia," 136 and *passim*.

there can be little doubt that Florentines already imagined the kings' exotic gifts and baggage trains as emblematic of the honor, trade, and wealth Cosimo brought the city.[20] These great cavalcades were financed in part by the government, which knew that the festival "demonstrated the city's all but negligible magnificence . . . , the honor of the Florentine *popolo* and the excellence of this city." On entering the city they stopped first at "Jerusalem" to honor the secular authority of Herod.[21] Then they proceeded past the Medici palace to "Bethlehem" in the Medici church of San Marco, where the Christ Child lay. The festivity of the Magi commented on the economic wealth of the city, asserted its citizens' noble character, and, over the years, established the royal pretensions of its leading family.[22]

The benefits to the Medici were much the same during the visits of real rather than play monarchs. From the time in 1434 when a kneeling Cosimo thanked the visiting Pope Eugenius for his support, Cosimo exerted himself to bring dignitaries to the city, ceremonially associating with them in time-honored Florentine fashion so as to participate in their charisma. Count Francesco Sforza came in 1435, the first of several dignitaries from this important family to honor the Medici as well as the city.[23] Cosimo's costly yet successful efforts to have the Council of Ferrara transferred to Florence in 1439 are well known, and when Pope Eugenius arrived in Florence for the occasion, it was Cosimo, elected Standard Bearer of Justice, who marched beside him and held the bridle of the papal horse.[24] Still, Cosimo was cautious not to upset his countrymen by too obviously manipulating these visits to his own ends. When the emperor Frederick III came to Florence in 1452, the first citizen remained in the background.[25] When Count Galeazzo Maria Sforza, son of the duke of Milan, came to Florence with Pope Pius II in 1459, Cosimo received them in his home, rather than take communal office to welcome them as he had Pope Eugenius in 1439.[26] And if, during a repeat visit, the count was domiciled in the Medici palace rather than in the official quarters that had been prepared for him, that was Sforza's choice, not the Medici's.[27] In the midst of the public panoply for which he was in part responsible, Cosimo knew how to appear domestic rather than political.

From the time the new Medici palace was completed in 1459, Cosimo and

20. On the identifications in paintings, see R. Hatfield, *Botticelli's Uffizi "Adoration"* (Princeton, 1976), 68–101. For a later, direct association between Medici wealth and that brought from the East, see Trexler and Lewis, "Two Captains."

21. The governmental rhetoric of 1428 and 1446 is cited in C. von Fabriczy, "Michelozzo di Barto-lomeo," *Jahrbuch der Königlich Preuszichen Kunst-sammlungen* XV (Beiheft; 1904), 93f.

22. By the last procession of the Magi in the later 1460s, both "Jerusalem" and "Bethlehem" were at San Marco, so that the roads to both secular and spiritual power passed the Medici palace to the Me-dici square; details in Trexler and Lewis, "Two Captains."

23. G. di Jacopo Morelli, *Cronica*, 141 (Nov. 15).

24. Cavalcanti, *Delle Carcere*, 244 (Moreni, citing a contemporary *priorista*).

25. See pages 310f, this volume.

26. Rab Hatfield continues to study the events of this year; for now see his "Some Unknown Descriptions of the Medici Palace in 1459," *Art Bulletin* LII (1970), 232–249.

27. On the 1467 reception, Trexler, *Libro*, 83; W. Ros-coe, *The Life of Lorenzo de' Medici, Called the Magnificent* (London, 1851), 425.

his successors used it in an ambiguous fashion. Certainly the immediate goal of official visitors to the city was the Palazzo della Signoria, and it was in this public square that the Florentines continued to witness and assess the ceremonies of welcome. Yet so many of these guests either resided in the new palace during their stay in Florence, passed it on their way to visit the famous image of the Annunziata, or visited its own wonders, that the palace became a new point on the itinerary of march for foreign visitors. Its existence therefore was modifying the public ritual space of the city.[28] Not dissimilar to a Renaissance church in shape, its womblike structure more hospitable than the male tower of the Palazzo della Signoria, the Medici palace competed with public buildings for worship, propitiation, and celebration, and seemed, in Ackerman's incisive phrase, "a grandiose stage for the performance of the rites of commercial and political leadership."[29] Adding to its public character, the palace had one of the few domestic chapels in Florence, and it was in this formal setting, surrounded by the Gozzoli painting of the *Journey of the Magi*, that Cosimo greeted visitors.[30] Amid a fabulous collection of books, cameos, plants, and young intellectuals who, in Roscoe's phrase, rewarded Cosimo's support by making his virtues the main subject of their discourses, the now elderly father received his foreign guests into the sacred setting.[31]

Thus the Medici palace cannot be said to have been a domestic or private residence in the modern sense. It was common knowledge that political decisions were made around the dinner table and it was evident that, like a public monument set in a broader ritual space, it embodied the victory of that thirst for family status and honor that was inherent among the citizens of the republic.[32] Yet the very essence of this public representation of status and honor was its domestic nature. Florentines knew that Cosimo was "at home" with worthy nobles when he was abroad, and that foreign nobles when in Florence were "at home" in Cosimo's palace. The very familiarity and domesticity of this formal representation signaled a slow shift in Florentines' perceptions of what was significant in their urban space and objects. Cosimo made the family residence a center of intimate ritual with public meaning, a type of princely camera; through that intimacy with princes he stood apart from his fellow citizens, but he snared his foreign bounty with his Florentine clients.

Cosimo cultivated the image of the simple father in a wondrous palace. The diplomat Lodovico Carbo told how Cosimo was discussing politics with Luccan ambassadors at home when he started to play with one of his grand-

28. See Trexler, *Libro*, 144 ("Palaces of Medici"). Visitors stayed in other palaces as well, though the Medici palace's preeminence as a tourist site and visitors' residence is unquestionable.

29. J. Ackerman, *The Architecture of Michelangelo* (London, 1966), 78, a view of the palace shared by F. Kent, *Household and Lineage*, 228f and *passim*. R. Goldthwaite, on the other hand, views the Renaissance palace in general, if not the Medici palace in particular, as a place for the "withdrawal of the family into a

new realm of privacy"; "The Florentine Palace as Domestic Architecture," *American Historical Review* LXXVII (1972), 988.

30. *Ibid.*, 1006; Rochon, *Jeunesse*, 74 (1459).

31. Roscoe, *Life of Lorenzo*, 63, 71.

32. On political discussions there, see Pius II and Cavalcanti, cited in Rubinstein, *Florentine Studies*, 459, 453. Recall that the municipal buildings of the fourteenth century were viewed as objects on which the emblems of private status could be placed.

children. Asked by the Luccans how he could mix play with the affairs of state, he is said to have replied, "Oh my mature brothers, are you not also fathers? Don't you know what it is to love sons and grandchildren? You're amazed that I played the bagpipe [with him]. You're lucky the child didn't ask me to sing a sonnet."[33] The theater of intimacy was much the same at Cosimo's country palace at Careggi, where he dined with Galeazzo Maria Sforza, who then wrote his father:

> We all dined together, except for Giovanni [di Cosimo], who would not sit or eat with us because he had so much to arrange. . . . When that was over, a charming little show was given by the ladies. The wives of Piero [di Cosimo] and of Giovanni, a grown daughter of Piero's, the wife of Pierfrancesco [di Lorenzo, brother of Cosimo], a young Strozzi . . . and a few country women took part in it. They all did dances in the Florentine manner, skipping and shifting in refined fashion.[34]

The bagpipe, the young Giovanni's table service, and the distaff dance were not, as some have thought, charming vestiges of republican simplicity but expressions of a sophisticated aristocratic ethos of public domesticity that had come to roost in Florence.[35]

Cosimo's contribution to the future ritual revolution in Florence was, therefore, the legitimation of domestic intimacy as a political instrument in a European ritual space. With that trace of noble superiority that European princes retained in their dealings with the best of Florentines, Francesco Sforza in a letter of 1463 spoke of the love that Cosimo's credit, wealth, and financial support had engendered in him:

> We have continually and singularly loved the magnificent Cosimo de' Medici of Florence because of his singular virtues. Or rather we are obliged and required to love all his things because he has reciprocally loved us and our things, and has served us in our needs.[36]

On Cosimo's death in the following year, Sforza's ambassador in Florence wrote his master of a purer, untrammeled familial affection that had bound the two men: "You lose a faithful friend and servant—thus he called himself. I don't doubt however that you would call him your father, for he had a father's affection for you, even though he held you his god on earth."[37]

There is much to be learned about Cosimo. Precisely because he cultivated the image of familial rather than political identity, his public personality continues to elude us. How did he walk the Florentine streets, and which groups attended him? At what distance did they follow him, in what order,

33. Rochon, *Jeunesse*, 48.

34. Buser, *Beziehungen*, 347 seq. (1459).

35. The idea that such performances were bourgeois simplicity itself may be found in C. Ady, *Lorenzo dei Medici and Renaissance Italy* (New York, 1962), 27. On domestic simplicity and intimacy as aristocratic qualities, see J. Huizinga, *The Waning of the Middle Ages* (Garden City, 1954), 54f, 128 seq., and as proof of friendship between princes, see page 445, this volume.

36. Fabroni, *Cosmi*, II, 246.

37. Buser, *Beziehungen*, 422f.

and with what gestures did they communicate with each other? The questions are better directed toward Lorenzo, whose record is fuller.[38] What role did Cosimo's ecclesiastical and secular buildings play in shifting Florentines' sense of significant space so that observers, on watching citizens flock to his palace to show him allegiance, could remark: "It was as if [Cosimo] were holding a church dedication at home"?[39] The subject needs a separate study. In what measure were Cosimo's motivations patriotic, defensive, and dynastic? This too is unclear, though as late as Savonarola, veterans of the Cosiminian age resisted the idea that he had calculatedly built a tyranny.[40] For all that is still to be learned, however, Cosimo's importance to the ritual history of the city is clear: Florence was now part of the *family* of Europe.

In the wake of Cosimo's passing, much appeared the same. Cosimo had behaved at home much like rich Florentines always had, only more; his funeral was typical of other Florentines', only less. The old man had forbidden any "pomps."[41] Florentine attitudes and behavior seemed little different than before. The Milanese ambassador wrote the duke that the Florentines' comportment toward him was as servile as always, and citizens seized the occasion of a Milanese victory over Genoa to rush to the Milanese embassy to congratulate the duke "as if they'd acquired [the victory] themselves."[42] These were traditional expressions, customary sentiments. Yet Cosimo had created a larger space for Florentine ritual action, as those people understood who, around Europe, attended the memorial Masses the branches of the Medici bank financed,[43] as those Florentines fathomed who saw the *pater patriae*'s burial tablet beneath the very cross of San Lorenzo:

> His prudence, his great wealth, the uses to which he applied it, and his splendid style of living, caused him to be beloved and respected in Florence, and obtained for him the highest consideration, not only among the princes and governments of Italy, but throughout all of Europe.[44]

38. A. Molho's projected biography of Cosimo should add much to the public picture of the man. The one possible quasi-realistic pictorial representation of Cosimo with his retinue is, or so W. Roscoe believed, in a painting (Plate 2) now attributed to Vecchietta, showing Bernardino of Siena preaching; W. Roscoe, *Illustrations, Historical and Critical, of the Life of Lorenzo de' Medici, called the Magnificent* (London, 1822), 90.

39. "In modo che pare abbia la sagra a casa"; Rubinstein, *Government*, 132f (1458). See F. Jenkins, "Cosimo de' Medici's Patronage of Architecture and the Theory of Magnificence," *Journal of the Warburg and Courtauld Institutes* XXXIII (1970), 162–170.

40. G. Pampaloni, "I Ricordi Segreti del Mediceo Francesco di Agostino Cegia (1495–1497)," *ASI*, CXV (1957), 222. Here, Cegia withdrew his support from Savonarola because the latter said Cosimo's *muraglie e*

fatte e limosine were *de' tiranni e vizi e difetti*. Cosimo's title of *pater patriae* was rescinded at this time, because in the government's view he had been a tyrant; Molho, "Cosimo," 32.

41. Piero's *ricordi*, cited in J. Ross, *Lives of the Early Medici as Told in Their Correspondence* (London, 1910), 78ff. Naturally, a funeral without pomp for such a man was "more" not "less," and a typical practice of great sovereigns. Cf. the burial "without pomp" of Philip the Bold of Burgundy (1404) in his magnificent monastery at Champmol; O. Cartellieri, *The Court of Burgundy* (New York, 1972), 35.

42. Buser, *Beziehungen*, 420 (Apr. 17, 1464); *ibid.*, 422f.

43. I have lost this particular reference. For the branches' annual celebration of the feast of SS. Cosmas and Damian, however, see n. 16.

44. Machiavelli, *History*, 318.

The Son

Lorenzo di Piero di Cosimo de' Medici was born on January 1, 1449, but no Florentine chronicler recorded the event.[45] The time had not yet come when historians thought the fate of Florence hung on the nativities of Medici children. Still, the circumstances of the boy's baptism, if not birth, and the events of his childhood and adolescence were special. The child Lorenzo stood under a new star: In the period from 1449 until the early 1470s, boy and family emerged as distinct ritual objects, prayed for and to by Florentines who loved them without necessarily knowing them personally. The age of abstract personalism began.

The entourage that accompanied Piero di Cosimo to the Baptistry on the feast of the Epiphany in 1449 was different from the neighbors and relatives who normally served as godparents for Florentine infants of the patrician class. This infant's sponsors were institutions.[46] The quarters of the city were evenly represented, and their presence was recorded by the scribe in the same sequence used in official communal documents. The representatives included the eight priors who had just left the office of the Signoria, nine of the current *accoppiatori* of the commune, and, from outside the communal government, three distinguished officials: the archbishop of Florence, the prior of the church of San Lorenzo, and a proctor for Federigo da Montefeltro, count of Urbino. Symbolically if not in law, the infant was sponsored by the structures of Florence, an innocent to be protected by abstract godparents. We have till now emphasized the cautious privateness of the Medici, but in the baptism of Lorenzo we find the family eliciting sentiment toward the innocent from public institutions.

One of the conventions of this abstract form of association, long common to feudal Europe but new to Florence, was that subjects prayed for their lords though they did not know them; the personal lives of others were important to strangers. It was a surprise to Piero di Cosimo to find that this was now true in Florence, and the tenor of his letter to his sick wife Lucrezia in 1467 brings to mind Cosimo's astonishment at new ritual developments:

> What must be attributed to the grace of God is that prayers have been said [for you] by those who do not know us, and whom you have never known. Truly [this is] a wondrous thing, more divine than human, and I steadfastly believe that owing to these prayers we shall receive the grace of God.[47]

To Lorenzo di Piero receiving such prayers was a matter of course, for he understood that in his person was reified, as in a sacred image, all that was

45. Rochon, *Jeunesse*, 59 (Lorenzo's *ricordo*).

46. The following summarizes my "Lorenzo and Savonarola," 294–297.

47. Ross, *Lives*, 116. Both this and Cosimo's earlier astonishment (pages 421f, this volume) refer to types of retinue. Cosimo's, however, had referred to a physical retinue. Piero spoke of that (doubtless he was speaking of people in chapels or churches praying for Lucrezia), but as well of the spiritual commitment to the family implied in the behavior.

credible and trustworthy about Florence. A priest present at young Lorenzo's joust in the Piazza Santa Croce in 1469 prayed for the latter's victory, confident that Lorenzo would reciprocate the favor once this stranger made it known to him.[48] For Lorenzo's credit was Florence's credit. Savonarola would remind his audiences how Lorenzo had insisted on participating in the profit of every commercial company,[49] and that was reasonable, for Lorenzo's credit was a part of any Florentine's investment. Jacopo Nardi wrote that simply by lending his name to a Florence firm, Lorenzo increased its credit, the city's prosperity, and of course Medici income—all without investing one florin.[50] The Florentine roots of this abstract personalism, so characteristic of the later Italian states and economies, lay in the age of the father, and were visible at the baptism of the child. Soon Luigi Pulci could explain to Lorenzo. "I had no money to spend for some time. So I've spent your reputation."[51]

THE CHILD IN THE TEMPLE

I am wax, and you can dispose of me and shape me as you want.[52]

The elders set the precious child into his Florentine manger, and taught him how to act while using his innocence as a ritual instrument. Lorenzo was only five years old when his grandfather thought it time to send him abroad, so he could "domesticate himself with the Duke [of Milan] and with his illustrious sons."[53] It was time as well to put him on the Florentine stage. With the duke of Anjou in town that same year, 1454, Lorenzo's teachers sent him out in public to greet the illustrious guest dressed up in French clothes, "surrounded by a crowd of children and adults, who followed us on our way to King René's son."[54] The boy was like an icon: Encased in a shell of foreign threads, yet, as his teacher Gentile Becchi pointed out, too grave in his comportment to be French,[55] he was distant yet very Florentine. In 1455, we find him made *messere* of the Bath while on vacation with his family.[56] Then during the public entertainments furnished the Milanese and papal visitors in 1459, ten-year-old Lorenzo shone as the *signore* of the festive brigade of the *armeggeria*. We recall the bystander's description:

48. So he said, at least, when he then approached Lorenzo asking that favor; B. Buser, *Lorenzo de' Medici als Italienischer Staatsmann* (Leipzig, 1879), 4ff.

49. *Amos e Zaccaria*, I, 224.

50. Nardi, I, 9; also A. von Reumont, *Lorenzo de' Medici. The Magnificent*, 2 vols. (London, 1876), II, 331. This important practice has apparently remained a secret to Florentine economic historians.

51. Pulci, *Lettere*, 69.

52. Lorenzo to the duke of Milan on the morrow of Piero's death in December 1469; Rochon, *Jeunesse*, 230, n. 108.

53. *Ibid.*, 103, n. 46.

54. Letter of Gentile Becchi to Piero, cited *ibid.*, 100, n. 4 (June 3).

55. "Multos tamen eo die fefellit, quos deinde illa sua gravitas minime habitui Gallico conveniens Laurentium esse docuit . . . "; *ibid*.

56. *Ibid.*, 73.

Everyone watches what he does. . . .
His dress surpasses easily that of
All those of whom we've spoken,
And well shows that he is signore.[57]

The public character of the boy at this time was not much different from what visitors to the Medici palace in this year saw on the chapel wall. In Gozzoli's famous fresco, Lorenzo seems portrayed as the youngest of the Magi, riding in a foreign aristocratic ambience; adults followed the child; they dressed him up—as nuns would Caterina de' Ricci—to adore him.[58]

The second phase of the boy's formal history stretched from 1465 to 1469. In these years the adolescent made three trips to foreign courts, intended to prepare him to assume power after the death of his ailing father. In 1465 he went to Milan, armed with detailed behavioral instructions from Piero, the first of a series of such little tracts on comportment prepared by Medicean fathers for their sons.[59] In choosing "what visits to pay and what to say," Piero wrote, Lorenzo was to follow the lead of the Medici bank manager in Milan. He should be "civil and alert, act as a man, not a boy," be splendid rather than parsimonious, for it was of the utmost importance that "you do yourself honor." Understanding that Medicean honor abroad was gained through submission, Piero admonished his son to consider himself always the servant of the duke, as did Piero, and as the court of Milan expected of the Medici.[60] These instructions project a clear sense of beginnings: "Show sense, industry, and manly endeavor," Piero added, "so that you may be employed in more important things, for this journey is the touchstone of your abilities."

In April 1466 Lorenzo was off to Rome and Naples, and this trip has left impressive evidence of the great attention family and courts paid to the details of Lorenzo's behavior. A letter Piero received from Gentile Becchi, for example, describes the interaction between the Neapolitan king Ferrante and the young Magus:

> In the moment we arrived in the hall, where there were many lords and barons, His Majesty the King came out of his room. I believe he planned [the timing] this way. Lorenzo stepped forward ostentatiously, and at his third reverence he threw himself at the feet [of the king] to kiss his knee. [The king] refused this with grave and benign manner, [and instead] received him [by permitting himself] to be kissed on the cheek. Then after [Lorenzo] had made his reverence to the duke of Calabria, His Majesty the King took him by the hand, and thus, [holding hands], he went [with Lorenzo] up to the cathedral, where he heard low Mass.[61]

57. See page 227, this volume.

58. The difference between the still-common practice of parents dressing children to affect themselves was that here Lorenzo was being dressed for society at large, and for diplomatic purposes. See the fine study of W. Brückner, *Bildnis und Brauch. Studien zur Bildfunktion der Effigies* (Berlin, 1966).

59. Ross, *Lives*, 93f (May 4).

60. The uncompromising demands of subservience Milan imposed on the Medici are evident in these words of Galeazzo Maria: "We are advised that Piero di Cosimo . . . speaks of us as he pleases. ` . . . If he were our equal we would have responded to him, but since he is not equal to us, we did not want to receive his words"; text in Rochon, *Jeunesse*, 103, n. 50 (1469).

61. *Ibid.*, 107, n. 99 (Apr. 14).

So affected was Piero by the contents of this letter that he wrote in the margin that he had read it three times.[62] He knew how important such a visit was, not only in Florence and Naples, but in Rome, where everyone wanted to know, as one correspondent wrote Lorenzo, "the particulars of the honors and fond reception which His Majesty the King [of Naples] accorded you."[63] Those anxious for such information assumed that Ferrante had meant to demonstrate his attitude toward the Medici through body language, and in answering Lorenzo's letter of thanks to him, the king said as much. His love for Lorenzo's father, for the family itself, and for the boy, said Ferrante, explained his behavior. This love "merited the greater demonstration."[64]

At least some of the witnesses to these Neapolitan ceremonies were not impressed with Lorenzo's performance at court, and hastened to pass on the news of Lorenzo's alleged failure to anti-Mediceans on the Arno, who used it to discredit the family. One such correspondent wrote with malicious delight: "Many fathers spend [money] to make their sons known, who would do better to spend [it] so they remained unknown."[65] In the following year this same correspondent denounced another ritual failure of a family member in the south, and drew a distinctly negative assessment from these Medicean trips abroad: "Piero butchers our city's reputation, by now reduced to vile estimation."[66] No longer a matter of mere family reputation, the behavior of the young Lorenzo could damage the community.

Any second thoughts the father may have had about Lorenzo's performances were squashed by his own weak physical condition, which made it imperative for the adolescent to continue his representations. Sent off to Milan in 1469, Lorenzo was by now an accomplished young lord. He stopped overnight at a hostel outside Lucca and, in the words of Becchi's report to Piero, "sat there in the open air of the piazza and received various visitors." Off for Milan the following morning, Becchi continued, "Lorenzo was followed by many citizens, for they wanted to accompany him and talk to him at length."[67] Again instructed by his father in the details of behavior—this time not to make a show and to remember that he went as a family member rather than as an ambassador—Lorenzo in his own memoirs expressed satisfaction with the outcome of the Milanese visit, giving us an insight into the young man's values at this time:

62. "Tre volte l'ho lecta per mia alegreza e piacere"; *ibid.*, 108, n. 112.

63. *Ibid.*

64. *Ibid.*, 108, n. 111. The scope of such visits was prearranged. In 1469, a Roman wanted to accord Lorenzo "a magnificent, quiet, or middling reception, according to your wishes"; Ross, *Lives*, 120. The mode of reception was also compared to the Magi story, as was evident when Giuliano visited Venice in 1472; Buser, *Lorenzo*, 128.

65. "Et tornando alla venuta di Lorenzo, molti padri spendono per fare cognoscere li figluoli loro che assai meglio seria spendere acciochè non fussono cognosciuti"; Rochon, *Jeunesse*, 108, n. 113 (May 6).

66. When Lucrezia went to Rome wife-hunting for Lorenzo, Jacopo Acciaiuoli wrote a friend: "Falla alla signorile e va lisciata come se fussi di 15 anni. Ecci chi si ride di lei ma più di Piero. . . . Tanto è che Piero fa notomia della riputazione della città nostra, ridutta horamai a vile extimatione"; *ibid.*, 51, n. 61 (Apr. 3, 1467).

67. Fabroni, *Laurentii*, II, 55.

> I was rendered great honors, more than anyone else who was there for the affair, even though certain of them were much more entitled to them than I. As was appropriate, we gifted the duchess with a gold necklace decorated with a big diamond which cost about three thousand ducats. The said lord [duke] because of this [gift] then expressed the wish that I be godfather to his subsequent children.[68]

Lorenzo had played the child and now, the brilliant adolescent *compare*, he had emerged as *persona grata* at the Italian courts. He had learned the importance of correct behavior and treasured, as had his predecessors, the smallest signs of foreign support for the family, quickly showing them off to an avid Florentine audience. Jousting for the hand of his fiancée not long before his father's death, Lorenzo showed himself to the Florentines as his father's heir apparent. He rode on a horse that was a present to him from the king of Naples; the citizens then saw him exchange this parade mount for a combat one, given him by the duke of Ferrara; preparing to enter the list, Lorenzo shed his coat to reveal armor presented to him by the duke of Milan.[69] At twenty, the boy still remained a wax icon shaped and dressed by foreign powers.

This joust of early 1469, Lorenzo's marriage feast with the Roman aristocrat Clarice Orsini in June of that year, the death of Piero on December 2 following, and the birth of Lorenzo's first son Piero in 1471 were the main events in Lorenzo's passage from adolescence to young manhood. Before, he had been abroad regularly as a child protected by his innocence; after 1471 the patterns of Lorenzo's adult behavior emerged. The intervening events offer us our first extended glimpse of Lorenzo in public in Florence, the character of his retinue, and the role his age and that of his *brigata* played in the emerging Lorenzan state.

As far as we can judge, Lorenzo's joust of February 7, 1469, was a competition the outcome of which was known in advance, not only by the participants and judges, but by the audience participating in the pious fraud. People prayed, of course. From Rome Clarice's mother wrote that her daughter planned to fast on the day of the joust. "as a service to you, so that God will preserve you and concede you victory,"[70] and on that day people prayed around the field of battle.[71] Lorenzo won, as Giuliano would win his joust in 1475.[72] Yet who could believe that he had won fairly? Machiavelli found it necessary to insist on it, but Savonarola recalled to a knowing audience how the tyrant had always arranged his victories in competitive games.[73] Certainly

68. Rochon, *Jeunesse*, 87. Piero's instructions are in Ross, *Lives*, 137. Lorenzo was also pleased that the king of France had allowed him to add the fleur-de-lis to the family crest, and recorded this for his sons; Roscoe, *Life of Lorenzo*, 425; Ross, *Lives*, 86; Buser, *Beziehungen*, 436.

69. The coats of arms of each of these powers were doubtless embossed on each of these objects to leave no question as to their source; Roscoe, *Life of Lorenzo*, 94.

70. The mother asked to know the exact day, implicitly so that the daughter's prayers would be efficacious; Rochon, *Jeunesse*, 136, n. 432.

71. See page 429, this volume.

72. P. Kristeller, "Un Documento Sconosciuto sulla Giostra di Giuliano de' Medici," *La Bibliofilia* XLI (1939), 405–417.

73. Machiavelli, *History*, 325; Villari and Casanova, *Scelta*, 376 (Savonarola, *Del Reggimento di Firenze*). In a

the prayers and the anticipation were genuine; preordained outcomes and competitiveness were no more mutually exclusive in the Florentine joust than they are in the Sienese *palio* today.[74] If Lorenzo had fallen from his horse, for example, the most biased of judges could not have named him the winner, and those prayerful souls asked less for Lorenzo's victory than that its preconditions not come undone. "Not yet having left adolescence," as an early biographer characterized Lorenzo in this year, the boy embodied the status of his ailing father, of his family, and the hopes of all those familiar and unknown people who prayed for him. His victory preserved and heightened Lorenzo's, and Florence's, honor.[75]

Lorenzo's marriage feast the following June gave Florentines their first formal view of their new lord at home. At its center was the groom, "young and thus a lover," skilled in the dances "suitable for gentlemen such as you, but not just for anyone." In the palace and streets around Lorenzo swirled a domestic ritual order that those present strained to observe and learn, and about which those absent from the city hastened to inform themselves.[76] One of the descriptions of these festivities has survived, an anonymous letter whose detailed and highly structured description of the scene gives unmistakable evidence that Florentines were reconstructing their ritual space around the exemplary figure of the young Lorenzo.[77] To gather his information the writer normally stood outside the Medici palace, regarding the inside as a holy of holies. Knowing that the feast should be emulated by all good Florentines, he supplemented his data on outside events with information from a *festaiolo* inside. The resulting letter to a compatriot in foreign parts is more than a quaint curiosity of domestic etiquette; it betrays the new spatial structures of Florence itself, and the new sense of political order that the young Medici master desired for his city.

From the first it was evident that this was no normal patrician marriage celebration. Friends brought gifts to the bride and groom, to be sure, but as in Lorenzo's baptism a generation earlier, some of the friends were political entities. "The principal towns, Pisa, Arezzo, and other communes, villas, and castles" gifted this private couple, much as on San Giovanni these parts of the Florentine dominion paid tribute to the government of Florence.[78] What

joust of 1427 the prize was given not to the winner, but to a jouster of the visiting Portuguese prince *per più honore;* Giovanni–Carnesecchi, Apr. 25. On other ways to win a joust, see page 504, this volume, and for family concern and strategy on its member's jousting, page 509.

74. On the pious fraud in the contemporary *palio* at Siena, see Dundes and Falassi, *Terra in Piazza,* 48–141.

75. On Lorenzo's continuing adolescence, Valori cited in Rochon, *Jeunesse,* 133, n. 396.

76. Such quotes emphasize the age expectancies attached to Lorenzo's behavior. Lorenzo as a dancer: Buser, *Lorenzo,* 119.

77. I am suggesting that Lorenzo was becoming an individual center with no previous parallel in Florentine history, except for religious images like Impruneta. The following description is based on the document in Ross, *Lives,* 129 seq.

78. The difference between the tribute of San Giovanni and these gifts is, of course, not negligible. Nor was it unknown for Florentine patricians to receive wedding gifts from villages and towns where their real estate holdings were extensive; see, for example, those received by the Rucellai mentioned in Giovanni's *Zibaldone,* 30. But for Lorenzo to receive gifts from the great cities of the dominion was a different matter, little different from a prince's trib-

followed was equally significant: Once the Medici had received the gifts, they redistributed them to some 800 citizens of Florence. Not only did Carlo de' Medici at his palace dole out hundreds of barrels of wine daily to any inhabitant, nor were the customary wedding alms at the main palace given only to the poor and the clergy. What Lorenzo in a private status had collected from the public entities of the dominion he redistributed to the citizenry. "You and I," wrote the anonymous spectator, "were among the number."[79] Lorenzo was the golden thread between two public entities, and shared his nuptial joy with grateful citizens. A significant modification in the ritual of urban exchange had taken place in the Medici palace; the wealth of the dominion reached the citizens through its first citizen.

Stationed beside the dance platform in the street outside, our observer carefully described the activities there because they could reveal the organization of the banquets inside. He knew that the fifty "dance maidens" sitting together outside dined with Clarice indoors, just as the thirty or more "male dancers" ate separately indoors, perhaps with Lorenzo.[80] The dance itself mattered little to the witness. Order and procedure did:

> The stage outside was decorated with tapestries, benches, and forms, and covered with large curtains of purple, green, and white cloth embroidered with the arms of the Medici and the Orsini. Every time a company came on to the stage to dance, they took refreshments once or twice which were suitable for that time of day. First came the trumpeters, then a great silver basin, then many smaller ones full of glasses, then small silver jars full of water, then . . . , then. . . . The account has not been drawn up [yet], but from five to . . . thousand pounds of sweetmeats and sugar plums were consumed.[81]

From the one banquet he attended and from what the *festaiolo* told him, the writer wove a rich tapestry, describing arrangements inside the palace, including the presence of the head of the family and of two relatives of the letter's recipient.[82] He specified the location of each table, the sex and age of those dining at each, the position of the forty elder marshals and the paired seneschals, the arrangement of the silver, and much more. The ritual of time seemed no less important. When the trumpets sounded and led the food in from the street, the writer noted, the stewards controlled the porters' speed in such a way that each serving going to the maidens' table in the distant garden arrived at the same instant it did at all other tables.[83] The writer was conscious in short of a master organization of space (evident in the four water-pourers at the center of the courtyard), time (the symmetry of serving), object (the same

---

ute. A fine example of the formal procedures through which towns offered the Medici gifts is in Ross, *Lives*, 269, where Clarice is the recipient.

79. We are not sure who either person was, though a library catalogue identifies the writer as Piero di Marco Parenti; Ross, *Lives*, 128. The recipient had relatives named Lorenzo, Agnolo, and Lodovico.

80. Interestingly, Lorenzo himself is nowhere men-

tioned in the description, though he was present for the festivities.

81. Compare this description to the dances analyzed on page 237, this volume.

82. Their names are given in n. 79.

83. It would seem that almost every movement was introduced by the sounds of music.

dish being eaten by everyone at any one time), and not least, of the organization of a specific moral lesson:

> The banquets were prepared for a marriage rather than for a magnificent feast, and I think this was done purposely as an example to others not to exceed the modesty and simplicity suitable to marriages, so there was never more than one roast.[84]

This was an unparalleled sentiment with an important future. In previous Florentine sources, we found the clergy giving example to the laity and, in the first half of the fifteenth century, the first indications of lay groups of adolescents giving example to older laymen. We even recall that young Florentines were encouraged to choose a distinguished older man to emulate.[85] But nowhere before do we encounter one boy staging domestic banquets, repeated five times until some 400 citizens had been able to attend, with the clear purpose of teaching comportment to the political class of the city. In absolutistic Europe, the every domestic act of a sovereign was viewed as didactic; here in the words of a fifteenth-century contemporary is that same understanding of the adolescent Lorenzo's behavior. Adolescents in confraternities and the young leader of the city seemed at one in showing their elders that there was another way.

This was heady stuff, and there were many citizens, perhaps even among those who attended these banquets, who resented such lessons from a young man still years away from the minimum legal age for holding any office, one who in fact would never reach the legal age for a Standard Bearer of Justice.[86] Here was a city being "led around here and there at the will of one adolescent," in the words of one anti-Medicean, "a *giovane* whose opinions and wishes prevailed over" those of the elders.[87] Worse, Lorenzo was said by some to be "governed by young men"[88] themselves too young for political office. Who were Lorenzo's friends in these years, wishing him well at his marriage feast, and watching his first steps in the political arena?

Lorenzo's friends were older than he was. Of eight persons Rochon found in the boy's inner circle at this time, only one was Lorenzo's contemporary, and the others ranged from seven to seventeen years older.[89] Though in the 1470s he added a few to the *brigata* who were more in his age cohort, the general picture of a *giovane* surrounded by older, although still often

84. Ross, *Lives*, 131. A similar description of another Lorenzan banquet is by the biographer of Michelangelo, Condivi, cited by Reumont, *Lorenzo*, II, 372.

85. See page 171, this volume.

86. That was forty-five; Lorenzo died at forty-three years of age.

87. In 1479 it made Rinuccini weep to think "ad unius adolescentis libidinem huc atque illuc circunduci"; F. Adorno (ed.), "Alamanni Rinuccini Dialogus de Libertate," *Atti e Memorie dell' Accademia Toscana di Scienze e Lettere 'La Colombaria'* XXII (1957), 282."Salli male ch'el parere et volere de uno giovane prevalga al suo"; G. Soranzo, "Lorenzo il Magnifico alla Morte del Padre e il suo primo Balzo verso la

Signoria," *ASI*, CXI (1953), 65 (Milanese report of 1470).

88. The French diplomat Commynes' assessment of Lorenzo in 1478; *Memoirs*, II, 393.

89. Bernardo Rucellai   b. 1448
Braccio Martelli   b. 1442
Dionigi Pucci   b. 1442
Gianfrancesco Ventura   b. 1442
Sigismondo Della Stufa   b. 1442
Guglielmo de' Pazzi   b. 1437
Piero Alamanni   b. 1434
Luigi Pulci   b. 1432
More on these early friendships in Lorenzo de' Medici, *Lettere*, I, 8, 20.

politically immature, *giovani*, still holds.[90] We may find it slightly surprising for the twenty-four-year-old Braccio Martelli to have "sinned together" with the seventeen-year-old Lorenzo; contemporaries would have been rather annoyed by the immaturity of the whole lot.[91]

On what terms did these fellows associate with the young master? The forms of address they used in writing him prove a disappointing avenue for answering that question. During the 1460s, for example, Lorenzo was addressed with the familiar *tu* not only by older but by younger men, by strangers as well as by friends.[92] In these letters, conventions of language and occupation seem to be just as important as relative intimacy in determining form. One correspondent wrote to Lorenzo as *voi* in the Italian language, for example, but addressed the sixteen-year-old as *tu* in the more formal Latin. A boy was expected to be *sotto governo*, and so most letters before 1470 asking favors requested only that the adolescent commend the writer to the elder Becchi.[93] After that date there was a decided shift toward the use of *voi* by both new correspondents and some older associates, including the significant change of Becchi himself.[94] Thus Lorenzo's age seems, in general, to have been the most important factor determining the form of address.

That factor certainly dictated the tone of discourse, which is best characterized as chummy obsequiousness. Typical of courtly behavior toward an adolescent, such playful obeisance was the rule whether Lorenzo was addressed as *tu* or *voi*, called a friend or a master. Giovanfrancesco Ventura could address the boy in 1468 as *dolce compare mio*, yet with the formal *voi*.[95] Luigi Pulci has always been cited as a (seventeen-year-older) friend who used familiar language with Lorenzo, but his words did not alter the subservient tone. Pulci might call Lorenzo *tu*, think of him "like a brother," but he knew that Medici was "like a superior to be honored," a "most distinguished youth" and "my most friendly superior."[96] When the Pazzi conspiracy of 1478 required all of Lorenzo's retinue to lay aside the playfulness and protest the most serious loyalty, Pulci was first in line to say: "I will always remain obligated to you in every way," "your servant or friend or *compare*, as I have long been." "I love you, revere you, and fear you."[97] In dozens of other

90. The "new friends" identified by Rochon (*Jeunesse*, 151 seq.) are

Bartolomeo Scala	b. 1428
Sforza Bettini	b. 1445
Niccolò Michelozzi	b. 1447
Matteo Franco	b. 1447
Angelo Poliziano	b. 1454

91. Martelli *ibid.*, 125, n. 312.

92. Examining the letters in Rochon, *Jeunesse*, one finds that among the older friends identified by Rochon, Pulci almost without exception used the familiar form throughout the sixties and seventies, as did Braccio Martelli and many others including the Pazzi. Yet Gianfrancesco Ventura used *voi* in 1468 and continued; Francesco Berlingueri did the same in 1466 and thereafter. Braccio Ugolini did the same, as did Matteo Franco when he replaced Luigi Pulci as Lorenzo's de facto buffoon. Among those using *tu*

with Lorenzo in these years whom Rochon does not identity as intimates are Niccolò Martelli, Pellegrino degli Agli, Cantalicio, Antonio degli Albizzi.

93. As is pointed out by Rochon, *Jeunesse*, 63, n. 218. A Latin letter of Francesco Berlingueri with *tu* is *ibid.*, 124, n. 300 (1466), an Italian with *voi* of the same year; *ibid.*, 70, n. 317.

94. An example of *tu*, *ibid.*, 128, n. 346 (1467). Of *voi*, *ibid.*, 61, n. 187 (1470); 287, n. 243 (1474); 63, n. 220 (1488).

95. *Ibid.*, 124, n. 294.

96. Cf. Pulci, *Lettere*, 40, 57, 62, 68.

97. *Ibid.*, 155. The hundreds of examples of chummy obsequiousness toward Lorenzo in these early years are comparable to the language Lorenzo and his father used in addressing foreign princes. Piero Vespucci would stop believing in Christ if Lorenzo did

letters from the time the message is the same: This was the court of an adolescent.

It was this unusual brigade of *giovani* who watched and perhaps encouraged the behavior their leader adopted toward his elders in the days and months after Piero's death. A citizen present at the funeral, in the first of many expressions of gratification that Lorenzo was going to act his age, reported that "Lorenzo . . . cried a great deal along the street."[98] True, some elders were ashamed when this mere boy all but commanded the elders (*vecchi*) to meet with him after the funeral, but there were many others who praised Lorenzo's stance as an orphaned adolescent in need of the protection and wisdom of paternal elders. One later writer said that Lorenzo in these crucial times treated citizens as fathers, and only later as servants; another praised him for having listened to the ancient counselors Soderini and Canigiani, "first of the knights," during these decisive days.[99] Contemporaries told the same edifying story of domestic humility: "Lorenzo continues to humble himself and to practice that style which pleases the *popolo*."[100] Among his elders, Lorenzo's behavior evoked that same sentiment of shame at the skills of children that the fathers showed toward the adolescent confraternities:

> Lorenzo comports himself in a fashion that shames the old and the dead. . . . Yesterday morning he collected in his own home twenty-five principal citizens to reveal his own thinking to them. He excused himself to them for having taken the liberty of convoking them.[101]

The Milanese ambassador Sagramoro, who believed he virtually monopolized the youth's instruction in formal presentation in these months, wrote his master: "In my judgment, Lorenzo comports himself very well, according to his age, and in true servitude toward Your Illustrious Signoria. And he is holding on to his friends."[102]

Students of Florentine political life have often viewed Lorenzo's behavior at this juncture as merely affected, that of an adult in boy's clothing manipulating credulous fathers. But Florentine elders were no fools, and seasoned diplomats like Sagramoro were not deceived. In fact, Lorenzo's performance

---

not help him; Buser, *Lorenzo*, 130. Elsewhere calling himself Piero de' Medici's "slave," Filippo Lippi in 1468 would do more for Lorenzo than anyone; Rochon, *Jeunesse*, 68, n. 300. Poliziano in 1470 wanted no God but Lorenzo; Ross, *Lives*, 156f. The *spedalungo* of S. Maria Nuova wanted to "bend my knee to your commands"; Passerini, *Storia*, 337. For northerners, such domestic subservience came naturally: A musician named Jacquet de Marville wished "God . . . give you the grace that on the first night that you sleep with your noble and illustrious wife, you can make a male child"; Rochon, *Jeunesse*, 352, n. 330.

98. Marco Parenti also gives the precise order of the funeral procession and Lorenzo's and Giuliano's position and accompaniment; Strozzi, *Lettere*, 608. Parenti also noted that Lorenzo stood in the middle of

his rank during the funeral procession.

99. Respectively Cambi, XXI, 68; "Laurentii Medicei Vita a Nicolao Valorio," in F. Villani, *Liber de Civitatis Florentiae Famosis Civibus* (Florence, 1847), 168 (hereafter Valori, *Vita*). Tommaso Soderini was born in 1403. Among the other older counselors Lorenzo is said to have relied on are Luigi (b. 1407) and Jacopo (b. 1422) Guicciardini, Bongianni Gianfigliazzi, Bernardo Del Nero, Antonio Pucci, and Girolamo Morelli. It does not seem that he was personally close to any of these oldsters, however

100. Filippo Sagramoro to the duke of Milan; Soranzo, "Lorenzo," 50 (Jan. 3, 1470).

101. Same to same; *ibid.* (Dec. 7, 1469).

102. *Ibid.*, 55.

affected both his audience and the boy himself, for age-specific behavior was part of Lorenzo's power. Sagramoro's insight was valid: Florence and the Medici were dependent on each other and on foreign approbation.[103] Lorenzo could only rule through keeping these friends. Maintaining those bonds required Lorenzo to act his age. Lorenzo succeeded, and his exquisite formal skills when combined with the interests of his domestic and foreign friends affirmed the young man's rule.

PALMS AND PASSION

And Lorenzo began to say for the salvation of the state he had offered up his brother and almost lost his own life.[104]

Little more than a year after the death of his father, the twenty-two-year-old Lorenzo was forced to change his behavior, and be a man. The expectation came from abroad, and the impact of Lorenzo's obedience to the demand was felt at home. After 1471, and as a consequence of Lorenzo's own behavioral evolution, far-reaching changes in Florentine behavioral mores appeared. They were accelerated, but not initiated, by the Pazzi conspiracy of 1478. We turn now to the Florentine ritual configuration in the later part of the Magnificent's life.

The first hint that the princes of Italy expected Lorenzo to grow up came in early 1471. Though assured by two ambassadors that the duke of Milan "loves you as himself" and that at Naples he was thought "unsurpassed and quite loved," Lorenzo was troubled to find that in Rome, circles of *signori et monsignori* had discussed his behavior and concluded that his reputation for carousing was not proper for a governor.[105] Defenders of Lorenzo in these Roman coteries insisted that "before you married there was perhaps something to that, but since, *omnia graviter . . . ,*" but the judges were unconvinced.[106] Lorenzo wanted the truth about his reputation in Rome, and Gentile Becchi responded, admonishing his lord with the skill of a courtly teacher:

One speaks of you here most honorably, and one hears no more about Tommaso [Soderini]. Up till now your reputation was painted; now it is sculpted, and stands

103. *Ibid.*, 48, for Milan's financial dependence on the Medici. Balancing the interminable expressions of Medicean devotion and subservience to Milan at this juncture is the cutting note in a letter of the Florentine ambassador in Milan to Lorenzo of June 2, 1470, speaking of Galeazzo Maria: "I will put him through the eye of a needle. . . . He would jump the rails for you"; Rochon, *Jeunesse*, 230, n. 108. An extreme example of scholars' disregard of the importance of forms is Rochon's simultaneous statement that in the League negotiations of 1470 Lorenzo followed every wish of Milan, and that Lorenzo's servile attitude toward its duke was affected and even comic;

ibid., 202.

104. "Et chominciò detto Lorenzo addire: Che per salvatione dello stato avea messo un fratello, ellui presso che la vita"; Cambi, XXI, 66.

105. Rochon, *Jeunesse*, 128, n. 346 (Becchi letter received Jan. 29, 1471). The Milanese assessment of 1470 is in Buser, *Lorenzo*, 16, the Neapolitan of 1471 in Pulci, *Lettere*, 93. Rochon, *Jeunesse*, 203 casts doubt on Pulci's perspicacity.

106. *Ibid.*, 128, n. 346 (Becchi, paraphrasing the defenders).

out. This was necessary. Some days past I asked the auditor [of the apostolic camera] how he thought you compared with his *messer* [Giovanni] Bentivoglio [of Bologna], you being of the same age [as he]. He replied that your competition was not *messer* Giovanni. Rather, you were expected to surpass Cosimo, and up until now you have passed the test, [for] you have already surpassed him as he was at your age. Nonetheless, he would like you to seem older in appearance, in dress, and in habits. [If you do so], he will then agree that you are the hope of this century, for here, where one keeps accounts of such things, one can't think of anyone better. He thought of Alfonso, Francesco Foscari, Cosimo, Duke Francesco, and of a Genoese. But [considering how each was] at your age, he would place them all behind you.[107]

As if to encourage Lorenzo to change his behavior, the elder mentor had now begun to address his master as *voi*.

The expectations of foreigners seem to be related to Lorenzo's subsequent behavior; appearing now in official functions, he slowly deserted the "things of children." In 1470 at the age of twenty-one he had discharged his first public ceremony at the behest of the Signoria, knighting the reigning Standard Bearer of Justice.[108] It was a clear manifestation of Lorenzo's authority, for he was neither a knight himself nor did he belong to that exalted company of popes, emperors, and other foreign dignitaries who had knighted previous heads of the republic.[109] Now in September 1471 he assumed the role of a communal ambassador for the first time, traveling to Rome with other emissaries to congratulate Pope Sixtus IV on his coronation. We do not know how the skeptical Romans judged him, but the Florentines thought the Magnificent, as he was now called, impressive indeed. Observing the conventions of his elders, Lorenzo left Florence for Rome when the stars were right, and with "many magnificences," as one eyewitness reported:

> Thirty-five horses and seven mules pulling wagons traveled with him, and he carried four hundred pounds of silver—which I saw packed—basins, various things, plates and saucers, and other silver vases. It was a beautiful apparatus whose departure we witnessed.[110]

We have seen that the month before, Lorenzo had "transformed the kingdoms" of the Florentine Magi. Now bedecked like the figure identified as Lorenzo in Botticelli's contemporary *Adoration of the Magi*, which possibly commemorates this embassy, Lorenzo was an almost Magian representative of his city.[111] In late 1472 he took one further step toward assuming his new political role, and formally withdrew from the city's confraternities as his age soon made necessary.[112]

107. "Solo desidera che voi ve avecchiate in apparentia, vestiri et modi, et poi v'appruova la speranza di questo secolo, chè qui dove si tiene tali conti non si sente meglio"; *ibid.*, 128, n. 346 (Feb. 14, 1471).

108. Roscoe, *Life of Lorenzo*, 115.

109. Knightings of the Standard Bearer were occasionally performed by visiting dignitaries; see, for example, Cambi, XX, 209. In April 1475, Lorenzo's brother Giuliano di Piero took his turn as syndic and

knighted another *gonfaloniere*; L. Morelli, 191; Salvemini, *Dignità*, 192; Hatfield, *Botticelli's Uffizi 'Adoration'*, 78.

110. "Dissesi che parte in quella hora per punto d'astrologia"; ser Giusto, ff. 99rv.

111. Neither Hatfield nor other students have considered this possibility. For Lorenzo's ceremonial caution at Rome, see his *Lettere*, I, 340f.

112. M. Del Piazzo, "Gli Autografi di Lorenzo de'

Lorenzo was of course only a youth, not an elder, and he comported himself as such. When the duchess of Ferrara visited Florence in 1473, Lorenzo was not too proud to serve as a squire with his younger brother Giuliano at a meal in her honor.[113] In 1475 the group that went to welcome a visiting Sforza condottiere had Lorenzo among the *giovani*, not the citizens.[114] Nor was Lorenzo beyond the age at which he could be excused from taking part in the fracas of Carnival (Plates 18, 19). Yet, as he explained in a comment of 1476, his heart was no longer in such frivolities: "For some time I had been quite alien to such festivities, and if they still pleased me sometimes, this came more from a certain normal wish to do like other *giovani* than from any great pleasure I derived from them."[115]

Giuliano stepped into the role of the "prince of youth" that Lorenzo slowly deserted, a noble, genial foil to his increasingly grave brother just as Giovanni had once been to Piero.[116] Lorenzo sent him to Genoa in 1471, where he was treated "more like a son than as the servant" the eighteen-year-old desired to be, to Venice in the following year where "those lords gentlemen who are humanity itself" (Becchi) behaved like so many Magi attending the Christ Child, showing that the Medici had "a different reputation abroad than at home."[117] Was this boy, who in confraternal orations moved grown men to tears, to become a cardinal? Lorenzo was advised to "dress [him] up as a protonotary" if he wished to increase his chances.[118] Or was he to become the warrior counterpart to his statesman brother? When it came time for Giuliano to have *his* joust in 1475, Lorenzo did his brother great honor. In the procession to the jousting field, the young play-warrior rode on a horse bristling with the gems and colors that Lorenzo had deserted. The older brother marched behind, one among the grave citizens honoring the youthful genius of Florence: "Many of our leading citizens followed [Giuliano], and especially Lorenzo his brother, the most worthy man of any his age, commended [Giuliano] to the *popolo* by his presence."[119]

Medici nell' Archivio di Stato di Firenze," *Rinascimento* VIII (1957), 226f (Dec. 12). In Sept. 1471 the maximum age for a *veduto* in a confraternity had been reset at twenty-five years; ser Giusto, f. 99r.

113. Information from her letter describing the "domestic collation" in C. Corvisieri, "Il Trionfo Romano di Eleonora d'Aragone," *Archivio della r. Società Romana di Storia Patria* X (1887), 655f.

114. A. Cappelli, "Lettere di Lorenzo de' Medici detto il Magnifico conservate nell'Archivio Palatino di Modena," *Atti e Memorie delle rr. Deputazioni di Storia Patria per le Provincie Modenesi e Parmensi* I (1863), 255 (Oct. 2).

115. Lorenzo, *Opere*, I, 35.

116. For the title, see Reumont, *Lorenzo*, I, 255; Rochon, *Jeunesse*, 26.

117. Rochon misunderstood Giuliano's reaction to his treatment in Genoa; *Jeunesse*, 27, 56, n. 132. In

Venice, Becchi noted that three gentlemen came to take Giuliano to dinner, "tutti di più età che e compagni chomegli anuntiati a' Magi"; Buser, *Lorenzo*, 127f (May 28).

118. As it was, Giuliano was too "unfinished" to assume such a dignity; Ross, *Lives*, 163, 169f (May 15, 1473). On Giuliano's orations, see Rochon, *Jeunesse*, 56.

119. "Multi deinde nostrorum civium proceres et presertim Laurentius eius germanus vir omnium sue etatis dignissimus sua presentia populo eum commendaverunt"; Kristeller, "Documento Sconosciuto," 414 (letter of Filippo Corsini). I have adopted Rochon's interpretation of this letter that Lorenzo and the other citizens were on foot (as *popolani* always were in such settings); *Jeunesse*, 259. An interesting sidelight on this joust is that one jouster was forced to take part; I. Del Lungo, *Florentia. Uomini e Cose del Quattrocento* (Florence, 1897), 397.

Yet if Lorenzo's public appearance was now *omnia graviter*, it did not have to be indistinguishable from that of other citizens. It was true that he wore the customary hat and coat "like other citizens," and that when in the company of older men he always accorded them the place of honor on his right. But Giovanni Cambi quickly added that Lorenzo was accompanied by a retinue of four citizens "for reputation" long before the attempt on his life in 1478 made such guards reasonable.[120] Thus although Lorenzo might march in burgher's clothes and without arms, his retinue, Cambi noted, carried swords and disdained the distinctive *capuccio* of the citizen.[121]

These formal modifications in Lorenzo's own behavior were one response to foreign expectations; the Magnificent's determined attack on other citizens' rights to public honor was another. A city of too many "delights and pleasures" in 1472, Florence after 1473 was to be more somber and dignified.[122] Doubtless with Lorenzo's approbation, the government in that year enacted a series of laws that not only severely restricted the outlays that citizens could incur for their families' ceremonial acts, such as funerals and baptisms, but struck at the patriciate's general life-style by restricting the expenses of any domestic meals to which outsiders were invited.[123] "All those things that had traditionally won support and reputation for the citizens. . . ," said Rinuccini, Lorenzo "damned both by example and by words."[124] Commune-wide festivities were of course one of the main settings for gaining such reputation, and here as well Lorenzo was on the offensive. The law of 1473 that restricted the government's outlays for the feast of San Giovanni merely formalized a Lorenzan disinterest in the feast that Luigi Pulci had already criticized the previous year.[125] The Baptist's feast in 1473 reflected the master's lack of support: Instead of the twenty-one floats characteristic of the Cosiminian and Petrine days, a mere seven festive floats rode through the streets.[126] Nor was Carnival immune from the effects of Lorenzo's disfavor, and a diarist recording the 1474 activities noted the decline: "They put together some festive mummeries, but not ones as beautiful as were done in the old days."[127]

Lorenzo's success in effecting these new departures in domestic ceremony must be taken as one reason the Magnificent was able to marshal the

---

120. "Detto Lorenzo andava il verno in mantello, et chapuccio paghonazzo, chome gli altri ciptadini, e quando era con ciptadini di più tempo di lui, sempre dava loro la mano ritta, e s'erano più di due, metteva in mezzo chi aveva più tempo; e la state andava in luccho chome gli altri. . . . Ma per aquistare riputatione si menava dirieto da principio 4 ciptadini cholle spade, in mantello, ma sanza chapuccio, da tre anni"; Cambi, XXI, 65, 67.

121. Cambi describes the changes in this bodyguard after the 1478 attack *ibid.*, 65. He is the only historian to make clear that Lorenzo had a bodyguard before this year; cf. Guicciardini, *History of Florence*, 36; Machiavelli, *History*, 371.

122. The 1472 characterization is in Rochon, *Jeunesse,* 336, n. 87.

123. References to these laws are on page 409, this volume.

124. "Tutte le cose che anticamente davano grazia e riputazione ai cittadini, come nozze, balli e feste e ornato di vestiri tutte dannava, e con esemplo e con parole levò via" Rinuccini, cxlviii.

125. See page 409, this volume.

126. Corvisieri, "Trionfo," 655.

127. "Non belle come già si sono fatte"; ser Giusto, f. 107v.

help or the neutrality of the great princely powers during the military crisis of 1478; these innovations demonstrated, while augmenting, Lorenzo's solid position as the single spokesman for the republic of Florence. At the same time, Lorenzo won the support of the princes by continuing the Medicean practice of liberal lending to them, a financial practice stemming from a theory of moral investment: "I could have invested capital," he once explained his failure to welcome a visiting cardinal to Florence, "without earning anything."[128] What Lorenzo hoped to earn through princely loans was less money than honor; that is, the noble's right to expect defense when weak. To "remain on good terms" with such princes, Piero had made loans to the duke of Burgundy, which were risky from a purely financial point of view. Lorenzo continued such practices, tying up large sums of money in the apostolic camera, for example, which could have been invested for better cash rewards.[129] Reputation, as one Medici banking agent defined it, was a "demonstration that one was in a position to do things," and there could be no greater thing than being associated with the great actions of princes.[130] Such dignitaries knew of course that they could not publicly press Lorenzo for loans, for any evidence that the Magnificent could not meet the requests of an ally would lead to his demise in Florence.[131] But Lorenzo was no less constrained for all that. As the Medici bank manager in Milan wrote, he could not withhold such loans from the Sforza "without losing favor and influence."[132] Curiously, in the world of princes and in Florence, the ability of a banker to lend to nobles measured the credibility of the lender—anxious to develop a reputation that could be spent—more than it did the borrower's.

These investments paid dividends, for when Lorenzo loaned beyond his capital, his debtors remained loyal to him. In Florence, Lorenzo found himself unable to deliver his clients all the offices they expected of him, yet in the wake of the Pazzi assassination of his brother in 1478, *compari* and strangers would rush to his aid. The Medici palace became a ritual center to defend the wounded Magnificent, so great was his brigade's belief that Lorenzo was loved abroad: "The reputation of the said Lorenzo is the estimation made of him by the potentates of Italy and by foreign lords. For without this, his stature in the city would not be what it is."[133] Abroad as well, as Raymond de Roover's study of the Medici bank has shown, Lorenzo was existing on equity, yet the potentates continued to honor him.[134] The bank branch in Lyon was already in deep financial difficulty in 1476 when the king of France

128. "Sampiero ad vincular fu a Firenze. Io lo ho fuggito perchè potevo mettervi di capitale che guadagnare"; Buser, *Lorenzo*, 179 (Sept. 11, 1487).

129. De Roover, *Rise and Decline*, 361, 370.

130. *Ibid.*, 465, n. 83 (1487).

131. Buser, *Lorenzo*, 21 (1472).

132. De Roover, *Rise and Decline*, 360 (1467).

133. Cappelli, "Lettere," 265 (Dec. 17, 1482). Buser believed that Lorenzo had overpromised; *Lorenzo*, 23.

On the response at the palace and elsewhere, see Guicciardini, *History of Florence*, 75f; Fabroni, *Laurentii*, II, 183, 204, 271. An extensive account by Giusto d'Anghiari of his actions at the palace has apparently escaped historians' notice; ser Giusto, ff. 122r–123r.

134. De Roover, *Rise and Decline*, 371. Unfortunately, De Roover never did squarely confront the broader nature of credit and equity, and views the banking difficulties as an unmitigated disaster without understanding the family's long-range success in purchasing honor and moral credit.

honored it with a visit, heralding the support that Lorenzo would receive in 1478. A hardheaded banker ecstatically trumpeted the profit that the Medici earned:

> The king . . . has been in your house here several times very domestically . . . , giving gifts . . . with his own hand . . . and in every way demonstrating that he holds you in great love. . . . At this moment the king has come here to the house and stayed a while to dine with us, as if he were some little lord. I repeat, great honor results from this.[135]

When the decisive conflict with the papacy broke out in 1478, Lorenzo announced his plight to all these monarchs and sought their aid. He did not, be it noted, do this by demanding his credits, but by protesting his humble servitude: to France, whose king in 1470 had insisted on being godfather to Lorenzo's daughter;[136] to Milan, whose duke had in 1472 required Lorenzo to be godfather to his child "so as to corroborate the spiritual bond of compaternity which we have with all of you through our other children";[137] to the king of Spain, whose letter of condolence on Giuliano's death, "the emotion evinced by so great a king," gave the Magnificent such comfort. He continued, "I commend myself forever to Your Majesty, oh my lord and king, and beg to be taken under the shadow of your wings."[138] Lorenzo's messages to the powers in these crucial months were always the same: "I beg your lordship to have faith in me."[139]

It was precisely the combination of the powers' unwillingness to side with Pope Sixtus in a war with Florence, and Lorenzo's own daring, that produced Lorenzo's implausible deliverance from catastrophe.[140] In late 1479 the Magnificent left Florence for the court of Naples, where he was received as an equal by Ferrante, Sixtus' one significant ally. Once again, Florentines heard of Lorenzo's flattering reception at a foreign court. This time, however, the impact was different. It was no longer a boy protected by innocence who had gone into the lion's den and tamed Ferrante, causing him to desert Sixtus, but a grown man. Lorenzo seemed led by a divine star. He was an image surrounded by a frame of great powers, who, like an image, showed a charismatic ability to move as well as to be moved. Lorenzo returned to Florence in early 1480 and was welcomed in his palace by able courtiers who, with tremulous awe, approached Lorenzo at the center of circles of arrayed admirers:

> How should I joy to touch Lorenzo's hand,
> Returning safely to his native land!

135. Buser, *Beziehungen*, 459 (May 22).

136. Rochon, *Jeunesse*, 231, n. 121.

137. Fabroni, *Laurentii*, II, 57.

138. Ross, *Lives*, 215.

139. Reumont, *Lorenzo*, II, 336f, a letter to Philippe Commynes, for whom in 1476 Lorenzo's agent in Lyon had urged a gift "because he's important, and because he merits it; it seems to me you owe him a beautiful and good exchange"; Buser, *Beziehungen*, 464f.

140. C. Ady points out that Medici's trip to Naples was not as daring in fact as it was perceived by the population; *Lorenzo*, 76.

> *But such the long and gratulating train*
> *That scarce his halls the joyful crowds contain.*
> *—Amidst the purpled senate, round him prest,*
> *He stands, in stature loftier than the rest.*
> *—Shall I approach?—the envious throng denies:*
> *—Or speak?—in fear the faltering accent dies:*
> *—Or see him?—to my share this sure may fall,*
> *For from the midst he overtops them all!*
> *Mark how th'entwining glories round him spread*
> *Pour their full radiance o'er his honour'd head!*
> *Whilst he salutes the friends that circling stand*
> *With cheerful looks, and nods, and voice, and hand.*
> *—Enough for me that with the rest array'd,*
> *My love is shewn, my duteous vows are paid.*
> *—Go then, my verse, salute the best of friends;*
> *And say, "These faithful lines Politian sends."*[141]

AN IDOL IN NEW SPACE

The geometric splendor of Poliziano's luminescent scene tells a new story. By the end of the Pazzi wars in 1481, contemporaries perceived Lorenzo de' Medici as a charismatic center that was transforming the traditional ritual spaces in which he moved. Medals announced that this survivor of the assassin's knife was the "salvation of the republic" (*salus publicus*), and martyr cults in Florentine churches candidly celebrated Lorenzo's birth while recalling Giuliano's martyrdom.[142] The language of a contemporary diplomat carries the same tone: "If those who rule had not had this idol," he wrote of Lorenzo in 1482, "there would have been no chance for a peace and league."[143] We have come to a decisive point in the description of the Florentine ritual revolution. Now our sources' interest in Lorenzo's every movement, and their perceptions of its impact on Florence, are abundant. Now we can study the full outlines of the new ritual order.

Starting with the chronicler's announcement of the birth of Giovanni de' Medici in 1475, contemporary scribes increasingly heralded the Magnificent's movements as Saint-Simon would herald the Sun King's.[144] Citizens kept a record of Lorenzo in the countryside (Landino noted the names of those who accompanied him out to the monastery of Camaldoli) and diarists pompously proclaimed his departures:

> On the twenty-sixth day [of April, 1490], Lorenzo de' Medici went to the baths of San Filippo. He rode off at exactly twenty hours. The Sienese did [him] great honor by providing him with a bodyguard richly dressed and ordered. He went to the said bath in 1490 with eight squadrons of soldiers and more than 500 soldiers.[145]

141. Poliziano, translated by Roscoe, *Illustrations*, 127.

142. Trexler, "Lorenzo and Savonarola," 297–301.

143. Cappelli, "Lettere," 265 (Dec. 17, 1482). Further instances of this wording: Machiavelli speaks of Lorenzo now being surrounded by a "halo of maj-

esty"; *History*, 382; a communal law passed shortly after the assassination calls Lorenzo the *lumen nostrae civitatis*; Fabroni, *Laurentii*, II, 114.

144. For the birth of Giovanni, see page 419, this volume.

145. Rossi, 251. For Landino, see Rochon, *Jeunesse*,

From the countryside Lorenzo's chaplain furnished a detailed description of the Medici entourage, and an almost liturgical account of Clarice's gift-giving and receiving forms.[146] In the city a diarist reported a rumor that Lorenzo, with more than 1500 persons attending, was near Impruneta holding a "beautiful hunt of leopards," and the fact that Lorenzo's son Piero was at Anghiari in a hunt with more than 100 hunters.[147] From Pistoia, Poliziano wrote home that the vacationing three-year-old Giovanni di Lorenzo "rides out on horseback, and the people follow him in crowds."[148]

Diplomats were no less meticulous in recording this rustic activity. We learn from one of their reports that the Spanish ambassador held a banquet "to top a dinner that the Magnificent Lorenzo served" at Careggi, and from another that Lorenzo had accompanied a condottiere out to his house at Caffagiola and then accompanied him every day he was there.[149] And as diplomats prepared statements on Lorenzo leaving the city, so they formally communicated his return to their principals: "Saturday the Magnificent Lorenzo arrived; all the ambassadors here went out to meet him."[150]

As far as the diplomats were concerned, the family palace to which Lorenzo returned was a public place. In 1485 the Ferrarese ambassador described a colleague who "never showed himself in public to talk with Magnificent Lorenzo, except yesterday when he publicly went to [Lorenzo's] house after eating, and spoke secretly for more than an hour." With still more significant language the same emissary wrote in 1488 that Lorenzo had held "a public dinner at home."[151] One Florentine chronicler thought it of public interest that the Magnificent had staged a "lovely meal" for the brother of the English monarch, and a foreign diplomat took pains to inform his principal that "today the Magnificent Lorenzo didn't leave his house, since his gout assaulted him. But he gambled and amused himself at home in the usual way."[152] Subsequent Florentine writers adopted a similar view of the public nature of the palace. Valori pictured Lorenzo teaching his fellows how to receive and give gifts there, and Michelangelo's biographer Condivi digressed from his subject to give a minute description of the seating order and rituals at Lorenzo's table. Still another near contemporary recorded Lorenzo's dictum that the more domestically a visiting dignitary was treated in the palace, the closer he was to the Magnificent.[153]

Yet at all times this public house retained its private mystery; in the future absolutistic state, the line between street formalism and domestic intimacy would be thoroughly obscured by the inscrutable prince. Suspected

40; Roscoe, *Life of Lorenzo*, 99f, and cf. *ibid.*, 69 for a similar list of those who had once accompanied Cosimo.

146. This long account is an important document for understanding gifting in this culture; Ross, *Lives*, 269.

147. Ser Giusto, f. 114r (Nov. 12, 1475), f. 137v (Nov. 18, 1480).

148. Roscoe, *Life of Lorenzo*, 273.

149. Careggi: Cappelli, "Lettere," 282. The condottiere: *ibid.*, 225–258 (Oct. 2, 1475).

150. *Ibid.*, 266 (Mar. 10, 1483).

151. Respectively *ibid.*, 274 (Nov. 27), 301 (May 29).

152. Respectively ser Giusto, f. 114v (Jan. 14, 1476), and Cappelli, "Lettere," 284.

153. Valori's tale is cited by Reumont, *Lorenzo*, I, 170, as is Condivi's description *ibid.*, II, 372. The oft-told tale of Lorenzo's domesticity with his guest Franceschetto Cibo in 1488 is *ibid.*, II, 373. Its first sure narration was by Vincenzo Borghini in the mid-sixteenth century; Del Lungo, *Florentia*, 437.

by some of being a house of magic, the Medici palace in fact contained a "stable" of cunning young geniuses like the precocious and mysterious Pico della Mirandola, pictured to the pope by Lorenzo as a type of arcane recluse "giving example to other men."[154] To its doors came the curious with letters of introduction, requesting they be permitted to see the rare antiquities in the garden and study. We have letters describing these foreigners being led through "the house, [its] medals, vases and cameos, and in sum everything including the garden . . . , everyone marvelling at the number of such good things."[155] Ambassadors spoke indistinctly of "visiting the churches and the house of Lorenzo, who showed [them] books, jewels, and figures"; the palace had become akin to the churches in the mystery of its contents, as much a stop on any foreigner's itinerary as the chapel of the Signoria or the cathedral of Florence.[156] In Galeazzo Maria Sforza's words, the Magnificent had collected the precious things of the whole world. In truth, the ancient Osirian dream of reconstructing all of history and power in the domestic soil of Florence seemed about to be realized in the Medici palace, around the figure of the *capo* or even in his person.[157] In one of his rings, went one story, Lorenzo held a genie prisoner whose mystic powers he used and controlled.[158]

The predominantly international and courtly character of this flood of reports on Lorenzo's palace activity is surely one of their most significant qualities. Neither the diplomats nor the domestic scribes found citizens' behavior in its ambience nearly as important as foreigners'. One later Florentine writer, it is true, praised Lorenzo for asking citizens to dinner there, but most contemporaries and subsequent biographers were more impressed by his unfailing invitations to visitors.[159] These Florentine biographers described exotica they loved, but had not mingled with: This psychic distance between Lorenzo and his fellow citizens, the perception of Florentine space as shaped by international charisma, is one of the most important qualities of a new ritual space. Citizens were out and courtiers in, as a letter to Lorenzo from his son describing one banquet for a foreigner makes clear: "The count [Pico] of Mirandola was here, messer Marsilio [Fici-

154. "He lives here with us most saintly, like a religious . . . , says the ordinary office of the priest, observes fasts and the greatest continence"; Fabroni, *Laurentii*, II, 291 (June 19, 1489); also Cappelli, "Lettere," 282. By this time young Michelangelo had joined the group; Trexler and Lewis, "Two Captains." Lorenzo used the word *stable* (*stalla*) to refer to his son's court; see page 458, this volume. On magic at Careggi, see Marcel, *Marsile Ficin*, 541f.

155. For the letters, see Ross, *Lives*, 316f; further Reumont, *Lorenzo*, II, 368. See Piero di Lorenzo's description of such a tour in Fabroni, *Laurentii*, II, 378. The Medici children could also be part of the scenery. See the tale of the German count who in 1482 saw them "collected" in a room, the boys on one side with Poliziano, the girls on the other with Cla-

rice; G. B. Picotti, *La Giovinezza di Leone X* (Milan, 1927), 46, n. 27, who correctly views this arrangement, if true, as "a carefully prepared scene meant to impress the illustrious guest."

156. Cappelli, "Lettere," 256.

157. "Quicquid sibique gentium pretiosum . . . ex tuto orbe collegerat"; Sforza, quoted by Lorenzo's biographer Valori, *Vita*, 168.

158. For more on this ring see page 458, this volume.

159. "Nemo unquam vir clarus aut Florentiam aut Florentinum agrum petiit, in quem non illa domus hoc magnificentiae genere usa sit"; Poliziano, cited by Rochon, *Jeunesse*, 353f, n. 355, with further comments on this subject.

no], messer Agnolo da Montepulciano. And in order to have a citizen, but only one who was a relative and a literary man, we chose Bernardo Rucellai."[160]

The occasional contact of Lorenzo with a foreign dignitary was the stuff of public record; the quotidian ranks of citizens who filled the palace court-yard to pay their respects and ask favors seemed less consequential. Yet to the individual citizen fortunate enough to gain access to the Magnificent, such a meeting was a moment in history, and he hastened to publicize it so as to make himself a public man. Tribaldo de' Rossi, for example, whose ances-tors had once hosted a thousand foreign knights in their palaces in Oltrarno, now filled the pages of his memoirs with news of his contacts with the allies and person of Lorenzo. A graphic report on the foundation of the Strozzi palace in 1489, for example, reverentially details how Filippo Strozzi with great ceremonial intimacy permitted Rossi to throw a coin in the foundation, and how Rossi fetched his children, dressed in their Sunday best, so they would remember this signal honor. He repeated much the same narrative in the following year when he contributed a coin to the foundation of the Gondi palace.[161] Rossi's contacts with Lorenzo, on the other hand, could be the alpha and omega of family identity, and, in a detailed report of 1490, he commemorated such a visit to the Medici palace.[162] The scene he painted, equal to Poliziano's poem in its structural clarity, is vivid evidence of the nature of the relations between Florentines and their leading citizen, first in the palace, then in the streets of Florence.

Rossi sets the scene by explaining his visit. For many years he had owned copper deposits but had not mined them. Now wishing to do so, he was afraid to gather the necessary work crews and capital, for that would have required publicizing the location of the deposits and thus put him in danger of being robbed. Certain that no governmental institution could protect his rights, but that only Lorenzo had such credit, he decided to approach the Magnificent. Rossi understood that this might entail Lorenzo participating in the profits, but the humble citizen was ready to share: "It occurred to me to reveal it only to Lorenzo de' Medici and not to trust a single other father's son, and to commend myself freely to him, in his hands only."[163] After speak-ing with Lorenzo's chancellor in the cathedral one day, Rossi was invited to the palace, and he describes how he approached it:

On the fifteenth day of the month [of December, 1490], I went there and ser Piero [the chancellor] said to me: "Wait for an hour and return, for [Lorenzo] wants to talk with

---

160. The 1490 visitor was the Venetian scholar Ermo-lao Barbaro; Fabroni, *Laurentii*, II, 378.

161. "When I had given him a lilied *quattrino*, [my son] threw it in, and I had him throw in a bunch of damask roses he had in hand, and I said: 'Remember this,' and he said: 'Yes,' and they were there together with Tita our servant [as witnesses]. . . . May this always be in the name of God"; see both fascinating

accounts in Rossi, 249, 253f. See also R. Goldthwaite, "The Building of the Strozzi Palace: The Construction Industry in Renaissance Florence," *Studies in Medieval and Renaissance History* X (1973), 113f.

162. The following is based on Rossi, 258–261.

163. The implication that Lorenzo might share in the profit is contained in these words.

you." I came back [later] and found a large group of citizens waiting to talk to him. I stayed from the twenty-third hour, after dinner, up till the time I became so uncomfortable about my shop that I left, with the idea of speaking to him at leisure on a feast day.

Rossi returned on December 21, feast of the Medicean St. Thomas, and resumed his account by first liturgically invoking that saint's augurs:

So in the eternal name of God and of the Virgin Mary, and of St. Thomas, I went after eating to the house of Lorenzo de' Medici and showed myself to ser Piero. He told me: "Don't leave, for he wants to talk to you." Lorenzo put on his coat and came down into the courtyard and gave audience. Ser Piero told me repeatedly to stay close to him, and that he would tell [Lorenzo] I was there, [we] being at the gate of the courtyard leading out [into the street]. Then ser Piero showed me to [Lorenzo]. Lorenzo called me. I began to tell him: "I gave ser Piero the sample of copper. . . ." And I had said just a little, and we were going hand in hand together up to the gate of the palace on the street side, when Lorenzo said to me: "Let me give audience to them"—for there were more than forty citizens there—"and then you will come with me." With that I removed myself down the street a few steps.

Rossi's account of many citizens waiting for a hearing in Lorenzo's palace is corroborated by other evidence of the time. It was difficult to obtain an audience with the Magnificent, who often kept clients waiting for hours before seeing them; citizens were servile, and some of them had to rely on non-Florentine courtiers to gain access to their fellow citizens.[164] Critics said that when Lorenzo finally did speak with his fellows, he was evasive, "responding shortly and ambiguously, so you have to understand him by the merest sign"; other contemporaries knew that all Florentines, and not just Lorenzo, "speak in hidden things and allusions . . . , with facial expressions . . . and in abbreviated phrases."[165] Rossi was one of them, and expected

---

164. As did Rossi on ser Piero da Bibbiena. Savonarola recalled Lorenzo's habits to a knowing audience: "The tyrant is very difficult to have audience with, and makes citizens stand and wait for four hours, and does the same with religious [persons]. He remains in his rooms with his friends and companions doing what he wants, and doesn't worry about who is waiting for him. And then when he comes out, he gives brief audiences"; *Amos e Zaccaria*, I, 226f. Rinuccini railed against the servility of the Florentines (*Ricordi*, cxlvii; *De Libertate*, 284), as did Cambi, XXI, 3, and page 502, this volume. But in the early sixteenth century, Lodovico Alamanni, while disagreeing with Rinuccini and Cambi on this question, agreed with both that Florentines' behavior had always been related to the ritual space in which they found themselves: "The Florentines are confirmed in a certain [habit], rather asininity than liberty: in Florence they don't deign to do reverence to anyone, even if he merits it, if not to their magistrates, and this they do *per forza* and with effort. They are so alien to the ways of the court, I believe few other [peoples] are so

[extreme]. None the less, when they are abroad they don't behave in this fashion. I believe it comes to this: in the beginning perhaps it seemed to them unadaptive behavior to lift their cap. Then this their laziness became custom, and from habit it became natural. And it is because of this [naturalness], I believe, that when they are outside the country and not in their [civil] clothing, it seems all the easier to them to converse with princes"; text in Albertini, *Staatsbewusstsein*, 370. Alamanni's analysis is the earliest Florentine attempt to understand the nature of the citizens' formal behavioral practices.

165. Respectively Savonarola, *Amos e Zaccaria*, I, 226f, and the Jewish mystic Alamanno describing the sixth quality of the Florentines: "They speak in two ways, by the wisdom of their voices and the action of their limbs, lest they be guilty in their speech which goes up upon their breath. But indeed they shall verily speak in hidden things and in allusions lest each one be seized by the appearances of his heart. Therefore they shall carefully guard their souls and with facial

Lorenzo to be cautious as any Florentine. When he finally did converse with the Magnificent, it was the latter's behavior that mattered and not his words:

> When [Lorenzo] had given audience to a few [citizens], he called me, and at our leisure we [left the palace and] went down the street alone together. Many followed in back as we talked together, up to that place past San Niccolò's in the Via del Cocomero, between the wax sculptors and [the church of] San Niccolò. There I took leave of him.

The precision of Rossi's ceremonial geography betrays the intent of his whole narration, which was to record the terms of a behavioral contract between Lorenzo and himself. Just as the Magnificent's retinue and passersby had witnessed their intimate association, so would history record that Lorenzo, who did not enter such contracts lightly, had publicly invested in Tribaldo de' Rossi, in the sight of St. Thomas, whose feast it was, to an extent measurable in the distance between the Medici palace and a certain point in the Street of the Watermelon. Rossi had sought something more solid than a paper contract protecting his mine. He wanted the public trust of a credible man, and proved by his description of shaped ritual spaces that he had won it.

Protected by laws of lèse-majesté, surrounded by twelve foreign toughs with swords drawn, and followed by a retinue of citizens, Lorenzo, in now moving out of the palace and into the streets of Florence, was a presence that bestowed worth and value on the city's several parts. The master of the cathedral school wrote the Magnificent, imploring him to deign to honor the schoolboys by his presence at one of their plays, and begging Lorenzo not to humiliate them by preferring other adolescents' theater.[166] In 1511 a one-time member of the boys' club of the Vangelista devoted a long memoir to his membership in the club in 1491: Lorenzo's son Giuliano had been the boys' *messere*, and the Magnificent had visited their Lenten performance of his play *SS. Giovanni e Paolo*; Bartolomeo Masi even recalled the clothing he and his brother wore on the stage for this audience.[167] The child Lorenzo had done much to foster the image of the young by his own renown. He had proven what one family surrounded by Florence's geniuses could produce, and thus intimated what other children could achieve. Somehow this iconic child of the 1450s had become a man, *omnia graviter*, without surrendering the attractiveness of youth. Once an abstract mirror of the socialized children of Florence,

---

expressions and with voices and words they will speak that which they desire. Also from this I learned hidden wisdom, to speak in abbreviated phrases"; J. Perles, "Les Savants Juifs à Florence à l'Epoque de Laurent de Médicis," *Revue des Etudes Juives* XII (1886), 254f. I am indebted for the translation from the Hebrew to Howard Jacobson, David Petersen, and Gary Porton.

166. Trexler, "Adolescence," 230f. On the toughs, Cambi, XXI, 65ff, with its evident implications for a

quasi-monarchical ritual space, and for the law of lèse majesté, see Cappelli, "Lettere," 255. Lodovico Alamanni offers an idyllic picture of Lorenzo "coming into the [public] square every day and giving audience easily and without charge [sic!] to whomever wanted it"; Albertini, *Staatsbewusstsein*, 368f. Alamanni contrasted the easily accessible Magnificent with a haughty later Medici, and thus the argument must not be taken at face value.

167. Masi, 15f.

he became the source of their genius by still bearing their genius in him. Visiting these confraternities as a sign of his favor, he placed his children in them so they too could partake of the confraternal pedagogy.[168]

The Magnificent's visits to the city's churches and monasteries were no less important to those institutions' stature. "These tyrants are always going from one church to another, and the other citizens and satellites come behind them," said Savonarola, and the friar's biographer told how Lorenzo on entering a monastery was followed about by fawning brothers desperate to please this living idol.[169] The Camaldolan general Delfin was one such monk. When Medici visited his monastery of the Angeli twice in 1487, Delfin was ecstatic. The monks of this order, he wrote Lorenzo, yearned for the latter's visit "like the patriarchs awaiting the Messiah in limbo"; the words that fell from the Magnificent's tongue during such visits became "revelation"; Giovanni di Lorenzo was nothing less than "a child come unto us."[170] Delfin knew that Lorenzo's visit to a religious house, and especially a cell-by-cell inspection of the kind he bestowed on one monastery in 1491, "raised its reputation" and, because of Lorenzo's influence upon government, perhaps lowered its tax assessment.[171]

Lorenzo's ability to visit value upon Florentine spaces, times, and objects was nothing new in principle for Florentine patricians, whose devotion had always been a foundation of objects' sacrality.[172] Yet the concentration of that value-giving authority in this single processional person represented something new in Florentine history, and had a decisive effect upon the Florentine behavioral universe. That his mere whim could raise the status of a hallowed monastery like the Angeli to the heights and that his neglect could condemn the feast of San Giovanni to relative inattention meant that not only fashions, but the sacred itself, was unstable. Until the Medici family developed its own sacral traditions, the normal rate of change in sacred spaces, times, and objects would be accelerated.[173] Furthermore, since devotion once visited upon images soon converts those objects into conceptually absolute *sacra*, which are thought first to sacralize devotees, Lorenzo's concentrated valuative authority came to seem little different from his sacrality; his magic seemed an object's magic. Lorenzo himself became a sacred ritual object, one charismatic figure visiting another and communing with it.

Nowhere is this penetration of Lorenzo's genius into the marrow of Florentine sacrality clearer than in the city's festivities during the Magnificent's later life. From the early 1470s until 1488 Lorenzo seems to have

168. On the visits, Trexler, "Adolescence," 230f. Giovanni di Lorenzo as well as Giuliano belonged to the boys' club of the Vangelista; F. Cionacci, *Rime Sacre del Magnifico Lorenzo de' Medici* (Bergamo, 1760), xvii.

169. "And barriers are put up on one side of them and the other when they circulate through [the churches]"; Savonarola, *Amos e Zaccaria*, I, 229; Ps.

Burlamacchi, 122 seq.

170. Schnitzer, *Delfin*, 92f, 97.

171. *Ibid.*, 91f.

172. See the analysis on pages 91 seq., this volume.

173. Some general ideas on the relation between fashion, religion, and power are in René König, *A La Mode* (New York, 1973), 122–133, 142.

suppressed important parts of the city's festive life, but in his last years he again lent them his favor. From 1488 till 1492 the streets of Florence were full of festive groups celebrating the Magnificent with Lorenzo's own words and forms. During Carnival, lower-class neighborhood and occupational groups performed skits and songs written by the forty-year-old *capo*.[174] A Company of the Star appeared on the scene to stage these increasingly elaborate productions, and it depended on Lorenzo for its inspiration.[175] Sycophants delighted each other with epistolary accounts of the master's plans for these events, and contemporary woodcuts suggest that Lorenzo actually took part in the festivities. An early printed edition of dancing songs has the name *Ballatette del magnificio Lorenzo de' Medici*, and its title page shows Florentine girls kneeling for alms before the author.[176] An engraving on another contemporary publication shows an unmasked Lorenzo tipping masked revelers; the text identifies those songs written by the Magnificent, but not those authored by others.[177]

How far Lorenzo had come in converting the traditional Florentine ritual world to one reflecting his own genius is, however, most significantly shown in the civic feast of San Giovanni, which underwent decisive changes in these years. At first the Magnificent's revival of this event, whose floats had not been part of the celebration since 1478, seemed to honor tradition; the 1488 *festa* featured the old biblical *edifizi* that told the story of Christ.[178] The celebration of 1491 told another salvational story, that of Lorenzo along with that of Christ. At the center of the former was the Triumph of the Roman consul Aemilius Paulus, an enormous pageant showing this fabled condottiere returning to Rome after conquering the East. It was Lorenzo as conceived by Lorenzo, as bystanders understood:

> Lorenzo de' Medici having conceived the idea, he had the Company of the Star construct fifteen *trionfi* designed by him. [They showed] Aemilius Paulus triumphing in Rome on returning [there] from a city with so much treasure that Rome's populace never paid taxes for forty or fifty years, so much treasure had he conquered. . . . There were fifteen *trionfi* with many, many ornaments. *As Aemilius Paulus had provided such booty at the time of Caesar Augustus, Lorenzo de' Medici provided it [now].* There were five richly caparisoned squadrons of horses in battle dress alongside the said *trionfi*, and [Lorenzo] had them brought from their stables to take part in this tribute [paid Aemilius Paulus]. Forty or fifty pairs of oxen pulled the said *trionfi*. It was considered the worthiest thing that had ever processed on San Giovanni.[179]

174. Lorenzo's *canti carnascialeschi* can be read in Lorenzo, *Opere*, II, 235–257, 313–324. See also Singleton, "Literature," who shows the direct and indirect fashions in which the songs often honored the Medici. On the refurbishing of festivities around 1488, see Fabroni, *Laurentii*, II, 386ff. The earliest datable Carnival song in the Florentine tradition is of 1488/1489, a song in a codex dated that year: A. Brandi (ed.), *Canzone del Carro delle Ninfe coi Poeti, Cantata in Firenze nel Carnevale del MCDLXXXVIII* (Arezzo, 1880); see Singleton, *Nuovi Canti*, 158.

175. Martelli, *Studi Laurenziani*, 39.

176. Reproduced in P. Toschi, *Le Origini del Teatro Italiano* (Turin, 1955), fig. 11. The sycophants may be read in Martelli, *Studi*, 38f.

177. Ferrari, "Canzone"; Singleton, "Literature," 58 seq.

178. Six *edifizi* were used; Fabroni, *Laurentii*, II, 388.

179. My italics; Rossi, 270ff.

Lorenzo's feast of the patron in 1491 was a stunning ritual departure on several fronts, not the least of which was its timing. Triumphs of Roman generals may have been staged during Florentine Carnivals before this date, but this spectacle may have been the first non-Christian show performed on the feast of San Giovanni.[180] The reader will understand that the narrow religious and iconographic implications of this shift from a "pagan" to a Christian theme are of secondary importance if understood in festive context; this Roman *trionfo* was but one further expression of a festive language that served the fundamental purpose of legitimating the city. The entrance of this Roman general was akin to the visits of the Magi and to those of real foreign dignitaries, and comparable as well to the ritual triumphs that Florentines offered their real victorious condottieres.[181] What should be stressed is that at a time when the visits of great foreign princes had abated, and in the same year Lorenzo's *sacra rappresentazione* of SS. *Giovanni e Paolo* implicitly compared the Magnificent to the emperor Constantine, the master's Triumph of Aemilius Paulus equated Florence's public identity with Lorenzo's authority. By comparing Lorenzo's actions with those of eternal Rome, it emphasized the international quality of his and Florence's identity, and trumped the Baptist's historic grace with the redemptive brilliance of Lorenzo's living star.[182]

The *trionfo* also proffered a moral that the simple diarist could understand. The city owed its wealth to Lorenzo, for it was his influence abroad that enriched the city. Florence had its own real Magus, at once an Augustus welcoming and a king bringing the wealth of nations.[183] Arranged about this ritual object, the city of Florence seemed about to inherit earth and history.

The Holy Spirit

> At this time the French called Piero de' Medici the Great Money-Changer, because he did not have any legitimate title of lord in Florence.

> Therefore lay aside all sorrow, and instead be happy and jubilant. . . . For in you will the promise be fulfilled.[184]

180. In previous San Giovannis, motifs like Augustus' Altar of Peace appeared, but within the biblical story and understood as part of prophetic history like the sibyls; see Palmieri's account of 1454 in Guasti, *Feste*, 21f. In a letter of 1467, Pulci tells Lorenzo that when he returns to Florence he wants "l'ombrello o il triumpho d'Emilio et di Cammillo"; *Lettere*, 64. But there is no evidence that such classicizing *trionfi* had actually been performed until that of Lorenzo in 1491.

181. See further Trexler and Lewis, "Two Captains."

182. The decline of visitors is clear in Trexler, *Libro*, 67f; on Constantine and Lorenzo, see W. Welliver, *L'Impero Fiorentino* (Florence, 1957), 220–225. Although Welliver noted the close correspondence of date with a threatening sermon of Savonarola's, he missed two other events contemporary to the Triumph that might well be part of its aetiology: just

one month before San Giovanni, a new coin had been minted that for a short time was thought would work miracles with the economy; Cambi, XXI, 60f. And only three days before the *festa*, the commune passed a law permitting citizens to pay off their debts to the commune at a fraction; Rossi, 272. As Rossi places this information immediately after his account of the festival, there is little doubt about the connection: Lorenzo was reducing poverty and helping his fellows.

183. Our one source for this description does not mention Lorenzo receiving the *triumphator*, but the ambivalent link between family and Triumph is unmistakable. On how both *triumphator* and receptor reflect the one glory of city government in ancient Rome, see Trexler and Lewis, "Two Captains."

184. "Il Gran Lombardo": Nardi, I, 12 (1494).

Urbs florentina was no longer the same. The great temple of San Giovanni had been "cleansed" of the republican paraphernalia of earlier ages, and the time of the Baptist was the imagination of one man's living genius.[185] In the Medici palace men's behavior now assumed the formal rigidity previously reserved for civic and ecclesiastical edifices; in the streets, the person of the Magnificent was a new object around which men arranged their formal presentations. The city was no longer ritually unified in the old fashion, but had become a plurality of neighborhoods, occupations, and social groups to whose hallowed grounds the master gave and took life by his visits or their absence. More than a republic united in its fear of personal charisma, Florence in 1490 seemed a kingdom whose several parts could develop idiosyncratic personalities because Lorenzo's itinerant charisma could now tolerate diversity. No longer a city defined only by its adult political males, Florence admitted the genius of its children, its workers, even at times its ladies, without deserting the claims of the ancient lineages to special place. The ritual configuration that linked Lorenzo with the margins of society is the most interesting phenomenon of the formal life of the later fifteenth century. Lorenzo stood at the center surrounded by the flattery of Europe, like a true prince androgynously embodying both growth and structure, passion and judgment, his standing among his fellow Florentines equivalent to his distance from them.[186] The Magnificent had become a personality of almost religious dimensions.

Florence had made him so. Its continuing need for trust, honor, and credit combined with the statist forces at work in fifteenth-century Italy to produce the charismatic republican citizen. Lorenzo's own life prepared him to assume this spiritual mantle. Sponsored by the city at baptism, his innocence an element of ceremonial politics from childhood, the *giovane* Lorenzo became a quasi-martyr after the Pazzi conspiracy, the *salus publicus*. Yet the truly decisive moment in the development of Lorenzo's sacred character remains to be examined: the elevation of his son Giovanni to the cardinalate.

"In your person we see the greatest dignity our house has ever had," Lorenzo humbly wrote his adolescent son after his consecration in 1492.[187] Florentines at the Magnificent's funeral recalled this honor more than any other: "He achieved what no citizen had been capable of doing for a long time, making his son a cardinal, ennobling not so much his family as the whole city." And once Giovanni attained the papacy in 1513, Lorenzo was

---

Another reason, Nardi added, was that the French tended to call all Italians Lombards. For the condolences to Cardinal Giovanni de' Medici on the death of his father Lorenzo, see Schnitzer, *Delfin*, 100.

185. The day after San Giovanni, 1484, a law ordered the removal of all *tavole*, paintings, and images, and all *ceri* and *palii* belonging to subjects, with the stated purpose of beautifying the church. Yet these symbols of history and civic dependencies were *cose pubbliche*, and many people were dissatisfied with the change, which may be viewed as the first step in the Medicean destruction of civic symbols; Rinuccini, cxxxviii,* and Landucci, 49.

186. Lorenzo's own personal predilection for rustic themes and feminine qualities is well known.

187. Roscoe, *Life of Lorenzo*, 467.

identified through his son: "Lorenzo de' Medici," people named him, "father of a pope."[188] Doubtless Lorenzo had attached great importance to preparing his oldest son Piero for succession to the family's secular leadership in Florence, but Giovanni's church dignity mattered still more to Lorenzo and the city. It institutionalized the family's foreign authority. Calling the child cardinal "servant and pillar of the republic" from the moment he received the purple, citizens knew that they had found that spiritual authority that was the heart of credit and trust.[189] The Triumph of Aemilius Paulus was possible in 1491 because Lorenzo had sired a spiritual prince in 1489.

Though at first glance Piero's domestication among the princes of Europe had the apparently independent goal of introducing the future ruler of Florence to the Italian courts, it also prepared the way for the accession of his younger brother Giovanni to the cardinalate. Lorenzo's instructions to his thirteen-year-old son for Piero's first official trip abroad, as an ambassador to Rome in 1484 to congratulate the new pope Innocent VIII, seem to have such an introduction in mind.[190] Guided at every step by the resident ambassador and by the cardinal Orsini, Piero was told by his father to be "well informed about all the ceremonies which are used" in Rome. He was to kiss letters patent before presenting them, and always to be careful not to take precedence over his seniors, for he was a Florentine citizen as were the other ambassadors. He had to respect age: "Deport yourself modestly . . . and humanely, and especially with gravity, with everyone. You ought the more exert yourself in these matters the less they are expected of someone your age." Assuming the classical role of Medicean innocent, Piero was to use "fitting, natural, unforced" words with everyone, and not wish to appear learned but rather "humane, sweet, and grave" in his language. The boy was to remind each cardinal of the particular obligation the Medici owed his house. To the Sforza cardinal, he spoke of "the ancient and natural obligations" he as a "natural Sforzescan and true servant" owed on behalf of *la cosa nostra*. With the son of the Neapolitan king, the subject was the great favors his father had done Lorenzo during the Pazzi wars, and Piero was told to say "that you have thought very seriously what would have been the condition of all my children if it had been otherwise . . . , and therefore . . . His Royal Majesty can sell you and loan you, and in effect treat you as their thing." To the Orsini cardinal, the fact that his family had "deigned to have us as their relatives" was conveyed; to cardinals related to the Orsini, the honor and "grace to be related to their most excellent houses, which we repute among the greatest ornaments of our house," were noted.

There is therefore no doubt that Lorenzo sent Piero to Rome as the heir to

188. Landucci, 65. Lorenzo was identified as such in editions of his own literary works: *Poesie Volgari Nuovamente Stampate, di Lorenzo de' Medici, che fu Padre di Papa Leone . . .* (Venice, 1554). He was identified in this fashion by Vasari (1550); Trexler and Lewis, "Two Captains."

189. The term is in Matteo Bosso, *Recuperationes Faesulanae* (Bologna, 1493), *epistola* CX.

190. In what follows I use the text in Roscoe, *Life of Lorenzo*, 464–467. Piero's visit to Milan in 1489 was also full of ritual detail; Reumont, *Lorenzo*, II, 292f; Fabroni, *Laurentii*, II, 295–298; Cambi, XXI, 39.

Medici family authority, great at home but less abroad. The son of an Orsini mother, Piero was more worthily born than his father—that much Lorenzo was willing to concede his son. But he was still a Florentine, and the Magnificent warned the boy to remind himself often of "who you are."[191] Also, "Their Most Reverend Lordships should get to know [the person] in whom the servitude of our house will continue." These were Lorenzo's own sentiments, and he assured his son that they were not said *per cerimonie*. His stated reason for having Piero meet the pope reflected Lorenzo's fundamental reverence for all the prelates and the powers they represented:

> I've sent you so that you begin at an early age to know His Beatitude as father and lord, and [so that] you have reason to continue in this devotion [to him] for a long time. [In such devotion] I nourish my other children as well, [and] I would not want them if they did not have this attitude.

Lorenzo's deep-seated conviction of his family's social inferiority, and his desire to help Piero overcome these disabilities so that he would be able to rule Florence, echo the sentiments that the Magnificent's own father had once directed to him.[192] Now, however, the stakes were higher, for Lorenzo wanted to make his second son a cardinal. The instructions now come to the point. Piero was instructed to draw the pontiff's attention to young Giovanni.

"Tell him I have made [Giovanni] a priest," Lorenzo wrote. The pope understood Lorenzo's verbal shorthand; the eight-year-old had taken the first steps toward a clerical career with the expectation he would one day gain the purple. Heir not to the material fortune of his father as much as to his star and spirit, the boy had received the four minor clerical orders in 1483 in the chapel of the family palace, and within a week his first ecclesiastical dignity, that of an apostolic notary.[193] Now addressed as messer Giovanni, the boy heard himself called a "noble and circumspect . . . boy," and was told that he descended "from a noble family"; the noble status the Medici would not allow their *capi* they permitted the second son.[194] In 1489 the long-awaited

191. "E ricordati spesso chi tu sei"; Roscoe, *Life of Lorenzo*, 467.

192. Lorenzo's expressions of social inferiority are legion. See, for example, Buser, *Lorenzo*, 76, 141, where Lorenzo in 1479 ruled out a marriage of his daughter to a Riario *gran maestro* because of his social condition; Cappelli, "Lettere," 293, where in 1487 Lorenzo was said to have promised not to marry any further daughters to foreign potentates "because of local unease"; Buser, *Lorenzo*, 165, where in 1485 an ambassador instructed Lorenzo on how to be patron of Lodovico il Moro by using submissive terms; Picotti, *Giovinezza*, 672, a capital instance of sensed inferiority, where Lorenzo writes the ambassador in Rome after the news of Giovanni's elevation: "It is something much above my merits"; Cappelli, "Lettere," 292, where Lorenzo tells the Ferrarese ambas-

sador in 1487 that he would not send mounted troops to the powers to announce his son's impending marriage to an Orsini, and would "leave such a ceremony to the *gran signori* and to *maggiori uomini* than he."

193. Picotti, *Giovinezza*, 652f. He took the first two major orders on Feb. 24, 1489; *ibid.*, 285, n. 65, but did not take priestly orders until he was elected pope; *ibid.*, 290, n. 103.

194. *Ibid.*, 651ff. Lorenzo himself recorded that after these ceremonies, "fu chiamato messer Giovanni"; Roscoe, *Life of Lorenzo*, 461. Accompanying this was Lorenzo's change in personal pronoun: he now addressed Giovanni as *messere*, and as *voi*; Picotti, *Giovinezza*, 89, 91. A cursory search suggests that Lorenzo was rarely addressed as noble. I find one case, a 1490 letter of the pope to Lorenzo; Fabroni, *Laurentii*, II, 79.

news reached Florence that Giovanni had been made a cardinal, though he would be consecrated in that dignity only when he was three years older.[195] The joy of the family and the city knew no bounds, for Lorenzo had effectively spiritualized his secular authority and thus the city's identity. The behavior of the Florentines at this time and again on March 10, 1492, when Giovanni entered Florence triumphantly after receiving the red cap at Fiesole, offers us further insight into the progressive transformation of the formal life of Florence.

Never had the city of Florence witnessed "a truer and more general happiness" than was expressed in the tumultuous celebration of 1489, or a more singular departure from tradition.[196] For along with the customary if outsized bonfires, *trionfi*, and processions that greeted the news, the Florentines "spontaneously" hung the Medici coat of arms from their homes and from the hostels of the city, converting the spaces of Florence into multiple altars of Medici sacrality.[197] This phenomenal festive departure, unwitnessed since the days of Walter of Brienne, was accompanied by a reorientation of patronal liens. The cathedral chapter, pride of the city's ecclesiastical establishment, chose the boy cardinal as its protector in Rome.[198] Other citizens shifted their sycophantic language from the father to the son. If Piero on mission for his father had been Christ sent to earth by God the Father, Giovanni became, in one prelate's words, "like Aaron called by the Lord. So will you in the future be a glowing light in the holy church. . . . [For] in you a child is given to us."[199]

Giovanni di Lorenzo had in truth become a "holy adolescent" (*sacer adolescens*) and this name, given him by a witness describing the boy-cardinal's triumphal entrance into Florence on March 10, 1492, may stand for all this boy meant to the city.[200] More was involved than imagining that Giovanni was the singular product of all the contemporary genius of Florence, as contemporary memorialists did.[201] As we watch him through the view of this eye witness, approaching the city on a donkey "in humble and simple cult . . . , a Joseph in continence, a Samson of strength, in holiness a Samuel, the very John of justice and religion," we can see that Giovanni de'

195. Lorenzo immediately ordered his Roman ambassador to prepare behaviorally for the interim: "This I would like to know. How we should govern ourselves in the future, and what [type of] life and style *messer* Giovanni should follow, both in dress and with his servants. . . . So advise me what we should do with him. For example, what signature or seal he should use if it should happen he would have to correspond. I send you his measurements in this [letter], but from yesterday morning on, he seems to be grown and changed"; Picotti, *Giovinezza*, 672.

196. The assessment is Lorenzo's, to the ambassador Lanfredini in Rome; Fabroni, *Laurentii*, II, 300. Further descriptions of the event in Picotti, *Giovinezza*, 198, and accompanying notes.

197. *Ibid.* On this phenomenon in 1513, see page 496, this volume, where Cambi adds that these Medici arms covered city arms. A similar phenomenon in the sphere of ritual sounds was noted by Rinuccini in 1478, when Florentines defending the Medici cried "'Palle, Palle!' nè mai fu chi dicesse loro che gridassin 'Marzocco!' o altro"; cxxviii. Note also that in 1488 when Franceschetto Cibo, son of the pope, came to Florence, the crowds cried "Cibo e Palle!"; Fabroni, *Laurentii*, II, 387. In 1520 the Medici coats of arms were mass produced by the Parte Guelfa for distribution on such occasions; *ASF, Parte Guelfa, numeri rossi*, 13, f. 24v (May 30).

198. Picotti, *Giovinezza*, 198.

199. Schnitzer, *Delfin*, 92f.

200. Bosso, *Recuperationes, loc. cit.*

201. Picotti, *Giovinezza*, 17.

Medici was like a processing icon of Florentine history, the embodiment and culmination of the Florentine journey toward foreign respect and domestic self-esteem. The material and spiritual genius of the city now combined in father and son. Hereafter, Florence had nothing to be ashamed of and could announce itself to the nations. Benedetto Dei, that uncrowned prince of patriotic arrivistes, prepared a special report on the entry of the new cardinal and sent it off in defiant pride "To the Venetians, to the Milanese . . . , and to everyone."[202]

We are told that Florentine citizens many years his senior fought to be part of the party of three hundred that went out to welcome the cardinal. This was a far cry, said Giovanni Cambi, from the normal foreigner's visit, when citizens had to be forced to do their duty.[203] Cambi's offhand observation betrays both the significance and the Florentine perception of this event: Giovanni de' Medici's welcome was the first reception ever accorded a Florentine as if he were a noble foreigner.[204] Citizens, the ambassadorial corps, and prelates went out to meet him, as they did foreigners. Past the *ambitiosissima pompa* at the city gate, Giovanni moved as had other cardinals before him to the Piazza della Signoria, where the Signoria greeted him, as one witness carefully noted, at the head of the Palace stairs.[205] On the following day the government sent gifts to the visitor at his residence, in the Medici palace.[206]

How unreal it must have seemed to anti-Mediceans to pay such obeisance to a Florentine boy, and yet how substantial was one witness's insight, that the gifts that the government bestowed on Giovanni completed a historical process of the deepest antiquity. The Medici supporter Benedetto Dei told the world that the medals the city now gifted its child were those the Signoria had accumulated over the years from emperors, kings, popes, infidels, and Christians.[207] Here was the wealth of nations that Florentine history had consumed into itself, but could not purify until it passed into the spirit. The Signoria's magnanimous gift to Cardinal Giovanni culminated all of history, the fancy of Dei intimated, for the medals had been coined, he said, "since the beginning of time on."[208] We earlier heard a Sforza prince remark that Lorenzo collected the precious things of all the peoples of the world in his home. Now in this grand gesture of the Florentine government, Florence itself seemed to complete the process of Osirian reconstruction in the person of the gilded cardinal Giovanni.[209]

202. *Ibid.*, 229, n. 143; 348, n. 59.

203. Cambi, XXI, 63.

204. The only comparable ritual might be that in which Florentine bishops of Florentine birth were first welcomed into the city to assume their duties. On the implications of Giovanni's reception, see my *Libro*, 67.

205. Rinuccini, cxlv; Ross, *Lives*, 331. Only Rossi mentioned that it rained; 277f. On the pomp, Bosso, *Recuperationes, loc cit.*

206. The boy used the gift reception for instructional purposes, refusing with good grace to accept gifts offered by the communes of the dominion, the Jews, or the citizens, and taking only those given by relatives; Ross, *Lives*, 331f; Cappelli, "Lettere," 311. On the Signoria's gifts, see Landucci, 63; Rinuccini, cxlv.

207. Cited in Picotti, *Giovinezza*, 318.

208. "Dal prencipio del mondo in qua"; *ibid.*

209. See page 446, this volume. In a practical vein, Piero Parenti also took account of what was happen-

Thus like a prince, Giovanni brought noble legitimation; as a prelate, he gave spiritual credit, and Florentine songsters at the event predicted he would one day be pope, the most credible of all human beings; and as an adolescent and one-time member of a boys' confraternity, he brought to the city the promise of youth's genius.[210] All this while guaranteeing benefices for Florentine merchants' sons, investments without risk, profits without end! Lorenzo de' Medici had brought the world to Florence, but his son had brought Florence to Florence.

Armed with a long didactic letter from his father on how to behave in Rome, the seventeen-year-old cardinal Giovanni left to assume his duties in Rome on March 12, 1492. The letter is well known, and continues the old traditions.[211] More than anything else, the boy was to act his age no matter how courtiers flattered him. Lorenzo advised Giovanni on the choice of a retinue or "stable," and urged him to prefer "some gentility of antique things and lovely books" to the jewels and silk that were inappropriate to the boy's age and social condition. Encased in this environment, the boy was to flee hypocrisy like infamy by projecting a moderate rather than an austere image in his "pomps." His ill and wasted father protested that he had given his son completely to the church and God, so that Giovanni was no longer fully a Florentine or a Medici: "[Yet] opportunity will not be wanting . . . to help the city and the house, because the city is tied to the church through [your office], and you ought to be the good chain in this. And our house's [fate] is the city's."[212]

On April 5, 1492, the sky darkened over Florence, and cracks of lightning struck the cathedral with destructive results. Three days later Lorenzo the Magnificent was dead, and there seemed no doubt that the harm visited on the city by the heavens was related to the demise of its first citizen.[213] One chronicler explained that Lorenzo, in extremis, had released the genie imprisoned in his ring, apparently thinking that the spirit that had aided him in the past had now turned against him. That release had caused the light of Florence to fade and the lantern of the cathedral to buckle.[214] An almost mystic spirit had passed. Borne into the city by his Company of the Magi, the

ing: "Il cardinale de' Medici, quali benefici vacavano, occupava; così tal cosa, usurpato havendosi lo ecclesiastico et il civile, oramai più sopportare non si poteano"; Schnitzer, *Quellen*, IV, 7. On Osiris, see page 60, this volume.

210. See page 450, this volume. The song, "Trionfo della Dea Minerva," ("ch'arai le tre corone e le duo chiave") was assigned this date by Singleton, "Literature," 55.

211. Text in Roscoe, *Life of Lorenzo*, 467–470.

212. "Nè vi mancherà modo con questo riservo d'aiutare la città et la casa; perchè per questa città fa l'unione della Chiesa, et voi dovete in ciò essere buona catena, et la casa ne va colla città. . . . Et più presto vorrei bella stalla, et famiglia ordinata et polita,

che ricca et pomposa . . ."; *ibid.*, 468f.

213. "The great importance was indicated by many signs"; Guicciardini, *History of Florence*, 70, and in the same vein Machiavelli, *History*, 407, and all other contemporaries.

214. "Dissesi, quando venne questa scurità del tempo, che fu che Lorenzo di Piero di Cosimo de' Medici lasciò andare uno spirito si diceva aveva tenuto legato in uno anello; el quale, si disse, lo liberò e lasciollo andare, in su quel punto che venne questa fortuna [delle saette]. El quale spirito, si diceva, aveva tenuto parecchi anni in detto anello; e perchè era malato grave in detto tempo, si dicie lo liberò"; Masi, 17. The report shows Masi's own uncertainty about the truth of the tale, but the importance he thought it deserved.

body of the Magnificent, after being viewed by all in the church of San Marco, was sealed away in the chapel in San Lorenzo that Cosimo had built.[215] When his remains were moved into Michelangelo's New Sacristy some sixty years later, Florentines had one further chance to gaze on Lorenzo. He was immaculate, Giorgio Vasari insisted at the time, his body like that of any saint untouched by the corruption of death.[216]

At death Lorenzo acted out the last exemplary ritual for his fellow Florentines. When the priest came into the bedroom with the viaticum, Lorenzo said a long prayer of greeting, which Poliziano copied down word for word when he recognized it had worked for the master. For now Lorenzo rose from his bed despite his pain, then fell to his knees to confess.[217] Passing through the valley of despair, he came to realize that God could indeed forgive any sin, and having attained this serenity, Lorenzo could then take communion; Poliziano noted that Lorenzo repeated "almost the same prayer" as before.[218] An ambassador witnessing the event wrote his principal with details of the instant of death, when Lorenzo seized "a certain image of Our Lady, which he kissed with his eyes full of tears. Then his head dropped and he passed away."[219] Lorenzo's death was a model for all Christians to imitate, religious specialists declared. The Magnificent was a St. Jerome, Benedetto Dei wrote, who "died with as much nobility, patience, understanding, and reverence to God, as the most religious man and divine soul could have shown."[220]

Prodigy, magician, idol, shepherd, martyr, savior, and finally exemplar of the good death, Lorenzo had doubtlessly combined in his person some of the religious qualities of the early modern monarch. He was still far from the finished product, however. First, as far as I can determine, citizens did not think that the fate of Florence depended on the intimate relations between God and the Magnificent, and no one is said to have asked him to intercede with the Almighty. Second, Lorenzo was not said to have had the thaumaturgic powers that were attributed to the later absolute kings of Europe, even if his genie was a source of occult power and affected others. Third, the Magnificent's fate after death was uncertain, and the theme of Lorenzo's apotheosis had to await a later age.[221] To be sure, one eulogist in Naples asserted that Lorenzo was in heaven protecting family and city, but the Florentine sources make no such claim.[222] In truth, it was only the elevation

215. For more details on the funeral, see Trexler and Lewis, "Two Captains."

216. *Ibid.*

217. The text in Roscoe, *Life of Lorenzo*, 471 seq. See also J. Schnitzer, "Mailändische Gesandtschaftsberichte über die letzte Krankheit Lorenzo de' Medici's," *Römische Quartalschrift für Christliche Altertumskunde und für Kirchengeschichte* XVI (1902), 152–169.

218. Ross, *Lives*, 337.

219. Schnitzer, "Mailändische," 169. Witnesses also were sure to record all the details of the crucifix Lorenzo had held during his ordeal; Roscoe, *Life of*

Lorenzo, 474; Ross, *Lives*, 343. Text criticism on which objects were used in Schnitzer, "Mailändische," 159.

220. Cited in Ross, *Lives*, 343; further sentiments of this type in Schnitzer, *Delfin*, 97.

221. The sculptural apotheosis, Lewis and I have argued, is in Michelangelo's Medici Chapel (1520–1534); "Two Captains." The closest contemporary association of Lorenzo to God came from his chaplain Guido's statement: "We owe everything to God, through Lorenzo his instrument"; Reumont, *Lorenzo*, II, 426.

222. Cited in Trexler and Lewis, "Two Captains."

of Lorenzo's son to the papacy in 1513 that would seal Lorenzo's spiritual identity, his place in heaven, and Florence's eternal blessedness. When Pope Leo X entered Florence in triumph in 1515, he would see a painting of his father looking down on him from an archway. The inscription on this portrait left no doubt about Lorenzo's spiritual legacy: "This is my beloved son."[223]

In the immediate wake of Lorenzo's death, opinions about him were more terrestrial; obituaries reviewed his earthly accomplishments rather than apotheosizing him. This practical assessment of the man, however, did not prevent writers from viewing his greatest success as an immaterial one. Lorenzo had gained respect and authority abroad. This was his crowning glory. Landucci and Masi, who thought Lorenzo "governed" Florence *and* Italy; Machiavelli and the Camaldolan Delfin, who said the Magnificent was honored "not only" by Florentines but by all Christian princes and even by barbarians; Guicciardini, who said that this Medici had enjoyed "friendship and credit . . . among many princes both in Italy and beyond"—all these men found Lorenzo's contribution to Florentine honor his most important quality.[224] Contemporaries also agreed on what best demonstrated Lorenzo's foreign credit: his ability to raise Giovanni to the cardinalate, and the fact that distant princes sent personal embassies to him with exotic gifts. It was not only the *popolano* Bartolomeo Masi who spent half his obituary recalling the sultan's gift of a giraffe to Lorenzo in 1487, but the learned patrician Guicciardini who evoked "the Grand Turk and . . . the Sultan, from whom in the last years of his life [Lorenzo] received a giraffe, a lion, and some geldings as gifts."[225]

Lorenzo's second achievement was that he had become, in Guicciardini's words, the arbiter of Florence.[226] He was that great precedence-setter whom Florence had never before dared to choose from among its own, a living image around whom the parts of the city could organize themselves in decent processional fraternity. The domestic cost of this development was clear to friend and critic. The citizen class of Florence had lost some of its rights, perhaps above all that pride that in earlier times, it was said, had prevented one father from demeaning himself before another.[227]

Of all the commentators, Rinuccini alone wondered if the domestic corruption that attended Lorenzo's magisterial position at home did not have its corollary abroad. In Florence, citizens knelt before Lorenzo to win honor, but abroad, Lorenzo stooped to conquer. Had Florence gained or lost by the leader's genuflections?[228] In the 1450s Luca Pitti had warned that the Medici's

Delfin's consolation letter to Cardinal Giovanni is about as close as any contemporary came; Schnitzer, *Delfin*, 100.

223. "Hic est filius meus dilectus"; Moreni, *De Ingressu*, 9ff.

224. Landucci, 65; Masi, 17; Machiavelli, *History*, 406; Schnitzer, *Delfin*, 97f; Guicciardini, *History of Florence*, 71ff, who repeats his assertion twice.

225. *Ibid.*, 71; Masi, 18. The enormous impact this visit had made is also recorded in Rinuccini, cxliii;

Landucci, 52f; L. Morelli, 197; Rossi, 246ff. On Anne of Brittany's request that Lorenzo give it to her as a gift, see Buser, *Beziehungen*, 272f, 521. Vasari painted the giraffe in the Sala di Lorenzo; Vasari–Milanesi, VIII, 114.

226. Guicciardini is cited by Rochon, *Jeunesse*, 195.

227. See Rinuccini, page 448, and Cambi, page 502, this volume.

228. Lorenzo himself perfectly understood the problem: "The more esteem one shows for others the less

willingness to do anything for Milan weakened the commune's sovereignty; now Rinuccini sensed that in the new ritual space created by the suppliant Lorenzo, not only the commune and its citizens but Lorenzo himself was at the mercy of that princely world that did not kneel. In his review of Lorenzo he bemoaned the government's declining authority over the provincial nobility that traditionally fought for the city: The commune continued to pay for the services of "every little tyrant and *signorotto*," but these petty lords now felt an obligation only to Lorenzo. Yet just how much stronger was Lorenzo? To obtain these obligations from foreigners, he had also paid a price, one which, as we have seen, Rinuccini thought was too high: "His ambition . . . induced him to never refuse anything to any foreigner, of even the lowest sort, as long as he believed [that foreigner] would speak well of him."[229]

Rinuccini was among those who believed that the Magi of this world came to Florence with empty coffers, and left with their trunks full of the city's wealth. Florence might be the "theater of the world," as some called it, but those who noticed that there seemed more foreigners at Florentine festivals than Florentines might well wonder if this High Renaissance city supplied more than the props and stage. Did Florentines still define the Florentine procession? Had Florence lost some of its sovereignty?[230]

For the moment, the answer was uncertain. The *sacer adolescens* who would one day guide that procession from afar was a boy in Rome who had taken the treasures of Florentine history with him. At home, the legacy of Lorenzo seemed equally in doubt. Piero di Lorenzo quickly bungled his communications with the Florentines in the ceremonial sphere. He paraded in the streets surrounded by the same bodyguard of foreign soldiers his father had used, as if to suggest that Florentines might kill this mere boy. Obviously, Piero had forgotten Lorenzo's admonition to remember who he was and where he was; his behavior "made the whole city want to throw up."[231] There was an explanation for Piero's gauche behavior, Piero Soderini would be made to say, one that questioned anew the price for the honor that fifteenth-century Florentines had so single-mindedly pursued, and pointed toward the reaction against Lorenzo's ritual universe that the Savonarolan period would bring:

> What could one hope for from Piero? Not only did he not have the greatest prudence, as you know; he was also not of that good nature and sweetness [common to] his father and grandfather, and ordinary in our nation. Nor is this any wonder, for being

is shown to one's self, and . . . one example entails others"; Ross, *Lives*, 278.

229. "Oltre a una immensa ambizione e vanagloria, la quale lo induceva che a nessuno estraneo di qualunche etiam estrema sorte negava alcuna domanda, purchè credesse che dicesse bene di lui"; Rinuccini, cxlix. The author's summary view: "E in somma si può conchiudere lui esser suto molti anni perniziosissimo e crudelissimo tiranno alla città nostra, e a quella aver fatto danno e diminuzione di reputazione quanto

facesse, già è grande tempo, alcuno cittadino"; *ibid.*

230. The contemporary view of Florence as theater is cited by Roscoe, *Life of Lorenzo*, 527; Rossi, 271 (1491), noted as had many previous chroniclers the large number of foreigners present in Florence for festivals; Masi, 144 compared them to the locals who were present in 1514 for San Giovanni.

231. "Stomachò a tutta la città"; Parenti, cited in Picotti, *Giovinezza*, 361.

born of a foreign mother, the Florentine blood in him was bastardized. His external comportment was degenerate, and [he was] too insolent and haughty for our way of life.[232]

The Prophetic Spirit

Florence is generated anew, not created. For the material is the same, though the form has changed. . . . Like a child he still has soft arms, and they have to be swaddled so as to anchor the members. Later we will clothe him in brocade and everything else.[233]

The fiery words of the Ferrarese prophet Savonarola and the French invasions of late 1494 were the immediate causes of the governmental coup of November 9, 1494, which ended in the exile of the Medici from Florence. The climax was ceremonial. Returning from an embassy to the advancing Charles VIII of France, Piero di Lorenzo proceeded to the Palazzo della Signoria to receive the customary thanks of the commune for a diplomatic task well done. On the steps of the Palace the Signoria required him, and Piero refused, to divest himself of his retinue before entering the Palace.[234] Humiliated before a large crowd of witnesses, Piero and his party left the city for exile. The very publicity and ceremoniousness of the ritual test demonstrated how significant was this break between the Medicean and Savonarolan periods of Florentine history. In search of a common prize, two contending parties now entered a long competition for spiritual authority. Championing the Medici party was the *sacer adolescens* in Rome; the prophetic spirit of Savonarola fed the hope of Medici opponents. Giovanni de' Medici offered the Florentines all the legitimation of the institutional church, whereas Savonarola promised a still more forceful external legitimation, his own unmediated contact with God. Both of these spirits struggled for the legacy of Lorenzo the Magnificent.

The competition between official and prophetic spirits had been long under way when Giovanni de' Medici entered Florence on a donkey in 1492. As early as 1472 a hermit had come to Florence to denounce the opulence of the city and the church. Dressed in tattered rags, dragging a life-size cross, and leading his donkey, he preached remorse and contrition to an enormous audience.[235] By the time Savonarola first preached in Florence in 1482, the lines of battle were forming between those who trusted in the official redemption offered by the rich curia and those who opened their ears to the dire predictions of itinerant prophets. When the Dominican returned to Florence in 1490, announcements of impending doom resounded throughout Italy, in

232. Guicciardini's *Del Reggimento di Firenze* (1521), cited by Rochon, *Jeunesse*, 270, n. 29.

233. Savonarola, *Salmi*, II, 106f.

234. Masi, 21ff; Rinuccini, clii; Nardi, I, 16, with references to other accounts, some of which suggest that Piero would have been murdered if he had entered the Palace. Cambi remembered that on entering the city for this dramatic confrontation, Piero and his party had incited the plebs and children in the Borgo San Frediano to cry *Palle, Palle!*; XXIII, 6. See further the Capponi and Gaddi documents in *ASI*, IV, pt. 2 (1853), 29f, 44ff.

235. Ser Giusto, f. 103v (Dec. 13).

PLATE 18. Lorenzo de' Medici et al.
Canzone per Andare in Maschera.
(Florence, sixteenth century.) Woodcut.

PLATE 19.   *Ballatete del Magnifico Lorenzo de' Medici e Messer Angelo Poliziano.*
(Florence, fifteenth century.) Woodcut.

PLATE 20. **Fra Roberto Caracciolo.** *Prediche Vulghare.*
(Florence, 1491.) Woodcut.

PLATE 21. **Francesco Granacci.** *The Entrance of Charles VIII into Florence.* **c. 1518.**
Florence, Palazzo Medici–Riccardi.

PLATE 22. Fra Girolamo Savonarola. *Compendio di Revelazione dello Inutile Servo di Jesu Christo.*
(Florence, 1496.) Woodcut.

PLATE 23. *The Execution of Fra Girolamo Savonarola.* Anonymous. c. 1498.
Text: "The aforesaid father died the twenty-third day of May."
Florence, Museo San Marco.

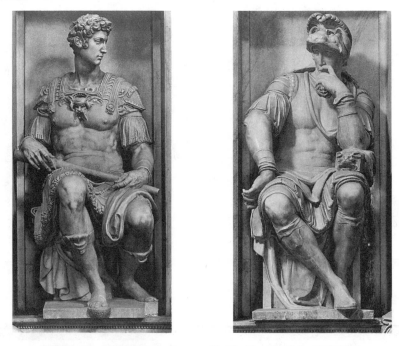

PLATE 24. Michelangelo Buonarotti. *The New Sacristy.* 1521–1534.
Florence, S. Lorenzo.

466

PLATE 25. *Coin of Pope Leo X.* 1514. Portrait text: "Leo X, Pontifex Maximus";
Magi text: "The True Light Shines in the Darkness."
New York, American Numismatic Association.

each city taking on a fitting individuality.[236] Florence was not immune, and in the midst of frightening omens associated with their city's significant places and times, citizens were prepared to believe the dire apocalypse Savonarola promised. During the St. John's celebration of 1488 the tarps over Piazza San Giovanni had been destroyed by the wind because, it was said, the government had shed blood on a feast, though the criminal's execution could have waited.[237] On the feast of Mary's Nativity in 1490 two boulders fell from the cathedral cupola at the place "where St. Thomas is," as one witness specified; Thomas was a Medicean saint.[238]

Unable to restrain the swell of prophecy, the Medici countered with promises of their own and, between Lent of 1491 and 1492, Florentines could choose their futures. While Giovanni de' Medici prepared to don the purple, his father's *sacra rappresentazione* of SS. *Giovanni e Paolo* suggested that the Magnificent was like Constantine and thus Florence was the heir to imperial riches. Enter the Triumph of Death. Scarcely nine days passed before Savonarola delivered his "terrifying sermon," which promised Florentines God's peculiar vengeance upon the city: It would no longer be called Florence but "turpitude and blood and a den of robbers."[239] Four months later Lorenzo staged his Triumph of Aemilius Paulus as if to reassure Florentines that the wealth of nations would ensure citizens a future without taxes. Events in April of the following year belied the Medici promise. An ancient Cassandra pierced the sacred space of Santa Maria Novella with fearsome prophecies of doom; this was the meaning of the new crash of cathedral boulders in the direction of the Medici palace.[240]

Before Lent of 1492 was over, Lorenzo was dead. Piero was soon expelled; the cardinal was in Rome. Savonarola seized the Lorenzan heritage by making a decisive change in his prophecy. There will be gloom and torment, to be sure, but then glory. Florence is elect, the prophet trumpeted, its future greater than the Magnificent's. From this city the Light will radiate abroad, to reform the church and convert the pagans. To its Light, as once pastors, Magi, and kings proved the Christ Child's dominion, will come the nations, and their wealth: *"Mihi alienigenae subditi sunt. 'Alienigenae,'* that is, from afar. That is, the Turks and the Moors will come from afar to this light."[241]

---

236. Weinstein, *Savonarola and Florence*, 84–98; C. Vasoli, "L'Attesa della Nuova Era in Ambienti e Gruppi Fiorentini del Quattrocento," in *L'Attesa dell'Età Nuova nella Spiritualità della Fine del Medioevo* (Todi, 1962), 377 seq.; D. Ruderman, "Giovanni Mercurio da Correggio's Appearance in Italy as seen through the Eyes of an Italian Jew," *Renaissance Quarterly* XXVIII (1975), 311. Weinstein, *loc. cit.*, carefully distinguishes between Savonarola's predictions of catastrophe in these years, and his visions, which date only from late 1494.

237. Rossi, 243f; Landucci, 55.

238. Rossi, 254.

239. The link between the two events is studied by Welliver, *L'Impero*, 220–229.

240. Ridolfi, *Studi Savonaroliani*, 262.

241. Savonarola, *Salmi*, II, 44, 190; note the association to the famous visit of the "Turks" to Lorenzo in 1487 mentioned in n. 225. The preacher, as far as I can determine, never made a direct link between the Magi theme and the riches that God would send to Florence, but the Isaian cast of his promise, with its inevitable Magian overlay, is unquestionable, for which see Trexler and Lewis, "Two Captains." Weinstein's otherwise excellent description of Savonarola's promise fails to appreciate this biblical under-

To soften God's ire and to hasten that millenial day when all Magian pilgrims would find the source of light in Florence, the Florentines must change the form of politics, the behavior of society, and thus the communications between inhabitants and God. To achieve these ends, three spaces in the city had to be purified and refashioned. First, a hall had to be built in the public Palace to house the newly constituted Grand Council. Savonarola shared with others the hope that this council would give the Florentine government a stability it had always lacked, and bestow upon the Palazzo della Signoria greater authority and majesty. Second, the city's churches and especially Savonarola's friary of San Marco had to be recognized as the primary stages of ritual efficacy and exemplary affect; the preacher proposed to end the similar role that the private palace, especially the Medici palace, had assumed, and return it to the houses of the religious specialists. Finally, the streets had to be cleansed and made ready for citizens' processional congregations there; as a republican and a prophet, Savonarola knew the streets expressed and created order and history through the inhabitants' passionate communication with each other, and thus with God. Those streets would witness his most radical inducement of the millenium, the processions of boys, and it was on these thoroughfares that he himself would be led to the pyre in May 1498. The following pages examine these three acts of the prophet's fateful journey.

From May 1495 on, Savonarola urged the building and rapid completion of the new Hall of the Grand Council as a divine imperative; it was God's will that it be built, so that in it men could act as his instruments.[242] Without this building, the friar warned, nothing of consequence could be achieved, and God wanted it done before all else. Though it had been hastily constructed, the preacher later assured those who feared the hall might collapse that the Sala was reliable. God would hold up the walls if they buckled, and the angels who even in the darkest days outnumbered the devils there would protect it as did swaddling the members of a new born child.[243] The form and activity of the government mattered more than building materials, and they were directed by God. If members of the council were unsure how to vote on a particular issue, they could draw straws and God would make the vote right.[244] If they voted wrong, God would change the color of their beans.[245] To those who wondered how there could be both yea and nay votes if men were directed by the Lord, Savonarola replied that this was done to prevent victors from being proud and losers from despairing.[246] Never in the history

pinning; *Savonarola and Florence*, 116, 132, 138–142. Note that Savonarola's promise is a continuation of Lorenzo's.

242. On this first reference, Steinberg, *Fra Girolamo*, 98.

243. *Amos e Zaccaria*, I, 257; *Giobbe*, I, 258; the simile of swaddling the child and building the Sala: *Salmi*, II, 106, 125; also Steinberg, *Fra Girolamo*, 95–98.

244. *Amos e Zaccaria*, I, 256.

245. *Ibid.*, III, 88; Placido Cinozzi, in Villari and Casanova, *Scelta*, 24. The awe at a unanimous vote could be such that people would cry *Santo partito!* In a case of 1527, all business was stopped, and the law was inscribed by a kneeling notary; Varchi, II, 23.

246. *Amos e Zaccaria*, I, 88.

of the republic had Florentines been so sure their government acted with cosmic validity. Magistrates of the city were "officials of God" or archangels served by angelic familiars.[247] Here was the myth of the representational group in a remarkably pure form: The government and the Grand Council were more than a profane assemblage of merchants. Florentine governmental bodies were the chosen instruments of God.[248]

Instruments of God may either enforce his will or model his virtue; the Grand Council of this age would not be moral exemplars. Savonarola did not view the Sala of the council as a school of example or manners; that perfervid attitude toward governmental space would only appear in the Last Republic.[249] No miracles emanated from it. The friar never lectured members on their duty to behave in a model fashion outside the council and, still more indicative of the curious profanity of the building and its counselors, he never ascribed to any member of the government an active ethical or exemplary role within the hall. On the contrary, the seamy behavior of elders in the Grand Council was one reason to keep their sons out, as Savonarola warned in July 1495:

> You want to put your son into the council so that you can procure him an office. . . . This leads him to want to live pompously, and he wants a servant, and someone else wants a servant, and [his wife] wants her domestic, and thus everyone wants his male and female servant.[250]

Florentine elders in the Grand Council would be enforcers, not moral beacons, and what reform was more pressing than to put an end to the pernicious influence that the *giovani* had had upon Medicean Florence? The Savonarolan republic turned its back on brilliance, and returned to gravity. Such elders would also see to it that the women were reformed, and that the children of Florence regained their manners.[251] They would be ruthless enforcers of morality as well as its legislators, and Savonarola urged them to think of themselves as quasi-sacerdotal figures:

> My lords the Eight . . . , I would like to see you make a lovely fire or two or three there in the piazza, of those sodomites male and female—women too pursue that criminal vice. Make, I say, a sacrifice to God, which He will accept as incense [honoring] His life.[252]

> Make a fire which the whole of Italy will smell.[253]

Yet for all their power, the politicians could not reform themselves; in the Savonarolan view, Florentine laymen retained that ethical feebleness that was their heritage. Groups outside government would have to provide an exam-

247. *Salmi*, I, 225; *Aggeo*, 418; also *Salmi*, I, 1.

248. On this ideal representational group, see page 19, this volume.

249. See pages 528f, this volume.

250. *Salmi*, II, 216.

251. The Savonarolan period saw laws regarding the reform of the women, and the reform of the children; there was no reform of the men.

252. *Salmi*, II, 124.

253. *Ibid.*, 168f.

ple, so as to guarantee the ritual efficaciousness of lay behavior. In the early period of his ministry, the friar proposed a reformed clergy for that task.

A SACERDOTAL UTOPIA

To understand the cure, the Florentines had to comprehend the disease. If the clergy were to be reformed correctly, citizens had to recognize the nature of the evil effect a corrupt clergy had had on the city; the laity had lost the ability to distinguish between the sacred and profane through the avarice and irreverence of the clergy. To an audience petrified by the godly omens and military disasters of the day, Savonarola explained that over the years, Florentines had grown old in the evils of Lorenzo's court,

> changing bad words to good. . . . And they have said that the virtues are sins and sins virtues, and that simple living is something for fools and the riffraff, and that it is hypocrisy to do good and go to church and act humbly.[254]

This lay inversion of Christian values was both exemplified in, and partially the product of, the way people interacted with each other, the prophet told his audiences. Although ceremonies were intended to produce sentiments and feelings between those participating in them, and toward God, they were now promoting idolatry rather than empathy.[255] The increasingly elaborate spectacles of the age might appear "beautiful and respectable," products of what seemed "a certain natural instinct," but when one looked closely, it was evident that these ceremonies in fact hindered the emotional life that was their goal.[256] For Florentine rituals were empty and cold, leaves without fruit or spirit, devoid of what Savonarola called "enamorative *virtù*."[257]

The clergy was responsible for both the elaboration and the emptiness of ritual life, because the laity merely followed the lead of the priests:

> Bad priests and religious . . . ruin true divine cult and good Christian life and every good government.[258]

> The priests have to be the mirror of the *popolo*, where each person sees and learns right living.[259]

> And thus, *popolo*, if you want to be good, try to get good priests.[260]

Commissioned to edify and give example to an ethically feeble laity, the Florentine clergy instead practiced both the very sin most characteristic of a

254. *Ruth e Michea*, II, 204. More on the breakdown of sacred–profane divisions in *Giobbe*, II, 126–130; *Esodo*, I, 261; II, 368.

255. On the mechanics of idolatry, *Amos e Zaccaria*, II, 26; also *Aggeo*, 38.

256. *Giobbe*, II, 243; Cinozzi, cited in Villari and Casanova, *Scelta*, 3.

257. "Non ci è drento la virtù innamorativa"; *Ezechiele*, II, 168; *Salmi*, I, 49, 296.

258. *Trattato*, in *Aggeo*, 466.

259. *Aggeo*, 220.

260. *Esodo*, I, 42.

merchant society—avarice—and the sin least admissible in the sacerdotal estate—irreverence at the altar. That segment of society charged with teaching ethics through reverential behavior was instead subverting the laity in the divine theater.

In countless sermons Savonarola described how a deceitful clergy imparted its attitudinal and ethical corruption to an often unsuspecting laity. The bells ringing for services did not call the faithful, he warned the people, but their money, bread, and candles.[261] Canons came to vespers for cash distributions, but avoided matins because they were unremunerative.[262] Poor priests deserted impoverished churches, and prelates sought out the ceremonies of rich temples to replenish their pockets.[263] Coming to the altar after a night with women or boys, the Florentine priest said Mass with altar boys who were girls, or with his prostitute in the choir.[264] How could the Florentines feel anything when the clergy felt nothing? The laity was little more than a source of income, to whom the priest sold Masses with no more sense of obligation than a baker selling a loaf of bread: "What do you want to give me, and I'll sing a Mass for you."[265]

"The altar has become the shop of the clergy," Savonarola roared to listeners who understood that sacrifice was different from contract.[266] Priests rushed through Mass if that was in their financial interest, either raising the host with tongue in cheek or even completely omitting the consecration of the host, while the gullible laity remained unaware of the deceit and sacrilege.[267] If more profit was to be had through increasing pomp, however, the clergy staged great ceremonies, the laity remaining oblivious to the emptiness they produced.[268] Polyphony, polyphony, polyphony, the preacher cried, and no spirit; organs, organs, organs, and the spirit is dead. Masses and more Masses, procession on procession, sermons at every turn, yet a wasteland without fraternity eroded the hallowed soil of Florence. Nothing was as it seemed![269]

Florentines felt they were not communicating with each other or with God, Savonarola was suggesting, because in its ceremonies the clergy did not reverentially represent the behavioral forms that provoked genuine feelings. Deceiving people into believing they were participating in sacrifice that contained such emotions, the clergy was in fact part of the merciless contractual world of merchant Florence. To correct this situation, two steps were necessary. First, the number of priests had to be decreased, which would decrease

261. *Esodo*, II, 367f.

262. *Ibid.*

263. His antiprelatial bias is best seen *ibid.*, I, 265.

264. *Amos e Zaccaria*, I, 330, 346; II, 22; *Ezechiele*, I, 233; *Esodo*, I, 262; II, 368.

265. *Ezechiele*, II, 30.

266. *Ibid.*, I, 267.

267. *Esodo*, I, 261, 42; also *Ezechiele*, I, 267.

268. Savonarola's greatest task was to convince his listeners that the ceremonialism of the age was not matched by an emotive value. This he did by asking the Florentines to reflect on what they gained, and by using the idea that they were duped by badly motivated priests. There is, of course, no clear evidence that the spiritual emptiness came first, and Savonarola as its result came second; that is, there is no evidence that, in fact, ritual had become routinized.

269. *Aggeo*, 115, 417; *Salmi*, I, 189; *Giobbe*, II, 135, 446; *Amos e Zaccaria*, II, 273f; III, 363f.

the number of ceremonies bad priests stimulated: "It is better to have a few good ministers than many bad ones, for the bad ones provoke the ire of God against the city."[270] Second, good priests had to be procured, and Savonarola painted for his listeners a picture of what the city could be like if this were done: "As we see every day, if Florence were free of bad priests and religious, it would return to living like the early Christians and would be a mirror of religion to the whole world."[271] The Florentine clergy, as Savonarola often said, would in the future be what only the friary of San Marco was now. San Marco was the mirror of things to come, the seedbed for the priests who would one day make Florence "like a holy friary."[272]

Florentine laymen showed a vivid interest in the behavior of the friars of San Marco during these years, and often recorded the edifying impressions these religious specialists left on them.[273] Here was a religious community that protected the city through its rituals, taught the laity how to act through its common life, and showed how the whole city would interact once the millenium had come. San Marco was a model of fraternity . . . which preserved hierarchy. Its division of labor on class lines meant that some tasks in the friary went to unlettered people, of course: cooks, shoemakers, beggars to accompany preachers, and the like were naturally poorer friars. Other offices required skills only the educated upper class possessed. Savonarola met the criticism of his predominantly elitist recruiting philosophy by asserting that the times required scholars and preachers more than simple tradesmen, and by making clear that fraternity did not imply a confusion of either labors or classes.[274] The division of labor was also basic for the friars' mission to the laity, because allowing each specialist to be good at his task, made possible the Dominicans' edifying representations to the people of Florence. Savonarola understood that lay society required that its own division of labor be reflected in the friars' activities, if with a fraternity impossible in the *saeculum*.

Savonarola's utopic vision of Florence under a reformed clergy was, therefore, surprisingly recognizable. It was nothing more than a city with good priests who continually held their latently "tepid" audiences in the grip of sacrifice through repeatedly representing correct attitudes and norms.[275] In the few glimpses of this future society that the friar afforded his listeners, we find no charismatic saints, no prophets, few teachers, but many priests. Having entered the ark of San Marco, legions of clean clergy would finish by peopling the altars first of Florence, then of Tuscany, and finally those of the infidels.[276] The good society of Florence would be full of good priests because

270. *Trattato,* in *Aggeo,* 466.

271. *Ibid.,* 469.

272. *Aggeo,* 82, 275; also Ps. Burlamacchi, 95.

273. Among many others, see Filipepi, cited in Villari and Casanova, *Scelta,* 477ff.

274. *Amos e Zaccaria,* III, 358; *Ruth e Michea,* I, 409, where Savonarola also makes clear that "the Lord mostly needs scholars" with languages because of the

coming evangelization of the Word by the friars of San Marco throughout the world. Savonarola's sense of class and labor division is in *Amos e Zaccaria,* III, 358f; *Ruth e Michea,* I, 58f.

275. The *tiepidi* were Savonarola's enemies, those who did not emotively respond to the representations of the preacher.

276. *Amos e Zaccaria,* III, 358.

the more cult was performed, the more attention and care God and the angels would bestow on the city.[277] In this sacerdotal model of utopia, the clergy would not wither away.

Nor would the laity avoid ceremony. In the present conditions, it was true, ceremonies hindered piety, less because they were hypocritical than because there were so many of them; the faithful spent their time running from one pomp to another instead of concentrating on developing "internal cult" in one setting.[278] Go to Mass every day, Savonarola urged his listeners, and imitate the early Christians by taking communion frequently.[279] But make each act count. Have only one Sunday Mass in the church rather than many, he pleaded, but make that one a three-hour-long solemn Mass.[280] The implications of these remarks are clear. Florentines would spend more time in church, not less; the city as friary would be a churchy place indeed. In the coming society, it is true, the priesthood would still preserve its powerful corporate identity at the head of the laity. But they would earn their keep. Priests would constantly respin that golden thread of feeling, which proved sacrifice and gave meaning to the human contacts of everyday.[281]

Fixing the blame for the city's crisis on the clergy appealed to the citizenry of Florence, but time showed that the reformation of the clergy was doomed to failure. Not only did this program of clerical regeneration arouse the implacable opposition of much of the Florentine and Roman clergy, but the laity was not responding to the example of the uncorrupt friars of San Marco, as they should have according to the friar's plan. There were many "tepid" adults, Savonarola came to realize, who were simply incorrigible. By early 1496 the friar's miscalculations were clear and, though he continued to demand that bad priests be expelled, he henceforth had little hope that the whole clergy could be reformed or that clerical reformation would necessarily transform the city. Guided by the Virgin, he now set out on a more radical and imaginative course. With the force of revelation, he began to preach that children and adolescents would save the city for the millenium.[282]

CHILD FLORENCE

It was a decisive moment in Savonarola's politics of salvation, and the prophet would be quick to develop all the behavioral and conceptual vistas

277. "Bisogna . . . ch'ella sia piena di buoni uomini, ministri dello altare: perchè, crescendo el culto divino e il bene vivere, è necessario ch'el governo si facci perfetto. Prima, perchè Dio e li angeli suoi ne hanno speziale cura. . . . Secundo, per le orazioni, che continuamente si fanno da quelli che sono deputati al culto divino e dall buoni che sono nella città ed *etiam* per le orazioni di tutto el popolo nelle sollennità"; *Trattato*, in *Aggeo*, 467.

278. *Amos e Zaccaria*, III, 220.

279. *Giobbe*, I, 396; *Ezechiele*, II, 332.

280. *Giobbe*, II, 135, 446. Savonarola himself was praised for saying such Masses: "Missas quas private celebrabat per trium horarum spatium saepe numero protrahebat"; *Bibl. Laurenziana, Chronica . . . S. Marci*, f. 73r.

281. This emotive transmission was exactly their task in the future, as it had been in the past, and present, when they are "thieves"; *Esodo*, I, 265.

282. The earliest reference to the boys having been reformed is in *Ruth e Michea*, II, 228 (Oct. 25, 1495). But the first indication of the boys as saviors is in February and March of 1496, on which see pages 477ff, this volume. On the whole question of these boys, see my "Adolescence."

his new advocacy of children revealed. Yet how reticently did he become their champion. Since 1488 it had been clear that, after a long hiatus in which boys' activities went unmentioned by our sources, the young were assuming an important public role as religiopolitical actors. In a Lenten sermon of that year, the Franciscan Bernardino da Feltre addressed thousands of boys gathered in the cathedral as his "soldiers" in the battle to start the Monte di Pietà in the city. Bernardino urged the boys to pray to God in public to inspire the Signoria to approve the new institution; instead, the boys proceeded to attack Jewish money lenders immediately after the sermon.[283] We have seen that in 1492 a Dominican suggested using boys in procession to assuage God's ire with the city. In the following year, a Franciscan chapter general meeting in the city culminated in a Burning of the Vanities being staged by the same Bernardino da Feltre, vanities presumably heaped on the *capannuccio* by the *fanciulli*.[284] In finally placing the boys in the limelight in 1496, therefore, Savonarola, though responding to the boys' own impetus, also followed an established tradition among both great Mendicant orders. Yet with characteristic zeal, he now developed them into a major communal force as police, processants, and churchgoers.

The first evidence that the boys of Florence were acting as civil "correctors" of morals comes from early 1496, and from then until the death of Savonarola in 1498 Florentine men and women on the approach of the boys would cry as they now did: " 'Here come the boys of the friar.' And everyone, every gambler no matter how tough, fled. And women dressed properly in the streets."[285] Prostitutes retreated to their brothels, homosexuals went in fear of their skins, boys' own recreations were regulated, and conventional morality in general was enforced with the tacit approval of the government.[286] There were excesses, of course, and the chroniclers' first report of such police activities concerns a group of boys who, on February 7, 1496, ripped the veils from a girl's head and caused a neighborhood disturbance.[287] Yet the use of force remained an exception. The boys generally heeded Savonarola's instructions to ask wrongdoers to hand over their vanities and, if they refused, to report them to the proper governmental authorities.[288] Though the friar recognized that the boys' very potential for violence deterred immorality, he counted on less violent inducements: the threat of official action, the shame perpetrators felt when they behaved immorally in the presence of children, and most significant, the example that the boys showed adults. In perfect marching order, small bands of innocents moved from place to place with saintly manners and dress, impressing their own innocence upon their elders. Here was no selfish juvenile rabble gather-

283. Rossi, 238f. The Monte was formed to offer low-interest loans to the needy.

284. *Ibid.*, 282; Masi, 18; Rinuccini, cl. See also page 122, this volume. Note also that when Piero de' Medici was not allowed in the Palace in 1494, he was immediately "perseguito da' fanciulli co' sassi"; Nardi, II, 16.

285. Landucci, 123.

286. On Savonarola's attacks on prostitution, see my "Prostitution," and in general my "Adolescence," 254f.

287. Landucci, 123.

288. As for example *Amos e Zaccaria*, I, 325f; *Ezechiele*, II, 277.

ing money for their own amusements by promising inviolability in exchange for a tip.[289] Gaining nothing for themselves, the Savonarolan boys acted for the welfare of the community at large in emptying the public space of Florence of the lewd products of a refined culture. While the correctors did their job, other boys called "cleansers" (*lustrelatori*) pursued the same end by searching for crosses and figures of saints in places where people urinated, cleaning them, and then removing them "so they would not be kept irreverently in similar places."[290] Now the people of Florence could traverse the streets of a purified city; now they could move in procession. The fundamental purpose of the boys' police activities was to prepare the ground for civil communication.

Cleaning the city was a traditional preface to adult procession.[291] The radical actions of the boys prepared Florence for their entry onto the processional stage. Only days after their police work was first recorded in the sources, the boys staged the first exclusively youthful procession in the history of Florence. For contemporaries, this procession of February 16, 1496, and the several that followed in the coming months and years crystallized the ritual and moral implications of the boys' police work. They made clear to God and man that a new Florentine community had been formed, that the boys were now part of this moral and processional community, and that for the first time, this lay community had within itself a social group that could give forms meaning: the incorporated pure boys of Florence.

The boys' explosion into the center of Florentine processional life in early 1496 must first be seen in the context of the processions that had been staged before that date. Since coming to influence in late 1494 Savonarola had been an outspoken proponent of these great public festivities, much to the consternation of those who expected his incessant attacks on "external ceremonies" to lead to their suppression. They were fools who said that such *feste* were only good for entertaining the public, the friar insisted, for processions could be used to gather money for the poor.[292] Processions could not only demonstrate the fraternity of those within them, he believed, but by redistributing wealth to those too shamed by their poverty to take part in them, they showed solidarity with these "shamed poor" (*vergognosi*). On the feast of Mary's Conception (December 8, 1494), the first such offertory procession was held with great success, money being gathered at every turn for later distribution to the shamed poor.[293] Another procession held on June 5, 1495, to ward off the threat of Charles VIII attacking the city, the procession of the Corpus Christi, and then that of San Giovanni of the same year, all repeated the same procedure with the same thought: If Florentines dressed in their poorest clothes and gathered alms during a procession, God would be likely to protect Florence.[294]

289. On the traditional exchange-extortions, see my "De la Ville à la Cour."

290. Ps. Burlamacchi, 123.

291. See page 76, this volume.

292. *Aggeo*, 138.

293. Landucci, 90; see also Trexler, "Charity," 95.

294. Landucci, 106f; *Salmi*, II, 89, 68f with references to the *vestacce cattive* which Florentines were to wear

To the best of our knowledge, children played no particular role in any of these offertory processions.[295] But now, on February 16, 1496, Savonarola chose what seemed the most improbable of strategies: Alms would again be gathered for the *vergognosi, during a Carnival procession of boys*. On the very feast of self-indulgence, Florentines would forget themselves and learn through their boys that charity and innocence would be fused in the utopic future. The lesson was irresistible. The procession of Carnival 1496 was an incredible success, and it set a precedent that would be repeated in Carnival processions of 1497 and 1498.[296] The same boys who on the eve of the normal Carnival blocked street corners to extort money now stood there with crucifixes and begged passersby to help the poor by giving "into their hands of holy purity," as one awed witness expressed it.[297] The very children who usually celebrated Carnival by having a stone fight and then burning a *capannuccio* full of insulting dolls and signs now organized a religious procession.[298] Demonstrating the discipline they had learned from Savonarola's associate fra Domenico da Pescia, the boys gathered in the Piazza degli Innocenti, placed themselves in ranks under the flags of each of their quarters, and joined hands. Adults who on previous Carnivals had been afraid to leave home for fear of the boys watched incredulously. In perfect order the boys first paid their respects to Our Lady of the Annunziata, then marched to San Marco, from whence, their approach heralded by the trumpets and flutes of the Signoria, they followed their parents' traditional processional route across the river and back, to end in a cathedral jammed with elders who awaited these saintly children. Now the children passed among them and took up a collection for the *vergognosi*. Coins, veils, table silver, and a host of other vanities filled their basins, visible evidence to adults and children alike of the fraternal force of a ritual community that included the young.[299]

The boys were now established as a central part of communal representation, and the Carnival processions of 1497 and 1498 drove that lesson home. Yet the boys' particular function as a processional facilitator of communal fraternity was destined to change. In 1496 a large part of the community had backed the friar and the boys, so an enormous demonstration of ritual charity was possible. In later Carnival processions, however, the boys represented only that narrowing part of the citizenry that continued to sustain Savonarola. In those conditions ridicule replaced charity as the dominant mode of *fanciulli* Carnival expression. Ridicule was a normal part of Carnival festivities, of course, and the very notion of holding a religious procession on Carnival in 1496 was intended to ridicule the devil.[300] But in 1497 the traditional Carnival

in these processions. When Savonarola condemned "external ceremonies," he meant to condemn more their riches and spiritual emptiness than their number. The major difference between the processional life of this period and that of earlier ones was the dress of the lay people, not the quantity of processions.

295. No account mentions their presence.

296. On which see my "Adolescence," 251, 262.

297. Landucci, 124.

298. Ps. Burlamacchi, 120, 123, for descriptions of these contemporary customs.

299. Landucci, 125; Trexler, "Adolescence," 256.

300. "In dispetto di Lucifero e sua seguacci"; Ps. Burlamacchi, 134.

bonfire or *capannuccio* reappeared, and was used again in 1498; the boys' procession ended not in the cathedral, but in the Piazza della Signoria where the *capannuccio* was; it mocked not only Satan, but the friar's opponents. The same types of goods that the Carnival boys of 1496 had converted to money for the poor were now heaped on the fire for these Savonarolan Burnings of the Vanities.

The *fanciulli* pushed their prophet to permit this sporting challenge of the tepid. Groups of young men rose to meet it.[301] On Carnival 1497 two squads of *giovani* tried to organize a ball game, apparently to incite disorders; they were humiliated when the Signoria lent its trumpeters to the *fanciulli*, and forbade the *giovani* their sport.[302] In 1498 another brigade of *giovani*, called the Compagnacci, organized Carnival festivities with the same purpose; they too failed to compete with the Burning by the *fanciulli*.[303] Thus in torching the symbols of the easy life, the Savonarolan boys in these tense festivals mocked the inability of the *tepidi* to gather retinue. These Carnival events of 1497 and 1498 were significant events indeed: nothing less than quasi-official tests to determine the formal identity of the whole community. The *fanciulli* reigned supreme, it seemed. Their ritual destruction of the city's riches was heralded by communal trumpeters, and witnessed by the Signoria from its Palace.

The Carnival procession of 1496, like that of the following year, was made up exclusively of *fanciulli* who performed for astounded adults.[304] Yet this first spectacle only began their conquest of the processional center of Florentine life. Once the boys had achieved a processional identity on the devil's own feast, they joined the processions of their elders and quickly transformed the traditional ecclesiastical feasts of the city. We possess descriptions of two general processions in which the boys took part, and of these, the famous Palm Sunday procession of 1496 was certainly the most important.[305] Performed only thirty-nine days after their stunning Carnival feat, it had an equally profound emotional impact upon the adult population; within the new processional community of Florence, the boys would lead the way, and represent the city before God.

The Palm Sunday procession of 1496 was held to celebrate the government's approval of the Monte di Pietà, and to collect donations for the capital of the new lending institution.[306] For weeks the boys had been prepared for the event. Savonarola told them that they were historical figures repeating

301. Direct evidence that the boys led Savonarola in this matter of *capannucci* is in the preacher's statement of Mar. 12, 1497, after Carnival of that year, that he understands the *fanciulli* want to "fare qualche festa," and were collecting vanities. He then approves their efforts; *Ezechiele*, II, 208.

302. Piero Parenti, cited in Schnitzer, *Quellen*, IV, 159ff.

303. A very interesting description of this group's activities in Cerretani, cited *ibid.*, III, 54–58. We will see that the Compagnacci played a key role in the demise of the Savonarolan regime.

304. The 1498 Carnival procession included other groups; Trexler, "Adolescence," 261f.

305. See *ibid.*, 251, n. 4 for all references. The other procession was that of the Corpus Christi, 1497, famous because of the open attack on the *fanciulli* by the *giovani* of the city; see Landucci, 150f. Note that the Palm Sunday procession of 1496 is the only general procession on that feast recorded in the annals of Florence. Note also that a Palm Sunday procession is a Christian Triumph; E. Kantorowicz, *Selected Studies* (Locust Valley, 1965), 45 and seq.

306. On which institution see my "Charity," 83ff.

specific events in the Old Testament; he flattered the role they were playing in the conversion of the city; he gave them detailed instructions for their behavior and comportment during the procession. The result was a spectacle the likes of which the city had never seen. At the head of the procession thousands of boys marched under the banners of their quarters, each group organized according to height. After that came a painting of Christ on an ass entering Jerusalem, covered by a baldachin. The girls of the city followed. Only then did the priests appear, trailed by communal officials. The procession closed with the grown men, and finally the matrons.[307]

At almost every step, this procession marked a new departure in the Florentine religious procession. Not the clergy, but the lay boys of the city led the way. They thus acted the part of a purified image of the adult political males. If in the traditional celebratory procession adult males were organized according to their wards, in this festival it was the *fanciulli* who assumed a political organization in God's sight; the adult males did not. I have previously noted that the behavior of the adult processants was also unparalleled: The sight of docile boys dressed in white with crowns of olives and red crosses in hand singing sweetly was so overpowering that grown men in the procession started dancing in the street and crying *Viva Christo!* Children could convert elders to holy madness.[308] This new ritual community marched through all parts of the city before returning to the cathedral, where the boys collected offerings from their elders, now almost a retinue to the childish center.[309]

It was in the cathedral where the boys' new role in Florentine ritual life could be witnessed as through a single lens. Savonarola and his aides had moulded the boys to perform on this stage as well, and the record makes clear that adults watched the boys' behavior in church as no laymen had ever been watched before. Diarists reported that the boys waited with perfect patience for hours before the beginning of services, that they sang angelic lauds to soothe their parents' spirits, that they received communion by the hundreds and thousands, that they took up the collections, and much more.[310] Never before in the city's history had a lay social group rivaled the priests and preachers as a source of edification and instruction in the church. What most impressed contemporaries, however, was that the boys sat together in church (as they now marched together in procession) in specially constructed stands seemingly designed to call attention to them. "In the guise of a theater," to use three independent sources' highly suggestive phrase, the *duomo* of Florence was now a stage for this part of the community.[311] It was "both ridicu-

---

307. See Savonarola's planning in *Amos e Zaccaria*, II, 433; III, 35, 71f, 123f, 139, 151–159, and for further references to the processors as Old Testamental figures, *Salmi*, I, 289–305 (procession of June 5, 1495). Descriptions in Ps. Burlamacchi, 127ff, and by G. Benivieni, in Manzoni, *Libro di Carnevale*, 186–227.

308. See page 339, this volume.

309. This image is the more appropriate since, as we have seen, only the male children were organized by

quarters, and not the adults. On the significance of an undifferentiated mass of dependents accompanying a categorized political group, see pages 266f, this volume.

310. See especially Ps. Burlamacchi, 120f, and Trexler, "Adolescence," 251.

311. Ps. Burlamacchi, 120; Nardi, II, 16, and a contemporary description sent to Venice in Sanuto, I, 78f.

lous and devout" to see the boys assembled together in church separate from their families, Piero Parenti remarked, still slightly bewildered by the novelty of the boys' ritual centrism.[312] It was as if one were watching the friars of San Marco themselves at their ritual work, as if the theater of children had been removed from the confraternal halls of the Medici period to this sacred place. Chroniclers like Parenti did not recognize the Medicean roots of this juvenile revolution.

The dominant import of the boys' activities was that a marginal lay group had culminated a century of development by seizing the center of Florentine representational life. True, the Grand Council of the adult political males acted for God, but not like his children, and they never marched as a group in a Florentine procession. The friars of San Marco were kept from this center by different constraints. Though the Dominican community was ritually effica-cious and edifying to God and citizenry, time ran out before it could fulfill Savonarola's prediction that it would become a ceremonial clergy, constantly stimulating the laity in the direct interaction of altar and procession. The boys of Florence alone could take to the streets and speak for the city. Leaving the friary of San Marco, where their general meetings were held, they resembled cloistered monks, so perfect was their innocence and discipline.[313] Heading the procession and passing before all eyes in church, they resembled a lay ceremonial clergy that represented the city, inspired their elders through reverential comportment, and facilitated communications between men and with God.[314] Organized into quarters identical to the political boundaries of the city and enforcing morality as their fathers had never had the will to do, they could be mistaken for an innocent government of the republic. The Savonarolan boys were a bona fide social and political phenomenon of the first rank. Their innocence of age, their governance, and their association with the prophet were the ultimate sources of their authority and impact on the city.

The extreme youth of the *fanciulli* was certainly their most important characteristic. The older boys ranged up to twenty years of age, usually belonged to the established adolescent confraternities as well, and held lead-ership positions within the movement.[315] But these *giovanotti* were outnum-bered by juniors as young as five or six years old. Thus the average age of all the boys was ten or eleven years, below the minimum age of admission to the adolescent confraternities.[316] We recall Franco Sacchetti's call for a new Herod to exterminate boys four to twelve years of age, so fearful was their racket.[317] Now for the first time Savonarola and his associates organized these

312. Parenti, cited in Schnitzer, *Quellen*, IV, 96.

313. On the similarity of the boys' internal discipline to that of the monastic clergy, see my "Adolescence," 245.

314. There is a striking similarity between the exem-plary role Savonarola said priests in church owed lay

people, and the reactions of the latter to the chil-dren's behavior.

315. On the whole question of age, see the more extensive documentation *ibid.*, 250–254.

316. *Ibid.*, 251.

317. See page 368, this volume.

preadolescent boys into religious groups, and their success was considered the friar's greatest achievement.

The social origins of these boys cannot be determined precisely with the information at our disposal, but the limited data are consistent in suggesting that leadership positions went to boys of good family and that it was they who did the police work, since wrongdoers feared these boys' fathers. The same class of boys was well represented at the base of the movement, but as a whole, children of lesser station were numerically superior.[318] The boys' movement, in short, probably resembled the social composition of the adult confraternities before the Medici had restricted the latter to the plebs of Florence.

When we examine the organization of the boys, however, we find that the question of social origins, as well as that concerning the relation of the movement to the established adolescent confraternities, are not as decisive as they might seem. The participating *fanciulli*, as we have seen, were organized according to the political geography of the city, and each of the four *compagnie* had its full complement of officials.[319] These *fanciulli* therefore owed primary allegiance to the company of the quarter in which they lived; the established adolescent confraternities, on the other hand, had scarcely any sectional allegiance. The implications of this geographic identity becomes quite evident when we understand that the juvenile officials of each quarter supervised not only the active members of the movement, but also all the boys of their respective quarters.[320] We recall how reticent the old republic had been to tolerate neighborhood social organizations and how the Medici had built such kingdoms to foster their subversive ends. Thus it is not surprising that Savonarola's determination to have such a constitution approved by the government enraged his opponents while it inspired his more dedicated supporters. The preacher clearly intended to build a type of juvenile political structure that would control all the city's *fanciulli*, a structure self-conscious enough to send its own ambassadors to the Signoria.[321]

"Woe to the city administered by *fanciulli*," cried an Augustinian preacher from his pulpit in Santo Spirito when, in March 1496, the government first considered approving the boys' constitution.[322] To do so would be equivalent to establishing "a small government of the republic," the friar

318. Trexler, "Adolescence," 252f, 264; Masi, 15f. These conclusions are validated by a document not previously used to answer these questions, a letter of fra Domenico da Pescia to the *fanciulli* of Sept. 3, 1497; J. Schnitzer, *Savonarolas Erzieher und Savonarola als Erzieher* (Berlin, 1913), 135–141.

319. Trexler, "Adolescence," 255.

320. *Ibid.*

321. On these embassies, *ibid.*, 254. Savonarola also recommended that an office of *paciere* be instituted in each quarter for making peace among men, and another in each quarter to regulate the women; *Salmi,*

II, 173. If we recall the earlier determination of one patron to found an adolescent confraternity in the quarter of Santo Spirito (page 373, this volume) and keep it there, the reader may question this book's thesis that political divisions were not affective neighborhood units. Doubtless this is a question of emphases over time, neighborhood pride and identity being markedly more evident in the later period; but as regards the history of confraternities, that Santo Spirito document is the only one from the earlier period that associates itself to a political division of the city.

322. Parenti, cited in Schnitzer, *Quellen*, IV, 112.

continued, and he expressed amazement "that the Florentines, who are considered so expert, [and] men of the most acute spirit, have come into such decline and lowness that the very children emerge with the upper hand and want to govern."[323] There was some truth in these words. Savonarola attempted to soothe this anxiety of some adults, and asked pointedly: "Tell me, are the boys magistrates? Are they of the Eight?"[324] The friar understood how sensitive the Florentines were to the ridicule on this score that came from abroad.[325] Yet such perorating was scarcely to the point, and when Savonarola did address the boys' role in society in relation to that of government, his views further disquieted his opponents. He seemed to be predicting the withering away of the elders' commune. When defending the boys' constitution, he could sound traditional enough in maintaining that the new juvenile structure would "begin to order the young in a good life-style, and from the tender years on [such a form] would show them how they will have to govern in the future. For it is of the utmost importance which habits they form."[326] But the friar did not mean, as had Traversari years before, that individual boys would utilize the lessons they had learned once they grew up and entered their fathers' government. These boys, Savonarola apparently believed, would never leave their companies, structures that the preacher knew to have not only the same divine approbation as the Grand Council but a creative charisma that government lacked.[327] Throughout his sermons after early 1496 there was the haunting suggestion that, active in their perfect "little republics," the incorporated innocents could force the world to become, and remain, young:

> I tell you boys that you have to be the good citizens who will enjoy the good which God has promised this city. A time will come when you will see many officials come to ask your advice on governing [the city]. And they will choose to govern as you govern yourselves.[328]

> I tell you, the Lord wants these boys. From among the elders he will take one here and there, [but] the others will be discarded. For they have become old in evil.[329]

As his own slaughter approached, the prophet of Florence still promised the sovereignty of the incorporated innocents.

THE FLORENTINE MARTYR

The prophet had brought a new urban salvational model to fruition. No longer were the clergy and the mature male laity at and near center; no longer did outsiders merely cry at the margins. The city was to be saved by those who grew, not by those who were grown. Now women and children were

323. *Ibid.*, 105.

324. Trexler, "Adolescence," 256, n. 3.

325. *Ibid.*

326. Parenti, cited in Schnitzer, *Quellen*, IV, 106.

327. This distinction is the decisive difference between the Consiglio and the boys as salvational media.

328. Trexler, "Adolescence," 249.

329. *Ibid.*

virile spirits, as Savonarola said, and the grave children of Florence stepped to the center of processional identity to claim the place of their fathers and of the clergy.[330] This new order had two meanings. First, the charisma of an outside or marginal social group became central to communal representations. Second, the individual magnetism of persons like Lorenzo and Savonarola grew commensurately, and was closely associated with the magnetism of the new ritual group. It is important to grasp the continuity of such men's personal charisma.

Savonarola's assumption of the Lorenzan heritage was as unmistakable as his critique of the tyrant.[331] We see it at the institutional level, where Savonarola continued to cultivate the neighborhood solidarities of nonpolitical social groups, but it is even more marked at the behavioral level. The friar may have eschewed Lorenzo's habit of visiting neighborhood groups and monuments so as to bestow value on them, but when he went to preach, a large retinue of armed men accompanied him, as they had Lorenzo, and great masses of men and women lined the streets "to see him, as if they had never heard him before."[332] Florentines also flocked to the friary of San Marco much as they had once streamed to the Medici palace, hanging upon every action and word of the leader and his brothers, even if some of the latter denounced their leader for conventual "tyrannies."[333] Finally, they venerated the friar with Magian rituals similar to those once accorded the Magnificent. If Lorenzo had been the Star of the Confraternity of the Magi, Savonarola held the Light to which the infidels would come; the imperial nature of Florence remained the same.[334] Savonarola alternately played the Christ Child, as when the Signoria visited him on Epiphany 1498 and kissed his hand, and the Magus, as in the great liturgical drama he staged in the church of San Marco.[335]

Thus iconographic similarities supplemented the institutional and behavioral continuities between the two leaders. All the time denouncing Lorenzo for having sought to make himself a prince, Savonarola carefully maintained the association of San Marco with the royal cult of the Magi, and propagandized a new regal cult, that of Christ the King, which was the Magi's logical successor. Why had the shepherds and the Magi come to visit the

330. On *fanciulli* and female virility, *Amos e Zaccaria*, II, 240.

331. As suggested by D. Cantimori in his review of Schnitzer's *Savonarola*, in the *Annali della r. Scuola Normale Superiore di Pisa*, ser. 2, I (1932), 93. A dissenting view is in Weinstein, *Savonarola and Florence*, 272f, who discounts the idea because Savonarola did not have the internal political base of the Medici.

332. Filipepi, cited in Villari and Casanova, *Scelta*, 475, saying that some seventy or eighty gentlemen plus friars accompanied him. Savonarola assured listeners that he had not asked for the bodyguard; *Ezechiele*, II, 354. But Parenti understood it was "per darsi più reputatione et mostrarsi nella terra amato et potente"; cited in Schnitzer, *Quellen*, IV, 169.

333. Weinstein, *Savonarola and Florence*, 273, notes the pilgrimages. Savonarola's "tyranny" (obviously with comparative Lorenzan overtones) is in Villari, *Storia*, cclviii.

334. Thus the Turks and the Moors would come to the Light; *Salmi*, II, 44 (as they had to Lorenzo's).

335. See the text of the latter report in ch. 6, this volume. On the Signoria visiting Savonarola, Schnitzer, *Quellen*, IV, 222 (Parenti). It is most suggestive that the famous 1496 sermon in which Savonarola summarized all the predictions he had made about Florence was delivered on the octave of Epiphany, the latter being that day of the year most associated with augurs and prophecies; *Salmi*, I, 41 seq.

Child, Savonarola asked, if not to show that Christ was King of the weak and the strong?[336] It was not clear, as the friar so often claimed, that Florence did not need a king. When the French king Charles VIII entered the city of Florence in November 1494 (Plate 21), he did not stay in Santa Maria Novella, as a truly restorative regime might have required. He bedded instead in the Medici palace and had his picture painted as if he had assumed possession.[337] After sixty years of Medici rule and a century of Magian dreams, the city could not be as it once had been.

From their beginnings these royal cults had expressed and formed the city's need for foreign acceptance, and Savonarola, like Lorenzo, had to embody the foreign recognition and credit that Florence had come to expect in and from its individual leaders. The friar sought to accomplish this through terrestrial diplomacy when he went on embassy in as effective and affective a manner as once Lorenzo had visited Ferrante in Naples· "I put myself in danger for your sake, for if what I told you [would happen] had not . . . , I would have been humiliated and would have had no place to flee."[338] And Savonarola attacked his task at the level of supernatural diplomacy as well. As "legate" to the divinities, the Dominican in his "embassies" to God and the Virgin received the promises of Florence's imperial future from these distant yet caring authorities.[339]

Here was a person by birth and calling outside the political order, as Lorenzo had been by age and private status, who was ready to suffer and die for the city though innocent of its sins. It was not that Savonarola likened himself to the Magnificent, though he did not hesitate to compare his abandonment by the Florentines to their defense of Lorenzo after the Pazzi conspiracy. Rather, the cult of charismatic innocence made the sacrifice of Savonarola a sequel to the assassination of Giuliano and the attempts on the life of Lorenzo de' Medici.[340] Florence would now test, and then offer up, its charismatic leader. The fire trial and burning of Savonarola were also part of the ritual revolution.

In the course of the year 1497, the string of fulfilled predictions through which Savonarola had maintained his credit ran out, and the friar no longer seemed capable of uniting the populace. On Corpus Christi of that year a gang of toughs seized the crosses carried by the *fanciulli* and publicly destroyed them, claiming that the crosses were in fact necromantic mandrakes in the service of Satan. This was awesome evidence that the city's ritual order was approaching crisis, for now some men feared to adore this Christian

336. *Salmi*, II, 190. On the development of regal cults, see further Trexler, "Magi Enter Florence," 155ff. That Florentines were aware of the political significance of this cult is clear from the attitudes toward it in the Last Republic; some suspected that Christ's reproclamation as king of Florence was a prelude to the government putting the city under the pope as that king's vicar; Roth, *Last Republic*, 90.

337. On this entry, see the bibliography in B. Mit-

chell (ed.), *Italian Civic Pageantry in the High Renaissance. A Descriptive Bibliography* (Florence, 1979), 35ff.

338. These words echo the selflessness attributed to Lorenzo after his visit to Ferrante; *Salmi*, II, 84f.

339. *Giobbe*, I, 269. See also Weinstein, *Savonarola and Florence*, 178.

340. The comparison is in *Esodo*, I, 29f.

symbol because they might be idolizing the devil.[341] The papacy encouraged such ideas, for it forbade citizens to frequent the friar's sacraments, processions, and sermons.[342]

Where lay the truth? Was it in the Rome of the Borgia pope and Medici cardinal, as local Franciscans proclaimed in increasingly bold sermons, or did the truth lie in the revelations that the prophet Savonarola received in his embassies to the divinities? By early 1498 it was a foregone conclusion among the city's counselors that the friar would "have to perform a miracle by which one would be forced to believe him, or he would have to leave."[343] Something had to be done, said another citizen, to "liberate this *popolo* and this city from such confusion." If Savonarola had his armed guard, so now did the Franciscans, the *giovani* Compagnacci whose nightly thuggeries made it seem that they, and not the government, were in control of the streets. Savonarola himself recognized the need for a great public miracle to determine "how this city is to be governed."[344] The result was a trial by fire.

As always, a public ceremony would express, test, and form the city's political structures; unique in Florentine history, this one would instantaneously answer ultimate questions of communal bonds and beliefs through one great game of chance in which equal competitors vied for God's lot. As Savonarola had once told his audience, the divinity played a hand in tilting equal chance; it was only necessary to recognize his will. So, on the eve of the trial, specialists developed an elaborate code through which men could read God's meaning from different possible outcomes of the trial, effectively informing God in advance of what his will would mean.[345] On that momentous April 7, 1498, the Dominicans came into the Piazza della Signoria in as large and pompous a procession as possible, all with the purpose, said one witness, of "striking fear into the hearts of" Savonarola's Franciscan opponents.[346] From grandstands erected in front of the Palace and from the windows all about the Piazza, the government and citizens of Florence watched this unprecedented spectacle. At one corner of the square communal soldiers stood ready to protect Savonarola, and at another the private youth group of the Compagnacci brandished the arms that would defend the Franciscans if the need arose. On either side of the government, each order

341. Ps. Burlamacchi, 135.

342. Trexler, *Spiritual Power*, 173–178. The pope had excommunicated Savonarola and threatened to interdict the city. This threat played an important role in weakening the friar's support.

343. Parenti, cited in Schnitzer, *Quellen*, IV, 201.

344. Savonarola, cited *ibid.*, IV, 251. The citizens' call for an end to confusion is in Ginori, cited *ibid.*, I, 102. One counselor thought the government should have been more occupied with the "inconvenienti che la nocte seguono de' giovani" than with Savonarola; C. Lupi, "Nuovi Documenti intorno a fra Girolamo Savonarola," *ASI*, ser. 3, III (1866), pt. 1, 57 (Mar. 30, Girolamo Capponi). On the Compagnacci's relation

to the Franciscans, see R. Ridolfi, *Vita di Girolamo Savonarola*, 2 vols. (Rome, 1952), I, 354. The assessment that *giovani* were in control is cited on page 515, this volume.

345. Weinstein, *Savonarola and Florence*, 286f. Savonarola's idea that God arranged the outcome of voting was referred to on page 469, this volume. Alternative methods of establishing truth were rejected; see these approaches in Schnitzer, *Quellen*, IV, 73, and Ps. Burlamacchi, 110f.

346. L. Randi (ed.), "Frate Girolamo Savonarola giudicato da Piero Vaglienti, Cronista Fiorentino," *Rivista delle Biblioteche* IV (1893), 59f (hereafter Vaglienti).

prepared its two champions for their walk across the burning embers and continued its attempts to make itself "more equal" by psychologically disarming the opponent. Thus the Dominicans prayed to St. Francis, one Franciscan declaimed, trying to have that saint desert his own order.[347] The Dominicans wanted to carry a host into the embers, but the Franciscans protested that this would give their opponents an unfair advantage, and they objected as well to the clothing the Dominicans wore, claiming that it was hexed so as to be fireproof.[348]

The test that the anticipatory Florentines had in advance nicknamed "the miracle" never materialized, but was aborted after continuing argument and a "miraculous" rainfall.[349] Inclined to blame Savonarola for its failure, many onlookers were ready to take the matter into their own hands, and as the friar headed up the route from the Piazza to San Marco, as if through the Red Sea, they prepared to stone him. They could not. For protection Savonarola now held over his head the host that he had earlier wanted his champions to carry into the fire. The murderous crowd, including one historian of these events, found itself powerless before the real presence. This aftermath carried a decisive message. If it was still unclear which party in the city was right— were not the Signori who left office on May 1 stoned as they made their way home?—it was now evident that Florentines would still unite under the host.[350] The body of Christ still had the power to prevent violence, still prevailed over men's passions in this weak and ignoble political community. Florence could still cohere without the charisma of living persons. A spectacle that had started by competing parties confidently offering their individual champions as proof of their fraternity ended by proving the continuing power of a civic contract beneath the host. It was because Florentines still worshiped the host that they could now execute their spiritual father.

On May 23, 1498, Savonarola and his two most devoted Dominican followers were burned after hanging. In the same square and perhaps on the same spot where great bonfires had consumed the vanities in two previous Carnivals, the fate that the friars had once demanded for homosexuals became their own. The city that had created this friar's awesome spiritual force would destroy it, and we see the terrible scene in an anonymous painting (Plate 23) of the execution.[351] Front and center on the large stage before the Palazzo della Signoria, ecclesiastics degraded the three friars of their clerical dignities and then handed them over to the secular authorities for burning as

347. Referred to on page 4, this volume, where the topos itself was examined. The presence of the *giovani* Compagnacci in the square in this quasi-public stance leaves little doubt as to the coercive power they had accrued; Cerretani, cited in Schnitzer, *Quellen*, III, 61.

348. Ps. Burlamacchi, 150; Schnitzer, *Quellen*, IV, 258; Vaglienti, 59.

349. Weinstein, *Savonarola and Florence*, 287; Ridolfi, *Vita . . . Savonarola*, I, 362.

350. For this dangerous procession see Vaglienti, 59f; Ps. Burlamacchi, 154, with references to the Red Sea. Venice heard the news of the stoning of the former priors from the Medici camp at Bologna; Sanuto, I, 955. Not surprisingly, the Florentine sources make no mention of it.

351. A variant is reproduced by Steinberg, *Fra Girolamo*, 111. See also S. Edgerton, "A Little-Known 'Purpose of Art' in the Italian Renaissance," *Art History* II (1979), pl. 28.

heretics, a three-hour service of disrobing and severance that one witness described as "a beautiful ritual."[352] Contrary to the curious emptiness shown in our painting, the square was jammed with people. Yet the area around the pyre was purposely empty. The government had determined to prevent the collection of relics and thus the Osirian reconstruction of the friar's body and myth.

Hanging from their posts, the martyrs seemed to be on crosses, and those who recalled another martyrdom cried, "Look, they want to crucify them!"[353] Other witnesses behaved as if it were Carnival. A group of boys stoned the friars as they would a mannequin, and hastened the friars' dismemberment and thus total cremation.[354] Was it Carnival or Calvary? Was Savonarola a saint or a fraud of genius, a man or an effeminate corruptor of boys, even a hermaphrodite whose grave manhood *and* chaotic womanhood were both exorcized in these flames?[355] One senses the anxiety over communal identity. City counselors rued the circumstance that had turned their meetings away from worthy questions of war and money to disputes over friars and were sure they were a shame to their fathers as well as "the laughingstock of the world."[356] Yet the act was now consummated. The government of Florence had been its one and only *festaiolo*.

How difficult it would be to find the equal of Savonarola's fire trial and execution at any other time or place in European history! It was phenomenal for a city to make a priest into a world historical figure, accept his visionary claim that Florence was unique in its godly identity and mission, and then publicly execute the man and, in a real sense, its own utopic identity. And yet, these events do not defy comprehension. They did culminate a recognizable direction in Florentine social and cultural life, and they clearly performed the same functions rituals had always served in the city's history. To understand these events historically and structurally, three questions must be addressed: Why was Savonarola kept in Florence? Why was he killed publicly? How did the fire trial and execution affect the city's processional structure?

Sovereignty was the decisive reason the Florentine government did not respect the pope's wishes and surrender Savonarola to Rome. The immediate concern was that the friar might reveal state secrets to the papacy and thus harm the commune's interests.[357] A further worry was that a hearing outside Florence could reveal that that government had forged the protocols of

352. Vaglienti, 61. The writer was moved by the art of the ceremony rather than venting his hate of Savonarola.

353. Landucci, 176. A correspondent writing to Venice thought it wondrous that Savonarola had been imprisoned at the beginning of Passiontime, and executed the eve of Ascension; Sanuto, I, 968.

354. Ridolfi, *Vita . . . Savonarola*, I, 405f. The contemporary Filipepi told how Savonarola's enemies set off firecrackers under the bodies, "and many of them went into the air just as happens with the *girandola* on

the evening of San Giovanni"; cited in Villari and Casanova, *Scelta*, 508.

355. See the homosexual accusations in my "De la Ville à la Cour." The hermaphroditic rumor is in Ridolfi, *Vita . . . Savonarola*, I, 383; Filipepi in Villari and Casanova, *Scelta*, 502.

356. Weinstein, *Savonarola and Florence*, 286.

357. A. Gherardi (ed.), *Nuovi Documenti e Studi intorno a Girolamo Savonarola* (Florence, 1887), 262; Ridolfi, *Vita . . . Savonarola*, I, 375, 384f, 380.

Savonarola's inquisition in which he had confessed to wrongdoing; the fact that the friar's prosecution was a matter of state and not of guilt might become all too evident.[358] Besides, the commune insisted to the pope, Savonarola should be punished in Florence as an example to others who might want to indulge "such arrogant and detestable undertakings."[359] The "dignity and honor" of the commune was at stake, and this stance became all the more imperative when Florentines heard a rumor that their government was considering trading Savonarola to the pope in exchange for the right to impose three tithes on ecclesiastical property. Here was a government that in the midst of combating a century of dependence upon charismatic external authority stood ready to bargain the highest matters of state for "thirty pieces of silver"![360] Evidently, only by keeping Savonarola could this petty government prove itself legitimate.

Exporting Savonarola was not the easy way out after all, nor did the government choose to let the friar die "accidentally" so as to avoid its responsibility and vendettas against its members.[361] Instead, it held the friar prisoner for a month and a half and then executed him publicly. The reasons for the deliberate and public activities went beyond the pedagogic benefits the government saw in such procedures. The execution itself had to be public because the pope insisted on this as a condition of his agreement to allow the Florentines to keep their friar. Just as the Signoria would demonstrate its authority by a public execution, so the papacy would show its rights and prerogatives by a public ceremony of ecclesiastical degradation.[362] More fundamentally, however, both the long trial and the public execution of Savonarola and his two colleagues must be seen together as a culminating test of governmental authority, and as a constitutive process.

In the wake of Savonarola's arrest on April 9, the Signoria's most immediate concern was the effect its action would have on its authority among the populace. From repeated reports on the situation, we can see that the priors were originally anxious on this score, but that they slowly assumed a more confident attitude. Original observations that the city was surprisingly quiet and that no one was voicing strong objections soon mixed with the view that through the execution of Savonarola, the government was increasing its authority among a "reunified" and "reintegrated" populace.[363] In a perverse fashion, the friar was still an image around which the Florentines could order and arrange themselves. Every day he sat in prison increased the authority of the commune that framed him with its coercive symbols. Public execution

---

358. *Ibid.*, I, 384; C. Lupi, "Nuovi Documenti," 75f.

359. Gherardi, *Nuovi Documenti*, 263; Lupi, "Nuovi Documenti," 76.

360. That is, $3 \times 10 = 30$; Landucci, 175. On the rumors, Gherardi, *Nuovi Documenti*, 255ff. Note also that the government purportedly used the trial to gain the support of the duke of Milan: "It did not dare kill" Savonarola, said a Venetian diplomat, until the duke had read and approved the trial; Sanuto, I, 947, 955.

361. One counselor did suggest life imprisonment, however, during which the friar could continue to inspire Christians with his writing; Ridolfi, *Vita . . . Savonarola*, I, 397.

362. The condition is printed in Gherardi, *Nuovi Documenti*, 265.

363. *Ibid.*, 231, 234, 236, 242ff.

was the supreme test of this growing authority; it was a decisive ritual means for forcing the populace to participate in the new order. This was the function and, in part, the purpose of the Florentine imprisonment and execution of Girolamo Savonarola. When the friar was arrested, a shaky and uncertain government held him amidst a surly populace. When he was sacrificed for the new order, a stronger executive and a different society had been constituted around the pyre, "from good to better, and with manifest sign of the reintegration and union of the citizens."[364]

The form and content of this modified processional society incorporated long-term trends in Florentine history even as the new government insisted it had returned to original republic purity. A personal political charisma of the Lorenzan and Savonarolan stamp, for example, proved irresistible. In the five years after the friar's execution a large number of rituals specifically designed to ridicule Savonarola were played out in the city, leaving no doubt that the citizens could not let the dead prophet lie. A charismatic political personality was now a rooted flash point of civic identity. There was no turning back to the anonymous civism of the past, and it did not take long for government itself to recognize this, and change its structure.[365] Accordingly, in 1502 the city decided to convert its highest office of Standard Bearer of Justice into a life appointment, and quickly surrounded the first tenant of that exalted station, Piero Soderini, with many of the accoutrements of official charisma long current among the doges of Venice.[366] If Florence was not to be led by a Magnificent *giovane* or a divine prophet, it seemed, it had to adopt the sacred political institutions of noble Venice.

The social composition of the Florentine procession also changed in the years after Savonarola's execution, in such a way as to affect both the visibility of marginal groups in public life and the position of the adult political males. Perhaps the increased evidence for the activity of the neighborhood festive groups called *potenze* is most interesting. They had grown under Medici patronage in the later part of the fifteenth century, suffered an eclipse during the rigorous Savonarolan period, to appear again after the friar's death. The *potenze*, as they are called from 1517 on, are now better documented. They are now mentioned by name in the narrative sources, and the classical groups of the sixteenth century can be identified.[367] Their patronage is also clearer, and it is characteristic of the political order as a whole. The *potenze* responded no longer to the will of only one family, but to those of the several Florentine clans that dreamed of inheriting the mantle of the Medici in this late republican, protoabsolutistic age. Increasingly disdaining their merchant heritage, these families used the different *potenze* to their own political ends, openly vaunting their individual families' honor. Such at least seems to be the use to which they were put between the Lorenzan age and the later Medicean age,

---

364. Characterization dated Apr. 21, 1498; *ibid.*, 244.

365. Trexler, "De la Ville à la Cour."

366. The ceremony was studied on page 337, this volume.

367. The *potenze* of Monteloro and of Melarancia are mentioned for the first time in 1501 by Cambi; for an analysis, see my "De la Ville à la Cour."

when that family again assumed the *potenze*'s unitary patronage. Much remains to be learned about the early history of the *potenze*, but it is already clear that as one marginal group in Florentine society, the *fanciulli*, was disgraced, another tended to move toward the center.

There is no doubt that a decisive element of the new processional order was the relative unimportance of boys in its midst. Not only did the Savonarolan organization of boys by quarter disappear, and with it their moral policing, but the boys of the traditional confraternities appeared in Florentine processions less frequently after their leaders' death.[368] They lost their central role in communal ritual, and clergy and laymen reassumed their dominant places. The execution of Savonarola represented an attempt to turn away from that type of personal charisma that had no base in Florentine governmental institutions; it also destroyed the claim of the innocent generation to speak for the commune.

Innocence had had its day and then forced its own martyrdom. In the long twilight of republican Florence, citizens had hoped to save their families and the old commune through making ritual figures of their children, who were the more effective and affective because they had not hurt anyone. They had combined this ritualization of their progeny first with a veneration of young Lorenzo de' Medici, who had not hurt anyone, and then by their worship of Savonarola, who was outside the communal identity. They were its fulcrum: immune yet dependent, illegitimate yet sanctioned by outside authority.

The age of innocence had now passed and, as in the funeral service where society kills the deceased so as to redefine the community, so in 1498 public martyrdom and human sacrifice were meant to bring to fruition a renaissance of the adult political males. Taking the blood of the martyr upon themselves, these men thought to cleanse the city of a nightmare of juvenility and vision. "Let us laden everything that is bad on this friar," said one counselor, "and rid the city of it all."[369]

---

368. An appearance of three *compagnie di fanciulli* is documented on Corpus Christi, 1522; Trexler, *Libro*, 129.

369. Ridolfi, *Vita . . . Savonarola*, I, 398.

Chapter 13

The Charismatic Center: Holy Father and Virile Youth

*Magistrates are not merchants.**

*So moved is this popolo, there is nothing but
devotion, procession, etc.*†

*The gioventù, who have their arms in hand, are
saying publicly and to a man that they will cut
even their own fathers to pieces if they would
consent to a condition inconsonant with freedom.*‡

*Anyone up high would have said: "Florence
burns, the whole city. . . ."*§

W e seek serenity after a storm, and rulers promise to
provide it though they, like their subjects, are the children of tempest. So it
was in Florence from Savonarola's death until the end of the republic in 1530.
In 1502 Piero Soderini was made Standard Bearer of Justice for life, a quasi-
signorial position unique in the constitutional history of the republic. Yet
Soderini's unprecedented official charisma did not prevent him from posturing as the restorer of old institutions.[1] After the Medici returned and expelled
Soderini in 1512, Giovanni de' Medici won the papacy, probably the first
Florentine to do so, yet Leo X would also say he only reformed his beloved
city. From 1527 until 1530, finally, the young men of Florence rose up against
the Medici and their fathers in the name of ancient Florentine purity. But who
could imagine *giovani* in politics as a restorative force? The fact was that the
ritual revolution continued, and there was no turning back to the *modo usato*,

*Oration of the youth Pierfilippo Pandolfini during the Last Republic; Busini, 63.

†Report to Venice during the Last Republic; Sanuto, LIII, 172.

‡Venetian ambassadorial report during the Last Republic; *Le Relazioni degli Ambasciatori Veneti al Senato*, ed.
E. Albèri, ser. II, tome 1 (Florence, 1859), 230.

§Report on the fires celebrating the election of Leo X in 1513; Landucci, 337.

1. On the debate whether Soderini was a "sincere"   Aspiring Prince or Civic Leader," *Studies in Medieval*
republican or not, see R. Cooper, "Pier Soderini: *and Renaissance History*, n.s. I (1978), 67–126.

or to the old actors. The present chapter brings to a conclusion the story of Florence's thrust toward a legitimate charismatic center.

Trust, honor, and credit, it is true, remained the basic requirements of civil life, and public exchange was still the primary means by which these values were created, maintained, and transformed. Public ceremony still played its part in expressing and forming political realities. The Florentine cosmology as well, the principles behind the processes by which inhabitants shaped the times, places, and objects that weakened and cemented bonds, persisted through these troubled times. Yet the specific times, spaces, and objects through which men competed and contracted, the ways in which they exchanged, and, most fundamentally, the identity of those who engaged in public exchange, continued to undergo important modifications.

It would be mere sloganing to brand this ritual process of the early sixteenth century a transition from republican to grand ducal forms. The period had a unity of its own in the midst of process, and we shall study this epoch so as to isolate that unity. This approach can also serve to highlight the changes Florentine public forms had undergone during the later fifteenth century. This chapter will describe three phases of the period after 1512 in terms of the three principal types of ritual: diplomatic, celebratory, and crisis. In the first phase the diplomatic behavior of the mid-1510s commands our attention, as it did that of contemporaries. We will examine the formal entries of this period, the festivities surrounding significant events abroad, and the ritual of the bestowal of the baton upon the captain-general of the republic. The second phase extends to 1527. Here the domestic celebrations of this period were and will be the focus of attention, with particular notice being given to the fate of the Florentine festive calendar, to the changes in the feast of St. John, and to the continuing incorporation of marginal groups into the city's festive identity. Finally, we shall look at the very different ritual of crisis developed by the commune when, after having expelled the Medici and granted unprecedented power and influence to its *giovani* in 1527, it withstood a long military siege until late 1530.

Inspired by its youth, the Last Republic made a final, desperate attempt to create an honorable and equal political order. The Medici Holy Fathers had brought the commune honors in abundance, but in doing so had subjected the political class. Now as citizen-soldiers, the *giovani* entered the official processional center for the first time. In this last fleeting moment of republican Florence, men could believe their commune was honorable through its military self-defense, yet equal because the youth were socialized. The collapse of this heroic attempt meant the final demise of the republic.

Diplomacy

Florence [speaks]: "Thanks to you I am raised up. For under you as my parent, I foresee [my] rule over land, sea, and air."[2]

2. Caption on a Roman festive representation celebrating the election of Leo X; Sanuto, XVI, 164.

The dominant fact of the ritual of diplomacy during this period was that Florentines rather than foreigners, the Medici instead of Milanese, Spaniards, or Germans, were ceremonially welcomed into the city. Historically a focal point of Florentine civic identity, the state entry was a procedure by which citizens judged their standing in the world and through which they organized themselves. Now this ritual became an instrument by which the first family, so great abroad, substituted itself for foreigners as a sufficient charismatic source at home. For the first time, the gates of Florence were a stage for an almost purely domestic ritual, a focus for the expression of internal order around domestic ritual objects. At the edge of the city the Medici tried to rule its heart, and the citizens either applauded or resisted the Magian monarchs.

The importance of Medicean behavior at the gates of the city was apparent from that moment in 1512 when youthful philo-Mediceans forced Piero Soderini to leave the city and invited the Medici to return from exile.[3] How would these darlings of the international community and of many Florentines choose to enter? The past offered the three leaders of the family both guidelines and options. As private persons, Giuliano di Lorenzo il Magnifico and the twenty-one-year-old Lorenzo di Piero del Magnifico found no precedent for any but the most anonymous of entrances. The cardinal legate Giovanni di Lorenzo, on the other hand, could claim the right to an official entry. It had been as a Roman dignitary that he had received diplomatic honors in March and May, 1492, the first entries of triumphal scope ever accorded a Florentine citizen.[4]

The particular circumstances, however, offered the Medici an option that went beyond the realm of law and custom. Since they were the masters of Florence, they might have entered the city with a total disregard for past constitution and present sensibilities. Here was the time, many thought, for the Medici to revenge the humiliations the family and its supporters had been subjected to. Now the inhabitants of Florence could be forced to honor the Medici as returning heroes. This was the optimal moment, in short, for that politics of force that one historian believes was characteristic of the postexilic Medici.[5] The Medici could have done as they pleased.

Instead, all three men respected civil forms. Chroniclers noted that Giuliano and Lorenzo entered the city "like citizens"; that both donned the somber coats or *lucchi* that were proper to their citizenship and to their age; once in the city, Giuliano proceeded to the Palazzo della Signoria to formally beg the Signoria to rescind its decree banishing family members.[6] Observers

3. A perceptive account of events is in J. Pitti, "Dell' Istoria Fiorentina," *ASI*, I (1842), 103f. Important details on the events are also in a letter of Bernardo da Bibbiena in Sanuto, XV, 57ff.

4. See page 456, this volume; Trexler, *Libro*, 97; and further on May 1494 in Picotti, *Giovinezza*, 381ff.

5. Gilbert, *Machiavelli and Guicciardini*, 130f.

6. "Not without some people laughing," Pitti adds, "at the idea that someone who had been the head of the city for sixty years, returning home with arms and

with the support of partisans after eighteen years of exile, would sit still for a diminution of his old authority"; J. Pitti, "Dell'Istoria," 103f; Cambi, XXI, 308–311; Landucci, 325; Paoli, in Rinuccini, clxxi; Nardi, V, 26, 53, 56. A letter from Ferrara says, erroneously, that Giuliano entered "con tanto triumpho che più non posso scrivere per non esser capaze"; Sanuto, XV, 30 (Sept. 4, 1512). On the mass of "friends" who greeted Giuliano at the Medici palace, however, see the eyewitness report *ibid.*, XV, 57ff, especially Bernardo da Bibbiena's measure of the returning Medi-

were no less interested in the entrance of the cardinal legate on September 14: Giovanni di Lorenzo refused the formal legatine procession that was his right, demurred at being accompanied to his residence by the official delegation of citizens, and turned back the same delegation when it came to accompany him to the Signoria the following morning.[7] Instead, the cardinal entered with a retinue of foreign men-at-arms and, though willing in legatine fashion to receive official visitors and gifts at the Medici palace, he nonetheless postponed visiting the Palace of the Signoria until the night of the fifteenth, "so as to have less ceremony."[8] Doubtless such a ritual stance was ambiguous, as were most formal presentations. Just as certainly, however, the victorious Medici understood the importance of their public behavior, and were determined to restrain their ritual claims upon the citizenry. This would cement rather than endanger their future in Florence.

In the coming years, Florence's traditional civic forms and procedures would continue to restrict the actions and thus the power of the Medici, even as they offered the family the possibility of enhancing that power. The ritual scene had always been a theater for testing individual in relation to communal identity. The paradox was as old as the republic itself: Although republican Florence always suspected and feared the representation of familial or individual charisma as a threat to the group rule of the political oligarchy, the city also needed the self-respect at home and honor abroad the Medici so clearly brought to the city. Lorenzo the Magnificent had first proposed an identity between himself and the commune. In 1513 the proposition was raised to a new level when the son of Lorenzo became the pope of Rome. The news caused wild celebration in Florence. It seemed that from now on, Florence would be but a creature of Medicean Rome.

There was no disputing the historic significance of March 11, 1513, the day the news of the election reached Florence. Men spoke ecstatically of the commercial promise of Leo's election, for now Florentine merchants could tap the great market of the curia under the wing of their fellow citizen; the pope's inexhaustible credit was now theirs.[9] Since Italians traditionally ascribed a pope's sacral nature to his family, the Florentines understood as well the impact the election would have on the authority of the Medici family. Entering Siena on his way to Rome for the coronation, the pope's brother was

cean's support among the Florentines: "E 'l bello era che noi da tutti eravamo conosciuti et ci chiamavano per nome, et noi pochissimi et quasi nessuno conosciavamo." On this ritual measure through unknowns who care, see page 428, this volume. Finally, note the Venetian ambassador's ritual measure of Giuliano's authority in a letter written six months later: "Li par magnifico Juliano sia signor di Fiorenza; sempre la sua anticamera e la camera è piena di cittadini, e cussì la camera dil cardinal: e quello voleno, fano. Il magnifico ogni matina va a palazo, e à driedo sempre da 100 citadini"; Sanuto, XV, 572ff (Feb. 19, 1513).

7. Cambi, XXI, 323f. On the diplomatic anticipation

as to the way Giovanni would enter: "Non sapea s'il dovea intrar come legato dil Papa over come cardinal semplice"; Sanuto, XV, 34 (letter of early September).

8. "Et disse, v'andre' di notte, per mancho cirimonie, et chosì fecie"; Cambi, 324. Yet according to Cambi the cardinal later used legatine rights "deceptively," visiting the Palace in order to seize control of it; *ibid.*

9. "In Firenze, della creazione del Papa si fece quella festa che si può stimare; e perchè li Fiorentini sono dediti alla mercatura ed al guadagno, tutti pensavano dovere trarre profitto di questo pontificata"; "Sommario della Storia d'Italia dal 1511 al 1527 composto da Francesco Vettori," *ASI, Appendice* VI (1848), 300.

received, as one gratified Florentine coppersmith recorded, "as if a great *signore*," and when Giuliano di Lorenzo reached Rome, Bartolomeo Masi added, he was welcomed "as if . . . the first lord of Italy."[10] Finally, contemporaries grasped the fact that this election represented a culmination of sorts in the search for Florentine identity. Now there could be no more talk of ignoble Florence, no longer a want of trust, honor, and credit at the heart of a republic *sub sigillo pescatoris*. A Florentine product had been transformed into a man–god![11]

Florentine flesh had been made Word, and the chroniclers reported the event in spiritual terms as if to show that Florence, like Giovanni de' Medici, had passed from a lower to a higher state. Landucci heralded the spiritual quality of the election by announcing that Florentines knew the news before it reached them: "Without knowing anything . . . , it seemed that the *popolo* had divined what had taken place, which was a wondrous thing. For the proverb is true:'Voice of the people, voice of God.' "[12] Bartolomeo Masi started and ended his account of the celebration with equally edifying statements:

> He was thirty-seven years old, and was created and made our pontiff peacefully and in holiness, as one ought to create and make a good pastor. . . .
> This came from nothing else than his fine reputation and his goodness, for [the election] was not at all done with simony or with other extortions, as had been the case with others at other times.[13]

And though a Savonarolan, Giovanni Cambi also wanted to believe in a triumph of Florentine honor and spirituality:

> God give him grace to govern the church well, for the honor of God, the salvation of his soul, and the good of his city of Florence, since he is the first Florentine pontiff, and was created with the grace of God, and without simony.[14]

Thus the city that, "crazy with happiness," set about organizing a three-day celebration of the news of the papal election "so as to feast and delight our pontiff," was a spiritual center. During this new age of diplomatic ritual, it could celebrate itself while participating in its fellow citizen's foreign glory.[15] Recognizably similar to past celebrations of this type, the election festivities that started on March 13 were different because they did not have to tailor their expressions of joy to avoid offending third parties. The Medici pope was, after all, the center of all Christendom. A joyous, unrestrained narcissism marks the four dominant events in this celebration.

---

10. Masi, 127f.

11. The theme of apotheosis of city and man is found in all the doggerel poetry of the time, as, for example, in Trexler, *Libro*, 55, 131ff; Singleton, "Literature," 44 seq. For Dei's image of Florence making Leo, see Picotti, *Giovinezza*, 17, 96.

12. *Diario*, 336.

13. *Ricordanze*, 119, 122.

14. *Istorie*, XXII, 6f.

15. The citations are from Masi, 120, 122. On the formal representation of "crazy" spontaneity, see page 283, this volume.

In the form of fagots, rockets, sparklers, and artillery, festive fires covered the city of Florence as they had never done before. The minute the news arrived, for example, youth started to tear down shop roofs so as to fuel great bonfires in the Mercato Nuovo, and it was the opinion of one chronicler that they would have dismantled the fronts of shops and houses if the government had not put a stop to the destruction on the morning of March 12.[16] The desire to burn was not, however, a mere excess of the youth, but an activity of all segments of the population. While fireworks lit the Piazza della Signoria and the palaces of Medicean partisans, the simplest men seized what was at hand and consumed it in flames:

> One burned innumerable fagots of brooms, sticks, baskets, barrels, and anything the poorest man had in his house. . . . It was an incredible thing, the number of fires there were in the city. The poorest creature had a fire at his door. . . . Anyone who had been up high would have said. "Florence burns, the whole city."[17]

Festive fires speak to men's general ability to destroy and be reborn, and a contemporary poem in describing the torching of a *girandola* called to mind the myth of Prometheus.[18] This city on fire was in fact, however, eradicating a very specific past in the interest of a definite future, and the Medici made sure this was well understood. Masi told how on three successive evenings, *trionfi* first of Discord, then of War, and finally of Fear were rolled through the streets up to the Medici palace and, after a chorus had sung a conjurative song, how each was burned until it was completely consumed.[19] These "beautiful" "gentilities," done *per magnificenze* (Masi), were then followed by a fourth *trionfo* of Peace, which, as the diarist Landucci pointed out, was not burned: "as if an end had been put to passions, leaving peace and triumphs."[20] The Medici seized the occasion, therefore, to drive home the specific myth of their first postexilic reign: Death had come with the passing of the Magnificent; purgatory was reflected in the city's long suffering while the Medici were in exile; their resurrection, in the person of the Magnificent's heirs, would reconcile the city.[21]

Thus these festive fires were more than a mere literary exercise of the Medicean intelligentsia. In a palpable fashion, the city itself helped destroy the old world, and we can see this in a second event of these festive days, the visual and aural transformation of the city. The historian Cambi tells us that the simplest citizens demonstrated their allegiance to the Medici by placing the family's coat of arms over their front doors. Public officials followed suit,

16. Landucci, 336f; also Masi, 120.

17. Landucci, 336f.

18. Guasti, *Feste*, 36.

19. Masi, 121.

20. Landucci, 337; also Masi, 122. This may be the date on which, as indicated on page 417, this volume, the Song of the Lovers of Peace was sung.

21. Much of the documentation for this idea is gathered in Trexler and Lewis, "Two Captains," where the New Sacristy of Michelangelo, titled *Of the Resurrection*, is placed in the more general context of Medici history. On the theme of the Golden Age, see Vasari–Milanesi, VI, 754; E. Gombrich, *Norm and Form. Studies in the Art of the Renaissance* (London, 1978), 29–34.

covering the civic coat of arms, the lilies of Florence, with the Medici balls (*palle*). Indeed, the horrified Cambi reported, the proud *palle* were to be found covering the very crucifixes of the churches![22] To accompany this astounding visual transformation of ritual space, there came an aural novelty. The Medicean cry of *Palle!* was on every lip, Cambi noted, and the traditional civil cry of *Marzocco!* could scarcely be heard, its utterance almost a challenge to the new Medicean order.[23] Though civic signs and sounds reappeared after these celebrations, they would be covered again in 1515 when the new pope visited his native city.[24] Florentines were ripe to accept a new civil banner. The celebration of the papal election had generated an amazing degree of civil identification with the Medici.

Within this city purged by fire, whose turrets and facades sported the ubiquitous *palle* as if they alone bound citizens together, the Medici palace became a ritual center in which to enact the great civil peace this family promised. In a third important event of these days, the prisons were opened and exiles were permitted to return to the city. A favor that the republic of Florence had once denied to an emperor because only communal laws could rightfully effect an amnesty from prison, it now conceded to the first family.[25] Most important, the Soderini family and its allies were returned to the city. This was an expression of confidence and liberality that made a deep impression on the Florentines: "Everyone says that there had never been a *magnificienza* as great as this one in the name of the Holiness of Our Lord Leo X."[26] "Good news," Cambi exulted, "with which [the families] could make peace with each other."[27] As in the early fourteenth century, when visiting foreign princes had reconstructed the commune through similar acts of amnesty and recommunication, so now the Medici assumed the task. And as if to seal the amity, a great wave of gift giving swept the city. This is the final occurrence that deserves our attention.

From the palaces of Medicean intimates, joyous politicos tossed enormous amounts of food, coin, and clothing to the crowds. For days on end inhabitants came to the Medici palace with flasks and baskets to vie for the mass of wine and bread, "nothing being said to anyone" who took these foods home to fill the larder.[28] Some 10,000 ducats in coin came tumbling down by the handful, the sack, and by the goblet, and the chronicler was careful to note that Giuliano di Lorenzo, Giulio di Giuliano, and their sisters and cousins took a direct part in disposing of their wealth.[29] Finally, the Medici threw a quantity of Giuliano's clothing to the crowd—types of secon-

22. Cambi, XXII, 48f, 73; XXIII, 8. On the Medici arms on SS. Annunziata, see Vasari–Milanesi, VI, 247f.

23. Cambi, XXIII, 8. At the time of the Pazzi conspiracy, however, Rinuccini noticed that *Palle!* was used rather than *Marzocco!*; Rinuccini, cxxviii.

24. See page 499, this volume.

25. On the refusal to Frederick III, see page 309, this volume.

26. Masi, 122; also Cambi, XXII, 8.

27. *Ibid.*

28. Masi, 122.

29. "E sopradetti danari ne gittava più persone: cioè ne gittava quando el magnifico Giuliano e quando messer Giulio, frategli del Papa, e quando loro sorelle e quando loro nipoti; e venivono alle finestre"; *ibid.*, 121.

dary relics from this brother of the pope and thus enchanted. Cambi chose this occasion to list all the relatives of Pope Leo he knew, as if they all gave themselves to the Florentines. "It would be a stupendous task," said Masi, "to narrate the magnificence and *festa* they made."[30]

The Medici had given a party, and everyone came. As the chroniclers took care to note, rich as well as poor, citizen but also noncitizen, celebrated the family. Florence partook of Medicean largess with an equality of distribution that is characteristic of absolutism: "Before one of the aforesaid goblets reached the ground, twenty-five hands went up, and it never left these hands until twenty-five pieces had been made of it."[31]

Still, this same total population gave as well as received, trading its support in exchange for the family's wealth. Contemporaries were aware that these great displays formed and tested the Florentines' adhesion to the papal family. What, after all, was the background to this great potlatch that had ended by sealing a new polity? Cambi tells us that the populace might have sacked the Medici palace (a common procedure in monarchical Rome on such occasions) if the family had not locked it up the minute the news of Leo's election arrived.[32] The magnificent largess that the Medici threw from this secured fortress was, therefore, a form of ersatz pillage that at once recognized the people's right to the family property, tested the order in a social fabric based on such exchange, and measured the good will of the Medici *and* their devotees.[33]

The celebration of the new pope's election illustrated the transformation of the ritual by which great foreign events were celebrated in Florence; the visit of Pope Leo to Florence in late 1515 and early 1516 shows the nature of entrance rituals under the sixteenth-century Medici. Earlier popes had been received in order to fill the city with the ennobling charisma of foreign nobles, but on this great occasion, Florence could show the world its own charisma. What was that? Was Florence distinct from the Medicean power and authority? No longer swept up in the euphoria of Leo's election, the commune in late 1515 would be more troubled by the Roman connection, and more determined to preserve its identity apart from the Medici, than it had earlier been.

If ever there were to be an occasion on which this ancient republic might think itself "proud and lordly" without anxiety over its lowly station, if ever it was to demonstrate to the world the "perfection of the work and the so unmeasured cost" of its public life, Florence had that right and opportunity during the visit of its native son Giovanni de' Medici.[34] The city had to be transformed into the worthy home of a spiritual monarch and, with incredible speed, the artisans set about converting all the material and artistic genius of a people into festive reality. The overhanging roofs and protruding stairs of the

30. Masi, 121; Cambi, XXII, 10f.

31. Masi, 121.

32. "In chasa e' Medici non si lasciavano entrare se non ciptadini amici loro, per paura di non andare a

saccho, chome si chostuma a Roma"; Cambi, XXII, 7.

33. On this type of exchange with the threat of sacking, see page 475, this volume.

34. The terms are Landucci's, 355, 353.

old city were destroyed: "Nothing was spared; they smashed things to pieces without moderation."[35] And a new, more beautiful city arose from these ashes. None but Florence could have brought this about, the diarist Landucci claimed: "No other city or lordship in the world could have done [this] or known how . . . it would have been difficult for any city to do."[36]

Yet what was the festive ideal Florence created, if not a semblance of Rome, whose monarchic charisma Florence had always envied? Carried aloft by a contingent of Florentine *giovani*, covered by a baldachin with *drappelloni* that "had no other coats of arms but those of the pontiff," as an observer noticed who was anxious to see if the pontiff preferred particular Florentine families, the returning son saw that his native town had been converted into a Medicean eternal city.[37] As in the celebrations of 1513, the *palle* covered every available urban space, but now many of these spaces had been transformed into a place in Rome. From the gate of San Piero Gattolino to the old papal quarters at Santa Maria Novella, Pope Leo passed under some twelve triumphal arches—apparently the first such festive arches the Florentines had ever erected for a visitor—and each was an imitation of a triumphal arch in Rome. One, for example, honored him as a laborer for Christianity; another showed him as a Florentine lion licking the wounds of the city's civil strife.[38] The most interesting legend has already been mentioned. It decorated a triumphal arch in the quarter of Santo Spirito, and featured a painting of the pope's father looking down on the papal presence beneath and saying, as had God the Father: "This is my beloved son."[39] Interspersed with these arches were copies of other well-known Roman monuments like the obelisk and Trajan's column, and the papal ceremonialist recorded each of them with its counterpart.[40] It is true that the Roman character of the pope's entry cannot be understood merely in terms of the Florentine experience, for Roman architectural copies were used in Rome itself and in other cities when a pope visited.[41] But the entry cannot be understood without Florence either. For to make this native son feel at home, burgher Florence surrounded him with the spaces and things of imperial Rome.

Revel though they might in the Roman authority the pope brought with him, the Florentines still feared the threat his visit posed to their independence. Through it the Medici family could gain almost princely authority, and

35. *Ibid.*, 359.

36. *Ibid.*, 353.

37. "Con l'arme del sopradetto ponteficie in ogni drappellone, e non v'era nessuna altra arme"; Masi, 165. Also Landucci, 352; Cambi, XXII, 87; Sanuto, XXI, 374f.

38. An anonymous source, cited in Moreni, *De Ingressu*, 9ff. The painting of the lion was on an arch at the Canto de' Carnesecchi, that to the "fidei cultori" at the Badia Fiorentina. New documentation on these contraptions is printed and glossed by J. Shearman, "The Florentine *Entrata* of Leo X, 1515," *Journal of the Warburg and Courtauld Institutes* XXXVIII (1975), 144–

153; see the bibliography on the entrance in Mitchell, *Italian Civic Pageantry*, 39–43.

39. The arch at S. Felice in Piazza, "dove era l'imagine di Lorenzo suo Padre con un verso, che diceva: "Hic est filius meus dilectus"; *ibid.*

40. "Et inter arcum et arcum erant variae structurae similes illis quae videntur in urbe Rome, videlicet obeliscus sicut in Vaticano, columna sicut in Campo Martio"; *ibid.* See also the descriptions in Landucci, 353f.

41. See, for example, the description "degli archi triumphali" made in Rome for Leo's coronation; Sanuto, XVI, 162–166.

the papacy itself could increase its power in Florence. Thus even as the pope moved through Roman festive spaces, the government of Florence put into action a policy of ritual distancing that it had adopted to counter the seemingly irresistible charisma of the Medici pope. To the chagrin of many curialists, the commune of Florence would maintain a distinct face in all its contacts with the papal party.

We first notice this policy of sovereign ceremonialism at the gates of the city. The papal master of ceremonies Paride de' Grassi demanded that the government of Florence offer Leo the keys to the city; he was rebuffed, for as always the commune would do no more than dismantle the gate for a pope.[42] When during his stay Leo prepared to visit the church of San Lorenzo so as to pray at the tomb of his father, the curialist Grassi wanted the government to accompany the pope; instead, the Signoria went directly to the church and awaited the papal arrival.[43] Finally, Grassi ordered the Signoria on several occasions to tip their caps and stand when the cardinals passed; the government uniformly refused to do so.[44]

The papal master of ceremonies was enraged by the "insupportable misery with which the Florentine *popolo* persecuted curialists, as if they were enemies," but the pope himself was more astute.[45] Long-term Medicean family interests made it dangerous to conflate the family with the papacy, he must have reasoned, and thus the identity of the commune of Florence had to remain distinct and separate from that of the papacy. Leo pointedly reminded Grassi that the Florentines should not be required to carry banners out to meet him, for that was proper only to subject towns in the Papal States.[46] Just as cautiously, the pope avoided putting himself or his family forward as a temporal lord of the city, and when he presented the government with a ceremonial sword to commemorate his stay, he publicly avowed that he offered it to the Signoria "as to his fellow citizens."[47] In the course of his visit to his native town, Pope Leo X accepted the honors his fellow citizens paid him because of his official status abroad, yet respected the restraints which a probing ritual of welcome imposed on him.[48] The ritual of visitation affirmed, and formed, the specific strength of the Medici–Florentine relationship.

Indoctrinated as they were with Savonarolan ideas, and more keenly aware now than they had been earlier of the price Florence paid for its papal son, *piagnoni* historians like Luca Landucci betrayed an ambivalent, troubled attitude toward the enormous display the city staged. Was it worth it?

> Know that I haven't written a tenth of what one could say and what I saw. And remember that for more than a month we had more than an estimated two thousand men at work—woodworkers, masons, painters, wagons, porters, sawers, and diverse trades—such that one figured a cost of 70,000 florins or more on these perishable

42. Moreni, *De Ingressu*, 7.

43. *Ibid.*, 27.

44. *Ibid.*, 5ff, 28.

45. *Ibid.*, 41, also 44f.

46. *Ibid.*, 5.

47. *Ibid.*, 29f.

48. For Leo's caution, see Albertini, *Staatsbewusstsein*, 35ff; also R. Devonshire Jones, *Francesco Vettori* (London, 1972), 136, 139f.

things that pass like shadows, which could have built a most beautiful temple to honor God and [given] glory to the city. Still, the poor artisans made good use of the earnings, for money was spread about somewhat.[49]

Landucci's assessment seemed to be that, on balance, ceremonies used wealth rather than created it. Yet there was a value created by this visit without which the city would be poorer; this was the sheer beauty of these arches and obelisks and false facades, itself a product of the genius of Florence's artisans. Landucci mourned their passing when they had to be taken down later: "So much did it please the eye, that one sorrowed to see it dismantled, these marvelous figures of good masters."[50]

This was as if to acknowledge that Florence's temporal achievements, all the things this city that aimed to please could do in an instant, were but fleeting moments in the affairs of men. Florence alas was not Rome, where the monuments were real, but was increasingly a mere "theater" of pretensions.[51] Did Landucci regret just a fake facade, or were his words an epitaph for a city whose genius only proved its impotence? Could the city withstand a European nobility that merely used the city to paint its sets? There were more foreigners in Florence, it seemed to one diarist of the celebrations of this decade, than there were Florentines.[52] Perhaps Florence, so zealous to consume foreign honor, was itself being consumed by these visiting Medici.

The acid test of such an eventuality would be the success of Lorenzo di Piero de' Medici and not the pope, a resident Medici and not his distant uncle, in using diplomatic ritual to alter Florentine identity. Who more than this private person could gain from the family's official stature, who was more likely to exacerbate the fears of distrustful Florentines than this arrogant young man? For Giovanni Cambi, Lorenzo was the son of a father "without civility" who, having grown up more a Roman Orsini than a Florentine, returned to Florence in 1512 "not used to civility, and thus aspiring to arms and dominion."[53] Cambi's evidence for this characterization was of course behavioral in nature. In his palace this unpleasant *giovane* maintained a group of "satellites and adulators" who "showed [Lorenzo] reverence" in courtly fashion. Perhaps these cronies called him *Magnifico* in public, Cambi conceded, but in private they addressed him as *padrone*.[54] Lorenzo had a personal chancellor from Pistoia named Goro di Gheri, our historian continues, who though a foreigner from "as low a family as possible" received a public adulation from Lorenzo's citizen-clients that was difficult for republicans to stomach:

49. Landucci, 359.

50. *Ibid.*, 355, also 356.

51. Interestingly, one of the creations for the entrance was called by a communal scribe the "teatro facto alla Chiesa di S. Trinita," that is in that church's square, but by the anonymous a "tondo tempio"; respectively Landucci, 354, n. 2; Moreni, *De Ingressu*,

9ff. Masi compared it to Hadrian's Tomb; 167. On the artists involved, see P. Minucci Del Rosso, "Curiosità Artistiche," *ASI*, ser. 4, III (1869), 472–482; C. von Holst, *Francesco Granacci* (Munich, 1974), 47f, 216f.

52. Masi, 144 (1514).

53. Cambi, XX, 27; XXII, 67.

54. *Ibid.*, 49f.

> At least three or four citizens accompanied him, then behind them [came] as many *giovani*, plus three or four familiars. And they lifted their hats when he passed, although such a thing was condemned by many. Since except for magistrates it was not the custom in the city to tip one's hat to any other citizen no matter how great he was reputed. And [Pistoia] was a land subject to Florence! Nor did [Goro] have any office![55]

Poor Florentines, who had so lost their dignity. Sad city, Cambi thought, whose gates in 1514 had to witness the haughty departure of Lorenzo for Rome with his uncle Giuliano. Ever the good citizen, the latter left quietly from his villa outside the city, but the former prepared an army of buffoons, hunting partners, and some 200 dogs to accompany him, so that "he really appeared a prince and nephew of the pope." Before Lorenzo left the Medici palace a group of citizens came to pay their respects: "All of them tipped their hats a little . . . , and such a thing had never been done in Florence to a private citizen."[56] This was the young man who, on August 15, 1515, received the military baton of the commune of Florence. In all previous Florentine history, only foreign field marshals had held the baton, and they had come to Florence for the ceremony; now for the first time, a Florentine assumed this office. The republicans of Florence feared the results.

In the ritual of the *presa di bastone*, the city legitimated a military authority it feared. Without such an office the commune was defenseless and without honor. Yet, as counselors pointed out in deliberating the matter in 1515, with it the Florentines assumed grave risks, especially when the condottiere was a native. The Romans had lost their freedom by bestowing military authority upon citizens, as had scores of medieval Italian towns.[57] Nevertheless the pope had decided to grant Lorenzo's wish to hold that office, and the counselors had to go along. The manner in which Lorenzo accepted the command, therefore, became of paramount importance. Would the papal nephew take the baton as a communal gift, or as a right? Once Lorenzo had that baton, could the city of Florence preserve its civil order?

The diarists who recorded the event were generally reassured by what they saw. True, Lorenzo showed definite signs of a disregard for traditional mores, refusing as would the pope four months later to be accompanied by mantled citizens to the *ringhiera*, which was a traditional recognition that the condottiere was a guest of the city. Instead, he chose to ride at his side a squadron of armed Florentine knights who called themselves, with feudal flourish, the "Barons of the Most Illustrious Captain."[58] Nor did Lorenzo's innovations stop there. At the critical moment when the Standard Bearer of Justice was to hand over the baton to the captain, one of Lorenzo's pages

---

55. *Ibid.*, 157.

56. *Ibid.*, 49f. The comparison of Lorenzo to Giuliano was a standard topos of the time; see especially Masi, 241; Trexler and Lewis, "Two Captains."

57. It is ironic that the Florentine government in charging Lorenzo also cited the *good* things that Roman citizens had accomplished leading Roman militias; A. Georgetti, "Lorenzo de' Medici Capitano Generale della Repubblica Fiorentina," *ASI*, ser. 4, XI (1883), 208.

58. Trexler, *Libro*, 118 (herald's account).

jumped forward and tried to hand it to his master.[59] Lorenzo obviously wanted to play down his dependence on the city.

In the midst of such breaches of decorum, however, observers could see that on balance Lorenzo did show proper respect for the sovereignty of the city:

> The captain sat down between the Standard Bearer of Justice and the Provost. But nevertheless, when the Standard Bearer spoke to him, the captain stood with his hat in hand.[60]
>
> [Lorenzo] said his words, thanking the excellent Signoria and the whole *popolo* for such an honor, promising to fulfill his duty with the greatest care and sincere love.[61]

No contemporary was foolish enough to believe that the Florentine government had been strengthened by Lorenzo's assumption of the baton, of course, and one retrospective view held that this ceremony had all but buried the commune:

> This deprived the city of whatever authority and force remained to it, and conferred so much honor upon [Lorenzo] that it seemed one could not legitimately contradict his will and actions. . . . Many noble Florentine youth who in the past had been soldiers or wanted to pursue this craft were made his gentlemen and bodyguards within diverse types of militia.[62]

In fact, however, Lorenzo's very restraint in the ritual suggests a different interpretation: That ritual, and the office itself, placed limits on the power Lorenzo had hoped to attain through them. Lorenzo's tenure confirms this view. Within three years of this ceremony, the grandson of the Magnificent came to realize that his efforts to establish a lordship in Florence were hampered by the public fashion in which he had submitted to the commune; the captain-generalcy of the Florentine army hurt more than it helped Lorenzo's aspirations. Though dissuaded by his mother, Lorenzo di Piero late in life seriously considered giving up the civic office and trying to rule Florence by other means.[63]

His desperation at achieving his goal through civic office led Lorenzo to a highly imaginative, almost revolutionary departure in the ritual of diplomacy, which summarizes, and frames, the modifications in this ritual we have examined. In late 1518, he decided to cast himself as a foreigner, and have the Florentines welcome him!

The occasion for this remarkable attempt to become a "lord with baton" (*signore a bacchetta*) through ritual means was Lorenzo's return from a private visit to the king of France. Doubtless counting on the authority he derived from his domesticity in the French court, he instructed his chancellor to meet

59. *Ibid.*, 118f.

60. Cambi, XXII, 75.

61. Trexler, *Libro*, 119, where Lorenzo also follows

the custom of the ritual kiss.

62. Niccolò Guicciardini, cited in Albertini, *Staatsbewusstsein*, 356f.

63. Vettori, "Sommario," 328.

with the solidly Medicean government and persuade it to send Florentine ambassadors out to meet him on his return. No Florentine had ever returned from a private trip to an official welcome, least of all one tendered by ambassadors.

Lorenzo's idea was motivationally translucent. He believed he could be welcomed "as if" a foreign lord. Purely in his capacity as a Medici, he could surround himself with the charisma Florentines historically reserved for their foreign betters, and thereby attain unquestioned power in the city. But Lorenzo aborted the ritual test he had arranged because the Florentine government, though led by philo-Mediceans like Lanfredino Lanfredini, steadfastly refused his request. For the historian Cambi, Lanfredini was a hero, "a most reputed, most favored, more practiced and best judge" who, echoing a measure of republican dignity from better times, had opposed the wishes of his master:

> It did not appear to [Lanfredini] that it would be fitting to send ambassadors, since [Lorenzo] was a citizen like the others, even if the first [among them]. [Lorenzo] could do what he wanted with the city if he retained the benevolence of these [citizens].[64]

It was an amazing climax to a history of ceremonial diplomacy that spanned two centuries. The city had long struggled with the difficulties of admitting visiting foreigners, and now found itself resisting a native family's attempts to go out citizens and come in lords. Until the end of the republic, the gates of Florence would be a stage where Florence fought for its identity in relation to that of others. Until the end, the formal life of diplomacy would encourage, yet restrain, the most forceful of suitors for the hand of Lady Florence.

Celebration

> Be sure that the family wins the prize, as it always has in this and other things. I remind you to look outside Florence for men skilled in jousting and its organization. Don't put confidence in the Florentines. Except in matters of articulating, they don't know what they're doing.[65]

> From 1494 until 1512 and then from 1527 to 1530 one used to solemnize the expulsion of the Medici. . . . Now one celebrates the feast of Saints Cosmas and Damian in [the church of] San Lorenzo in their honor.[66]

It is an anonymous chronicler of the 1530s who, when the ashes of the Florentine republic had barely turned to dust, summarized one important trait of the ritual of celebration in the later Florentine republic: Medicean family pomps became the stuff of official joy, even as official civil feasts

64. Cambi, XXII, 150.   Bossi VI (Milan, 1817), 225 (1514).
65. W. Roscoe, *Vita e Pontificato di Leone X*, ed. L.   66. Biagi, "Per la Cronica," 74.

underwent a Medicean personalization. In his accounts of other festivities of this epoch, another anonymous chronicler makes a second crucial observation on the city's domestic celebrations: The *potenze* and *giovani* of Florence now approached the center of Florentine ritual space in their thirst to honor the Medici and be honored by them.[67] The nonpolitical, marginal segments of Florentine society continued their historic march toward festive incorporation. Let us review each of these developments separately.

Our first chronicler recalled previous generations when the family saints brought together only Cosimo's branch of the family, "their close friends and servants, with the associates of their commercial companies and shops."[68] Other Florentines who adopted the cult had worshiped on their own, visiting the chapels of Cosmas and Damian that Cosimo de' Medici set up in the city and provided with divine services.[69] Cosimo had feared the charge of arrogance, and Lorenzo the Magnificent had resisted demands among his followers that the feast be made official; now, the latter's papal son feared no such suspicion. On September 27, 1513, a formal procession made its way to the Medicean parish church of San Lorenzo, with the Signoria of Florence in its train.[70] At the behest of Leo X, the city now honored the saints of its first family.

The Mediceanization of Florentine sacred time soon led to the sacralization of Medici time. As early as 1434 Cosimo had encouraged the celebration of his return from exile by favoring its anniversary on the feast of St. Thomas, and to celebrate his own coeval birthday, Lorenzo the Magnificent had instituted special divine services on the octave of St. Stephen. But only once, in 1458, had the family actually tried to celebrate Medici biography without a justification in the sacred calendar.[71] This latter procedure now became common. From 1514 onward, for example, Florentines streamed to the church of San Lorenzo to celebrate the anniversary of the election of Pope Leo, and similar processions and fireworks were staged after 1523 to record the election of Clement VII de' Medici.[72] Such world historical events were not the only Medicean celebrations to receive an official stamp. Family funerals and weddings became indistinguishable from civic celebrations, since the government of Florence took an active part in them.[73] Even a minor family event could be perpetually commemorated. Thus after visiting his parish church in late 1515 to pray publicly at the tomb of his Magnificent father, Giovanni de' Medici provided a papal indulgence to those who would pray for Lorenzo at San Lorenzo on the anniversaries of that papal visit.[74]

---

67. *Ibid.*, 77 and seq.

68. "Questa festa di S. Cosimo e S. Damiano cominciò da Cosimo Medici privatamente, solo co' loro domestici e famigliari, e co' compagni delle loro ragioni di traffichi e botteghe"; *ibid.*, 73.

69. See page 423, this volume.

70. Cambi, XXII, 31.

71. See page 423, this volume.

72. As traditional in Florence, the celebrations were for "the news of the creation" and not for the creation itself; examples in *ASL*, provisional nn. 2368, f. 104r (1518 celebration of Pope Leo); *ibid.*, 1939⁷, f. 2v (1530 celebration of Pope Clement); see also Biagi, "Per la Cronica," 74f.

73. There are extensive accounts of Giuliano's and Lorenzo's funerals, for example, in both of which the government was represented; Trexler and Lewis, "Two Captains"; Trexler, *Libro*, 124ff.

74. *ASL*, provisional n. 2371, f. 2r (visit of Dec. 2).

European princes had long encouraged their cities to celebrate royal saints, births, and honors as a way of strengthening the contractual and emotive ties of city dwellers with their courts; the Medici actions in this direction, therefore, aped the family's betters. In the sixteenth century, however, these same princes set about a more delicate task, that of dismantling or reorienting the major urban festivals of Europe so as to weaken their chthonic and civic character. In this area of festive polity, the Medici would be in the vanguard.[75] It was not difficult for them to monopolize the Carnival festivals, of course, for we have seen that they had a private patronal character that Lorenzo the Magnificent had already largely monopolized.[76] The great official feast of San Giovanni was another matter, however, and the methods the family used to redirect its civic character require our particular attention. For in the structures, ideology, motivations, and sociology of the feasts of the Baptist from 1513 to 1516, we see a protomonarchic thrust, which yet preserves the competitive and contractual character of an urban festive community. We witness a festival creating a new order, using social forces that could destroy that order.

The San Giovanni feast of 1513 was the first to be celebrated after the return of the Medici, and the new regime promptly tested the strength of the citizens' attachment to tradition by omitting the *edifizi* or biblical floats that were the pride of the city's confraternities and a standard part of the celebration. Criticism of this move on religious grounds was not long in coming, for the absence of the floats robbed the feast of the city patron of one of its central spiritual motifs.[77] In subsequent years they returned, and thereafter remained part of the feasts. Although there is no proof that civic dissatisfaction at their absence was responsible for this reversal, circumstantial evidence does suggest that the *festaioli* had hoped to destroy the *edifizi* because they were associated with republican traditions.

This is evidenced in the one decisive change in the San Giovanni festival during these years: the destruction during the festival of 1514 of the *ceri* with which for centuries the territorial subjects of the commune of Florence had paid their ancient tribute and made their annual oaths of obligation to the city. These colorful painted castles that once children had taunted as they were borne from the Piazza della Signoria to the Baptistry had long since been thought to mar the beauty of that temple, and had not been stored there since 1484. Now they would no longer even be carried there, for the *festaioli* of 1514 kept them in the Piazza della Signoria, where they were destroyed by the children.[78] "Toys of children," the *festaioli* called them, "a disgrace to the feast" so out of step with the finer fashions of the time that they were best used to light "a lovely fire [which would] lend magnificence to the festival."[79]

75. For this process in northern Europe, see the references in the Introduction, this volume.

76. See pages 224 seq., this volume, and for Carnivals of this period, pages 450f.

77. "Cheffù una festa tutta bestiale, et lasciorono stare le feste spirituale, chessi solevano fare per S. Giovanni cerano 4 o 6 edifici bene a hordine di raprexentatione di Santi, in modo, che S. Giovanni era disonorato, et none honorato"; Cambi, XXII, 24.

78. *Ibid.*, XXII, 69; Landucci, 345; Masi, 142.

79. Cited in Guasti, *Feste*, 27f; more on their reputation in Vasari–Milanesi, III, 203 (*Vita* of Cecca).

Though the regime soon promised to build new *ceri* to serve the festival more worthily, the damage was done.[80] The *ceri* were not like the annual *girandola* whose sole purpose was to light the night sky of Florence, but were historic structures that for generations had expressed, and formed, the relations between Florence, its patron, and the dominion. The Medici had long since destroyed inner simplicity, the Savonarolan Cambi said in mourning this event. Now with the destruction of the *ceri*—"that antiquity of simple things"—external simplicity had fled as well.[81] It was as if fire, which had always re-created the commune, had lost its charm.

Instead, it was a Medicean Resurrection that the festivals announced; the San Giovanni celebrations of these years were pervaded by direct and highly literary ideological communications that equated the Medici with divinities and divine histories. Florence, of course, was not Rome. Here, "young cardinals and other prelates" could not be theatrically lowered from the roof to the floor of a church full of clients "to represent the descent of the Holy Ghost upon the apostles," as happened on the Tiber in 1519.[82] But with the pope as its leader, the family affirmed its divinity in less dramatic fashion. It was said that Florence was protected by two lions now—Pope Leo and the Florentine Marzocco—as well as by two Johns—the Baptist and Giovanni de' Medici.[83] The family let its intellectuals give flight to their fancy and state its destiny in unequivocal terms.

One driving force behind the festive ideology of these years was that each celebration of San Giovanni should, when possible, have as its justification an event in family history, rather than the commemoration of the total civic past and present. We find such motivations cited for the feast of 1513, which was observed, Cambi tells us, "to thank God for giving [Florence] a pope," and for the feast of 1516, when in the wake of a military victory by Lorenzo di Piero, "a chorus declared . . . that the said *trionfi* were made to honor *signore* Lorenzo de' Medici."[84]

Once the celebration was cast in this mould, it was child's play to combine the old festive machines of San Giovanni with new ones that told Medicean history. What was the city before the Medici, the great presentation of 1514 seemed to ask, but a Ship of Fools that Florentines saw pulled through the streets:

> *The happy city exults at the curious sight,*
> *For on its soil one sees launched*
> *A formidable ship raised to the sky,*
> *Where sits the violent mob.*
> *Here one [person] stupidly insults the other*
> *And gives convincing proof of their madness.*[85]

80. Cambi, XXII, 69f; Guasti, *Feste*, 27f.

81. Cambi, XXII, 69f, who points out that although the old *ceri* were each borne by subjects of the respective *terre*, the new ones were pulled by oxen "like triumphal *carri*."

82. Sanuto, XXVII, 273 (May Day, 1519).

83. This was the decoration on the "theater" in the

Piazza S. Trinita when Leo entered in 1515; Moreni, *De Ingressu*, 9ff.

84. Cambi, XXII, 23ff; Masi, 204–207; Rinuccini, clxxxi.

85. Guasti, *Feste*, 33; Cambi, XXII, 44f; Sanuto, XVIII, 313; Trexler, "De la Ville à la Cour." See also page 255, this volume.

Was not the ancient *edifizio* of St. Michael, that "celestial prince of arms" who confounded the bad angels who had tried to establish a kingdom of darkness, in 1513 meant to celebrate the victory of Lorenzo di Piero over a contemporary conspiracy?[86] Did not the famous "monument" or *madia* of Limbo and Resurrection now tell the story of Medicean survival as well as Christ's?[87] We cannot be sure and it would be treacherous to push the matter further as it regards specific festive machines. Yet the general theme of Medicean resurrection in the representations of these years is unmistakable. The vehicle might be the story of the Golden Age or the descent of Hercules into hell or, as in the orations, songs, and poems, a more direct association of Christ's resurrection with the family's survival.[88]

Perhaps the most direct festive representation of the theme of resurrection was the Triumph of Camillus, an enormous show that delighted and disturbed the Florentines on June 23, 1514. As the song that accompanied its seventeen carts explained for all to hear, Lorenzo di Piero's return to Florence in 1512 was comparable to the return of the exiled Camillus to the despoiled city of Rome, his contribution to Florence's rebirth similar to Camillus' salvation of the Eternal City, his rescue of the Florentines from their wrongheaded alliance with the French before 1512 akin to Camillus' victories over the Gauls.[89] We recall that in 1491 Lorenzo the Magnificient had compared himself to Aemilius Paulus. Now his grandson easily transcended the rough beginnings of absolutistic theater that the Magnificent had dared: Through war, struggle, exile, and suffering, Florentine history had made the Medici supreme, and given the Florentines serenity in a spiritual father and a temporal lord, Giovanni and Lorenzo de' Medici.[90]

I would summarize the thrust of Medicean ideology in the St. John festivals as follows: True to the principles of their ancestors, the early sixteenth-century Medici historicized the San Giovanni festival and made their fate that of the commune. San Giovanni now told more about the history of Florence than about its structures. It represented the violence and individuality, the natural and biological forces that had helped make the state, instead of subsuming history and individuality into a representation of the "commune that cannot die."[91]

---

86. Guasti, *Feste*, 33, for the characterization of St. Michael. The conspiracy was that of Pier Pagolo Boscoli, on whom see ch. 7, this volume.

87. In his edition of Masi, Corazzini said he could not find another reference to the *edifizio* of La Madia mentioned by Masi in 1514; 142. A letter to Venice describing the same San Giovanni shows that it was another name for Il Monumento, and describes the representation: "E la madia non vi machò over munimento: sussitando Christo, estrasse e Santi Padri del nymbo [sic]", that is, limbo; Sanuto, XVIII, 313.

88. For Hercules, see Sanuto, *loc. cit.* For many other references on the theme, see Trexler and Lewis, "Two Captains." Given the broad evidence of the theme in many areas of representational life, the cult of the Resurrection at this time clearly deserves a separate study.

89. Singleton, "Literature," 32; *Canti*, 251f. The song is by Jacopo Nardi. In its original form it was so anti-French that curialists insisted it be purged before its presentation; Roscoe, *Vita . . . Leone*, VI, 224f (letters of June 8 and seq.).

90. On Aemilius Paulus, see page 451, and for the beginning of Florentine historical representations, see 375, this volume.

91. See Dati's quote, page 334, this volume.

These were the barely concealed world views that most annoyed anti-Mediceans when they saw them filtering through the festive forms of San Giovanni. To Cambi and Landucci, for example, the *caccie* or hunts that were a standard part of the celebrations of these years (after not having been seen in Florence since 1459) were not repulsive in themselves; the chroniclers described the slaughter of bulls and the instigation of animals to bloody fights without disapprobation. But when the *festaioli* of the hunt of 1514 put an estrous mare into the ring of the Piazza della Signoria with stallions, "so that anyone who didn't know how to, learned" the sexual act (through which, we might add, the commune *actually* reproduced itself), these men were horrified: "a most abominable thing, that . . . 40,000 women and girls could see their dirty acts."[92] Again, after watching the festive siege or tournament of San Giovanni in 1513, Giovanni Cambi did not object to the form per se; such battles were not unknown in past Florentine festivities. What Cambi thought "bestial" was that this mock defense of Florence ended with many participants being wounded. This was the predictable result of a battle that did not, as in the traditional tournament, pit the city's professional soldiers against each other, but rather placed a group of Florentine *giovani* against an equally amateurish squadron of *contadini* besiegers, who battled with bricks as well as wooden arms.[93] Behold Florentine history, the *festaioli* seemed to say, a result of bloody conflict, from now on to be acted out by Florentines rather than by surrogates. Florentine history was the result of copulation, birth, and death no different than in the animal world. The Medici "had the balls" (*palle*) to make the Florentines' testicles hurt, a contemporary pun ran, if the citizens could not accept a sweeter yoke.[94]

The effect of the Medicean theater was alienation among the viewers. The direct, highly literary propaganda of these festivals; their destruction of the *ceri* "so as to amuse"; the Medicean motivations for the festive celebrations; perhaps the Ships of Fools that emphasized the ridiculousness of republican life; certainly the curious representation of Florentine history as blood and passion—all this must be related to the unmistakable distance

---

92. Landucci, 346. According to a description sent to Venice, the three horses were not planned, but substituted for a lion and a bear when complications arose; Sanuto, XVIII, 315. Cambi's horror is in his *Istorie*, XXII, 47. The conversion of the Piazza into a wood, with trees and plants, and the chronicler's conception of the surrounding stands as part of the natural scene ("Nè credere che città al mondo potessi avere tanta copia di legniame"; Landucci, 346) points to the phenomenon Mona Ozouf has studied, the creation of a natural setting for purposes of social reorganization; "Le Cortège et la Ville. Les Itinéraires Parisiens des Fêtes Révolutionnaires," *Annales E.S.C.* XXVI (1971), 894f, 899.

93. "Feciono chonbattere un chastello grande quadro, che girò più di braccia 80. E drento vi missono da 80 uomini, ch'erano el forte Fiorentini, ch'erano cierti bravi, e di mala vita, e di fuori erano da 400 uomini

soldati di nostro tenitorio, e aveano tutti arme da hoffendere di faggio, ed arientate a modo d'arme buone, e in efetto quelli di fuori ne fu ghuasti assai, e di que' di drento quaxi nessuno, e benchè si disse nonne morì nessuno, pure s'andò a grandissimo pericholo"; Cambi, XXII, 24. Landucci insisted that people had died, and adds that bricks were used; 340.

94. "Li arrabiati abasseranno il colo al suave jugo de le clementissimo Palle, *aliter* gustarano qual sia el dolor de' testiculi"; Sanuto, LIII, 466 (letter of the bishop of Nocera, Aug. 9, 1530). A suggestion of the direct dependence of city history on the risk of Medici violence is in Lorenzo di Piero's willingness to joust even though he governed the state. In trying unsuccessfully to dissuade him from the joust, his mother pointed out that from Piero di Cosimo on, no Medici *capo* had jousted; Roscoe, *Vita . . . Leone*, VI, 226 (1514).

510 The Ritual Revolution

that characterizes the lengthy reports on the feasts by both anti- and pro-Mediceans.

Through the words of the diarists, these celebrations appear as events to which people came, rather than ones they made. The chroniclers now for the first time regularly list the *festaioli* or stage managers of the San Giovanni celebrations.[95] They often report the "meanings" of different parts of the shows, as if to bridge the distance they themselves felt in viewing them.[96] They betray a conscious interest in the grandstands and specify who exactly was in them, especially foreign visitors.[97] Now the price of tickets is mentioned with some consistency.[98] Finally, diarists now detail how they were taxed to defray the expenses of the festivals, as if this was taxation without representation.[99] All this adds up to a perception of these activities as a formal, theatrical presentation in which the diarists were not directly involved. It is this subtle change in reportage that helps explain Giovanni Cambi's attitude that these spectacles were beautiful, but "without spirit."[100]

Yet the San Giovanni festivals had *not* reached a new stage in theatricalization; the public life of the 1510s can *not* be viewed as an objectification of a previously participatory reality. The change that we observe in the chroniclers was due instead to their position in the festival: The literate, middle-class diarists and chroniclers of Florence, our primary sources through all of Florentine history for the details of its public life, had now become part of the audience instead of participants. Conversely, the illiterate noncitizens of the *potenze*, and the prepolitical *giovani* of the city, had moved to the center of processional attention. We shall look at the history of both these groups after 1494, and show how each fit into the festive panoply of postexilic Florence.

Unlike their Medicean sponsors, the plebeian festive confraternities of Florence survived their repression during the Savonarolan period and became an important festive force in the interregnum. They were, in fact, the beneficiaries of a factious political order whose parties seem to have used these marginal political forces to their own ends. The neighborhood groups that had received a formal identity and been brought under a single aegis by the Medicean Magi now played for various patrons and threatened the equilibrium of a troubled city. We hear of a Carnival in 1499, for example, in which "plebeian" festive groups led by *messeri* of good families planned to engage in stone fights around fifteen pyres set up in different parts of the city; these groups may be none other than the comparable number of total *potenze* we encounter in later records.[101] For their part, the mounted *potenze* of the

95. Rinuccini, clxxx; Masi, 141, 204; Cambi, XXII, 44.

96. For example, "La similitudine che l'era: [cioè] che detti difizi erono fatti in lalde del signiore Lorenzo de' Medici"; Masi, 205.

97. For example, Cambi, XXII, 48; Landucci, 346; Masi, 144.

98. See, for example, *ibid.*, 142ff. The only previous record I know of the price of tickets is in ser Giusto, f.

76r: "Spesi io soldi dodici pe' miei figliuoli acciòchè potessino stare a vedere" (Apr. 29, 1459).

99. Masi, 143; Landucci, 346.

100. Cambi, XXII, 45 (1514).

101. See page 410, this volume. Different neighborhoods were by now so formally identifiable as productive units that publications appeared with their colophon. For the colophon *Stampata nella Inclita*

sixteenth-century festive order first emerge in clear profile during these years. Thus on May Day 1501 Monteloro and Melandristi are named as those "companies of *armeggiatori*" that performed "customary" *armeggerie* in the Piazza della Signoria in honor of the entering and departing priors.[102] In 1511 we find the government permitting its domestics to serve the Emperor of the Meadow, the first unequivocal reference to this third and most important of the mounted *potenze*. And in a carnival song perhaps written at about the same time these three neighborhood groups and the Città Rossa are described as fighting battles with each other, and then celebrating a festive peace.[103] Thus in the period before the return of the Medici in 1512, four of the five mounted *potenze* were actively involved in mock neighborhood battles for the delectation of the carnival crowds and the honor of the Signoria. The lesson is clear. These *potenze* were sustained by a faltering republican political order; they were not merely instruments of a (banished) first family that could create and dissolve them at will.

One of the main reasons for the weakness of the Soderinian regime was the tremendous pressures of the Italian Wars, which left Florence no surcease from the threat of attack, and it is quite possible that the vitality of these festo-military *potenze* during this time is related to the city's first attempt to build an indigenous army for defense. The Carnival season of 1506 was one in which Charles Singleton noted a concentration of festive activity among groups that would later be classified as foot *potenze*;[104] it was also a feast during which the commune first showed off its new militia:

> And on the fifteenth day of February 1506, a review was held in the Piazza of 400 soldiers who had been formed by the Standard Bearer of Justice [Soderini] from among our *contadini*. And he gave them each a white doublet, a pair of white and red liveried stockings, and a white beret and shoes, and an iron chestplate and lances, and to some of them guns. And they will be called battalions. And he gave them a constable who would guide them and teach them to use arms. And these were [foot soldiers], and they stayed at home, obliged to come together when they were needed. And [Soderini] ordained that many thousands of them be made in the whole *contado* so that we would no longer need foreigners. And this was considered the most beautiful thing that had ever been ordained for the city of Florence.[105]

For the city, but not of it. Despite the personal preference of Soderini's secretary Niccolò Machiavelli, an urban militia was not established at this time, since the fear of mounting the city's *giovani* and arming its plebs was too strong.[106]

Could the city's *potenze* have been so active at this time for want of

Monarchia di Città Rossa, see C. Guasti (ed.), *Il Sacco di Prato e il Ritorno dei Medici in Firenze* (Bologna, 1880), xiv.

102. Cambi, XXI, 159f.

103. Gori, *Feste,* 305; Del Badia, "Compagnia della Gazza," 25f. "Canzone degli Amatori di Pace" by Gianfrancesco Del Bianco (fl. 1510); Singleton, *Canti,* 231; "Literature," 207.

104. *Ibid.,* 81f.

105. Landucci, 273.

106. C. Bayley, *War and Society in Renaissance Florence* (Toronto, 1961), 255; N. Machiavelli, *Arte della Guerra e Scritti Politici Minori,* ed. S. Bertelli (Milan, 1961), 79–84, 96.

something better? In a commune deeply preoccupied with military matters and edging more and more toward the idea of national defense, the city's *potenze* may have given expression to a dangerous wish—the arming of the marginal males of the city of Florence—while the *potenze*'s festive counterparts in the *contado*, the so-called *signorie*, grew alongside the rural militias.[107] Here is an idea in search of evidence to be sure, but one whose synthetic imagination is irresistible. The mock arms of the Florentine *potenze* in festival are a trick image of a commune gravely learning to defend the nation through its youth and workers. When for the San Giovanni festival of 1513 Lorenzo de' Medici arranged the bloody battle of bricks and mock weapons (the traditional arms of the later *potenze* entertainments) between *contadini* and inhabitants of the city, he was using a republican idea of self-defense to his own ends.[108] When he reinstituted the Machiavellian militia in the *contado* at the same time, and made "noble Florentine youth . . . [into] various types of militias" in 1515, he once again responded to a central need of the Florentine commonwealth for the representation of indigenous military honor.[109] In the years leading up to the return of the Medici in 1512, the republic showed a comic face to the grave national problem of self-defense. Country bumpkins marched in tandem with plebeian *potenze* in both hilarious and earnest array.

From the moment the Medici reentered the city in 1512, the evidence of the *potenze*'s almost official status in the Florentine festive sphere multiplied, as the family took all necessary steps to bring their wooden arms under its control. Some of the carnival songs must have been done by *potenze* to honor Lorenzo di Piero. In one, an oriental shah, having conquered Persia and Syria, wants to rule Egypt and Turkey, so he hires a valorous captain from Florence and sends him a great embassy laden with gold and silver. What can this be but a festive re-creation of Pope Leo's appointment of Lorenzo as condottiere, the Magian organization of fifteenth-century Florentine confraternities still reverberating in the *potenze*'s Persian cavalcades?[110] The same can be asked of the 1514 Triumph of Camillus performed in honor of Lorenzo di Piero. In it three companies of mounted soldiers and then another group of fifty foot soldiers paraded in the honored position immediately before the great Camillus. Since the latter group was fitted out with wooden arms, must not it as well as the riding companies have been *potenze* of Florence?[111]

The *potenze*'s participation in the festivities surrounding Pope Leo's visit

107. On the latter, see Del Badia, *Signorie o Potenze;* the author traces their beginnings to the early sixteenth century.

108. On that battle, see page 509, this volume; on Lorenzo's reorganization of the *contado* militia, see G. Canestrini, "Documenti per Servire alla Storia della Milizia Italiana dal XIII secolo al XVI," *ASI*, XV (1851), 328–336.

109. See the quote on page 503, this volume.

110. "Canzone della Nuova Milizia del Soffi"; Singleton, *Canti*, 183.

111. "Venivano drieto a questi [pregioni] circha 200 cavali, ch'era da 80 homeni d'arme compartiti per hordine benissimo in tre parte, ch'eran tre compagnie che hanno di poi servito a la zostra. . . . Apresso poi a le gente d'arme con loro stendardi e ogni arnese necessario seguiva 50 a piedi vestiti tutti di panno azuro con certe arme di legno, con certi fassi di verge d'oro a quelle aste ligate in capeglii con girlande de lauro in testa. Ultimamente ne veniva . . . Camillo"; Sanuto, XVIII, 314. It will be recalled that the *potenze* were often called standards.

in 1515–1516 is not in doubt, for Cambi tells us that the pope himself— perhaps during the Carnival he had organized—bestowed individual banners on each of the foot *potenze*. This is the earliest reference to a classic custom of the later Medici.[112] In 1518, the Mediceo-centric celebrations of the *potenze* are again in evidence: "all the *potenze* of Florence," says one source, came to the palace to celebrate Lorenzo di Piero's marriage.[113] By 1522 the festive position of the *potenze* was so exalted that Cardinal Giulio de' Medici watched the *palio* of San Giovanni from the home of the Emperor of the Meadow.[114] Thus when in the following year the news of Giulio's election as pope reached the city, it was to be expected that the plebeian *potenze* of Florence would march to the family palace to *concelebrare* the family's good news, and receive tips for its efforts.[115]

The *potenze* had definitely assumed their classic forms and functions by this time, even if we must wait until May Day 1532 to view them in ensemble. On that day, the five *potenze* of *armeggiatori* would perform their festive trade: first outside the Medici palace, then at the homes of the citizens of their choice (probably those who had loaned them fine clothes for the day and otherwise supported them), and finally before "all those plebs and *potenze* who had made decorations in their neighborhoods."[116] Thus the precedentially superior mounted *potenze* who specialized in cavalcades and *armeggerie* and may have been the same groups that graced the cavalcades of an earlier date, honored their subject foot *potenze* in the neighborhoods. The latter specialized not only in marching and stone fights but in theatrical productions, as we

112. "Tutte le potentie di Chamaldoli, e tintori e tessitori di prebei ch'avavano nomi di Signori e bandiere aute da Papa Leone, e chonpagnie d'armegiatori"; retrospective from 1523 in Cambi, XXII, 249f. On Pope Leo's Carnival presentation, see page 544, this volume. The custom is detailed in 1532: All the flags of the *potenze* being displayed outside the Medici palace, each of these confraternities marched to that palace in precedential order and received its banner from the head of the family; Cambi, XXIII, 117. The European political powers' growing involvement, associated to the plebs, in Carnival activities can be compared to the use of the same feast during the early Reformation; B. Scribner, "Reformation, Carnival, and the World Turned Upside-Down," *Social History* III (1978), 303–329. The possibility that the Florentine distinction between mounted *potenze* and unmounted *potenze* with signorial titles may reflect divisions between the four or five great powers and the *signori* of the several smaller regions of Italy may be pursued in writings of Benedetto Dei, printed in G. F. Pagnini (ed.), *Della Decima e di Varie altre Gravezze imposte dal Comune di Firenze. Della Moneta e della Mercatura de' Fiorentini fino al secolo XVI*, II (Lisbon and Lucca, 1765), 277–280 ("Una Risposta al Gran Turco fatta 1463"), and in a presently unpublished chronicle: M. Phillips, "A Newly Discovered Chronicle of Marco Parenti," *Renaissance Quarterly*

XXXI (1978), 158 and seq., where, as does Dei, Parenti names the *signori* of north and central Italy region by region.

113. "Tutte le Potenzie di Firenze andorno a rallegrarsi al palazzo di detto duca . . . , quelle potenzie che armeggiano . . . e le potenzie che non armeggiano"; Masi, 237. This is the earliest use of the term *potenze* unequivocally referring to a structured fraternal system.

114. "Per amore del corso del palio . . . monsignior Iulio [andò] in casa lo imperadore del Prato"; Trexler, *Libro*, 130.

115. Masi, 274. Note that in this context Masi repeats his distinction between "tutte le . . . potenze che armeggiano . . . et . . . tutte l'altre potenze che non armeggiano," whereas describing the same events, Cambi, as we saw above in n. 112, distinguishes *potenze* and the *chonpagnie d'armegiatori*.

116. "E armeggiorono la mattina di chalen di Maggio, in prima nella via largha al palazo del prefato Duca, dexinato che ebbe a ore 16, e dipoi per la città a que' cittadini pareva loro, e a tutte quelle prebe, e potentia, che aveano fatti aparati ne' paexi loro"; Cambi, XXIII, 117. On the clothes loaned them for the day, Cambi, XXI, 159f; XXIII, 129.

surmised they did in the fourteen triumphal arches of the papal visit of 1515.[117] Perhaps it was these foot *potenze* who in 1533 performed "comedies" in the courtyard of the Medici palace while the mounted *potenze* of Florence did their equestrian tricks outside.[118]

Our first notice of a *libro di confini* that, kept by the Emperor of the Prato, regulated the neighborhood borders of each *potenza*, comes only later.[119] Only after the end of the republic do we have evidence proving that the Medici actually appointed the urban Emperor of the Prato, as they did the *signori* of the *contado* groups, and that they won popular support by rescuing these festive lords from pauperism. But by the end of the second period of Medici rule in 1527, the eminently familial power that the *potenze* served was clear to all. In recommending their suppression after the revolt of that year, Donato Giannotti had recent history on his side: "for they are all things that decrease the reputation of the public [sphere] and increase that of private persons."[120]

Giannotti's judgment is solid, yet too simple. The *potenze* were more than instruments of private power, as our history of these groups has shown. The public sphere in Florence had always needed the acclamation and retinue of private persons, and in the May Day celebrations of 1501 we could document the *potenze* performing for the government of Florence *before* we had equally decisive documentation that they did the same for families like the Medici. The *potenze* rose and flourished in part because they were necessary to the honor of the government when the great families of the commune, pushed by Lorenzo the Magnificent, ceased to maintain their public ritual face through personal participation in festival.[121] As the children of Florence had assumed the task of communal representation during the Savonarolan period, and as the city's *giovani* would do the same during the Last Republic, so in this period did the *potenze* honor the commune even as they provided retinue for the first family. We see them in city and countryside in 1536 welcoming Emperor Charles V as once their ancestors had welcomed the Magi, "to the honor of the city" as well as that of the Medici.[122] The lower classes of Florence maintained the republic and its honor even as they raised the Medici up on festive shields. For a weakened patriciate and an ambitious family, the day of the workingman had come.

This was a fact that dispossessed citizens found hard to accept, not Giannotti with his reductionist distinction between public and private, not Cambi with his simple distinction between spirited and those "without spirit." With an exuberance unmatched since the Ciompi revolt of 1378, the lesser artisans and laborers now marched in the streets to their own drummer. The

117. See page 499, this volume.

118. Cambi, XXIII, 117.

119. Ricci, 223 (1577).

120. For the full quote, see page 413, this volume. The Medicis' appointment of the Emperor of the Meadow is mentioned by Del Badia, *Signorie o*

Potenze, 26; Doni's story of Alessandro de' Medici bailing out an emperor who had spent everything on a festival is in *L'Illustratore Fiorentino*, III (Florence, 1837), 52.

121. See page 410, this volume.

122. Del Badia, *Signorie o Potenze*, 13f.

potenze had taken upon themselves an almost customary right to honor a merchant culture that loved the noble trappings of horse and triumphant arch, yet with Medici backing they insisted on the validity of nobility *and* work. Dressed like toys and in borrowed clothes, the politically excluded male populace of Florence finally allied with the Medici because there was no place for them in the bourgeois republic. What self-respecting merchant Standard Bearer of Justice would have watched the palio from the home of a weaver, as did a Medici cardinal? The first family had arrived. It honored the workingman, and was legitimated by a festive emperor.

The popular *potenze* were the structural element of society that the Medici were able to win to their side in the years after their return to Florence in 1512; the city's *giovani* provided a generational element. We have seen that the roots of this youthful adhesion to the family lay in the Lorenzan period, and that the ultimate thrust of these young men into the center of Florentine public life came in the Last Republic. It was in the interim that Florentine youth first became a major political force, as it was also at this time that the vitriolic generational hatreds that were so characteristic of the last years of the republic first showed their face. In the period up to the second exile of the Medici in 1527, the youth celebrated the family when they were not attacking the whole established gerontocratic order. In the crisis of the Last Republic, they would save, then bury, the republic itself.

From the death of Lorenzo the Magnificent until the return of the Medici in 1512, the youth of Florence bore the brunt of blame for almost every disaster that befell the commune. Why had Piero de' Medici lost the support of the politicians and been driven from the city in 1494? In one historian's opinion, it was because "he furthered the youth and minor lords, and favored them against the will of some elderly *principali* and men of mature age. It seemed to such older men that [Piero] did not appreciate them."[123] Why had Savonarola failed? In part, said Jacopo Nardi, because once admitted to the Grand Council, "the degenerate youth" had allied themselves with the preacher's older opponents and proved to be enemies of the council.[124] Could anyone doubt that the youth were out of control from then on? The youth group of the Compagnacci had openly attacked the saintly *fanciulli* of the friar, had tried to use festive competitions to stimulate riots, and had gone so far as to besmirch the pulpits and altars of the churches.[125] It was the youth of the Compagnacci and not the constituted oldsters of Florence, one foreign power believed, who were in practical control of the city during Savonarola's trial and after his death.[126] Raucous at the seat of power in the postprophetic

123. Parenti, cited in Weinstein, *Savonarola and Florence*, 121.

124. Nardi, II, 25. Confirmed by the well-informed Parenti, in Schnitzer, *Quellen*, IV, 245.

125. Trexler, "Adolescence," 259f; Parenti in Schnitzer, *Quellen*, IV, 270, 286; Landucci, 190; Cambi, XXI, 119, 135, 252.

126. "Una certa conpagnia nuovamente facta fra 500 giovani et più, di quelli che sono di buono sangue et poveri, et tenuti già fuori del governo, se ànno quasi vendicato il dominio di questa terra"; C. Lupi, "Documenti Pisani intorno a fra G. Savonarola," *ASI*, ser. 3, XIII (1871), 188 (letter of Pisan Anziani of Apr. 17, 1498); Sanuto, I, 935; II, 407, 541; III, 95; Ridolfi, *Vita . . . Savonarola*, I, 276, 354, 360, 365 and seq. The

years, the *giovani* turned the streets of the city into a "hell" that lasted for years.[127] They ridiculed those who had followed Savonarola, staged mock judicial trials of those they disliked and hung them in effigy, and even defiled the quarters of resident ambassadors when the mood suited them.[128] Small wonder that communal counselors in these years considered "the correction of the inconveniences caused by the *giovani* at night" to be a matter of the first priority, even if, there being as many as nine hundred youth involved in these affairs, the government was for a time unable to prosecute them.[129] Clearly, such people could not be allowed into the militia in 1506 if the fathers were ever to know peace; instead, they had to be excluded from all public life. Thus in 1510 the Soderinian government refused to renew the privilege of twenty-four-year-olds to enter the Grand Council, and it sharpened the antihomosexual laws so as to persecute a generation whose support it could not claim.[130]

Youth led the final attack on the Soderinian regime in late August 1512. They invaded the Palace of the Signori and demanded that all those who had been admonished for homosexuality be reinstated.[131] Some *giovani* favored the return of the Medici, said Jacopo Nardi, for then they could pay their debts and pursue their insatiable appetites.[132] When on September 1 of that year Giuliano de' Medici reentered Florence, he came with the youth. Observers displayed that attention to age that was to be so typical of the period when they noted that the thirty-three-year-old scion of the house of Medici was "accompanied by [twenty-six-year-old] Antonfrancesco di Luca degli Albizzi, an audacious young man," and followed by relatives and friends, "especially the *giovani*."[133]

Contemporaries had no doubt that the youth were the bedfellows of authoritarianism. In early January 1513 a correspondent wrote that Giuliano and Lorenzo de' Medici had each instituted a company of standard from among their youthful cohorts so as to celebrate the coming Carnival. This society took it as an article of faith that youth loved show and would follow anyone who offered such an opportunity. Could there thus be any doubt that the "noble and grave *giovani*" over twenty years of age in Lorenzo's Company of the Broncone, while delighting the Carnival crowds with the *trionfi* of the Four Ages of the World, also served as a personal bodyguard for their patron?

150 youth were the swing vote in the council, Parenti says, "talchè dove questi giovani con i loro favori s'indirizavano, quivi era lo augumento"; Schnitzer, *Quellen*, IV, 245.

127. Giles of Viterbo was finally brought in in 1502 to try to end the disorders; *ibid.*, 300.

128. The Florentine chroniclers do not, of course, report this indecorous judicial and diplomatic behavior. The information comes from Sanuto, II, 378, 407. The reigning Standard Bearer of Justice, Guido Antonio Vespucci, was "convicted" of *crimen lesae majestatis* and an effigy torched in front of his home; the Milanese ambassador's residence was walled up

with manure. These acts of ridicule were unknown to me when I wrote "De la Ville à la Cour."

129. Lupi, "Nuovi Documenti," 57. "Et non poteno rimediar per esser tanto numero"; Sanuto, II, 407.

130. Cambi, XXI, 239, with a long diatribe against the *giovani*. See my interpretation of these laws in "Prostitution."

131. Cambi, XXI, 309; Nardi, V, 55.

132. *Ibid.*, V, 29.

133. *Ibid.*, V, 56; also Cambi, XXI, 308 with Albizzi's age, 311 with Lorenzo di Piero's.

Or that the Barons of the Most Illustrious Captain performed the same function when they accompanied Lorenzo to the *ringhiera* in 1515 to receive the communal baton?[134] We have seen that contemporaries understood the generational politics of that latter ritual. Lorenzo was now able to arm those "many noble Florentine youth" who wanted to pursue military honor. He could now make these prepolitical males "his gentlemen and bodyguards within diverse types of militias."[135] At a stroke, Lorenzo violated one of the oldest Florentine tabus and armed the youth. Evidently the Medici, different from the old oligarchy, did not fear youth any more than it feared the lower classes. Within the year, Florentine military captains serving Lorenzo became a common sight in Florentine festive life, bearing the flags and threads of nobility with a public pomp few could have earlier imagined.[136] Lorenzo di Piero had brought about a fundamental change in Florentine ceremonial life; the city's youth in pursuit of military glory now had reason to praise the Florentine government!

Yet in the midst of all this evidence of an affinity between the youth and the Medici, events transpired that prohibited an easy equation of the two. Within a month of the Carnival festivities of 1513, a conspiracy was uncovered whose perpetrators were uniformly referred to as youth and whose object was nothing less than the murder of the Medici chieftains. Many contemporaries dismissed Pier Pagolo Boscoli and his fellows as isolated bankrupts without a following, but others set about immortalizing their sacrifice as an act of heroism; their passion and execution would become a heroic example to others who yearned for the republic.[137] In 1522 another youthful conspiracy was uncovered, this one said to have aimed at assassinating the Medici cardinal while he marched in the procession on the feast of S. Zanobi.[138] The fact was that the Medici competed with republicans for the favor of the twenty-year-olds. The *giovani* of Florence were developing a political and social mentality of their own, and claiming a rightful role in civic life.

With a swiftness paralleled only by the speed with which the city's

---

134. On the institution of the Standard Companies of the Broncone and Giuliano's Diamante, see the letter of Jan. 8, 1513, in Del Lungo, *Florentia*, 414; for their representations of the Ages of the World, see Cambi, XXII, 2. The requirements for membership in the Broncone may be read in the draft of their statutes in G. Palagi (ed.), *I Capitoli della Compagnia del Broncone* (Florence, 1872), 9, 16. On the Barons, see page 502, this volume. On the Carnival of 1513, see the bibliography in Mitchell, *Italian Civic Pageantry*, 38f.

135. For the quote, see page 503, this volume.

136. In the very ritual of the *presa di bastone*, a correspondent in Florence wrote of a section "tutti gioveni fiorentini che hora cominciono dare principio a l'arte militare, armati a la leggiera *cum* saioni de velluto et barde coperte de raso a la livrea de sua signoria";

Sanuto, XX, 531.

137. Yet Pier Pagolo Boscoli was thirty-one, Agostino Capponi forty-three years of age. For Boscoli's presumed relation to the coterie at the Rucellai Gardens, see Busini, 85.

138. The victims of 1522 were Jacopo di Giovanbattista da Diacetto, a *giovanetto* of nineteen; G. Spini, *Tra Rinascimento e Riforma* (Florence, 1940), 27; and the soldier Luigi di Tommaso Alamanni. Diaccetino and the two authors of the plot, Zanobi di Bartolomeo Buondelmonte (thirty-one) and Luigi di Piero Alamanni (twenty-seven) were frequenters of the Rucellai Gardens. For the procession plan, Sanuto, XXXIII, 297, and in general, C. Guasti (ed.), "Documenti della Congiura fatta contro il Cardinale Giulio de' Medici nel 1522," *Giornale Storico degli Archivi Toscani* III (1859), 216–232.

fanciulli had been processionally incorporated into the civic structure in the 1490s, Florentines now revolutionized their ideas about political structures, and announced that the political divisions in the city were generational before they were economic or social in nature. The most fundamental division in the *res publica* was between the old and the young! The chorus was incessant, largely limited to Medicean youth in the period before 1527 and to the family's opponents thereafter, and its message was unmistakable: Anyone who wanted to rule had to begin by understanding age differences and build on that foundation.

Among the pro-Medicean youth, no one was outdone in his frankly generational view of politics by Niccolò Martelli, who addressed a memorandum to the Medici on ruling Florence after the conspiracy of 1522.[139] Society was divided between the old and the young, Martelli said. There were three types of elders (*vecchi*) whom the Medici had to control, he argued, and they were paralleled by three groups of *giovani:* budding merchants sprung from merchant parents, those who wanted to be soldiers, and those who preferred to pursue their studies. The Medici would have to satisfy the needs of each. As for the young merchants, the matter was easy enough; all they wanted were wives and the capital to start a business. The challenge began when the regime addressed itself to more ambitious youth.

How could the scholars be made to serve the interests of the regime? Martelli had an ingenious answer. First of all, the city needed the best professors money could buy so as to attract students and keep them occupied with studies and out of politics. To sweeten the pie, the Medici should supply tutors, degrees, and generous financial support. Finally, Martelli urged his patrons to recruit ten thousand foreign students who would come to the city with the financial support of the *signore*. There they should be armed by the family, and thus form a bastion of academic loyalty to their patron, and a deterrent to their Florentine colleagues who might dream of revolt.[140]

Finally there were those youth who "desired the militia," that is, who wanted to pursue a military career. Martelli recognized that such youth were to be found among enemies as well as among friends of the ruling family, yet he urged it to recruit both zealously by playing on their common desire for military glory. Dispersing anti-Medicean youth into garrisons outside Florence while keeping pro-Medicean *giovani* at his side in the city, the Medicean *capo* would make the well-dressed martial youth hostages of the princely order by persuading them they were fighting either for their own honor or for that of their country.[141]

The rough brilliance of Martelli's almost utopic project is complemented

---

139. The following is based on the text printed *ibid.*, one which Albertini's important *Staatsbewusstsein* neglected, though it is as significant as the tracts he did study.

140. "Huomini e in tutte le scientie peritissimi . . . affine [i giovani] havessino altra delectatione d'a-

nimo, che pormi mente alle mani e allo stato mio. . . . Diecimila scolari . . . acciochè sempre mi fussin favorevoli contro a' ciptadini"; *ibid.*, 221, 226.

141. "Sott'ombra di tenergli per soldati, mi servissino per statichi, e che fussino sempre una briglia a' padri e parenti loro, quando pur pensassino machinarmi contro"; *ibid.*, 225, 221.

peaks at the top

by the polished thought of Lodovico Alamanni, another Medicean youth who in 1516 prepared a practical manual for ruling Florence. Stark generational antagonism marked his whole approach to the problem of cowing the disgruntled political oligarchy of the pre-1512 period:

> The [republican] fantasies of the *vecchi* can never be eliminated. But [the *vecchi*] are wise, and the wise do not have to be feared, because they never do anything. The *giovani* can easily be weaned of this *civiltà* and will grow accustomed to the ways of courtiers, if the prince desires.[142]

Much more than Martelli, who showed little grasp of the complexity of socializing the youth, the twenty-eight-year-old Alamanni understood both the ritual mechanisms and the intergenerational dynamism that were involved. To make youth into courtiers, he said,

> one must specifically designate and elect all those *giovani* in our city who should be honored because of their own qualitites or those of their father or house. One should be sent for, and then another, each being told that you are pleased that they come to stand by you. Each should be given the position and pay which suit him. No one will refuse, and once they have come to do you service, their civilian dress should be removed and replaced with courtly attire, as are all your others. . . . You will have at your side men who by their manner and presence will render you as much honor as is rendered any nation on earth. Besides this, and more considerable, this will divest them of the *civiltà* so foreign to their vestments. For those who doff the [courtier's] cap and discard the [burgher's] headgear for Your Excellency will renounce the republic and make profession of your order. And they will never again have any hope of civilian preferment or popular benevolence. . . . If it should ever happen that in uncertain times it were necessary to go abroad with [the *giovani*], the politicians of your state [within the city] will keep their troth. This is because all those who stay at home in the government will be either the fathers or uncles or fathers-in-law of these *giovani*, and either for love or fear of them they will remain firm and faithful. If as the years go by one by one, the same procedure is adhered to of electing and calling to oneself those coming *giovani* who are today's *fanciulli*, and placing in the government of the city those who now are *giovani* but then will be *vecchi*, having been nursed and bred in your school, it will transpire that in our city people will not be able to live without a prince to entertain them, whereas now it appears impossible.[143]

Here was a young man who grasped the politics of formal procedures: Akin to a rite of passage, a ceremonial change of clothes would "divest" *civiltà* and sever youth from oldsters; the cohesion they would develop in Lorenzo's "order," to use Alamanni's paramonastic metaphor, would convert the youth's fathers into retinue for this new processional order. Still, the sociopolitical transformations Alamanni saw resulting from society's new face were not meant to strengthen merely the Medici, but the nation. Through youth's "manner and presence" Lorenzo as a person might be rendered as much

142. Albertini, *Staatsbewusstsein*, 370.
143. *Ibid.*, 370f. The view that controlling the *giovani* forced the *vecchi* to submit was held by Martelli (n. 141), and others; *ibid.*, 357. F. Gilbert sees the youthful emphasis on force as deriving from the bitter experiences of the invasions. The young men were the "prophets of force"; *Machiavelli and Guicciardini*, 129.

honor "as any nation," but the honor of the nation would also be served by the valor of the youth and other nonpolitical groups. If only the procession were a military parade—if only a shamed nation, faced with the humiliations of the Italian Wars, would learn the lessons of the past:

> We owe our forefathers very little. Subverting Italy's good order, they reduced it to the governance of priests and merchants. It is they who by introducing a mercenary militia have brought it to its present ignominy and servitude. Our fathers still do not want to admit that this is the reason for our illness. Instead they attribute everything that has happened either to our sins or to fate. Reason, however, shows otherwise. . . . And when our elders are forced to admit this, they say Florentines are constrained to use mercenary militia because the populace is not good at fighting, and because tumults would often result if arms were given to the common people.[144]

It was a lesson both the Medicean youth and their republican opponents taught; the identity of the city had to be broadened to include its marginal groups if its honor was to be redeemed. "These wise old men of yours," said the republican Machiavelli in that bitter antipaternal tone of the age, had presided over the demise of the city's honor. It remained for his youthful audience to resurrect it through arms:

> I think we should follow the Venetian practice of the youngest speaking first. For since this [militia] is an exercise of the *giovani*, I am persuaded that the *giovani* are better able to discuss it, as they are readier to execute it. . . . I believe that the *gioventù* are greater friends of things military and readier to believe what I will say. Those others, because their hair is already white and their blood cold, are in part traditional opponents of war, and in part incorrigible, like those who believe that the times and not bad customs force men to live in this way.[145]

This is the language of the *engagé,* whether Medicean or republican, and not the balanced judgment of the tractatist whose bloodless words we have avoided throughout this work. These are the reflective perceptions of youth and their supporters who, observing the contemporary scene of mixed ritual spaces in which they themselves acted, chose two different centers around which to build a better center: the one around the Medici palace, the other about the Palazzo della Signoria. Both were united in believing that out of the contemporary strife would come an order in which youth would be at center.

Events conspired to give the lead to the republican youth. Lorenzo di Piero died in 1519, Pope Leo in 1521, and when Giulio de' Medici was elected pope in 1523, he had to leave the city in the hands of Medicean children and a foreign cardinal who could not command the city's loyalty. The Medicean youth's vision of a world in which charismatic political leadership allied with brilliant youth for the good of the city proved a chimera; the martyrology that the liberal youth had cultivated after the execution of their cohorts in 1513 and 1522 had a future. Faced in 1527 with the threat of sacking by foreign armies,

144. *Ibid.,* 372.
145. Machiavelli, *Arte,* 398, 334. In Florence older men spoke first; page 394, this volume. Machiavelli wrote this in 1523.

the family's government and its youth proved incapable of defending the *patria*.[146]

The liberal youth clamored for arms. They were not the Savonarolan *fanciulli* grown to *gioventù*, but a generation that had been born after the prophet's demise and grown up during the Medicean restoration.[147] They were intensely patriotic, but no saints. Called, from the beginning of party formations in 1527, the Rabids (Arrabiati) or Compagnacci, as had been Savonarola's youthful enemies, these "libertine" youth resisted paternal authority *and* religious hypocrisy, rejecting the impotence of their fathers *and* their priests:

> Our city is greatly in debt to this *gioventù*. . . . These *vecchi* who made and make such professions of civic wisdom. . . . Living of their own free will under the tyranny they have made. . . . They say the *giovani* should not discuss public affairs, but pursue their sexual needs. . . . say[ing] that a *giovane* of twenty-five years [is] still a *fanciullo*. . . . believing that the *giovani* have the same defects they do. . . . I want to stop talking about the perversity of [these *vecchi*], because every time I think about their evil ways, I get very sick to the stomach.[148]

The Medicean Nerli understood the revolution of these virile saviors. It appeared to him that with the encouragement of some older men, the *gioventù* "had taken upon itself the protection of the whole *popolo*." Opposed to the young men stood the *vecchi*.[149] The Last Republic had begun.

Crisis

> To hear it was a miracle. In the midst of the roar of our [artillery] from the walls [against the besiegers] . . . , no one in the city moved. Rather, at every corner one heard silence, as if each person slept in the most secure place he could desire.[150]

The great siege of Florence lasted from spring 1529 until the city capitulated in August 1530. No survivor ever forgot the experience, not Michelan-

146. On this background, Roth, *Last Republic*, 1–31.

147. A sixteen-year-old in the Savonarolan processions of 1497 was forty-six in 1527, a ten-year-old was forty years of age. Here are the ages of some of the better known liberal *giovani* of the Last Republic in the year 1527:

Jacopo Alamanni, 22; *ASI*, I (1842), 137.
Baccio Cavalcanti, 24; Albertini, *Staatsbewusstsein*, 167.
Pierfilippo d'Alessandro Pandolfini, 28; *ibid.*, 127.
Dante di Guido da Castiglione, 24; L. Passerini in A. Ademollo, *Marietta de' Ricci* (Florence, 1845), 506.
Salvestro di Piero Aldobrandini, 28; *ibid.*, 1676.
Piero Vettori, 28; Albertini, *Staatsbewusstsein*, 144.
Giovanni Rignadori, 24 (about); Nerli, II, 97.
Lodovico Martelli, 23; Ademollo, *Marietta*, 374.
Carlo Aldobrandini, 25 (about); *Francesco Ferruccio*, 420.
Giovanni Bandini, 25 (about); *ibid*.

148. Composite from Giannotti, *Opere*, 158, 229, 230, 182, 242, 159. Cecil Roth remarked the "very modern spirit" of Giannotti's remarks, but did not develop the idea further; *Last Republic*, 215, n. 3. The oft-blurred line between Savonarolan and Rabid youth is clearly marked in L. Guicciardini, *Del Savonarola, ovvero Dialogo tra Francesco Zati e Pieradovardo Giachinotti il Giorno dopo la Battaglia di Gavinana* (Florence, 1959), 100, 134f, 161. This is a conversation between a member of each group.

149. "Sotto tale così velato colore era favorita quella gioventù da tutta quella parte de' cittadini, che pareva avessero preso la protezione universale del popolo. . . . [Altri] molto vecchi . . . concorrevano, così vecchi, vivamente con messer Matteo Niccolini . . . e con tutta quella parte di cittadini che della mutazione dello stato e del governo popolare più temevano"; Nerli, II, 24f.

150. Sanuto, LII, 379.

gelo who fortified the walls that so long excluded the foreigners, not the dumb princes of latter-day Naples, not even the heroes of the Risorgimento, who could see in this epic conflict the tragic beginning of the long struggle for Italian national unity. For those in the midst of the siege as well, it was as if history had started in 1527, so total and so numbing was the experience of that year and a half. It took a real effort to remember how Florence had collectively responded to the crises of earlier times. The permanent crisis had arrived.

Yet as we begin the behavioral analysis of this crisis, we must recall the forms of the past. To placate an angry God, the adult political males had once placed their women in back of them and a brilliantly dressed clergy at the head of the procession. These marginal groups had called God the Father's attention to the saintly redistribution of property that their "great and small, rich and poor" men, the reformed social order, carried out in the midst of the procession. Then Savonarola had modified this classic crisis procession, placing innocent lay children and not priests in front so as to save the city; an emphasis on growth and the future seemed better suited to crisis solution than the institutional processions of the past. Yet as Florentine society in 1527 entered the last great test of its republican political order, no one could recall a procession, or part of one, that had been made up of *giovani*. Impotence, not the honorable virility of youth, the prepotence of children and not the sagacious belligerence of their older brothers, remained the one and only face of a humble commune in crisis.

The military crisis of the Last Republic changed that. The aging fathers relied on their sons to man the walls, and were thus forced to cede them a place at the center as well; governmental ceremonialists and religious specialists had to integrate the *giovani* into representations of the city. The place of the youth in a besieged republic, in turn, was but one part of the larger problem of organizing all urban resources to confront the enemy. Workingmen and young girls, political males and mature women, children and youth, all had to pray together and, each group in its own way, fight together in a processional order that would both dishearten the enemy and delight a vengeful God. Throughout Florentine history it had been axiomatic that a city honorably at arms was one where the equality of the governing class could not endure. Throughout these centuries as well, republican governors had resisted marginal groups' attempts to develop their own independent cultic face. Would war, which in Machiavelli's words was "a thing of *giovani*," save, or terminate, the republic? Would the procession of the total city at arms end in violence and civil war, or move men to a new type of brotherhood? How adaptable was this city to be in defending itself against the massed forces of early absolutistic Europe?

THE FORMS OF CRISIS GOVERNMENT

One month before the events that drove the Medici from the city, a delegation marched toward the Palazzo della Signoria to demand that the

Medicean government take steps to defend the *patria* against approaching armies. The procession was dramatic, yet its form seemed traditional enough. Armed youth went in front, followed by their "fathers" in the place of honor, a proper embassy of oldsters ready to lay their grievances before their cohorts in government. Perceptive observers, however, knew that the retinue was at center, that the youth led, rather than simply accompanied, the grave elders of Florence. Ready to defend the Medici palace while their sons wanted to defend their country, the oldsters had apparently been offered the choice: Either take the place of honor in a march to the Palazzo or be branded *grandi* and lose all political rights.[151] Like Parthian kings in golden chains entering ancient Rome, the fathers of Florence assumed their wonted position in the civic procession.

Invading the Palace, the youth leading this procession soon showed who was in control, to the horror of the worthy elders in their wake. The *giovani* threw the robes of the Medicean Standard Bearer of Justice out the window, and the *gonfaloniere* himself was wounded by none other than his godson.[152] Now twenty-four-year-old Baccio Cavalcanti stepped forward as spokesman for the youth and presented his cohorts' demands for the reproclamation of the republic.[153] Could there be any doubt that the youth acted as a self-conscious political group and that they, not the *vecchi* who then issued the reproclamation, were in absolute control of the situation? Could anyone not see that it was the youth who were "sincere," the elders who would do anything for peace and quiet? When Medici reinforcements arrived at the city hall to expel the revolutionaries, the *vecchi* rushed home to lock up their shops; the *giovani* stood and fought the tyrants' mercenaries.[154] The first act of the Last Republic, this "Tumult of Friday," had begun and ended with the glory of the young and the humiliation of the old.

The circumstances of the definitive Medicean withdrawal from Florence one month later were entirely different. This time the Medici contingent, forced to evacuate because of the Sack of Rome and the imprisonment of the Medici pope Clement VII, had the decency to hand over control of the city formally to the governmental "fathers."[155] They would conduct communal business as usual, under new management. The government in office, it was decided, would serve out its term even though it was riddled with Medicean creatures. There was no need to rush to reopen the Grand Council, the elders said, and anyway, it would take a month to organize this revered republican body and prepare the Great Hall for the event.[156] Effervescence had to be excluded at all costs. Reasonable men of all persuasions understood what the call for calm meant: to reestablish a businesslike form of government, the youth had to be depoliticized.

151. The eyewitness account of Nardi shows the youths' domination of events; VIII, 8–9. Bernardo Segni's *Life* of his uncle Niccolò Capponi accords the *gonfaloniere*-to-be a more flattering role; Segni, *Vita*, 914. On the choice of the fathers, J. Pitti, "Dell'Istoria," 137.

152. Roth, *Last Republic*, 26f.

153. Varchi, II, 23.

154. Nardi, VIII, 10–15; letter of Marco Foscari to Venice in Sanuto, XLIV, 580ff.

155. Roth, *Last Republic*, 42–45.

156. Varchi, III, 9.

In a remarkable description of the political spectrum in Florence at this time, the Venetian ambassador Foscari explained what was involved. *Piagnoni* devotees of the martyr Savonarola controlled government and council, but they were ready to ally themselves with the Grays (Bigi), those Mediceans who could live with the republic. These two groups comprised the prudent men of the city. The third political force in the city, the *giovani*, was another matter. These Arrabiati or Compagnacci, Foscari reported,

> represent the interests of the poor bankrupt *giovani* and persons without father and without governance, of poor quality, as one says in Florence. These are also of goodly number, perhaps eight hundred. The majority are ignoble, that is, of the lesser gilds; in short, they are the scum of Florence, or so they say.[157]

The youth had emerged as an independent force in Florentine politics. Some *vecchi* were associated with them, to be sure, but Foscari saw that the oldsters "supported" the young rather than vice versa, "in order to win the favor of these *giovani*" instead of the other way around.[158] It was this party of youth that the responsible men of Florence had to keep out of the Grand Council and otherwise repress. The *giovani* only wanted to "sack, ruin, and do every evil," the grave elders said of this "raw and bankrupt lot." A relative of the first Standard Bearer of Justice during the Last Republic summarized the attitude of the elders with a paternalism worthy of the ancient republican gerontocracy:

> One cannot say that one lives more freely in this city than before, for the authority of the republic has fallen to a few *giovani* who are rabid rather than strong, partisan instead of civil, rapacious and libidinous not just or temperate. I do not so much sorrow at such a manifestly vituperate thing as marvel that it has been tolerated for so long.[159]

Clearly, age, piety, and experience once more had to triumph over the virile anarchy of youth, if the republic was to be saved.

The *giovani* were enraged at this attempt to send them back to private life the instant the Medici left the city. "It appeared to them," Foscari continued, "that they were the authors of the new government, and [yet] were perse-

157. *Relazioni*, ser. 2, I, 69f.

158. *Ibid.*, 72. Some pro-Medicean youth remained in the city, of course. For their demonstrations of affection when the thirty-year-old Medicean archbishop of Florence left the city, see Sanuto, XLV, 156; a strict Medicean account of Last Republic events is by Francesco di Giovanni Baldovinetti, edited by E. Londi, *Appunti di un Fautore dei Medici durante l'Assedio di Firenze del 1529–1530* (Florence, 1911). And from the beginning a group of "better qualified" youth favored the new *piagnone* (pro-Savonarolan) Standard Bearer Capponi; Nerli, II, 29, 39, 58; also Busini, 14. Yet despite Nerli's statement (II, 88) that "youth were

divided as were also the first citizens of the government," the pro-Capponi youth played no significant public role until late 1528 and early 1529; *ibid.*, 24. Segni explains this in terms of the Standard Bearer's belief that if a legitimate leader favors youth, he will become a tyrant ("se si cominciava dalla sua parte a favorir gioventù, e dare animo a persona in favor suo, che gli bisognava di principe legittimo divenir tiranno"); Segni, *Storie*, 130. Yet Segni himself points out that Capponi's age and limited funds were other factors explaining his reticence; *ibid.*, 76.

159. Segni, *Storie*, 193, in the context of events of 1529. For the evil goals of the youth, *Relazioni*, 72.

cuted by the *piagnoni*."[160] What could be the motivations behind such self-righteousness, they asked, and a sinister response was not long in coming:

> If one wanted to pursue the matter and punish the *giovani* who in their zeal for liberty had in youthful heat somewhat exceeded civil procedure, this was nothing else than to desire to change the state and readmit the Medici.[161]

No, the liberty that the youth had conquered was too precious to lose to the businessmen who had negotiated the transfer of the state. If the latter were telling each other that, like the ancient Romans, they had to defend liberty even "against their very own sons," the former warned these oldsters that the youth would cut their own fathers to pieces if they acted "inconsonant with freedom."[162] Youth were the defenders of liberty and must participate. Government must be spirited and pursue ideals. This essence of the youth platform was perfectly typified in an address of the twenty-nine-year-old Pierfilippo Pandolfini to the elders of government, delivered during these months:

> I want to ask you in the name of [the *gioventù*] to not consider them presumptuous for making such requests of such optimal and sage citizens our lords. It might not appear reasonable to you that the *giovani*, who have no position at all, come before the oldest, constituted by the *popolo* in the supreme honor, [and] commend to them the public welfare. . . . But . . . in each person, even if young and inexperienced, one can find something of use to the public good. . . . You can well recognize our spirit for what it is, and with what intent we say these things, by looking us in the face and seeing that we have always been sincere, and that we intend to perpetually maintain liberty and the well-being of this republic.[163]

The youth demonstrated their power so as to formalize their menacing presence in the counsels of government. Clamoring *giovani* forced the vestigial Medicean government to resign despite the protests of their honored fathers.[164] They stupefied their elders and the city at large by personally preparing the venerated Hall of the Grand Council—"purifying it," as was said, of Medicean "filth"—with such zealous speed that the government had no choice but to accede to youthful threats.[165] It moved up the council's first meeting by a full month and allowed the youth to attend its first two meetings despite their prepolitical age.[166]

160. *Ibid.*

161. Assessment of the second Standard Bearer of the Last Republic Francesco Carducci, in 1529; Nerli, II, 97.

162. *Relazioni*, 230; the admonition to the fathers to defend liberty was by, among others, Niccolò Guicciardini, cited in Albertini, *Staatsbewusstsein*, 384f.

163. Attributed to Pandolfini by Segni, *Storie*, 77f. This radical is portrayed by his later accusers as the classical young Momus: he corrupted young minds, was unpredictable, chastised and struck his parents, and so on; J. Pitti, "Dell'Istoria," 170f.

164. Nardi, VIII, 21.

165. "Netta e purgata la sala da ogni lordura, fu eziandio purgata e espiata da' sacerdoti con l'aqua santa, secondo l'uso delle cerimonie sacre"; Nardi, VIII, 21; Varchi, III, 9; Roth, *Last Republic*, 49f.

166. "Fatto mezzo il tempo dell'uficio suo per satisfare al popolo, et a' giovani, et fu conceduto a' giovani da 24 in 30 anni trovarsi a fare el Gonfaloniere; il che fu acconsentito sì per satisfazione di detti giovani, et sì per arte, e industria di chi sperava da loro favore"; L. Morelli, 246.

Apparently intended to reward the youths' contribution to the city's liberty, this flattery did not defuse their vigilance in the defense of liberty. Terrorizing philo-Mediceans in the city, the *giovani* all but forced their exclusion from government councils and offices.[167] Youth spied on Niccolò Capponi, the new Standard Bearer of Justice, because they doubted his dedication to liberty from the Medici, and posted a guard around the Palace to prevent enemies of the republic from entering. The august elders of the commune were, in one outraged elder's words, surrounded by "a pack of children"; the youthful guard in the Piazza della Signoria became one of the striking formal scenes of the Last Republic.[168] Still, the elders refused to open the Grand Council to the regular attendance of the young, and decided to maintain the age of twenty-nine for admission.[169] Unwilling to have them in council, they were just as determined to resist the youths' second demand: their formation into an official city militia.[170] As the dust settled on these hectic months of mid-1527, it seemed that the impetus of the young for incorporation into the commune had been stayed.

From within the Capponi government the secretary of the Ten, Donato Giannotti, continued to warn his patrons not to set themselves up as a bulwark against youth. The times called for elders to assume a qualitatively new attitude toward youth, Giannotti insisted, one that would permit the *vecchi* both to politicize and to militarize this great untapped resource in their own interest. Partly implemented and partly discarded, Giannotti's views portended a radical new face for a better commune of Florence, and they deserve our close attention. Among his contemporaries, only Giannotti's mentor Machiavelli understood as well as he the important role that ritual had to play in modifying social and political structure.[171]

Liberal commentators like the secretary of the Ten agreed with their conservative colleagues on the youths' basic predicament. Florence had never had a government, said Niccolò Giucciardini, that "encouraged *giovani* to make themselves egregious and excellent." The city was willing to support youthful mechanics and merchants, he continued, but it had little to offer "liberal" youth.[172] As things were, Machiavelli had written, when a liberal youth no longer wanted to obey his father he had no choice but to go abroad and become a soldier or, as Giannotti said, stay at home and perpetrate all manner of licentiousness.[173] This was not, however, a given of political and social life, but something that, Giannotti believed, could be changed.

167. *Ibid.*; Varchi, III, 9; Nerli, II, 9; Cambi, XXII, 318ff.

168. Varchi, VII, 13.

169. Roth, *Last Republic*, 49; Dorini, "Ragguagli," 58f, 61. But see page 527, this volume.

170. See page 529, this volume.

171. For Giannotti's background, R. Starn, *Donato Giannotti and His Epistolae* (Geneva, 1968), 17–31. Our main source for Giannotti's thought is his *Della Repubblica Fiorentina*, finished in exile shortly after the end of the republic, Nov. 14, 1531, and published in his *Opere*. It justifies the Last Republic, and projects a reborn one. Hereafter we shall assume that the relevant ideas in this work are the same ones Giannotti pushed during the Last Republic, especially since they uniformly agree with those of the "Discourse" written in 1529, and edited by Sanesi.

172. Albertini, *Staatsbewusstsein*, 394, 396.

173. Machiavelli, *Arte*, 100, 344; Giannotti, *Opere*, 170 (speaking of the rich *giovani*), 227ff.

Like his mentor Machiavelli, the secretary saw no absolute dividing line, no final psychological impasse between youth and age. It might be, for example, that today war could only be pursued by those eighteen to thirty-five years of age, but that was because older men became unnecessarily flaccid; it did not have to be so.[174] Perhaps *giovani* did cut up when they were allowed into council—in one case, years before, they made such a noise with their feet on the parliamentary benches that the Grand Council had to be dismissed—but that too was the result of an imperfect social order.[175] Why not make one in which "youth would exert themselves to be old men before being young; this would be most beautiful in a republic"?[176] Experience was the key, not age. In the future Florentine republic, Florentine counselors would be "experienced, whether they be young or old."[177]

To gain this experience, youth, in Giannotti's view, had to be encouraged to express their political opinions as part of their workaday occupations. Not only would the *giovani*'s preoccupation with political events leave them little time for private matters, which were the source of faction and rancor, but it would make them expert in public matters, to the benefit of the republic.[178] Giannotti dismissed those *vecchi* who ridiculed his suggestions, for they were the very same wise men who had been responsible for the Medici tyranny, in which neither they nor their sons could open their mouths.[179]

Armed with this practical knowledge of political affairs, youth should be made members of the Grand Council at the earliest possible stage, Giannotti thought:

> Before the *giovani* arrive at their twenty-fourth year, they should commence going to the council, so that they begin to taste the sweetness of the republic. If they become wise at a tender age, they will not be able to forget the republic, and they will then be the more ferocious and ardent in defending it. . . . So that the *giovani* begin at once to pursue public affairs, the Venetians have a certain law by which they annually give a certain number of those between twenty and twenty-five years faculty to be able to go to the council. Whence, if one wanted to imitate the Venetians, one could ordain that each year all the *giovani* between twenty and twenty-five years would be voted upon in the Grand Council, and those who got a majority could go to council.[180]

In early 1528, the government does seem to have relaxed along these lines. By a law of May of that year it set twenty-four years as a minimum age rather than the previous twenty-nine. Still, policemen were stationed within the council to preserve gravity, and to exclude those below twenty-four.[181] No one ever seriously considered the possibility of twenty-year-olds entering this august chamber. Florence was not Venice.

174. Giannotti, "Discorso," 22.

175. That case is documented in Sanuto, III, 95 (1500).

176. Giannotti, *Opere*, 182.

177. *Ibid.*, 141.

178. *Ibid.*, 230.

179. *Ibid.*

180. *Ibid.*, 182. At every stage, Giannotti compared the Florentine constitution unfavorably with the Venetian, which among other things could incorporate the young as Florence's could not.

181. Varchi, VI, 10.

The second recommendation of Giannotti for the political participation of the young was much more radical, and less successful. The *giovani*, he believed, should have access to the offices and magistracies of the republic and not just to the council. There were Scipios and Corvinuses among those of tender age, he said, whose talents the republic could ill afford to lose.[182] Each year the older members of the Grand Council should vote on all their colleagues who were still below the twenty-nine-year-old minimum for these offices, Giannotti suggested, with those achieving a certain vote being given access to office:

> Such an ordinance would admirably inflame the spirits of youth toward *virtù*, [since they] would see that they could accede to those honors in youth that render others glorious in old age. And as the *vecchi* are more impelled by avarice than by glory, so the *giovani* are incited by glory more than any other thing. If from an early age they begin to taste glory, they will give themselves over entirely to those means that they believe will allow them to obtain it.[183]

The reaction of the councilors to such a suggestion was predictably negative. The elders' determination to maintain a monopoly of offices was an established part of Florentine political life, even more inflexibly insisted upon by the lesser citizens than by the upper classes.[184] When in mid-1528 the minimum age for the Grand Council was dropped to twenty-four, the minimum age for offices was kept at twenty-nine.[185] Some *giovani* might be in the council of the commune, but all were refused access to what contemporaries called "the honors."

How would the *giovani* behave in the Grand Council and what should be done to guarantee gravity in the Great Hall? It was at this point that Giannotti first displays his sensitivity to the forms that politics took. Unlike Savonarola, our secretary believed that government institutions could serve as examples to the citizenry at large; through its formal structure as much as through the substance of debate, the Grand Council would educate the young man in civility:

> I believe it necessary to seek out every means by which the *giovani*, and the *vecchi* as well, remain grave in the place where the council is held. The Venetians arrange the Capi de' Dieci and the Avvocatori and some other magistrates in some eminent places, so that their awesomeness brakes youthful levity. If this procedure seems good, we could still easily imitate it, disposing some of the highest magistrates in the most conspicuous places of the hall. One could also ordain that the benches would be distinct according to the wards, and that each ward sit on assigned benches. Whoever was honored with some magistracy would sit in the place assigned for that magistrate. . . . It would follow from this arrangement that the *giovani* would be forced to be grave, sitting [as they would be] next to their fathers and to the other *vecchi* who would be in each ward.[186]

182. Giannotti, *Opere*, 231.

183. *Ibid*.

184. See page 391, this volume.

185. Busini, 64f.

186. Giannotti, *Opere*, 181f. Florentine *pratiche* were traditionally arranged according to age and honor; Varchi, X, 19. Seating and voting in the Grand Council was arranged according to benches (*panche*); Cambi, XXI, 182; Lupi, "Nuovi Documenti," 27–75.

Giannotti's view that formal structures created moral virtues would pervade his military and religious, as well as his political, thought; similar ideas had informed the world view of Niccolò Machiavelli.[187] Like the parade of a militia, so the Grand Council too was a theatrical school of manners. Here in the political procession old men acted and dressed their age so as to educate the young in gravity, and ultimately the whole society in reverence. From the halls of government, Giannotti foresaw, the moral force of the good republic of youth and adults would radiate outward and create a new attitude toward age. All the magistrates would wear distinguishing uniforms, but so would the more revered elders who were not in government. In Giannotti's plan, not just the *vecchi* in government, but the elderly men in society at large, would thus receive proper deference.[188]

As far as we know, such arrangements were never put into effect. In general, Giannotti's aim of incorporating the youth into the political structure of the city met with indifferent success. The secretary had in essence warned his masters that only the *giovani* could save the commune, but at the political level, the fathers of Florence refused to act on his message. Nor were things much different at the military level, since for more than a year, we are told, "generally all the *vecchi*" opposed the idea of mobilizing the *gioventù*.[189] Many councilors must have seen the seeming contradictions in the secretary's plan. He said the *giovani* would be submissive to their fathers in the council, yet that that very council would "inflame their spirits," "incite" them, and make them "ferocious and ardent" in the military defense of their country. It was enough to frighten anyone. Ferocity had no place anywhere in the city; it was the enemy of all civil life.

When the elders deserted this view in November 1528 and passed a law instituting an urban militia of the *gioventù*, they did so for reasons having little to do with Giannotti's grand idea of a citizen soldiery and more to do with regaining the dignity of the government of the *vecchi*.[190] Through all this time, a standing guard of youth had circled the Palazzo not so much to protect as to spy on their fathers. A private creation of the *gioventù* rather than an official body, the guard was a constant humiliation to the government. Now the Standard Bearer Capponi decided that a militia of all youth with fathers in the Grand Council would prove more friendly than the single-minded Rabids who watched his every move with suspicion. He promptly sponsored a bill for the creation of such a militia.[191] This recommendation was quickly

187. See the famous passages on cult in the Discourses; *Il Principe e Discorsi*, ed. S. Bertelli (Milan, 1960), 153–173 (I, 9–14). See also the passage on ceremonies in his *Asino d'Oro*, cited by Bayley, *War and Society*, 296. For Machiavelli on the importance of oaths, see page 536, this volume.

188. Giannotti, *Opere*, 229f.

189. Varchi, V, 19; VII, 12. A law of June 11, 1527, had allowed the Nine of the Militia to enroll an urban militia, but only if the Signoria and Ten agreed, which they did not. Jacopo Pitti thought this law was

a maneuver of the *ottimati* to prevent such a militia; J. Pitti, "Dell'Istoria," 158. Niccolò Guicciardini approved this sidetracking and rebuked Giannotti for his radical proposals; Albertini, *Staatsbewusstsein*, 388; Starn, *Giannotti*, 31.

190. The text of the militia law of Nov. 6, 1528, is in *ASI*, I (1842), 397–409. A modifying law of Dec. 14, 1528, is in Canestrini, "Documenti," 337–341.

191. Varchi, VII, 12–13. The last Standard Bearer of the republic is said to have widened the social character of the militia to the same conservative ends;

adopted, but any thought of further political concessions to the youth was discarded. The militia would regiment the youth under the government, the *vecchi* now believed, and would not, as Giannotti had hoped, serve as but one part of a seamless web of youthful participation in civil life. On November 6, pro-Capponian councilors leaving the hall after passing this decisive law taunted the youth guarding the Palace: "God be thanked. Now we will be rid of this pack of children."[192]

The youthful defenders of freedom were right in viewing Capponi's turnabout on the militia issue as a move to crush them; they closed ranks in the Confraternity of the Faithful from which had come their original impetus, determined to maintain their dedication to the libertarian ideals and forestall the leveling influence of the broader *gioventù*.[193] But the resentment at Capponi was not limited to these youth; many older citizens suspected that the Standard Bearer wanted to suppress the youth so as to be able to subvert the city's liberty.[194] The attempt to neutralize the radical youth failed, and when these *giovani* discovered Capponi exchanging correspondence with the Medici pope in clear violation of the law, the die was cast. The old man fell from power on April 17, 1529.[195]

The scene was reminiscent of others. A wrathful *gioventù* invaded the Piazza after discovering the letter and demanded that Capponi be tried by torture. There they were met by a rival band of Capponian *giovani* who defended the disgraced official's right to civil procedure. The first threat of a direct confrontation between different parties of *giovani* loomed. At this instant a marvelous thing happened. In order to secure a fair trial for his predecessor, the government ordered the mobilization of the *milizia della gioventù*, and the new *gonfaloniere* Francesco Carducci ordered three of its units to take over the guard in front of the Palace. They received complete obedience from all the agitated youth.[196] It was clear to all that the promptitude with which the youth obeyed this summons saved Florence from tumult, and that the institution of the militia was mainly responsible for their salvation.[197] With the fall of Niccolò Capponi, the appointment of a new Standard Bearer with impeccable anti-Medicean credentials, and with this first call to arms of the whole militia, the ceaseless violence and vigilance, the repeated eruptions of the *giovani* into the political arena, passed their apex. The city prepared for a siege. In the midst of the hardship that lay ahead, it was the miracle of disciplined youth, fighting without wages for their *patria*, that would stand out against the failure of the *vecchi*.

Bayley, *War and Society*, 293, 304f. But for other reasons, see subsequent pages.

192. Varchi, VII, 13. The exact words of Alfonso Capponi vary in different accounts, but not their meaning.

193. On the Fedeli, see *Relazioni degli Ambasciatori Veneti*, ser. 2, V (Florence, 1858), 412; J. Pitti, "Dell'Istoria," 168. The group's title was presumably used by contemporaries to designate faith in Savonarola's prophecies; Canestrini, "Documenti," 357f; Busini,

30. Perhaps this confraternity is that group of Fedeli founded in 1522 whose statutes and matriculation are extant; *Bibl. Laurenziana, Acquisti e Doni*, 11, kindly brought to my attention by Ronald Weissman.

194. J. Pitti, "Dell'Istoria," 165f.

195. Roth, *Last Republic*, 124–129.

196. *Ibid.*, 125; Segni, *Storie*, 140.

197. Varchi, VIII, 7; Segni, *Storie*, 151; J. Pitti, "Dell'Istoria," 177; Busini, 70; Sanuto, LII, 137f, 379, 585.

THE FORMS OF THE MILITIA

The Florentine cavalry . . . on parade was like a moustached toy soldiery mounted on she-goats. I never saw anything like it. In truth it was [more like] a funeral dirge mourning a people who have abandoned their slippers, burgher-caps, and usury. Atop their mares, well armed and wearing pompous under- and outerclothing, they looked like gallow bums who, silent, wailed: "I surrender."[198]

In my adolescence I saw fathers and mothers take and remove every type of arms from the rooms of their young boys as best they knew how, so that they would be better disciplined and as little delinquent as possible. Since that time I have myself seen more than one father still in his *gioventù*, enrolled in the aforesaid militia, go to the *mostra* or parade, even to the skirmishes outside the gates, accompanied by two of his small sons who were no more than fifteen or sixteen years old. And similarly I have seen sisters arm their brothers, and mothers and fathers send their sons happily off to the encounters of war, blessing them and commending them to God.[199]

The *milizia della gioventù* was in arms from November 1528 until August 1530, when the city surrendered to imperial forces. Although the defense of the Florentine dominion was consigned to rural militias and to foreign mercenaries, that of the city was given to the urban youth and a sizable body of mercenaries. Defending the city meant guarding the gates from surprise attacks and patrolling the streets; although the occasional sallies the *gioventù* made beyond the walls were psychologically important, they had little direct military significance.[200] The militia was doubtless a crucial element in Florence's ability to withstand the enemy for so long, but actual combat was a low priority. Derisive punsters taunted the youth with the accusation that their militia was pro forma, and there was something to that.[201] But the form was one means by which the city cohered during the siege.

To a remarkable extent, this form set the militia apart from the civilian population much as Lodovico Alamanni had once recommended to the tyrant. The young men were in effect interned in a "school."[202] First of all, the *giovani* were subject to military as well as civil law and were consequently exposed to harsher penalties than their fathers. Second, the magistracy in charge of military affairs, the Nine of the Militia, consciously sought to tighten the working relationship between the militia and the mercenary troops in the city; the idea was not only to ensure the loyalty of the mercenaries or increase the military skills of the urban *gioventù*, but also to alienate the latter from the city's sectarian politics.[203] To dilute further the youths' attach-

198. A foreigner's characterization of the Medici militia in 1516; Sanuto, XX, 564.

199. Nardi, VIII, 55.

200. This has been the opinion of experts since Canestrini, "Documenti," cxix; Roth, *Last Republic*, 194–197.

201. Varchi, XI, 29. Giannotti himself praised the militia for preventing tumult in the city, not for its military prowess; *Opere*, 157. The insult that the militia was "una prospettiva, et non da combattere," was

one reason for the famous single combat between loyal and pro-Medicean youth of 1530; G. Milanesi (ed.), "Cartelli di Querela e di Sfida . . . al Tempo dell'Assedio di Firenze . . . ," *ASI*, n.s., IV, pt. 2 (1857), 11.

202. As the "schools" of various *condottieri* also trained professional soldiers; see Alamanni's view, page 519, this volume. Giannotti noted that the militia was set apart from the city; *Opere*, 238–241.

203. See the 1528 law in *ASI*, I (1842), 407f; Roth, *Last Republic*, 270; *Francesco Ferruccio*, 414.

ment to the city's private unions, each four companies of the militia stood under the immediate command and discipline of a non-Florentine sergeant appointed by the Nine, so that an equitable discipline free of familial influence could be maintained.[204]

Neighborhood loyalties had to be undermined as well, and the Nine came up with a shrewd approach. Though using the sixteen traditional wards of the city to organize the militia, the Nine recruited the members of each company from across the city.[205] This was different from Giannotti's recommendations for the Grand Council, therefore, where youth were to be socialized by being surrounded by their elder neighbors. In Cleisthenian fashion, neighboring youth in arms had to be kept in different companies.

Finally, the vigilance of the Nine is seen in their decision to separate age cohorts. In the original militial law of late 1528, each of these sixteen units was to be constructed from equal numbers of those eighteen to twenty-four, twenty-four to thirty, and thirty to thirty-six years of age.[206] From this provision we can also surmise that the majority of these youth were unmarried, as they had been in Machiavelli's *contado* militia before 1512, and as Giannotti had wanted them to be for offensive duties.[207] There is no reason not to credit Jacopo Nardi's Hectorian image of fathers marching off to war with their sons, of course. Yet the sight would have been more common in late 1529 and early 1530 when, as the desperate straits of the city became evident, the maximum age for the militia was raised first to fifty and then to sixty years of age.[208] Until a complete reconstruction of the militia is undertaken, we must assume that most *giovani* were not heads of households. As one critic wrote in 1530–1531, these were boys who had enjoyed military service because at home, "they could command their fathers and other brothers who were not fit for arms."[209]

For more than a year from its inception, the militia recruited its youth exclusively from those "beneficed" families that belonged to the Consiglio Maggiore; it thus reflected the propertied sociology of that group, which ranged from the patriciate to the established artisanate.[210] When in December

204. According to the 1528 law the four sergeants could be either Florentine or foreign, but the first four were foreigners (Varchi, VIII, 7), and the Venetian ambassador understood that foreigners were to be the disciplinarians of the militia; Sanuto, XLIX, 114f, and that ambassador's *Relazione*, V, 427. On the other hand, the militiamen elected their own flag-bearers, drummers, and (ten-membered) squadron heads; a rough calculation shows that a militia of 3000 men yielded honorifics for about 380 *giovani*.

205. Giannotti, *Opere*, 238–242, who knew that in an ideal republic, natural neighborhood alliances could be honored without fear.

206. J. Pitti, "Dell'Istoria," 158.

207. Machiavelli in 1507: "La maggior parte, immo quasi tutti questi nostri scritti, sono figliuoli di famiglia; perchè tale esercizio si espetta a' giovani, e

non a quelli che sono di età provetti"; *Opere di Niccolò Machiavelli*, ed. S. Bertelli, IX (Milan, 1970), 383. "As many bachelors as possible"; *ibid.*, 303 (1506). See also Giannotti, "Discorso," 22.

208. Roth, *Last Republic*, 195, 298. But many of these were for long not armed, but only enrolled; see below.

209. *ASI*, I (1842), 437.

210. The legal makeup of the council depended on its families' previous right to offices in the republic; another ancient requirement—not to be in tax arrears—was waived at times to obtain a quorum. For this complicated question, see N. Rubinstein, "I Primi Anni del Consiglio Maggiore di Firenze," *ASI*, CXII (1954), 154–229, 321–347, and Roth, *Last Republic*, 47ff.

1529 a serious need for more militiamen arose, the government, with extreme reluctance, enrolled *giovani nonbenefiziati* in the ranks, and thus formally broadened the militia's social composition to include families that had no political investment in the regime because they were not part of the Grand Council.[211] However, it is not clear that these same youth were armed at this time. Only in late July 1530 did the elders of Florence, in extremis, give weapons to these youth—the same desperate point at which the whole male population of the city had to be armed.[212] If the fathers had been able to avoid it, no *giovane* would have borne arms. But they far preferred arming their own sons to replacing with steel the wooden arms of the plebs of Florence.

By all accounts, these battalions of Florentine youth gave the Last Republic a lease on life it would otherwise not have had. In the twilight of a republican culture, the brilliant, frightful, and dangerous youth of Florence saved this city from its fate not through military exploits, but through parades, not by destroying the order of the besiegers, but by reinvigorating the ritual order within the walls of Florence. How did the youth achieve this miracle of civil preservation? The answer lies first in the creation of a completely new ritual presentation by the *giovani* in arms, which we may call the ceremony of the oath. What follows is a composite picture of this youth ritual in the Last Republic.

The Orations

To teach the militiamen obedience and unity and to impress upon them the solemnity of the oaths the youth took to defend the city, the government of Florence established two cycles of orations to be delivered on successive days in the four quarter churches of Florence. One cycle was to culminate with a citywide oration on February 9, the feast of the election of Christ as king of Florence, and the other was to end with a similar general oration on May 15, vigil of the anniversary of the Medicean expulsion from the city.[213]

The texts of these orations have drawn the attention of past students; their contexts, and the behavior of the youthful orators have not. Yet it was specifically these details that had such resonance at the time.[214] What an

211. *Ibid.*, 195, 298.

212. *Ibid.*, 298; Sanuto, LIII, 389 (July 23).

213. The law of June 26, 1529, ordained the orations of Feb. 9 and May 15, and the details were spelled out in a law of Sept. 7 following; P. Falletti-Fossati, *Assedio di Firenze*, 2 vols. (Palermo, 1885), I, 433–437. The orations in the quarter churches were provided for in the original militia law. For orations on the feast of the Holy Savior, see Roth, *Last Republic*, 197, who mistakes the age limitations for council orators.

214. The surviving records of actual orations vary from the legal timetables. Here is a reconstruction:
1529:
Jan. 25, S. Spirito; Giovanbattista Nasi or Domenico Simoni

Jan. 26, S. Maria Novella: as above
Jan. 27, S. Lorenzo: Pierfilippo Pandolfini
Jan. 28, S. Croce: Luigi Alamanni; Landucci, 368; Busini, 63; Albertini, *Staatsbewusstsein*, 133.

1530:
Feb. 3, S. Spirito: Baccio Cavalcanti
Feb. 4, S. Croce: Lorenzo Benivieni
Feb. 5, S. Maria Novella: Piero Vettori
Feb. 6, S. Giovanni: Pierfilippo Pandolfini
Feb. 8, Sala del Gran Consiglio: Giovanbattista Nasi
May 15, Sala del Gran Consiglio: Baccio Cavalcanti; Varchi, X, 74; Busini, 73; "Diario d'Incerto," 32; *Raccolta di Prose Fiorentine* VI (*Orazioni*) (Florence, 1731), 42; Albertini, *Staatsbewusstsein*, 404; Cambi, XXIII, 60; Sanuto, LII, 585. Albertini's examination of these ora-

unprecedented sight it was! On the days of the orations in the quarter churches, the four companies of the particular quarter marched into their church in full battle array to take their seats. They were led by their weaponed orator, who ascended the pulpit, and looked out beyond his colleagues to the rear of the church. It was filled with a crowd of older citizens, also armed, who had come to hear his martial words.[215] It was as if Florence at large watched its most powerful confraternity perform the most sacred, and cunning, rite. From the words of the orator they would hear the secrets that were to save the city, and in the disciplined action of the armed youth they sensed a dedication that made the city invulnerable.

The orator spoke, and how fiercely he rejected the Florentine past! "How can it be that our fathers (they will pardon me) have been so shortsighted," Luigi Alamanni asked his fellow *giovani* while the fathers listened. They spend their life accumulating, and this mercantile avocation has made them greedy, their women licentious, their young men effeminate, the political class tired, aged, and incapable of defending itself.[216] The orators constantly implied, when they did not actually say it, that the *vecchi* thought governing was little more than a business, involving "this deal or that," whereas right-minded persons knew that magistrates are not merchants, and that liberty could not be maintained by a political culture that had no standards beyond the mere accumulation of wealth.[217] Clearly, the ideals that now motivated both urban and mercenary youth could not have come from their fathers, but were a direct gift of God:

> O glorious and high God, you have always given particular attention to this city, and one can see this [in the fact] that you did not want to completely destroy this miserable *popolo*. For you have ignited in the breasts of these valorous soldiers that ancient *virtù*, hidden and buried for so long. . . . For you have generated such open spirits and such resolute hearts in this *bella gioventù* that they throw themselves so ardently into every danger to save our sweet liberty and give vent to a just ire against the enemy.[218]

Humbled, perhaps even contrite *vecchi* watched in awe as the militia responded to such words, not with uncontrolled rage against the fathers, but

tions may fairly be characterized as verbocentric; *Staatsbewusstsein*, 167–178.

215. Orators, troops, and spectators came to the churches armed; Busini, 73. Interestingly, citizens attending the orations in the Sala del Gran Consiglio could not carry arms; Varchi, X, 74.

216. "Come esser può che i nostri padri (et perdoninmi loro) abbian veduto sì poco avanti"; Canestrini, "Documenti," 342ff. Pandolfini spoke of the plutocrats creating social friction *ibid.*, 362. Vettori also referred to dishonestly acquired goods; Albertini, *Staatsbewusstsein*, 406. Cf. their mentor Giannotti: "Doubtless the elders, *popolani* as well as *grandi*, are all occupied in abject and vile thoughts, because all have no other goal than to accumulate money"; *Opere*, 170f.

217. Busini summarized Pandolfini's oration: "Diceva che i Magistrati non fossero Mercanti, e non facessero questo Appalto e quello, e così successivamente"; Busini, 63. Vettori spoke of the "male educatione ch'annighittisce et addormenta ogni generoso spirito col nutrirlo in opere abiette et meccanice"; Albertini, *Staatsbewusstsein*, 406. The charge of buying and selling the state was heard in council: "Questo non essere un compromesso della Mercanzia"; Varchi, X, 22. Another such reference in Roth, *Last Republic*, 185.

218. Albertini, *Staatsbewusstsein*, 407 (Vettori). More on this theme in Canestrini, "Documenti," 351 (Pandolfini); *ibid.*, 346 (Alamanni). Baccio Cavalcanti says God illuminated the spirits of the *giovani*'s fathers; *Raccolta*, 44.

with sweet understanding. They marveled at the orator's ability to control his audience through his actions as well as through his words, much as they might have viewed "the action" as well as the "oration" of a preacher.[219] The content of Piero Vettori's oration was excellent, a witness remembered, "but the action, that is the pronunciation and the gestures, pleased no one."[220] Baccio Cavalcanti's "beautiful gestures and enthusiasm," on the other hand, were guaranteed to move the crowd, another observer thought, because "the eloquence of his words was perfectly accompanied by voice and manners."[221]

All listened as the orators explained how their peers could best fulfill their godly mission of saving the city. Brotherhood was the first necessity, and only by repressing their mutual enmities could the *giovani* succor tired and weak parents and rescue the city: "From good rules are born good friendship, from friendships are born reliable confederations, from confederations results the power of the provinces which cannot be easily assaulted by foreigners."[222] Next came discipline, a science greater than any art or profession: The recruits had been given a terrible power over the lives of the citizens, and the welfare of everyone depended both on the civility of the youth and on their willingness to avoid excess.[223] Finally there was the virtue of obedience. The orators left no doubt that this meant obeying the government of the elders: "The principal and most necessary of [political habits]," said one speaker, "is to obey the magistrates with great reverence and do that entirely which the law ordains."[224]

If the youth observed fraternity, discipline, and obedience in their mutual and civil behavior, they would be all the more ferocious against the enemy; the ideal of an almost schizophrenically placid youth in arms was alive and well. Though the militia was *giovane et inexperta,* one orator was pleased to suggest, had these *fortissimi giovani* not already proven themselves through their *virtuosi fatti* in defense of the city? One day, he went on, the militia of the youth would burst the imposed bonds of the siege, pass from defense to offense, and build an empire. The militia would give birth to "incredible acquisitions."[225] In these ceremonial orations of a heroic, dying republic, we hear again the golden promise of the Magian empire of Florence, this time from the mouths of its civil, warrior youth. The future utopia seemed to abide in the honor of the young.

The Oath

From the earliest plans for the creation of a militia, orations were viewed in the context of the oaths that the soldiers would take to the commune of

219. The formulation is Varchi's, X, 74.

220. *Ibid.*

221. Busini, 62, 73; also Segni, *Storie,* 86f.

222. From the oration attributed to Filippo Parenti; Albertini, *Staatsbewusstsein,* 137. See also Canestrini, "Documenti," 348 (Alamanni), 355 (Pandolfini); *Raccolta,* 53f (Cavalcanti), and especially on vengeance in Albertini, *Staatsbewusstsein,* 408f.

223. *Raccolta,* 57f. Lack of discipline was all the more unjustified because the *giovani* had elected their own officers; Albertini, *Staatsbewusstsein,* 405, 408 (Vettori). More on discipline in Canestrini, "Documenti," 348 (Alamanni).

224. Albertini, *Staatsbewusstsein,* 408f, 404f (Vettori).

225. *Ibid.*

Florence. In Machiavelli's 1506 militia law for the *contado*, for example, the newly organized militiamen were to congregate in the village church the morning after a parade and hear the Mass of the Holy Ghost. This Mass was to be followed by an oration delivered by a deputated member. Then each *giovane* was to come forward, hear a recitation of all the crimes for which capital punishment could be levied on him, and immediately after take a fearsome oath, "solemnizing the oath with all those words found most efficacious in being obligatory upon soul and body."[226]

This key phrase had two meanings. First, it assumed that certain words had the effect of controlling behavior better than others; second, and more significant, it said that violation of those words was a sin. Florentine subgovernmental corporations, in keeping with the canon law, usually discouraged oaths whose violation was a sin. Except in the most extreme circumstances, they preferred words whose violation merely invoked the threat of confraternal displeasure.[227] These were not usual times, however, and subsequent militial reforms preserved the idea that such perjury was sinful. Like Machiavelli's oath (*sacramento*) "obligatory upon soul and body," therefore, that of the Last Republic also relied on the coercive force of divine displeasure. "Jesus Christ, Lord of the Armies" would receive the oaths of the *giovani*. The militiamen were warned that if they violated this *religione del sacramento*, they or their descendants would reap godly as well as civil wrath.[228] So sacred was the community of the *giovani* in arms, so serious was the threat to the city.

While incorporating Machiavelli's basic model for oath taking, the Last Republic's first militia law of 1528 also ordained that the new militia's first ceremony was to be held on separate days in each of the four quarter churches, so that the citizenry and the magistrates could witness all the oaths.[229] In the following year Donato Giannotti suggested a procedure for incorporating each successive class of eighteen-year-old recruits. There should be a "solemn pomp and ceremony" in the cathedral, he believed, that would provide a centralized, highly motivating spectacle for the youth and the whole city:

> I would like this ceremony to be done in the following way. On the feast days of San Giovanni, on a certain designated day, the Signoria should have a solemn Mass sung in Santa Reparata, at which they should be present. And all the wards will have gathered there those youth of their *gonfaloni* who had reached their eighteenth year. The Mass having been sung, each [ward] *gonfaloniere* would present his [*giovani*] to the Signoria, one by one, and each would be given a piece of offensive arms. . . . And as soon as one had taken arms, he would present himself before the altar, and with great reverence take the oath from the priest who had sung the Mass: to defend the honor

226. "Aggravando il giuramento con tutte quelle parole obbligatorie dell'anima e del corpo, che si potranno trovare più efficaci"; test in Machiavelli, *Arte*, 111.

227. See the typical language in Doren, *Arti*, II, 135.

228. Albertini, *Staatsbewusstsein*, 408ff. Cambi indicates that the oath was to Christ, King of Florence; XXIII, 60. The Roman military oath was often the object of humanistic admiration; Bayley, *War and Society*, 213ff, 258.

229. *ASI*, I (1842), 402f; Segni, *Storie*, 86f.

of God, the liberty of the *patria,* and always to be obedient to the magistrates, and never to use those arms to other ends than those ordained by his superiors. The arms having been given, His Excellency the Standard Bearer [of Justice] would deliver an oration, in which he would exhort them to [do] the aforementioned things. And then the Signoria would leave, and would be accompanied by the other magistrates to the Palace by the said *giovani.* This would be a beautiful ceremony and very useful to the republic, because through it the spirits [of the *giovani*] would admirably exert themselves toward *virtù* and the defense of the *patria.* And nothing moves tender spirits more than seeing themselves associating with and honored by public magistrates. And tied to religion, one cannot imagine how many admirable results this [ceremony] would produce.[230]

This was one recommendation of Giannotti's that was fully executed; the city of Florence did build a great new ceremonial contract around the oath of the youth. The *giovani* marched to the cathedral in all three years, each ward led by its flag—the section emblem on a field of youth's green color.[231] In the square between the cathedral and the Baptistry stood the great silver altar customarily used in important communal solemnities, adorned "as richly as possible" in keeping with the government's wishes.[232] Astonished oldsters who were accustomed themselves to taking terrible oaths to the *buon comune* to ward off civil war, now saw grave young men do it for them. Giovanni Cambi described one setting, in which "all the relics of San Giovanni and the relics of the chapel of the cross of Santa Maria del Fiore, and the head of San Zanobi"[233] stood on the altar, and over against the main door of the cathedral sat the highest officials of the government in their magnificent tribunal. Nardi remembered the occasion as if it were yesterday:

> Then the whole of the militia coming in order, and arriving before the altar, each of the *giovani,* with suitable acts and gestures, first made his reverence to [the altar], and then turned to the Signoria and did the same. And placing their hands upon the sacred and holy book of the Evangelists which was carried to them at each corner of the altar by one of the principal priests, they took the solemn oath, according to a certain formula of words ordered just for the occasion.[234]

The Parade

Throughout the fifteenth and early sixteenth century, *giovani* had mixed with elders in the great urban festivals; now they commanded the streets in their own ritual, while the city watched. On the way to the cathedral to take their oath, and especially afterward when they marched from the cathedral to the meadow of Ognissanti, the *milizia della gioventù* treated spectators to a review or procession—the military and religious terms were both used—that

230. "A tutti quelli a' quali, dopo la prima universale descrizione, per virtù della età si dessino l'armi, sarí ben darle con solenne pompa e ceremonia"; Giannotti, "Discorso," 26.

231. Landucci, 368; Cambi, XXIII, 61.

232. Falletti-Fossati, *Assedio,* I, 435 (law of Sept. 7, 1529).

233. Cambi, XXIII, 61 (oaths of May 16, 1530).

234. Nardi, VIII, 32 ("questa prima rassegna, o mostra che si vogliamo dire"—uncertain date, perhaps Feb. 5, 1529). "E a dì 5 di febraio, s'apiccò 16 bandiere verde, co' loro sengni de' gonfaloni, in piazza, che erono fatte di nuovo pe'la sopradetta milizia"; Landucci, 368.

left witnesses all but speechless.[235] If in the traditional procession of crisis priests had marched in splendor to bear witness to the eleemosynary altruism of the elders, the lay *giovani* of Florence now bore the incredible wealth of a city on their backs. If the military review had once been the preserve of foreign mercenaries, Florence's own youth now marched alongside the instruments of war. One contemporary diarist had difficulty distinguishing between arms and clothing: "The general parade . . . was a very beautiful thing, with twelve big pieces of artillery and twenty-eight hundred *giovani* in perfect order, both arms and garments."[236] Three historians who when young marched in these processions recalled their opulence as well, fusing arms and clothing in their memory of events:

> No one could believe either the good effects that the militia gave birth to or with how much spontaneity and ease it became perfect. No one should think that a more beautiful spectacle can be seen than that made by the Florentine *gioventù* when they gathered, both by the precision of their drills and by [the fact that] they were no less usefully armed than pompously dressed. . . . But mostly by a certain concord and union which appeared marvelous. One could not discern which was greater, the modesty of the captains in commanding or the promptness of the commanded in obeying. And I, who in that time . . . was one of them, repeatedly saw and heard even old soldiers beside themselves with wonder.[237]

> They were sumptuously adorned both in vestments and in weaponry.[238]

> With such beautiful weapons, and in such abundance, that seeing [the squadrons] and considering their cost brought the greatest wonder and delight and great confidence to [the spectators'] spirits.[239]

There can be no accident that so many contemporaries recorded the parade of the *giovani* as if the individual militiaman was a mannequin dressed in arms and cloth. Certainly men were awed by the Florentines' ability to prove their wealth and charity in the midst of the greatest crisis, and just as surely they were consoled by the sight of their youth defending them. But there was more. These youth were the docile, socialized bearers of the city's future. With all their rejection of merchandising, the *giovani* yet embodied the hope for a future in which men could sell cloth in the midst of an armed, erotic, and honorable youth.

The Mock Battle

The older generation of the friends of youth must have been delighted at the feigned battles that were performed once these youthful icons had congregated in the Prato. Long ago Antonio Brucioli had told frequenters of the Rucellai gardens that children should not waste time with foolish games, but rather spend their energy in military exercises, "teaching them through

---

235. E. Albèri, *L'Assedio di Firenze* (Florence, 1840), 142f.

236. Letter of June 24, 1529, in Falletti-Fossati, *Assedio*, I, 437.

237. Varchi, VIII, 7.

238. Nardi, VIII, 32.

239. Segni, *Storie*, 86.

feigned battles to excel in real ones."[240] Niccolò Machiavelli in the same setting had praised the Romans for training young people not in the army but first in the city. Once adept in the "imaginary militia," he said, they would easily fit into a real one.[241] Now Donato Giannotti continued this tradition. In 1529 he recommended that the militiamen drill on Sundays and after work during the week, "as an exercise, as one plays soccer and other games of the *giovani.*"[242]

Savonarola had thought of games as necessary wastes of precious time, but Giannotti and other patrons of the militia watched the military salvation of the commune. To disarm the enemy the same *giovani* might at one moment stage an ostentatious soccer match in the Piazza Santa Croce as if Florence was without cares, and then organize in the Prato for a mock battle.[243] To reward the winner with prizes ranging from bagatelles to statues, the units, and the commune itself, had contributed to a fund.[244] But more important, there was the gratitude of a consoled commune to stimulate the *giovani*: "This imagination and semblance of an encounter gave such a pleasure and marvel to whomever saw it . . . , almost as if it had been an actual conflict."[245]

The Banquet

Among the several parts of the military ritual of the *giovani*, only its concluding meal cannot be shown to have taken place during the Last Republic; we possess only Giannotti's contemporary recommendations that one be held. Yet the banquet that the secretary believed should follow the *fatto d'arme* in the public square was motivated by the same behavioral pedagogy as those parts of the ritual we know were performed, and it deserves our attention for that reason. The setting was to be the sacred Hall of the Grand Council, where the magistracy would annually host its youth. Filing into this room where on other days the hierarchically ordered elders made laws, the *giovani* would seat themselves in their one hierarchy, dressed for war, arms at their sides. Their magisterial hosts would eat with them, but on platforms raised above and circling about the young men, "so that by submitting each person to the eyes of the magistrates, each would reverentially refrain from any jocularity."[246] Here was no rowdy attack on viands, Giannotti clearly

240. D. Cantimori, "Rhetoric and Politics in Italian Humanism," *Journal of the Warburg and Courtauld Institutes* I (1937–1938), 97.

241. "Assuefatti in modo nella finta milizia, che potevano facilmente adoperarsi nella vera"; Machiavelli, *Arte*, 352. Is it possible that the *finte arme* of the *potenze* mentioned above were related to the games of the *giovani*?

242. Giannotti, "Discorso," 24.

243. For the soccer match, Varchi, XI, 21. The colors were white and green, and thus may have represented a contest between younger and older youth. At one point having heard of an imperial joust at Bologna, "ancora loro sopra la piaza di Giovanin ha

fatto un'altra tela et vogliano *etiam* loro giostrare, sichè fanno sì poco conto del papa et di l'imperatore"; Sanuto, LII, 306. The church of S. Giovannino was next door to the Medici palace. Thus such a joust was a classical insult similar to those performed around the walls of a besieged city, mentioned at the beginning of this volume.

244. *ASI*, I (1842), 404, 451. Humanistic attention to awards is described in Bayley, *War and Society*, 206, 238, and in *Della Vita Civile di Matteo Palmieri. De Optimo Cive di Bartolomeo Sacchi detto il Platina*, ed. F. Battaglia (Bologna, 1944), 253 (Platina).

245. Varchi, VIII, 32.

246. Giannotti, *Opere*, 265f; "Discorso," 18f.

believed, no egalitarian taking and passing of foods, but an occasion for learning the ritual practices of the community without which there could be no brotherhood. In the secretary's scheme, one government official would stand after the meal and address these youthful saviors at his feet. He would praise the practice of eating together, Giannotti continued, "showing how useful it was to the republic that men occasionally recognize each other as brothers."[247]

FROM CRISIS PARADE TO CRISIS PROCESSION

"It is a thing worthy of memory to see arms and religion together," contemporaries wrote on seeing the youth parade to take their oath. Their observation cautions us against separating violence and prayer.[248] Granted, the *milizia della gioventù* did not undergo religious conversion during the Last Republic as had the *fanciulli* in the Savonarolan period, nor did anyone imagine they had been morally regenerated in the conventional religious sense. Hypocrisy was a vice of those over thirty-five, Giannotti said; the reason the freethinker Brucioli was banished, Busini and Varchi added, was that the responsible priors were all over fifty-eight years old and *piagnoni*.[249] As we shall see, society ceded a certain moral latitude to the *giovani* in exchange for the services they provided.

The *milizia della gioventù* was anything but a profane body of killers hired for dirty work, however; the sacrality of a social group results from its role, rather than from the comportment of its individual members. A product of Florentine society organized to save all Florence's people, the militia appeared to be nothing less than a "sacrosanct" body, whose members, whatever their individual behavior, deserved no less respect than that due the holy talismans of the Mass.[250] What preacher had ever done more to calm a distraught city? There was but one association contemporaries could make in trying to describe what they saw, and it was a religious one; the militia was a *religione*, it was said, its comportment comparable only to a "most Observant order of St. Francis."[251]

Like friars, the youth cut their hair during the mobilization of the militia. Their fashionable lovelocks were too feminine, it was said, and beards were more suited to a race of warriors.[252] Like celibates, it was feared that in defeat they, not just the virgin girls of the city, would be raped by the victors.[253] Like

247. *Ibid.*

248. Sanuto, LII, 379.

249. "Avenne che fu una Signoria, che il più giovane aveva 58 anni"; Busini, 30. "Al tempo di questi medesimi Signori, i quali erano tutti vecchi e tutti piagnoni"; Varchi, VIII, 30; Giannotti, *Opere*, 237.

250. "Ma siete in mente, che non con men riverenza et candidezza di animo si conviene a te di venire a questo sacratissimo esercizio, che al trattar le divine cose"; Canestrini, "Documenti," 346 (oration of Luigi Alamanni).

251. "As if this numerous militia was the most Observant branch of the friars of St. Francis"; Sanuto, LII, 345 (Dec. 3, 1529). "Never was a holy religion formed with such holy customs"; Canestrini, "Documenti," 348. The humanistic comparison of the Roman legions to "Observant religious" is in Palmieri, cited in Battaglia, *Della Vita Civile*, 98.

252. Landucci, 371; Varchi gives the classical description of conversion from wastrel lives to martial vigor, if not religion; IX, 49.

253. The *gonfaloniere* Carducci's fear: "Ultimamente,

the good women of Florence, finally, the *giovani* of the militia—on the command of the government—appeared at the communion rail en masse. Unheard of![254] All this was evidence that youth, *bella gioventù* at the barricades, was no longer an uncivil interlude between childish innocence and elderly *gravità*, but a positive and crucial civic generation that had to be ritually incorporated into the Florentine procession. The crisis of the Last Republic would place the greatest demands on the religious specialists of Florence, charged as they were with uniting the city, disarming the enemy, and charming an angry God through their processional organization of the city. The incorporation of the armed youth into those processions would not be the least of their innovations.

How remarkable, and yet how recognizable, are the reports of processional life in these desperate years. Once again, as in Savonarola's day, men and women stood separate in church, when the latter were not excluded.[255] Blasphemers and sodomites met death in this new wave of moral reform, and the Eucharist was received on a scale and with a frequency unparalleled in Florentine history.[256] In the churches the Signoria went barefoot to the altar, and in the streets they wore the brown of remorse.[257] The streets groaned beneath the weight of processions: "In adversities and dangers the lords of Florence turn to God, processions and prayers. . . . They automatically held processions every Friday with the greatest devotion."[258] As the siege began in earnest and the very real danger of a sack was the alternative to endurance, there were daily processions, processions every Saturday, a solid week of processions.[259] "In this city," the Venetian ambassador wrote in these dire days, "there is nothing else but devotions, processions, etc."[260]

The echoes of countless past reports in this stunned tone sound in our ears, yet when we listen carefully, we discover that the processions of the Last Republic were not the same as the classic crisis processions of earlier times. The situation had changed. An examination of the resulting proces-

---

con infinito danno e vergogna nostra e con perpetuale infamia e biasimo vostro, violare le sacre vergini, svergognare le caste donzelle, sforzare le maritate, corrupere le vedove e, quello che io non posso nè pensare senza orrore nè proferire senza lagrime, strupare i giovani, e uccidergli insiememente"; Varchi, XI, 109.

254. "Addì 29 di luglio [1530] andò uno bando che ogni huomo si confessassi et la domenica vegnente si dovessi communichare"; "Diario d'Incerto," 150. As far as is known, this was the first time communion was used as an official instrument of propitiation in Florence. The edict specifically urged the *giovani* of the militia to receive communion; Ademollo, *Marietta*, 1892. Observers were struck by the participation of the *giovani*: "Ogni festa vedesi comunicar le genti, et non meno la militare che l'altra"; Sanuto, LII, 585 (letter of Feb. 2, 1530).

255. "Diario d'Incerto," 147; Varchi, XI, 67. Segni also records that stands were erected in all the main

churches so people would not wander about during services; *Vita*, 929.

256. Roth, *Last Republic*, 140f, 272.

257. *Ibid.*, 309.

258. *Relazioni*, I, 24.

259. Eight days of fasting and procession, and for two months daily processions in the parish churches; Sanuto, LII, 215 (late 1529). Lent, 1530: procession every Friday; *Relazioni*, I, 280. Processions every Wednesday during Lent in single parishes, and every Friday during Lent a general procession; Cambi, XXIII, 52. Procession on Ash Wednesday and the first Sunday in Lent; Varchi, XI, 28. May 11: animal procession; see subsequent pages. May 12: solemn procession; "Diario d'Incerto," 147. June 24: solemn procession; *ibid.*, 148. July 31: general procession; *ibid.*, 150. This compilation excludes military parades and oath ceremonies.

260. Sanuto, LIII, 18 (Mar. 1, 1530).

sional experiments will show us the better commune that the city promised God on the eve of the dissolution of the republic.

Certainly one of the most striking innovations in the processions of these years was brought on by the danger of starvation. Food was still reasonably available in May 1529 when a discussion in council as to whether the miraculous image of Impruneta should be carried over the fields of the *contado* to help the crops or brought into the city to console and unite the citizens ended with the decision to do the latter.[261] But a year later things were different. When two cargoes of sheep, cows, goats, and other edibles miraculously escaped the enemy embargo and managed to reach the city, the Dominican friars were sure that only a procession of these animals could properly show God the city's gratitude. On May 12, 1530, the procession of animals made its way through the city heralded by trumpets and led "by four angels and a St. John and a Christ, who were children of the city dressed as they do in the confraternities for the processions of San Giovanni."[262]

Writing his *History of Florence* many years after the event, Benedetto Varchi remembered this marvelous procession with evident distaste: It was hard for him to admit, as did the procession, that the city of Florence had once represented itself by alimentary and biological, as much as by political orders.[263] Children dressing as angels to accompany animals; women interpreting their visions for city elders;[264] friars doing basic research on the city's plight, and reporting their findings to the government in open session;[265] girls and armed boys kneeling at the communion rail—every single element from the margins of Florence participated in the procession to save the city, whereas Varchi, a militiaman himself, preferred to remember the heroic past of his *giovani* alone. It was indeed a time of miracles. The procession of the chickens was only the most extreme example of a city ready to use all its processional resources in this death march of the republic.

Two specific experiments in organizing the city's human population in procession are worthy of particular attention. The first was the unparalleled geographic decentralization of the procession during this time, as if the single parishes of the city were ritual units in themselves, the total force of the city's prayers only the summation of its neighborhoods' plaints. We have seen that Florence's long preserved ritual unity had begun to weaken only during the later fifteenth century; the rise of neighborhood confraternities and the beginning of processions in designated quarters of the city were two evidences of this shift.[266] Now in the late 1520s the sources abound with references not

261. "Item andando el tempo sinistro per le ricolte, pensassimo se fusse da fare venir la tavola della Impruneta o farla andare supra li monti"; cited in Roth, *Last Republic*, 153. The first indication that Florentines went to accompany Our Lady "su per quei monti" seems to be in 1474; ser Giusto, f. 108r. But for the much older custom of *contadini* around the village of Impruneta carrying her over the crops, see *Capitoli . . . Impruneta*, 25f.

262. "Diario d'Incerto," 146f.

263. Varchi, XI, 55.

264. On suor Maddalena before the chancellor, see Parenti, in Schnitzer, *Quellen*, IV, 174.

265. See the charge and extensive report in Varchi, XI, 53–54.

266. See pages 399 seq., this volume.

only to quarters, but also to parishes and parish churches as processional units, their marches sometimes but not always culminating in a great general procession of the whole city. In 1530 alone, we hear of two months of daily processions in the churches of the parishes and of weekly processions staged each Wednesday in their neighborhoods.[267] Doubtless the fact that in the previous annals of the city there is scant reference to parish processions does not mean that they were unknown;[268] their repeated documentation during the Last Republic does mean that they were now politically significant. The city of Florence was being sacrally deconstructed; the neighborhoods were important to the unity of the city, and to the one true God.

The second experiment by the religious specialists of the city also paid witness to the decentralized civic identity that, first fostered by the Medici, had become an unavoidable burden of the best of republican governments. I am speaking of two remarkable processional cycles of the Last Republic, in which each of the ages and sexes of the population was given a day when its procession monopolized the streets. For all the previous history of the republic, the political males had been both the objects and the center of the crisis procession, even during the Savonarolan period when the *fanciulli* had led their sinful fathers. Now in these last days, the *vecchi* marched on one day, and each of the marginal groups marched on other days of the cycle. The Last Republic ended after recognizing the separate ritual identity of its several members.

The first of these cycles was held in late October and early November 1529 and was led off with a procession of the Signoria and magistracy. On the following day the venerable elders (*vecchioni*) of the city marched, then on the third day the whole militia. On the fourth day all of the women took their turn, and on the fifth the *fanciulli*; three other days of processions completed this cycle, but our source does not say who was in them.[269] Then in March 1530 the Dominican friar Benedetto da Foiano conceived a similar "penance," this one to be executed on seven consecutive Fridays, with each procession being led by the miraculous Cross of the Bianchi, to be carried by its confraternity. On the first day the Signoria and magistracy marched in the quarter of Santa Croce. On the second the cross was followed by the (male) *popolo* of Florence into the quarter of Santo Spirito. The third day found all the women of Florence in the quarter of Santa Croce. On the fourth Friday, finally, "all the *giovani* of the Florentine militia" "who guarded the city during the siege," marched in the quarter of Santa Maria Novella.[270]

These processions were the first in Florentine history in which the *giovani* marched as a unit in order to propitiate God and, just as amazing, they were the first in which the women of Florence had achieved their own distinct ritual character.[271] Was it not wondrous that the group if not class margins of

267. See n. 259.

268. A rare reference to three days of procession, "ciaschuna chiesa nel popolo suo," is in Panciatichi, f. 160r (1390).

269. Sanuto, LII, 585.

270. Again, Cambi does not say who marched on the latter days; XXIII, 52f.

271. A foot race for *fanciulle* on the feast of St. Mary

society walked for God on an equal footing with the political males? Who was not awed to watch man then woman, warrior then pious peacemaker, child then adult independently comingling prayers and gestures for a city's salvation? "We hope," the Signoria had announced to the city in November 1529, "that the arms of our militia when accompanied by prayer and divine help will always gain victory." Thus, the government decreed,

> Every time our soldiers come to battle with the enemy, all those . . . persons unable or unsuited to bear arms [like priests, friars, monks, nuns, children, and women of all ages] are required to kneel . . . , and say continual prayers as long as the battle continues.[272]

With these processions of grief and repentance, in which the liminal populations were incorporated into the processional community with distinct identities, the ritual revolution had reached its logical conclusion. At the center of this total ritual population stood the virile saviors of the militia. In their charismatic persons, the republic had made its ultimate attempt to infuse honor into a base political order.

The End of the Republic

In the great swell of popular support for the militia, the opposition of some citizens to the growing authority of the *giovani* was muted. The Florentines had harnessed fire itself, and few wanted to suggest that the city might be scorched for fear of being branded Mediceans. Yet as the crisis of the Last Republic moved toward its final denouement, the danger of the militia became too evident to be ignored. From its beginnings and in the course of its history, this salvational army had been granted privileges that distinguished it from the rest of the citizenry. In the final months of the republic, those privileges gave the young men a de facto control over city and government.

Machiavelli had known how dangerous yet unavoidable these warrior privileges were. "Because of military service," the Nine wrote to a field commissioner of the *contado* militia in 1507, these *contadini* "ought to have somewhat more license than others." They might not curse God, the magistrates continued, but cursing the saints ought not be prosecuted (during the Last Republic, one contemporary would condemn the blasphemies of the militiamen as impeding the salvation of the city).[273] Machiavelli's successor

---

Magdalene is documented, however, in 1475; see page 394, and note also the presence of *fanciulle* in one procession of the Savonarola period, page 479, this volume. A variegated age- and sex-specific public activity was first seen in Florence during three days of Carnival, 1516, when Pope Leo X staged races of "uomini vecchi, e quale a garzoni, e quale a fanciulle" in addition to those of horses, asses, and so on; Masi,

188f. Masi noted their derivation from the Roman Carnival of the popes, and in fact this form can be traced back to its innovator, Paul II; Pastor, *Geschichte*, II, 314.

272. The entire decree cited in Roth, *Last Republic*, 220.

273. Paolo Paoli, cited in *Francesco Ferruccio*, 437; "Per

Giannotti was just as flexible in this regard, and the 1528 law of the militia accorded the *giovani* the right to livery and to exceed sumptuary regulations.[274] To one critic, privilege was the real reason the young liked the militia:

> The *giovani* had this pleasure of being enlisted and of carrying arms. Through this means they were successful in satisfying their desire to eat and drink well, to dress beyond the laws, to have women and other things with more facility, to rule the roost at home, to incur debts without paying.[275]

Thus when in the extremities of the siege the *giovani* ate meat while citizens ate cats, asses, and horses, and the soldiers could imbibe wine, because the citizens drank water, more was involved than military necessity. The *giovani* had from the beginning had a privileged position, not the least example of which was their ritual centrality. The extreme state of the city in the last days of the regime made the matter worse. Unable to offer the militiamen political rewards, the government began to use the *giovani* as privileged enforcers of its edicts and maintainers of its order. "In Florence," our best source wrote, "the fear and confusion of the citizens grew. Nevertheless the magistrates maintained their reputation through the order and *virtù* of the militia, because suspects were kept in check."[276] How changed things were when the elders depended on the youth for the maintenance of a regime! The Venetian ambassador now saw the militia as a handmaiden of the government in terrorizing citizens: "[The militia] has kept in terror and fear those who desired and wanted to change things, for they did not dare raise a finger. And this is the reason that everyone acquiesces in what the government does."[277] By summer 1530 there was no longer any concealing the facts, even in the Grand Council of the *vecchi*. It was time, one councilor had already proclaimed to his fellow citizens, that the militia "either heals or kills the city."[278]

The city was desperate, and its only hope was for the urban troops to break out into the countryside and attack the camp of the enemy. It was decided that the Standard Bearer of Justice himself would lead the army.[279] There would be a great parade of the whole militia and then one last massive procession during which the *gioventù* would take communion together.[280] The city provided first for God, and then for man.

When on August 6, 1530, Malatesta Baglione, the commander of all the

lo esercizio militare egli abbino qualche larghezza più che li altri; non però tale che si offenda Iddio"; Machiavelli, *Opere*, IX, 383.

274. *ASI*, I (1842), 403f.

275. Francesco Vettori cited in Albertini, *Staatsbewusstsein*, 411. For his similar formulation, see *ASI*, I (1842), 437.

276. Busini, 70. Nerli charged that the Standard Bearer Carducci used a section of the militia as en-

forcers; II, 73. On the alimentary privileges of the soldiers, see Sanuto, LIII, 172; fra Giuliano Ughi, cited in *Francesco Ferruccio*, 426; Roth, *Last Republic*, 196, 270.

277. Sanuto, LII, 137f.

278. View quoted in Falletti-Fossati, *Assedio*, I, 429 (Feb. 18, 1530).

279. Roth, *Last Republic*, 299.

280. *Ibid.*, 299, 309; Sanuto, LIII, 477.

troops in the city, refused the command to lead this sortie, the government relieved him of his command. The test of the militia had come: Would the young men "heal or kill" the city? Would they obey the government or their general? In a unique situation, the head of the government seized at straws. The Standard Bearer left behind much of the solemn retinue that was his due and rushed to the different units in the city. On street corners rather than at the Baptistry, he would once more require each militia member to swear ceremoniously the oath of loyalty to the government of Florence.[281] This penultimate public test of formal order in republican Florence failed. Militial solidarity dissolved.

In the Piazza Santo Spirito across the river, a group of about four hundred young men allied itself with the traitorous captain-general and with his subordinate Stefano Colonna, commander of the *milizia della gioventù*. It was the first illegal assemblage of the youth since the beginning of the siege, the decisive violation of that *"religione del sacramento* which they had taken so many times and in so many ways."[282] Varchi's dramatic and tragic words still shatter our complaisance. Commanded to order the *giovani* to disperse, Baglione instead proclaimed "that he stood by these *giovani*, and that he knew no other lord."[283]

Either the militia would obey the magistrates, or the republic would collapse. The government decreed that the militia was to assemble in the Piazza della Signoria. Our mind's eye flashes back through Florentine history to "the first procession, when forty-day-old Christ was presented in the temple . . . . Anne was there with much company [and] behind them went . . . Mary . . . [and] . . . Joseph with their retinue."[284] The Florentines stood ready to witness the last formal assembly of the republic. A loyal member of the militia described its last bid for civil contract:

> We were a squadron of about eight hundred or a thousand *giovani*, for no more appeared. . . . But . . . in the moment that news spread among us that . . . Malatesta had occupied the gate, and that those other [*giovani*] . . . were in Santo Spirito to favor the worthy Malatesta, of the eight hundred or a thousand of us, not more than two hundred or less remained. For out of fear some went home, while others (and these were the richer and less satisfied) [went] to Santo Spirito to be pardoned.[285]

The republic was in ruins. On August 11, the day after San Lorenzo's, a settlement with the besiegers was almost at hand. "Praise be to God," one of them wrote, "and to lord Lorenzo, that is of the Medici, patron of the house on the eve of whose birth one laid the foundation of this most holy peace."[286]

281. Varchi, XI, 130.

282. *Ibid.*

283. *Ibid.*

284. *Capitoli . . . Impruneta*, 16.

285. Busini, 160f.

286. "Laudato Dio et signor Lorenzo, *idest* de' Me-

dici, patrono de la casa nel cui dì natalicio heri si butò il fondamento di questa santissima pace"; Sanuto, LIII, 460. The sacrality of time was obviously alive and well. Cf. to a commentator at the time of Savonarola's death: "Et questo è *mirum*, che dicto fra Hironimo, el zorno di la dominica di l'olivo, ch'è principio di passione, fue preso, et la vezilia di l'asensa passoe di questa vita"; *ibid.*, I, 968.

The following day, the city capitulated. There had been limits to youthful conviction, solidarity, and obedience, for the siege had become unbearable, and it had eaten away at the proud fraternity of the militia. The bitterness of defeat would be intolerable. Was it true that the *giovani* who headed the platoons had betrayed their subordinates, or was the blame to be fixed on the rich *giovani* who had misled the poorer youth? Perhaps age had been decisive, with the older *giovani* corrupting the younger members:

> Never in the world had there been a greater terror than in those two months that I remained in Florence from the change of government until my banishment. The youth were most hateful to one another. The elders were mocked by the lower class.[287]

Florence had not followed the example of Saguntum, as it had so often sworn to do. "Here Lay Florence" never recorded a Tuscan landscape in whose hallowed spaces men and women had once formed themselves about venerated things.[288] Florence continued. Yet to the returning Miceans, the *giovani*'s break with the conquering family seemed complete. Francesco Guicciardini wrote that the *giovani* hated the Medici so deeply that it would be a century before the family could rule in peace.[289] Francesco Vettori thought that the libertine nobility under thirty-five were irreparably lost to the restored tyrants.[290] Luigi Guicciardini warned against establishing chairs in philosophy, for "they were the means for all those *giovani* to congregate who, poorly domesticated to the regime, had risen up in 1527."[291] Before all else, he urged, the Medici must win these *giovani* to their side. *Vecchi* were slow to act; *giovani* were poisonous.[292] The republican historian Varchi closed the book on this era of intense generational awareness, on a republic that to the last made and unmade itself in public:

> If the *vecchi* had comported themselves during the whole siege as the *giovani* behaved, they would have doubtless merited more praise than they received, and perhaps they would have had a better fate than they did.[293]

287. Busini, 166. On the squadron leaders deserting, Segni, *Storie*, 283. On age as a factor, Varchi, XI, 130. Of interest is that four of the known *giovani* oratori deserted the colors; Busini, 157, 160f, 164.

288. For this "Last Days mood" and the comparison to Saguntum, see Varchi, IX, 16; XI, 129.

289. "Abbiamo per inimico un popolo intero, e più la gioventù che i vecchi, in modo che ci è da temere per cento anni"; *ASI*, I (1842), 455.

290. *Ibid.*, 437.

291. Albertini, *Staatsbewusstsein*, 169.

292. "Perchè dei vecchi tengo men conto assai, per essere più freddi all'imprese, nè tanto velenosi"; *ibid.*, 460 (attributed to Francesco Guicciardini).

293. Varchi, X, 73.

Chapter 14

Epilogue and Prolegomenon: The Pasts and Futures of Urban Forms

The wealth of nations shall come to you. . . .
They shall bring gold and frankincense,
And shall proclaim the praise of the Lord.*

How quickly Florence forgot. Abroad, the exiled Donato Giannotti might still fantasize revived republics to come, and in Rome Michelangelo could yet recall the political heritage of his youth. But in mid-sixteenth-century Florence the poisonous heroes of the Last Republic had become pliant elders of the Grand Duchy of Tuscany.[1] They had long since discarded citizens' clothes, carefully forgotten the republican roots of the new princely culture, and consigned to ignominy the indecorous haggling that had gone into the foundations of this new Athens. Admirers of Michelangelo escorting visitors through the master's *New Sacristy* (Plate 24) at this time were at a loss to explain its meaning.[2] Pope Leo X (Plate 25) had started this Chapel of the Resurrection in 1521 to represent the journey of Florence and the Medici family toward eternity: the *New Sacristy*, we believe, was meant to summarize a political culture.[3] Now it was merely, if triumphantly, beautiful. Within a generation, the Medici chapel as a historical document had ceased to exist. At the conclusion of this book, let us recapture the journey of Magian Florence with the sculptor as our guide.

---

* Isaiah 60: 5–6.

1. See Cochrane, *Florence in the Forgotten Centuries,* 13–92.

2. Antonfrancesco Doni's account is paraphrased in

Trexler and Lewis, "Two Captains."

3. *Ibid.* Note that Leo X's coin (Plate 25) intimates that he was the culmination of the journey of the Magi.

Facing the head of the chapel, we see on our left Lorenzo, grandson of the Magnificent, sitting above his sarcophagus with its figures of Day and Night, and to our right Giuliano, son of the Magnificent, towers over Dawn and Dusk.[4] Lorenzo bears the condottiere's baton, recording that ceremony of 1515 in which the republic gave him the civil command; Giuliano, heeding the Florentine fear of foreign rulers and their generals, holds only the cloth (*mappa*) of the Roman consul to represent his command of the papal army. These two captains, as Michelangelo called them, look toward the head of the chapel where Mary and Child, flanked by Sts. Cosmas and Damian, sit upon the graves of Lorenzo the Magnificent and his brother Giuliano. It is a classic, seemingly static, scene, where scattered warriors beneath triumphal arches pay tribute to a distant stone Child.

A closer look, a willingness to view this chapel in its Florentine historical context, and the chapel resurrects the noise and smell, the touch and movement of a historical procession. Almost concealed beneath the baton of the Florentine captain are gold coins falling from Lorenzo's hand; now we recognize the object beneath Giuliano's elbow as an incense box; the doctor–saints at the head of the chapel surely hold in their medicine vessels the myrrh of eternal preservation so appropriate to a funeral chapel. These are the gifts of kings! We are swept into a Magian procession, and enter a more animated space. Now Lorenzo and Giuliano are great puppets atop creaky festive *trionfi*. The Times of Day at their feet like gypsum giants beneath the heroes of carnival *trionfi*, these noble servants wheel toward a manger at the head of the sacristy where lie their apotheosized Medici lords: Lorenzo the Magnificent, Giuliano his brother, and Cosimo *pater patriae* represented by his patrons Cosmas and Damian.[5] The Medici chapel speaks of Florence's processional history. It opens a road for comprehending the traditional European city. And, as we devotees move about Our Lady's image and honorable Medicean frame, the chapel emphasizes our own processional identity.

Florentine history rests encapsuled in this chapel. If we step toward the hushed manger with its luminescent Lady, we search out the specific context of the Florentine cult of the Madonna, and recall Machiavelli's commentary on the events of the 1340s. The burghers had discredited the city's aristocracy at that time, this contemporary of our sculptor recorded, and with its demise had gone the generosity of feeling and the military virtue peculiar to a privileged order; the *popolo*, Machiavelli assumed, was incapable of such noble virtues.[6] For a time some imagined that a mere public bank could furnish all the credit a merchant city desired, but the author of *The Prince* knew better. Institutions only enforce credit; persons create and sustain it.

Who were these persons to be? Historically, Florentines looked to the entourage of Our Lady to solve that dilemma, for it was there where citizens jockeyed for position so as to participate in her credit. Yet the commune

4. Our identification of the captains is the reverse of the traditional one; *ibid.*

5. Cosimo is actually buried at the cross in the body

of the church of S. Lorenzo.

6. See page 18, this volume.

dissuaded its fellows from pasting family coats of arms on civic images, just as it refused to endow its fellows in government with the serene aura of the Venetian doges. In the later fourteenth century, communal condottieres and Florentines with great positions abroad tried to court the civic gods. But Florence resisted the triumphal entry of all lords for fear of insurrection. The trust necessary to civil and diplomatic life, and the credit that was a foundation of this crippled Croesus' political and economic activity were values that only the world of princes could bestow in sufficient quantity, yet Florence would not welcome them.

The Ciompi revolt of 1378 weakened this resolve, and in its wake the political class turned more and more toward the leadership of a native elite that bought knighthood from Teutonic lords and got on with Christly vicars. Florence would be ennobled by insiders who could attract outsiders' honor. Our Lady needed a more honorable frame.

In the neofeudal world of fifteenth-century Europe, where powerful lay and ecclesiastical lords threatened to overwhelm Lady Florence, she chose honor, developing a seductive vocabulary of processional forms and groups to ward off ravishment. Mock Magi came to town till real royal visitors converted this gate-city into a courtier's paradise. A single family succeeded best in bringing foreigners to the Florentine show, so astutely courting them that in the end, the Medici visiting Florence sufficed to prove the city's nobility. In that celebration of the city's newfound respectability, a fundamental change in civic representation took place: first boys, then plebs, youth, and at last even women entered the city's self-representation as distinct groups, threatening, as do we in this Magian chapel, to breathe a different life into processional marble.

The famous festivals of fifteenth-century Florence were no mere bread and circuses for children, youth, and workers; a vulgar functional analysis of public activity will not do. These groups appeared in the festivals because of the increasing impotence of the republic of grave men, who recognized their need for new civic clienteles to bolster their waning authority publicly. Flattered by the families that manipulated them, these liminal groups also manipulated their betters in the politics of the public procession. Once allied with the dazzling energy of Medicean youth, they slowly pushed apart the old ritual order and created new sacred images, times, and places. The Savonarolan and Soderinian regimes, as well as the Last Republic, were but the last acts of an ancient constitutional script; the republic of grave men ultimately acquiesced to a native family that brought them foreign credit and social peace. Sixteenth-century Florence was graced by an absolutistic prince who honored a plurality of neighborhoods, occupations, generations, and sexes, while decorating his throne with the arms of noble if subject families.

Stepping back now so as to encompass the captains and the Times of Day in our view, we hear the clamor of their history and realize the relevance of the procession to the understanding of the past. These statues ask us to study European urban culture through its formal behavioral structures. From the earliest pages of this book, we have seen the Florentines assemble their living theater simultaneously to define while projecting their political and social order. The streets, squares, churches, and palaces were legitimating stages to which varied classes and groups sent "embassies" that, witnessed by the city, foreign lords, and deities, formed and transformed civil, diplomatic, and religious bonds. Public life in the city was, is, a political process, and should be studied as such. Here in the streets there is not only noise and odor, but meaning.

This study has shown how abundant the source materials are for uncovering the meaning of public life in traditional European cities. The student of urban politics need not, therefore, dismiss the legitimating action of the public sphere. Nor should the student of past religion explain pious behavior wholly as right or wrong expressions of dogma. The student of past artifacts dare not, finally, view them as above, or outside, the ceremonial procession of the historic city. Much of the abyss between social and cultural history may be spanned, in short, by watching urban populations behave in their sacred and profane places.

The present work only starts the task of studying urban formal structures, and betrays the crudity of beginnings. My sources rarely mention the Jews of Florence in a formal behavioral context; I have had to neglect them.[7] The same sources tend to conflate the behavioral functions of boys, youth, plebs, and women; I have at times placed these liminal groups indifferently around the classical male center. Not satisfied with studying the relation between individual identities and group dynamics among adult males, I have presumed to attribute meanings to the actions of liminal groups whose members have left few narrative records. Clearly, much remains to be done; everything needs refinement. This work only creates a series of formal structures, cartographs, so to speak, with which to view the meaning of public action.

Finally, I have chosen to ignore political and religious dogma, preferring to study meaning through the unreflective perceptions of contemporary narrative sources.[8] This only postpones the question of the relation between ideas and actions. This strategy may, it is true, help clear the way for a better understanding of the problem; guided by the idea that reflection determines action, writers have ever identified hypocrisy and altruism and called this analysis, seldom reckoning that a coherent set of ideas is itself a reverential deception. Still, such coherent bodies of thought do effect and modify behavior. In still unclear ways, such culture does shape human society. The Times of Day ponder the effects of culture beneath their captains, vestiges of a society past. In this work, honor and credit have remained only ethologic facts.

---

7. Florentine narrative sources do not even contain a description of a converted Jew's baptism, for example. See, however, page 256, this volume.

8. The character of the chosen sources was described early in ch. 2.

A final step back out of the charmed Magian retinue of the Medici chapel, and we may regard the processional traces our own presence has left in that space. Like the Florentines who fled the city to avoid the plague's infection, the modern viewer may find that there is no escaping the common journey of society, for it is the circle of our public solidarities that gives us identity. Today's devotees touch these stone giants much as centuries ago other Florentines crowded about great visitors and Virgins to attach their coats of arms. We give them audience through reverence or deny it through blasphemy. We play their games, but can yet make them ours.

Bibliography

Manuscript Sources

I. *Archivio Arcivescovile, Florence:*
Atti Straordinari
Beneficiali
Contratti
Filza Cartapecore

II. *Archivio del Convento di San Marco, Florence:*
Liber Vestitionum

III. *Archivio di Stato, Florence:*
Acquisti e Doni
Arte della Lana
Camera del Comune
Carte di Corredo
Carte Strozziane
Catasto
Compagnie Religiose Soppresse, Capitoli
Consulte e Pratiche
Deliberazioni della Signoria. Speciale Autorità
Diplomatico
Manoscritti
Miscellanea Repubblicana
Missive, Prima Cancelleria

Notarile Antecosimiano
Otto di Guardia
Provvisioni, Registri
Tratte
Ufficiali dell' Onestà
Ufficiali della Notte

IV. *Biblioteca Laurenziana, Florence:*
Acquisti e Doni
Archivio di San Lorenzo
Biblioteca di San Marco

V. *Biblioteca Nazionale, Florence:*
Carte Palagi
Conventi Religiosi Soppressi
Custode
Magliabechiana
Panciatichi

VI. *Biblioteca Riccardiana, Florence:*
ms. Moreniana
ms. Riccardiana

Printed Sources

Alberti, Leon Battista, *I Libri della Famiglia*, eds. R. Romano and A. Tenenti (Turin, 1969).
Albizzi, Rinaldo degli, *Commissioni di Rinaldo degli Albizzi per il Comune di Firenze dal MCCCXCIX al MCCCCXXXIII*, ed. C. Guasti, 3 vols. (Florence, 1867–1873).
Aliotti, Hieronymus, *Epistolae et Opuscula*, ed. G. Scarmali, 2 vols. (Arezzo, 1769).
Allessio, "Due Responsi Astrologici dell'anno 1382 resi da maestro Allessio da Firenze concernante due Pistoiesi," ed. A. Chiappelli, *Bolletino Storico Pistoiese* XXIV (1922), 133–138.
Altoviti, Francesco, *In Defensione de Magistrati, et delle Legge et Antiche Cerimonie al Culto Divino della Citta di Firenze contro alle Invettive et Offensione di fra Girolamo* (Florence, 1497).
Ammirato, Scipione, *Istorie Fiorentine*, 11 vols. (Florence, 1824–1827).
Archivio Storico Italiano (ASI).
Arditi, Bastiano, *Diario di Firenze e di Altre Parti della Cristianità (1574–1579)*, ed. R. Cantagalli (Florence, 1970).
Aretino, Pietro, *I Ragionamenti*, ed. A. Foschini (Milan, 1960).
Arlotto Mainardi, *Motti e Facezie del Piovano Arlotto*, ed. G. Folena (Milan, 1953).
Baldovinetti, Francesco, *Appunti di un Fautore dei Medici durante l'Assedio di Firenze del 1529–1530*, ed. E. Londi (Florence, 1911).
Battistini, M. (ed.), *La Confrérie de Sainte-Barbe des Flamands à Florence. Documents relatifs aux Tisserands et aux Tapissiers* (Brussels, 1931).
Benvenuti Papi, A., "L'impianto Mendicante in Firenze, un Problema Aperto," *Mélanges de l'École Française de Rome. Moyen Age, Temps Modernes* LXXXIX (1977), 597–608.
Bernardino of Siena, St., *Le Prediche Volgari*, ed. C. Cannarozzi, Florentine sermons, 1424: 2 vols. (Pistoia, 1934); Sienese and Florentine sermons, 1425: 5 vols. (I–II, III–V) (Florence, 1940–1958).
———, *Le Prediche Volgari*, ed. P. Bargellini, Sienese sermons, 1427 (Milan, 1936).
Biagi, G. (ed.), "Per la Cronica di Firenze nel secolo XVI," *Rivista delle Biblioteche e degli Archivi* XVII (1906), 70–128.
Boccaccio, Giovanni, *Opere*, ed. C. Segre (Milan, 1966).
Boncompagno da Signo, "Cedrus," in L. Rockinger (ed.), *Briefsteller und Formelbücher des Eilften bis Vierzehnten Jahrhunderts* I (Munich, 1863).

Bonvesin de la Riva, "De Quinquaginta Curialitatibus ad Mensam," in *Le Opere Volgari*, ed. G. Contini (Rome, 1941).

Bosso, Matteo, *Recuperationes Faesulanae* (Bologna, 1493).

Bracciolini, Poggio, *Two Renaissance Book Hunters. The Letters of Poggius Bracciolini to Nicolaus de Niccolis*, ed. P. Gordan (New York, 1974).

Brucker, G. (ed.), *The Society of Renaissance Florence. A Documentary Study* (New York, 1971).

Filippo Brunelleschi, l'Uomo e l'Artista. Mostra Documentaria (Florence, 1977).

Buonarotti, Michelangelo, *Le Lettere*, ed. G. Papini (Lanciano, 1913).

Burchiello, Domenico di Giovanni, called il, *I Sonetti*, ed. A. Viviani (Milan, 1940).

Burlamacchi, Pseudo-, *La Vita del beato Ieronimo Savonarola, scritta da un Anonimo del secolo XVI e già Attribuita a fra Pacifico Burlamacchi*, ed. P. Ginori Conti (Florence, 1937).

Busini, Giovanni Battista, *Lettere di Gio. Batista Busini a Benedetto Varchi, sugli Avvenimenti dell'Assedio di Firenze* (Pisa, 1822).

Cambi, Giovanni, *Istorie di Giovanni Cambi, Cittadino Fiorentino*, in *Delizie*, XX–XXIII.

Campanella, Tommaso, *The City of the Sun*, in F. White (ed.), *Famous Utopias of the Renaissance* (New York, 1955).

Canestrini, G. (ed.), "Documenti per Servire alla Storia della Milizia Italiana dal XIII secolo al XVI," *ASI*, XV (1851), 1–550.

Canti Carnascialeschi del Rinascimento, ed. C. Singleton (Bari, 1936).

Canti Carnascialeschi del Rinascimento (*Nuovi*), ed. C. Singleton (Modena, 1940).

Canzone del Carro delle Ninfe coi Poeti, Cantata in Firenze nel Carnevale del MCDLXXXVIII, ed. A. Brandi (Arezzo, 1880).

"Canzone per Andare in Maschera per Carnasciale facte da più Persone," ed. S. Ferrari, *Biblioteca di Letteratura Popolare Italiana* I (1882), 5–62.

I Capitoli del Comune di Firenze, eds. C. Guasti and A. Gherardi, 2 vols. (Florence, 1866–1893).

I Capitoli della Compagnia del Broncone, ed. G. Palagi (Florence, 1872).

Capitoli della Compagnia della Madonna dell'Impruneta, ed. C. Guasti (Florence, 1866).

Cappelli, A. (ed.), *See* Medici, Lorenzo de'.

Capponi, Gino, "Ricordi," ed. R. Sereno, *American Political Science Review* LII (1958), 1118–1122.

Carnesecchi, Baccio, "Storia di Firenze dal 1526 al 1529," ed. U. Dorini, *Rivista Storica degli Archivi Toscani* III (1931), 100–112, 196–207.

Castiglionchio, Lapo da, *De Hospitalitate*, in *Tractatus Universi Iuris, duce et auspice Gregorii XIII . . .* , XIV (Venice, 1585).

Castiglionchio, Lapo da (Junior), *see* Scholz.

Cavalcanti, Giovanni, *Della Carcere, dell'Ingiusto Esilio e del Trionfal Ritorno di Cosimo, Padre della Patria*, ed. D. Moreni (Florence, 1821).

———, *Istorie Fiorentine*, ed. G. Di Pino (Milan, 1944).

———, *The "Trattato Politico-Morale" of Giovanni Cavalcanti (1381–c. 1451)*, ed. M. Grendler (Geneva, 1973).

Cegia, Francesco, "I Ricordi Segreti del Mediceo Francesco di Agostino Cegia (1495–1497)," ed. G. Pampaloni, *ASI*, CXV (1957), 188–234.

Cennini, Piero, "Il Bel S. Giovanni e le Feste Patronali di Firenze descritte nel 1475 da Piero Cennini," ed. G. Mancini, *Rivista d'Arte* VI (1909), 185–227.

Cerretani, Bartolomeo, *Storia Fiorentina*, in Schnitzer, *Quellen*, III.

Cianfogni, P. (ed.), *Memorie Istoriche dell'Ambrosiana r. Basilica di S. Lorenzo di Firenze*, with the *Continuazione* of D. Moreni, 3 vols. (Florence, 1804–1817).

Cinozzi, Placido, "Epistola," in Savonarola, *Scelta*.

Commynes, Philippe de, *The Memoirs*, ed. S. Kinser, 2 vols. (Columbia, S.C., 1969–1973).

Compagni, Dino, *Cronica delle Cose Occorrenti ne' Tempi suoi*, ed. F. Pittorru (Milan, 1965).

Corti, G. (ed.), "Consiglio sulla Mercatura di un Anonimo Fiorentino," *ASI*, CX (1952), 114–119.

"La Cronaca del Convento Fiorentino di San Marco," ed. R. Morçay, *ASI*, LXXI (1913), 1–29.

Cronache e Memorie sul Tumulto dei Ciompi, ed. G. Scaramella, in *RIS*, XVIII, pt. 3.

Cronichette Antiche di Varii Scrittori del Buon Secolo della Lingua Toscana, ed. D. Manni (Florence, 1733).

Dati, Gregorio, *Istorie di Firenze di Gregorio Dati dall'anno MCCCLXXX all'anno MCCCCV* (Florence, 1735).

──────, *Memoir*, in *Two Memoirs of Renaissance Florence. The Diaries of Buonaccorso Pitti and Gregorio Dati*, ed. G. Brucker (New York, 1967).

Davidsohn, R. (ed.), *Forschungen zur Geschichte von Florenz*, 4 vols. (Berlin, 1896–1908).

Dei, Benedetto, *Dalla Cronica*, in G. F. Pagnini della Ventura (ed.), *Della Decima e di varie altre Gravezze Imposte dal Comune di Firenze. Della Moneta e della Mercatura de' Fiorentini fino al secolo XVI*, II (Lisbon and Lucca, 1765).

Del Corazza, Bartolommeo di Michele, "Diario Fiorentino di Bartolommeo di Michele Del Corazza, anni 1405–1438," ed. G. Corazzini, *ASI*, ser. 5, XIV (1894), 233–298.

Delizie degli Eruditi Toscani, ed. I. da San Luigi, 24 vols. (Florence, 1770–1789).

Della Casa, Giovanni, *Galateo, ovvero de' Costumi*, ed. D. Provenzal (Milan, 1950).

Della Robbia, Luca, *La Morte di Pietro Paolo Boscoli*, ed. R. Bacchelli (Florence, 1943).

Diario d'Anonimo Fiorentino dall'anno 1358 al 1389, in *Cronache dei secoli XIII e XIV*, ed. A. Gherardi (Florence, 1876).

Diario di anonimo fiorentino (1382–1401), Alle Bocche della Piazza, eds. A. Molho and F. Sznura (Florence, 1986).

"Diario d'Incerto del 1529 e 1530 per l'Assedio di Firenze," ed. U. Dorini, *Rivista Storica degli Archivi Toscani* IV (1932), 30–45, 140–152.

Dominici, Giovanni, *On the Education of Children*, ed. A. Coté (Washington, 1927).

Dorini, U. (ed.), "Ragguagli delle Cose di Firenze dal 1524 al 1530," *Rivista Storica degli Archivi Toscani* III (1931), 53–67.

Filarete, Antonio, *Filarete's Treatise on Architecture, Being the Treatise by Antonio di Piero Averlino known as Filarete*, ed. J. Spencer, I (New Haven, 1965).

Filarete, Francesco, see *Libro Cerimoniale*.

Filipepi, Simone, "Cronaca," in Savonarola, *Scelta*.

Flora, F. (ed.), *Storia di fra Michele Minorita* (Florence, 1946).

Francesco da Barberino, *Del Reggimento e Costumi di Donna*, ed. C. Baudi di Vesme (Bologna, 1875).

──────, *I Documenti d'Amore*, ed. F. Egidi, 4 vols. (Rome, 1905–1927).

Francesco Ferruccio e la Guerra di Firenze del 1529–1530. Raccolta di Scritti e Documenti Rari pubblicati per cura del Comitato per le Onoranze a Francesco Ferrucci (Florence, 1889).

Garin, E. (ed.), *L'Educazione Umanistica in Italia* (Bari, 1949).

──────, *Il Pensiero Pedagogico dello Umanesimo* (Florence, 1958).

Gaye, G. (ed.), *Carteggio Inedito d'Artisti dei secoli XIV, XV, XVI*, 3 vols. (Florence, 1839–1840).

Gherardi, A. (ed.), *Nuovi Documenti e Studi intorno a Girolamo Savonarola* (Florence, 1887).

Giannotti, Donato, "Un Discorso Sconosciuto di Donato Giannotti intorno alla Milizia," ed. G. Sanesi, *ASI*, ser. 5, VIII (1891), 3–27.

──────, *Donato Giannotti and His Epistolae*, ed. R. Starn (Geneva, 1968).

──────, *Opere Politiche e Letterarie*, ed. F. Polidori, I (Florence, 1850).

Ginori, Tommaso, *Libro*, in Schnitzer, *Quellen*, I.

Giordano da Pisa [Rivalto], *Prediche del beato fra Giordano da Rivalto dell'Ordine dei Predicatori: Recitate in Firenze, dal MCCCIII al MCCCVI*, ed. D. Moreni, 2 vols. (Florence, 1831).

──────, *Prediche Inedite del beato Giordano da Rivalto dell'Ordine de' Predicatori, Recitate in Firenze dal 1302 al 1305*, ed. E. Narducci (Bologna, 1867).

──────, *Quaresimale Fiorentino, 1305–1306*, ed. C. Delcorno (Florence, 1974).

Giulini, G. (ed.), *Memorie spettanti alla Storia, al Governo, ed alla Descrizione della Città, e della Campagna di Milano, ne' secoli bassi*, 12 vols. (Milan, 1760–1771).

Grassis, Paris de, *De Ingressu Summi Pont. Leonis X Florentiam Descriptio*, ed. D. Moreni (Florence, 1793).

Grazzini, Antonio Francesco (Il Lasca), *Tutti i Trionfi, Carri, Mascherate o Canti Carnascialeschi andati per Firenze, dal Tempo del Magnifico Lorenzo Vecchio de Medici* (Florence, 1559).

Guasti, C. "Documenti della Congiura fatta contro il Cardinale Giulio de' Medici nel 1522," *Giornale Storico degli Archivi Toscani* III (1859), 185–232, 239–267.

────── (ed.), *Le Feste di S. Giovanni Batista in Firenze Descritte in Prosa e in Rima da Contemporanei* (Florence, 1884).

──────, *Il Sacco di Prato e il Ritorno de' Medici in Firenze nel MDXII* (Bologna, 1880).

————, *Santa Maria del Fiore. La Costruzione della Chiesa e del Campanile secondo i Documenti tratti dall'Archivio dell'Opera Secolare e da quello di Stato* (Florence, 1887).

Guazzo, Stefano, *De Civili Conversatione domini Stephani Guazzi Libri Quatuor* (Strassburg, 1614).

Guicciardini, Francesco, *The History of Florence*, trans. M. Domandi (New York, 1970).

————, *Storia d'Italia*, ed. L. Felici, 5 vols. to date (Rome, 1967–).

Guicciardini, Luigi, *Del Savonarola, ovvero Dialogo tra Francesco Zati e Pieradovardo Giachinotti il Giorno dopo la Battaglia di Gavinana*, ed. B. Simonetta (Florence, 1959).

Hasenohr-Esnos, G. (ed.), "Un Recueil Inédit de Lettres de Direction Spirituelle du XVe siècle," *Mélanges d'Archéologie et d'Histoire* LXXXII (1970), 401–500.

Hatfield, R. (ed.), "Some Unknown Descriptions of the Medici Palace in 1459," *Art Bulletin* LII (1970), 232–249.

Hippocrates, *On Joints*, trans. W. Jones (Cambridge, Mass., 1959).

Ivánka, E. von (ed.), *Europa im XV. Jahrhundert von Byzantinern Gesehen* (Graz, 1954).

Jacopo da Varagine, *Leggenda Aurea*, trans. C. Lisi (Florence, 1952).

Johannes von Hildesheim, *La Storia dei Re Magi*, ed. A. di Nola (Florence, 1966).

Kendall, P., and Ilardi, V. (eds.), *Dispatches with Related Documents of Milanese Ambassadors in France and Burgundy, 1450–1483*, 2 vols. (Athens, Ohio, 1970–1971).

Kristeller, P. (ed.), "Un Documento Sconosciuto sulla Giostra di Giuliano de' Medici," *La Bibliofilia* XLI (1939), 405–417.

Landucci, Luca, *Diario Fiorentino dal 1450 al 1516, continuato da un Anonimo fino al 1542*, ed. I. Del Badia (Florence, 1969).

Lanza, A. (ed.), *Lirici Toscani del '400*, I (Rome, 1973).

Lapini, Agostino, *Diario Fiorentino dal 252 al 1596*, ed. G. Corazzini (Florence, 1900).

Leonardo da Vinci, *The Notebooks*, ed. J. Richter, 2 vols. (New York, 1970).

The Libro Cerimoniale of the Florentine Republic by Francesco Filarete and Angelo Manfidi. Introduction and Text, ed. R. Trexler (Geneva, 1978).

Libro degli Ordinamenti de la Compagnia di Santa Maria del Carmino, scritto nel 1280, ed. G. Piccini (Bologna, 1867).

Luiso, F. (ed.), *Firenze in Festa per la Consecrazione di Santa Maria del Fiore* (Lucca, 1904).

Lupi, C. (ed.), "Documenti Pisani intorno a fra Girolamo Savonarola," *ASI*, ser. 3, XIII (1871), 180–190.

————, "Nuovi Documenti intorno a fra Girolamo Savonarola," *ASI*, ser. 3, III (1866), 3–77.

Machiavelli, Niccolò, *Arte della Guerra e Scritti Politici Minori*, ed. S. Bertelli (Milan, 1961).

————, *History of Florence and of the Affairs of Italy, from the Earliest Times to the Death of Lorenzo the Magnificent*, intro. F. Gilbert (New York, 1960).

————, *Opere*, ed. S. Bertelli (Milan, 1968–).

————, *The Prince and the Discourses*, trans. L. Ricci (New York, 1950).

————, *Il Principe e Discorsi sopra la Prima Deca di Tito Livio*, ed. S. Bertelli (Milan, 1960).

Magnani, R. (ed.), *Relazioni Private tra la Corte Sforzesca di Milano e Casa Medici, 1450–1500* (Milan, 1910).

Manetti, Giannozzo, "Oratio . . . de Saecularibus et Pontificalibus Pompis in Consecratione Basilicae Florentinae habitis," in *Umanesimo e Esoterismo*, eds. E. Garin *et al.* (Padua, 1960).

Manfidi, Angelo, see *Libro Cerimoniale*.

Manzoni, L. (ed.), *Libro di Carnevale dei secoli XV e XVI* (Bologna, 1881).

Martène, E., and Durand, U. (eds.), *Veterum Scriptorum et Monumentorum Historicorum, Dogmaticorum, Moralium, Amplissima Collectio* III (Paris, 1724).

Martin, Gregory, *Roma Sancta (1581)*, ed. G. Parks (Rome, 1969).

Masi, Bartolomeo, *Ricordanze di Bartolomeo Masi, Calderaio Fiorentino dal 1478 al 1526*, ed. G. Corazzini (Florence, 1906).

Maspes, A. (ed.), "Prammatica pel Ricevimento degli Ambasciatori Inviati alla Corte di Galeazzo Maria Sforza, Duca di Milano (1468—10 Dicembre)," *Archivio Storico Lombardo*, ser. 2, XVII (1890), 146–151.

Mazzei, Lapo, *Lettere di un Notaro a un Mercante del secolo XIV, con altre Lettere e Documenti*, ed. C. Guasti, 2 vols. (Florence, 1880).

Medici, Lorenzo de', *Lettere* eds. R. Fubini and N. Rubinstein, 3 vols. to date (1977–).

————, "Lettere di Lorenzo de' Medici detto il Magnifico conservate nell'Archivio Palatino di Modena," ed. A. Cappelli, *Atti e Memorie delle rr. Deputazioni di Storia Patria per le Provincie Modenesi e Parmensi,* I (1863), 231–320.

————, *Opere,* ed. A. Simioni, 2 vols. (Bari, 1939).

————, *Poesie Volgari nuovamente Stampate, di Lorenzo de' Medici, che fu Padre di Papa Leone, col Commento del Medesimo sopra alcuni de' suoi Sonetti* (Venice, 1554).

————, *Rime Sacre del Magnifico Lorenzo de' Medici, il Vecchio, di Madonna Lucrezia sua Madre, e d'altri della stessa Famiglia,* ed. F. Cionacci (Bergamo, 1760).

Milanesi, G. (ed.), "Cartelli di Querela di Sfida . . . al Tempo dell' Assedio di Firenze," *ASI,* n.s., IV, pt. 2 (1857), 3–25.

Minerbetti, Pseudo-, *Cronica Volgare di Anonimo Fiorentino dall'anno 1385 al 1409, già attribuita a Piero di Giovanni Minerbetti,* ed. E. Bellondi, in *RIS,* XXVII, pt. 2.

Minucci Del Rosso, P. (ed.), "Curiosità Artistiche," *ASI,* ser. 4, III (1879), 475–482.

Molinari, C. (ed.), "La Rappresentazione di S. Bartolomeo," *Annuali della Scuola Normale Superiore di Pisa,* ser. 2, XXIX (1960), 257–283.

Monaldi, Guido, *Diario,* in *Istorie Pistolesi, ovvero delle Cose avvenute in Toscana dall'anno MCCC al MCCCXLVIII, e Diario del Monaldi* (Florence, 1733).

Morelli, Giovanni di Jacopo, *Cronica,* in *Delizie,* XIX.

Morelli, Giovanni di Pagolo, *Ricordi,* ed. V. Branca (Florence, 1956).

————, "In Search of Father. The Experience of Abandonment in the Recollections of Giovanni di Pagolo Morelli," ed. R. Trexler, *History of Childhood Quarterly* III (1975), 225–252.

Morelli, Lionardo di Lorenzo, *Cronaca,* in *Delizie,* XIX.

Moreni, D. (ed.), *Mores et Consuetudines Ecclesiae Florentinae* (Florence, 1794).

Morini, U. (ed.), *Documenti Inediti o Poco Noti per la Storia della Misericordia di Firenze (1240–1525)* (Florence, 1940).

Naddo da Montecatini, *Memorie Storiche,* in *Delizie,* XVIII.

Nardi, Jacopo, *Istorie della Città di Firenze,* ed. A. Gelli (Florence, 1858).

Neri di Bicci, *Le Ricordanze,* ed. B. Santi (Pisa, 1976).

Nerli, Filippo de', *Commentari dei Fatti Civili occorsi dentro la Città di Firenze dall'anno 1215 al 1537,* 2 vols. (Trieste, 1859).

Palmieri, Matteo, *Della Vita Civile di Matteo Palmieri. De Optimo Cive di Bartolomeo Sacchi detto il Platina,* ed. F. Battaglia (Bologna, 1944).

————, *Historia Fiorentina,* ed. G. Scaramella, in *RIS,* XXVI, pt. 1.

Paolo da Certaldo, *Libro di Buoni Costumi,* ed. A. Schiaffini (Florence, 1945).

Papanti, G. (ed.), *Facezie e Motti dei secoli XV e XVI inediti* (Bologna, 1874).

Parenti, Piero, *Historia Fiorentina,* in Schnitzer, *Quellen,* IV.

Passerini, L. (ed.), *Modi di Dire Proverbiali* (Rome, 1875).

Paoli, Paolo, *Priorista,* in Rinuccini, Filippo, *Ricordi.*

Pieri, Paolino, *Cronica di Paolino Pieri Fiorentino delle Cose d'Italia dall' anno 1080 fino all'anno 1305,* ed. A. Adami (Rome, 1755).

Pierozzi, Antoninus, St., *Chronica domini Antonini Archipraesulis Florentini . . . ,* 3 vols. (Lyon, 1543).

————, "The Episcopal Constitutions of Antoninus of Florence," ed. R. Trexler, *Quellen und Forschungen aus Italienischen Archiven und Bibliotheken* LIX (1979), 111–139.

Pitti, Buonaccorso, *Memoir,* in *Two Memoirs of Renaissance Florence. The Diaries of Buonaccorso Pitti and Gregorio Dati,* ed. G. Brucker (New York, 1967).

Pitti, Jacopo, "Dell'Istoria Fiorentina," *ASI,* I (1842), 1–203.

Pius II, Pope, *I Commentari,* ed. G. Bernetti, 5 vols. (Siena, 1972–1976).

Pucci, Antonio, *Centiloquio,* in *Delizie,* III–VI.

————, "Guerra Pisana," in *Delizie,* VI.

Pulci, Luigi, *Lettere di Luigi Pulci a Lorenzo il Magnifico e ad Altri,* ed. S. Bongi (Lucca, 1886).

Quintilian, *Institutio Oratoria,* ed. H. Butler (London, 1922).

Raccolta di Prose Fiorentine VI (Florence, 1731).

Razzi, Serafino, *Vita di Santa Caterina de' Ricci con Documenti Inediti Antecedenti l'Edizione,* ed. G. di Agresti (Florence, 1965).

Redditi, Bartolomeo, *Breve Compendio* . . . , in Schnitzer, *Quellen*, I.

Relazioni degli Ambasciatori Veneti al Senato, ed. E. Alberi, 15 vols. (Florence, 1839–1863).

Renaudet, A. (ed.), *Le Concile Gallican de Pise–Milan. Documents Florentins (1510–1512)* (Paris, 1922).

Rerum Italicorum Scriptores, n.s. (*RIS*) (Città di Castello, 1900–).

Ricci, Caterina de', St., *Cronache-Diplomatica-Lettere Varie*, ed. G. di Agresti (Florence, 1969).

Ricci, Giuliano de', *Cronaca (1532–1606)*, ed. G. Sapori (Milan, 1972).

Ricordi di Firenze dell'anno 1459, ed. G. Volpi, in *RIS*, XXVII, pt. 1.

Rinuccini, Alamanno, "Dialogus de Libertate," ed. F. Adorno, *Atti e Memorie dell' Accademia Toscana di Scienze e Lettere "La Colombaria"* XXII (1957), 265–303.

Rinuccini, Filippo, *Ricordi Storici di Filippo di Cino Rinuccini dal 1282 al 1460, colla Continuazione di Alamanno e Neri, suoi Figli, fino al 1506, seguiti da altri Monumenti Inediti di Storia Patria Estratti dai Codici Originali e Preceduti dalla Storia Genealogica della loro Famiglia e della Descrizione della Cappella Gentilizia in S. Croce*, ed. G. Aiazzi (Florence, 1840).

Ross, J. (ed.), *Lives of the Early Medici as Told in Their Correspondence* (London, 1910).

Rossi, Tribaldo de', *Ricordanze*, in *Delizie*, XXIII.

Rucellai, Giovanni, *Zibaldoni. I: Il Zibaldone Quaresimale*, ed. A. Perosa (London, 1960).

Sacchetti, Franco, *Opere*, ed. A. Chiari (Bari, 1938).

———, *Il Trecentonovelle*, ed. V. Pernicone (Florence, 1946).

Sacchi, Bartolomeo (Il Platina), *see* Palmieri.

Salimbene de Adam, *Cronica*, ed. G. Scalia, 2 vols. (Bari, 1966).

Salutati, Coluccio, *Epistolae*, ed. J. Rigaccio, 2 vols. (Florence, 1741–1742).

———, *Epistolario*, ed. F. Novati, 4 vols. (Rome, 1891–1911).

Salviati, Jacopo, *Cronica*, in *Delizie*, XVIII.

Santa Maria Novella, "Necrologio" di S. Maria Novella. Testo Integrale dall'Inizio (MCCXXXV) al MDIV, ed. S. Orlandi, 2 vols. (Florence, 1955).

———, "Venerabilis Coenobii Sanctae Mariae Novellae de Florentia Chronica," *Analecta Sacri Ordinis Fratrum Praedicatorum* VIII (1906), 428–447, 507–510; VIII (1907), 120–125; IX (1909), 125–128, 197–200; XII (1915–1916), 41–57, 116–122, 168–186, 238–251, 308–316, 383–395, 469–480, 536–548, 623–642, 707–724, 799–816; XIII (1916), 364–376, 430–438.

Sanuto, Marino, *I Diarii di Marino Sanuto (MCCCCXCVI–MDXXXIII)*, eds. R. Fulin *et al.*, 58 vols. (Venice, 1879–1903).

Savonarola, Girolamo, *Edizione Nazionale delle Opere*, genr. ed. R. Ridolfi (Rome, 1955–). *Prediche sopra Aggeo con il Trattato circa il Reggimento e Governo della Città di Firenze. Prediche sopra Amos e Zaccaria*, 3 vols; *Esodo*, 2 vols; *Ezechiele*, 2 vols.; *Giobbe*, 2 vols.; *Ruth e Michea*, 2 vols.; *Salmi*, 2 vols.

———, *Scelta di Prediche e Scritti di fra Girolamo Savonarola con Nuovi Documenti intorno alla sua Vita*, eds. P. Villari and E. Casanova (Florence, 1898).

Schnitzer, J. (ed.), "Mailändische Gesandschaftsberichte über die letzte Krankheit Lorenzo de' Medicis," *Römische Quartalschrift für Christliche Altertumskunde und für Kirchengeschichte* XVI (1902), 152–169.

———, *Quellen und Forschungen zur Geschichte Savonarolas*, 4 vols. (Munich and Leipzig, 1902–1910).

Scholz, R. (ed.), "Eine Humanistische Schilderung der Kurie aus dem Jahre 1438," *Quellen und Forschungen aus Italienischen Archiven und Bibliotheken* XVI (1913), 108–153.

Schubring, P. (ed.), *Cassoni*, 2 vols. (Leipzig, 1923).

Segni, Bernardo, *Storie Fiorentine di messer Bernardo Segni Gentiluomo Fiorentino dall'anno MDXXVII al MDLV, colla Vita di Niccolò Capponi*, 3 vols. (Livorno, 1830).

Soranus, *Gynecology*, ed. O. Temkin (Baltimore, 1956).

Sozomeni Pistoriensis Presbyteri Chronicon Universale, ed. G. Zaccagnini, in *RIS*, XVI, pt. 1.

Statuta Populi et Communis Florentiae, 3 vols. (Fribourg, 1778).

Statuti della Repubblica Fiorentina, ed. R. Caggese, 2 vols. (Florence, 1910–1921): I. *Statuto del Capitano del Popolo degli anni 1322–1325*. II. *Statuto del Podestà dell'anno 1325*.

"Statuto della Parte Guelfa di Firenze compilato nel MCCCXXXV," ed. F. Bonaini, *Giornale Storico degli Archivi Toscani* I (1857), 1–41.

Stefani, Marchionne di Coppo (Bonaiuti), *Cronaca Fiorentina*, ed. N. Rodolico, in *RIS*, XXX, pt. 1.
Strozzi, Alessandra Macinghi negli, *Lettere di una Gentildonna Fiorentina del secolo XV ai Figliuoli Esuli*, ed. C. Guasti (Florence, 1877).
Ambrosii Traversarii Generalis Camaldulensium aliorumque ad ipsum, et ad alios de eodem Ambrosio Latinae Epistolae, ed. L. Mehus, 2 vols. (Florence, 1759).
————, *Hodoeporicon*, in A. Dini-Traversari, *Ambrogio Traversari e i suoi Tempi* (Florence, 1912).
Trexler, R. (ed.), *Synodal Law in Florence and Fiesole, 1306–1518* (Vatican City, 1971).
Ubaldi, Piero degli, *Tractatus super Canonica Episcopali, et Parochiali*, in *Tractatus Universi Iuris, duce et auspice Gregorii XIII . . .* , XV, pt. 2 (Venice, 1584).
Ughi, Giuliano, *Della Cronica di Firenze*, ed. F. Frediano, in *ASI, Appendice* VII (1849), 113–274.
Vaglienti, Piero, "Frate Girolamo Savonarola Giudicato da Piero Vaglienti, Cronista Fiorentino," ed. L. Randi, *Rivista delle Biblioteche* IV (1893), 49–63.
Valori, Niccolò, "Laurentii Medicei Vita," in F. Villani, *Liber de Civitatis Florentiae Famosis Civibus ex Codice Mediceo Laurentiano* (Florence, 1847).
Varchi, Benedetto, *Storia Fiorentina*, 2 vols. (Florence, 1963).
Vasari, Giorgio, *Le Opere*, ed. G. Milanesi, 9 vols. (Florence, 1973).
————, *Le Vite de' Più Eccelenti Pittori, Scultori, e Architettori*, ed. K. Frey, I (Munich, 1911).
Velluti, Donato, *La Cronica Domestica di messer Donato Velluti, scritta fra il 1367 e il 1370, con le Addizioni di Paolo Velluti, scritte fra il 1555 e il 1560*, eds. I. Del Lungo and G. Volpi (Florence, 1914).
Verde, A. (ed.), *Lo Studio Fiorentino, 1473–1503. Ricerche e Documenti*, 3 vols. (Pistoia, 1977).
Vespasiano da Bisticci, *Vite di Uomini Illustri del secolo XV*, ed. G. Vita (Florence, 1938).
Vettori, Francesco, "Sommario della Storia d'Italia dal 1511 al 1527," *ASI, Appendice* VI (1848), 287–382.
Vigo, P. (ed.), *Una Confraternità di Giovanetti Pistoiesi a Principio del secolo XVI (Compagnia della Purità)* (Bologna, 1887).
Villani, Giovanni, *Cronica di Giovanni Villani a Miglior Lezione Ridotta, coll'Aiuto de' Testi a Penna*, ed. F. Dragomanni, 4 vols. (Florence, 1844–1845).
————, Giovanni, Matteo, and Filippo, *Croniche di Giovanni, Matteo, et Filippo Villani, secondo le Migliori Stampe e Corredate di Note Filologiche e Storiche . . .* , 2 vols. (Trieste, 1857).
Zafarana, Z. (ed.), "Per la Storia Religiosa di Firenze nel Quattrocento," *Studi Medievali*, ser. 3, IX (1968), 1017–1113.

Secondary Works

Ackerman, J., *The Architecture of Michelangelo* (London, 1966).
Ademollo, A., *Marietta de' Ricci, ovvero Firenze al Tempo dell' Assedio*, ed. L. Passerini, 3 vols. (Florence, 1845).
Ady, C., *Lorenzo dei Medici and Renaissance Italy* (New York, 1962).
Alberi, E., *L'Assedio di Firenze* (Florence, 1840).
Albertini, R. von, *Das Florentinische Staatsbewusstsein im Übergang von der Republik zum Prinzipat* (Bern, 1955).
Artusi, L., and Gabbrielli, S., *Feste e Giochi a Firenze* (Florence, 1976).
Banfield, E., *The Moral Basis of a Backward Society* (Chicago, 1958).
Barash, M., "Der Ausdruck in der Italienischen Kunsttheorie," *Zeitschrift für Ästhetik und Allgemeine Kunstwissenschaft* XII (1967), 33–69.
Bargellini, P., Morozzi, G., and Batini, G., *Santa Reparata, La Cattedrale Risorta* (Florence, 1970).
Baron, H., *The Crisis of the Early Italian Renaissance. Civic Humanism and Republican Liberty in an Age of Classicism and Tyranny* (Princeton, 1966).
Bateson, G., *Steps to an Ecology of the Mind* (New York, 1972).
Battara, P., *La Popolazione di Firenze alla Metà del Cinquecento* (Florence, 1935).

Baxandall, M., *Painting and Experience in Fifteenth-Century Italy. A Primer in the Social History of Pictorial Style* (Oxford, 1972).

Bayley, C., *War and Society in Renaissance Florence. The De Militia of Leonardo Bruni* (Toronto, 1961).

Bec, C., *Les Marchands Ecrivains. Affaires et Humanisme à Florence, 1375–1434* (Paris, 1967).

Becker, M., *Florence in Transition*, 2 vols. (Baltimore, 1967–1968).

Bellah, R., reviewed in the Symposium on ʾCivic Religion, in *Journal for the Scientific Study of Religion* XIV (1975), 385–414.

Bensa, E., *Francesco di Marco da Prato. Notizie e Documenti sulla Mercatura Italiana del secolo XIV* (Milan, 1928).

Bercé, Y.-M., *Fête et Révolte. Des Mentalités Populaires du XVIe au XVIIIe siècle* (Paris, 1976).

Bernard, F., *Les Fêtes Célèbres de l'Antiquité du Moyen Age et des Temps Modernes* (Paris, 1878).

Berner, S., "Florentine Society in the Late Sixteenth and Early Seventeenth Centuries," *Studies in the Renaissance* XVIII (1971), 203–246.

Berry, B., and Harris, C., "Central Place," *International Encyclopedia of the Social Sciences* II (1968), 365–370.

Bertelli, S., "Constitutional Reforms in Renaissance Florence," *The Journal of Medieval and Renaissance Studies* III (1973), 139–164.

———, and Ramakus, G. (eds.), *Essays Presented to Myron P. Gilmore*, 2 vols. (Florence, 1978).

Bettanini, A., "Note di Cerimoniale Diplomatico," in *Studi dedicati alla Memoria di Pier Paolo Zanzucchi dalla Facoltà di Giurisprudenza*, ed. E. Albertario (Milan, 1927).

Bevan, E., *Holy Images. An Inquiry into Idolatry and Image-Worship in Ancient Paganism and in Christianity* (London, 1940).

Bloch, M., *Les Rois Thaumaturges. Etude sur le Caracter Surnaturel Attribué à la Puissance Royale, particulièrement en France et en Angleterre* (Strassburg, 1924).

Bocock, R., *Ritual in Industrial Society. A Sociological Analysis of Ritualism in Modern England* (London, 1974).

Boissevain, J., *Saints and Fireworks. Religion and Politics in Rural Malta* (New York, 1965).

Borella, P., "Corpi Santi in Milano e Diocesi," in *Studi in Onore di Carlo Castiglioni, Prefetto dell'Ambrosiana* (Milan, 1957).

Borsook, E., "Art and Politics at the Medici Court. I: The Funeral of Cosimo I de' Medici," *Mitteilungen des Kunsthistorischen Institutes in Florenz* XII (1965), 31–54.

———, "Decor in Florence for the Entry of Charles VIII of France," *ibid.*, X (1961–1962), 106–122, 217.

Bouwsma, W., "The Renaissance and Drama of Western History," *American Historical Review* LXXXIV (1979), 1–15.

Bowsky, W., *The Finance of the Commune of Siena, 1287–1355* (Oxford, 1970).

Bredekamp, H., "Renaissancekultur als 'Hölle': Savonarolas Verbrennungen der Eitelkeiten," in *Bildersturm. Die Zerstörung des Kunstwerks*, ed. M. Warnke (Munich, 1973), 41–64.

Brentano, R., *Two Churches. England and Italy in the Thirteenth Century* (Princeton, 1968).

Browe, P., *Die Verehrung der Eucharistie im Mittelalter* (Munich, 1933).

Brown, A., "The Humanistic Portrait of Cosimo de' Medici, *Pater Patriae*," *Journal of the Warburg and Courtauld Institutes* XXIV (1961), 186–221.

Brown, P. "A Dark-Age Crisis: Aspects of the Iconoclastic Controversy," *English Historical Review* LXXXVIII (1973), 1–34.

———, "The Rise and Function of the Holy Man in Late Antiquity," *The Journal of Roman Studies* LXI (1971), 80–101.

———, "The View from the Precipice," *New York Review of Books* (Oct. 3, 1974), 3f.

Brucker, G., *The Civic World of Early Renaissance Florence* (Princeton, 1977).

———, *Florentine Politics and Society, 1343–1378* (Princeton, 1962).

——— (ed.), *People and Communities in the Western World* (Homewood, Ill., 1979).

Brückner, W., *Bildnis und Brauch. Studien zur Bildfunktion der Effigies* (Berlin, 1966).

Brunt, P., "*Amicitia* in the Late Roman Republic," in *The Crisis of the Roman Republic*, ed. R. Seager (Cambridge, 1969), 199–218.

Burckhardt, J., *The Civilization of the Renaissance in Italy*, 2 vols. (New York, 1958).

Buser, B., *Die Beziehungen der Mediceer zu Frankreich während der Jahre 1434–1494, in ihrem Zusammenhang mit den Allgemeinen Verhältnissen Italiens* (Leipzig, 1879).

——, *Lorenzo de' Medici als Italienischer Staatsmann* (Leipzig, 1879).

Butters, H., "Florentine Politics, 1502–1515" (diss. Oxford Univ., 1974).

Cantimori, D., "Rhetoric and Politics in Italian Humanism," *Journal of the Warburg and Courtauld Institutes* I (1937–1938), 83–102.

——, review of Schnitzer, *Savonarola*, in *Annali della r. Scuola Normale Superiore di Pisa*, ser. 2, I (1932), 90–104.

Cartellieri, O., *The Court of Burgundy* (New York, 1972).

Casanova, E., "L'Astrologia e la Consegna del Bastone al Capitano Generale della Repubblica Fiorentina," *ASI*, ser. 5, VII (1891), 134–144.

Chadwick-Jones, J., *Social Exchange Theory: Its Structure and Influence in Social Psychology* (London, 1976.)

Chambers, D., *The Imperial Age of Venice, 1380–1580* (London, 1970).

Chevalier-Skolnikoff, S., "Kids," *Animal Kingdom* LXXXII, n. 3 (July, 1979), 11–18.

Chojnacki, S., "Political Adulthood in Fifteenth-Century Venice," *American Historical Review* XCI (1986), 791–810.

Cochrane, E., *Florence in the Forgotten Centuries, 1527–1800* (Chicago, 1973).

Cohn, S., "Community and Conflict in the Renaissance, 1340–1530" (diss. Harvard Univ., 1978).

——, "Rivolte Popolari e Classi Sociali nella Toscana del Rinascimento," *Studi Storici* XX (1979), 747–758.

Cooper, R. "Pier Soderini: Aspiring Prince or Civic Leader," *Studies in Medieval and Renaissance History*, n.s., I (1978), 67–126.

Corvisieri, C. "Il Trionfo Romano di Eleonora d'Aragone," *Archivio della r. Società Romana di Storia Patria* X (1887), 629–687.

Cox, H., *The Secular City. Secularization and Urbanization in Theological Perspective* (New York, 1965).

Cranach, M. von, and Vine, I. (eds.), *Social Communication and Movement. Studies of Interaction and Expression in Man and Chimpanzee* (London, 1973).

D'Ancona, A., *Origini del Teatro Italiano. Libri Tre con Due Appendici sulla Rappresentazione Drammatica del Contado Toscano e sul Teatro Mantovano nel secolo XVI*, 2 vols. (Turin, 1891).

Davidsohn, R., *Firenze ai Tempi di Dante* (Florence, 1929).

——, *Storia di Firenze*, 8 vols. (Florence, 1956–1968).

Davis, N. Zemon, "Deforming the Reformation," *New York Review of Books* (April 10, 1969), 35 seq.

——, "The Sacred and the Body Social in Sixteenth-Century Lyon," *Past and Present*, no. 90 (1981), 40–70.

——, *Society and Culture in Early Modern France* (Stanford, 1975).

——, "Some Tasks and Themes in the Study of Popular Religion," in Trinkaus, *Pursuit*, 307–336.

Dawkins, R., *The Selfish Gene* (Oxford, 1976).

De Coulanges, F., *The Ancient City. A Study on the Religion, Laws, and Institutions of Greece and Rome* (Garden City, 1956).

De la Roncière, C., "La Place des Confréries dans l'Encadrement Religieux du Contado Florentin: l'Exemple de la Val d'Elsa," *Mélanges de l'Ecole Française de Rome* LXXXV (1973), 31–77.

——, "L'Influence des Franciscans dans la Campagne de Florence au XIVe siècle (1280–1360)," *ibid.*, LXXXVII (1975), 27–103.

DeMause, L. (ed.), *The History of Childhood* (New York, 1974).

De Roover, R., *The Rise and Decline of the Medici Bank, 1397–1494* (New York, 1966).

Del Badia, I., "La Compagnia della Gazza. I suoi Capitoli e le sue Tramutazioni," *Miscellanea Fiorentina di Erudizione e Storia* II (1902), 92–109.

——, *Le Signorie o le Potenze Festeggianti del Contado Fiorentino* (Florence, 1876).

Del Lungo, I., *La Donna Fiorentina del Buon Tempo Antico* (Florence, 1906).

——, *Florentia. Uomini e Cose del Quattrocento* (Florence, 1897).

——, "Una Vendetta in Firenze il Giorno di San Giovanni del 1293," *ASI*, ser. 4, XVIII (1886), 355–409.

Del Migliore, F., *Firenze Citta' Nobilissima Illustrata* (Florence, 1684).

Del Piazzo, M., "Gli Autografi di Lorenzo de' Medici nell'Archivio di Stato di Firenze," *Rinascimento* VIII (1957), 212–260.

Devlin, D., "Corpus Christi: A Study in Medieval Eucharistic Theory, Devotion, and Practice" (diss. Univ. of Chicago, 1975).

Dillon, W., *Gifts and Nations. The Obligation to Give, Receive, and Repay* (The Hague, 1968).

Doren, A., *Le Arti Fiorentine*, 2 vols. (Florence, 1940).

——, *Deutsche Handwerker und Handwerkerbruderschaften im Mittelalterlischen Italien* (Berlin, 1903).

Dorini, U., "Il Culto delle Memorie Patrie nella Repubblica di Firenze," *Rassegna Nazionale* CLXXIX (1911), 3–25.

Douglas, M., *Natural Symbols: Explorations in Cosmology* (New York, 1973).

——, *Purity and Danger: An Analysis of Concepts of Pollution and Taboo* (London, 1970).

Dundes, A., "Into the Endzone for a Touchdown: A Psychoanalytic Consideration of American Football," *Western Folklore* XXXVII (1978), 75–88.

——, and Falassi, A., *La Terra in Piazza: An Interpretation of the Palio of Siena* (Berkeley, 1975).

Edgerton, S., "A Little-Known 'Purpose of Art' in the Italian Renaissance," *Art History* II (1979), 45–61.

——, *Pictures and Punishment: Art and Criminal Punishment during the Florentine Renaissance* (Ithaca, 1985).

Eibl-Eibesfeldt, I., *Love and Hate. The Natural History of Behavior Patterns* (New York, 1972).

Erikson, E., *Toys and Reasons. Stages in the Ritualization of Experience* (New York, 1977).

——, *Young Man Luther. A Study in Psychoanalysis and History* (New York, 1962).

Fabbri, M., Zorzi, E., and Tofani, A. (eds.), *Il Luogo Teatrale a Firenze: Brunelleschi, Vasari, Buontalenti, Parigi* (Exhibition Catalogue) (Milan, 1975).

Fabriczy, C. von, "Michelozzo di Bartolomeo," *Jahrbuch der Königlich Preuszichen Kunstsammlungen* XV (Beiheft, 1904), 34–110.

Fabroni, A., *Laurentii Medicis Magnifici Vita*, 2 vols. (Pisa, 1784).

——, *Magni Cosmi Medicei Vita*, 2 vols. (Pisa, 1788–1789).

Falletti-Fossati, P., *Assedio di Firenze*, 2 vols. (Palermo, 1885).

Fanelli, G., *Firenze, Architettura e Città*, 2 vols. (Florence, 1973).

Ferguson, W., *The Renaissance in Historical Thought. Five Centuries of Interpretation* (Cambridge, Mass., 1948).

Fiske, A., *Friends and Friendship in the Monastic Tradition* (Cuernavaca, 1970).

Fiumi, E., "La Demografia Fiorentina nelle Pagine di Giovanni Villani," *ASI*, CVIII (1950), 78–158.

Flamini, F., *La Lirica Toscana del Rinascimento Anteriore ai Tempi del Magnifico* (Pisa, 1891).

Flavell, J., *The Developmental Psychology of Jean Piaget* (Princeton, 1963).

Fleming, J., "The Hugfords of Florence," *Connoisseur* CXXXVI (1955), 106–110, 197–206.

Fowler, J., "The Life and Miracles of St. William of York," *Yorkshire Archeological and Topographical Journal* III (1875), 198–348.

Galante, A., "Per la Storia Giuridica della Basilica di San Marco," *Zeitschrift der Savignystiftung für Rechtsgeschichte, Kanonistische Abteilung* XXXIII (1912), 283–298.

Gardner, L., "Deprivation Dwarfism," *Scientific American* (July, 1972), 76–82.

Garin, E., *Medioevo e Rinascimento. Studi e Ricerche* (Bari, 1966).

Geary, P., *Furta Sacra: Thefts of Relics in the Central Middle Ages, 800–1100* (Princeton, 1978).

Geertz, C., *The Interpretation of Cultures. Selected Essays* (New York, 1973).

Geertz, H., "An Anthropology of Religion and Magic. I," *Journal of Interdisciplinary History* VI (1975), 71–109.

Gennep, A. van, *The Rites of Passage* (Chicago, 1960).

Gilbert, C., "The Archbishop on the Painters of Florence, 1450," *Art Bulletin* XLI (1959), 75–87.

Gilbert, F., *Machiavelli and Guicciardini. Politics and History in Sixteenth-Century Florence* (Princeton, 1965).

Giorgetti, A., "Lorenzo de' Medici, Capitano Generale della Republica Fiorentina," *ASI*, ser. 4, XI (1883), 194–215.

Gluckman, M. (ed.), *Essays on the Ritual of Social Relations* (Manchester, 1962).

Goffman, E., *Asylums. Essays on the Social Situation of Mental Patients and Other Inmates* (Garden City, 1961).

——, *Frame Analysis. An Essay on the Organization of Experience* (Cambridge, Mass., 1975).

——, *Interaction Ritual. Essays on Face-to-Face Behavior* (Garden City, 1967).

——, *The Presentation of Self in Everyday Life* (Garden City, 1959).

Goldthwaite, R., "The Building of the Strozzi Palace: The Construction Industry in Renaissance Florence," *Studies in Medieval and Renaissance History* X (1973), 97–194.

——, "The Florentine Palace as Domestic Architecture," *American Historical Review* LXXVII (1972), 977–1012.

Gombrich, E., *Norm and Form* (London, 1978).

Goody, J., "Religion and Ritual: The Definitional Problem," *The British Journal of Sociology* XII (1961), 142–164.

Gori, P., *Le Feste Fiorentine attraverso i secoli. Le Feste per San Giovanni* (Florence, 1926).

Gougaud, L., *Devotional and Ascetic Practices in the Middle Ages* (London, 1927).

Gouldner, A., *The Coming Crisis of Western Sociology* (New York, 1970).

Gray, H., "Renaissance Humanism. The Pursuit of Eloquence," *Journal of the History of Ideas* XXIV (1963), 497–514.

Green, L., *Chronicle into History. An Essay on the Interpretation of History in Florentine Fourteenth-Century Chronicles* (Cambridge, 1972).

Greenacre, P., "Crowds and Crisis. Psychological Considerations," *Psychoanalytic Study of the Child* XXVII (1973), 136–155.

Greenewalt, C., *Ritual Dinners in Early Historic Sardis* (Berkeley, 1978).

Gudeman, S., "The *Compadrazgo* as a Reflection of the Natural and Spiritual Person," *Proceedings of the Royal Anthropological Institute of Great Britain and Ireland for 1971*, 45–71.

Guerri, D., *La Corrente Popolare nel Rinascimento. Berte, Burle, e Baie nella Firenze del Brunellesco e del Burchiello* (Florence, 1931).

Hale, J. (ed.), *Renaissance Venice* (London, 1973).

Hall, E., *The Silent Language* (Garden City, 1973).

Hall, M., "The *Tramezzo* in Santa Croce, Florence, Revisited," *Art Bulletin* LVI (1974), 325–341.

Hardison, O., *Christian Rite and Christian Drama in the Middle Ages. Essays in the Origin and Early History of Modern Drama* (Baltimore, 1965).

Hastings, J. (ed.), *Dictionary of the Bible* (New York, 1963).

Hatfield, R., *Botticelli's Uffizi "Adoration." A Study in Pictorial Content* (Princeton, 1976).

——, "The Compagnia de' Magi," *Journal of the Warburg and Courtauld Institutes* XXXIII (1970), 107–161.

Hauser, P., and Schnore, L. (eds.), *The Study of Urbanization* (New York, 1965).

Heers, J., *Le Clan Familial au Moyen Age. Etude sur les Structures Politiques et Sociales des Milieux Urbains* (Paris, 1974).

——, *Fêtes, Jeux, et Joutes dans les Sociétés d'Occident à la fin du Moyen Age* (Montreal, 1971).

Hefele, C. von, *Conciliengeschichte*, 9 vols. (Freiburg, 1873–1890).

Herde, P., "Politische Verhaltensweisen der Florentinischen Oligarchie, 1382–1402," in *Geschichte und Verfassungsgefüge. Frankfurter Festgabe für Walter Schlesinger*, ed. K. Zernack (Wiesbaden, 1973), 161–249.

Herlihy, D., "Mapping Households in Medieval Italy," *Catholic Historical Review* LVIII (1972), 1–24.

——, "Vieillir à Florence au Quattrocento," *Annales E.S.C.* XXIV (1969), 1338–1352.

——, and Klapisch-Zuber, C., *Les Toscans et leurs Familles. Une Etude du Catasto Florentin de 1427* (Paris, 1978).

Hocart, A., *Kings and Councillors: An Essay in the Comparative Anatomy of Human Society* (Chicago, 1970).

Holst, C. von, *Francesco Granacci* (Munich, 1974).

Hubert, H., and Mauss, M., *Sacrifice: Its Nature and Function* (Chicago, 1964).

Huizinga, J., *The Waning of the Middle Ages. A Study of the Forms of Life, Thought, and Art in France and the Netherlands in the XIVth and XVth Centuries* (Garden City, 1954).

Hunt, J. McV., *Intelligence and Experience* (New York, 1961).

Huxley, J. (ed.), "A Discussion on Ritualization of Behavior in Animals and Man," *Philosophical Transactions of the Royal Society of London*, ser. B, CCLI (1966), 247–526.

L'Illustratore Fiorentino, 3 vols. (Florence, 1835–1838).

Jacob, E. (ed.), *Italian Renaissance Studies. A Tribute to the late Cecilia M. Ady* (London, 1960).

Jacobson, D., *Itinerant Townsmen. Friendship and Social Order in Urban Uganda* (Menlo Park, N.J. 1973).

Jacquot, J., and Konigson, E. (eds.), *Les Fêtes de la Renaissance. Etudes Réunies et Présentées*, 3 vols. (Paris, 1956–1975).

Jenkins, F., "Cosmo de' Medici's Patronage of Architecture and the Theory of Magnificence," *Journal of the Warburg and Courtauld Institutes* XXXIII (1970), 162–170.

Jones, R. Devonshire, *Francesco Vettori, Florentine Citizen and Medici Servant* (London, 1972).

Kantorowicz, E., *The King's Two Bodies. A Study in Medieval Political Theology* (Princeton, 1957).

———, *Laudes Regiae. A Study in Liturgical Acclamations and Mediaeval Ruler Worship* (Berkeley, 1946).

———, *Selected Studies* (Locust Valley, 1965).

Kent, D., "I Medici in Esilio: una Vittoria di Famiglia ed una Disfatta Personale," *ASI*, CXXXII (1976), 3–63.

———, *The Rise of the Medici. Faction in Florence, 1426–1434* (Oxford, 1978).

Kent, F., *Household and Lineage in Renaissance Florence. The Family Life of the Capponi, Ginori, and Rucellai* (Princeton, 1977).

Kernodle, G., *From Art to Theatre. Form and Convention in the Renaissance* (Chicago, 1944).

Kirshner, J., *Pursuing Honor While Avoiding Sin. The Monte delle Doti of Florence* (Milan, 1978).

Kirshner, J., *see* Molho.

Klapisch, C., "L'Attribution d'un Prénom à l'Enfant en Toscane à la fin du Moyen-Age," in *L'Enfant au Moyen-Age. Actes du Colloque d'Aix-en-Provençe, Mars, 1979* (Aix-en-Provençe. Cahiers du C.U.E.R.-M.A., 1980).

Klapisch-Zuber, C., "Parenti, Amici, e Vicini: il Territorio Urbano d'una Famiglia Mercantile nel XV secolo," *Quaderni Storici* XXXIII (1976), 953–982.

Klapisch-Zuber, C., *see* Herlihy.

König, R., *A la Mode. On the Social Psychology of Fashion* (New York, 1973).

Krailsheimer, A., *Rabelais and the Franciscans* (Oxford, 1963).

La Fontaine, J. (ed.), *The Interpretation of Ritual. Essays in Honour of A. I. Richards* (London, 1973).

La Sorsa, S., *La Compagnia d'Or San Michele* (Trani, 1902).

Ladner, G., "The Gestures of Prayer in Papal Iconography of the Thirteenth and Early Fourteenth Centuries," in *Didascaliae. Studies in Honor of Anselm M. Albareda, Prefect of the Vatican Library*, ed. S. Prete (New York, 1961), 245–275.

Laín Entralgo, P., *The Therapy of the Word in Classical Antiquity* (New Haven, 1970).

Langer, S., *Mind*, 2 vols. (Baltimore, 1967–1972).

Lanternari, V., "La Politica Culturale della Chiesa nelle Campagne: la Festa di San Giovanni," *Società* XI (1955), 64–95.

Lasky, M., "One Nation, Divisible," *New York Times Magazine* (Sept. 22, 1974), 20 seq.

Law, J. Easton, "Age Qualifications and the Venetian Constitution: The Case of the Capello Family," *Papers of the British School at Rome* XXXIX (1971), 124–137.

Leroi-Gourhan, A., *Le Geste et la Parole*, 2 vols. (Paris, 1964–1965).

Levine, D., "Integration, Cultural," *International Encyclopedia of the Social Sciences* VII (1968), 372–380.

Levine, S., "The Location of Michelangelo's *David*: The Meeting of January 25, 1504," *Art Bulletin* LVI (1974), 31–49.

Lippi, L., *Il Malmantile Racquistato di Perlone Zipoli*, ed. P. Minucci, 2 vols. (Florence, 1788).

Little, L., *Religious Poverty and the Profit Economy in Medieval Europe* (Ithaca, 1978).

Luotto, P., *Il Vero Savonarola e il Savonarola di L. Pastor* (Florence, 1897).

Manzi, G., *Discorso di Guglielmo Manzi sopra gli Spettacoli, le Feste, ed il Lusso degl'Italiani nel secolo XIV* (Rome, 1818).

Marcel, R., *Marsile Ficin (1433–1499)* (Paris, 1958).

Martines, L., *Lawyers and Statecraft in Renaissance Florence* (Princeton, 1968).

———, *The Social World of the Florentine Humanists, 1390–1460* (Princeton, 1963).

——— (ed.), *Violence and Civil Disorder in Italian Cities, 1200–1500* (Berkeley, 1972).

Masi, G., "La Pittura Infamante nella Legislazione e nella Vita del Comune Fiorentino (secc. XIII–XVI)," in *Studi di Diritto Commerciale in Onore di Cesare Vivante,* eds. A. Rocco *et al.,* II (Rome, 1931), 627–657.

———, "Schiavi, Servi, e Manomessi nel Comune Fiorentino," *Il Marzocco* XXVIII, no. 6 (Feb. 11, 1923), 2ff.

Mauss, M., *The Gift. Forms and Functions of Exchange in Archaic Societies* (New York, 1967).

Mauss, M., *see* Hubert.

Meiss, M., "An Early Altarpiece from the Cathedral of Florence," *The Metropolitan Museum of Art Bulletin,* n.s., XII (1954), 302–317.

———, *Painting in Florence and Siena after the Black Death. The Arts, Religion, and Society in the Mid-Fourteenth Century* (New York, 1964).

Mitchell, B. (ed.), *Italian Civic Pageantry in the High Renaissance. A Descriptive Bibliography* (Florence, 1979).

Molho, A., "The Brancacci Chapel: Studies in Its Iconography and History," *Journal of the Warburg and Courtauld Institutes* XL (1977), 50–98.

———, "Cosimo de' Medici: *Pater Patriae* or *Padrino?*" *Stanford Italian Review* I (1979), 5–33.

———, *Florentine Public Finances in the Early Renaissance, 1400–1433* (Cambridge, Mass., 1971).

———, and Kirshner, J., "The Dowry Fund and the Marriage Market in Early Quattrocento Florence," *Journal of Modern History* L (1978), 403–438.

———, and Tedeschi, J. (eds.), *Renaissance Studies in Honor of Hans Baron* (De Kalb, 1971).

Molinari, C., *Spettacoli Fiorentini del Quattrocento. Contributi allo Studio delle Sacre Rappresentazioni* (Venice, 1961).

Monti, G., *Le Confraternite Medievali dell'Alta e Media Italia,* 2 vols. (Venice, 1927).

Morçay, R., *Saint Antonin, Fondateur du Couvent de Saint-Marc, Archevêque de Florence, 1389–1459* (Paris, 1914).

Moroni, G., *Dizionario di Erudizione Storico-Ecclesiastica da S. Pietro sino ai nostri Giorni,* 103 vols. (Venice, 1840–1861).

Morrison, K., *Europe's Middle Ages, 565–1500* (Glenview, 1970).

Muir, E., *Civic Ritual in Renaissance Venice* (Princeton, 1981).

———, "Images of Power: Art and Pageantry in Renaissance Venice," *American Historical Review* LXXXIV (1979), 16–52.

Munichi, A., *La Fazione Anti-Medicea detta "Del Poggio"* (Florence, 1911).

Munn, N., *Walbiri Iconography: Graphic Representation and Cultural Symbolism in a Central Australian Society* (Ithaca, 1973).

Najemy, J. "Guild Republicanism in Trecento Florence: The Success and Ultimate Failure of Corporate Politics," *American Historical Review* LXXXIV (1979), 53–71.

———, "The Guilds in Florentine Politics, 1292–1394" (diss. Harvard Univ., 1972).

Ohm, T., *Die Gebetsgebärden der Völker und das Christentum* (Leiden, 1948).

Origo, I., "The Domestic Enemy: Eastern Slaves in Tuscany in the Fourteenth and Fifteenth Centuries," *Speculum* XXX (1955), 321–366.

———, *The Merchant of Prato, Francesco di Marco Datini, 1335–1410* (New York, 1957).

———, *The World of San Bernardino* (New York, 1962).

Otto, R., *The Idea of the Holy. An Inquiry into the Non-Rational Factor in the Idea of the Divine and Its Relation to the Rational* (New York, 1958).

Ozouf, M., "Le Cortège et la Ville. Les Itinéraires Parisiens des Fêtes Révolutionnaires," *Annales E.S.C.* XXVI (1971), 889–916.

Pampaloni, G., "Fermenti di Riforme Democratiche nella Firenze Medicea del Quattrocento," *ASI,* CXIX (1961), 11–62, 241–281.

———, "Nuovi Tentativi di Riforme alla Costituzione Fiorentina visti attraverso le Consulte," *ASI,* CXX (1962), 521–581.

Paoli, C., "Della Signoria di Gualtieri Duca d'Atene in Firenze," *Giornale Storico degli Archivi Toscani* VI (1862), 81–121, 169–286.

Paoli, G., *Mercato, Scritta, e Danaro di Dio* (Florence, 1895).

Passerini, L., *Storia degli Stabilimenti di Beneficenza e d'Istruzione Elementare Gratuita della Città di Firenze* (Florence, 1853).

Pastor, L. von, *Geschichte der Päpste seit dem Ausgang des Mittelalters*, 16 vols. (Freiburg, 1955–1961).

Penlikäinen, J., *The Nordic Dead Child Tradition* (Helsinki, 1968).

Peristiany, J., *Contributions to Mediterranean Sociology. Mediterranean Rural Communities and Social Change* (*Acts of the Mediterranean Sociological Conference, Athens, July 1963*) (Paris, 1968).

——— (ed.), *Honour and Shame: The Values of Mediterranean Society* (Chicago, 1966).

Perles, J., "Les Savants Juifs à Florence à l'Epoque de Laurent de Médicis," *Revue des Etudes Juives* XII (1886), 244–258.

Petrocchi, M., *Una "Devotio Moderna" nel Quattrocento Italiano? ed altri Studi* (Florence, 1961).

Peyer, H., *Stadt und Stadtpatron im Mittelalterlichen Italien* (Zurich, 1955).

Pfandl, L., *Philipp II. Gemälde eines Lebens und einer Zeit* (Munich, 1938).

Pfleger, L., "Die Stadt und Rats-Gottesdienste im Strassburger Münster," *Archiv für Elsässische Kirchengeschichte* XII (1937), 1–55.

Phillips, J., *The Reformation of Images: Destruction of Art in England, 1535–1660* (Berkeley, 1973).

Phillips, M., "A Newly Discovered Chronicle of Marco Parenti," *Renaissance Quarterly* XXXI (1978), 153–160.

Phythian-Adams, C., "Ceremony and the Citizen in the Communal Year at Coventry," in *Crisis and Order in English Towns, 1500–1700. Essays in Urban History*, eds. P. Clark and P. Slack (London, 1972), 57–85.

Piana, C., "La Posizione Giuridica del Terz'Ordine della Penitenza a Firenze nel secolo XIV," *Archivum Franciscanum Historicum* L (1957), 49–73.

Picotti, G. B., *La Giovinezza di Leone X* (Milan, 1927).

Pinto, G., "Il Personale, le Balie, i Salariati dell'Ospedale di San Gallo di Firenze negli anni 1395–1406. Note per la Storia del Salariato nelle Città Medievali," *Ricerche Storiche* IV (1974), 113–168.

Pipponier, F., *Costume et Vie Sociale. La Cour d'Anjou, XIVe–XVe siècles* (Paris, 1970).

Plesner, J., *L'Emigration de la Campagne à la Ville Libre de Florence au XIIIe siècle* (Copenhagen, 1934).

Pocock, D., "Sociologies: Urban and Rural," *Contributions to Indian Sociology* IV (1960), 63–81.

Postan, M., and Rich, F. (eds.), *The Cambridge Economic History of Europe from the Decline of the Roman Empire* III (Cambridge, 1963).

Preuss, J., "Machiavelli's Functional Analysis of Religion: Context and Object," *Journal of the History of Ideas* XL (1979), 171–190.

Preziosi, D., *The Semiotics of the Built Environment* (Bloomington, 1979).

Puccinelli, P., *Istoria dell'Eroiche Attioni d'Ugo il Grande, Duca della Toscana, di Spoleto, e di Camerino . . . con la Cronica dell'Abbadia di Fiorenze* (Milan, 1664).

Pullan, B., *Rich and Poor in Renaissance Venice. The Social Institutions of a Catholic State to 1620* (Cambridge, Mass., 1971).

Queller, D., *Early Venetian Legislation on Ambassadors* (Geneva, 1966).

———, *The Office of Ambassador in the Middle Ages* (Princeton, 1967).

Quilici, B., "La Chiesa di Firenze dal Governo del 'Primo Popolo' alla Restaurazione Guelfa," *ASI*, CXXVII (1969), 265–337, 423–460.

Ransel, D. (ed.), *The Family in Imperial Russia: New Lines of Historical Research* (Urbana, 1978).

Rappaport, R., "The Sacred in Human Evolution," *Annual Review of Ecology and Systematics* II (1971), 23–44.

Redfield, R., *The Little Community, and Peasant Society and Culture* (Chicago, 1960).

Reumont, A. von, *Lorenzo de' Medici the Magnificent*, 2 vols. (London, 1876).

Richa, G., *Notizie Istoriche delle Chiese Fiorentine, divise ne' suoi Quartieri*, 10 vols. (Florence, 1754–1762).

Ridolfi, R., *Studi Savonaroliani* (Florence, 1935).

———, *Vita di Girolamo Savonarola*, 2 vols. (Rome, 1952).

Rochon, A., *La Jeunesse de Laurent de Médicis (1449–1478)* (Paris, 1963).

Rodolico, N., *I Ciompi. Una Pagina di Storia del Proletariato Operaio* (Florence, 1971).

———, *La Democrazia Fiorentina nel suo Tramonto (1378–1382)* (Bologna, 1905).

Rondini, G., "I 'Giustiziati' a Firenze," *ASI*, ser. 5, XXVIII (1901), 209–256.

Roscoe, W., *Illustrations, Historical and Critical, of the Life of Lorenzo de' Medici, Called the Magnificent* (London, 1822).

———, *The Life and Pontificate of Leo the Tenth* III (Liverpool, 1805).

————, *The Life of Lorenzo de' Medici, Called the Magnificent* (London, 1851).

————, *Vita e Pontificato di Leone X*, ed. L. Bossi, 12 vols. (Milan, 1816–1817).

Rosenberg, P., review of Goffman, *Frame Analysis*, in *New York Times Book Review* (Feb. 16, 1975), 21.

Roth, C., *The Last Florentine Republic* (London, 1925).

Rothkrug, L., "Popular Religion and Holy Shrines. Their Influence on the Origins of the German Reformation and Their Role in German Cultural Development," in J. Obelkevich (ed.), *Religion and the People, 800–1700* (Chapel Hill, 1979), 20–86.

————, "Religious Practices and Collective Perceptions. Hidden Homologues in the Renaissance and Reformation," *Historical Reflections* VII (1980).

Rubinstein, N. (ed.), *Florentine Studies: Politics and Society in Renaissance Florence* (London, 1968).

————, *The Government of Florence under the Medici (1434–1494)* (Oxford, 1966).

————, "The Piazza della Signoria in Florence," in *Festschrift H. Siebenhüner*, eds. E. Hubula and G. Schweikhart (Würzburg, 1978), 19–30.

————, "I Primi Anni del Consiglio Maggiore di Firenze," *ASI*, CXII (1954), 151–194, 321–347.

Ruderman, D., "Giovanni Mercurio da Correggio's Appearance in Italy as Seen Through the Eyes of an Italian Jew," *Renaissance Quarterly* XXVIII (1975), 309–322.

Russell, J., *Medieval Regions and Their Cities* (Bloomington, 1972).

Rutenburg, V., *Popolo e Movimenti Popolari nell'Italia del '300 e '400* (Bologna, 1971).

Saalman, H., *The Bigallo. The Oratory and Residence of the Compagnia del Bigallo e della Misericordia in Florence* (New York, 1969).

Salvemini, G., *La Dignità Cavalleresca nel Comune di Firenze e altri Scritti* (Milan, 1972).

Sanesi, E., "Canonici Fiorentini dal secolo XIII al secolo XV," *Atti della Società Colombaria di Firenze (1928–1929)* (Florence, 1930), 37–51.

————, *Vicari e Canonici Fiorentini e il 'Caso Savonarola'* (Florence, 1932).

Santini, E., *Firenze e i suoi "Oratori" nel Quattrocento* (Milan, 1922).

Sapori, A., *Studi di Storia Economica (secoli XIII, XIV, XV)*, 3 vols. (Florence, 1955–1967).

Scaglione, A., *Nature and Love in the Late Middle Ages* (Berkeley, 1963).

Schapiro, M., *Words and Pictures. On the Literal and the Symbolic in the Illustration of a Text* (The Hague, 1973).

Schevill, F., *Medieval and Renaissance Florence* (New York, 1961).

Schnitzer, J., "Die Flugschriften-Literatur für und wider Girolamo Savonarola," in *Festgabe Karl Theodor von Heigel zur Vollendung seines Sechzigsten Lebensjahres*, eds. T. Bitterauf *et al.* (Munich, 1903), 196–235.

————, *Peter Delfin, General des Camaldulenserordens (1444–1525). Ein Beitrag zur Geschichte der Kirchenreform Alexanders VI und Savonarolas* (Munich, 1926).

————, *Savonarolas Erzieher und Savonarola als Erzieher* (Berlin, 1913).

Schwimmer, E., *Exchange in the Social Structure of the Orokaiva. Traditional and Emergent Ideologies in the Northern District of Papua* (London, 1973).

Scribner, B., "Reformation, Carnival, and the World Turned Upside-Down," *Social History* III (1978), 303–329.

Seigel, J., *Rhetoric and Philosophy in Renaissance Humanism. The Union of Eloquence and Wisdom, Petrarch to Valla* (Princeton, 1968).

Sennett, R., *The Fall of Public Man* (New York, 1976).

————, "Two on the Aisle," *New York Review of Books* (Nov. 1, 1973), 29–31.

Shaughnessy, J. (ed.), *The Roots of Ritual* (Grand Rapids, 1973).

Shearman, J., "The Florentine *Entrata* of Leo X, 1515," *Journal of the Warburg and Courtauld Institutes* XXXVIII (1975), 136–154.

Shklar, J. (ed.), *Hypocrisy, Illusion, and Evasion*, in *Daedalus* (Summer, 1979).

————, "Let Us Not Be Hypocritical," *Daedalus* (Summer, 1979), 1–25.

Silverman, S., "On the Uses of History in Anthropology: The *Palio* of Siena," *American Ethnologist* VI (1979), 413–436.

Simmel, G., *Soziologie. Untersuchungen über die Formen der Vergesellschaftung* (Berlin, 1968).

Singleton, C., "The Literature of Pageantry in Florence during the Renaissance" (diss. Univ. of California, Berkeley, 1931).

Soboul, A., "Religious Sentiment and Popular Culture during the Revolution," in *New Perspectives on the French Revolution. Readings in Historical Sociology*, ed. J. Kapplow (New York, 1965), 338–350.

Soranzo, G., "Lorenzo il Magnifico alla Morte del Padre e il suo primo Balzo verso la Signoria," *ASI*, CXI (1953), 42–77.

Spagnolo, A., *Le Scuole Accolitali in Verona* (Verona, 1904).

Spini, G., *Tra Rinascimento e Riforma* (Florence, 1940).

Stegemann, V., "Giovanni Villanis Historische Charakterbilder und die Astrologischen Texte der Planetarischen Anthropologie," in *Lebenskräfte in der Abendländischen Geistesgeschichte* (Festschrift Walter Goetz), eds. B. Bischoff *et al.* (Marburg, 1948), 125–199.

Steinberg, R., *Fra Girolamo Savonarola, Florentine Art, and Renaissance Historiography* (Athens, Ohio, 1977).

Stephens, J., "Heresy in Medieval and Renaissance Florence," *Past and Present*, no. 54 (1972), 25–60.

Storia di Milano. Fondazione Treccani degli Alfieri per la Storia di Milano, 16 vols. (Milan, 1953–1962).

Strauss, G., *Luther's House of Learning. Indoctrination of the Young in the German Reformation* (Baltimore, 1978).

Swanson, G., *Religion and Regime. A Sociological Account of the Reformation* (Ann Arbor, 1967).

———, reviewed in "Reevaluating the Reformation: A Symposium, *Journal of Interdisciplinary History* I (1971), 379–446.

Thomas, K., "An Anthropology of Religion and Magic, II," *Journal of Interdisciplinary History* VI (1975), 91–109.

———, *Religion and the Decline of Magic. Studies in Popular Beliefs in Sixteenth and Seventeenth Century England* (London, 1971)

Thompson, E. P., "The Moral Economy of the English Crowd in the Eighteenth Century," *Past and Present*, no. 50 (1971), 76–136.

———, "Patrician Society, Plebeian Culture," *Journal of Social History* VII (1974), 382–405.

Thorndike, L., *A History of Magic and Experimental Science*, 8 vols. (New York, 1923–1958).

Tiger, L., *Men in Groups* (New York, 1969).

Tillich, P., *Love, Power, and Justice; Ontological Analyses and Ethical Applications* (New York, 1954).

Tilly, C., "The Routinization of Protest in Nineteenth-Century France," Working Paper no. 181, *Center for Research on Social Organization* (Univ. of Michigan).

———, "The Web of Collective Action in Eighteenth-Century Cities," Working Paper no. 74, *Center for Research on Social Organization* (Univ. of Michigan).

Toschi, P., *Le Origini del Teatro Italiano* (Turin, 1955).

Trexler, B., "Hospital Patients in Florence: San Paolo, 1567–1568," *Bulletin of the History of Medicine* XLVIII (1974), 41–59.

Trexler, R., "Le Célibat à la Fin du Moyen Age: les Religieuses de Florence," *Annales E.S.C.* XXVII (1972), 1329–1350.

———, "Charity and the Defense of Urban Elites in the Italian Communes," in *The Rich, the Well Born, and the Powerful. Elites and Upper Classes in History*, ed. F. Jaher (Urbana, 1973), 64–109.

———, *Church and Community, 1200–1600: Studies in the History of Florence and New Spain* (Rome, 1987).

———, "De la Ville à la Cour. La Déraison à Florence durant la Republique et le Grand Duché," in *Le Charivari. Actes de la Table Ronde organisée par le Centre Nationale de Recherche Scientifique et l'Ecole des Hautes Etudes*, eds. J. Le Goff and J.-C. Schmitt (Paris, 1981), 165–176.

———, "The Episcopal Constitutions of Antoninus of Florence," *Quellen und Forschungen aus Italienischen Archiven und Bibliotheken* LIX (1979), 244–272.

———, *Famiglia e potere a Firenze nel Rinascimento.*

———, "Florence, by the Grace of the Lord Pope . . . ," *Studies in Medieval and Renaissance History* IX (1972), 115–215.

———, "Florentine Religious Experience: The Sacred Image," *Studies in the Renaissance* XIX (1972), 7–41.

———, "The Foundlings of Florence, 1395–1455," *History of Childhood Quarterly* I (1973), 259–284.

———, "Infanticide in Florence: New Sources and First Results," *History of Childhood Quarterly* I (1973), 98–116.

————, "Lorenzo de' Medici and Savonarola, Martyrs for Florence," *Renaissance Quarterly* XXXI (1978), 293–308.

————, "The Magi Enter Florence. The Ubriachi of Florence and Venice," *Studies in Medieval and Renaissance History*, n.s., I (1978), 127–218.

————, "A Medieval Census: The *Liber Divisonis*," *Medievalia et Humanistica* XVII (1966), 82–85.

————,"La prostitution florentine au XVe siècle: Patronages et clientèles," *Annales E.S.C.* XXXVI (1981), 983–1015.

————, "Ritual Behavior in Renaissance Florence: The Setting," *Medievalia et Humanistica*, n.s., IV (1973), 125–144.

————, "Ritual in Florence: Adolescence and Salvation in the Renaissance," in Trinkaus, *Pursuit*, 200–264.

————, *The Spiritual Power. Republican Florence under Interdict* (Leiden, 1974).

————, and Lewis, M., "Two Captains and Three Kings. New Light on the Medici Chapel," *Studies in Medieval and Renaissance History*, n.s., IV (1981), 91–177.

Trilling, L., *Sincerity and Authenticity* (Cambridge, Mass., 1972).

Trinkaus, C., with Oberman, H. (ed.), *The Pursuit of Holiness in Late Medieval and Renaissance Religion* (Leiden, 1974)

Truffi, R., *Giostre e Cantori di Giostre. Studi e Ricerche di Storia e di Letteratura* (Rocca S. Casciano, 1911).

Turner, V., "The Center Out There: Pilgrim's Goal," *History of Religions* XII (1972), 191–230.

Van Der Leeuw, G., *Religion in Essence and Manifestation*, 2 vols. (New York, 1963).

Vasoli, C., "L'Attesa della Nuova Era in Ambienti e Gruppi Fiorentini del Quattrocento," in *L'Attesa dell'Età Nuova nella Spiritualità della Fine del Medioevo*, ed. G. Ermini (Todi, 1962), 370–432.

Vauchez, A., "La Commune de Sienne, les Ordres Mendiants et le Culte de Saints. Histoire et Enseignements d'une Crise." *Mélanges de l'Ecole Française de Rome. Moyen Age, Temps Modernes* LXXXIX (1977), 757–767.

Vedovato, G., *Note sul Diritto Diplomatico della Repubblica Fiorentina* (Florence, 1946).

Venturi, L., "Le Compagnie della Calza (secc. XV–XVI)," *Nuovo Archivio Veneto* [*Archivio Veneto*, ser. 3, XVI–XVIII] (1908), 161–221, 140–233.

Villari, P., *La Storia di Girolamo Savonarola e de' suoi Tempi, con l'Aiuto di Nuovi Documenti*, 2 vols. (Florence, 1926).

Viviani Della Robbia, E., *Nei Monasteri Fiorentini* (Florence, 1946).

Wallerstein, I., *The Modern World-System. Capitalist Agriculture and the Origins of the European World-Economy in the Sixteenth Century* (New York, 1974).

Warburg, A., *Gesammelte Schriften*, 2 vols. (Leipzig, 1932).

Weber, M., *The City*, eds. D. Martindale and G. Neuwirth (Glencoe, Ill., 1958).

Weinstein, D., *Savonarola and Florence. Prophecy and Patriotism in the Renaissance* (Princeton, 1970).

Weissman, R., "Community and Piety between Renaissance and Counter-Reformation. Florentine Confraternities 1200–1600" (diss. Univ. of California, Berkeley, 1978).

————, *Ritual Brotherhood in Renaissance Florence* (New York, 1982).

Welliver, W., *L'Impero Fiorentino* (Florence, 1957).

Wheatley, P., *The Pivot of the Four Quarters: A Preliminary Enquiry into the Origins and Character of the Ancient Chinese City* (Chicago, 1971).

Wilcox, D., *The Development of Florentine Humanist Historiography in the Fifteenth Century* (Cambridge, Mass., 1969).

Wirth, J., "Sainte Anne est une Sorcière," *Bibliothèque d'Humanisme et Renaissance* XL (1978), 449–480.

Wissowa, G., *Religion und Kultus der Römer* (Munich, 1912).

Wittgenstein, L., *Philosophical Investigations* (New York, 1953).

Wolf, E. (ed.), "Social and Political Processes in the Western Mediterranean," *Anthropological Quarterly* XLII, no. 3 (1969).

Yates, G., *Giordano Bruno and the Hermetic Tradition* (New York, 1969).

Zdekauer, L., "Il Giuoco in Italia nei secoli XIII e XIV," *ASI*, ser. 4, XLIII (1886), 20–74.

Index

neighborhoods and parishes, 9, 12–13, 48–49, 170, 173, 220, 262, 273, 341–342, 396–398, 400–418, 451, 481, 483, 510–511, 514, 532, 542–543, 551
palaces and squares
Alberti, 229
Episcopal, 264, 352
Giustizia, 209
Gondi, 447
Grano, 208
Innocenti, 477
Medici, 9, 396, 412, 424–426, 430, 433–435, 442–449, 453, 457, 469, 483–484, 494, 497–498, 520, 523
Parte Guelfa, 233
Podestà (Bargello), 30, 199
S. Ambrogio, 400
S. Croce, 234, 258, 381, 396–398, 401–402, 429, 539
S. Firenze, 250
S. Felice, 355–356, 358
S. Giovanni, 247, 252, 322, 468
S. Piero Maggiore, 51, 249, 262
Signoria, 9, 49–50, 52, 66, 82, 237, 250, 258–259, 266, 315–318, 321–323, 346, 356–358, 376, 425, 457, 462, 478, 485–487, 506, 509, 511, 516, 520, 522–523, 529–530, 546
and the Palace's Chapel, 31, 47, 50, 322, 446
Hall of the Grand Council, 469–470, 523, 525, 539–540
ringhiera, 49–50, 250, 315–318, 356, 369, 502–503
Udienza, 322–323
S. Spirito, 398, 546
Strozzi, 447
quarters and wards, 9, 12–14, 170, 181, 183, 217, 219, 221–222, 249–252, 255–257, 267, 271, 284, 336, 344–346, 354, 373, 397, 403, 428, 477, 479–481, 499, 528, 532–533, 536, 542–543
streets
Borgo Pinti, 51
Borgo S. Jacopo, 250
Canto degli Stampatori, 322
Canto de' Tornaquinci, 323
Cerretani, 250
Cocomero, 449
Corso de' Tintori, 220
Ghibellina, 51, 220
Giustizia, 207
Gondi, 250
Larga, 399, 416
Maggio, 416
Por San Maria, 250
Proconsolo, 250
S. Gallo, 51, 342
Tornabuoni, 250
Vacchereccia, 250, 315
university, 272
walls and boundaries, 10, 47–48, 250, 344, 363, 400–401, 409, 450, 514, 522
Florentines abroad, 12, 42–43, 280–283, 288, 300–301, 328, 390
and Florence, characterized, 9, 18, 29, 40, 43, 150, 169, 279–280, 293, 304, 313, 328–330, 335, 349, 358, 365, 368, 380, 391, 422, 438–439, 441, 448–449, 453–455, 473–474, 482, 487, 492, 499, 504, 521, 526, 531, 534–535, 540–541
Foreigners, resident in Florence, 14, 404, 411, 414, 448
Foscari, Francesco, 439
Venetian ambassador, 524–525
Foundlings and orphans, 164–167, 170, 256, 356, 369–370, 437
Frames and fences, 46, 49, 85–128, 160, 179, 238–239, 248, 271, 278, 443–444, 450, 551
France, 41, 150, 221, 281–282, 285, 287–289, 293, 295, 299, 319, 429, 442–443, 503, 508
Charles VI of, 288
Charles VIII of, 286–287, 309–310, 351, 462, 476, 484
Francis I of, 43
Louis XII of, 282
Louis XIV of, 444
Philip IV of, 297
Francesco da Barberino, 40, 91, 100, 102, 104–105, 107–112, 179, 291
Francesco d'Argenta, 99
Fraticelli, 198, 205, 207
Frescobaldi, Giovanni, 398–399
Friars, 4, 31–35, 71–72, 187–190, 540
Friar Secretary, 32
Friendship, 28–29, 56, 72, 104–107, 131–158, 163, 167–169, 171, 199, 226–227, 266, 298, 316, 327, 435–438, 460, 535
Friuli, 180

G

Gaits, 295, 315–316, 430, 434
Games, 51–52, 71, 74, 76, 120, 192, 208, 232, 315, 381, 385, 445, 475, 539, 553
ball-(Calcio), 374, 398–399, 478, 539

Library of Congress Cataloging-in-Publication Data

Trexler, Richard C., 1932–
    Public life in Renaissance Florence / Richard C. Trexler.
        p.   cm.
    Originally published: Academic Press, 1980, in series: Studies in
social discontinuity.
    Includes bibliographical references (p.   ) and index.
    ISBN 0-8014-2694-4 (cloth : alk. paper). — ISBN 0-8014-9979-8
(paper : alk. paper)
    1. Florence (Italy)—History—1421–1737. 2. Church and state—
Italy—Florence. 3. Florence (Italy)—Social conditions.
I. Title.
DG737.4.T66   1991
945′.5105—dc20   91-55259